The Conduct of Hostilities in International Humanitarian Law, Volume I

The Library of Essays in International Humanitarian Law
Series Editors: Michael N. Schmitt and Wolff Heintschel von Heinegg

Titles in the Series:

The Development and Principles of International Humanitarian Law
Michael N. Schmitt and Wolff Heintschel von Heinegg

The Scope and Applicability of International Humanitarian Law
Michael N. Schmitt and Wolff Heintschel von Heinegg

The Conduct of Hostilities in International Humanitarian Law, Volume I
Michael N. Schmitt and Wolff Heintschel von Heinegg

The Conduct of Hostilities in International Humanitarian Law, Volume II
Michael N. Schmitt and Wolff Heintschel von Heinegg

Detention and Occupation in International Humanitarian Law
Michael N. Schmitt and Wolff Heintschel von Heinegg

The Implementation and Enforcement of International Humanitarian Law
Michael N. Schmitt and Wolff Heintschel von Heinegg

The Conduct of Hostilities in International Humanitarian Law, Volume I

Edited by

Michael N. Schmitt

US Naval War College, USA

Wolff Heintschel von Heinegg

Europa-Universitat Viadrina, Germany

Routledge
Taylor & Francis Group
LONDON AND NEW YORK

First published 2012 by Ashgate Publishing

2 Park Square, Milton Park, Abingdon, Oxfordshire OX14 4RN
711 Third Avenue, New York, NY 10017

Routledge is an imprint of the Taylor & Francis Group, an informa business

First issued in paperback 2018

British Library Cataloguing in Publication Data
The conduct of hostilities in international humanitarian law.
Volume I. – (The library of essays in international humanitarian law)
1. Humanitarian law. 2. Combatants and noncombatants (International law) 3. War–Protection of civilians.
4. War, Maritime (International law) 5. Air warfare (International law)
I. Series II. Schmitt, Michael N. III. Heintschel von Heinegg, Wolff.
341.6'7 015–dc23

Library of Congress Control Number: 2011946157

ISBN 978-0-7546-2935-1 (hbk)
ISBN 978-1-138-37862-9 (pbk)

Contents

Acknowledgements

The editors and publishers wish to thank the following for permission to use copyright material.

Air Force Law Review for the essay: W. Hays Parks (1990), 'Air War and the Law of War', *Air Force Law Review*, **32**, pp. 1–225.

Cambridge University Press for the essays: A.P.V. Rogers (2000), 'Zero-Casualty Warfare', *International Review of the Red Cross*, **82**, pp. 165–82. Copyright © 2000 International Committee of the Red Cross; Kenneth Watkin (2005), 'Assessing Proportionality: Moral Complexity and Legal Rules', *Yearbook of International Humanitarian Law*, **8**, pp. 3–53. Copyright © 2005 Kenneth Watkin and TMC Asser Press.

Copyright Clearance Center for the essay: Wolff Heintschel von Heinegg (1994), 'The International Law of Mine Warfare at Sea', *Israel Yearbook on Human Rights*, **23**, pp. 53–76. Copyright © 1994 Israel Yearbook on Human Rights.

Wolff Heintschel von Heinegg (2005), 'Naval Blockade', *International Law Studies*, **75**, pp. 203–30. Copyright © 2005 Wolff Heintschel von Heinegg.

Oxford University Press for the essay: Hans Blix (1978), 'Area Bombardment: Rules and Reasons', *British Year Book of International Law*, **49**, pp. 31–69. Copyright © 1978 Hans Blix.

Royal Institute of International Affairs for the essays: A. Pearce Higgins (1920–21), 'Submarine Warfare', *British Year Book of International Law*, **1**, pp. 149–65; G.G. Fitzmaurice (1945), 'Some Aspects of Modern Contraband Control and the Law of Prize', *British Year Book of International Law*, **22**, pp. 73–95.

UBC Press for the essay: W.J. Fenrick (1986), 'The Exclusion Zone Device in the Law of Naval Warfare', *Canadian Yearbook of International Law*, **24**, pp. 91–126.

Every effort has been made to trace all the copyright holders, but if any have been inadvertently overlooked the publishers will be pleased to make the necessary arrangement at the first opportunity.

Series Preface

Over half a century ago, Sir Hersch Lauterpacht, then Whewell Professor of International Law at the University of Cambridge, observed that 'if international law is the vanishing point of law, the law of war is at the vanishing point of international law'. He was wrong. While it is true that the law of war, or international humanitarian law as it has become known, is particularly vulnerable to the vagaries of political, social and economic influences, it has nevertheless proven itself a robust normative regime that positively shapes man's most destructive undertaking – warfare. No other body of law can be credited with saving more lives or alleviating as much suffering.

These six volumes comprise a collection of particularly significant works on humanitarian law. They are intended for use by scholars, practitioners and students who seek to better understand the topics addressed herein, together with their lineage. Just as importantly, they allow users to begin to separate the wheat from the chaff. The proliferation of publications in the field, in part a sad reflection of the fact that armed conflict remains so horribly pervasive, as well as the digitization that facilitates access to journals that would not otherwise be readily available, often results in information overload. A Ministry of Defence legal adviser looking for background material to address a situation involving belligerent occupation will, for instance, uncover scores of articles. The student writing a dissertation on the law of targeting or a scholar penning an article on detention will find him- or herself buried in material. Unfortunately, some of what they unearth will prove misguided, out of context or simply wrong. This collection will not break down these obstacles in their entirety. But it does afford a useful starting-point by offering topically arranged humanitarian law journal essays that have been thoroughly vetted by many of the top experts in the field.

In this regard, a few words on the process used to choose the essays are helpful. It began with the selection of those subjects that we believed comprised the *sine qua non* of international humanitarian law – development, principles, scope, application, conduct of hostilities, detention, occupation, and implementation and enforcement. We then contacted over 60 recognized humanitarian law experts, both academics and seasoned legal advisers. They were provided the topics and asked in a very open-ended fashion to identify pieces they considered 'classics', believed to be 'essential' in a compilation of this nature, have found to be especially influential, used regularly in their work or deserved greater attention on the basis of their quality and insights. The experts were asked to pay particular attention to those essays that may have been 'forgotten' over time, but merited 'rediscovery'. Many of them responded in depth. We also benefited from the work of a five-member team from Emory Law School's International Humanitarian Law Clinic which conducted an exhaustive literature review to locate essays relied on regularly by writers – the 'usual suspects', if you will. Finally, as editors we took the liberty of adding a few pieces to the pool *sua sponte*.

Armed with a daunting inventory of candidates for inclusion, we began the difficult task of whittling it down. Many essays proved to be consensus choices among the experts; often the Emory team had also identified them. These provided the skeleton for the project. We then fleshed out the collection based on two key factors: quality assessments by the experts and topic coverage. The latter criterion proved particularly central to the process, for our objective was to produce a collection that not only contained thoughtful and influential works, but also addressed most key humanitarian law topics.

Beyond esteem factors and topical relevance, some essays were selected on account of their temporal significance, that is, having been written at key junctures in the development of international humanitarian law. As an example, the collection includes pieces written in the immediate aftermath of the First and Second World Wars and the attacks of 11 September 2001. Others were published soon after adoption of the 1949 Geneva Conventions or the 1977 Additional Protocols. We hope they both afford insight into the perspectives at play as humanitarian law was evolving and provide a context for understanding the genesis of contemporary norms.

In the end, we were unable to include many insightful and influential works. Exclusion was frequently a mere matter of being cursed with too many good choices on a particular topic. Although no reader is likely to be entirely satisfied with the essays included, or comfortable with the omission of others, we hope the rigorous selection process has resulted in a collection that is both useful and enlightening.

This project would not have been possible without the help of many supporters. We are, of course, deeply indebted to the many international experts who took time from their busy schedules to offer recommendations and comments over the course of the three-year effort. Although we cannot possibly name them all, particular appreciation is due to Ken Anderson, Yutaka Arai, Louise Arimatsu, Laurie Blank, Gabriella Blum, Bill Boothby, Ove Bring, Claude Bruderlein, Knut Dörmann, Alison Duxbury, William Fenrick, Dieter Fleck, Steven Haines, Agnieszka Jachec-Neale, Dick Jackson, Marie Jacobsson, Claus Kress, William Lietzau, Noam Lubell, Lindsay Moir, John Murphy, Sean Murphy, Mary Ellen O'Connell, Bruce Oswald, Hays Parks, Stephen Pomper, Jean-Francois Queguiner, Noelle Quenivet, Adam Roberts, A.P.V. Rogers, Peter Rowe, Joseph Rutigliano, Robert Sloane, Dale Stephens, Ken Watkin and Sean Watts.

We are equally indebted to the brilliant group of young scholars at Emory Law School, whom we dubbed our 'IHL Detectives' – Flora Manship, Carmel Mushin, Jeannine Privat, Nandini Rao and, in particular, Benjamin Farley. Their ability to identify and locate 'lost treasures' of humanitarian law was awe-inspiring. All have since graduated, and we wish them the very best in their professional careers.

Three people deserve special mention and gratitude. Laurie Blank, Director of the Emory's International Humanitarian Law Clinic, ably and tirelessly supervised her team. Beyond supervision, she also devoted an enormous amount of her own time to the substance and administration of the project. At European University Viadrina, Kaya Kowalski took on the task of collating materials and later working with us as we made the final selections for the collection. She was unflappable in the face of our long and sometimes contentious deliberations and always exceptionally good-natured and professional. Finally, we thank our editor at Ashgate, Valerie Saunders, who showed the patience of Job throughout.

We hope this collection proves valuable in the years to come. For our part, it was a fascinating endeavour.

MICHAEL N. SCHMITT
Newport, Rhode Island, USA

and

WOLFF HEINTSCHEL VON HEINEGG
Frankfurt (Oder), Germany

Introduction

This is the first of two volumes on the 'conduct of hostilities'. The phrase refers to military operations during an armed conflict that involve the application of force. Conduct of hostilities rules governing methods and means of warfare have traditionally been labelled 'Hague Law', a reference to the fact that many of the early treaties in the field were adopted at the Hague Peace Conferences of 1899 and 1907. Notable in this regard is Hague Convention IV on the Laws and Customs of War on Land, and in particular its annexed Regulations, which the Nuremberg Tribunal and the International Court of Justice have recognized as reflective of customary international law. Hague Law is to be distinguished from 'Geneva Law', a designation that derives primarily from the Geneva Conventions of 1864, 1906, 1929 and 1949. Geneva Law sets forth specific protections for various categories of persons and property, such as civilians, prisoners of war and the wounded and sick.

Today, the distinction has lost much of its relevance. Most significant in this regard is the fact that the 1977 Additional Protocols, especially Protocol I on international armed conflict, combine elements of both aspects of international humanitarian law (IHL). This is a sensible approach, for the distinction has proven artificial in practice. The humanitarian purposes of IHL are realized not only by explicit protections afforded to particular persons and property, but also through limitations on the methods and means that can be employed on the battlefield. These two volumes address issues that are the subject of both of the traditional categories of international humanitarian law.

What is most apparent in these volumes is that all of IHL reflects a balance between the intent of states to retain the ability to engage in actions that are militarily necessary and a desire to pursue humanitarian ends, if only to protect their own citizens and soldiers from the effects of warfare. Nowhere is this balancing more evident than in the law framing the conduct of hostilities. The quintessential example is the principle of proportionality, which permits incidental harm to civilians and civilian objects during attacks on combatants and military objectives so long as the expected harm is not excessive relative to the anticipated military advantage to be gained. Virtually every issue examined in these two volumes is the subject of an analogous balancing of military necessity and humanitarian considerations. The thoughts and opinions expressed by the authors are, in essence, attempts to more appropriately balance the two values.

Of course, as shall become evident, one's perspective inevitably influences arguments as to the correct balance. Those responsible for prosecuting warfare tend to be more sensitive to the realities of the battlefield, either in terms of mounting effective operations or in limiting behaviours that heighten the risk to their soldiers, sailors and airmen. By contrast, individuals and organizations dedicated to ensuring the well-being of the civilian population, such as the International Committee of the Red Cross or non-governmental organizations, are more attuned to the humanitarian considerations at play in the balance. Such differences are healthy, for they fuel a dialectical process through which an optimal balance can be better reached. The essays chosen for these volumes have exerted, and continue to exert, influence on that process. They offer us a glimpse of the genesis of contemporary IHL, while affording us a sense of its possible future vector. Volume I addresses three broad topics: distinction, maritime warfare and air warfare.

Distinction

The four essays in Part I explore aspects of the principle of distinction. Distinction is IHL's seminal notion. It has been codified in Additional Protocol I, Article 48, which requires parties to a conflict to 'at all times distinguish between the civilian population and combatants and between civilian objects and military objectives and accordingly ... direct their operations only against military objectives'. This rule reflects customary international law in both international and non-international conflict. It has been operationalized in such subsidiary norms as the prohibition of indiscriminate attacks, the rule of proportionality and the requirement to take precautions in attack.

'Protection of Civilians against the Effects of Hostilities' (Chapter 1) is Waldemar Solf's survey of the protection civilians enjoy under customary law and Additional Protocol I. Solf was uniquely positioned to comment on the subject, having served as a US army officer, as civilian Chief of International Law for the US army and as a member of the US delegation to the Diplomatic Conference on International Humanitarian Law (1974–77) that produced Additional Protocols I (international armed conflict) and II (non-international armed conflict). What is particularly interesting about his essay is that it was written the year before US President Reagan notified the Senate of the administration's opposition to the ratification of Protocol I on the basis that the treaty was 'fundamentally and irreconcilably flawed'. The President supported ratification of Additional Protocol II, but to date the Senate has not ratified the instrument. In 2011 Secretary of State Clinton notified the Senate that the Obama administration was again seeking advice and consent to its ratification.

In his essay, Solf explores the historical development of restraints on methods and means of warfare, the customary status of some of the norms and the relationship between customary and treaty law, paying particular attention to the core treaties in the field – the Hague Conventions of 1907, the Geneva Conventions of 1949 and the 1977 Additional Protocol I. His discussion of the historical lineage of this law is particularly rich, with examples that illustrate the genesis of principles such as discrimination and proportionality drawn from the writings of, *inter alia*, Sun Tzu, Shakespeare, Vitoria and Lieber.

Tellingly, Solf identifies the tensions inherent in the balance between considerations of necessity and humanity. He notes that the 1907 Hague Conventions omitted the reasons unpinning the rules based on 'the belief of humanitarian scholars that a humanitarian instrument should provide what is to be spared, and should not explicitly authorize violence' (p. 7). Unfortunately, 'this restraint sacrificed clarity' because 'military men tended to consider permissible any measure not expressly prohibited' (pp. 7–8). Solf rejects this perspective, arguing, correctly, that customary law retains its validity in the face of treaty law except as modified thereby. In particular, he points to the Martens Clause of the 1899 and 1907 Hague Conventions, which was subsequently included in Additional Protocol I. By the clause, 'the inhabitants and the belligerents remain under the protection and rule of the principles of the law of nations, as they result from the usages established among civilized peoples, from the laws of humanity, and the dictates of the public conscience', whenever there is no express rule on point. Solf also highlights the dynamic by which treaty law, or at least the general principle set forth therein, can mature into customary law binding even non-parties, the two paradigmatic examples being the 1907 Hague Regulations and the 1949 Geneva Conventions.

The essay is noteworthy for its discussion of the development of post-Second World War conduct of hostilities law. Interestingly, in the aftermath of the war and the adoption of the four 1949 Geneva Conventions, the new United Nations International Law Commission was asked to begin a codification of IHL. It declined, in its report to the General Assembly, on the ground that '"[w]ar having been outlawed, the regulation of its conduct has ceased to become relevant"' (p. 10). Sadly, the Commission could not have been more wrong.

The development of new weaponry, especially that associated with air warfare, nevertheless provided an impetus for development of the law. In this regard, Solf notes that four elements are inherent in the foundational juxtaposition of the necessity and humanity principles:

> (1) there are limitations on the methods and means of warfare; (2) these limitations are expressed in binding international law; (3) loss of life and destruction of property must have some rational tendency to the prompt achievement of a definite military advantage; and (4) such casualties and damage must not be disproportionate or excessive in relation to the military advantage anticipated. (p. 14)

Additional Protocol I, according to Solf, responds to these elements in a variety of ways. It contains provisions which 'revitalize and strengthen the distinction between military objectives and civilians/civilian objects', 'clarify the legal regulation of attacks', 'define in detail the precautionary steps that both the attackers and defenders must take' and set forth prohibitions on attacking particular persons and objects (p. 15). He suggests that the treaty does not create new law, but rather draws on existing customary law, with the exception of the prohibition on reprisals. Thus, he concurs with the International Committee of the Red Cross's self-assessment that in proffering the draft Protocol, the organization 'remained steadfast to the spirit in which, since 1864, it has demanded, for the benefit of individuals, guarantees consistent with the dictates of humanity whilst bearing in mind the realities of national defense and security' (p. 21). Obviously, in light of the non-party status of key war-fighting nations such as the United States and Israel, not all states and commentators have agreed with him.

Chapter 2, 'The Principle of Discrimination in 21st Century Warfare', builds on these foundations by examining how the principle of discrimination is likely to fare in the face of the ever-evolving nature of warfare. Written at the turn of the millennium by one of the editors these volumes, Michael Schmitt, while a military officer just recently graduated from the Naval War College, the essay addresses the impact of the 'revolution in military affairs' (RMA) on the law and vice versa (p. 23).

Schmitt observes that law and war exist in a symbiotic relationship. When changes in warfare occur, new law emerges, old law falls into desuetude or new interpretations of the law that are more attuned to the contemporary battlefield gain traction. These adjustments play themselves out on future battlefields, thereby creating a feedback loop that influences the further development of law. The classic example of this process was adoption of the 1949 Fourth Geneva Convention Relative to the Protection of Civilian Persons in Time of War following the horrendous suffering of civilians during the Second World War, and the subsequent decision to update them with the Additional Protocols.

In his essay, Schmitt identifies certain trends of the RMA and offers suggestions as to how they might affect the principle of discrimination. He begins by noting an 'accentuation of global divisibility' into the military (and economic) 'haves' and 'have nots' (p. 33). The trend continues, with the United States becoming increasingly dominant in military wherewithal as its underfunded allies and other states, with the key exception of China, slip further and further behind. The result is asymmetrical warfare, dramatically illustrated in Afghanistan and Iraq. Disparity on the battlefield results in a dangerous dynamic that 'encourages' the disadvantaged side to dispense with the extant legal norms in order to acquire its own asymmetrical advantage over states that remain committed to the norms of international humanitarian law.

The RMA also results in a 'blurring of the lines between protected persons and objects and valid military targets' (p. 38). Schmitt suggests that the blurring is the product of the militarization of previously protected entities and individuals, such as civilians who serve as military contractors. When this happens, '[t]here will be measurable pressure to interpret the universe of targetable objects and individuals more liberally … because each side will seek to deny its opponent potential advantage' (p. 41).

A further phenomenon of the RMA is the transformation of battlefields into 'battlespaces'. Because of the range of modern weaponry and the sophistication of intelligence, surveillance and reconnaissance assets, advanced militaries can today strike anywhere they wish into an enemy's territory. As a result, the protection of distance from the frontlines that civilians historically enjoyed has disappeared. This new reality dramatically heightens the centrality of the rule of proportionality and the requirement to take precautions in attack.

The 'advent of precision engagement' also affects IHL's implementation (p. 42). Precision attacks have the positive effect of minimizing collateral damage in comparison to strikes employing unguided systems. However, the fact that the 'have' states field precise systems when their opponents do not effectively creates relative legal obligations in the context of the IHL requirement to take precautions in attack, specifically in terms of the choice of methods and means. This may tend to weaken allegiance to IHL norms, for although IHL is not designed to ensure a 'fair fight', the willingness of states to accept legal limits on their activities has always been partly based on a sense that their opponents would be equally constrained. Further, the availability of precision weaponry renders many more targets lawful because they may now be struck without violating the requirement of proportionality. This is particularly true in urban environments. To the extent that more targets are legally targetable, the total collateral damage during a conflict, as distinct from the collateral damage caused by a particular strike, may rise.

Finally, Schmitt draws attention to the existence of 'disparate cognitive approaches' (p. 50). In light of technological asymmetry and the civilianization of the battlefield, advanced states have an incentive to limit the range of lawful targets to those that are strictly military.

This is because they rely heavily on the civilian sector, are generally adept at protecting their forces and can easily penetrate enemy defences. On the other hand, a lesser equipped belligerent, unable to get through its opponent's defences, will probably begin to perceive the enemy's civilian population and civilian objects as fruitful targets, not only because its opponent relies on them, but also because targeting the civilian population may turn popular sentiment against the conflict.

It must be conceded that the term 'revolution in military affairs' has fallen into disfavour as a result of the conflicts in Afghanistan and Iraq, which seem to hark back to classic counterinsurgencies. However, reports of the death of the RMA are greatly exaggerated. Precision strikes by unmanned aerial drones flown from hundreds, even thousands, of miles away against insurgent fighters located through cellphone intercepts serve to remind us that the RMA is alive and well.

Schmitt concludes by cautioning against responding to asymmetry through relaxation of the IHL's norms, reminding readers that 'war is a political decision for which the average citizen bears the burden, but not the responsibility' (p. 62). But he also cautions that military necessity must continue to be accounted for in the law if it is to retain the commitment of states.

The latter point lies at the heart of A.P.V. Rogers's essay, 'Zero-Casualty Warfare' (Chapter 3). Rogers, former Director of the British Army's Legal Services and a Fellow at Cambridge's Lauterpacht Centre, uses the 1999 NATO air campaign during the Kosovo conflict as a point of departure for examining the legal obligations attendant to collateral damage. The twentieth century has witnessed a dramatic rise in the risk of collateral damage for a number of reasons. Air power has made possible strikes deep into enemy territory where civilians are located. The size and mechanization of twentieth-century armies has increased military dependency on civilian-operated industrial production and logistics facilities, thereby making them advantageous targets. Since such entities tend to be based near population centres, attacking them has necessarily resulted in high levels of civilian casualties. Guerrilla warfare, especially prevalent in the post-Second World War era, places civilians at risk because guerillas typically operate among the people. And '[t]he understandable modern attitude of military commanders that they will not expose their subordinates to unnecessary risks tends to increase the danger to civilians' (p. 66). This attitude corresponds with 'growing pressure, especially in the West, to reduce military casualties to a minimum, otherwise public support for the campaign is likely to fall away' (ibid.) The consequence of these trends has been 'a steady increase in the ratio of civilian to military casualties in armed conflict despite the efforts of diplomats and international lawyers to emphasize the principle of civilian immunity' (p. 67).

Some commentators and war-fighters looked to 'smart weapons' – that is, those with highly accurate guidance systems – as the solution to this dilemma. Rogers correctly notes that expectations exceeded reality. Enemy air defence can affect accuracy by frustrating delivery, unreliable intelligence can lead to very accurate attacks on the wrong target, and human error can never be ruled out. A tragic incident during the Kosovo air campaign illustrates the problem. In order to stay outside the threat envelope of enemy surface-to-air missiles, NATO aircraft typically released their weapons from 15,000 feet. During one such attack, a group of civilian vehicles was attacked after being mistaken for a military convoy.

What must be understood is that honest mistakes do not violate international humanitarian law so long as the attacker took adequate precautions to minimize civilian casualties when planning and executing the attack. The law requires an attacker to do everything feasible to verify that the target is a lawful military objective, select weapons and tactics with an eye to reducing collateral damage (without forfeiting military advantage) and, when possible, issue warnings of attack. In cases of doubt as to the status of a potential target, it must be presumed to be civilian. To comply with the principle of proportionality, the expected collateral damage to civilians and civilian objects must not be excessive relative to the military advantage anticipated to accrue from the attack.

Rogers identifies the key dilemma facing those who conduct attacks – that measures taken to limit collateral damage may involve greater risk to an attacker. Nevertheless, he argues that '[m]ilitary necessity cannot always override humanity. In taking care to protect civilians, soldiers must accept some element of risk to themselves' (p. 75), although he acknowledges that the 'rule of proportionality is unclear as to what degree of care is required of a soldier and what degree of risk he must take' (ibid.). Applying his practical experience to the law, Rogers suggests a rule of engagement that might read as follows: 'Are you sure that the target is a military objective? If you are in any doubt, would you or friendly forces be placed in danger if the attack were not carried out? If not, the attack is NOT to be carried out' (p. 77).

Significantly, he points out that situations 'will occur when members of the armed forces will not be able to make … cool calculations' (p. 78). Therefore, the risk posed to the attacker is an important factor in assessing the proportionality principle in a case involving individual responsibility. Those making the assessment 'would have to put themselves in the position of the armed forces member concerned, taking all the surrounding circumstances into account, so as to experience the situation as he experienced it at the time, before considering the question of culpability' (ibid.).

As should be clear, the law governing attacks is replete with moral, operational and legal issues. For no rule is this truer than for that of proportionality, a topic explored by Kenneth Watkin, former Judge Advocate General of the Canadian forces and current Stockton Professor at the US Naval War College, in his essay 'Assessing Proportionality' (Chapter 4). When he wrote the essay, Canadian forces were heavily involved in combat operations in Afghanistan – a fact that lends the piece particular resonance.

Reflecting his practical experience, Watkin rejects narrow interpretations of the rule that civilians who directly participate in hostilities lose their protection from attack for such time as they so participate. He points out that 'for a state and its military forces waiting to react to an attack from such "civilians", such a narrow interpretation appears dramatically inconsistent with the nature of the threat presented by such members of armed groups' (p. 91).

That said, Watkin highlights the fact that the standard for targeting individuals differs from that which applies to strikes against military objectives. The latter is much more permissive. For instance, although workers in a munitions factory are fully civilians, the factory itself qualifies as a military objective. The workers may not be attacked directly, and any harm to them during an attack on the factory must be factored into the proportionality calculation. This example illustrates how 'humanitarian law can be interpreted to place a higher premium on life than on the damage or destruction to "objects"' (p. 91).

As with the debate over the scope of the notion of direct participation, disagreement prevails regarding the law governing attacks on objects. The most significant of these surrounds the meaning of the term 'military objective'. The United States interprets the term to extend to 'war-sustaining' entities, particularly those that provide the means to finance the war effort, such as oil exports. Most other countries limit it to war-fighting or war-supporting objects. Watkin notes that the US approach 'has been criticised as being too easily open to interpretation that could justify unleashing the type of indiscriminate attacks that occurred during World War II' and as a '"slippery slope" where every economic activity might be interpreted as indirectly sustaining the war effort' (p. 95). Thus, he concludes that '[t]he meaning to be given to this term introduces fundamental questions regarding the goals of armed conflict, how campaigns are waged and the impact of the levels of warfare on "proportionality"' (ibid.).

The rule of proportionality, and IHL more generally, traces its roots to the early Christian doctrine of 'double effect' which served to reconcile the absolute prohibition on attacking non-combatants with the need to fight effectively. In other words, it attempted to balance humanitarian considerations and military necessity. The doctrine provided that:

> ... it is permissible to perform an act that has 'evil' consequences if four conditions are met: the act is good in itself or at least indifferent; the direct effect is morally acceptable; the intention of the actor is a good one and the evil effect is not one of the ends or a means to an end; and the 'good effect' is sufficiently good to compensate for any evil outcome. (p. 104)

But application of this principle, as translated into the legal notion of distinction, is subject to varying analytical frameworks – pacifism, human rights, tactical-level control and the strategic approach. What one sees depends on where one stands.

Watkin concludes that 'it is not clear if any of them provides the sole means by which proportionality can be assessed' (p. 125) since each has strengths and weaknesses. He suggests that the protection of civilians can be enhanced

> ... if the principle of distinction is reinforced by more clearly identifying who can be targeted; greater accountability is demanded regarding the approach of considering attacks as part of a whole in addition to the attention often paid to tactical level effects; the importance of the right to life is emphasised; and those principles are applied rigorously at all levels of warfare. (p. 125)

He further urges the establishment (or reinforcement) of what he labels 'a culture of "due diligence"' (p. 125). Accordingly, he emphasizes the importance of a command climate in realizing both moral and legal ends.

Maritime Warfare

Maritime warfare is the focus of Part II of this volume. Unlike the principle of distinction, which was only codified in a meaningful way in the second half of the twentieth century, the law of maritime warfare has long been the subject of treaty law. At the 1907 Hague Peace Conference, for instance, conventions were adopted on the status of merchant ships, conversion of merchant ships into warships, the laying of automatic submarine contact mines, naval bombardment, hospital ships, the International Prize Court, and the right of capture and neutrality. In 1913 the Institute of Internal Law adopted a Manual on the Laws of Naval Warfare (the Oxford Manual) in preparation for a later peace conference (which was never held). After the First World War, the five victorious powers adopted a treaty on submarine warfare at the 1922 Washington Conference, although, due to the failure of France to ratify the instrument, it never entered into force. In 1928 a Convention on Maritime Neutrality was adopted, which largely reiterated the provisions of its 1907 Hague Conference counterpart. Two years later, the powers that concluded the abortive 1922 treaty on submarines adopted the Treaty of London for the Limitation and Reduction of Naval Armaments. Although most of the treaty expired six years later, the provision on submarines remained in force. During the Spanish Civil War, nine powers agreed, in the Nyon Agreement, to collective measures in the face of submarine attacks against merchant vessels. The last major treaty on naval warfare was the 1949 Geneva Convention (II) for the Amelioration of the Condition of Wounded, Sick and Shipwrecked Members of Armed Forces at Sea.

In an effort to capture changes in the customary law of naval warfare during and following the Second World War, as well as to reaffirm the earlier law that had survived, the International Institute of Humanitarian Law in San Remo convened a series of Round Tables between 1988 and 1994 attended by a group of international legal and naval experts. The resulting 'San Remo Manual' provides a restatement of the then existing international law applicable to armed conflicts at sea. Although non-binding, the San Remo Manual has become a touchstone for those working in the field.

Nevertheless, maritime operations continue to evolve. The twenty-first century has witnessed a resurgence of piracy, unprecedented international cooperation in addressing threats such as transnational terrorism and weapons of mass destruction and, most significantly from the perspective of the law of naval warfare, the use of blockades. In light of these developments, it is a propitious time to reflect upon the origins and content of the norms governing the conduct of hostilities at sea.

The first essay in Part II, 'Submarine Warfare' (Chapter 5), deals with a topic that has been at the forefront of the law of naval warfare since the turn of the twentieth century. It remains relevant in light of, for instance, the growth of the Chinese submarine fleet. Published in the aftermath of the controversial employment of submarines during the First World War and as the Washington Conference was looming by A. Pearce Higgins, then Whewell Professor of International Law at the University of Cambridge, it argues that the extant law adequately addresses the issues that arose during the conflagration, but urges greater enforcement efforts.

The law was relatively simple. Enemy warships could be attacked without visit or opportunity for surrender, while enemy merchant ships were liable to visit and capture, but steps had to be taken to ensure the safety of the crew. Captured ships were subject to prize proceedings, but could be destroyed on account of unseaworthiness, likelihood of recapture or impracticality of passage to a port. Merchantmen were permitted to be armed in self-defence, but if they forcefully resisted capture, they became subject to attack. Citing both customary and treaty law, Higgins confirms that a 'warship was not allowed to make the merchantman's possible strength the excuse for a surprise attack, or for sinking at sight' (pp. 137–38). Confirmed by the London Protocol of 1936, this generally remains the law today.

Yet, during the First World War such incidents periodically occurred; in the Second World War, they were common.

Neutral merchantmen were also subject to visit and search. In the event of carriage of contraband, attempted breach of blockade or the performance of other non-neutral service, they became liable to capture. Whether they could lawfully be destroyed was, according to Higgins, unsettled.

Submarines tested these requirements. As noted in a 1915 British Declaration to neutral states, German submarines could not put a prize crew on board captured vessels to sail them to a port, did not take captured vessels to prize courts, had difficulty distinguishing neutral from enemy vessels and did not bring aboard the crew of those they sank. The US Secretary of State made the same points, arguing that '"[m]anifestly submarines cannot be used against merchantmen ... without an inevitable violation of many sacred principles of justice and humanity"' (p. 143).[1]

For Higgins, the key legal obstacle lies in the inability to ensure the safety of the crew of captured or destroyed merchantmen. He rejects claims that 'the introduction of new weapons and new conditions of warfare demands the modification or alteration of the old rules' (p. 145), pointing out that other new means and methods, such as torpedoes, have been fielded without having to discard existing norms. In a proposition equally applicable to contemporary technological developments such as unmanned systems and cyber operations, Higgins emphasizes that '[w]ar is not conducted on the analogy of handicapping rules at race meetings ... New weapons are illegitimate if their use necessarily entails violation of fundamental principles' (p. 146).

As to claims that German actions might be characterized as reprisals against alleged British violations of the law, Higgins, without labelling them as such, reminds readers of the requirement that reprisals be proportionate. For Higgins, '[i]t is enough to say that no reprisals directed against enemy and neutral ships alike can be permitted which violate fundamental laws of humanity involving the certainty of death or mutilation to non-combatants, neutral as well as enemy' (p. 147).

Rejecting calls for abolition of the right to capture of private property at sea, ransom and bonding, Higgins concludes that:

> The attack on a merchant ship without previous warning is illegal and officers guilty of violating the rule are guilty of a war-crime. Submarines are legitimate means of attacking enemy commerce only if they conform to the laws of naval warfare hitherto observed by surface warships. (p. 150)

Reiterating a maxim as relevant today as it was then, he points to Article 22 of the 1907 Hague Regulations to remind readers that '[a]ll is not fair in war; in sea warfare as in land warfare, '"belligerents have not an unlimited right as to the choice of means for injuring the enemy"' (p. 151).

In 'The International Law of Mine Warfare at Sea' (Chapter 6), Wolff Heintschel von Heinegg, co-editor of these volumes, addresses a naval warfare technology that has similarly presented legal challenges. Although naval mine warfare stretches back well over a century,

---

1 Citing Mr Bryan, US Secretary of State, in a dispatch to the US Ambassador in Berlin, 18 May 1915.

the sole international instrument governing its use is the 1907 Hague Convention VIII. Given subsequent technical developments, he queries whether 'this treaty may still be considered adequate for securing the principle that the right of the parties to the conflict to chose methods and means of warfare is limited' (p. 155).

Treaty negotiations always reflect the particular national interests of the states involved. Hague Convention VIII was a post Russo-Japanese War accommodation between major sea powers such as Great Britain, which opposed the technology out of concern that it might compromise its naval superiority, and the majority of other states, which saw naval mines as a relatively cheap and effective means of countering enemy warships. The compromise adopted in the treaty involved a differentiation between anchored and unanchored mines. Unanchored mines had to become harmless within one hour; anchored mines were required to become harmless if they broke loose from their moorings.

With the Second World War's unrestricted mine warfare still fresh in the minds of commentators, post-war debates questioned the continued applicability of the restrictions. Von Heinegg holds that the convention has achieved customary status, but notes that it is unclear whether its provisions apply to bottom mines, modern anchored mines or remote-controlled minefields since they do not explode on contact, but rather react to magnetic and acoustic signatures or changes in water pressure. Mine warfare therefore offers an interesting case study in the applicability of weapons treaties to technology that has developed beyond that envisaged.

The essay is a *tour de force* on the present international law of mine warfare. Of particular importance are the geographical limits of the activity. Naval mines may only be laid in the general area of naval operations. They may not be placed in the territorial, internal or archipelagic waters of a state that is not party to a conflict and may not prevent passage between neutral and international waters. Parties laying mines must have 'due regard' for the rights of coastal states, such as those attaching in the exclusive economic zone. Importantly, von Heinegg notes that despite the unlimited mine warfare of the Second World War, state practice since then has established the principle that 'unless free and safe passage for peaceful shipping is provided for, the mining of the high seas is contrary to international law' (p. 162) and that closure of an international strait by mining 'will be legitimate only in exceptional cases and may not last indefinitely' (p. 163).

Von Heinegg stresses that, in mine warfare, 'the general principles of the (maritime) *jus in bello* equally apply, in particular the principle of distinction' (p. 164). He goes on to explore additional duties and prohibitions: effective surveillance, risk control, warning, precautionary measures, mine-laying with the sole object of intercepting commercial shipping and the removal or rendering harmless of mines at the close of an armed conflict.

When belligerents fail to meet their legal obligations, questions arise regarding the right of neutrals to take self-help measures to protect their shipping, such as removing free-floating mines. According to von Heinegg, consensus exists on the authority to do so beyond territorial waters, either based on the inherent right of self-defence or to enforce freedom of navigation. The more difficult legal issue is whether such an action is permissible in an international strait, which by definition overlaps territorial waters. Recall that in 1949 the International Court of Justice deemed Great Britain's removal of mines from Albanian waters a violation of international law in the *Corfu Channel* case. Von Heinegg argues that the present law of the sea transit passage regime supplants the holding. Accordingly, if belligerents engage in illegal mining and no alternative route of similar convenience exists, third states may remove the mines to effect their right of passage.

Naval mines illustrate how legal regimes can fail to keep up with emerging technologies. While it is often possible to interpret extant regimes fairly in changed circumstances, sometimes new law would ease the interpretive burden. In this particular case, von Heinegg concludes that '[t]he only promising means of achieving this aim is an international codification of the laws of naval warfare' (p. 176).

In 'Some Aspects of Modern Contraband Control and the Law of Prize' (Chapter 7), Sir Gerald Fitzmaurice, former Legal Adviser to the Foreign Office and Judge of the International Court of Justice (*inter alia*), examines contraband control, 'the aggregate of the techniques whereby a belligerent in a position to enforce such control by naval action seeks to prevent supplies from overseas reaching his enemy' (p. 177). The principal technique for doing so is:

> ... interception of the ships at sea, their diversion into port, the examination of their cargoes, and the seizure and placing in Prize ... of any consignments suspected on reasonable grounds of having enemy destination – to be eventually followed either by their final condemnation as prize by the Prize Court, or by their release if the case against them cannot be sustained. (p. 177)

The essay bears not only on the narrow topic of contraband and prize, but also on the dynamic of law's adaptation to the shifting realities of warfare. Fitzmaurice notes that the law of prize upon commencement of the Second World War was basically that in place at the end of the Napoleonic Wars. Yet, 'enormous changes had occurred both in the field of international commerce and in methods of warfare, changes not merely of scale and degree, but of kind' (p. 178). The British government, therefore, 'was obliged to have frequent recourse to the [Prize] Court, not merely to obtain the actual condemnation as Prize of ships and goods that had been seized, but also in order to test, directly or indirectly, its right to effect any seizure at all in novel cases' (ibid.).

One point that appears to have been clarified by practices during the war involved a distinction between condemnation and seizure of goods. In the nineteenth century, seized goods had to be condemned. Otherwise, if released for any reason, the goods might find their way to the enemy because the law did not prevent reshipment. However, by *Falk*, a 1921 decision of the Privy Council, the release of seized goods in the United Kingdom did not relieve the owner of legal obligations attendant to their 'export', which might result in denial of an export licence in the event that there was a chance of subsequent trans-shipment to the enemy.

Practice during the war also established the principle that the owner of goods seized in Prize was often entitled only to their fair market value, and not the goods themselves. In some cases, they (or the vessels transporting them) were sold or requisitioned before the Prize proceedings to preclude, for instance, the chance that they might find their way to the enemy. Fitzmaurice concludes that:

> The theory underlying the sale or requisitioning of seized goods is (*a*) that it would be unreasonable that goods the preservation of which was difficult or impossible, or which were urgently required

> for national use, should have to be kept *in specie* to await the outcome of the proceedings, and (*b*) that the rights of the claimant are not prejudiced since, if an order for release is made in his favour, he will obtain, if not the goods themselves, their value. (p. 185)

Another method of contraband control was, and remains, the 'navicert' system, whereby a belligerent authority issues a certificate that indicates a lack of objection to the cargo in question. Institution of the system raised legal questions as to its legal basis. Today, Fitzmaurice's explanation is universally accepted:

> The system … rests…on the ordinary and acknowledged right of a belligerent to intercept any vessel at sea, to divert her into port for examination, to seize any items of cargo suspected on reasonable grounds of being enemy-owned or of having an enemy destination, and in certain circumstances to seize the ship also. In instituting a navicert system a belligerent in effect announces that, subject to a general reservation of his rights, he will not in practice exercise them if certain specified requirements are fulfilled by ship and cargo, and if certificates to that effect are issued by his competent authorities. (p. 187)

The absence of a navicert is not per se grounds for seizure of a vessel; nor are belligerents obliged to issue them. Fitzmaurice, therefore, hesitantly justifies the British 1940 Reprisals Order permitting seizure of vessels without a navicert as 'a legitimate act of reprisals, to simplify the conduct of the blockade' (p. 193).

A third method of contraband control is 'rationing' which is based on the precept that it is 'only by limiting neutrals who have land communications with enemy territory to their own strict necessities in the matter of overseas imports that it is possible to ensure that no substantial proportion of these will reach the enemy' (p. 193). In other words, if a country imports more than it requires, a rebuttable presumption attaches that the excess will go to the enemy. In rationing, the belligerent fixes the amount of reasonable necessities, blocking imports exceeding the figure.

Fitzmaurice points to the problems inherent in the system. Even if it can be assumed that imports are excessive, for example, there is no way of determining that any goods seized are actually bound for the enemy. Absent other evidence supporting such a system, Fitzmaurice opines that Prize Courts will be hesitant to condemn the goods, although he suggests that statistical evidence of excessive imports is a ground for the initial seizure. Obviously, this third method of contraband control is on normatively thin ice.

In light of the controversial Israeli blockade of Gaza, as well as its earlier blockade of Lebanon, issues surrounding the legality and lawful execution of naval blockades are again attracting attention. The law of naval blockade is also proving highly relevant with regard to the possible normative framework for aerial and cyber blockades. In 'Naval Blockade' (Chapter 8), Wolff Heintschel von Heinegg, who was one of the key drafters of the San Remo Manual on International Law Applicable to Armed Conflict at Sea, examines the law governing blockades in its contemporary context.

A blockade is 'a belligerent operation to prevent vessels and/or aircraft of all nations, enemy as well as neutral, from entering or exiting specified ports, airfields, or coastal areas belonging to, occupied by, or under the control of an enemy nation' (p. 201). Although blockades were historically employed as a means of economic warfare since the Second World War, the more common practice is to employ them as part of a military strategy designed to deprive the enemy of external support.

Clearly, blockades mounted during an armed conflict must comport with the maritime *jus in bello*. However, the relationship of blockade law to other legal regimes remains somewhat unsettled. As von Heinegg points out, the 'extent [to which] the *jus ad bellum* also serves as a yardstick for naval blockades is a highly disputed issue' (p. 202).

Following a comprehensive discussion of the historical background of blockade law, he turns to contemporary practice. Recent state practice has discredited any suggestion that blockades have become obsolete. In particular, '[b]lockade remains an especially efficient method for subduing the enemy in limited armed conflicts' (p. 211). It is similarly effective in cutting off enemy exports that provide the funding necessary to prosecute a conflict.

While the traditional requirements that a blockade be declared, notified and impartial are easily met during modern blockade operations, disagreement exists over the fourth – effectiveness. All commentators agree with the general premise that modern technology has relieved blockading states of any obligation to deploy its forces close to the blockaded coastline or ports. Modern technology makes it possible to enforce blockades from great distances because of the speed and observation capabilities of platforms and the range and precision of weapons. Von Heinegg sagely concludes that naval blockading forces 'may choose a combination of legitimate methods and means of warfare provided this combination does not result in acts inconsistent with the other rules and principles of the maritime *jus in bello*' (pp. 212–13). These can include aircraft, submarines and naval mines, although mines, in light of the current state of the technology, may not be used alone to maintain a blockade because certain categories of vessels cannot be barred from passing through the blockaded area. He further concludes that a blockade need not exclusively serve either a military or an economic purpose.

Von Heinegg rejects the application of the doctrine of continuous voyage, which the US *Commander's Handbook on the Law of Naval Operations* adopts. By this doctrine, a vessel or aircraft can be intercepted at any point on its voyage so long as the ultimate destination is the blockaded area, regardless of whether an intermediate port of call is in neutral territory. Von Heinegg argues that the doctrine would render meaningless the requirement of effectiveness if belligerents were permitted to enforce a blockade far from a blockaded area:

> As long as neutral merchant vessels are situated outside the range of operations of the forces maintaining the blockade, and as long as they do not carry contraband or act in a way that makes them liable to attack, the freedoms of navigation and overflight supersede the belligerents' interest in a comprehensive prohibition of imports to their respective enemies. (p. 214)

The extent to which the rules governing blockade apply to a blockade mandated by the UN Security Council remains unsettled. Perhaps most importantly, von Heinegg takes the position that 'in the case of enforcement measures under Chapter VII, there is no room for neutrality' (p. 216). As a result, third states can be affected to whatever extent envisioned in the mandate. The mandate may even authorize interception at great distances from the blockade area, thereby obviating von Heinegg's rejection of the doctrine of continuous voyage. And since these blockades are ordered by the Security Council, there is no requirement for effectiveness. Nevertheless, because UN blockades rely on states' armed forces for enforcement, the rules of the maritime *jus in bello* apply.

In 'The Exclusion Zone Device in the Law of Naval Warfare' (Chapter 9), William Fenrick, then with the Canadian Forces as Director of International Law and later Senior Legal Adviser at the International Criminal Tribunal for Yugoslavia, deals with a area of maritime operations that was used in both World Wars and in the Iran–Iraq conflict. However, its use came to international attention with the sinking of the Argentinean cruiser, the *Belgrano*, outside the British-declared exclusion zone during the Falklands conflict. The sinking was widely, and counter-normatively, criticized as a violation of international law.

As a general matter, belligerents may conduct combat operations on the high seas, including the exclusive economic zone, and in the territorial and internal waters of belligerent states. Within the immediate area of naval operations, they may restrict or prohibit neutral vessel presence. An exclusion zone, as examined by Fenrick, is 'an area of water and superjacent air space in which a party to an armed conflict purports to exercise control and to which it denies access to ships and aircraft without permission' (p. 230). As such, it interferes with the navigational rights vessels enjoy pursuant to the law of the sea.

Fenrick sets forth a rich historical account of zone practices, as well as attacks on merchantmen, including an analysis of the trial of Admirals Doenitz and Raeder before the International Military Tribunal at Nuremberg. Practices throughout the Second World War did not crystallize the law regarding exclusion zones. Some post-war writers argued that zones which present a risk of ships being attacked on sight are illegal. Others accepted them, but imposed requirements of effective control over the zone and set out measures necessary to avoid imperilling neutrals and non-combatants. Still others claimed that the zones could be enforced by a sink-on-sight policy as to neutral and belligerent shipping that was incorporated into the belligerent war effort.

Drawing on the experience of the complicated series of zones established by Argentina and the United Kingdom during the Falklands conflict, Fenrick offers a number of important conclusions. First, he dispenses with arguments that 'one party to a conflict can only attack another party's warships, naval auxiliaries, and military aircraft within certain circumscribed areas in a limited conflict' by noting that 'the evidence of such an obligation in customary law is insufficient. Any restrictions concerning attacks on an opponent's warships, naval auxiliaries, and military aircraft outside neutral waters or territory, which are observed by a party to a limited conflict, are voluntary self-limitations' (p. 253).

Fenrick looks to the Iran–Iraq tanker war in his assessment of attacks on neutral shipping. Both sides declared exclusion zones in the Persian Gulf, designed to impede their opponent's oil exports. In the Iraqi zone, most targets were neutral tankers proceeding to and from oil-loading facilities in Iranian territory (Kharg Island), some of which were convoyed by Iranian warships and therefore subject to attack. As to the others, Fenrick concludes that:

> It is debatable whether or not unconvoyed neutral tankers can be considered as incorporated into the Iranian war effort. The tankers are unarmed and are not integrated into the Iranian intelligence system. It is, however, possible to argue that the tankers are essential to the Iranian war economy

> and, just as oil refineries and trains may be attacked in war on land, so may targets be legitimately attacked at sea. (p. 259)

The illegality of many Iranian attacks was clearer, since Iran attacked neutral vessels in transit to and from neutral ports outside the exclusion zones, sometimes even in neutral waters. Fenrick observes that '[e]ven if one concedes that the other Gulf states are providing financial support to Iraq, it does not appear possible to consider the neutral ships engaged in traffic with these states to be incorporated into the Iraqi war effort' (p. 259).

Various factors will inevitably influence perceptions of legality as to particular exclusion zones. Belligerents should 'publicly declare the existence, location, and duration of the zones, what is excluded from the zone, and the sanctions likely to be imposed on ships and aircraft entering the zone without permission, and also provide enough lead time before the zone comes into effect to allow ships to clear the area' (p. 262). Like blockades, they should be 'effective', and the minimum steps to enforce them, such as seizure rather than attack, should be employed. Measures must be taken to properly identify vessels entering a zone, there must be a nexus between the zone and the belligerent's defensive needs, and if the zone is in an area of high traffic, special routes should be provided for merchant shipping. The legality of the zone will also depend on its size, location, duration and purpose.

Air Warfare

The final two essays, comprising Part III, address air warfare. This issue regained prominence in the post-Second World War era with the Coalition air campaign against Iraq in 1991, a massive country-wide bombardment that laid the groundwork for the 100-hour ground campaign. The 'shock and awe' air attacks against Iraq in 2003 further heightened international sensitivity concerning the law of aerial operations. More recently, the use of unmanned aerial vehicles (UAVs) in counter-insurgency and counter-terrorist operations has drawn the attention of the international humanitarian law community. What is unique about the law of air and missile warfare is that no treaty specifically addresses air warfare as such. Rather, treaty law deals with the subject only indirectly (as in prohibiting or restricting the use of certain weapons that may be air-delivered, like incendiaries, cluster munitions or anti-personnel mines) or in a limited fashion (as in Additional Protocol I's limitation to air-to-ground attacks).

Instead, the law of air warfare consists primarily of soft-law instruments. The 1923 Hague Rules of Air Warfare, which were produced by a Commission of Jurists established by the Washington Conference on the Limitation of Armament, are authoritative, but non-binding. In 2004, Harvard University's Program on Humanitarian Policy and Conflict Research (HPCR) launched a multi-year project to capture the customary law applicable to air warfare. The resulting 2009 *Manual on International Law Applicable to Air and Missile Warfare* is the sole comprehensive contemporary treatment of the subject. It, too, is non-binding.

In his essay, 'Area Bombardment' (Chapter 10), Hans Blix, then Minister of Foreign Affairs for Sweden, examines the 1977 Additional Protocols as they relate to air attack. Published in 1978, the essay is important in the sense that it came immediately on the heels of the Diplomatic Conference convened to draft the Protocols and was authored by a representative of a state highly supportive of them. Although the title seemingly limits coverage to area attacks, the piece relates to air attacks more generally.

The Protocols were adopted at a particularly important time in the history of air warfare. The mass bombing campaigns of the Second World War had raised the question of the scope of international law governing such operations. After all, no treaty on point existed. Moreover, the International Military Tribunal at Nuremberg had dealt with no cases involving aerial bombing. The Vietnam War, which involved thousands of air strikes, again drew widespread international attention. Many scholars and states highlighted the absence of *lex scripta* and called for the Diplomatic Conference to fill the void.

Blix surveys the provisions of Additional Protocol I, which was limited in application to air-to-ground operations (as distinct from air-to-air, air-to-sea and sea/ground-to-air), relevant to air attacks. The Protocol prohibits direct attacks on civilians, attacks intended to terrorize the civilian population and indiscriminate attacks. Commenting on these prohibitions, Blix rejects the notion of 'quasi combatants', such as workers in armament factories, pointing to Article 51(3), which only deprives civilians of protection when they are direct participants in hostilities.

It must be emphasized that the morale of the civilian population is not a lawful military objective – even of factory workers and others indirectly involved in the war effort. Blix is careful to highlight the fact that the prohibition on acts or threats of violence that have a 'primary purpose' of spreading terror among the civilian population only bans attacks where the intent is to terrorize, as distinct from those with a military purpose but which incidentally cause fear among the civilian population. Perceptively, he notes that '[i]t is an odd result of the text that it would seem permissible to carry out acts which have "terror" as a secondary purpose' (p. 282). This appears to be an acknowledgement that attackers can hope that civilian morale will be affected so long as their main intent is to harm military objectives, combatants or civilians directly participating in the hostilities.

Blix deconstructs the prohibition on indiscriminate attacks into three key elements:

> (a) that targets must be *identified* with some certainty as military objectives;
> (b) that attacks must be *directed* to such identified targets, and
> (c) that the weapons and methods must be such that the target may be hit with some degree of likelihood. (p. 284, emphasis in original)

At the Conference, Blix argued that some weapons were themselves indiscriminate (rather than subject to indiscriminate use), citing as an example the German V-1s. Other delegates rejected this position, leading Blix to surmise that 'this attitude was taken to foreclose any discussion of the question whether nuclear weapons are inevitably indiscriminate' (p. 286).

The remainder of the essay deals with area bombardment, the subject of Article 51(5)(a) of Additional Protocol I. That article prohibits 'bombardment by any methods or means which treats as a single military objective a number of clearly separated and distinct military objectives located in a city, town, village or other area containing a similar concentration of civilians or civilian objects'.

Blix struggles with the legality of bombing of cities during the Second World War, cataloguing the various views on the subject. He does identify one common thread in the debate – 'legitimate military objectives may be so *concentrated* in a single area that the whole area can be regarded as a military objective' (p. 293, emphasis in original). The final formulation of Article 51 amounted to a compromise between those who wished to limit the provision to urban areas, on the one hand, and delegations which sought to extend it to any area at all, on the other.

The issue of military objectives not in close proximity proved contentious. Some delegates wanted to expressly state that the prohibition applied when it was reasonably possible to separately attack the objectives. But this was rejected as affording too much latitude to the attackers. Usefully, Blix explains the difference between the terms 'separate' and 'distinct'. 'Separate' refers to distance. 'Distinct', by contrast, has to do with whether they can be attacked individually. In other words, if an attack on a military objective employs weapons which have a blast effect reaching other military objectives, those objectives are not distinct. Blix perceptively points out that 'with the development of "smart bombs" guided by laser or other devices, which allow precision attacks, perhaps more targets become "distinct"' (p. 302).

The final essay is W. Hays Parks's classic 'Air War and the Law of War' (Chapter 11). Written while Parks was Chief of the International Law Team for the US army, just prior to the massive air campaign against Iraq that commenced in 1991, it is a sweeping survey of the history and law of aerial warfare. Just as importantly, it is an incisive commentary on the state of international humanitarian law at the time, particularly Additional Protocol I.

The first section of the essay deals with the norms governing air warfare prior to and during the Second World War and whether these norms were observed by the belligerents. Parks concludes that:

> An air planner in any nation in the interwar era as well as during World War II ... would have found it impossible to find clear, well-defined, express language prohibiting or permitting the actions he was contemplating ... He would have been unable to find a comprehensive list of objects that legitimately could be considered military objects; and, in particular, he would not have been able to find appropriate language explaining the distinction between combatants and noncombatants ... (p. 356)

Although a prohibition on indiscriminate attack existed,

> [a] longstanding practice of nations was that collateral civilian casualties were not only an inevitable result of bombardment, but the cost to a nation of engaging in war; their avoidance was the principal responsibility of the defender, who had exclusive control over the civilian population. (p. 357)

Moreover, the term 'indiscriminate' was 'without legal definition' (p. 358).

Parks usefully describes the standard of 'careful distinction' during operations as 'one of ordinary care by a reasonable man under the same or similar circumstances' (pp. 358–59) and suggests that '[n]o greater standard of care has been proposed in the years that have passed since World War II' (p. 359). Typical of his very practical approach to international humanitarian law, he also notes that since 'the law of war is not a suicide pact … [i]t does not require that an attacker employ the most discriminate force available to him' (p.360).

Of course, the watershed event in the post-Geneva Conventions development of international humanitarian law was the adoption of Additional Protocol I. Parks offers a scathing critic of the Protocols. While he concedes that Additional Protocol II on non-international armed conflict represented 'a minor advance in the protection of innocent civilians … Protocol I diminished rather than advanced the law of war' (p. 400). He highlights two key issues to substantiate this characterization.

First, Protocol I prohibits reprisals against the civilian population or civilian objects. As a legal term, reprisals are illegal acts undertaken for the purpose of compelling the enemy to desist in its own illegal activity. As such, they 'have proved necessary and effective in preventing violations of the law of war' (p. 401), as in the case of Roosevelt's threat to employ chemical weapons if Germany resorted to them.

Second, Parks criticizes Article 44(3) of the Protocol, which requires combatants to 'distinguish themselves from the civilian population' (a historical obligation), but relieves them of the obligation where, 'owing to the nature of the hostilities', they cannot do so. In such cases, the combatant need only carry arms openly during military engagements and while deploying to such when visible to the enemy. Parks contends that 'automatically to deny combatant status [and therefore prisoner-of-war status if captured] to a guerrilla served as a disincentive to that individual to comply with the law of war' (p. 404). For Parks, the removal of the distinction requirement permits 'an organization to assert a claim as a legitimate belligerent while ignoring its law of war obligations' (p. 407).

Parks harbours many other concerns. For instance, although there is universal agreement with the general principle of distinction, he questions:

> (a) use of the term 'attack;' (b) the definition of who is a civilian and who is a combatant; (c) the definition of what is a military objective as opposed to a civilian object; (d) the placing of equal emphasis on the protection of civilian objects as is provided civilians and, commensurately, a diminishment of the value of the lives of one's own combatants; and (e) assignment of responsibility for collateral civilian casualties between attacker and defender. (p. 419)

He finds that the principle of proportionality is undeniably an element of customary international law, but takes issue with its expression in the Protocol, arguing that it is vague, requires the 'assumption of risk by an attacker for the action or inaction of the defender' (p. 481) and focuses on results rather than intent.

For Parks, the Protocol 'fail[s] to consider what Clausewitz referred to as the friction of war' (p. 488). He concludes:

> Cloaked in a humanitarian guise, the articles of Protocol I were drafted with a view to off-setting any military advantage a superior enemy force might have – particularly an air power – in attacking another nation within that other nation's territory. (p. 524)

MICHAEL N. SCHMITT

Part I
Distinction

[1]

PROTECTION OF CIVILIANS AGAINST THE EFFECTS OF HOSTILITIES UNDER CUSTOMARY INTERNATIONAL LAW AND UNDER PROTOCOL I

Waldemar A. Solf*

INTRODUCTION

Humanitarian law is the outgrowth of centuries of warfare from which the rules and customs governing the conduct of hostilities have developed. Its development was stimulated by military men who recognized that violence and destruction, which are superfluous to actual military necessity, are not only immoral and wasteful of scarce resources, but are also counter-productive to the attainment of the political objectives for which military force is used.

The purpose of this presentation is to outline the historical development of restraints on the methods and means of warfare, their acceptance as customary law binding on all states, and the relation of customary law to the codifications of international law in the Hague Conventions of 1907,[1] the Geneva Conventions of 1949,[2] and the 1977

* Adjunct Professor of Law, Washington College of Law, The American University; Member, U.S. Delegation to the Diplomatic Conference on International Humanitarian Law, 1974-1977.

This Article is based on a speech delivered by the author at a Seminar for Diplomats on Humanitarian Law sponsored by the American Red Cross and The American University, Washington College of Law in June, 1985. The editors and staff of the *American University Journal of International Law and Policy* have provided supplementary footnotes for this Article.

1. Hague Convention No. IV of 18 October 1907, Respecting the Laws and Customs of War on Land, 36 Stat. 2227, T.S. No. 539 [hereinafter cited as Hague Convention No. IV] and the annex thereto, embodying the Regulations Respecting the Laws and Customs of War on Land, 36 Stat. 2295 [hereinafter cited as Hague Regulations]; Hague Convention No. V of 18 October 1907, Respecting the Rights and Duties of Neutral Powers and Persons in Case of War on Land, 36 Stat. 2310, T.S. No. 540 [hereinafter cited as Hague Convention No. V]; Hague Convention No. IX of 18 October 1907, Respecting Bombardment by Naval Forces in Time of War, 36 Stat. 2351, T.S. No. 542 [hereinafter cited as Hague Convention No. IX].

2. Geneva Convention for the Amelioration of the Condition of the Wounded and Sick in Armed Forces in the Field of 12 August 1949, 6 U.S.T. 3114, T.I.A.S. No. 3362, 75 U.N.T.S. 31 [hereinafter cited as First Geneva Convention of 1949]; Geneva Convention for the Amelioration of the Condition of the Wounded, Sick and Shipwrecked Members of Armed Forces at Sea of 12 August 1949, 6 U.S.T. 3217, T.I.A.S. No. 3363, 75 U.N.T.S. 85 [hereinafter cited as Second Geneva Convention of 1949]; Geneva Convention Relative to the Treatment of Prisoners of War of 12 August 1949, 6 U.S.T. 3316, T.I.A.S. No. 3364, 75 U.N.T.S. 135 [hereinafter cited as Third Geneva Convention of 1949]; Geneva Convention Relative to the Protection of Civilian Persons

Protocol I additional to the Geneva Conventions.[3]

I. THE HISTORICAL DEVELOPMENT OF THE PRINCIPLES OF RESTRAINT ON THE METHODS AND MEANS OF WARFARE

Throughout history, men have preached about the restraints on the methods and means of warfare. As early as the fourth century B.C., Sun Tzu's classic, *The Art of War*, noted that there was an obligation to care for the wounded and prisoners of war.[4] He observed that atrocities infuriated the enemy, stiffened their resistance and increased their fighting ability instead of paralyzing them with terror.[5]

In 634 A.D., Caliph Abu Bakr exhorted the first Moslem Arab Army invading Christian Syria to learn certain rules by heart:

> Do not commit treachery, nor depart from the right path. You must not mutilate, neither kill a child or aged man or woman. Do not destroy a palm tree, nor burn it with fire and do not cut any fruitful tree. You must not slay any of the flock or the herds or the camels, save for your subsistence. You are likely to pass by people who have devoted their lives to monastic services; leave them to that to which they have devoted their lives.[6]

Shakespeare quotes Henry V, instructing his army on the march to Agincourt in 1415: "[W]e give express charge, that in our marches through the country, there be nothing compelled from the villages, nothing taken but paid for, none of the French upbraided or abused in disdainful language; for when lenity and cruelty play for a kingdom, the gentler gamester is the soonest winner."[7]

In 1923, Admiral William L. Rodgers, an acute observer of war, wrote in a lead article in the *American Journal of International Law*:

> It pleases us to call rules of war humanitarian, but really they fulfill a double object: as toward the individual enemy these restrictive rules are humane; as towards one's own organized forces these restrictives promote discipline and efficiency, and so help to shorten war through earlier and more complete victory over the hostile state . . . [T]hus these so called humane rules are advantageous

in Time of War of 12 August 1949, 6 U.S.T. 3516, T.I.A.S. No. 3365, 75 U.N.T.S. 287 [hereinafter cited as Fourth Geneva Convention of 1949] [all four hereinafter collectively cited as the Geneva Convention of 1949].

3. Protocol Additional to the Geneva Conventions of 1949, and Relating to the Protection of Victims of International Conflicts (Protocol I), *opened for signature* Dec. 12, 1977, *reprinted in* THE LAWS OF ARMED CONFLICTS 551 (D. Schindler & J. Toman 2d rev. ed. 1981) [hereinafter cited as Protocol I].

4. SUN TZU, THE ART OF WAR 75-76 (S. Griffith trans. 1963).

5. *Id.*

6. M. KHADDURI, WAR AND PEACE IN THE LAW OF ISLAM 102 (1955).

7. W. Shakespeare, *The Life of Henry the Fifth*, act III, sc. vi (1599).

simultaneously to both sides.[8]

Most of the early rules of war were in the form of orders issued by sovereign authorities for the regulation of their own armed forces. In time, various practices of civilized nations, all of whom imposed similar limitations on their own actions, became regarded as rules binding on them all.

The Catholic Church exercised significant influence in the development of restraints in war from the fourth century A.D. The early Christians were extreme pacifists who considered military service incompatible with Christian principles.[9] As a minority and dissident sect with no responsibility for the security of the empire, they could savor their moral superiority and venerate their martyrs to the cause of pacifism.[10] But when Caesar became a Christian, the Church, as an accommodation, developed the Just War Doctrine which accepted the necessity of going to war for a just cause.[11] The Just War Doctrine dealt primarily with the conditions justifying resort to war: the *jus ad bellum*; it also held that the conduct of the just war, *jus in bello*, must conform to the principles of discrimination and proportion.[12]

The principle of discrimination prescribed the immunity of the innocent from direct attack. Who are the innocent? Francisco de Vitoria, the noted theologian and jurist, included women, children, "harmless agricultural folk," "the rest of the peaceable civilian population," and "clerics and members of a religious order."[13] Realizing that collateral casualties among the innocent must be expected, theologians recognized the rule of "double effect," distinguishing intended killing of combatants from unintended, accidental killing of civilians.[14] The latter is excusable. But what about a situation where it is expected that there will be unintended killings? Vitoria concludes: "[I]t is never right to slay the guiltless, even as an indirect and unintended result, except when there is no other means of carrying on the operations of a just war . . . . "[15] In such a case the principle of proportion becomes dominant.[16]

8. Rodgers, *Suggestions as to Changes in the International Law for Maritime Warfare*, 17 AM. J. INT'L L. 1, 4 (1923).
9. S. BAILEY, PROHIBITIONS AND RESTRAINTS IN WAR 2 (1972).
10. *Id.* at 1-2.
11. *Id.* at 3-5.
12. *Id.* at 12.
13. F. DE VITORIA, DE INDIS ET DE IURE BELLI RELECTIONES 179 (J. Bate trans. 1917 of 1696 ed.).
14. *Id.* at 179; *see also* BAILEY, *supra* note 9, at 12-13.
15. VITORIA, *supra* note 13, at 179.
16. BAILEY, *supra* note 9, at 13-14. "For if little effect upon the ultimate issue of the

The principles of restraint and the influence of the natural law principles of discrimination and proportion virtually disappeared in the unrestrained savagery of the Thirty Years War from 1618-1648. The Peace of Westphalia[17] also diminished the influence of the Church by recognizing the absolute sovereignty of princes, each of whom had a direct pipeline to God. In 1625, Hugo Grotius published his masterwork, *The Law of War and Peace*, in which he analyzed the practice of states over the centuries in order to outline systematically how that practice had hardened into the law of nations.[18]

The 18th century Age of Reason was an era of limited wars during which the restraints of the *jus in bello* became well known to the professional soldiers of the time. Armies were relatively small and very expensive; limited violence was an exercise of prudent self interest. Various nations entered into bilateral treaties, addressing in advance particular questions which might arise in the event of war between the parties. The subjects commonly covered were the rights of alien citizens, the rules of naval prizes, the status of diplomats, the limitations of legitimate military targets and the protection of prisoners of war.

The Napoleonic war and the French Revolution put an end to the era of limited warfare. Thereafter, wars were fought by nations in arms. The entire population was mobilized for the war effort, blurring the distinction between combatants and civilians, putting great strain on the customary law of war. As Winston Churchill commented: "When democracy forced itself upon the battlefield war ceased to be a gentleman's game."[19] Nevertheless, the customary *jus in bello* survived, taking modest account of changed conditions of warfare. The mobilization of mass armies necessitated precise codified rules which would serve as instruction to citizen armies.

---

war is to be expected from the storming of a fortress or fortified town wherein are many innocent folk, it would not be right, for the purpose of assailing a few guilty, to slay the many innocent by use of . . . means likely to overwhelm indifferently both innocent and guilty." VITORIA, *supra* note 13, at 179. The principle of proportion also holds that it is forbidden to use weapons which would cause unnecessary suffering or superfluous injury. "The aim [of the this element of the modern rules] was not primarily to spare civilians, but to avoid causing suffering to combatants in excess of what is essential to place an adversary *hors de combat*." BAILEY, *supra* note 9, at 79-80. *See also infra* note 78 and accompanying text (discussing the rule of proportionality).

17. Treaty of Peace Between Sweden and the Empire, signed at Osnabruck (Peace of Westphalia I), 24 Oct. 1648, 1 Consol. Treaty Series 119; Treaty of Peace Between France and the Empire, signed at Munster (Peace of Westphalia II), 24 Oct. 1648, 1 Consol. Treaty Series 271.

18. H. GROTIUS, DE JURE BELLI ET PACIS LIBRI TRES (F. Kelsey trans. 1925 of 1625 ed.); BAILEY, *supra* note 9, at 25.

19. Winston Churchill, *quoted in* Ford, *Resistance Movements and International Law*, 8 INT'L REV. RED CROSS 43 (1968).

II. ACCEPTANCE AND CODIFICATION OF THE RESTRAINTS ON THE METHODS AND MEANS OF WARFARE

The first systematic codification of the restraints on the methods and means of warfare was the *Instructions for the Government of the Armies of the United States in the Field*, prepared by Professor Francis Lieber in 1863 during the American Civil War.[20] The Lieber Instructions took into account the needs of a nation in arms and the influence of the Industrial Revolution. Lieber's treatment of the principle of military necessity is significant: "Military necessity, as understood by modern civilized nations, consists in the necessity of those measures which are indispensable for securing the ends of the war, and *which are lawful according to the modern law and usages of war*" (emphasis added).[21] Lieber outlined in considerable detail those measures which were permitted and those which were prohibited by customary law. Among the measures prohibited was "any act of hostility which makes the return to peace unnecessarily difficult."[22] To promote understanding, the Lieber Instructions stated the reasons for each rule. In this respect it was a fairly accurate reflection of the customary law of war as it was understood in 1863.

The Lieber Instructions stimulated efforts to codify the law applicable to armed conflict, culminating in the Brussels Conference of 1874,[23] which laid the groundwork for the Hague Conventions of 1899[24] and 1907.[25] The Hague Conventions were not as comprehensive as the Lieber Instructions. The Hague Conventions omitted the reasons for the rules,[26] and with few exceptions, limited the text to prohibitions without stating what was permitted. This practice was based on the belief of humanitarian scholars that a humanitarian instrument should provide what is to be spared, and should not explicitly authorize violence.[27] Frequently, this restraint sacrificed clarity; military men

20. U.S. DEP'T OF WAR, INSTRUCTIONS FOR THE GOVERNMENT OF THE ARMIES OF THE UNITED STATES IN THE FIELD, GENERAL ORDERS No. 100 (1863) (Lieber Instructions), *reprinted in* THE LAWS OF ARMED CONFLICTS 3 (D. Schindler & J. Toman 2d rev. ed. 1981) [hereinafter cited as Lieber Instructions].

21. Lieber Instructions, *supra* note 20, at art. 14.

22. *Id.* at art. 16.

23. Project of an International Declaration Concerning the Laws & Customs of War, Brussels Conference of 1874, *reprinted in* 1 AM. J. INT'L L. Supp. 96-103 (1907).

24. Hague Convention No. II of 29 July 1899, with Respect to the Laws and Customs of War on Land, 32 Stat. 1803, *reprinted in* 1 AM. J. INT'L L. Supp. 129-53 (1907).

25. Hague Convention No. IV, *supra* note 1.

26. *Cf.* Martens Clause, *infra* notes 28-29 and accompanying text.

27. In the debates concerning article 18 of the First Geneva Convention providing

tended to consider permissible any measure not expressly prohibited. This was in error, for customary law remained in full force, except to the extent modified by conventional law.

The preambles to the Hague Convention No. II of 1899 and the Hague Convention No. IV of 1907 each contain a Martens Clause[28] the latter of which states:

> [T]he High Contracting Parties clearly do not intend that unforeseen cases should, in the absence of a written undertaking, be left to the arbitrary judgment of military commanders.
>
> Until a more complete code of the laws of war has been issued, the High Contracting Parties deem it expedient to declare that, in cases not included in the Regulations adopted by them, the inhabitants and the belligerents remain under the protection and rule of the principles of the law of nations, as they result from the usages established among civilized peoples, from the laws of humanity, and the dictates of the public conscience.[29]

The rules of the 1907 Hague Regulations were negotiated with military necessity in mind, and cited necessity expressly to justify derogations from certain prohibitory rules.[30] Necessity, however, is not defined. The reluctance to express what is authorized under customary law made it necessary for military manuals to fill in the lacunae, including a statement as to the meaning and limitations of military necessity.

The First Geneva Convention of 1864[31] became the first multilateral

---

for the role of the civilian population in collecting and caring for the wounded and sick, the drafting committee rejected a proposal that the civilian population could not withhold the wounded and sick they had collected from possible control by the military authorities. While recognizing that the authorities had the undoubted right to issue regulations establishing such control, the committee did not believe this should be mentioned in a humanitarian instrument. INT'L COMM. OF THE RED CROSS, COMMENTARY: GENEVA CONVENTION FOR THE AMELIORATION OF THE CONDITION OF WOUNDED AND SICK IN ARMED FORCES IN THE FIELD 190 (J. Pictet ed. 1952); *see also* M. BOTHE, K. PARTSCH & W. SOLF, NEW RULES FOR VICTIMS OF ARMED CONFLICTS: COMMENTARY ON THE TWO 1977 PROTOCOLS ADDITIONAL TO THE GENEVA CONVENTIONS OF 1949 322 (1982) (concerning objections voiced in the 1974-77 Diplomatic Conference about the departure from tradition in the definition of military objectives).

28. The Martens Clause is named after Fyodor Martens, the Russian diplomat and jurist who drafted it. A similar formula appears in each of the 1949 Geneva Conventions and in the 1977 Protocols. *See* First Geneva Convention of 1949, *supra* note 2, at art. 63(4); Second Geneva Convention of 1949, *supra* note 2, at art. 62(4); Third Geneva Convention of 1949, *supra* note 2, at art. 142(4); Fourth Geneva Convention of 1949, *supra* note 2, at art. 158(4); Protocol I, *supra* note 3, at art. 1(2); Protocol Additional to the Geneva Conventions of 1949, and Relating to the Protection of Victims of Non-International Armed Conflicts (Protocol II), *opened for signature* Dec. 12, 1977, preamble, *reprinted in* THE LAWS OF ARMED CONFLICTS 621 (D. Schindler & J. Toman 2d rev. ed. 1981).

29. *See* Hague Convention No. IV, *supra* note 1, at preamble (Martens Clause).

30. Hague Regulations, *supra* note 1, at art. 23(g).

31. Geneva Convention for the Amelioration of the Condition of the Wounded in

treaty governing land warfare. The resulting Law of Geneva protected wounded in armies in the field, medical personnel, units and transports. Through the stimulus of the International Committee of the Red Cross (ICRC),[32] the Law of Geneva was updated in 1899,[33] 1906,[34] 1929,[35] 1949,[36] and 1977,[37] expanding its protection to additional victims of war. In particular, the Fourth Geneva Convention of 1949 extended protection to civilians under the control of the opposing party.[38]

Although treaties, as contractual instruments, are binding only upon the contracting parties, the principles and rules of treaties which are declaratory of customary international law are also binding on non-parties. New development of principles of treaties, if widely practiced by parties and non-parties alike, may become customary international law. For example, the 1907 Hague Convention No. IV included a general participation clause which provided that its regulations were binding only if all participants to a war were parties to that Convention.[39] Thus, the 1907 Hague Convention, as a treaty, was not applicable in either World War because not all belligerent states were parties to the Convention. Similarly, the 1929 Geneva Prisoner of War Convention[40] was not applicable between Germany and the Soviet Union because the Soviet Union had never ratified it. But when the Nazi defendants in the Nuremberg trials raised the non-applicability of the Hague and Geneva Conventions as a matter of defense, the International Military Tribunal held that the general principles of these Conventions had passed into general international law and were thus binding on Germany.[41] In *The High Command Case*,[42] however, the International Military Tribunal

---

Armies in the Field of 22 August 1864, 22 Stat. 940, T.S. No. 377.

32. *See* INT'L COMM. OF THE RED CROSS, INTERNATIONAL RED CROSS HANDBOOK 407 (1983) (discussing the Statutes of the International Red Cross which set out the organizational structure of the Red Cross).

33. Hague Convention No. III for the Adaptation to Maritime Warfare of the Principles of the Geneva Conventions of 22 August 1864, 32 Stat. 1827, T.S. No. 453.

34. Geneva Convention for the Amelioration of the Condition of the Wounded and Sick in Armies in the Field of 6 July 1906, 35 Stat. 1885, T.S. No. 464.

35. Geneva Convention for the Amelioration of the Condition of the Wounded and Sick in Armies in the Field of 27 July 1929, 47 Stat. 2074, T.S. No. 847; Geneva Convention Relative to the Treatment of Prisoners of War of 27 July 1929, 47 Stat. 2021, T.S. No. 846.

36. Geneva Conventions of 1949, *supra* note 2.

37. Protocol I, *supra* note 3.

38. Fourth Geneva Convention of 1949, *supra* note 2, at art. 4.

39. Hague Convention No. IV, *supra* note 1, at art. 2.

40. Convention Relative to the Treatment of Prisoners of War, July 27, 1929, 47 Stat. 2021, T.S. No. 846, 118 L.N.T.S. 343.

41. 1 TRIAL OF THE MAJOR WAR CRIMINALS BEFORE THE INTERNATIONAL MILITARY TRIBUNAL 253 (1945).

42. United States v. Von Leeb (The High Command Case), *reprinted in* 11 TRIALS

stated that in holding "that the Hague and Geneva Conventions express accepted usages and customs of war, it must be noted that certain detailed provisions pertaining to the care and treatment of prisoners of war can hardly be so designated. Such details it is believed could be binding only by international agreement."[43]

At the present time, 161 states are parties to the 1949 Geneva Conventions.[44] In view of the universality of the Geneva Conventions, it may be concluded that their general principles, although not all the detailed rules implementing these principles, are now customary law binding on non-parties. As previously noted, the law relative to the protection of war victims has been updated periodically and has grown as a direct result of the patient and impartial work of the International Committee of the Red Cross through its dedication to the protection of individual victims of war against the abuse of authority and indifference to human suffering. The law of the Hague, however, was not updated from the turn of the century until 1977, with the exception of the Geneva Gas Protocol.[45] During this period, there was no agency like the International Committee of the Red Cross to ensure that the law of the Hague was respected and periodically updated.

While the 1949 Diplomatic Conference was putting the finishing touches on the four Geneva Conventions, the newly established United Nations International Law Commission (ILC) was asked to codify the law dealing with the conduct of hostilities. It declined the task reasoning that, "[w]ar having been outlawed, the regulation of its conduct has ceased to be relevant" and that undertaking such a project at the beginning of the ILC's existence would evince a lack of confidence in the efficacy of the U.N. Charter's means for maintaining peace.[46]

In 1956, the International Red Cross made an effort to revise the badly outdated 1907 Hague Regulations.[47] This effort was met with enthusiasm by humanitarians and "Ban the Bomb" activists. Governments, however, reacted with polite inaction, most likely because the proposed drafts were too restrictive of air power. In 1968, the United

OF WAR CRIMINALS BEFORE THE NUREMBERG MILITARY TRIBUNAL 462 (1950).

43. *Id.* at 535.

44. 25 INT'L REV. RED CROSS 60 (1985).

45. Protocol for the Prohibition of the Use of Asphyxiating Poisonous or Other Gases, and of Bacteriological Methods of Warfare of 17 June 1925, 26 U.S.T. 571, T.I.A.S. No. 8061, 94 L.N.T.S. 65.

46. Report of the International Law Commission to the General Assembly on the Work of the First Session, 1949 Y.B. INT'L L. COMM'N 281 (1950).

47. Int'l Comm. of the Red Cross, Draft Rules for the Limitation of the Danger Incurred by the Civilian Population in Time of War, (2d ed. Geneva 1958), *reprinted in* THE LAWS OF ARMED CONFLICTS 187-93 (D. Schindler & J. Toman 2d rev. ed. 1981).

Nations Conference on Human Rights,[48] meeting in the shadow of the Vietnam conflict, decided that updating the law of armed conflict was a suitable project for the United Nations' attention.

The interest of the United Nations human rights community stimulated the International Red Cross into action. The International Committee of the Red Cross began a process to update and clarify the four Geneva Conventions and to modernize the rules of methods and means of warfare.[49] The new instruments were designed to supplement rather than replace the existing Geneva Conventions, codifying the newly developed and emerging customary international law. The ICRC began a series of consultations and conferences with government and Red Cross experts. As a result of these consultations and conferences, the ICRC drafted two protocols, one on international armed conflict and another on internal armed conflict. These protocols formed the single negotiating text for a Diplomatic Conference convened by the Swiss Government in 1974. After four annual sessions in Geneva, attended by 135 States, the Conference adopted the two protocols on June 10, 1977.[50]

III. THE CODIFICATION OF THE RULES FOR PROTECTION OF CIVILIANS AGAINST THE EFFECTS OF HOSTILITIES

The 1907 Hague Regulations dealing with the conduct of hostilities on land were designed to apply to the immediate combat zone where hostile land forces confront each other. To the extent that they protected civilians against the effects of hostilities, they contemplated

48. United Nations International Conference on Human Rights, Res. XXIII, 12 May 1968, *text published in* Final Act of the United Nations International Conference on Human Rights, U.N. Doc. A/Conf. 32/41, U.N. Sales No. E.68.XIV.2 (1968), *reprinted in* THE LAWS OF ARMED CONFLICTS 197-98 (D. Schindler & J. Toman 2d rev. ed. 1981); G.A. Res. 2444, 23 U.N. GAOR Supp. (No. 18) at 50-51, U.N. Doc. A/7218 (1968) [hereinafter referred to as U.N. General Assembly Resolution 2444].

49. *See* Baxter, *Perspective: The Evolving Laws of Armed Conflict*, 60 MIL. L. REV. 99 (1973) (discussing the International Red Cross' participation in drafting humanitarian law documents); *see also* XXIst International Conference of the Red Cross, Resolution XIII, Reaffirmation and Development of the Laws and Customs Applicable in Armed Conflict, Istanbul, Turkey, 1969.

50. Protocol I, *supra* note 3; Protocol Additional to the Geneva Conventions of 1949, and Relating to the Protection of Victims of Non-International Armed Conflicts (Protocol II), *opened for signature* Dec. 12, 1977, *reprinted in* THE LAWS OF ARMED CONFLICTS 619 (D. Schindler & J. Toman 2d rev. ed. 1981).

As of November, 1985, 51 states were parties to Protocol I and 44 states were parties to Protocol II. The People's Republic of China is the only permanent member of the Security Council to be a party to both Protocols. France is a party to Protocol II only and is the only State to be a party to Protocol II without also being a party to Protocol I. Cyprus, Vietnam, Zaire, Cuba, Mexico, Mozambique, Syria and Angola are parties to Protocol I but not to Protocol II. 25 INT'L REV. RED CROSS 61-62 (1985).

bombardment and sieges of defended cities and towns and required a warning — unless the element of surprise was necessary — so that civilians might leave or take shelter. Bombardment of undefended places, i.e., places open to occupation without resistance, was recognized as unnecessary and was thus prohibited. Pillage was prohibited, even after an assault of a besieged city. Although the emergence of air power was dimly recognized, air bombardment was thought to be feasible only for the close support of ground forces — a sort of supplement to artillery. In bombarding defended towns, precautions were required as to educational, scientific, religious and cultural objects, which were not to be attacked if properly marked.[51] With the exception of military objectives in undefended ports, the hinterland was believed to be secure from the effects of hostilities. It was recognized, however, that military objectives located in undefended ports might be attacked by naval gunfire. The Hague Convention No. IX concerning Bombardment of Naval Forces recognized that collateral civilian casualties might result and urged that precautions be taken to avoid or minimize them.[52] The Hague Conventions and the Hague Regulations applied through World Wars I and II, during which time air power shattered any illusion about the security of the hinterland.

The Fourth Geneva Convention of 1949, Part II, provided new rules for the protection of the civilian population of the countries in conflict. Articles 13 through 26, *inter alia*, specify that civilian hospitals, medical transports and medical personnel are immune from attack.[53] Articles 14 and 15 provide for the establishment of safe refuges to protect certain classes of civilians from the effects of war.[54] Article 14 contemplates the deliberate and preplanned establishment of hospital and safety zones in rear areas for military and civilian wounded, sick and aged persons, children under fifteen, expectant mothers and mothers of children under seven. These zones may be established by unilateral action but agreement as to the mutual recognition of such zones is encouraged. Article 15 provides for the establishment by mutual agreement of neutralized zones in areas where fighting is taking place.[55]

51. Hague Regulations, *supra* note 1, at arts. 25-28.
52. Hague Convention No. IX, *supra* note 1, at art. 2.
53. Fourth Geneva Convention of 1949, *supra* note 2, at arts. 13-26.
54. *Id.* at arts. 14-15.
55. *Id.* at art. 15. The 1982 Falkland Islands conflict presented an opportunity to test the efficacy of article 15. As the British drew close to Port Stanley-Puerto Argentino on the Falkland-Malvinas Islands, the Argentine and British authorities agreed, at the suggestion of the ICRC, to establish a neutralized zone in the center of town. The zone was never actually established, however, because active hostilities came to an end shortly after the agreement was concluded. S. JUNOD, PROTECTION OF THE VICTIMS OF

These zones serve as refuges for the wounded and sick and for civilians who take no part in the hostilities and who, while they reside in the zone, perform no work of a military nature.

By 1968, the development of air power and the increased destructiveness of modern weapons necessitated the formulation of new rules for the protection of civilian populations. The basic principles of customary law were expressed in the 1968 U.N. General Assembly Resolution 2444, *Respect for Human Rights in Armed Conflicts*:

> a. [T]he right of the parties to a conflict to adopt means of injuring the enemy is not unlimited;
> b. [I]t is prohibited to launch attacks against the civilian population as such;
> c. [A] distinction must be made at all times between persons taking an active part in the hostilities and members of the civilian population to the effect that the latter be spared as much as possible.[56]

The statement of the first abstract principle requires some explanation of the layers of limitations on the choice of methods and means of warfare. First, there are specific prohibitions and restrictions as expressed in the "rules of international law applicable in armed conflict."[57] For example, there are specific prohibitions against the use of poison or poisoned weapons: the employment of weapons and methods of warfare of a nature to cause superfluous injury or unnecessary suffering, perfidious killing, wounding or capturing of enemy combatants, denial of quarter, the murder of prisoners of war or other detained persons, attacks on civilians, attacks on specifically protected objects, and misuse of protective signs.[58]

Next, there are conditional prohibitions against certain acts for which exceptions may be made in cases of urgent or imperative necessities of war. The most important of these is the prohibition against seizure or destruction of the enemy's property in the absence of urgent military necessity.[59]

ARMED CONFLICT FALKLAND-MALVINAS ISLANDS (1982) 33-34 (1984).

56. U.N. General Assembly Resolution 2444, *supra* note 48. The 1968 resolution, adopted unanimously, borrowed its provisions from a 1965 International Red Cross Resolution. *See* 20th International Conference of the Red Cross, Resolution XXVIII, Protection of Civilian Populations Against the Dangers of Indiscriminate Warfare, Vienna, Austria, 1965, *reprinted in* THE LAWS OF ARMED CONFLICTS, *supra* note 3, at 195; Hague Regulations, *supra* note 1 (first provision reaffirming the well-established Hague principle embodied in article 22 of the Hague Regulations); Protocol I, *supra* note 3 (Article 35(1) of Protocol I also reaffirms the principle embodied in article 22 of the Hague Regulations).

57. Protocol I, *supra* note 3, at art. 2(b).

58. Hague Regulations, *supra* note 1; Protocol I, *supra* note 3, at arts. 37-42, 51-56.

59. Regulations, *supra* note 1, at art. 23(g); Fourth Geneva Convention of 1949, *supra* note 2, at art. 53.

Finally, there are prohibitions inherent in the complementary principles of necessity and humanity which underlie the law governing the conduct of hostilities. The principle of necessity justifies only those measures of military violence not forbidden by international law that are relevant and proportionate to securing the prompt submission of the enemy with the least possible expenditure of economic or human resources.[60] The principle of humanity complements the principle of necessity by forbidding those measures of violence that are not necessary, i.e., not relevant or proportionate to the achievement of a definite military advantage.[61]

Inherent in the principles we have discussed are the following elements: (1) there are limitations on the methods and means of warfare; (2) these limitations are expressed in binding international law; (3) loss of life and destruction of property must have some rational tendency to the prompt achievement of a definite military advantage; and (4) such casualties and damage must not be disproportionate or excessive in relation to the military advantage anticipated.[62] Necessity, like its components of relevance and proportionality, is a relational concept. To speak of necessity, or the lack thereof, is to raise the question: necessary or unnecessary for what?[63]

A. Analyzing the Components of Necessity: Relevance and Proportionality

Relevance means a rational tendency to the prompt achievement of a definite military advantage. Proportionality means not excessive in relation to the military advantage anticipated. When viewed from the standpoint of national-strategic planning, the necessity must be judged in relation to the attainment of the object for which the armed conflict is waged. From the viewpoint of the field commander and his tactical planners, necessity, relevance, and proportionality must be judged in relation to the attainment of a definite military advantage. Definite means concrete and perceptible, rather than hypothetical or speculative. It is in this sense that the term necessity is used in Protocol I in the articles dealing with the protection of the civilian population.[64]

60. Lieber Instructions, *supra* note 20, at arts. 14-16; M. McDougal & F. Feliciano, Law and Minimum World Public Order: The Legal Regulation of International Coercion 525-30 (1961); M. Bothe, K. Partsch & W. Solf, *supra* note 27, at 194-95.

61. M. McDougal & F. Feliciano, *supra* note 60, at 525.

62. M. Bothe, K. Partsch & W. Solf, *supra* note 27, at 195.

63. M. McDougal & F. Feliciano, *supra* note 60, at 525.

64. Protocol I, *supra* note 3, at arts. 51(5)(b), 52(2), 57(2)(a)(iii).

B. Protecting the Civilian Population

Protocol I reaffirms and supports the customary principles that prohibit the attack on civilians and civilian objects, and that require that distinctions be made between the treatment of combatants and civilians. In furtherance of these principles, Protocol I includes detailed implementing rules, most of which reaffirm or clarify the customary rules designed to protect civilians against the effects of attacks.

The articles adopted in Protocol I utilize four different approaches to reinforce the customary norms. First, there are the provisions designed to revitalize and strengthen the distinction between military objectives and civilians/civilian objects. Second, are provisions which clarify the legal regulation of attacks. Particularly, these incorporate the rule of proportionality and a prohibition against indiscriminate attacks. Third, are a group of provisions which define in detail the precautionary steps that both the attackers and defenders must take to avoid or minimize civilian casualties and damage to civilian objects. Finally, in an effort to provide more objective legal protection for the civilian population, there are specific provisions that limit or prohibit attacks on particular objects and on specified areas.

1. Strengthening the Distinction Between Civilian and Military Objects

The provisions of Protocol I do not preclude attacks that may cause civilian casualties. The Protocol does, however, require that parties to the conflict direct their military operations only against military objectives. Accordingly, article 48 requires that a commander have some coherent military objective in mind when he decides upon an attack, and his plan of attack must be directed toward destroying, neutralizing or capturing that military objective.[65]

Article 52 defines military objectives as those objects: which by their nature, location and use make an effective contribution to the enemy's military action; and (2) whose destruction, capture or neutralization, "*in the circumstances ruling at the time*, offer a definite military advantage."[66] For the first time, article 52 gives an explicit definition of military objectives, thus providing guidance in distinguishing civilian

65. Protocol I, *supra* note 3, at art. 48. *See also* U.N. General Assembly Resolution 2444, *supra* note 47 (Article 48 paraphrasing the basic rules stated in paragraphs 2-3 of the resolution).

66. Protocol I, *supra* note 3, at art. 52(2) (emphasis added).

objects from military objectives.[67] This distinction between civilian and military objects is further clarified through explicit definitions of civilians and the civilian population.[68] In addition, there are presumptions regarding the treatment of civilian houses, schools, places of worship and other objects normally dedicated to civilian use.[69] To the extent that Protocol I clarifies and implements the principle of civilian immunity and the principle of distinction, its provisions should be considered customary law.

2. Clarifying Regulations of Attacks

Further efforts to strengthen customary law are reflected in the provisions of Protocol I which clarify and develop the regulation of attacks. Article 51 prohibits making civilians the object of an attack, although civilians may lose such protection in event of their direct participation in the hostilities with the intent to cause physical harm to enemy personnel and objects.[70] Indiscriminate attacks are also prohibited and illustrated as including broad area-wide attacks on several clearly separated military objectives located among concentrations of civilians, and disproportionate attacks.[71] Finally, reprisal attacks on civilians are prohibited.[72] Additionally, these provisions place duties upon armed forces toward civilians under their control by prohibiting the use of civilians to shield military objectives or to shield, favor or impede military operations.[73] In general, article 51 reaffirms existing customary law prohibiting attacks against civilians as such.

It should be noted, however, that under article 52 civilian objects lose their protection if they are used to make an effective contribution

67. Earlier efforts to provide an explicit definition had failed, primarily because such definition was considered inappropriate in a humanitarian instrument. *See supra* notes 27-29 and accompanying text (discussing the lack of clear definitions of prohibited conduct). Article 52 overcomes the traditional objections in two ways. First, article 52 states the rule in the traditional prohibitory manner, and defines civilian objects in the negative as "all objects which are not military objectives as defined in paragraph 2." Second, article 52 limits attacks to objects that meet its two-pronged test. Protocol I, *supra* note 3, at art. 52.

68. Protocol I, *supra* note 3, at art. 50(1)-50(2).

69. *Id.* at art. 51(2)-51(3).

70. *Id.* at art. 51(4)-51(5).

71. *Id.*

72. *Id.* at art. 51(6). Reprisals are acts of retaliation in the form of conduct which would otherwise be unlawful, taken as a last resort by one party to a conflict against enemy personnel or property in response to a manifest and serious violation of the law of armed conflict, for the sole purpose of enforcing compliance with the rules of that law. Reprisals must be proportionate to the accomplishment of their intended purpose, and must be halted when the enemy's unlawful conduct has ceased.

73. *Id.* at art. 51(7).

to enemy military action and if their destruction, capture, or neutralization offers a definite military advantage.[74] This is a lesser standard than that which causes loss of protection to civilian persons. Thus, while a civilian may not lose his protection against individualized attack while working in a munitions plant, he assumes the risk of collateral injury when he is in the vicinity of the munitions plant, although he continues to retain full protection while at home.

Articles 51 and 52 provide prohibitions against reprisals or retaliatory attacks against civilians and civilian objects.[75] These prohibitions break new ground and thus cannot be considered reaffirmation of customary law. The 1949 Geneva Conventions prohibit reprisals against the wounded, sick and shipwrecked, as well as against medical personnel, units and establishments and transports, prisoners of war, and protected civilians.[76] It should be noted that the term "protected persons" includes only civilians in the power of a party of which they are not nationals. Thus, the population of a party under the control of that party is not protected against reprisals.[77]

Articles 51 and 57 contain the first codifications of the rule of proportionality. The rule prohibits attacks that may be expected to cause incidental civilian casualties or property damage which would be excessive in relation to the concrete and direct military advantage anticipated.[78] If viewed as a restatement of the basic principle of military necessity, i.e., relevance and proportionality, this would undoubtedly be considered a reaffirmation of customary law. Whether the other illustration, that demonstrating the prohibition against treating a number of clearly separated and distinct targets as a single military objective, constitutes a new development or a reaffirmation of existing law depends on how one construes the term "clearly separated." If it is construed as meaning separated at such a distance and under such circumstances that the military targets can be attacked separately, it is probably a reaffirmation of customary international law.

3. Emphasizing Precautionary Measures

Precautionary measures intended to avoid or minimize civilian casu-

---

74. *Id.* at art. 52(2).
75. *Id.* at arts. 51(6), 52(1).
76. First Geneva Convention, *supra* note 2, at art. 47; Second Geneva Convention, *supra* note 2, at art. 47; Third Geneva Convention, *supra* note 2, at art. 13(1); Fourth Geneva Convention, *supra* note 2, at art. 33(3).
77. *Id.* at art. 4; *see also* Convention for the Protection of Cultural Property, 14 May 1954 249 U.N.T.S. 340, art. 4 (prohibiting reprisals against cultural property).
78. Protocol I, *supra* note 3, at arts. 51(5)(b) and 57(2)(iii).

alties and damage to civilian property, which both the attacker and defender must take, are emphasized in articles 57 and 58, as well as in an extensive codification of rules pertaining to civil defense in articles 61-67.

Under the provisions of article 57, commanders and their planning staff are required to take all feasible measures to verify that targets of an attack are military objectives. Moreover, they are required to take all feasible precautions in the choice of methods and means of attack to avoid or minimize collateral injury to civilians or damage to civilian objects. They must refrain from launching any attack which may be expected to cause collateral civilian casualties or damage to civilian objects excessive in relation to the concrete and direct military advantage.[79] If it becomes apparent during an attack that the objective is not a military one or that disproportionate civilian casualties or damage to civilian property may result, the attack must be cancelled or suspended.[80] Furthermore, where an attack may affect the civilian population, advance warning is required unless the circumstances preclude such action by the necessity of surprise.[81] To the greatest extent possible, the party controlling the civilian population should endeavor to evacuate civilians from the vicinity of military objectives, to avoid locating military objectives within or near densely populated areas, and to take any additional precautions, such as the provision of shelters and civilian defense programs, to protect the civilian population against the danger resulting from military operations.[82]

4. Providing Special Legal Protection

Although the provisions on the regulation of attacks are more detailed than those of prior law, they remain to a large extent general principles which require subjective judgment in specific situations. Recognizing this subjectivity, the diplomatic conference developed the fourth approach to achieving improved protection for the civilian population, *viz.*, specific provisions regulating attacks on particular objects and specific areas.

Article 53 prohibits acts of hostilities against culturally important historic monuments, places of worship and works of art, and at the same time prohibits use of such objects to support the military effort.[83]

79. *Id.* at art. 57 (2)(a)(iii).
80. *Id.* at art. 57(2)(b).
81. *Id.* at art. 57(2)(c).
82. *Id.* at art. 58.
83. *Id.* at arts. 53(a)-53(b).

Customary international law, as reflected in article 27 of the 1907 Hague Regulations, prohibits attacks on a variety of cultural and religious objects *provided* they are not used at the time for military purposes. The 1954 Hague Convention, however, which provides for the protection of cultural property, permits derogations, even in the case of very important cultural objects, where imperative military necessity demands such attacks.[84] As article 53 of Protocol I is made subject to both of these relevant conventions, it is not yet clear whether customary international law is as broad as article 53 seems to be.

By prohibiting the starvation of civilians as a method of warfare, article 54 establishes a substantially new principle which is not yet customary international law.[85] The customary practice, as illustrated by article 17 of the Lieber Instructions, declares that "war is not carried out by arms alone. It is lawful to starve the hostile belligerent, armed or unarmed, so that it leads to the speedier subjection of the enemy."[86] This principle was modified somewhat by article 23 of the 1907 Hague Regulations, but the prohibition was subject to derogation for military necessity.[87] As a policy, general devastation or a "scorched earth" was permitted if there was an honest belief that urgent military necessity required such action.[88] Article 23 of the Fourth Geneva Convention modified this principle modestly by requiring relief for only that portion of the civilian population presumed incapable of making a substantial contribution to their country's war effort, e.g., children under fifteen and expectant mothers.[89] Similarly, the provisions of Protocol I do not depart entirely from customary practice as the protections granted are not absolute. The specific prohibition against attack, destruction, removal or rendering objects useless under article 54 pertains only to action taken for the specific purpose of denial for its sustenance value, not for any collateral effect the action may have on the civilian population.[90]

Articles 35 and 55 of Protocol I prohibit the use of methods and means of warfare which are intended or may be expected to cause

84. Convention for the Protection of Cultural Property in the Event of Armed Conflict of 14 May 1954, arts. 4(2), 11, 249 U.N.T.S. 240, *reprinted in* THE LAW OF ARMED CONFLICTS 664 (D. Schindler & J. Toman 2d rev. ed. 1981).

85. Protocol I, *supra* note 3, at art. 54(1).

86. Lieber Instructions, *supra* note 20, at art. 17.

87. Hague Regulations, *supra* note 1, at art. 23(g).

88. United States v. List (The Hostage Case), *reported in* 11 TRIALS OF WAR CRIMINALS BEFORE THE NUREMBERG MILITARY TRIBUNAL 1230, 1233, 1295-97 (1950).

89. Fourth Geneva Convention of 1949, *supra* note 2, at art. 23.

90. Protocol I, *supra* note 3, at art. 54(2).

"widespread, long-term and severe" damage to the natural environment and thereby prejudice the health or survival of the population.[91] It should be noted that the terms "widespread, long-term and severe" are in the conjunctive, whereas in the Environmental Modification Treaty (ENMOD Treaty)[92] the comparable terms are in the disjunctive. Furthermore, the negotiating record of articles 35 and 55 of Protocol I demonstrates that "long-term" is construed to involve decades, whereas in the ENMOD treaty, "long-lasting" is construed to involve seasons.[93] Although the formulation is new, and the protections granted by Protocol I are greater, this prohibition is so basic that it must be construed as being inherent to a general principle of law and thus, general international law.

Special protection for dams, dikes and nuclear-electric generating stations is provided by article 56, which prohibits attacks on these works and installations, and on military objectives located in their vicinity if such attack may cause the release of dangerous forces and consequent severe losses among the civilian population.[94] Some limited exceptions to this protection exist. For example, the protection in article 56 does not apply when the installation or military objective is used in regular and direct support of military operations and if such attack is the only feasible way to terminate such support.[95] Yet even if the special protection is lost, the general protection of the Protocol and the rule of proportionality remain in effect. It would require an extraordinarily important target and a very significant military advantage to outweigh the severe civilian losses which might result from the dangerous forces released by the destruction of a dam, dike, or nuclear power station. The practice of states has previously indicated great restraint in the attacks of dams and dikes, the breach of which would cause such severe civilian losses. Article 56 thus differs little from customary international law.

---

91. *Id.* at arts. 35(3) and 55.

92. *See generally* Convention on the Prohibition of Military or Any Other Hostile Use of Environmental Modification Techniques, signed at Geneva May 18, 1977, 31 U.S.T. 333, T.I.A.S. No. 6839.

93. SWISS FED. POLITICAL DEP'T, *Berne Report of Committee III*, CDDH/215/Rev.1, ¶ 27 (1975); 15 OFFICIAL RECORDS OF THE DIPLOMATIC CONFERENCE ON HUMANITARIAN LAW 268 (1978); *Understandings Regarding the Convention on the Prohibition of Military or Any Other Hostile Use of Environmental Modification Techniques*, Report by Committee of the Conference on Disarmament 1976, *reprinted in* U.S. ARMS CONTROL AND DISARMAMENT AGENCY, ARMS CONTROL AND DISARMAMENT AGREEMENTS 197 (1982); M. BOTHE, K. PARTSCH & W. SOLF, *supra* note 27, at 346-48.

94. Protocol I, *supra* note 3, at art. 56.

95. *Id.* at art. 56(2).

Article 59 essentially clarifies and details the customary law prohibition of attacks on undefended places in the immediate combat zone which are open to occupation without resistance.[96] It is thus a clear declaration of well-established customary international law. By agreement, states may provide special protection for certain demilitarized zones under article 60; these are then declared off-limits to attacks and any other form of military operation, so long as the agreement remains in effect.[97]

Among the group of articles discussed, the only sharp changes from customary international law are the prohibitions against reprisals in articles 51-56 and the prohibition against starvation of civilians as a method of warfare in article 54. The other changes merely clarify and refine existing restraints, most of which will be recognized as either emerging or established customary international law.

CONCLUSION

Protocol I accomplishes its purpose by modernizing and clarifying the 1907 Hague Regulations in response to the danger presented by modern warfare to the civilian population. The articles of Protocol I are very complex in comparison with the simple statements of principle in the Hague Regulations. Except for the prohibition of reprisal attacks, however, the new rules are generally reaffirmations of existing customary law which is itself complex. In reaffirming customary law, Protocol I defines such essential matters as military objectives and codifies the rule of proportionality. Although these matters add to the complexity of the text, they promote better understanding and simplify their application on the battlefield.

In general, Protocol I reflects the attitude of the International Committee of the Red Cross when it prepared the Draft Protocols:

> In drawing up the Draft Protocol . . . the ICRC believes that it has remained steadfast to the spirit in which, since 1864, it has demanded, for the benefit of individuals, guarantees consistent with the dictates of humanity whilst bearing in mind the realities of national defense and security.[98]

96. *Id.* at art. 59.
97. *Id.* at art. 60.
98. INT'L COMM. OF THE RED CROSS, DRAFT PROTOCOLS ADDITIONAL TO THE GENEVA CONVENTIONS OF 12 AUGUST 1949 AND RELATING TO THE PROTECTION OF VICTIMS OF ARMED CONFLICTS 2 (1973).

[2]

The Principle of Discrimination in 21st Century Warfare

by Michael N. Schmitt*

I. INTRODUCTION

¶1 The premise that warfare is a constantly evolving phenomenon is axiomatic. In this century alone, consider the dramatic transmutations caused, for instance, by the machine gun, tank, airplane, radar, guided missile, and nuclear weapon. Change in the nature of warfare can also arise from major shifts in political-economic-societal structures, such as the rise of the nation-State or industrialization.[1] When the resultant shifts, whatever their cause, prove fundamental, a "revolution in military affairs" (RMA) occurs. Many argue that the global community is in the midst of an RMA today, a revolution generated by both technology and a dramatically altered geopolitical environment.[2]

---

* Professor of International Law, George C. Marshall European Center for Security Studies, Garmisch-Partenkirchen, Germany. Faculty, International Institute of Humanitarian Law, San Remo, Italy. The views, opinions, and conclusions in this article are those of the author and should not be construed as an official position of the United States Department of Defense, Marshall Center or any other organization. A version of this article was previously published in the Israel Yearbook on Human Rights as *Future War and the Principle of Distinction.*

1. Colin Gray has cited seven "historical transformations of warfare" since the fall of Rome: (1) fifth century cavalry, which "ushered in a long period of advantage for soldiers who could fight on horseback"; (2) the military revolution of the sixteenth and seventeenth centuries which "was led by the adoption of firearms for siege and open warfare"; (3) the "Nation in Arms," a "concept of popular warfare, increasingly armed and sustained by industrially and agriculturally modern states"; (5) mechanized warfare, signaled in 1916 by use of the tank in the Battle of the Somme and large scale aerial battles over Verdun; (6) nuclear warfare; and (7) information warfare. Colin S. Gray, *The Influence of Space Power upon History*, 15 COMP. STRATEGY 293, 297 (1996); *see also* Eliot A. Cohen, *A Revolution in Warfare*, FOREIGN AFF., Mar.-Apr. 1996, at 37 (discussing how technology has engineered a revolution in military affairs).

2. On the "revolution in military affairs," see SECRETARY OF DEFENSE, ANNUAL REPORT TO THE PRESIDENT AND THE CONGRESS ch. 13 (1998); Dennis M. Drew, *Technology and the American Way of War: Worshipping a False Idol?*, AIR FORCE J. LOGISTICS, Winter 1987, at 21; James R. Fitzsimonds, *The Coming Military Revolution: Opportunities and Risks*, PARAMETERS, Summer 1995, at 30; Dan Goure, *Is There a Military-Technical Revolution in America's Future?*, WASH. Q., Autumn 1993, at 175; Andrew F. Krepinevich, *Cavalry to Computer: The Pattern of Military Revolutions*, *in* STRATEGY AND FORCE PLANNING 430 (Naval War College Faculty eds., 2d. ed. 1995); Kenneth F. McKenzie, *Beyond Luddites and Magicians: Examining the MTR*, PARAMETERS, Summer 1995, at 15; Abhi Shelat, *An Empty Revolution: MTR Expectations Fall Short*, HARV.

¶2 RMAs encompass far more than simply strategic and tactical concerns. They often signal dramatic turns in the effects of warfare on civilians and their property. During the Second World War, as an example, each side directed aerial bombardment at their opponent's civilian population, usually with horrendous humanitarian consequences.[3] It was only the RMA wrought by aircraft that made possible the targeting of civilians at such a distance and with such effect. Perhaps more consequential still in terms of placing civilians at risk was the RMA spawned by the advent of nuclear weaponry.[4] At the height of the Cold War, entire populations were held hostage to the threat of counter-value targeting.[5] Even though the risk of massive nuclear exchanges has dissipated, the continued threat they pose to the global populace has led the International Court of Justice to recently declare that the use of nuclear weapons is contrary to the principles of *humanitarian* law except, perhaps, in "extreme circumstances of self-defense, in which [the State's] very survival would be at stake."[6]

¶3 The protection of civilians and civilian objects during armed conflict is a core purpose of humanitarian law, a branch of international law also known as the law of armed conflict and the law of war. It applies in situations of armed conflict, whether that conflict occurs during a solely internal conflagration or crosses geopolitical borders. Although, humanitarian law has traditionally had its greatest impact in the latter case, there has been increasing normative attention paid to the case of internal armed conflict.[7] Humanitarian law does not apply in situations not

INT'L REV., Summer 1994, at 52.

3. For instance, approximately one million German civilians were killed or wounded by bomber attacks. The attacks also destroyed one-fifth of German homes and rendered 7.5 million people homeless. *See* CHRISTOPHER C. HARMON, "ARE WE BEASTS?": CHURCHILL AND THE MORAL QUESTION OF WORLD WAR II "AREA BOMBING" 3 (1991).

4. For a discussion of the nuclear RMA, see Martin C. Libicki, *Information & Nuclear RMAs Compared*, NAT'L DEF. U. STRATEGIC F., No. 82 (July 1996) (visited Apr. 15, 1999) <http://www.ndu.edu/inss/strforum/forum82.html>.

5. Counter-value targeting is directed against cities and industrial areas; the premise is that one targets that which the opponent values most. Counter-force targeting, by contrast, is the targeting of the enemy's military, most commonly his strategic assets (such as an intercontinental missile force or strategic bomber bases).

6. Advisory Opinion on the Legality of the Threat or Use of Nuclear Weapons, ¶ 97, *reprinted in* 35 I.L.M. 809, 830 (July 8, 1996). The Court did not address the use of the weapons in belligerent reprisal, i.e. an unlawful act in response to a prior unlawful act, which is designed to force the opposing belligerent to desist in its unlawful conduct. On the case, see Richard A. Falk, *Nuclear Weapons, International Law and the World Court: A Historic Encounter*, 91 AM. J. INT'L L. 64 (1997); Robert F. Turner, *Nuclear Weapons and the World Court: The ICJ's Advisory Opinion and Its Significance for U.S. Strategic Doctrine*, *in* THE LAW OF MILITARY OPERATIONS 309 (Michael N. Schmitt ed., 1998); Michael N. Schmitt, *The International Court of Justice and the Use of Nuclear Weapons*, NAVAL WAR COLLEGE REV., Spring 1998, at 91.

7. Internal armed conflict is governed by Common Article III to the four 1949 Geneva Conventions and Protocol II Additional to the Geneva Conventions. *See* Geneva Convention for the Amelioration of the Condition of the Wounded and Sick in Armed forces in the Field, Aug. 12, 1949, art. 3, 6 U.S.T. 3114, 75 U.N.T.S. 31; Geneva Convention for the Amelioration of the Condition of the Wounded, Sick and Shipwrecked Members of the Armed Forces at Sea, Aug. 12, 1949, art. 3, 6 U.S.T. 3217, 75 U.N.T.S. 85; Geneva Convention Relative to the Treatment of Prisoners of War, Aug. 12, 1949, art. 3, 6 U.S.T. 3316, 75 U.N.T.S. 135; Geneva

amounting to armed conflict, such as riots, strikes, demonstrations, isolated acts of violence, or traditional criminal activity, even if military forces are employed to address them. In such cases, domestic and international human rights law tempers the violence.[8]

¶4 There are two complementary components of humanitarian law, the *jus ad bellum*, which some view as a separate body of law altogether, and the *jus in bello*. The former sets forth the criteria for the use of force as an instrument of national policy, asking *when* a State may use force. The *jus in bello*, by contrast, addresses *how* force may be used in an armed conflict, regardless of the propriety of the decision to resort to it.

Two primary purposes underlie the *jus in bello*. The first is a desire to ratchet down the level of violence that occurs in armed conflict, a goal expressed most clearly in instruments that prohibit use of particular weapons[9] or forbid the creation of unnecessary suffering.[10] Restrictions responsive to this objective are usually framed in terms of limits on "methods or means" of warfare and over time have been labeled "Hague Law."[11] The second purpose of the *jus in bello* is to shield those who are not directly participating in the conflict from its effects. Classic examples are the limitations on targeting civilians and civilian objects, the protection of medical personnel and facilities, and norms regarding the treatment of prisoners of war. Restrictions emanating from this goal tend to be framed in terms of the protected person or object at issue and are colloquially know as "Geneva Law."

¶5 Because evolution in the conduct of warfare affects the individuals and objects which humanitarian law seeks to shelter, it is not surprising that law has proven responsive, both proactively and reactively, to warfare's changing nature.[12] In the last century alone, advances in

---

Convention Relative to the Protection of Civilian Persons in Time of War, Aug. 12, 1949, art. 3, 6 U.S.T. 3516, 75 U.N.T.S. 287 [hereinafter "Geneva Convention IV"]; Protocol Additional to the Geneva Conventions of August 12, 1949, and Relating to the Protection of Victims of Non-International Armed Conflicts, June 8, 1977, U.N. Doc. A/32/144, Annex II (1977), *reprinted in* 16 I.L.M. 1442 (1977).

8. There is "bleed over" because human rights law, particularly its non-derogable components, can apply during periods of armed conflict.

9. *See, e.g.*, Final Act of the United Nations Conference on Prohibitions or Restrictions of the Use of Certain Conventional Weapons, Oct. 10, 1980, 1342 U.N.T.S. 7, *reprinted in* 19 I.L.M. 1523 (1980).

10. Among the first formal expressions of the principle was the St. Petersburg Declaration of 1868, which provided that "the only legitimate object which states should endeavor to accomplish in war is to weaken the military force of the enemy," and that "this object would be exceeded by employment of arms which use aggravate the sufferings of disabled men, or render their death inevitable." Declaration of St. Petersburg, 1868, *reprinted in* Official Documents, 1 AM. J. INT'L L. 95 (Supp. 1907).

11. The designation "Geneva Law" refers to that portion of the law of armed conflict addressing protected classes of persons: civilians, prisoners of war, the sick or shipwrecked, and medical personnel. It is distinguished from "Hague Law," which governs methods and means of combat, occupation, and neutrality. For a discussion of the international instruments which fall into each category, and of those which display elements of both, see FREDERIC DEMULINEN, HANDBOOK ON THE LAW OF WAR FOR ARMED FORCES 3-4 (1987).

12. Proactive efforts seek to head off negative consequences before they occur. For instance, Protocol IV of the Conventional Weapons Convention prohibited the use of

humanitarian law have tracked major conflicts with great regularity. The Geneva Convention of 1906 and the Hague Conventions of 1907 followed closely on the heels of the 1905 Russo-Japanese War. World War I, in great part, served as the impetus for the 1925 Gas Protocol and the 1929 Geneva Convention. The enormous devastation of the Second World War led to humanitarian law's greatest leap forward in the form of the four 1949 Geneva Conventions, as well as the 1954 Cultural Property Convention. In the aftermath of World War II, bipolarity and wars of national liberation dominated inter-State conflict, while new technologies and sensibilities led to heightened concerns over the methods and means of warfare. The Additional Protocols to the Geneva Conventions, Environmental Modification Convention, Biological Weapons Convention, Conventional Weapons Convention, and Landmines Convention resulted.[13] So too did numerous arms control treaties designed to limit the testing, possession, and spread of nuclear weapons, the unprecedented power of which had been so dramatically illustrated at Nagasaki and Hiroshima.[14]

¶6 The symbiosis between change, war, and law lends itself to reflection on normative futures. Through projections about the nature of future war, it is possible to draw tentative conclusions about those megatrends therein that might place existing law under greater stress, strengthen its impact, or move it in new directions. Of course, predictive endeavors in the soft sciences are tentative, and should cause some trepidation in those who embark on them.[15] This is certainly true in the case of predicting the face of future war or, even more presumptuously,

permanently blinding lasers before they were fielded by any armed force. *See* Additional Protocol to the Convention on the Prohibitions or Restrictions on the Use of Certain Conventional Weapons Which May be Deemed to be Excessively Injurious or to Have Indiscriminate Effects, Protocol on Blinding Laser Weapons (Protocol IV), Oct. 13, 1995, 35 I.L.M. 1218 (1996). By contrast, most of humanitarian law is reactive; the best example is the establishment of the International Committee of the Red Cross (ICRC) following Henri Dunant's account of the bloody Battle of Solferino during the Italian War of Unification. *See* HENRI DUNANT, SOUVENIR DE SOLFERINO (1862).

13. Each of the aforementioned instruments may be found at the ICRC's website: www.icrc.org/unicc/ihl_eng.nsf/web?OpenNavigator. Except for the Landmines Convention, they are also reprinted in THE LAWS OF ARMED CONFLICTS (Dietrich Schindler & Jiri Toman eds., 1988), at 301, 53, 115, 325, 373, 745, 621, 163, 137, and 179, respectively.

14. *See, e.g.*, Treaty Banning Nuclear Weapons Tests in the Atmosphere, in Outer Space and Under Water, Aug. 5, 1963, 14 U.S.T. 1313, 480 U.N.T.S. 43; Treaty for the Prohibition of Nuclear Weapons in Latin America (Treaty of Tlatelolco), Feb. 14, 1967, 634 U.N.T.S. 281, 6 I.L.M. 521 (1967); Treaty on the Non-Proliferation of Nuclear Weapons, July 1, 1968, 21 U.S.T. 483, 729 U.N.T.S. 161; Treaty on the Prohibition of the Emplacement of Nuclear Weapons and Other Weapons of Mass Destruction on the Seabed and the Ocean Floor and in the Subsoil Thereof, Feb. 11, 1971, 23 U.S.T. 701, 10 I.L.M. 145 (1971).

15. The range of variables that will determine the future are vast. For instance, which States are likely to be core adversaries in the next century? What types of conflicts will predominate? How effective will the "revitalized" United Nations system be? Which political, religious, and ethnic forces will prove most powerful? Indeed, even technological predictions are suspect. *See* Herb Brody, *Great Expectations: Why Technological Predictions go Awry*, TECH. REV., July 1991, at 39. For an extremely interesting effort to identify current trends relevant to the use of force, see Anthony D'Amato, *Megatrends in the Use of Force*, *in* THE LAW OF ARMED CONFLICT: INTO THE NEXT MILLENNIUM 1 (Michael N. Schmitt & Leslie C. Green eds., 1998).

speculating on what future war portends for global prescriptive norms. Nevertheless, if we are to affect the vector that evolving law is to take, the effort must be made to grasp the future and proactively respond to it.

¶7 This essay undertakes that task vis-à-vis what can fairly be characterized as the pith of humanitarian law, those prescriptive norms of the *jus in bello* mandating discrimination between civilians (and their property) and legitimate targets.[16] It begins with an analysis of the current state of the principle of discrimination. Once this context has been set forth, the essay will turn to a description of projected aspects of warfare in the first half of the next century, which some characterize as an RMA, most likely to stress, strengthen, or impel change in the concept of discrimination. Specifically, suggestions will be offered on how possible changes may affect the existing normative milieu.[17] Because most such aspects will be driven by changes in U.S. military strategies, tactics, and capabilities, this discussion will necessarily take on a U.S.-centric tenor.[18] Receiving particular attention will be the expectation that States will not share equally in the revolution, as some are not financially or technologically capable of participating, and the particularly insidious normative dynamic this "have/have-not" dichotomy may create. Finally, to the extent possible in such a speculative undertaking, several tentative suggestions will be offered on how to soften the impact of any potentially negative trends.

II. The Principle of Discrimination

¶8 The principle of discrimination is bifurcated.[19] On the one hand, it limits the use of weapons that are by nature indiscriminate, that is, incapable of discriminating between lawful (combatants and military objectives) and unlawful (noncombatants and civilian objects) targets. Most often, the prohibition is expressed in terms of the ability to aim the weapon in question. For instance, a long-range missile with no, or only a rudimentary, guidance system would be objectionable because it is too indiscriminate. So too would biological weapons that spread contagious diseases, for such weapons are incapable of afflicting only combatants and difficult to control.[20]

16. This principle most clearly expresses humanitarian law's balancing of State-centric interests in resorting to force against the more broadly based human interest in shielding non-participants from the effects of what is, at best, an unfortunate necessity.

17. For discussion of *implementation* in future conflict, see Louise Doswald-Beck, *Implementation of International Humanitarian Law in Future Wars*, *in* Schmitt & Green, *supra* note 15, at 39; and Howard Levie, *An Optimist Looks at the Law of War in the Twenty-First Century*, *in id.* at 311.

18. Though the RMA certainly will not be limited to the United States, most core participants are States traditionally aligned with the United States. For instance, a disproportionate share of the most technologically advanced militaries are NATO members.

19. For a comprehensive review of the principle, see generally ESBJÖRN ROSENBLAD, INTERNATIONAL HUMANITARIAN LAW OF ARMED CONFLICT: SOME ASPECTS OF THE PRINCIPLE OF DISTINCTION AND RELATED PROBLEMS (1979).

20. Protocol I Additional to the Geneva Conventions expresses the prohibition thusly:

¶9 By contrast, the second facet of the principle precludes indiscriminate *use* of weapons, regardless of their innate ability to discriminate.[21] The SCUD missiles launched by the Iraqis in the 1990-91 Persian Gulf War aptly illustrate the difference. SCUDS are not inherently indiscriminate. For example, if employed in the vast expanses of the desert against troops, military equipment, or bases far removed from population centers, little danger of random destruction of protected persons or objects exists. However, Iraqi SCUD attacks against Israeli and Saudi cities (the issue of use against a non-belligerent State aside) clearly constituted indiscriminate use,[22] for whatever the actual intent of the Iraqis may have been, the likelihood of harming lawful targets was far outweighed by that of striking protected persons or objects.

¶10 This latter aspect of discrimination itself consists of three components—distinction, proportionality, and minimizing collateral damage and incidental injury.[23] Each is found in customary law and codified in Additional Protocol I to the Geneva Conventions. Although certain countries, most notably the United States, have failed to ratify the Protocol, they generally concur that its core provisions on discrimination express customary principles of international law.[24]

¶11 Distinction prohibits direct attacks on civilians or civilian objects. Article 48 of the Protocol expresses the basic rule that Parties to a conflict

---

> Indiscriminate attacks are. . .(b) those which employ a method or means of combat which cannot be directed at a specific military objective; or (c) those which employ a method or means of combat the effects of which cannot be limited as required by this Protocol; and consequently, in each such case, are of a nature to strike military objectives and civilians or civilian objects without distinction.

Protocol Additional to the Geneva Conventions of August 12, 1949 and Relating to the Protection of Victims of International Armed Conflict, June 8, 1977, ¶ 4, art. 51.4(b-c), U.N. Doc. A/32/144, Annex I (1977), *reprinted in* 16 I.L.M. 1391, 1413 (1977) [hereinafter "Additional Protocol I"]. Unguided missiles exemplify the former, biological weapons the latter.

21. The provision cited in the previous footnote incorporates this prohibition as attacks which "are not directed at a specific military objective . . . ." *Id.*, art. 51.4(a).

22. U.S. DEPARTMENT OF DEFENSE, REPORT TO CONGRESS ON THE CONDUCT OF THE PERSIAN GULF WAR (Title V Report to Congress) (1992), at 621-22, *reprinted in* 31 I.L.M. 612 (1992).

23. The typology of law of war principles varies. For instance, the U.S. Air Force employs the categories of military necessity, humanity, and chivalry, with proportionality as an element of necessity, whereas the U.S. Navy uses necessity, humanity and chivalry. In substantive effect, though, there is no real difference between the typologies. The law is the same; only the verbiage differs. *Cf.* DEPARTMENT OF THE AIR FORCE, INTERNATIONAL LAW—THE CONDUCT OF ARMED CONFLICT AND AIR OPERATIONS (AF Pamphlet 110-31, 1976), at 1-5—1-6, *with* U.S. NAVY/MARINE CORPS/COAST GUARD, THE COMMANDER'S HANDBOOK ON THE LAW OF NAVAL OPERATIONS (NWP 1-14M, MCWP 5-2.1, COMDTPUB P5800.7), 5.1 (1995). This article adopts the typology of discrimination set forth in Christopher Greenwood, *The Law of Weaponry at the Start of the New Millennium, in* Schmitt & Green, *supra* note 15, at 199-202.

24. Unofficial, but probative compilations of the United States' views on the Additional Protocol I by then State Department attorneys can be found in: Michael J. Matheson, *Session One: The United States Position on the Relation of Customary International Law to the 1977 Protocols Additional to the 1949 Geneva Conventions*, 2 AM. U. J. INT'L L. & POL. 419 (1987); Abraham D. Sofaer, *Agora: The U.S. Decision Not to Ratify Protocol I to the Geneva Conventions on the Protection of War Victims*, 82 AM. J. INT'L L. 784 (1988).

must "distinguish between the civilian population and combatants and between civilian objects and military objectives and accordingly direct their operations only against military objectives."[25] Military objectives are "those objects which by their nature, location, purpose or use make an effective contribution to military action and whose total or partial destruction, capture or neutralization, in the circumstances ruling at the time, offers a definite military advantage."[26]

¶12 This seemingly straightforward principle often proves difficult to apply in practice.[27] The dilemma lies in the extent of nexus required between the object to be attacked and the military operation. In others words, the subjectivity inherent in the terms "effective" and "definite" invites disparate interpretation. Some entities, such as the International Committee of the Red Cross (ICRC), define the concepts narrowly. In the ICRC's *Commentary* on the Protocol, effective contribution includes objects "*directly used* by the armed forces" (e.g., weapons and equipment), locations of "*special importance* for military operations" (e.g., bridges), and objects *intended* for use or *being used* for military purposes.[28] The Commentary interprets the phrase "definite military advantage" to exclude those attacks offering only "*potential or indeterminate* advantages."[29] Civilians are legally protected from attack unless they take a "*direct* part in the hostilities."[30] The ICRC defines such participation as "acts of war which by their nature or purpose are likely to cause actual harm to the personnel and equipment of the enemy armed forces."[31] Doubt as to the character of an object or individual is resolved in favor of finding civilian status.[32]

¶13 Others take a less protective approach to the limitations.[33] The United States, for example, would include economic facilities that "*indirectly but effectively* support and sustain the enemy's war-fighting capability" within the ambit of appropriate targets.[34] Similarly, some have

---

25. Additional Protocol I, *supra* note 20, art. 48. The *Commentary on the Protocol*, citing the St. Petersburg Declaration, includes members of the armed forces in the term "military objectives." COMMENTARY ON THE ADDITIONAL PROTOCOLS OF 8 JUNE 1977 TO THE GENEVA CONVENTIONS OF 12 AUGUST 1949 [hereinafter "COMMENTARY"], at 635 (Yves Sandoz et. al. eds., 1987). The prohibition is also expressed in Article 51.2 ("The civilian population as such, as well as individual civilians, shall not be the object of attack.") and Article 52.2 ("Attacks shall be limited to strictly military objectives."). *See* Additional Protocol I, *supra* note 20, arts. 51.1, 51.2.

26. Additional Protocol I, *supra* note 20, art. 52.2. According to the *Commentary*, the term "object" encompasses combatants. *See* COMMENTARY, *supra* note 25, at 635.

27. The *Commentary* notes that "[t]he text of this paragraph certainly constitutes a valuable guide, but it will not always be easy to interpret, particularly for those who have to decide about an attack and on the means and methods to be used." *See id.*.

28. *Id.* at 636 (emphasis added).

29. *Id.* (emphasis added).

30. Additional Protocol I, *supra* note 20, art. 51.3 (emphasis added).

31. COMMENTARY, *supra* note 25, at 619.

32. Additional Protocol I, *supra* note 20, arts. 50.1 (for civilians) and 52.3 (for civilian objects).

33. *See, e.g.*, W. Hays, *Air War and the Law of War*, 32 AIR FORCE L. REV. 1, 113-145 (1990).

34. *See* U.S. NAVY/MARINE CORPS/COAST GUARD, *supra* note 23, at 8.1.1. This assertion is labeled a "statement of customary international law." The *Handbook* cites General Counsel, Dep't of Defense, Ltr. of Sept. 22, 1972, *reprinted in* 67 AM. J. INT'L L. 123 (1973), as the basis for

cited mission-essential civilians working at a base during hostilities, even though not directly engaging in acts of war, as legitimate targets.[35] Thus, while there is general agreement that the Protocol accurately states customary law principles, notable disagreement persists over exactly what those standards are.

¶14 The second component of the prohibition on indiscriminate use is the principle of proportionality, codified in Articles 51 and 57 of the Protocol.[36] Proportionality enjoins attacks which "may be expected to cause incidental loss of civilian life, injury to civilians, damage to civilian objects, or a combination thereof, which would be excessive in relation to the concrete and direct military advantage anticipated."[37] As with Article 48, terminological imprecision, specifically as to the phrase "concrete and direct," invites subjective interpretation and application.[38] The Commentary indicates that the "expression . . . was intended to show that the advantage concerned should be substantial and relatively close, and that advantages which are hardly perceptible and those which would only appear in the long term should be disregarded."[39]

¶15 Proportionality differs from distinction in terms of *scienter*. Whereas the restriction to military objectives seeks to preclude attacks in which protected persons or object are themselves targets, or where the attack is made with culpable disregard for the civilian consequences, proportionality operates in scenarios in which incidental injury and collateral damage are the foreseeable, albeit undesired, result of attack on a legitimate target. This renders the discrimination decision matrix much more complex. With the first tier of discrimination analysis, the question is: "May I lawfully target an object or person?" With proportionality, an additional query must occur: "Even if I conclude that targeting the person or object is unlawful, may I nevertheless knowingly cause him or it injury or damage in my attack on a legitimate objective?"

¶16 When performing proportionality calculations, the actor must not

---

this characterization.

35. *See* Letter from DAJA-IA [Department of the Army, Judge Advocate, International Affairs] to Counselor for Defense Research and Engineering (Economics), Embassy of the Federal Republic of Germany (Jan. 22, 1988), *cited in* Parks, *supra* note 33, at 134 n.400.

36. Additional Protocol I, *supra* note 20. On the issue of proportionality generally, see William J. Fenrick, *The Role of Proportionality and Protocol I in Conventional Warfare*, 98 MIL. L. REV. 91 (1982), and Judith Gail Gardam, *Proportionality and Force in International Law*, 87 AM. J. INT'L L. 391 (1993).

37. Additional Protocol I, *supra* note 20, art. 51.5(b). A similar prohibition, in the context of precautions in attack, is found at *id.*, art. 57.2(a)(iii). Military advantage is evaluated in terms of the entire campaign/war, not simply the immediate advantage from which attacking forces benefit. On this point, see generally Stefan Oeter, *Methods and Means of Combat*, *in* THE HANDBOOK OF HUMANITARIAN LAW IN ARMED CONFLICTS 105 (Dieter Fleck ed., 1995).

38. Indeed, the ICRC *Commentary* notes that "the criticism [in the Diplomatic Conference and thereafter] was directed particularly at the imprecise wording and terminology. . . . Such criticisms are justified, at least to some extent. Putting these provisions [subparas. 4 and 5] into practice . . . will require complete good faith on the part of belligerents, as well as the desire to conform with the general principle of respect for the civilian population." COMMENTARY, *supra* note 25, at 625.

39. *Id.* at 684.

only struggle with issues of inclusiveness (what are the concrete and direct consequences?), but he must also conduct a difficult jurisprudential balancing test. Optimally, balancing tests compare like values. However, proportionality calculations are heterogeneous, because dissimilar value genres—military and humanitarian—are being weighed against each other. How, for example, does one objectively calculate the relative weight of an aircraft, tank, ship, or vantage point in terms of human casualties?

¶17 Further compounding the elusiveness of definitive proportionality calculations is the multiplicity of "valuation paradigms" that affect the weight accorded particular military or humanitarian occurrences.[40] Context often determines value. For example, destroying command, control, and communications (C^3) facilities in circumstances in which the outcome of a conflict is uncertain is essential to operating within an opponent's decision loop. Destroying these assets as efforts are underway to negotiate termination of hostilities may, by contrast, prove counter-productive.

¶18 Valuation paradigms may also be experientially determined. On an immediate individual basis, of course, there is no distinction in the value placed on life by different societies. It would be absurd, for instance, to suggest that a Belgian valued the life of a loved one any more or less than a Somali. Yet, in some societies, death, poverty, and deprivation tragically are so widespread that their population can become desensitized to death in the more general sense. In much the same way that a doctor becomes less personally affected by death over time, or a criminal defense attorney learns to react somewhat impersonally to the crimes of her client, those who have the misfortune to live amongst death-filled circumstances may become inured to death when it is not personally relevant. This notion flies in the face of the objective valuation of life sought by humanitarian law, but represents an unfortunate reality that shades proportionality calculations. Among makers of proportionality calculations, therefore, the value attributed to the human suffering caused by a military operation may very widely with social or cultural background.

¶19 Conceptually determined valuation paradigms are yet a third complicating factor. As an example, there is growing recognition of the need to protect the environment during armed conflict. However, proportionality calculations made in the attempt to do so will be determined in great part by whether one values the environment in and of itself (intrinsic valuation), or in terms of what it offers humankind (anthropocentric valuation).[41] Lastly, valuation paradigms may be temporally determined, that is, evolving over time. Again, using the environment as an example, fifty years ago there was hardly a whimper as

40. The issue of valuation paradigms in the context of environmental damage during armed conflict is explored more fully in Michael N. Schmitt, *War and the Environment: Fault Lines in the Prescriptive Landscape*, ARCHIV DES VÖLKERRECHTS, March 1999, at 25.

41. This theme is developed in Michael N. Schmitt, *Green War: An Assessment of the Environmental Law of International Armed Conflict*, 22 YALE J. INT'L L. 1 (1997).

war wrought horrendous environmental consequences. Today, military leaders and policy-makers increasingly evidence environmental consciousness by factoring environmental damage into their proportionality calculations.[42]

¶20 The final component of discrimination is the requirement to select the method or means of attack likely to cause the least collateral damage or incidental injury, all other things being equal, relative to the military advantage obtained. Whereas the first two components of discrimination focused on whether a target could be struck, this requirement, codified in Article 57 of the Protocol,[43] disallows injury or damage that the attacker can reasonably avoid. Consider an attack on a command and control facility in a population center. Obviously, the center is a legitimate target. Additionally, though civilian casualties and damage are likely to result from a proposed attack by aircraft employing unguided bombs, the anticipated extent of the damage and injury is clearly outweighed by the military advantage that will inure to the attacker. However, if guided munitions would lessen the expected loss and damage without increasing the risk to the aircrew or decreasing the expected damage to the target, and the guided munitions are readily available, then the attacking force should employ them.

III. THE POSSIBLE IMPACT OF FUTURE WAR

¶21 As noted, predictive efforts are inherently replete with uncertainty. Yet, certain possible, or even likely, trends in military affairs can be identified based on technological advances, geopolitical events, and logical shifts in strategy and tactics. Together, they suggest the presence of an RMA for the new millennium. Moreover, they will surely influence the existing understanding of the principle of discrimination. What follows are predictions about the possible future changes in warfare and the context in which it occurs, together with their potential consequences for the principle of discrimination.[44]

---

42. An excellent example of the military's concern with environmental damage was the 1995 international conference on the topic sponsored by the United States Naval War College. The proceedings of that conference are published in 69 U.S. NAVAL WAR COLLEGE INTERNATIONAL LAW STUDIES, PROTECTION OF THE ENVIRONMENT DURING ARMED CONFLICT (Richard Grunawalt et al. eds., 1996).

43. Additional Protocol I, *supra* note 20, art. 57.2(a)(ii) ("With respect to attacks, the following precautions shall be taken . . . take all feasible precautions in the choice of means and methods of attack with a view to avoiding, and in any event to minimizing, incidental loss of civilian life, injury to civilians and damage to civilian objects . . . .").

44. Much of the analysis offered herein draws on JOINT CHIEFS OF STAFF, CONCEPT FOR FUTURE JOINT OPERATIONS: EXPANDING JOINT VISION 2010 (1997). The principle of discrimination will evolve in the face of changes in the nature of warfare, for, much as water seeks a constant level, law inevitably endeavors to fill normative lacunae or dispense with contextually irrelevant or unresponsive standards.

A. Accentuation of Global Divisibility

¶22 There are significant forces at work that contain within them the potential for sharpening global division. In particular, the gap between the developed and lesser developed States may widen as advantaged States continue to leverage their comparative economic and technological advantages to control increasing shares of the global economy.[45] Their relative ability to do so will grow with the swelling importance of technologically intense sectors of the market, such as information management.[46]

¶23 Today, economic strength translates into potential military strength to a degree that is perhaps unprecedented in history. Most notably, the military budgets of the United States and its closest allies dwarf those of most of the rest of the world. For instance, in 1997 the United States spent $259 billion on defense, over a third of the world's total defense expenditures, and five times that of the number two defense spender, Japan. Indeed, U.S. defense expenditures exceed those of the next eight spenders combined. Perhaps more determinative with regard to future war is the fact that the United States spent seven times more money on defense-related research and development than its next closest competitor, France.[47] Such disparities have practical consequences.

¶24 As an example, consider aircraft carriers. In 1998, only nine States possessed these dominant naval warships.[48] The United States, with the largest economy, had twelve, more than the remainder of the world

45. Statistical trends in long-term development are set forth at WORLD BANK, WORLD DEVELOPMENT INDICATORS 1998 (CD-Rom), tbl. 1.4. While the disparities in annual average percentage of growth are not huge, since the developed States start with a much larger economy, the percentages translate into significant differences in actual growth. A particular dilemma is that as the comparative disadvantages of the "have-nots" grow, these States are ever more aware of their status due to the spread of mass communications in lesser developed States. This awareness, and the inflated expectations that are likely to result therefrom, can be a source of instability. Interestingly, though the relative gap may widen, the number of "haves" may increase in the twenty-first century due to the diffusion of advanced technology. One possible danger of this situation is that more States will have the economic and technological wherewithal to develop indigenous weapons production capabilities, thereby exacerbating the problem of weapons proliferation. For a discussion of the proliferation threat, see OFFICE OF THE SECRETARY OF DEFENSE, PROLIFERATION: THREAT AND RESPONSE (1996).

46. For data illustrating differences in the distribution of the gross world product, see generally UNITED NATIONS, TRENDS IN INTERNATIONAL DISTRIBUTION OF GROSS WORLD PRODUCT (1993). Between 1960 and 1994, the per capita income disparity between the richest and poorest fifths of the world's nations grew from 30 to 1, to 78 to 1. The problem may continue to increase because many lesser-developed countries have a birth rate that outpaces their economic growth. *See* Steven Sinding, *Now We Can Be Serious about Population Politics*, INT'L HERALD TRIB., Feb. 8, 1999, at 8.

47. *See* ECONOMIST, June 20, 1998, at 120, tbl. In 1997, the top 10 defense spenders were: United States, Japan, France, Germany, Britain, Russia, Italy, Saudi Arabia, South Korea, and Brazil.

48. United States, France, Italy, Spain, United Kingdom, Russia, India, Thailand, and Brazil. *See generally* THE INTERNATIONAL INSTITUTE FOR STRATEGIC STUDIES, THE MILITARY BALANCE, 1997/98 (1997) [hereinafter THE MILITARY BALANCE].

combined.[49] Similarly, consider the United States Air Force's new Air Expeditionary Force (AEF) concept. The Air Force will build 10 deployable packages of 175 aircraft and 2,600 support troops. Each will be capable of deploying on short notice worldwide for missions ranging from combat to disaster relief.[50] Just one would be able to outfight the air forces of many nations.

¶25 Conclusions as to the future relationship between economic wherewithal and military strength must be carefully drawn. Most significant are issues of quantity versus quality. In the not too distant past, defense spending roughly tracked quantitative relationships between militaries. Thus, the more a country spent on defense, the larger its armed forces. This is changing. Although the United States spends a far greater amount on defense than any potential competitor, it has only the third largest military.[51] The reason is simple: high technology weaponry is expensive, while personnel, particularly in lesser developed countries, are cheap. As an example, the cost estimate of the Army's Theater High Altitude Area Defense (THAAD) system, which is being developed to guard against missile attacks, is 14 billion dollars.[52] To place this figure in context, the projected cost of this *single* U.S. system roughly equals or exceeds the defense budgets of China, which has the largest military in the world, and such technologically advanced States as Canada and Israel.[53]

¶26 The gap between States in ability to field new military technologies must surely expand as technology costs rise in relative terms. Aircraft represent an excellent example. Tomorrow's main-line U.S. fighter will be the F-22 Raptor. Produced by Lockheed-Martin, the proposed package of 442 aircraft is expected to cost $71.6 billion.[54] What the future may hold, then, is a trend towards efforts by developed States, faced with continuing demands to reduce the size of their militaries, to leverage their comparative economic and technological advantages by fielding high-tech weaponry in compensation for numerical weakness.

¶27 The United States has recognized these advantages in *Joint Vision 2010*, an official document that sets forth in broad terms how it intends to fight in the twenty-first century.[55] This publication describes the goal of

49. *See id.* at 20.

50. Described by Major General Dennis Gray, ANG (visited Apr. 15, 1999) <aflsa.jag.af.mil/GROUPS/NATIONAL_GUARD/ANG/AEFGray.html>.

51. *See* THE MILITARY BALANCE, *supra* note 48, at 291-97, tbl. 53 (current as of 1996 and excluding reservists or paramilitary forces).

52. *See* Bradley Graham, *Anti Missile Systems' Costs Test U.S. Ability to Pay, General Says*, WASH. POST, Sept. 3, 1998, at 4.

53. Figures for national military expenditures are available on-line. *See* SIPRI Military Expenditure Database (visited Apr. 15, 1999) <http://www.sipri.se/projects/Milex/Introduction.html>. The defense budget calculation for the Chinese military is based on the officially reported budget, but in fact, funds available to the Chinese military exceed this figure.

54. *See* U.S. Government Accounting Office, *Tactical Aircraft: Concurrency in Development and Production of F-22 Aircraft Should Be Reduced* (1995) (visited Apr. 27, 1999) <http://frwebgate.access.gpo.gov/cg. . .txt&directory=diskb/wais/data/gao>.

55. U.S. JOINT CHIEFS OF STAFF, JOINT VISION 2010 (1996) [hereinafter JOINT VISION 2010] (also available at http://www.dtic.mil/doctrine/jv2010/jv2010.pdf). Each military service in

"full spectrum dominance," i.e., the ability to dominate warfare in any environment and at any level of conflict, from military operations other than war to large scale international armed conflict.[56] To achieve this goal, the United States will take advantage of technological innovations and information superiority to out-maneuver, out-target, and out-defend the opponent. With its military partners, it will enjoy greater situational awareness of the battlefield and be capable of reacting to threats and opportunities thereon more quickly and more definitively than the enemy.[57]

¶28 Warfare along these lines is asymmetrical in that the opposing sides approach the battlefield from very different perspectives, perspectives which are in great part the product of economic and military disparity between the "haves" and "have-nots" (or at least, "have-lesses").[58] The former group is illustrated by States such as the United States, Canada, most western European countries, Japan, and, in light of its military wherewithal and potential, possibly China; the latter group would include lesser and undeveloped States such as the bulk of those in Africa. If the gap between the "haves" and "have-nots" continues to widen, warfare will become increasingly asymmetrical as technologically advanced States play to their strengths to defeat numerically superior forces.[59] And, as demonstrated in the 1990-91 Persian Gulf War, the obverse is unlikely: asymmetry in the form of sheer numbers is unlikely to offset technological inferiority. Thus, technologically impaired forces must seek low-cost, low-tech methods of asymmetrical warfare. In terms of the principle of discrimination, the risks posed by asymmetry are dangerous.

¶29 Recall first that discrimination prohibits the use of indiscriminate weapons. Two categories of low-cost, low-tech weaponry, which could be used with great effect against better equipped forces, are chemicals and biologicals. The core reason chemicals and biologicals are prohibited is that they are inherently indiscriminate; their dissemination is subject to such unpredictable influences as weather or the travel patterns of those afflicted. Moreover, the capability to use them in a discriminatory fashion depends on the delivery system's complexity, the ability of the user State to develop non-persistent strains of toxins, and the scientific savvy of those employing them. Unfortunately, the "haves/have-nots" premise suggests

---

the United States has published a complementary service-specific vision: U.S. NAVY, FORWARD . . . FROM THE SEA (1994); U.S. ARMY, ARMY VISION 2010 (1996); U.S. AIR FORCE, GLOBAL ENGAGEMENT: A VISION FOR THE 21ST CENTURY (1996).

56. *See*The concept of "full spectrum dominance" is set forth in JOINT VISION 2010, *supra* note 51, esp. 20-23; CONCEPT FOR FUTURE JOINT OPERATIONS, *supra* note 40, esp. 50-51.55, at 25-26.

57. *See id.* at 20-23; JOINT CHIEFS OF STAFF, *supra* note 44, at 50-51.

58. The United States specifically cites asymmetric challenges as one of four national security threat categories. The others are regional dangers, transnational dangers, and wild cards (unanticipated threats). *See* White House, *A National Security Strategy for a New Century* (1997) (visited Apr. 27, 1999) <http://www.jya.com/nss.htm>.

59. On the issue of leveraging technology to compensate for size, see generally Anthony H. Cordesman, *Compensating for Smaller Forces: Adjusting Ways and Means Through Technology*, 1992 U.S. ARMY WAR C. THIRD ANN. CONF. ON STRATEGY 1.

that those States least likely to possess such attributes are the very ones most likely to resort to this non-discriminatory form of warfare.

¶30 All of the potential adversaries and allies of the United States in the Middle East are developing chemical and/or biological warfare capability.[60] As a result of the 1993 Chemical Weapons Convention[61] and the 1972 Biological Weapons Convention,[62] most of the developed States against which they might be used have either destroyed or are destroying their chemical and biological weapons arsenals.[63] The consequent inability of developed States to respond in kind provides a significant incentive for lesser equipped militaries to resort to such weapons. Perhaps the only credible deterrent against their doing so (aside from any likelihood that the State employing them would nevertheless lose the conflict) is the threat of nuclear retaliation, a threat which proved effective during the Gulf War.[64] The dilemma is that the use of nuclear weapons is itself under normative attack, the most recent salvo being the 1996 Advisory Opinion of the International Court of Justice mentioned above.[65]

¶31 Disparity also provides an incentive for "have-nots" to define the concept of military objective broadly. If they cannot hope to match their opponent on the battlefield, they must look elsewhere for targets. Since economic facilities undergird the "haves'" superiority, these facilities will become particularly attractive targets. For instance, the notion of attacking

---

60. The Institute for National Strategic Studies has noted the following capabilities in the Middle East: Algeria (infrastructure for the production of chemical weapons, base of experts for biological weapon production); Libya (production of chemical weapons, possible research on biological weapons); Egypt (production of chemical weapons, base of experts for biological weapon production); Syria (production of chemical weapons, possible production of biological weapons); Iraq (infrastructure for the production of chemical weapons if decision is made to produce, infrastructure for the production of biological weapons); Iran (production of chemical weapons, possible production of biological weapons); Jordan (base of experts for chemical weapons production, technical base for biological weapons production); Israel (possible production of chemical weapons, infrastructure for production of biological weapons if decision is made to produce). *See* INSTITUTE FOR NATIONAL STRATEGIC STUDIES, STRATEGIC ASSESSMENT 1996, at 202 (1996).

61. Convention on the Prohibition of the Development, Production, Stockpiling and Use of Chemical Weapons and on Their Destruction, Jan. 13, 1993, U.N. Doc. CD/CW/WP.400/Rev. 1, *reprinted in* 32 I.L.M. 800 (1993) [hereinafter "Convention on Chemical Weapons"].

62. Convention on the Prohibition of the Development, Production and Stockpiling of Bacteriological (Biological) and Toxin Weapons and on Their Destruction, *opened for signature* Apr. 10, 1972, U.N. Doc. A/RES/2826, *reprinted in* 11 I.L.M. 309 (1972).

63. Among the developed States that have ratified, acceded, or succeeded to the Biological Weapons Convention as of August 1998 are France, Germany, Japan, Russia, United Kingdom, and United States. Iraq is not a party, though it is a signatory. Each of these is also a party to the Chemical Weapons Convention, while, again, Iraq is not.

64. Judge Schwebel of the International Court of Justice discusses this episode in his dissenting opinion in the *Nuclear Weapons Case*. *See* Nuclear Weapons Case, *supra* note 6, Dissenting Opinion of Judge Schwebel, at 11; *see also* INSTITUTE FOR NATIONAL STRATEGIC STUDIES, *supra* note 60, at 203. The problem of countering weapons of mass destruction has drawn attention in military circles. *See, e.g.*, Robert W. Chandler, Counterforce: Locating and Destroying Weapons of Mass Destruction (Aug. 1998) (USAF Academy Institute for National Security Studies Occasional Paper 21).

65. *See* Nuclear Weapons Case, *supra* note 6.

financial entities, such as a stock market or financial system, readily surfaces in discussions of information warfare.[66] These are not military objectives under the present humanitarian law. However, nations outclassed on the battlefield certainly have an incentive for viewing them as such, regardless of the narrower approach advocated by entities such as the ICRC.

¶32 Much more frightening is the prospect that relative disadvantage will drive the "have-nots" to abandon the principle of discrimination altogether. If a State cannot hope to win on the battlefield, then perhaps it will elect to carry the battle beyond it. After all, this is precisely what terrorists do. The State-sponsored terrorism witnessed over the past decades is but a step away from State terrorism, a fact well-illustrated by the Iraqi plot to kill former President Bush in 1993. This propensity may even become prevalent in conventional warfare. Facing an overwhelmingly dominant force during the Gulf War, the Iraqis chose to target Israeli cities, classic forbidden targets even if Israel had been a belligerent, in an effort to splinter the coalition it faced. Despite the mandates of humanitarian law, the incentive to alter the cost-benefit calculations of an opponent by targeting its civilians and civilian property, thereby violating the principle of distinction, increases in proportion to one's own military disadvantage.

¶33 Disparity also aggravates the application of the proportionality principle by distorting its various valuation paradigms. In the first place, the mere fact that one faces significant disadvantages creates a context very different from that in which a more technologically sophisticated opponent operates. Because of the disadvantages, the calculation of military advantage likely to result from an operation will be greater, for the issue is not the objective value of a target, but rather the target's subjective value to the attacker. To an attacker facing impending defeat, the destruction of any of the enemy's capability is invaluable; to one certain of victory, there may be very little value added in the destruction of further targets, at least relative to the likelihood of civilian loss. Even the destruction of *valid* targets with negligible civilian loss when victory is at hand can draw international condemnation, as demonstrated by the criticism over the "Highway of Death" incident during the Gulf War.[67] Thus, military disadvantage may serve to "exaggerate" military advantage calculations at the expense of avoiding civilian harm.

¶34 Similarly, it is reasonable to conclude that two adversaries at clearly distinguishable stages of development may draw differing conclusions as to what value to assign to civilian objects, and possibly even civilians. Thus, though the opponents may actually be making a

---

66. On information warfare in an *ad bellum* context, see Michael N. Schmitt, *Computer Network Attack and the Use of Force in International Law: Thoughts on a Normative Framework*, 37 COLUM. J. TRANSNAT'L L. 885 (1999).

67. A concise legal analysis of this incident is offered by Professor Françoise Hampson in *Proportionality and Necessity in the Gulf Conflict*, PROC. 86TH ANNUAL MEETING AM. SOC'Y INT'L L. 45, 53-54 (1992).

calculation at the same time, from the perspective of their development as a modern State, they operate within divergent valuation paradigms. This phenomenon is evident, for example, in the increased casualty aversion of more developed countries compared to lesser-developed States.[68] Whether civilian or military casualties are involved, anecdotal evidence suggests that the more developed a country, the less fatalistic its populace. The greater the disparity, then, the further we move away from an objectively determinable proportionality balancing. Regrettably, this situation is self-catalytic: the wider the chasm between competing standards of balance, the greater the likelihood that the side that advances the higher standard will ratchet its calculations downward in response to an opponent's actions.

¶35 Beyond the dynamics of relative economic wherewithal and its military consequences, the global community is at risk of fragmentation from other forces. Of particular divisiveness is a growing tendency towards religious and ethnic discord.[69] During the Cold War, such discord was somewhat muted by the umbrella of bipolar competition. Today, however, ethnic and religious violence, both internal and international, has become widespread. Unfortunately, in the passion of morally or ethnically charged violence, humanitarian principles, particularly those requiring discrimination, may be discarded. From Nagoro-Karabakh and Sarajevo to Belfast and the remote villages of Rwanda, internecine conflict in the post Cold-War era has assumed a particularly brutal, and often indiscriminate, visage.

¶36 The unprecedented willingness of the international community to create war crimes tribunals in the cases of Yugoslavia and Rwanda and to move towards the creation of a permanent International Criminal Court demonstrates the alarm that these tragedies have finally begun to raise. Unfortunately, little reason exists to believe that war crimes will be relegated to the dust bin of history anytime in the near future.

B. A Blurring of the Lines Between Protected Persons and Objects and Valid Military Targets

¶37 As was noted in the previous section, the "haves/have-nots" dichotomy may encourage "have-not" States to blur the line between civilians and civilian objects on the one hand, and valid military objectives on the other. This is driven by the desire to compensate for weakness on

---

68. The clearest recent example of casualty aversion occurred following the October 1993 shoot-down of two U.S. Army helicopters that were involved in operations to capture the Somali military leader, General Aideed. Eighteen U.S. servicemen, along with hundreds of Somalis, perished in the incident. The uproar this incident caused in the United States led to the withdrawal of all U.S. troops by March 1994. *See* Gary Anderson, *UNOSOM II: Not Failure, Not Success*, *in* BEYOND TRADITIONAL PEACEKEEPING 267, 273 (Donald C.F. Daniel & Bradd C. Hayes eds., 1995).

69. Samuel Huntington has argued that future global discord will be based in culture rather than economics or ideology. *See generally* Samuel P. Huntington, *The Clash of Civilizations?*, FOREIGN AFF., Summer 1993.

the purely military front. However, blurring may also result from a much more subtle phenomenon—the militarization of previously protected entities and individuals.

¶38 Widespread involvement of the citizenry in war can be traced back at least to the nineteenth century. The Napoleonic wars signaled the "popularization" of warfare beyond a select group of professional soldiers, and the Industrial Revolution made possible the arming and equipping of the mass armies first seen on a grand scale during these wars. Success in combat arguably became as dependent on the capability of a State to mobilize its economy to equip huge armies as on the professional acumen of its officer corps. In an unprecedented way, factories, factory workers, and certain other civilian facilities and individuals had a tangible effect on the course of a conflict. That being so, it is not surprising that by the Second World War, belligerents attacked them directly. The appropriateness, or lack thereof, of those attacks informs much of the current debate over the reach of the term "military objective" in Article 48 of Protocol I and, more generally, customary international law.

¶39 The concept of military objective will remain beleaguered as civilian activities are further militarized, and military activities are increasingly civilianized, especially in technologically advanced States. With regard to the former trend, it is becoming ever more difficult to determine when an object, and the facility that makes it, is military. Because the "full spectrum dominance" heralded by the United States necessitates operating within an opponent's decision loop, a capability relying largely on advanced information technology, this is especially true for developed States.[70] The problem is that the technology able to perform these functions differs little, if at all, from that used in the civilian community. How is one to distinguish, as an example, a computer chip manufacturer that sells its chips only to civilian end-users from one that has a number of military contracts?[71] Obviously, such quandaries multiply the difficulty of discrimination.

¶40 Complicating matters is a push to lower costs by purchasing "off-the-shelf" products designed for civilian use, and then adapting them to

---

70. The concept of operating within an opponent's OODA (observe, orient, decide, act) loop implies being able to make decisions faster and better than an opponent so as to force him to react. Enjoying that capability in the twenty-first century will require advanced computer technology to manipulate and operate next-generation sensors and then quickly sort through the resulting data in search of that information relevant to a particular end-user (a commander, unit, or individual soldier).

71. Former Vice-Chairman of the U.S. Joint Chiefs of Staff, Admiral William Owens has highlighted this trend:

> Today, the center of technological acceleration in each of these technologies [battlespace awareness, C^4I, and precision use of force] lies generally in the commercial, non-defense sectors. Our ability to accelerate the fielding of systems, on which we will base our future military superiority, thus depends on our capacity to tap into developments taking place for the most part outside the existing Department of Defense laboratory and development infrastructure.

William A. Owens, *The Emerging System of Systems*, PROCEEDINGS, May 1995, at 36, 38.

military purposes. If military officers use Microsoft Word as their word processing software of choice, for example, does a Microsoft plant become a valid target? Along these same lines, the military increasingly utilizes civilian facilities and activities in order to minimize costs. Such arrangements range from sharing office space, runways, or port facilities, to using the Internet or pursuing partnerships with commercial space entities and consortiums.[72] In the search for savings and efficiencies, such practices dilute the prescriptive effect of the belligerents' obligations to "avoid locating military objectives within or near densely populated areas" and to "take the other .necessary precautions to protect the civilian population, individual civilians[,] and civilian objects under their control against the dangers resulting from military operations."[73] At the same time, there will be pressure from those who wish to target such entities and activities to lower the threshold for judging a target lawful.

¶41 Finally, there is an increased proclivity, again often for fiscal reasons, to contract out many activities which previously were performed by military personnel, and which are integral to the effective conduct of military operations. The U.S. military, for example, has at times contracted out aircraft maintenance, security, transportation of troops and supplies, housing, and even training in basic combat functions. When civilians perform support functions, the line between non-combatants and combatants inevitably blurs. Are civilians who perform these support functions targetable? If so, which functions rise to the requisite level of support to combat operations necessary to render them subject to attack? Even if one accepts the argument that such individuals are targetable, these activities place *all* civilians at greater risk because of the difficulty an attacking force will have in distinguishing civilian participants from civilian non-participants. In fact, this very concern drew objections to the Protocol I provisions relaxing the requirement that combatants distinguish themselves from the civilian population.[74]

¶42 Clearly, if the trend towards militarizing civilian activities and

---

72. The U.S. Space Command is actively seeking partnerships with commercial entities and consortiums, sometimes multinational in nature, as well as with civilian governmental agencies involved in space operations, such as NASA. Indeed, "Global Partnership" is one of Space Command's four operational concepts. U.S. SPACE COMMAND, VISION for 2010 (1997). On the legal issues involved with such activities, see generally Peter Jankowitsch, *Legal Aspects of Military Space Activities, in* SPACE LAW: DEVELOPMENT AND SCOPE 143 (Nandasiri Jasentuliyana ed., 1992); and Richard A. Morgan, *Military Use of Commercial Satellites: A New Look at the Outer Space Treaty and "Peaceful Purposes,"* 60 J. AIR L. & COMM. 237 (1994). The implications of this practice are momentous. If a country uses civilian airliners for military purposes during a war, to what extent do the carrier's aircraft, maintenance facilities, and control centers become lawful targets? What about the regional air traffic control system? Are commercial satellites that provide positioning data to military, commercial, and private aircraft and ships targetable? What about those that provide weather data to both military planners and emergency response organizations? Does the military's use of the Internet make it a target?

73. Additional Protocol I, *supra* note 20, art. 58 (b-c).

74. These objections have come from the United States, among others. *See* 1 U.S. AIR FORCE, OFFICE OF THE JUDGE ADVOCATE GENERAL, OPERATIONS LAW DEPLOYMENT DESKBOOK, tab 12, ¶ 1.7.6.1 (objecting to the provision).

civilianizing military ones continues, the consequences for the principle of discrimination are grave. There will be measurable pressure to interpret the universe of targetable objects and individuals more liberally than today simply because each side will seek to deny its opponent potential advantage. Any such calls for relaxing the criteria for valid targets should be, as discussed *infra*, resisted. Moreover, as a practical matter the difficulty of determining who and what is, in fact, supporting the military effort will complicate discrimination. Today, the Internet, stock markets, economic infrastructure, and other primarily civilian entities do not constitute lawful targets, regardless of who the attacker is. The tie to direct and concrete military advantage is simply too attenuated. Yet, as integration expands it will prove ever more difficult to determine with any precision the relationship of a potential target to the military effort. Nevertheless, humanitarian principles dictate that any consequent urge to simplify legal criteria by relaxing them should be opposed.

C. From Battlefield to "Battlespace"

¶43 In battles past, combat was generally linear. Opposing forces faced each other across fairly distinct, geographically articulable lines. Objects susceptible to being struck, either directly or collaterally, tended to be those closest to the forward edge of the battle area. Civilians were usually absent from the battlefield, either because the battle occurred in relatively unpopulated areas or because they had fled prior to its onset.

¶44 In the twentieth century, this linearity has diminished severely. Blitzkrieg warfare as practiced by the mechanized German Army in 1939-40, for instance, was based on maneuver so fluid that the forward edges of battle areas became transitory. Similarly, strategic bombing did away with linearity altogether in the aerial realm. The result of this revolution in speed and reach was that civilians found themselves at growing risk. In many cases, it became difficult to escape the onslaught of combat by simply fleeing the battlefield, because the battlefield moved too quickly and too unpredictably. Furthermore, the ability to apply force beyond the immediate area of military operations rendered the heretofore de facto enforcer of the principle of discrimination —distance—impotent. The novel technologies meant that new, yet still valid, military target sets far beyond the battlefield could be struck, but because they were often located near civilians and civilian objects, the likelihood of collateral damage and incidental injury increased.

¶45 In twenty-first century warfare, this tendency will be exacerbated many-fold, as "battlespaces," virtual and non-linear loci of combat, replace battlefields. Future wars will involve technologically advanced militaries applying carefully synchronized force from an array of precision platforms against targets identified and located by advanced sensors.[75] The question

75. *See generally* DOMINANT BATTLESPACE KNOWLEDGE (Stuart E. Johnson & Martin C. Libicki eds., 1995).

for civilians will be less one of *where* combat is occurring as *when*, for there will be few sanctuaries from its effects.

¶46 Notions of battlespace further complicate application of the principle of discrimination. After all, the humanitarian effect of the ability to strike anywhere and anytime necessarily increases the extent to which civilians and civilian objects are intermingled with military objectives. This intermingling results not from the presence of more civilians and civilian objects in the target area, but rather from the fact that valid targets which could not feasibly be struck in the past now become vulnerable. To the extent that the universe of strikeable targets multiplies, so too does the potential for collateral damage and incidental injuries. This actuality, *sans plus*, does not complicate the making of proportionality calculations, but it does dramatically increase the frequency with which the most difficult ones (those involving intermingling) will have to be made. It will also require greater attention to the attacker's obligation to chose that method or means of warfare least likely to cause collateral damage or incidental injury, while still achieving military objectives.

D. The Advent of Precision Engagement

¶47 In the next century, the operational concept of "precision engagement" will underlie military tactics and strategy. Set forth in *Joint Vision 2010*,[76] precision engagement "will consist of a system of systems that enables military forces to locate the objective or target, provide responsive command and control, generate the desired effect, assess [the] level of success, and retain the flexibility to re-engage with precision when required."[77]

Thus, precision takes on new meaning. Rather than being the ability to strike a designated target; it becomes a qualitatively improved holistic combat methodology.[78] Two capabilities are key to achieving precision engagement: information dominance, particularly surveillance and reconnaissance, and the ability to apply just the right amount and kind of force to accomplish the objective. Information dominance implies the transparency of an opponent's actions and intentions, and the concealment of one's own. Improved and new technologies will enable quantum leaps in intelligence gathering, surveillance, and reconnaissance.[79] For example,

76. Precision engagement is one of four key concepts in the enabling of *full spectrum dominance*, as articulated in *Joint Vision 2010*. The others are *dominant maneuver*, "the multidimensional application of information, engagement, and mobility capabilities to position and employ widely dispersed joint air, land, sea, and space forces"; *full dimension protection*, which will use information technology to better protect U.S. forces; and *focused logistics*, the "fusion of information, logistics, and transportation technologies to provide rapid crisis response, to track and shift assets even while en route, and to deliver tailored logistics packages and sustainment directly at the strategic, operational, and tactical levels of operations." JOINT VISION 2010, *supra* note 55, at 20, 23, 24.

77. *Id.* at 21.

78. *See generally* JOINT CHIEFS OF STAFF, *supra* note 44, at 51.

79. Space satellites serve as an apt example. By the early twenty-first century,

micromachining offers fantastic new possibilities, many of which involve the production of tiny sensors that an adversary may detect only with great difficulty.[80] Technology also will promote greater transparency of an enemy even at the level of an individual soldier.[81]

¶48 Data gathering technologies are supplemented by systems that make possible the effective use of that data. Given the capabilities of sensor assets, the mountain of information that will be available to the decision-maker will, in most cases, be unmanageable in its unprocessed form. Therefore, new data processing systems employing artificial intelligence are being developed to rapidly fuse, sort, evaluate and disseminate information in user-friendly form.[82] Analogous decision-

---

reconnaissance satellites will offer 24-hour worldwide coverage, with improvable resolution of two to three meters. Even more astonishing, in future wars, satellites may be capable of detecting normal conversations on earth with sound sensor technologies. *See* Jeffrey E. Thieret et al., *Hit 'Em Where it Hurts: Strategic Attack in 2025*, *in* 3 AIR UNIVERSITY, 2025, WHITE PAPERS 173, 187 (1996). Consider this possible future scenario from one U.S. Air Force study:

> In the year 2025, sensor collection provides enough data for a virtual 3-D model of the [target] to include its composition, internal structure, baseline characteristics, and tendencies.... Sensors determine the building's exact dimensions and floor plan. They then highlight soft spots. Sensors distinguish between rooms containing biological agents, test equipment, sleeping quarters, and even the snack bar. Target acquisition sensors also construct a baseline, or living archive, of data concerning routine activity and environmental conditions. Examples include the average number of people who enter and exit each day, the number of vehicles in the parking lot, and the level of noise generated by the facility.

Id. at 185-86. Using this information, targeters can determine where to strike the building, with what, and when the building can best be attacked without causing extensive civilian casualties.

80. For instance, some futurists envision minuscule "robots" with optical and communications capabilities, which would be disguised as insects for use in jungles where present day sensors are often ineffective. *See* Pat Cooper, *U.S. Develops Army of Tiny Robots*, DEF. NEWS, Nov. 11-17, 1996, at 4. Future sensors may be the size of dust mites and seedable by unmanned aerial vehicles, and could be sucked into the air conditioning system of facilities to be monitored. *See id.* Sensors' "senses" would not necessarily be limited to sight and hearing. Certain ones might be sensitive to particular chemical make-ups, thus allowing the identification of chemical weapons or metal objects like armor or aircraft. *See* Thieret et al., *supra* note 74, at 187-88.

81. Most notably for the not-too-distant future, the proposed Land Warrior Modular Fighting System will equip soldiers with a helmet-mounted computerized display tied to an improved weapon, thermal sensor for night vision, and an image enhancer. The system will allow the soldier to "see around corners" and transmit data up the chain of command. There are even suggestions that soldiers will have access to eye-sized real time picture map displays to enhance situational awareness. *See* Art Pine, *Revolutionary High-Tech Military Isn't Ready for the World's Battlefields*, PROVIDENCE J., Jan. 5, 1997, at D3; Barbara A. Jezior, The Revolutionized Warfighter Circa 2025 (1997) (unpublished manuscript on file with the Naval War College Library); *see also Infantry System Turns Soldier into High-Tech Urban Warrior*, NAT'L DEF., Apr. 1997, at 24.

82. An excellent example being developed for the U.S. Navy by Johns Hopkins University is the Force Threat Evaluation and Weapon Assignment System. It will collate data from radar systems aboard the ships of an entire battle group and then fuse it to generate a three-dimensional graphic display of the threat environment for the battle manager. The system will even evaluate threats and suggest which to engage and when. *See* Douglas Waller, *Onward Cyber Soldiers*, TIME, Aug. 21, 1995, at 38, 41.

making enhancement systems will be available at the operational (theater) and strategic levels as well. The real-time nature of these "C^{4}ISR"[83] technologies will for the first time make planning as events unfold possible. In terms of operations tempo, this is a quantum leap over the present practice of planning in advance of execution or in response to enemy action.

¶49 Complementing the revolution in information systems are equally impressive advances in weapons capabilities. Inaccurately hailed as the first "smart" war,[84] the 1991 Persian Gulf War popularized the capabilities of precision guided munitions. Though the accuracy and effectiveness of smart weapons in that war may have been exaggerated through coverage in the popular media, the weapons of future wars will be more than smart—they will be "brilliant." Inertial navigation technologies, the incorporation of global positioning data, and other improvements in guidance systems will permit weapons to regularly strike within centimeters of the desired point of impact.[85] Accuracy will be further enhanced by improvements in the overall "weapon system," which consists of the weapon, launcher, and other external components that make the attack possible.[86] Not only will technology allow better target identification

---

83. Command, control, communications, computers, intelligence, surveillance, and reconnaissance.

84. Despite impressive film footage of precision guided munitions (PGMs) being employed during the conflict, the Gulf War was actually dominated by conventionally delivered munitions. Only eight percent of the weapons used were precision guided. A General Accounting Office study of 20 major targets found that Coalition forces used at least two laser-guided weapons against each. Twenty percent of the targets were struck with at least six weapons, while 15 percent were hit by eight or more. The need to strike targets repeatedly is persuasive evidence that such weapons were no panacea. *See* Tony Capaccio, *GAO Questions U.S. Air Power Impact on Gulf War*, DEF. WK., June 30, 1997, at 1; *see also* Barton Geldman, *U.S. Bombs Missed 70% of the Time; "Smart" Munitions Far More Accurate*, WASH. POST, Mar. 16, 1991, at A-1. Since the Gulf War, the United States has invested heavily in precision weaponry. For example, the two U.S. carriers deployed to the Persian Gulf in February 1998 carried with them more smart weapons than all six of the carriers deployed during the war. *See* Bradley Graham, *New Weapons Give Navy Top Air Role This Time*, WASH. POST, Feb. 12, 1998, at A-1, 25.

85. Inertial navigation is dead reckoning performed automatically by a device that continuously integrates acceleration and direction from a know point of departure in order to ascertain location. Its advantage is that it is completely passive and self-contained; therefore, its users are not subject to electronic signal monitoring or electronic countermeasures. Some warheads will actually count walls penetrated to ensure that the warhead explodes within the desired room. This capability is particularly useful in strikes against biological or chemical facilities in which the goal is to destroy toxins without releasing them into the atmosphere. *See* William Matthews, *New Bombs Penetrate, Incinerate*, AIR FORCE TIMES, Feb. 16, 1998, at 6. To place this degree of accuracy in historical perspective, during World War II, one-half of all bombs dropped landed over one mile from their intended target. *See All Things Considered* (National Public Radio broadcast, Feb. 13, 1998).

86. For instance, combat aircraft today use information provided by on-board sensors or verbal communications with other aircraft, such as the Airborne Warning and Control System (AWACS), or ground controllers. In the not-too-distant future, by contrast, fighters and bombers will have direct access to data gathered by space- and ground-based sensors, unmanned reconnaissance aerial vehicles, and aircraft other than specialized platforms like the AWACS. *See* USAF SCIENTIFIC ADVISORY BOARD, NEW WORLD VISTAS: AIR AND SPACE POWER FOR THE 21ST CENTURY 11 (summary vol. 1995). On the ground, the U.S. Army may

and accuracy, but those weapons that strike the target will be more effective in achieving the desired level of destruction or damage.[87]

¶50 Non-lethal weapons technologies will also provide fighting forces with a means more precisely tailored to achieve a desired effect.[88] In many "military operations other than war" situations, for example, the use of deadly force may be counterproductive. The prevailing scenario involves crowd control in circumstances where troops are trying to stabilize civil unrest. New non-lethal technologies on the drawing board may offer field commanders less irreversible ways to handle such situations than using traditional armed force.[89]

¶51 In a perfect universe, these advances in information acquisition/dissemination and weapons accuracy/suitability would result in an impressive concentration of precision firepower that could be brought to bear in a transparent and well-understood battlespace against easily identifiable targets. Despite its impressiveness, however, technology contains within it the potential to thicken the Clausewitzian fog of war rather than clear it.[90] To begin with, new stealth technologies may defeat

---

field a "brilliant" anti-armor submunition that will be fired by the Army Tactical Missile System. The munitions will use acoustic and infrared sensors to identify a formation of vehicles, single one out for attack, and destroy it. *See* Owens, *supra* note 71, at 37.

87. Today, a weapon usually destroys through penetration of the target and explosion. This approach will predominate in the next century, but be much improved. Microtechnology will allow weapons to be much smaller, thereby permitting more of them to be carried aboard delivery platforms. *See* Thieret et al., *supra* note 79, at 189. Consider hardened targets. Today they are best attacked with at least a two-thousand pound guided bomb unit; in the future they may be attacked with a 250 pound weapon just as effectively. Moreover, microexplosive technology will make it possible for minute quantities of explosive to destroy a target, further facilitating miniaturization and limiting the collateral damage and incidental injury produced by larger explosions. *See* USAF SCIENTIFIC ADVISORY BOARD, *supra* note 86, at 9-10.

88. The term non-lethal is somewhat controversial because death is possible in the case of many such weapons; it is simply less likely. Therefore, these weapons are increasingly being labeled "less-lethal" rather than non-lethal. On non-lethal weapons, see generally James C. Duncan, *A Primer on the Employment of Non-Lethal Weapons*, 45 NAVAL L. REV. 1 (1998).; James W. Cook III et al., *Non-Lethal Weapons: Technologies, Legalities, and Potential Policies*, AIRPOWER J., Special Ed. 1995, at 77; James C. Duncan, *A Primer on the Employment of Non-Lethal Weapons*, XLV NAVAL LAW REVIEW 1 (1998).

89. Consider acoustic and microwave weapons. The former generate sound frequencies that cause pain and nausea, while the latter cause discomfort or seizure by raising the target's body temperature. *See* Douglas Pasternak, *Wonder Weapons*, U.S. NEWS & WORLD REP., July 7, 1997, at 38. Other technologies being considered include sleep agents, "slick-ums," which coat surfaces with an anti-traction substance that renders them difficult to walk or drive on, and "stick-ums," a sticky foam that can immobilize individuals without killing them. *See* Greg R. Schneider, Nonlethal Weapons: Considerations for Decision Makers 9-10, 27 (Jan. 1997) (Arms Control, Disarmament, and International Security Occasional Paper, University of Illinois at Urbana-Champaign). Other potential non-lethals that some have suggested for use against enemy equipment include electro-magnetic pulse weapons that produce radio-frequency wavelengths damaging to electrical equipment, *see id.* at 14, super-caustics and embrittling agents that can be sprayed from aircraft or delivered by shells to corrode or weaken surfaces such as bridges, optical lenses, tires, etc., *see id.* at 20-22, microbes that eat rubber, silicon, electronics, and oil, *see* Jezior, *supra* note 81, at 16, and "super-glue," an air-dispensable substance that fouls equipment and weapons, *see* Schneider, *supra*, at 9-10.

90. The Naval War College's Mackubin Owens has questioned the current "obsession" with technology. According to Owens, there is a

> recrudescence of a McNamara-like worship of technology in some part of

transparency.[91] At a more basic level, information dominance may yield little more than information overload, a situation in which so much information is provided that the decision-maker becomes stressed and confused and begins to make worse decisions than he otherwise would have.[92]

¶52 Perhaps most potentially troublesome is the fact that every information dependency becomes an information vulnerability.[93] This fact has fostered the growth of a relatively new form of combat, information warfare. In information warfare, the enemy's information systems are targeted to deny or distort the information on which he relies. One technique, computer network attack, presents a particular problem for high-tech militaries which depend on computers for everything from deployment planning and intelligence dissemination to transmitting air tasking orders.[94] Militaries that train in an information rich environment may be crippled by the disabling of their computer systems. More troubling is the prospect that the information on which they depend could be altered. Using this tactic, the attacker can essentially take control of its opponent's deliberative processes. A frightening variant of this scenario is one in which the victim is made to target its own forces or even civilians

---

> the Pentagon, a worship that ignores the principal lesson of military history: as long as war involves humans, no technology can completely eliminate friction, ambiguity and uncertainty, thereby ensuring that a military organization will function at 100 percent efficiency.... The question is, who is more relevant in the real world: Clausewitz, who observed that "everything is simple, but the simplest thing is difficult. The difficulties accumulate and the end by producing a kind of friction that is inconceivable unless one has experienced war"; or those who reject him, explicitly or implicitly, assuming that technology will render friction in war obsolete?

Mackubin T. Owens, *Planning for Future Conflict: Strategy vs. "Fad,"* STRATEGIC REV., Summer 1996, at 5, 6. For a fascinating account of how a combatant might fight against a technologically superior military, see generally Charles J. Dunlap, Jr., *How We Lost the High-Tech War of 2007: A Warning from the Future,* WKLY. STANDARD, Jan. 29, 1996, at 22.

91. As an example, the removal of the pilot and cockpit in "uninhabited combat aerial vehicles" may allow novel design features that reduce the radar cross section by a factor of two. *See* USAF SCIENTIFIC ADVISORY BOARD, *supra* note 86, at 8.

92. *See* R.L. DiNardo & Daniel J. Hughes, *Some Cautionary Thoughts on Information Warfare,* AIRPOWER J., Winter 1995, at 69, 75.

93. *See, e.g.,* Neil Munro, *Our Electronic Achilles' Heel,* WASH. POST WKLY. ED., Aug. 14-20, 1995, at 24.

94. The U.S. military has over 2.1 million computers and 10,000 local area networks. *See* Thomas E. Ricks, *Information-Warfare Defense is Urged,* WALL ST. J., Jan. 6, 1997, at 1; B2. Computer network attack can take many forms, most commonly through introduction of a "virus." For example, "logic bombs" can be transmitted to a computer where they sit idle until activated by a specific event or at a set time. They might be used, for example, to attack such targets as air defense or air traffic control systems. Other techniques include flooding a system with so much data it cannot process it, or the use of "sniffer" programs to gather access codes allowing entry into target systems. In many instances, the attacks may occur without the knowledge of the victim. On the threat posed by information warfare from the U.S. perspective, see OFFICE OF THE UNDER SECRETARY OF DEFENSE FOR ACQUISITION AND TECHNOLOGY, REPORT OF THE DEFENSE SCIENCE BOARD TASK FORCE ON INFORMATION WARFARE DEFENSE, Nov. 1996, at app. B (Threat Assessment).

and civilian targets.[95]

¶53 Despite countervailing trends, the various aspects of precision engagement generally bode very well for implementation of the principle of discrimination. The Gulf War may serve as a preview of things to come. Although only eight percent of the munitions employed in that conflict were precision guided,[96] and despite isolated claims to the contrary, the use of advanced information systems, delivery techniques, and improved weaponry led to a dramatic decrease in the extent of civilian casualties and damage to civilian objects relative to the scope and intensity of the campaign.[97] Technology made these results possible.[98] When compared to urban air attacks of past wars, the Desert Storm bombing effort was astonishingly discriminate

¶54 In the future, discrimination capabilities certainly will improve. Collateral damage and incidental injury generally result from the interplay of three factors: uncertainty as to what is being hit, inability to precisely meter the amount of force applied, and the lack of absolute certainty that the target can be hit. The technologies described above will dramatically diminish the effect of each of these limiting factors. Simply put, in the conflict of tomorrow, technologically advanced forces will be able to strike what they want with near one hundred percent accuracy using techniques in which significant collateral damage and incidental injury will be the exception, not the rule.[99]

---

95. Reports of a war game held at National Defense University several years ago portray one hypothetical future war scenario. Set in the year 2000, it involved an OPEC meeting that goes awry when Saudi Arabia opposes Iranian demands for an oil production cutback in order to drive prices up. Iran mobilizes and conducts several attacks on Saudi warships. It also begins to conduct information warfare operations to destabilize the Saudi regime and keep the United States and United Kingdom out of the fray. A Saudi refinery is destroyed when computer malfunctions in its control mechanisms cause a fire, a "logic bomb" placed in the computer system running U.S. railways causes a passenger train to derail, computer "worms" begin to corrupt the U.S. military's classified deployment database, and a "sniffer" disrupts fund transfers in the Bank of England. *See* Steve Lohr, *Ready, Aim, Zap*, N.Y. TIMES, Sept. 30, 1996, at D1. The civilian consequences of these and similar operations are self-evident.

96. *See* discussion *supra* note 84.

97. For criticism of the coalition's actions during the 1991 Gulf War, see generally HUMAN RIGHTS WATCH, NEEDLESS DEATHS IN THE GULF WAR (1991); and Roger Normand & Chris Jochnick, *The Legitimization of Violence: A Critical Analysis of the Gulf War*, 35 HARV. J. INT'L L. 387 (1994). The proceedings of a panel chaired by Professor Oscar Schacter at the 1992 meeting of the American Society of International Law offer a more balanced approach. Panelists included Professors Frits Kalshoven, Françoise Hampson, Yoram Dinstein, Ruth Wedgwood, and Colonel Fred Green. *See Implementing Limitations on the Use of Force: The Doctrine of Proportionality and Necessity*, PROC. 86TH ANNUAL MEETING AM. SOC'Y INT'L L. 39 (1992). The United States' position on the subject is set forth in U.S. DEP'T OF DEFENSE, *supra* note 22, at 611-17.

98. For instance, in the first night's attacks against central Baghdad, only highly precise F-117 Nighthawk aircraft and Tomahawk land attack missile (TLAM) cruise missiles were employed in order to minimize collateral damage and incidental injury. While almost forty-eight key targets in and near Baghdad were struck in the first twenty-four hours of the campaign, direct civilian casualties were minimal. *See* U.S. DEP'T OF DEFENSE, *supra* note 22, at 116-18, 177-78.

99. Expectations will shift accordingly. For instance, speaking of his decision to order

¶55 Should this prognosis become reality, understanding of how to apply the rule of proportionality may shift subtly, but meaningfully. If first-tier collateral damage and incidental injury (i.e., damage and injury directly caused by the kinetic force of the attack) become rarer, it is probable that humanitarian attention will increasingly dwell on subsequent-tier, or reverberating, effects. As an illustration, since electrical grids will be attackable with highly surgical strikes, proportionality analysis in future war may well center on derivative consequences, such as unintended but foreseeable denial of power to medical facilities.[100] Given the increase of dual-use technologies and facilities, described above, the risk of subsequent-tier damage and injury may actually increase because of the greater interconnectivity of valid target sets with civilian activities. This is especially true with regard to information warfare. Imagine, for instance, information warfare attacks on railroad switching computers, air traffic control systems, or telephone exchanges. The civilian fallout would be monumental and severe. Of course, reverberating effects were theoretically always calculated when assessing proportionality. However, it is only now that the means exist to limit dramatically direct collateral damage and incidental injury that we are being sensitized to reverberation.[101] Improved capabilities inevitably lead to heightened humanitarian expectations.

¶56 The one exception to the advent of precision engagement is non-lethal weapons. As conceived of today, technologies such as acoustic or microwave weapons are fairly indiscriminate; as "area" weapons, they are difficult to direct with any precision. Of course, their discriminatory capabilities can be expected to improve in the future. Additionally, as in other cases, the issue is discriminatory *use* rather than discriminatory *capability*. The real danger is that non-lethals will be used in situations or locations, such as urban settings, that do not permit sufficient discrimination. However, their use might still be both appropriate and proportionate because the lesser lethality of such weapons will compensate for their increased coverage. In other words, proportionality may be measured less in terms of scope than in terms of severity.

¶57 Paradoxically, precision engagement capabilities have the potential to make discrimination *more* difficult to achieve. Three possibilities are particularly threatening. The first is that the ability to easily identify and

---

attacks in August 1998 against a suspected secret chemical plant in Sudan, President Clinton stated that "I didn't want some person who was a nobody to me, but who may have a family to feed and a life to live, and probably had no earthly idea what else was going on there, to die needlessly." Tim Weiner & Steven L. Myers, *Flaws in U.S. Account Raise Questions on Strike in Sudan*, N.Y. TIMES, Aug. 29, 1998, at A-1. Thus, highly precise cruise missiles were used to strike the plant at a time when it would not be filled with employees.

100. On these attacks, see James W. Crawford, *The Law of Noncombatant Immunity and the Targeting of National Electrical Power Systems*, FLETCHER F. WORLD AFF., Summer/Fall 1997, at 101.

101. The limited criticism of the Gulf War air campaign that has been voiced evidences this growing sensitization, for it was predominately based on allegations that coalition attacks did not pay adequate attention to subsequent-tier effects.

target military assets may encourage the practice of placing them in the vicinity of civilians and civilian objects so as to cause attackers to hesitate lest they cause disproportionate damage or injury. Although the use of civilians or other protected persons as shields violates Geneva Convention IV and Protocol I and constitutes a Grave Breach,[102] attackers remain obligated to perform proportionality calculations.[103] This fact makes civilian shields appealing when an opponent might otherwise target your assets with great impunity. Saddam Hussein used this tactic with unfortunate regularity. Recall the Iraqi placement of foreign and Kuwaiti hostages at military sites, the dispersal of helicopters to residential areas, placement of surface-to-air missiles in a school located in Kuwait City, basing of fighter aircraft next to the Temple of Ur, and the decision not to evacuate Baghdad despite having practiced just such a civil defense operation.[104] As technologies improve even further, and in light of the fact that "have" States will disproportionately possess them, condemnable practices may recur.[105]

¶58 Second, and equally troubling, is the prospect that because proportionality valuation paradigms are conceptually determined, there is a risk that the "haves" will face pressure to readjust their proportionality balance calculations to account for the other side's malfeasance. This pressure would result from treating humanitarian law as if it were designed to ensure a fair fight rather than protect non-participants from the effect of hostilities, a dangerous trend from the humanitarian perspective.

¶59 Finally, when facing an adversary that enjoys the capability to render one's actions transparent, the incentives to engage in perfidy and the disincentives to distinguish oneself from the civilian population swell. The blurring of the line between combatants and non-combatants was discussed earlier. Here, the blurring is intentional, almost a form of camouflage. Although these practices are unlawful,[106] the same decisional dynamics set forth above regarding placement will be at play, both as to the attacker and the target forces. In fact, Protocol I has recognized this reality to some extent in its relaxation of the requirement that combatants

---

102. *See* Geneva IV, *supra* note 7, arts. 29, 149; Additional Protocol I, *supra* note 20, arts. 75.2(c), 85.2.

103. *See* Additional Protocol I, *supra* note 20, art. 51.7-8.

104. *See* U.S. DEP'T OF DEFENSE, *supra* note 22, at 607-08, 613-15.

105. And, in fact, have. Since the Gulf War, Iraqi citizens have occupied potential targets on multiple occasions to shield the targets against threatened air attacks by the multinational forces still patrolling Iraqi skies. The ability of the Iraqi Air Force or air defense to deter such attacks is minimal; thus, the resort to civilian shields.

106. Perfidious acts are those "inviting the confidence of an adversary to lead him to believe that he is entitled to, or is obliged to accord, protection under rules of international law applicable in armed conflict, with intent to betray that confidence." Protocol I, *supra* note 20, art. 37. Typical examples involve misuse of the Red Cross, Red Crescent, or the surrender flag. Such practices are also proscribed by the Annexed Regulations to Hague IV. *See* Hague Convention IV Respecting the Laws and Customs of War on Land, with Annexed Regulations, Oct. 18, 1907, art. 23(F), *reprinted in* Schindler & Toman, *supra* note 13, at 63, 83. The combatant/noncombatant distinction is found in varying formats in Hague Convention IV, *id.*, art. 1; Geneva IV, *supra* note 7, art. 4A(2); and Additional Protocol I, *supra* note 20, art. 44.

distinguish themselves. Aware that they will not do so when it would be suicidal, Protocol I now provides that when "owing to the nature of the hostilities an armed combatant cannot distinguish himself," he need only carry his arms openly during the engagement and be visible to his opponent while deploying in preparation for the launching of the attack.[107] Similar pressures to relax standards may well surface in the future as distinguishing oneself becomes ever more foolhardy, at least from the perspective of those facing technologically advanced foes.

E. Disparate Cognitive Approaches

¶60 The inherent complexity of the principle of discrimination should by now be apparent. At the most basic level, targeting civilians and civilian objects is prohibited. Additionally, there are certain situations in which all reasonable actors would agree on the proportionality balance. No one would suggest, for example, that capturing a single low-ranking soldier would justify the death of hundreds of civilians. Similarly, the military advantage of destroying a command and control center would seldom be outweighed by damage to an uninhabited building. The complexity emerges when one moves from these extremes along the proportionality continuum toward the center. It is here that dissimilar valuation paradigms clash. Despite the resulting dissonance, however, at this point parties may still agree that they should all be judged by objective standards; they simply disagree as to what those standards should be.

¶61 Normative relativism began to slip into humanitarian law with the Protocol I, Article 57 prohibition of avoidable damage and injury. Beyond an objective level of requisite discrimination, different States will be subject to different standards based upon their capabilities. There is little serious question that some degree of subjective application is merited. The quandary lies in translating this subjectivity into affirmative actions. Must a State use precision guided munitions if it possesses them?[108] Assuming it does, what are the requirements for their use? May it hold them in reserve until the course of the battle becomes clear? To what extent does a State's ability to replenish its supply of such munitions bear on the appropriate rate of employment? Do States have to acquire them if they have the economic wherewithal to do so? Or consider non-lethals. When must a State use non-lethals if conventional weaponry is likely to have more

107. *See* Additional Protocol I, *supra* note 20, art. 44.3. As noted *supra* note 24, the United States opposes this provision. According to the Rapporteur, the Additional Protocol I provision exception "recognized that situations could occur in occupied territory and in wars of national liberation in which a guerrilla fighter could not distinguish himself throughout his military operations and still retain any chance of success." XV Official Records of the Diplomatic Conference on the Reaffirmation and Development of International Humanitarian Law Applicable in Armed Conflicts, Geneva, 1974-1977, at 453, CDDH/407/Rev. 1, ¶ 19.

108. For an argument that it need not, see Danielle L. Infeld, *Precision-Guided Munitions Demonstrated their Pinpoint Accuracy in Desert Storm; But is a Country Obligated to Use Precision Technology to Minimize Collateral Civilian Injury and Damage?*, 26 GEO. WASH. J. INT'L L. & ECON. 109 (1992).

definitive effect? Must a State arm its military with non-lethals if it has the economic resources to do so?

¶62 The major premises advanced in this essay spotlight these issues. Assuming the "haves/have-nots" dichotomy holds, the "haves" will suffer most from the blurring of the line between civilians/civilian objects and military objectives because they are the ones taking greatest advantage of the economies and efficiencies offered by an advanced civilian economy. Moreover, they will dominate the battlespace through the precision engagement made possible by systems only they can afford. Given these realities, their approach to the issue of normative relativism in discrimination should logically be to advocate raising the *objective* level of requisite discrimination, while holding firm against enhanced *subjective* obligations. If a technologically-advanced military can easily defeat an opponent on the battlefield, would it not seek to keep the fight there by legally immunizing areas beyond it from attack? While an expansive view of the term "military objective" made much sense when facing a huge Soviet military-industrial complex across the Fulda gap, in the unipolar setting of the twenty-first century, advanced States likely will play to their advantages by taking a narrower view. Of course, the flip side of this equation is that technologically-advanced States logically will object to expanding *subjective* obligations because those obligations will fall most heavily on their shoulders.

¶63 By contrast, the technologically-impaired States' cognitive approach toward prescriptive evolution likely will oppose expanding the objective understanding of discrimination, for doing so might deprive them of the only targets and strategies likely to hold any promise for success. In many cases, their only hope is not to prevail in combat, but rather to raise the costs for their opponents to an unacceptable level. The fewer targets the States with lesser technology are permitted to strike, the less opportunity they will have to impose costs on their advantaged opponents. By the same token, the more limits placed upon their opponents, the greater the advantage to these States. Normative relativism will drive up costs, both monetarily and in terms of efforts expended, for their opponents, and will limit damage and injury to their own people and facilities. Therefore, it will most often operate to their benefit.

IV. Assessing the Prospects for the Future

¶64 It is essential when assessing the future prospects for humanitarian law to maintain focus on the foundational purposes of this body of law. The goal is not to manipulate prescriptive norms to one's advantage, a particularly insidious form of *realpolitik*, nor is it to ensure a "fair fight" on the battlefield by ensuring that neither side enjoys advantages unavailable to the other. Instead, the purpose is *humanitarian*, to place a human face on a particularly inhuman activity.

¶65 Humanitarian law accomplishes this objective in two ways. First, it strives to limit the level of violence by restricting certain methods and means of warfare, thereby benefiting both participants and non-participants in the conflict. Recognizing that States will hesitate to forego effective techniques and instruments for achieving military objectives, humanitarian law operates at the margins by limiting only the most egregious alternatives (e.g., chemical and biological weapons). Second, it seeks to shield non-participants (primarily civilians) from the conflict by extending certain protections and immunities to them. Discrimination norms represent the archetypal example of this effort. For instance, the proportionality principle recognizes the unfortunate, yet inevitable existence of organized violence in inter-State relations, but attempts to narrow the scope of such violence to the destruction and physical suffering necessary to achieve valid military objectives.

¶66 Assuming, arguendo, the validity of the analysis proffered in this essay thus far, the future seems to bode ill for the principle of discrimination. The major positive trend lies in the area of precision engagement; however, the technology necessary to conduct operations of this complexity is unlikely to be widespread, at least for the foreseeable future. More important, the disparity between the "haves" and "have-nots" reflected in the predictions set forth herein may actually do violence to the principle, for the "have-nots" may well seek that plane of conflict on which they can viably, and asymmetrically, face their high-tech opponents. Other trends either provide disincentives to rigorous application of the principle or encourage its violation. Several simply obfuscate the application of discrimination, even for those who might seek to conduct themselves in accordance with its principles.

¶67 Are the assumptions and motivations underlying the threats to the principle valid, and what approach should States take toward potential deterioration in the principle's normative impact? Optimally, any attempt to arrest or prevent negative trends should reflect commitment to the purposes informing humanitarian law. Yet, the very concept of the State, and related principles such as sovereignty and territoriality, resonates with self-interest, rather than selflessness. States need not operate from within a zero-sum paradigm in making policy choices, but ultimately, most States are rational actors making rational, cost-benefit decisions. Humanitarian law, by forbidding certain actions, limits the options legally available to the State to advance its own interests.

¶68 At first glance, then, neither the "haves" nor the "have-nots" appear to have a logical reason for assuming further humanitarian obligations—each seeks "fairness" (or advantage) and unless the burdens fall with equal weight on all parties, that criterion is breached. The "have-nots" fear that more stringent *objective* standards may deprive them of potential tactics against an enemy that is better placed to operate in the face of these normative constraints on acceptable targets. Arguably, the goal of the "have-not" States should be to relax objective standards so as to take advantage of asymmetrical possibilities. The "haves," on the other hand, view the possibility of *subjective* standards as unfairly biased in a world of theoretical sovereign equality. Why should they be held to a higher standard than other States?

¶69 From a humanitarian standpoint, the appropriate perspective is one that aspires to raise (or at least preserve) *both* the objective and subjective bars, for doing so will foster protection of non-participants. Whether such aspirations are realistic ultimately depends on the cost-benefit calculations made by rational States. Before rejecting this possibility out of hand, it must be recognized that *all* humanitarian law limits the conduct of States in armed conflict. The very existence of this body of law, and the fact that in most conflicts, most military forces comply with it, is testament to the fact that States are willing to accept some legal limits, even when limitations may deny them immediate advantages. They do so for a number of reasons. Abiding by humanitarian law encourages reciprocal adherence by the other side, and compliance avoids the risks of negative domestic and international reaction. As illustrated by the political and public fallout from the My Lai atrocities during the Vietnam War, such reaction may directly affect the course of an armed conflict. Moreover, adherence to humanitarian norms facilitates war termination and restoration of the peace.[109] While States conduct a cost-benefit analysis in determining whether or not to abide by a prescriptive norm, the calculation is far more complex than simply quantifying immediate and direct benefits of compliance.

¶70 Thus, State practice belies the validity of any broad assertion that efforts to enhance humanitarian law are futile because they would limit State prerogatives in combat. The question then becomes whether, given the disparate cognitive perspective of States, the specific humanitarian law principle of discrimination can be strengthened, or at least withstand efforts to weaken its requirements. That, assuming the accuracy of the rational actor characterization, depends on whether States see that it is in their interest to maintain or fortify the principle. Although States are driven by altruistic motivations at times, self-interest tempers even the policies of those States that harbor the worthiest of intentions.

¶71 To assess the prospect, it is first necessary to understand the dynamics, vis-à-vis discrimination, of objective and subjective standards. Recall that discrimination has three components: proportionality, distinction, and minimizing collateral damage. It is theoretically possible to raise the objective demands of discrimination with regard to the first two. The third, by contrast, is inherently contextual and subjective because it requires selecting the most discriminatory option *available to the actor*, all other things being equal.

¶72 To begin with, and despite the inherently subjective contextual,

---

109. The difficulties of returning to normalcy in the States formed from the former Yugoslavia and the continuing mistrust and isolation of Iraq are in no small part the product of war crimes committed during those conflicts. For obvious reasons, negotiating and implementing agreements made with a foe that committed such breaches is difficult at best. By contrast, consider the ease with which Argentina and the United Kingdom returned to relative normalcy following the Falklands/Malvinas war, in which compliance with humanitarian law was widespread.

experiential, and temporal valuation paradigms discussed earlier, in a sense there is an objective proportionality standard because at some distinct point along the continuum of proportionality, an attack becomes disproportionate. The standard could be heightened through adverbial supplementation, as in "military advantage must greatly outweigh" or "significantly outweigh" collateral damage and incidental injury. In an era of precision weaponry, one could argue that doing so would be reasonable.

¶73 The principle of distinction could also be enhanced objectively by expanding the universe of forbidden targets. This might be accomplished either by clarifying the generalized standard, as in expressly resolving the differences over the necessary nexus with military operations before civilians or non-military objects may be attacked in favor of immunity, or by creating additional prohibitions on certain targets, as was done in Protocol I with respect to dams, dikes, and nuclear electrical power generating stations.

¶74 Although some "haves" have resisted similar efforts (the United States, for example, opposes the limit on striking targets likely to release dangerous forces), as noted above, the "have-nots" are more likely to oppose raising objective standards because they then would be deprived of potential targets beyond the battlefield. The "have-nots" may well seek relaxation of the standards so as to secure greater opportunities to fight asymmetrically. From their perspective, the present objective standards disproportionately aid the "haves."

¶75 Of course, from a strictly humanitarian point of view, the issue of which side benefits from an enhanced norm is irrelevant so long as non-participants and their property are shielded from the conflict to a greater degree. That said, only humanitarian approaches that take the existence of inter-State competition into account can succeed. Can the humanitarian and political/military impulses be reconciled?

¶76 They can. Although it is not immediately self-evident, any approach that endeavors to lower the objective bar is short-sighted because the gains are minimal or non-existent. In fact, nearly universal agreement exists among military experts that harm to civilians or civilian property during an international armed conflict is usually counterproductive.[110] It strengthens civilian and military resolve, in part by exacerbating negative images of the enemy. There is no evidence, for instance, that either the bombing of civilian targets by both sides or the use of indiscriminate weapons such as the V-2 during the Second World War yielded tangible returns.[111] Additionally, it may decrease domestic support for the conflict

110. As Adam Roberts has noted, "[t]here is a need to place more emphasis on the idea that this body of law is intensely practical—that it represents, at least in part, a set of professional military standards and bargains among States; that its origins are as much military as diplomatic; and that its implementation can have consequences which are for the most part compatible with the interests of those applying it." Adam Roberts, *Implementation of the Laws of War in Late-Twentieth-Century Conflicts*, *in* Schmitt & Green, *supra* note 15, at 359, 381.

111. On this issue, and aerial warfare generally, see the excellent article by Hays Parks, *The Protection of Civilians from Air Warfare*, 1997 ISRAEL Y.B. HUM. RTS. 65, 77-84.

(as in My Lai) and engender unfavorable international opinion (as did, for example, Iraqi hostage taking and environmental terrorism).

¶77 In fairness, it can be asserted that the counterproductive nature of attacks on civilians and civilian objects is "have" specific. The strategic calculus for a "have-not" State facing a "have" is arguably different, for the potential gains of attacking civilian institutions or individuals are greater. As demonstrated in Vietnam, developed nations have displayed a strong reluctance to continue military action if the conflict imposes a large burden on their civilian population, is taking place in a distant venue, and does not resonate strongly with the average citizen.

¶78 Recent history, however, suggests the futility of "have-not" attacks on civilians or civilian objects. The classic example (although not in the context of international armed conflict) of "have-nots" targeting "have" civilians in order to raise costs and force a change in policy is terrorism. Yet, terrorism usually results in abhorrence and a hardening of will by the target state.[112] Terrorism may draw the attention of the international community to an issue, but there is minimal evidence that it affects either the victim State or its population in a way useful to the terrorist. While it is true that in Vietnam and other such conflicts, public pressure in the United States to withdraw resulted from a sense that the population was bearing unnecessary burdens, the difference is that there the United States itself, and the policies it pursued, was seen as the cause of the hardship, rather than the enemy. Thus it is not the extent of the burden, but rather its perceived source, that is determinative. To the extent that "have-nots" attack "have" civilians, they will be correctly viewed as culpable, thereby causing any cost-benefit calculations on the part of the "haves" to be skewed accordingly.

¶79 A good example is an information warfare attack on a stock market. For obvious reasons, the more developed a State's economy, the greater impact a successful attack against its stock market (or one in which it is involved) would have. Seemingly, then, a stock market would present an attractive target to a "have-not" State frustrated on the battlefield. However, consider the cost-benefit calculus. The attack will have minimal immediate effect on the war-making capability of the target State. In fact, because it is primarily the civilian population and civilian infrastructure that will suffer, public opinion likely will turn against the source of their suffering, the attacker. Moreover, given globalization of the world's economies, an attack on any one stock market will have measurable reverberating effects internationally. This will hardly advance the "have-not" cause from the perspective of non-participants in the conflict (or even that of some supporters of the "have-not" effort). Clearly, in such a case, the costs far-outweigh the benefits (such as emboldening public opinion at home through a daring blow at one's enemy) of such an operation.

¶80 The harder question involves targeting objects or individuals with

---

112. Consider, for example, the U.S. response to the La Belle Disco bombing in Berlin in 1986, the crystallization of British attitudes towards the Northern Ireland issue following IRA bombings, or Israeli reaction to the Intifada.

shared civilian/military character, for by definition their destruction does yield some degree of military advantage. If "have-nots" gain nothing by lowering the objective bar to authorize attacks on civilians and civilian objects, might they nevertheless suffer if it is raised to protect targets which lie on the civilian-military margin? In many cases, they may not, for the prohibition that protects their enemy also protects them, and as a disadvantaged State they are unlikely to enjoy a redundancy of assets or productive capability equal to that of their opponent. Moreover, to the extent that such targets are less than obviously military in nature, their destruction will result in proportionally diminished returns with respect to the potential for prevailing in the conflict. For example, even assuming that Iraq set Kuwati oil wells ablaze and released oil into the Persian Gulf in order to foil coalition air and amphibious operations, the net effect on coalition combat operations was minimal. Thus, the "have-nots" should not exaggerate the benefits asymmetrical operations will yield them in the long term.

¶81 "Have-nots" must realize that the key is not the availability of targets to strike, but rather the net gain derived from their destruction. Arguably, there is little benefit to relaxing objective distinction standards, and probably less to fear in strengthening them than might appear at first glance. In fairness, these premises ring less true with regard to proportionality. Augmentation of the proportionality requirements might well limit "have-not" options, particularly given their relative disadvantage in the realm of precision weaponry. Nevertheless, the loss would be offset to some degree by the fact that as the weaker party to a conflict, military advantage calculations for a given operation are generally greater. Moreover, the international political capital acquired through avoidance of incidental injury and collateral damage is not insignificant. Simply put, despite the threat to objective discrimination standards present and future trends pose, upon deeper reflection neither "have" nor "have-not" States have much net incentive to dispense with or negatively adjust them.

¶82 Any "have" concern regarding the imposition of more stringent subjective discrimination requirements is similarly overstated. It is simply beyond credulity to suggest that the acceptability of striking a particular type of target or causing a certain amount of collateral damage or incidental injury might one day depend on the characteristics of the attacking State. On what basis would such distinctions be made: GNP? Population? Size of military? Technological prowess of the military? Of course, it is theoretically possible to assert that a powerful State should not be able to strike at the variety of targets its disadvantaged opponents can or that it should cause less collateral damage or incidental injury in pursuit of its military objectives. But even if one accepted such an equalizing approach despite its incongruency with existing humanitarian law purposes, given the complexity of their differences, there is no practical way to draw the necessary distinctions between States. Proportionality already accounts for contextual considerations in calculating military advantage; this is the best that can be expected in imposing "subjective" discrimination standards.

¶83 An exception lies in application of the third component of discrimination, that requiring selection of the option causing the least collateral damage or incidental injury, all other things being equal. As noted, this standard is already subjective in a sense, for there is no equity clause in humanitarian law that allows a State chose a more destructive option if its opponent could do no better in conducting the same option. The real question is whether a State should be obligated to *create* options for itself by, for example, acquiring and fielding more precise, less destructive weaponry. No such obligation exists under current humanitarian law; one takes fielded militaries as one finds them.

¶84 Arguably, States should be willing to expend reasonable resources to acquire weaponry necessary to limit collateral damage and incidental injury. Since the goal is not equality between opposing sides, reasonableness should not be measured in terms of an opponent's efforts, but rather by a subjective standard based on one's own valid competing demands (such as well-being of the population). Further, "reasonableness" does not require the unreasonable; thus, "have" States should not fear the substantive effect of such a requirement. The problem resides, as it so often does, in the practicalities. By what standard should one measure reasonableness? How might a State evaluate the relative weight of a return on investment in primary education or elder care against collateral damage or incidental injury avoided due to employment of a precision munition? How would disparate valuation paradigms be addressed? Normative relativity in the fielding of military weaponry is a noble aspiration, but perhaps the issue is best left to the moral realm.

¶85 To summarize, while it is true that the principle of discrimination is at great risk from current and future trends in war and warfare, all is not lost. It is possible for States to be committed to the humanitarian ends of this body of law without severely disadvantaging themselves. Commitment depends on a State's ability to avoid opportunistic and reflexive reaction to change, and instead take a longer, more holistic, view of the principle of discrimination and how compliance or deviation therefrom will affect the State's *overall* objectives. There is little real long-term advantage to anyone in lowering the objective bar of discrimination, and the costs of raising it are in all probability less than most would initially anticipate. Unfortunately, although imposing heightened subjective standards on those capable of achieving them would also advance humanitarian results, the effort would pose great practical difficulties. Nevertheless, maximizing one's ability to avoid collateral damage and incidental injury represents an aspirational norm to which responsible and humane States should aspire.

V. Fostering Humanitarian Ends In Future War

¶86 While the purpose of this essay is to identify possible future fault lines in the application of the principle of discrimination, rather than to suggest *lex ferenda* or new normative schema, several generalized thoughts on the subject can be offered to spark reflection and discourse. First and foremost, before the global community can hope to stop backsliding from current respect for humanitarian law norms, international implementation mechanisms must be improved. In other words, potential malfeasors have to believe that their violations of humanitarian law will come at a cost. If future war may increase the allure of violations, their cost must be raised to at least a corresponding degree. This requires international criminalization of undesirable conduct, impartial and credible fora in which to try offenders, comprehensive jurisdiction over offenses, and the means physically to bring offenders to trial.[113]

¶87 An International Criminal Court (ICC) holds the greatest promise for altering the cost-benefit analysis of potential violators. Though most responsible States agree on the need for such a judicial body, some of them maintain that the Court's Statute, adopted in July 1998, is dysfunctional. The objections are both substantive and procedural, and they have led the seminal player in the process, the United States, to reject the Statute.[114] While this is not the place to debate the merits of the ICC Statute, there can be little doubt that the notion of a permanent tribunal to try war criminals is, *in abstracto*, a very positive one. There can also be little doubt that for such a tribunal to be maximally effective, U.S. participation is essential. This is especially true in light of the "haves/have-nots" dichotomy. Since the United States is the "have" State most likely to be involved in an asymmetrical conflict in which its opponents revert to tactics and strategies that challenge the principle of discrimination, its inclusion in the Court's implementation efforts is key. Without it, the Court is destined to be little more than a "permanent *ad hoc*" tribunal in the mold of those for the former Yugoslavia and Rwanda — useful, but limited in both reach and effect.

¶88 Strengthening the role of international organizations and coalitions of States in enforcing humanitarian standards may also serve to enhance implementation, and thereby create disincentives for normative regression. Inclusivity of enforcement efforts is a positive feature. To begin with, as a general rule, the more States that are engaged in an enforcement action, the greater the sanction available against the miscreant and the greater the deterrent effect. Of course, certain notable failures, such as UNOSOM or UNPROFOR,[115] argue against broad international enforcement actions.

---

113. On jurisdiction, see Yoram Dinstein, *The Universality Principle and War Crimes*, *in* Schmitt & Green, *supra* note 15, at 17. On war crimes generally, see Theodor Meron, *War Crimes Law for the Late Twenty-First Century*, *in id.* at 325.

114. For a discussion of the U.S. rationale for opposition by the Ambassador who led the US Delegation, see David J. Scheffer, *The United States and the International Criminal Court*, 93 AM. J. INT'L L. 12 (1999). On the ICC more generally, see Mahnoush H. Arsanjani, *The Rome Statute of the International Criminal Court*, 93 AM. J. INT'L L. 22 (1999); Ved P. Nanda, *The Establishment of a Permanent International Criminal Court*, 20 HUM. RTS. Q. 413 (1998); and American Society of International Law, *Bibliography on International Criminal Court* (visited Apr. 15, 1999) <http://www.asil.org/crmctbib.htm>.

115. United Nations Operation in Somalia (I & II) and United Nations Protection Force. These operations are discussed in UNITED NATIONS, THE BLUE HELMETS: A REVIEW OF UNITED NATIONS PEACE-KEEPING 285-318, 511-42 (3d ed., 1996).

Nevertheless, while it may sometimes be militarily more sensible to send in forces with focused national identity who have trained and operated together in the past, it should not be forgotten that the mere existence of an international implementation effort, aside from the success thereof, has normative valence. Therefore, the greater the inclusivity of response to a violation of humanitarian principles, the less likely it is to be seen as prescriptively precedential. At least *from this vantage point*, UN or regional organization efforts to induce compliance should be favored over unilateral or limited multilateral operations.

¶89 Inclusivity is valuable beyond implementation. As noted above, disparity in military strength creates much of the potential dissonance surrounding the principle of discrimination. Standing alone, a State's relative military weakness vis-à-vis an opponent may drive it to extremes to which it would not otherwise resort. Inclusivity in the form of collective security regimes helps remedy this dynamic in two ways. First, it narrows the universe of likely opponents, particularly because security regimes tend to be regional in nature and one's natural enemies are often on one's borders. Intra-alliance conflict is simply far less likely to happen than extra-alliance hostilities. That Greece and Turkey have not gone to war against each other in the past fifty years is testament, for example, to the stabilizing influence of NATO membership. Moreover, alliance membership compensates for weaknesses of individual members. For example, knowledge that the United States can provide strategic and tactical airlift capability to its allies allows them to divert resources they would otherwise devote to acquiring mobility capability to technologies such as precision weaponry. In other words, alliance structures offer members synergy through task-based divisions of labor. This improves the military prowess of the membership as a whole, thereby helping alleviate any concerns members may harbor about raising the objective standards of humanitarian law, especially its discrimination component. Thus, to the extent politically and militarily feasible, and when the aims of the alliance are apolitical, alliance expansion, such as that underway in NATO, tends to be useful from the humanitarian perspective.

¶90 Arms control efforts also foster reassurance. To address the incentives described earlier with respect to the use of indiscriminate weapons, such efforts should concentrate on the weaponry to which States would likely resort if facing defeat at the hands of overwhelmingly superior foes.[116] Nuclear, biological, and chemical (NBC) weapons are the most prominent examples. Consider the situation in Iraq. As empirically demonstrated in 1991, Saddam Hussein's chances of prevailing over a western coalition are minimal in the foreseeable future. However, his possession of NBC weapons would demonstrably alter the equation in his

116. One interesting proposal is that when the sales of arms "to relatively poor nations are unavoidable, international law should require the sellers to actually subsidize the price of sophisticated weaponry that can be used with greater likelihood of distinguishing between combatants and noncombatants." R. George Wright, *Noncombatant Immunity: A Case Study in the Relation Between International Law and Morality*, 67 NOTRE DAME L. REV.335, 337 (1991).

favor. Therefore, the value of the UNSCOM effort to seek out and destroy Iraqi NBC capabilities extended beyond keeping Saddam Hussein too weak to viably threaten his neighbors; the indiscriminate nature of the weapons infused the effort with humanitarian import.[117] An identical purpose underpins the need to support the inspection and verification efforts of the Organization for the Prohibition of Chemical Weapons[118] in implementing the 1993 Chemical Weapons Treaty.

¶91 That said, arms control is not necessarily good in and of itself. It must emphasize those weapons which pose the greatest risks *in the context in which they operate*. The effort to have the International Court of Justice declare the use of nuclear weapons a violation of international law is an excellent example of this premise.[119] Clearly, most uses of these weapons would be unlawful as either directly indiscriminate (as in counter-value targeting) or as violative of the principle of proportionality. However, when properly limited, they retain some utility. Reconsider Saddam Hussein's threats to use chemical and biological weapons in the Gulf War. But for possession of nuclear weapons, how could the coalition effectively have deterred his resort to them? Indeed, had he used them early in the war against Turkish, Arab, or Israeli population centers, the conflict might have taken a very different course. Would the fragile coalition have held together if Israel had entered the fray?[120] Would the Turkish government have permitted attacks on Iraq from Turkish bases in Operation Proven Force if the cities of Southeast Turkey had been placed at risk? Might the Arab States have been willing to accept the annexation of Kuwait into Iraq to stave off severe civilian casualties? These queries are not meant to suggest that the nuclear powers should retain their nuclear arsenal. Instead, the point is simpler—one must be careful what one wishes for. Banning or limiting weapons does not inevitably lead to either the protection of the civilian population or a ratcheting down of combat intensity. Each case must be evaluated in the global context in which it occurs.

---

117. United Nations Special Commission (UNSCOM).

118. Convention on Chemical Weapons, *supra* note 61, art VII. The OPCW maintains an informational website. *See* Organization for the Prohibition of Chemical Weapons, *The Chemical Weapons Convention Home Page* (visited Apr. 15, 1999) <http://www.opcw.nl/pts.home.htm>.

119. *See generally* Schmitt, *supra* note 6.

120. This point does illustrate one possible "valid" motivation for a "have-not" State to strike directly at enemy civilians or civilian objects. In the case of a coalition force consisting of "strange bedfellows," potential cracks in the coalition may be exploited by taking this tact. Saddam Hussein certainly tried this with his Scud attacks on Israeli population centers, and with some effect. Much of the U.S. air effort was redirected to finding mobile Scud launchers in the hope that they could be destroyed, thereby foreclosing the need for the Israelis to enter the fray. The immediate military benefit, however, of destroying the Scuds was minimal. Instead, it was a "political" operation, for had the Israelis attacked Iraqi forces, it was not certain that the coalition, which included opponents of Israel such as Syria, would have held together. That said, the circumstances under which such a scenario might recur are fairly unlikely, and certainly not sufficient alone to justify a "have-not" State in opting out of a more stringent humanitarian regime because of fear that it might lose a valuable option open to it when facing superior forces in the future.

¶92 Finally, discrimination can be fostered not only by controlling weapons, but also by limiting the universe of legal targets. For instance, there has been much debate over the past decade regarding whether the environment should be protected during armed conflict by a convention specifically addressing the topic. Similarly, as information operations increasingly dominate future war, calls for protecting civilians from their effects through the codification of use restrictions should be anticipated. As with arms control, the prospect that future war will strain the principle of discrimination constitutes ample reason to redouble efforts to codify (with high degrees of inclusivity) limits on what can be attacked in armed conflict. However, and again as with arms control, such limits are not inherently beneficial. To safeguard the environment at the expense of human protection does a disservice to the principle of discrimination. Similarly, to absolutely restrict strikes on particular information targets makes little sense if the only alternative to neutralizing their military value is conventional strikes against related facilities that, albeit proportional, cause greater civilian suffering. The point is that although codification can advance valid humanitarian ends, and should be pursued when it has that potential, any such effort must be evaluated in the greater scheme of things.

VI. CONCLUDING THOUGHTS

¶93 It is important to emphasize that the notional future posited in this essay is simply that — notional. However, it is a future that many see as plausible, even probable.[121] Tomorrow's war may potentially place the principle of discrimination, which lies at the core of humanitarian law, under great stress. Sadly, it may lead some to adopt positions that challenge the very foundations of humanitarian law. One commentator has even suggested that

> [i]nternational law in its present form shows more concern with antiquated concepts of chivalry among combatants than with the modern reality of mass destruction. The rules of war do not adequately reflect the reality of warfare between a third-world country and a superpower. Compliance with the rules of war is a prescription for disaster. This lesson was learned a long time ago in places such as Vietnam and Afghanistan. To assert that massive aerial bombardment—with its inevitable civilian casualties—complies with the international laws of warfare, but the reciprocal efforts by a third-world country to put civilian populations at risk violate international law reveals one's own political interests. One

121. As noted earlier, the future described is particularly dependent on official U.S. publications such as *Joint Vision 2010*, *supra* note 55; *National Security Strategy for a New Century*, *supra* note 58; *National Military Strategy*, *supra* note 58; and *Concept for Future Joint Operations*, *supra* note 44.

> cannot take this position and realistically expect the international system to gain the respect of countries that are more likely to be the victims than the allies of great powers. . . . The international law that governs the conduct of war is ultimately a system designed to protect the self-interests of the more powerful states. Rules that do not treat all lives equally cannot, in the long run, support the international system.[122]

¶94 The author has lost sight of the prize. Humanitarian law is designed to limit the reach and intensity of armed conflict, not to protect the interests of the "haves." Quite to the contrary, the major instruments of humanitarian law resulted from concern over the tragic humanitarian consequences of conflict between powerful States. The dilemma is that current trends may seem to require deviation from humanitarian norms if weaker States are viably to compete in international armed conflict. One would certainly hope that those who share humanitarian commitment would not advocate sacrificing the all-too-limited protection non-participants in armed conflict enjoy, merely to render war more equitable. They must not forget that war is a political decision for which the average citizen bears the burden, but not the responsibility.

¶95 The challenge for the future is to approach this dilemma with an appropriate cognitive perspective, one that comprehends and works towards the humanitarianism that underlies humanitarian law. Doing so will require a normative sophistication that all too often escapes both those focused on minutiae while insensitive to the ultimate aim of the law, and those who fail to grasp the fact that the idealism law represents must eventually play itself out in a real world. In order to continue to advance the aims of discrimination, it will be necessary to see both the forest *and* the trees. Whether the global community will have the maturity to master this challenge remains to be seen.

122. Paul W. Kahn, *Lessons for International Law from the Gulf War*, 45 STAN. L. REV. 425, 437 (1993). Note that to some extent his analysis mixes, compares, and contrasts *ad bellum* and *in bello* issues. This detracts from the persuasiveness of the argument.

[3]

Zero-casualty warfare

by
A. P. V. ROGERS

There can be no doubt that the political and military planners of the NATO air campaign in the Kosovo conflict of 1999 were determined that it should be carried out strictly in accordance with the law of armed conflict.

"The targets were exclusively military — every effort was made to avoid collateral damage — planes only fire at targets when we are confident that we can strike accurately — some aircraft in the first operation returned without dropping ordnance. Targets are carefully selected and continuously assessed to avoid collateral damage."[1]

"Others, and I have said continually this week that our aim is to hit the target and not to cause collateral damage to any surrounding areas. You have seen the effects of the bombs that we have dropped and the missiles that we have launched. We need to put those on the target, so if someone is in the cockpit and he has got to see the target all the way down to the ground he has to make sure that he can see that target and if he doesn't he is professional enough to not hit that target and bring his bombs back."[2]

"Rules of engagement and concerns about collateral damage placed on us by our political masters are, rightly, very tautly drawn. The discipline of our people is such that they will not drop their weapons unless they have clearly identified their assigned target and know precisely what they're doing."[3]

A. P. V. ROGERS is a Fellow of the Lauterpacht Research Centre for International Law, University of Cambridge, and a former Director of Army Legal Services, United Kingdom.

These are sentiments that experts in the law of armed conflict would heartily endorse.

Despite problems caused by cloud cover, care was taken to ensure that only military objectives were hit. There were, inevitably, some instances of collateral damage.[4] But, by and large, things seemed to go well until an attack on a vehicle column by NATO aircraft operating at 15,000 feet raised an important question about the law of armed conflict: what is the precise legal obligation on an attacker to identify the target as a military objective before he launches his attack?

Background

Until the development of air power in this century, wars tended to be fought by opposing armies or navies in a series of short but bloody battles. While civilians suffered from the effects of armies on the march and from evacuation, billeting and requisitioning, they were rarely directly affected by the fighting unless they were inhabitants of a besieged town.[5] During the static trench warfare of the First World War, they were usually evacuated from the front line area and out of range of artillery fire.

Air power enabled the belligerents to strike well behind enemy lines, at the lines of communication and logistics that kept enemy armies supplied. By cutting them off from reinforcements, fuel, food and ammunition, their ability to fight was severely curtailed. However, this meant striking at areas that were likely to be populated by civilians, thus increasing the risk of civilian casualties. In the First World War military casualties were still extremely heavy, since the tank

1 Jamie Shea, at the NATO press briefing on 26 March 1999, website: www.nato.int.

2 Air Commodore David Wilbey, at the NATO press briefing on 1 April 1999.

3 Air Chief Marshal Sir Richard Johns, "Air power in a new era", *Royal Society of Arts Journal*, 3-4 of 1999, p. 99.

4 As when a bomb fell 600 metres short of the target, at Aleksinac. There was also the incident on 12 April when missiles were fired at a railway bridge near Leskovac, just as a train from Belgrade to Thessaloniki was crossing it.

5 Indeed, the preamble to the Declaration of St. Petersburg of 1868 proclaimed that the only legitimate object of war was to weaken the military forces of the enemy and that, for this purpose, it was sufficient to disable the greatest possible number of men.

was in its infancy and only sheer weight of numbers — allowing for such losses — could win through against the hail of enemy shrapnel and machine-gun bullets; civilian casualties were relatively light.[6] This was about to change. The senior commanders of the war, of course, deeply regretted the death, wounds and sickness of their men, but the sense of military duty to defeat the enemy at any cost seemed to prevail. The more junior commanders, who would rise to high rank in the next war, were determined to ensure that in future military casualties would be reduced.

Things were to change in other ways too. The heavy demands of the large but mobile conscript armies that were put into the field in the Second World War and their increasing reliance on mechanization meant that civilians had to be employed in factories producing weapons, warships and military aircraft, their armaments and components, and in installations producing the fuel to drive vehicles and the raw materials such as steel needed to build ships. The emphasis of targeting was shifting away from enemy combatants to the equipment and supplies on which they depended, but at great cost to the enemy's civilian population. Though still protected by the law of armed conflict from direct attack, they were not protected from incidental damage caused as a by-product of attacks on war production facilities. Bombing was still far from precise.

Guerrilla warfare, in which fighters merge with the civilian population, tends to increase civilian casualties. It has taken its sad toll in many post-1945 conflicts. Guerrillas prefer to launch attacks out of civilian anonymity at the enemy's weak points, often using tactics such as ambush very successfully. Finding it hard to identify and grapple with the guerrillas, their adversaries, the regular forces, are inclined to overreact with their countermeasures or with heavier weapons, in either case to the detriment of the civilian population. The situation is exacerbated when guerrillas, partisans, freedom fighters or other armed factions are engaged in combat in towns or populated areas.

6 For the British Empire forces, 908,371 military battle deaths and 2,090,212 military wounded out of a mobilized military strength of 8,900,000. See the table in the *British Army Review*, August 1996, p. 79.

Regular forces are unable to deploy their armoured vehicles to best advantage and their opponents, from the cover of civilian buildings, can deploy light weapons and anti-tank grenades very effectively at short range. Such fighting entails severe casualties, not only for the troops involved but also for the civilian inhabitants who get caught up in the hostilities. In circumstances like that, the Russian proposal to set up safe corridors to allow the civilian population to escape the fighting in Grozny is in keeping with the principles of the law of armed conflict. Of course, those corridors must genuinely be safe and, preferably, monitored by international organizations such as the ICRC or OSCE.

The understandable modern attitude of military commanders that they will not expose their subordinates to unnecessary risks tends to increase the danger to civilians. This attitude is not limited to the West. After the casualties suffered by the Russian army in its attempts to invade the Chechen capital in January 1995, it tried new tactics in its campaign of 1999. Marshal Igor Sergeyev, the Russian Defence Minister, was reported as saying that Russia was relying on the massive use of firepower to keep down its casualties and that artillery and air force was being used to "destroy the Chechen gangs and their camps". It was estimated that Russia had deployed 100,000 troops against President Maskhadov who had 20,000 to 30,000 experienced guerrillas with light weapons.[7]

There has also been growing pressure, especially in the West, to reduce military casualties to a minimum, otherwise public support for the campaign is likely to fall away. Indeed, there is almost an expectation now of few, if any, casualties, especially if the country is not directly threatened by military operations. The British task force suffered 256 military battle deaths and 777 military wounded out of a mobilized military strength of 9,500 in its campaign to retake the Falkland Islands in 1982.[8] This was tolerated by the British public, perhaps because it was thought that British interests were at stake. But there would have been lower tolerance in the Gulf War of 1991 or in

7 *The Independent*, 4 November 1999.

8 *Op. cit.* (note 6), p. 80.

RICR MARS IRRC MARCH 2000 VOL. 82 N° 837

the Kosovo conflict of 1999, since neither directly affected the British people. In the event, the casualties were slight. There were 17 British military battle deaths in the Gulf;[9] there has been none yet in Kosovo.[10]

The result of these trends has been a steady increase in the ratio of civilian to military casualties in armed conflicts despite the efforts of diplomats and international lawyers to emphasize the principle of civilian immunity.[11] There has been growing public awareness, possibly since the Vietnam War, of these civilian casualties. Media reports, often broadcast at the same time as events unfold in a campaign, have a very immediate impact and influence on the public. This is known as "the CNN factor". The public are shocked by images of women and children killed or injured in war and are likely to have a low tolerance of such casualties, especially, again, if they perceive that national interests are not at stake. The situation is probably exacerbated by their unduly high expectations of the accuracy of smart weapons. As the NATO air campaign in Kosovo went on and mistakes occurred, there was an almost tangible sense of public discomfort. This could have led to pressure to call off the air strikes.

Requirements concerning methods and means of warfare

So the political and military imperative is for weapons and tactics that, so far as possible, prevent own casualties, hit military

9 *Ibid.* According to Erik Durschmied, *The Hinge Factor*, Hodder & Stoughton, 1999, Iraqi military losses were over 100,000 whereas Coalition forces suffered a total of 192 killed, of whom 35 died from "friendly fire" and two were killed dismantling a bomb. "In military terms, such a ratio is called the *Zero Factor*."

10 "NATO won the Kosovo conflict without a single life lost in combat operations on its own side (...) for just two aircraft lost", Nick Cook, "War of extremes", *Jane's Defence Weekly*, 7 July 1999. Two Gurkha engineers, Lt. Gareth Evans and Sgt. Balaram Rai, were killed dealing with unexploded ordnance during the operation.

11 According to the Swiss Federal Office for Civilian Protection, the ratio of the First World War was 200 military: 1 civilian; in the Second World War nearly 1:1 and in the Vietnam War, 1 military: 20 civilians. See M. Sassoli/A. Bouvier, *How Does Law Protect in War?*, ICRC, Geneva, 1999, p. 145.

objectives accurately and reduce incidental death, injury and damage to an absolute minimum.[12] It has been said that:

"The next key requirement [for air power in a new era] is to increase stand-off capability for weapons which have pinpoint delivery accuracy to achieve maximum strategic effect, with minimum collateral damage and minimum risk to the weapon carrier and launcher."[13]

Smart weapons, a universal panacea?

In the Gulf War of 1991, Royal Air Force (RAF) Tornado aircraft were used initially to attack Iraqi airfields by dropping JP233 bombs from a low altitude above the target. Low-altitude attacks were meant to defeat enemy radar and increase the element of surprise. But the RAF suffered the loss of five aircraft in seven days and so aircraft were switched to dropping 1,000lb iron bombs from 20,000 feet where they were out of range of anti-aircraft guns but from where the bombing was less accurate.[14] In response to demands for smart technology, the RAF used Buccaneer aircraft fitted with laser target designators to pinpoint targets, along with Tornados carrying laser-guided weapons in order to minimize collateral damage. The thermal imaging and laser designation pod (TIALD) was rushed into service. These changes dramatically improved targeting accuracy.[15]

Some argue that stand-off weapons remove any element of humanity from warfare, which is reduced to a cold and ruthless

12 "While such errors were inevitable, observers contend, widespread public faith early on in the campaign in the ability of modern surveillance systems and smart weaponry to restrict collateral damage heightened reaction against the bombing campaign when civilian casualties did occur and led to intense pressure at times on politicians to call a halt to the attacks ... If politicians insist on minimum — and perhaps even zero — attrition rates among their military personnel in future air campaigns, a range of new weapons, up to and including UCAVs, will need to be introduced as soon as the technology allows. The alternative for the military is to brace civilians — politicians, media and public alike — for the realities of attrition in parallel with an increased investment in equipment and tactics that support manned close air support and battlefield air interdiction missions at low as well as high altitudes." Cook, *op. cit.* (note 10).

13 Johns, *op. cit.* (note 3), p. 96.

14 Charles Allen (ed.), *Thunder and Lightening*, HMSO, 1991, p. 74, 80.

15 *Ibid.* p. 81/2.

RICR MARS IRRC MARCH 2000 VOL. 82 N° 837 171

activity carried out with clinical precision. The further from the target an attack is launched, the less the attacker is aware of the human cost involved because he does not see the effects of the attack. It is sometimes said that this results in a dehumanization of warfare. It may be thought that because personnel launching stand-off weapons are attacking inanimate objects, such as airfields or bridges, but do not know of the destruction and misery that is being caused on the ground, they are not so aware of the problem of collateral damage.[16] This is not always true in the case of smart technology. The laser designator system used by the Buccaneers had a built-in video camera that recorded what appeared on the navigator's screen as he guided the laser designator on to the target. As a result, air crews and ground staff could see exactly what was happening.[17]

Media reports of allied bombing during the Gulf War and Kosovo air campaigns gave the impression that the weapons deployed were mainly smart weapons and that these weapons were unerringly accurate. Of course, that is far from the truth. Smart weapons are capable of delivery with considerable accuracy, but that capability is only one of many factors that affect accurate targeting. The effects of air defence measures, which can deflect missiles from their course; the strains under which air crew may be operating at the time of weapons release, such as avoiding surface-to-air missiles; the quality of intelligence about the identity of the proposed target;[18] the technical problems of identifying and hitting targets on the ground from the air; the possible failures of guidance systems; the limitations of target recognition techniques;[19] and ordinary human fallibility can all affect the

16 *Ibid.*, p. 137: "Aircrew usually had the comfort of being remote from the destruction caused by their bombs or rockets."

17 *Ibid.*, pp. 113-114: "That really brought it home (...) we were actually killing people "

18 According to Wing Commander Greg Bagwell, "Precision weapons", *Royal Air Force Air Power Review*, Spring 1999, p. 7, the Al Firdos bunker in Baghdad was assessed as a communication node but, unknown to allied intelligence, it was also being used as a civilian air raid shelter. The Chinese Embassy in Belgrade was hit by mistake on 7 May 1999 owing to the use of faulty intelligence at the planning stage which went unnoticed through subsequent checks. See the report in *The Independent*, 11 May 1999.

19 Where thermal, acoustic or radar "blueprints" of enemy military equipment are programmed into a weapon's memory. *Op. cit.* (note 18), p. 7.

outcome of an attack. Guidance and reconnaissance systems are usually affected by cloud, rain or smoke.[20] Furthermore, even if the target is accurately hit, that does not mean that there will be no collateral damage.[21]

In view of the cost of smart weapons,[22] they tend to be used sparingly. Only about 9% of the total tonnage of air delivered weapons during the Gulf War consisted of precision munitions and these were delivered mainly at strategic or operational level targets.[23]

Autonomous weapons,[24] such as cruise missiles, may seem to be the perfect answer to the problem of accurate targeting, but they generally provide no imagery of the attack and they also suffer from a serious drawback: they cannot adjust to last-minute changes of circumstances. Even against static targets that can be extremely problematic, for instance when a civilian refugee column crosses a bridge just as the autonomous weapon strikes. This is a scenario that can be avoided where the weapon is being guided by line of sight to the target. Against mobile targets, such as enemy troops on the ground, autonomous weapons are not easy to deploy effectively. Older systems like Paveway are more flexible in these situations.[25]

It seems that smart weapons are not as yet the solution to the problem of incidental damage nor are they as good as the public

20 Apart from the new US joint direct attack munition (JDAM) which can be deployed from altitudes above cloud cover. See *Joint Statement on the Kosovo After Action Review*, Department of Defense, 14 October 1999.

21 *Op. cit.* (note 14), p. 81: "... in reality you cannot have a surgical war. There is no such thing. For a bomb to go down an elevator shaft is just luck. It probably has a CEP — a computer error probability — of maybe 30-40ft. That can make the difference between hitting the place you're aiming for and the one next door which is full of civilians." Incidentally, other authors define CEP as "circular error probable", i.e. the radius of a circle centred on the target within which 50% of all bombs dropped will land. Bagwell, *op. cit.* (note 18), p. 14. Bagwell, p. 8, also comments that "the explosive force of a 500lb warhead does not constitute keyhole surgery!"

22 *Ibid.*, p. 13, quotes $9,000 for a simple GPS guided bomb and $500,000 for a Block III Tomahawk missile.

23 *Ibid.*, p. 3.

24 Defined by Bagwell, *op. cit.* (note 18), p. 14, as those requiring no human input during the final phase of flight.

25 At the NATO press briefing on 18 April 1999, an account was given of how a pilot launched an attack against a radar and, noticing that the site was close to a church, pulled his weapon off the target so that it exploded harmlessly in a wood.

may have been led to believe. They are certainly more capable of accurate delivery than dumb bombs, but there are various other factors affecting possible incidental damage, not least the "circular error probable" which means that this risk, while much reduced, is not eliminated, especially in populated areas. Autonomous weapons bring with them a degree of inflexibility that means that the human element in guiding weapons on to the target will remain necessary in many cases in the foreseeable future.

The Incident of 14 April 1999

In the Kosovo conflict of 1999, pilots minimized danger to themselves by attacking from an altitude of 15,000 feet, where they were out of range of most hand-held surface-to-air missiles and anti-aircraft artillery,[26] until the Yugoslav air defences had been degraded to such an extent that they could safely fly at lower altitudes.[27]

On 14 April 1999, NATO pilots, flying at 15,000 feet and apparently looking for opportunity targets in Kosovo, attacked what they thought was the lead vehicle of a column of military vehicles. The following day there were numerous media reports that a refugee column had been attacked near Djakovica. Pictures on BBC World[28] showed scenes of carnage near the village of Meja. According to Serb reports, 64 civilians were killed, including three Serb policemen who were escorting them. The Serb-run Media Centre in Pristina claimed that a second, smaller column was hit on the road from Prizren to Djakovica in which six people were killed and 11 wounded. On 15 April, the NATO spokesman, Jamie Shea, expressed deep regret at the daily press briefing for loss of life to civilians from the attack the previous day on a convoy travelling between Prizren and Djakovica.[29]

There was some confusion about the incident in the days that followed. Survivors referred to a low-level attack by a MiG aircraft

26 *Op. cit.* (note 10).

27 Lord Robertson, *Kosovo: An Account of the Crisis*, Ministry of Defence, London, 1999, p. 13.

28 At 1800 hours BST on 17 April 1999.

29 NATO press briefing, 15 April 1999.

and reporters talked about machine gun or cannon fire. Robert Fisk, one of NATO's fiercest critics, visited three reported strike locations on the Prizren-Dakovica road: at Velika Krusa, Gradis and Terezifki,[30] he collected munitions parts and noted serial numbers. At Gradis, he said, there was evidence of strafing, similar to A10 strikes in the Gulf War, as well as bombing.[31] At the NATO press briefings reporters tried to ascertain precisely which attack Jamie Shea had been referring to, as there were at least two attacks on convoys in the area. A tape was played describing an attack on a column of three vehicles near Djakovica, but it was later stated that this did not relate to a refugee convoy.

General Marani answered press questions about attacks from an altitude of 15,000 feet. He said that target identification was more complex and was carried out correlating more information, not only what the pilot could see but other information he had before leaving and before arriving in the area, which he received from other aircraft, from other weapons systems not necessarily on board his aircraft. In other words, it was, he said, very much a team effort and not a case of a single pilot acting on his own initiative.

A full explanation was given on 19 April by Brigadier-General Dan Leaf.[32] He described two incidents on 14 April, both involving the use of 500lb laser-guided bombs. The first was north-west of Djakovica and involved an attack at 11:10 GMT on a vehicle whose crew were considered to be responsible for the burning of houses. This was followed at 11:48 GMT by an attack on a group of vehicles in a courtyard. That produced a secondary explosion consistent with the igniting of a gasoline store. The second incident involved a large convoy of more than 100 vehicles on a major road south-east of Djakovica. The first 20 vehicles were uniform in shape and colour and they maintained a set pace and spacing, indicative of military movement. The possibility of IDPs (internally displaced persons) being in the convoy was discussed but intelligence material indicated that this

30 Or possibly Terzick Most Zrze.

31 *The Independent*, 17 April 1999.

32 To be found on www.fas.org/man/dod/docs99/s990419b.htm.

RICR MARS IRRC MARCH 2000 VOL. 82 N° 837 175

was a military convoy. The lead vehicles of the convoy were attacked by F-16 and Jaguar aircraft, starting at 12:19 GMT. Not all the attacks were successful. Some anti-aircraft fire was encountered. Doubts began to assail the military planners because it was unusual for the Serbian forces to travel in such large convoys, so A-10 aircraft, which are slower and more stable than F-16s, were called in to check and further attacks on the convoy were suspended at 13:00 GMT. On reports that the convoy consisted of both military and civilian vehicles, all attacks were cancelled and aircraft withdrawn at 13:20 GMT.

What are the legal requirements?

For States party to Geneva Protocol I of 1977,[33] the duty, before carrying out an attack, is to "do everything feasible to verify that the objectives to be attacked are (...) military objectives".[34] Feasible precautions may be defined as those which are "practicable or practically possible, taking into account all circumstances ruling at the time, including humanitarian and military considerations".[35]

Humanitarian considerations would require a pilot to get close to the target to identify it properly; military considerations would require the pilot to fly at a safe height to be at reduced risk from anti-aircraft fire. This is a conflict that cannot be resolved easily.

Also relevant here is the rule of doubt. In case of doubt whether a person is a civilian or whether an object is normally dedicated to civilian purposes, the Protocol lays down a presumption of civilian status.[36]

33 At the time of the Kosovo conflict, for example, the USA and France were not party to Protocol I but Germany and the UK were.

34 Protocol I, Art. 57, para. 2(a)(i).

35 The United Kingdom made a declaration of understanding to this effect when ratifying Protocol I. See *IRRC*, No. 322, March 1998, pp. 186 ff. — The Conventional Weapons Convention of 1981 contains similar language in the Amended Mines Protocol of 1 May 1996, Art. 3, para. 10.

36 Protocol I, Arts 50, para. 1, and 52, para. 3. With regard to Art. 50, para. 1, the United Kingdom, on ratification of the Protocol, made a statement of understanding that the rule applied "only in cases of substantial doubt still remaining after the assessment (...) has been made, and not as overriding a commander's duty to protect the safety of troops under his command or to preserve his military situation, in conformity with other provisions of the Protocol." *Ibid.*

For States not party to the Protocol, customary law nevertheless requires their forces to attack only military objectives and that means distinguishing them from civilian objects. The precise standard of care is not clear. It is certainly not higher than the "do everything feasible" standard imposed by Protocol I. At the very least, customary law would require those responsible for attacks not to attack persons or objects which they know or believe to be civilian.

Responsibilities in attack[37]

Whether or not a State is party to the Protocol, its armed forces are required to respect the customary rule of proportionality which attempts to balance military and humanitarian considerations. In applying this rule, the military decision-maker has to consider various factors when deciding what weapon or tactics to use, the object being to neutralize the military target with the least possible incidental damage or loss:

a. the importance of the target and urgency of the situation;

b. intelligence about the proposed target, i.e., what it is being, or will be, used for and when;

c. what weapons are available, their range, accuracy and radius of effect;

d. conditions affecting accuracy of targeting such as terrain, weather, night or day;

e. factors affecting incidental loss or damage, such as the proximity of civilians or civilian objects in the vicinity of the target or other protected objects or zone and whether they are inhabited, or the possible release of hazardous substances as a result of the attack;

f. the risks to his own troops posed by the various options open to him.[38]

37 This passage is adapted from the author's text in the *Model Manual on the Law of Armed Conflict*, ICRC, Geneva, 1999.

38 The United Kingdom, on ratification of Protocol I, declared that "Military commanders and others responsible for planning, deciding upon, or executing attacks necessarily have to reach decisions on the basis of their assessment of the information from all sources which is reasonably available to them at the relevant time." *Loc. cit.* (note 35).

Smart weaponry, if available, has increased the options open to the attacker. From a legal point of view, he needs not only to assess what feasible precautions can be taken to minimize incidental loss, but also to make a comparison between different tactics or weapons so as to be able to choose the least damaging course of action compatible with military success.

Application of the principle of proportionality is more easily stated than applied in practice, as by adopting a method of attack that would reduce incidental damage, the risk to the attacking troops may be increased. The law is not clear as to the degree of care required of the attacker and the degree of risk that he must be prepared to take.[39]

As the author has written previously: "... Military necessity cannot always override humanity. In taking care to protect civilians, soldiers must accept some element of risk to themselves. The rule [of proportionality] is unclear as to what degree of care is required of a soldier and what degree of risk he must take. Everything depends on the target, the urgency of the moment, the available technology and so on."[40]

This approach is reflected in British defence doctrine:

> "*Targeting.* A key issue for commanders and planners is deciding what constitutes a legitimate target and how it may be attacked. This revolves around the principles of distinction and proportionality. Attacks should be limited to combatants and other military objectives. The civilian population and civilian objects must not be deliberately targeted; the morale of an enemy's civilian population is not a legitimate target and attacks designed to spread terror among the civilian population are expressly prohibited. Even military objectives should not be targeted if an

39 Bagwell, *op. cit.* (note 18), p. 9, thinks that this should be dealt with in rules of engagement: "... some targets could require such guaranteed accuracy that the aircraft/platform might be placed at increased risk to enemy defences. In this case the ROE will need to make the desired identification criteria extremely clear so that crews, who are effectively judge and jury, will be able to take the right course of action."

40 A. P. V. Rogers, "Conduct of combat and risks run by the civilian population", *Military Law & Law of War Review*, 1982, p. 310.

attack is likely to cause (collateral) civilian casualties or damage which would be excessive in relation to the direct military advantage which the attack is expected to produce. The law stipulates that the military worth of the target needs to be considered in relation to the circumstances at the time. Therefore, a commander needs to have an up-to-date assessment of the significance of a target and the value of attacking it. If there is a choice of weapons or methods of attack available, a commander should select those which are most likely to avoid, or at least minimize, incidental civilian casualties or damage. However, he is entitled to take into account factors such as his stocks of different weapons and likely future demands, the timeliness of attack and risks to his own forces. Nevertheless, there may be occasions when a commander will have to accept a higher level of risk to his own forces in order to avoid or reduce collateral damage to the enemy's civil population."[41]

Responsibilities in defence

It is not only the attackers who have a responsibility for protecting civilians from the effects of armed conflict. This is a general responsibility which falls not only on the armed forces but also on the civilian administration and political leadership. For States party to Protocol I this specifically requires, so far as possible, the removal of civilians from the vicinity of military objectives, avoiding locating military objectives in or near densely populated areas as well as taking steps like the provision of shelters to protect civilians.[42] Unfortunately, there is evidence to suggest that some States do not merely fail to comply with these requirements of international law, but deliberately put military assets close to protected objects or place civilians in military locations with the intention of protecting military objectives from attack or even in the hope of attracting international condemnation of the enemy if civilians are killed or civilian objects destroyed. Those

41 *British Defence Doctrine* (JWP 0-01) issued by the British Minster of Defence in 1996.

42 Protocol I, Art. 58.

carrying out attacks in such circumstances are not relieved of their obligation to attack military objectives only and reduce incidental damage as much as possible, but in considering the rule of proportionality, any tribunal dealing with the matter would be obliged to weigh in the balance in favour of the attackers any such illegal activity by the defenders.[43]

Applying the legal requirements in practice

It seems, at least in some cases of aerial attacks against targets on the ground, that the question of the risk to the attacker is not such an important consideration in practice.

If the target is sufficiently important, higher commanders may be prepared to accept a greater degree of risk to the aircraft crew to ensure that the target is properly identified and accurately attacked. No-risk warfare is unheard of. Risks may be taken, for example, to rescue pilots who have been shot down or in deploying forces on reconnaissance or target identification missions in enemy-held territory.

However, if the target is assessed as not being worth that risk and a minimum operational altitude is set for their protection, the aircrew involved in the operation will have to make their own assessment of the risks involved in verifying and attacking the assigned target. If their assessment is that (a) the risk to them of getting close enough to the target to identify it properly is too high, (b) that there is a real danger of incidental death, injury or damage to civilians or civilian objects because of lack of verification of the target, and (c) they or friendly forces are not in immediate danger if the attack is not carried out, there is no need for them to put themselves at risk to verify the target. Quite simply, the attack should not be carried out.

Rules of engagement could make this clear with a test like: "Are you sure that the target is a military objective? If you are in any doubt, would you or friendly forces be placed in danger if the attack were not carried out? If not, the attack is NOT to be carried out."

43 See A. P. V. Rogers, *Law on the Battlefield*, Manchester University Press, 1996, p. 79.

Individual responsibility

Of course, cases will occur when members of the armed forces will not be able to make such cool calculations reminiscent of a jury in a criminal trial. In the heat of the moment, they may release their weapons even if not sure that the target is a military objective and even if not in danger themselves. Any tribunal considering the matter subsequently would be concerned with the proportionality principle. They would be assessing the importance of the target in relation to the incidental damage expected. However, the risk to attacking forces is an important factor to be taken into consideration when applying the proportionality principle. In dealing with the case, the tribunal would have to put themselves in the position of the armed forces member concerned, taking all the surrounding circumstances into account, so as to experience the situation as he experienced it at the time, before considering the question of culpability.

Operational reality is recognized in the Statute of the International Criminal Court. This makes the infliction of incidental loss or damage an offence only if the attack is launched intentionally in the knowledge that it will cause incidental civilian loss of life, injury or damage which would be clearly excessive in relation to the concrete and direct military advantage anticipated.[44] The use of the word "clearly" ensures that the court would be involved only in cases where the excessiveness of incidental damage was obvious, not in cases that involved errors of judgement by commanders in the field.[45]

A member of the armed forces doing his level best in difficult circumstances to comply with the law of armed conflict would have nothing to fear from a subsequent inquiry, even if he made a mistake under pressure.

Conclusion

The law does not demand that there be no casualties in armed conflict. However, the law, political expediency and public

44 Statute of the International Criminal Court, Art. 8, para. 2(b)(iv).

45 Roy S. Lee (ed.), *The International Criminal Court*, Kluwer Law International, 1999, p. 111.

sentiment combine to demand that casualties, whether among members of the armed forces or among the civilian population, should be reduced to the maximum extent that the exigencies of armed conflict will allow. An important element of this endeavour is verification of the target, because attacking the wrong target is likely to lead to unnecessary casualties. Target verification requires reasonable care to be exercised. The precise degree of care required depends on the circumstances, especially the time available for making a decision. In the event of doubt about the nature of the target, an attack should not be carried out, with a possible exception where failure to prosecute the attack would put attacking forces in immediate danger.

[4]

ASSESSING PROPORTIONALITY: MORAL COMPLEXITY AND LEGAL RULES[1]

Kenneth Watkin[2]

2. Brigadier-General Ken Watkin is the Judge Advocate General for the Canadian Forces. The opinions expressed in this article are solely those of the author and do not necessarily reflect the views of the government of Canada.

4 *K. Watkin*

'Weapons, however terrible, however destructive, however automatic, are in themselves dead machines; everything depends on the heart of men that use them.'[3]

1. INTRODUCTION

There may be no other term in international humanitarian law (hereinafter, IHL) which evokes such debate or controversy as 'proportionality'. In part, this debate is a result of the nature of the term itself. The broad use of the term 'proportionality' in international law,[4] combined with images of an almost scientific balancing of opposing interests on finely tuned scales of humanitarian justice, masks a much more complex and unclear reality. The degree to which contemporary discussion and, with it, the law camouflages the complex moral issues underlying the targeting 'proportionality' test is reflected in the fact that conventional law does not actually use the term. Rather, the question 'at law' is whether a loss of civilian life or damage to civilian property during the conduct of hostilities is 'excessive in relation to the concrete and direct military advantage anticipated'.[5]

The difficult questions presented when assessing proportionality during targeting arise in part because society is required to face the reality that '[i]n any armed conflict people are injured or killed and property is damaged or destroyed.'[6] Even more fundamentally, the assessment of 'excessive' killing or damage forces a qualitative assessment by 'civilised' peoples of the value of human life not only in relation to other humans but also with respect to property and ultimately politically-driven objectives related to the conduct of hostilities.[7] Ultimately, the goal of warfare is to change the 'mind' of another state or other political entity.[8] Yet, forcing one's will on another state by violent means inevitably results in civilians

---

3. J.L. Kunz, 'The chaotic status of the laws of war and the urgent necessity for their revision', 45 *AJIL* (1951) pp. 37 at 41.

4. See J.G. Gardam, 'Proportionality and force in international law', 87 *AJIL* (1993) p. 391 ('Proportionality is a fundamental concept of the law on the use of force and the law of armed conflict.').

5. See 1977 Protocol Additional to the Geneva Conventions of 12 August 1949, and Relating to the Protection of Victims of International Armed Conflicts (Protocol I), Art. 57(2)(a)(iii) and 51(5)(b) 51 (5)(b) (hereinafter, AP I). The four 1949 Geneva Conventions are: 1949 Geneva Convention (I) for the Amelioration of the Condition of the Wounded and Sick in Armed Forces in the Field (hereinafter, GC I); 1949 Geneva Convention (II) for the Amelioration of the Condition of Wounded, Sick and Shipwrecked Members of Armed Forces at Sea (hereinafter, GC II); 1949 Geneva Convention (III) Relative to the Treatment of Prisoners of War (hereinafter, GC III); and 1949 Geneva Convention (IV) Relative to the Protection of Civilian Persons in Time of War (hereinafter, GC IV).

6. W.J. Fenrick, 'The rule of proportionality and Protocol I in conventional warfare', 98 *Mil. LR* (1982) pp. 91 at 92.

7. See Carl Von Clausewitz, *On War*, translated by M. Howard and P. Paret (Princeton, Princeton University Press 1986) p. 87 ('When whole communities go to war – whole peoples, and especially *civilized* peoples – the reason lies in some political situation, and the occasion is always due to some political object.').

8. See J.M. Spaight, *Air Power and War Rights*, 3rd edn. (London, Longman Green and Co. 1947) ch. X, p. 2, where it is noted war is fought 'in order to bring about a change of mind in another state'.

being put at risk 'not because anyone set out to attack them, but only because of their proximity to a battle that is being fought against someone else'.[9]

William Fenrick has noted that '[s]ince the quantities being measured, civilian losses and military advantage, are dissimilar, it is not possible to establish any reasonably exact proportionality equation between them.'[10] The difficulty of being forced, in fact or by law, to weigh the relative value of such different concepts is reflected in the moral roots of this dilemma. The almost antiseptic verbiage of 'proportionality' is the contemporary expression of the medieval moral doctrine of 'double effect',[11] where authority is provided to 'perform an act likely to have evil consequences (the killing of noncombatants) … .'[12]

Traditionally, IHL did not address such matters, 'with the cruelest decisions to be made by men on the spot with reference only to their moral notions or the military traditions of the army in which they serve'.[13] However, the post World War II efforts to re-establish the principle of distinction[14] have not only seen the development of targeting precautions[15] but also the criminalisation of conduct that breaches legal proscriptions regarding 'proportionality'.[16] By the close of the twentieth century, the Rome Statute of the International Criminal Court provided that a war crime is committed during an international armed conflict by intentionally launching an attack that will cause incidental civilian casualties, damage to civilian objects or widespread, long-term and severe damage to the natural environment 'which would be clearly excessive in relation to the concrete and direct overall military advantage anticipated'.[17]

While no similar crime is enumerated in that statute regarding non-international conflicts, the 'proportionality' standard can be found in other limited treaty law and is recognised as part of customary international law applicable to both international and non-international armed conflict.[18] Further, in respect of contemporary 'three block wars', non-combatant evacuation operations, peace enforcement operations and the other small conflicts of the twenty-first century, there has developed a practice by some states of applying a 'spirit and principles' approach in

9. M. Walzer, *Just and Unjust Wars* (New York, Basic Books 1977) pp. 151-152
10. See Fenrick, *supra* n. 6, p. 102.
11. See Walzer, *supra* n. 9, pp. 152-153.
12. Ibid., p. 153.
13. Ibid., p. 152.
14. See H. Lauterpacht, 'The problem of the revision of the law of war', 29 *BYIL* (1952) pp. 360 at 364, where, in respect of the principle of distinction, he noted 'whatever may have been the original merits of that distinction, the phenomenon of total war has reduced it, in most respects, to a hollow phrase'.
15. See Art. 57 AP I.
16. See Art. 85(3)(b) AP I.
17. See Art. 8(2)(b)(iv) Rome Statute of the International Criminal Court 1998,
18. For example, Art. 3, para. 8 of the 1996 Amended Protocol II to the Convention on Certain Conventional Weapons 1996 (the 'proportionality' test is set out in the context of what constitutes an indiscriminate attack). See J.-M. Henckaerts and L. Doswald-Beck, *Customary International Humanitarian Law* (Cambridge, Cambridge University Press 2005) pp. 48-49.

6 *K. Watkin*

applying humanitarian law, which would inevitably include the proportionality principle.[19]

The legal proscriptions regarding proportionality reflect the secularisation of older 'just war' principles.[20] Perhaps more significantly for contemporary society, the goal of holding planners and decision makers accountable for the force used in maintaining social order is an important aspect of the 'rule of law'.[21] These legal obligations are now attracting significant scrutiny by criminal courts,[22] prosecutors,[23] human rights tribunals and courts,[24] non-governmental organisations[25] and the academic community,[26] with a variety of approaches being taken towards the assessment of proportionality.

---

19. See Canadian Forces doctrine manual, *The Law of Armed Conflict at the Operational and Tactical Level*, B-GJ-005-104/FP-021 (August 2001) p. 17-1, para. 1702 <www.forces.gc.ca/jag/training/ publications/loac_man_e.asp>; the United Nations Secretary-General's Bulletin, 'Observance by United Nations Forces of international humanitarian law', 38 *ILM* (1999) p. 1656; and DoD Law of War Program, Department of Defense Directive, Number 5100.77 4 (December 1998) para. 5.3.1 <www.dtic.mil/whs/ directives/corres/pdf/d510077_120998/d510077p.pdf>.

20. See M.R. Ishay, *The History of Human Rights: From Ancient Times to the Globalization Era* (Berkley, University of California Press 2004) pp. 60-61.

21. I. Brownlie, *The Rule Of Law In International Affairs* (The Hague, Marinus Nijhoff Publishers 1998) pp. 213-214. The elements of the rule of law are identified as: the powers of officials must be based on authority conferred by law; the law must conform to standards of substantial and procedural justice; the powers of the executive, the legislature, and the judicial function must be separated; the judiciary should not be subject to the control of the executive; and all legal persons are subject to the rules of law. See also *Reference re Secession of Quebec* [1998] 2 *SCR* 217, 257-58.

22. See, e.g., *Prosecutor* v. *Galić*, Case No. IT-98-29-T, Judgement, Trial Chamber, 5 December 2003, paras. 36-61; and *Prosecutor* v. *Kupreškić*, Case No. IT-95-16-T, Judgement, Trial Chamber, 14 January 2000, paras. 513, 524.

23. See Final Report to the Prosecutor by the Committee Established to Review the NATO Bombing Campaign Against the Federal Republic of Yugoslavia <www.un.org/icty/pressreal/nato061300.htm> (hereinafter, ICTY Final Report).

24. See, e.g., *Ergi* v. *Turkey*, Judgement of 28 July 1998, 31 *EHRR* (1998) p. 388. See also *Isayeva, Usupova and Bazayeva* v. *Russia* (Application nos. 57947-49/00), Judgement of 24 February 2005; and *Isayeva* v. *Russia* (Application no. 57950/00), Judgement of 24 February 2005.

25. See, e.g., Human Rights Watch Report, 'Civilian Deaths in the NATO Air Campaign' (February 2000) <www.hrw.org/reports/ 2000/nato/>; 'Nato/Federal Republic Of Yugoslavia: "Collateral Damage" Or Unlawful Killings? Violations Of The Laws Of War By NATO During Operation Allied Force' (June 2000) <www.amnesty.org/ailib/intcam/kosovo/docs/nato_all.pdf > (hereinafter, 'Collateral Damage or Unlawful Killing'); and Human Rights Watch Report, 'Off Target: the Conduct of the War and Civilian Casualties in Iraq' (2003) pp. 9, 18-20 <www.hrw.org/reports/2003/usa1203/usa1203.pdf> (hereinafter, 'Off Target').

26. See, e.g., W.J. Fenrick, 'Targeting and proportionality after Operation Allied Force: A view from the outside', 3 *YIHL* (2000) p. 53; A. Laursen, 'NATO, the war over Kosovo, and the ICTY investigation', 17 *Amer. Univ. ILR* (2002) pp. 765 at 795; M. Sassoli, 'Targeting: The scope and utility of the concept of "military objectives" for the protection of civilians in contemporary armed conflicts', in D. Wippman and M. Evangelista, eds., *New Wars, New Laws? Applying the Laws of War in 21st Century Conflicts* (New York, Transnational Publishers 2005) p. 181; P. Benvenuti, 'The ICTY Prosecutor and the review of the NATO bombing campaign against the Federal Republic of Yugoslavia', 12 *EJIL* (2001) pp. 503 at 515-516; and M. Bothe, 'Protection of the civilian population and NATO bombing on Yugoslavia', 12 *EJIL* (2001) pp. 531 at 534.

In addition, with an estimated 95 percent of contemporary conflict comprising non-international armed conflict,[27] it has become increasingly necessary to assess the direct interface between international human rights law and humanitarian law. As Ward Thomas has noted, '[t]he bombings in Chechnya – and similar attacks on villages by the governments of Sierra Leone and Sudan in civil wars in those countries – also raise the question of what effect the norm has in an internal, rather than an interstate, war.'[28]

The purpose of this article is to explore the issue of 'proportionality' in order to outline a number of factors that might be considered regarding its application to the complex security operations of the twenty-first century. The article is divided into three parts. First, the contemporary definition, its relevance to the overall legal framework governing targeting, and the 'moral' roots of the proportionality principle will be explored. This will include an outline of the doctrine of 'double effect'; the effect of its incorporation into IHL; the interface between law and politics; and interpretative challenges. Secondly, four themes that impact on the application of the proportionality principle to targeting, one of which is just now emerging from human rights-based tribunals, will be considered. These approaches are referred to as the 'pacifism and pacificism', 'human rights', 'tactical level control' and 'strategic impact' analytical frameworks. Finally, the article will outline a number of general principles that might be considered when attempting to apply the legal test for proportionality.

2. PROPORTIONALITY: THE TEST AND THE CHALLENGES

In order to understand the challenges confronting commanders, planners and those seeking to hold them accountable regarding the application of the proportionality principle, it is first necessary to set out a definition of the term and then situate the principle within the broader legal framework governing targeting. This, in turn, raises a number of complex moral, policy and legal questions which will be placed in their historic context by outlining the doctrine of 'double effect'.

2.1 Excessive by any other name?

A commonly accepted definition of 'proportionality' is set out in Article 57(2)(a)(iii) of Additional Protocol I (hereinafter, AP I), which states:

> '(2) those who plan or decide upon an attack shall:

27. See *Human Security Report 2005: War and Peace in the 21st Century* (New York, Oxford University Press 2005) p. 23 <www.humansecurityreport.info/HSR2005_PDF/Part1.pdf>.

28. W. Thomas, *The Ethics of Destruction: Norms and Force in International Relations* (Ithaca, Cornell University Press 2001) p. 177.

> (iii) refrain from deciding to launch an attack which may be expected to cause incidental loss of civilian life, injury to civilians, damage to civilian objects, or a combination thereof, which would be excessive in relation to the concrete and direct military advantage anticipated.'

It is also part of the definition of what constitutes an indiscriminate attack found in Article 51(5)(b) AP I. The ICRC study on customary international humanitarian law (hereinafter, CIHL Study) indicates that the proportionality principle is reflected in a number of military manuals, including those of the United States (which is not a party to Protocol I). [29] Further, that Study states that the principle is part of customary international law although not necessarily with the exact wording found in Additional Protocol I.[30]

As has been noted, one of the most striking elements of the Additional Protocol I definition is the lack of any reference to 'proportionality'. During the negotiations of the Protocol it appears that the term 'disproportionate' was rejected because of its subjectivity.[31] In its place the term 'excessive' is used, although since 'excessive' means 'more than necessary, normal or desirable'[32] it is not clear that the issue of subjectivity has been resolved. Yoram Dinstein has suggested excessive 'means the disproportion is clearly discernible: the adverb 'clearly' is explicitly added in the Rome Statute'.[33] The fact that the word 'clearly' was added to the offence in that statute relating to the excessive use of force reflects a concern over the quantum of collateral damage that might attract criminal sanction.

2.2 Proportionality and the targeting framework

2.2.1 *The principle of distinction*

A key requirement in assessing 'proportionality' is to remember that this test does not operate in isolation from other principles of IHL. For example, the principle of

29. Henckaerts and Doswald-Beck, *supra* n. 18, p. 47 n. 8. Examples of countries which make such references include Australia, Canada, Belgium, Germany, Israel, Indonesia, France, Spain, Sweden, the United Kingdom and the United States. See also *Annotated Supplement to the Naval Commander's Handbook on the Law of Naval Operations* (1997) para. 8.1.2.1 at 8-4 to 8-5 and n. 17, where reference is made to 'excessive' incidental injury or collateral damage. The basis for the 'proportionality' test is identified in footnote 19 as AP I, Arts. 51(5)(b) and 57(2)(a)(ii)-(iii) <www.nwc.navy.mil/ILD/ Annotated%20Supplement%20to%20the%20Commander's%20Handbook.htm>.

30. See Henckaerts and Doswald-Beck, *supra* n. 18, pp. 46-50. Rule 14 states: 'Launching an attack which may be expected to cause incidental loss of civilian life, injury to civilians, damage to civilian objects, or a combination thereof, which would be excessive in relation to the concrete and direct military advantage anticipated, is prohibited.'

31. Fenrick, *supra* n. 6, p. 106.

32. C. Soanes, ed., *Oxford English Dictionary* (2002) p. 284.

33. See Y. Dinstein, *The Conduct of Hostilities Under the Law of International Armed Conflict* (Cambridge, Cambridge University Press 2004) p. 120.

distinction has a fundamental impact on the proportionality principle.[34] The assessment of what constitutes excessive collateral damage or loss of life is dependent first on identifying valid military objectives. People and property that constitute 'military objectives' may be attacked and destroyed.[35] As Additional Protocol I states, civilian objects[36] and the 'civilian population as such, as well as individual civilians, shall not be the object of attack'.[37] The International Criminal Tribunal for the former Yugoslavia (hereinafter, ICTY) noted in the *Prosecutor* v. *Galić*[38] decision that once the military character of a target has been ascertained, commanders must apply the proportionality principle.[39]

However, perhaps one of the controversial aspects of the proportionality principle has been that although civilians are not to be directly made the object of an attack, humanitarian law accepts that they may be killed or civilian property may be damaged as a result of an attack on a military objective. The application of the principle of distinction is further complicated by the different nature of the obligations regarding the identification of persons and objects and by the complex fact situations that can present themselves during armed conflict.

Combatants are required to distinguish themselves from the civilian population while they are engaged in an attack or operations preparatory to an attack.[40] While such an obligation has been interpreted as extending to vehicles, aircraft and vessels used by combatants, no similar requirement exists in respect of visually distinguishing other military objects (e.g., bridges, factories, oil production facilities) from either civilians or civilian objects.[41] However, humanitarian law does provide for the identification of specially protected persons and objects by unique emblems, signs, signals or symbols.[42]

As will be discussed in the next two subsections, the differences in the application of humanitarian law in respect of people and objects does not end with this general observation on the principle of distinction.

2.2.2 *Targeting people*

The targeting of state and non-state participants in contemporary conflict has attracted particular controversy in the post 9/11 security environment because of the potential geographic breadth of the operating environment and the spectacular

34. See *Prosecutor* v. *Galić*, *supra* n. 22, para. 58.
35. See Art. 52(2) AP I.
36. See Art. 52(1) AP I.
37. See Art. 51(2) AP I.
38. *Prosecutor* v. *Galić*, *supra* n. 22.
39. Ibid., para. 58.
40. See Art. 43(3) AP I.
41. See Dinstein, *supra* n. 33, p. 38.
42. See, e.g., GC I, ch VII: The distinctive emblem; GC II, ch. VI: The distinctive emblem; AP I, Art. 18 and section II: Medical Transportation (medical personnel, aircraft and establishments); AP I, Art. 56 (dams, dykes and generating stations); AP I, Art. 66 (civil defence organizations); and Art. 20 Convention for the Protection of Cultural Property in the Event of Armed Conflict 1954.

technical capability of advanced armed forces to locate and target individual opponents using satellites, unmanned drones and air delivered weapons. Although battles still do occur where opposing forces line up against one another, often fighting from trench lines,[43] there has also been a significant expansion of the twenty-first century battlespace. Attacks in Yemen,[44] Pakistan,[45] Iraq[46] and the Palestinian Occupied Territories[47] all bear witness to this new capability. As Michael Schmitt has noted, 'current technologies have transformed the linear battlefield into a battlespace, with combat operations often occurring simultaneously on the ground and high seas, in the air and space and through cyberspace'.[48] It has raised significant moral issues as targeting can conceivably result in the death of a targeted person's spouse, children or neighbours far from the traditional perspective of what constitutes the 'frontlines' if an enemy leader is attacked at home.

The criteria used to identify 'persons' as targets are different from those applied to 'military objects'. Humanitarian law provides that only persons 'taking a direct part in hostilities' are valid targets. This test for participation in combat is clearly linked in Additional Protocol I to 'combatants'[49] and applies to 'civilians' who act like combatants, i.e., who take a direct part in hostilities. Yet, disturbingly, given the existence of the direct participation criteria for a quarter century, there is much about the Additional Protocol I test that remains unresolved. Attempts to clarify the meaning of the term are complicated by the existence of other phrases in humanitarian law describing such participation,[50] the reality that participation in hos-

43. P. Biles, 'Ethiopia's push north', BBC News online, 20 May 2000 (In flying over a recently evacuated Ethiopian/Eritrean battlefield it is noted 'below us were the trenches, long snaking lines in the brown earth, stretching for mile after mile, broken only by small bunkers and dugouts.') <news.bbc.co.uk/1/hi/ programmes/ from_our_own_correspondent/756845.stm>.

44. D. Johnston and D.E. Sanger, 'Fatal strike in Yemen was based on rules set out by Bush', in *The New York Times*, 6 November 2002, p. A16.

45. D. Priest, 'Covert CIA program withstands new furor', in *The Washington Post*, 30 December 2005, p. A01 (reporting the killing of an Al Qaeda planner, Hamza Rabia) <www.washingtonpost.com/wp-dyn/content/article/2005/12/29/AR2005122901585.html>; and D Priest, 'Surveillance operation in Pakistan located and killed Al Qaeda official', in *The Washington Post*, 15 May 2005, p. A25 (reporting the killing of an Al-Qaeda leader, al-Yemeni) <www.washingtonpost.com/wp-dyn/content/article/2005/05/14/ AR2005051401121.html>.

46. W. Murray and Major General R.H. Scales, Jr., *The Iraq War: A Military History* (2003), pp. 154-157, for an account of the attack on Saddam Hussein on 20 March 2003 starting the Iraq War.

47. 'Hamas founder killed in Israeli airstrike: Car hit by rockets as Yassin left mosque', CNN.com, 22 March 2004 <www.cnn.com/2004/WORLD/meast/03/21/yassin/>.

48. See M. Schmitt, 'War, technology, and international humanitarian law', Occasional Paper Series No. 4, Summer 2005, pp. 53-54 <www.hpcr.org/pdfs/OccasionalPaper4.pdf>.

49. Art. 43(2) AP I.

50. See, e.g., Arts. 45(3), 65, 67(1)(e) AP I; Art. 21 GC I; Art. 34 GC II; and Art. 19 GC IV ('acts harmful to the enemy'); Art. 3 GC I to IV ('take no active part'). See also M. Schmitt, 'The principle of distinction in 21st century warfare', 2 *Yale HR & DLJ* (1999) p. 149.

tilities is inherently a 'group' activity,[51] and a lack of consensus that 'people' fall solely into one of two groups: 'lawful combatants' and 'civilians'.[52]

Efforts to limit the distinction principle to 'lawful' combatants and civilians results from a strict reading of Article 50(1) AP I.[53] While such an approach provides a simple theoretical construct, it does not reflect the reality that 'unlawful combatants' or 'unprivileged belligerents' have been and remain a part of warfare.[54] Ultimately, 'combatants' and 'civilians' are defined in Additional Protocol I in a manner which can have a significant impact on the application of the proportionality principle.[55] Civilians who participate in hostilities *de jure* retain their status but not the protection associated with that status. As a result, they become military objectives and can be killed. Maintaining the title of 'civilian' while participating in conflict carries significant potential for the erosion of the protected status of other uninvolved civilians. It also represents a not so subtle weakening of the prohibition that all 'civilians' cannot be targeted.

It appears to have been a concern over perpetuating the World War II view that some civilians could be viewed as 'quasi-combatants'[56] which resulted in the expansion of 'civilian' status to cover quite active participants in hostilities. The concept of 'quasi-combatant' has been rejected,[57] and personnel such as factory work-

51. See C. McKeogh, *Innocent Civilians: The Morality of Killing in War* (New York, Palgrave 2002) p. 1 ('War is a purposeful act of lethal force on the group level.'); C. Gray, *Another Bloody Century: Future War* (London, Weidenfeld & Nicholson 2005) p. 30, where war is defined as 'organized violence threatened or waged for political purposes'; and K. Watkin, 'Canada/United States military interoperability and humanitarian law issues: Land mines, terrorism, military objectives and targeted killing', 15 *Duke JCIL* (2005) p. 281 at 311-313 (arguing that the performance" of a combatant like function by a "civilian" who is a member of a non-state armed group would result in that person being treated like a combatant).

52. See Dinstein, *supra* n. 33, p. 29.

53. See AP I, Art. 50(1): 'A civilian is any person who does not belong to one of the categories of persons referred to in Article 4 A (1), (2), (3) and (6) of the Third Convention and in Article 43 of this Protocol.' See also *Prosecutor* v. *Blaškić*, Case No. IT-95-14-A, Judgement, Appeal Chamber, 29 July 2004, paras. 111-114, where the Appeals Chamber appeared to divide a population into 'combatants' meeting the requirements of lawful combatants and 'civilians' <www.un.org/icty/blaskic/appeal/judgement/bla-aj040729e.pdf>.

54. See L. Nurick and R.W. Barrett, 'Legality of guerrilla forces under the laws of war', 40 *AJIL* (1946) p. 563; *Ex Parte Quirin*, 317 *US* 1 (1942); R.R. Baxter, 'So-called "unprivileged belligerency": Spies, guerrillas, and saboteurs, 28 *BYIL* (1951) p. 323; G.I.A.D. Draper, 'The status of combatants and the question of guerrilla warfare', 45 *BYIL* (1971) p. 173; and K. Watkin, 'Warriors without rights? Combatants, unprivileged belligerents, and the struggle over legitimacy', Occasional Paper Series No. 2, Winter 2005, pp. 45-72 <www.hpcr.org/pdfs/OccasionalPaper2.pdf>.

55. See Art. 44(4) AP I. Otherwise lawful "combatants" who fail to meet even the relaxed criteria for combatancy loose their right to be a prisoner of war. In effect they do not have one of the key privileges of lawful combatancy.

56. See J.M. Spaight, 'Non-combatants and air attack', *Air LR* (1938) p. 372 at 375 ('International law should...classify such [armament] workers as *quasi-combatants.* Unless they are clearly separated from ordinary non-combatants their treatment may set the pace for the treatment of all non-combatants.').

57. See Sassoli, *supra* n. 26, pp. 201-202.

ers cannot be targeted.[58] However, the participation of civilians in providing support to armed forces, their location near military objectives and their employment in support of the defence effort (i.e., defence scientists) makes the *de facto* nature of their involvement often difficult to assess.[59] Furthermore, accounting for civilian participation in military operations has presented a challenge since the earliest efforts to codify IHL.[60] Their sometimes unique status is reflected in the Third Geneva Convention of 1949, where some civilians are provided prisoner-of-war status.[61]

The increased use by states of civilian government and contract employees to support their operations,[62] as well as private military firms to maintain security,[63] further clouds the nature of civilian involvement. This, in turn, has the potential to impact on the application of the proportionality principle. The large-scale involvement of civilians in the emerging highly technical disciplines such as computer network operations also raises questions as to the nature of their participation.[64] At some point it becomes extremely difficult to argue that civilians paid to provide direct support to military forces, and who are often physically integrated into military operations or present in the vicinity of military objects (e.g., aircraft maintainers located at an enemy airfield), should have a significant limiting impact on the proportionality equation, although taking steps such as altering the timing of an attack may offer a way of limiting civilian casualties.

---

58. See M. Bothe et al., *New Rules for Victims of Armed Conflicts* (Dordrecht, Martinus Nijhoff Publishers 1982) p. 303 ('civilians providing only indirect support to the armed forces, such as workers in defence plants or those engaged in distribution or storage of military supplies in rear areas do not pose an immediate threat to the adversary … .'). See also ICRC Commentary, Art. 51, para. 1945: 'There should be a clear distinction between direct participation in hostilities and participation in the war effort.' <www.cicr.org/ihl.nsf/COM/470-750065?OpenDocument>.

59. See W. Hays Parks, 'Memorandum of Law: Executive Order 12333 and assassination', *The Army Lawyer* (1989) p. 6.

60. See Art. 50 of the Instructions for the Government of Armies of the United States in the Field 1863 (hereinafter, Lieber Code), and Art. 13 of the Hague Land Regulations 1907.

61. See Art. 4A(4)-(5) GC II. However, see also R.R. Wilson, 'Treatment of civilian alien enemies', 37 *AJIL* (1943) p 30 at 31, where following World War I a German-American Mixed Claims Commission refused a claim for damages to health and loss of personal effects made by the civilian master of a vessel of the United States Army Transport Service because damages were only awarded to civilians and 'the test for determining who were civilians involved the question of whether their activities were at the time aimed at the direct furtherance of a military operation against Germany and her allies.'

62. See Major L.L. Turner and Major L.G. Norton, 'Civilians at the tip of the spear', 51 *Air Force LR* (2001) p. 1; and Major M.E. Guillory, 'Civilianizing the force: Is the United States crossing the Rubicon', 51 *Air Force LR* (2001) p. 111.

63. See A. McDonald, 'The legal status of military and security contractors', in R. Arnold and P.-A. Hildebrand, eds., *International Humanitarian Law and the 21st Century Conflicts* (Lausanne, Editions interuniversitaires Suisse-Edis 2005) p. 215; and M. Schmitt, 'Humanitarian law and direct participation in hostilities by private contractors or civilian employees', 5 *Chicago JIL* (2004) p. 511.

64. See Schmitt, *supra* n. 48, p. 54, where it is noted that there is increasing civilianization due to the introduction of advanced technology.

The potential for confusion regarding when civilians must be protected is further increased if the 'unless and for such time as' temporal limitations of direct civilian participation are interpreted too narrowly. Suggestions that 'civilians' should be targeted only when they are carrying weapons or explosives can create a 'revolving door'[65] concept that would allow members of armed groups to plan or prepare further attacks free from the threat of being targeted. The idea of 'immunity' for such part-time participants is reflected in the writing of Colm McKeogh when he states that 'they could move from the category of combatant to the category of civilian (and back again) depending upon their activity at any given time'.[66] The idea that someone has to carry a weapon in order to be targeted was rejected in respect of 'lawful combatants' by the ICTY Appeals Chamber decision in *Prosecutor* v. *Blaškić*.[67] However, there remains a school of thought which prefers the narrower interpretation in respect of 'part-time' civilian participants in hostilities.[68] If this approach were adopted, the 'civilian' status of such participants could theoretically render an otherwise valid target immune from attack if those 'civilians' were factored into the proportionality test. Yet for a state and its military forces waiting to react to an attack from such 'civilians', such a narrow interpretation appears dramatically inconsistent with the nature of the threat presented by such members of armed groups.

The test for targeting people (e.g., taking a direct part in hostilities) is and must be different from that applied when identifying military objects. As will be noted in the next section, 'military objectives' can constitute a much broader set of targets than 'combatants', lawful or otherwise. It is the narrower 'people' test that results in civilian factory workers supporting the war effort being viewed as civilians and therefore not subject to direct attack even though the factory they work in constitutes a military objective.[69] Such an interpretation provides an example of where humanitarian law can be interpreted to place a higher premium on life than on the damage or destruction to 'objects'. Despite debate over whether human rights have a hierarchical structure, the right to life stands out as part of an irredu-

65. See the comments of W. Hays Parks, 'Air war and the law of war', 31 *Air Force LR* (1990) pp. 1 at 118-120, where he refers to the 'initial problem with establishment of combatant or civilian status lies in the new revolving door provided for in Protocol I'. See also D. Kretzmer, 'Targeted killing of suspected terrorists: Extra-judicial executions or legitimate means of defence?', 16 *EJIL* (2005) pp. 171 at 193-194, for a discussion of this issue in respect of transnational terrorist groups.

66. See McKeogh, *supra* n. 51, p. 140.

67. See *Prosecutor* v. *Blaškić*, Case No. IT-95-14-A, Appeals Chamber, para. 114 ('the specific situation of the victim at the time the crimes are committed may not be determinative of his civilian or non-civilian status. If he is indeed a member of an armed organization, the fact that he is not armed or in combat at the time of the commission of crimes, does not accord him civilian status.').

68. See A. Cassese, 'Expert opinion on whether Israel's targeted killings of Palestinian terrorists is consonant with international humanitarian law', Public Committee Against Torture in Israel, pp. 7-8 <www.stoptorture.org.il/eng/images/uploaded/publications/64.pdf>; and the Amnesty International Report, 'Israel and the Occupied Territories: State assassinations and other unlawful killings' (2001) <web.amnesty.org/aidoc/aidoc_pdf.nsf/Index/MDE150052001ENGLISH/$File/MDE1500501.pdf>.

69. See K. Watkin, 'Humans in the cross-hairs: Targeting, assassination and extra-legal killing in contemporary armed conflict', in Wippman and Evangelista, *supra* n. 26, p. 159.

cible core of non-derogable rights.[70] The primacy of that right is reflected in the view that '[w]hen life is deprived, it is impossible to enjoy any fundamental freedom.'[71]

2.2.3 *Attacking objects*

In terms of the distinction principle, another casualty of military operations during World War II was the protection afforded to civilian 'objects'. Aerial warfare tactics such as area bombing,[72] attacks on those parts of cities where workers lived,[73] and the effort to erode the morale of the civilian inhabitants,[74] combined with insufficiently precise bombing capability,[75] seriously degraded the distinction between military and civilian objects. However, even with a more precise targeting capability the definition of what constitutes a military object continues to have a significant impact on the civilian population. For instance, an attack on an oil production facility not only endangers workers but potentially also the civilians living nearby since such facilities are often located in or near inhabited areas. The location of objects identified as valid military targets in cities and far beyond traditional ideas of the frontlines impacts directly on the amount of potential collateral damage.

The post World War II initiatives to re-establish the distinction principle led to renewed efforts to define 'military objects', with the most generally accepted definition being set out in Article 52(2) AP I:

> 'In so far as objects are concerned, military objectives are limited to those objects which by their nature, location, purpose or use make an effective contribution to military action and whose total or partial destruction, capture or neutralization, in the circumstances ruling at the time, offers a definite military advantage.'

70. See T. Meron, 'On a hierarchy of international human rights', 80 *AJIL* (1986) pp. 3 at 11.

71. See Y. Dinstein, 'Terrorism as an international crime', *Israel YB HR* (1987) pp. 55 at 63.

72. See Thomas, *supra* n. 28, p. 132.

73. See, e.g., S. Lindqvist, *A History of Bombing* (New York, The New Press 2001) p. 110; and Major J. D. Reynolds, 'Collateral damage on the 21st century battlefield: Enemy exploitation of the law of armed conflict, and the struggle for a moral high ground', 56 *Air Force LR* (2005) pp. 1 at 13 (quoting from J. Ellis, *Brute Force: Allied Strategy and Tactics in the Second World War* (New York, Viking 1990) p. 180, for references to targeting locations where factory workers lived).

74. See Thomas, *supra* n. 28, p. 132 (relying on T. Davis Biddle, 'The British and American approaches to strategic bombing: Their origins and implementation in the World War II combined bomber offensive', in John Gooch, ed., *Airpower: Theory and Practice* (London, Frank Cass 1995) p. 117 ('In February 1942 an RAF directive formally endorsed "the morale of the enemy population" as the primary objective of the bombing campaign, specifying that bombers should aim for "built-up" areas of German cities in an attempt to "render the German industrial population homeless, spiritless, and, in so far as possible, dead.')).

75. Ibid., p. 133. In respect of American efforts with quite capable technology, such as the Norden bombsite, it is noted 'even under optimal conditions, U.S. bombing was too inaccurate to be described as "precise"'.

The CIHL Study states that this definition 'is a norm of customary international law in both international and non-international armed conflict'.[76]

As with the 'direct participation' test, the question of how to assess what constitutes a military object is the subject of considerable debate. This has led to contemporary discussion as to whether the general statement found in Additional Protocol I is sufficient or if a list-based approach is required in order to provide greater clarity.[77] It has been suggested that a general definition 'was presumably, intended to, at a minimum, shift targeting decision-makers away from a list-oriented approach ... towards a situation-dependent, criterion-oriented approach'.[78] However, in practical terms the identification of 'types' of targets is often part of legal analysis.[79] Further, 'target sets' such as 'railways and bridges', 'nuclear, biological, and chemical facilities', 'electric power' and 'oil facilities' are used in applying targeting doctrine.[80] Whatever method of analysis is agreed upon, it has to reflect the reality of how military campaigns are waged and targets are selected.

The terms 'nature', 'location', 'purpose' or 'use' are themselves the subject of significant contemporary debate. Suffice it to say that 'objects' subject to attack are diverse, including areas of land, factories and transportation facilities. Military objectives can also include industries with both military and civilian use and involve

76. See Henckaerts and Doswald-Beck, *supra* n. 18, p. 29.

77. Dinstein, *supra* n. 33, pp. 83-84, where the general definition is criticized as being too abstract and for failing to provide a workable definition. It is suggested to use 'a composite definition – combining an abstract statement with a non-exhaustive catalogue of concrete illustrations ...'.

78. See W.J. Fenrick, 'Targeting and proportionality during the NATO bombing campaign against Yugoslavia', 12 *EJIL* (2001) pp. 489 at 495.

79. See ICRC Commentary, AP I, Art. 52, n. 5 <www.cicr.org/ihl.nsf/COM/470-750067?OpenDocument>. The 1956 Draft Rules for the Limitation of Dangers Incurred by the Civilian Population in Time of War contained a list of types of targets. As would be expected, that list contained references to armed forces, traditional military installations and equipment. However, it also referred to factories; lines and means of communication (such as railway lines, roads, bridges, tunnels and canals); energy producing installations; and broadcast and television stations as well as telephone and telegraph exchanges. For a criticism of the ICRC list and its use by the ICTY Review Committee assessing the 1999 Kosovo bombing campaign, see Benvenuti, *supra* n. 26, pp. 515-516. However, see also the ICTY Final Report, *supra* n. 23, para. 78, where the objects identified as part of Yugoslav command and control network included transmission towers and control buildings of the Yugoslav radio rely network (related to controlling the army, repressive police forces and the air-defence network); the command and control assets of the Yugoslav Army; the electricity grids supplying those networks; and other radio and TV sites and command posts.

80. See M.W. Lewis, 'The law of aerial bombardment in the 1991 Gulf War', 97 *AJIL* (2003) pp. 481 at 488. See also *Air Warfare*, Air Force Doctrine Document 2-1, United States Air Force (January 2000) p. 3 ('the strategist devises a joint campaign plan to answer them, with a joint force air operation as part of it. This involves transforming broad goals into specific military objectives, identifying the *target sets* that need to be affected (not necessarily destroyed) to attain those objectives, and then converting the whole into a coordinated operations order (OPORD) that can be implemented by the military forces involved.') (emphasis added) <www.dtic.mil/doctrine/jel/service_pubs/afd2_1.pdf> (hereinafter, *Air Warfare*); and *British Airpower Doctrine*, 3rd ed. (1999) AP 3000 at 2.6.7 ('Target sets identified by campaign planning tools may include the machinery of government, military forces, infrastructure and research and production facilities.') <www.raf.mod.uk/downloads/ap3000.html> (hereinafter, *British Airpower*).

those providing products and services essential to the civilian population (e.g., oil production facilities, electricity generation facilities and grids). Often referred to as 'dual use' facilities, this term is problematic for two reasons. First, like proportionality, 'dual use' is not a term set out in the law. This can complicate analysis in an area that is already fraught with definitional challenges. Secondly, the term 'dual use' may inadvertently mask the nature of the decision being made. The object is either a valid military target or it is a civilian object. This distinction is reflected in the test for identifying military objectives where there is no 'undistributed middle between the categories' with the result that 'civilian' objects may include installations that are not actually civilian 'in the dictionary meaning of the word'.[81]

It should also be noted that the wording used in the Additional Protocol I definition of military objects does not reflect the approach taken by all states. While the US Army and Air Force reflect the Additional Protocol I wording,[82] the Navy[83] and more recent Department of Defence documents[84] substitute 'enemy's war-fighting or war-sustaining capability' for 'military action'. As the CIHL Study notes, this wording 'reflects its [the United States'] position that this definition is a wide one which includes areas of land, objects screening other military objectives and war-supporting economic facilities'.[85]

However, the fact that the US wording may reflect a different approach to identifying 'military objects' than that found in Additional Protocol I cannot be understated. In this respect, it has been noted that '[b]ombing has always been a mode of warfare predominately limited to a relative small number of powerful states.'[86] The concern that such states and their allies may have over narrow legal interpretations of the rules governing the conduct of air warfare is not limited to the fact that relatively few states practice this method of warfare but includes the possibility that the norms might be applied 'strategically to handcuff a more powerful foe'.[87] Overly narrow interpretations of military objectives or the proportionality test itself may serve to reinforce that concern.

There is a general acknowledgment that 'war-fighting' and 'military action' are substantially the same.[88] Further, there may be no substantial difference between

81. See Dinstein, *supra* n. 33, p. 114.

82. For the Air Force definition, see *The Military Commander and The Law*, 8th ed. (Maxwell AFB, AFJAGS Press, 2006) p. 614 <http://milcom.jag.af.mil/milcom2006-complete.pdf>; and *The Law of Land Warfare*, FM 27-10 (1976) ch. 2, para. 40 c <http://atiam.train.army.mil/portal/atia/adlsc/view/ public/296783-1/fm/27-10/Ch2.htm#s4>.

83. *United States Commander's Handbook on the Law of Naval Operations*, 21 NWP 1-14M (October 1995) para. 8.1.1 at 8-1 <www.nwc.navy.mil/ILD/NWP%201-14M.htm>.

84. See Department of Defence Military Commission Instruction No. 2, 30 April 2003, para. 5 D 3 <www.dod.gov/news/May2003/d20030430milcominstno2.pdf>.

85. Henckaerts and Doswald-Beck, *supra* n. 18, p. 31.

86. See Thomas, *supra* n. 28, p. 176.

87. Ibid., p. 175, where the examples provided include Iraq and Serbia when confronted by the United States and its allies.

88. See H.B. Robertson, Jr., 'The principle of the military objective in the law of armed conflict', 72 *Int. Law Studies* (1998) pp. 197 at 209.

the wording of Additional Protocol I and the US wording as long as it is accepted the Protocol wording is to be broadly interpreted.[89] When that approach is used, the differences in interpretation appear to hinge to a significant extent on whether exports financing the war effort can be targeted.[90] However, the 'war sustaining' wording has been criticised as being too easily open to interpretation that could justify unleashing the type of indiscriminate attacks that occurred during World War II.[91] It has also been identified as a 'slippery slope' where every economic activity might be interpreted as indirectly sustaining the war effort.[92]

The difference between 'war-sustaining' and 'military action' appears to be central to the assessment of the 'military advantage' a particular attack may produce. Interestingly, 'military advantage' is found in both the definition of military objects and the proportionality test. The meaning to be given to this term introduces fundamental questions regarding the goals of armed conflict, how campaigns are waged and the impact of the levels of warfare on 'proportionality'. It is to those issues that the analysis will now turn.

2.2.4 *Military advantage*

Given that one goal of humanitarian law is to provide a normative framework to be applied by all participants in warfare, there are aspects of Additional Protocol I that at first glance do not lend themselves to easy application. One example is the term 'military advantage' that is found in the proportionality test, a test for indiscriminate attack and the definition of military objects.[93] It has been noted that 'the notion of "military advantage" is not singularly helpful'.[94] The two criteria, 'military advantage' and making 'an effective contribution to military action', in the definition of military object are seen as being inevitably linked.[95] Various modi-

89. Ibid., pp. 210-211, and Dinstein, *supra* n. 33, p. 87.

90. See Robertson, *supra* n. 88, pp. 210-211.

91. L. Doswald-Beck, 'The San Remo Manual on International Law Applicable to Armed Conflicts at Sea', 89 *AJIL* (1995) pp. 192 at 199. For a criticism of this view, see Robertson, *supra* n. 88, p. 210. However, see also F. Kalshoven, Noncombatant persons: A comment to chapter 11 of the Commander's Handbook on the Law of Naval Operations, 64 *Int. Law Studies* (1991) pp. 300 at 310.

92. See Dinstein, *supra* n. 33, p. 87.

93. See Arts. 51(1)(5), 52(2) and 57(2)(iii) AP I.

94. Dinstein, *supra* n. 33, p. 86.

95. Ibid., p. 85 (referring to M. Sassoli and A.A. Bouvier, *How Does the Law Protect in War? Cases, Documents and Teaching Materials on Contemporary Practice in International Law* (ICRC 1999) p. 161).

fiers, such as 'definite'[96], 'distinct'[97] and 'concrete and direct',[98] are used in relation to military advantage. The use of 'concrete and direct' conveys the idea of 'a concrete and perceptible military advantage rather than a hypothetical and speculative one'.[99] The ICRC Commentary to AP I suggests 'that the words "concrete and direct" impose stricter conditions on the attacker than those implied by the criteria defining military objectives in Article 52'.[100] Yet it is not evident why that should be the case.[101]

While repetitive, there are significant practical reasons for having the same standard for assessing military advantage in both the definitions of military objects and proportionality. The requirement to conduct targeting in stressful, time constrained situations does not lend itself to nuanced interpretations of multiple tests for assessing military advantage in respect of the same target. Further, including 'military advantage' in the Article 57(2)(iii) AP I proportionality test introduces this standard to the targeting process applied to attacks against people since it applies to the targeting of both persons and objects. Unlike the Article 52(2) definition of military objects, the provisions relating to the targeting of persons do not refer to military advantage. Ultimately, the requirement to identify a military advantage appears to be primarily an articulation of the 'military necessity' aspect of humanitarian law insofar as the purpose of the proportionality rule 'is aimed at establishing an equitable balance between humanitarian requirements and the sad necessities of war'.[102]

The modifying words 'concrete and direct' have spawned considerable debate, with tension existing between an approach that would primarily restrict such advantage to attacks directed at traditional military objectives (e.g., troops, naval ves-

---

96. Art. 52(2) AP I.

97. See Dinstein, *supra* n. 33, p. 85 ('There is no apparent difference in the present context between the adjectives "distinct" and "definite" or, for that matter, several other alternatives pondered by the framers of Article 52(2).'). See also Art. 24(1) Hague Rules of Air Warfare 1923, where reference is made to an 'obvious' military advantage; and ICRC Commentary, AP I, Art. 52, *supra* n. 79 ('It should be noted that the expression "a definite military advantage" is very similar to the terms used in Articles 51 (Protection of the civilian population), paragraph 5(b) and 57 (Precautions in attack), paragraph 2(a)(iii) and (b). These articles use the expression "concrete and direct military advantage anticipated". (17) In the draft the ICRC had used the same expression in both articles: "distinct and substantial military advantage".').

98. Arts. 51(5)(b), 57(2)(a)(iii) AP I.

99. See Dinstein, *supra* n. 33, pp. 85-86 (relying on Bothe, *supra* n. 58, p. 325).

100. ICRC Commentary, AP I, Art. 57, para. 2218 <www.cicr.org/ihl.nsf/COM/470-750073?OpenDocument>. See also ICRC Commentary, AP I, Art. 52, *supra* n. 79, para. 2028 ('In the case of Article 52 there must be a definite military advantage for every military objective that is attacked. In the case of Article 57 (Precautions in attack) this condition must also be fulfilled, but in addition, the military advantage which should also be concrete and direct must be weighed against the civilian losses and damage which could result from an attack.').

101. See ICRC Commentary, AP I, Art. 52, *supra* n. 79, para. 2027 ('The documents of the Diplomatic Conference do not contain any indication about the reasons why different expressions were preferred. One is therefore left to analyze the meaning of the words used.').

102. ICRC Commentary, AP I, Art. 57, *supra* n. 100, para. 2219.

sels, aircraft, supplies)[103] and other views that recognise the broader strategic objectives of the parties to the conflict.[104] Concern over the potential limiting effect of the words 'concrete and direct' prompted a number of nations to state that 'the expression "military advantage" refers to the advantage anticipated from the military attack considered as a whole and not only from isolated or particular parts of that attack'.[105] This broader perspective on military advantage is reflected in Article 8(2)(b)(iv) of the ICC Statute, which refers to 'the concrete and direct *overall* military advantage anticipated'.[106] Such wording emphasises the strategic impact of an attack although it has been noted '"an attack as a whole" must be viewed as a finite event, not to be confused with the entire war'.[107]

In order to assess how broadly 'military advantage' might be interpreted, it is necessary to take into consideration the nature of warfare and how wars are fought. As Clausewitz so famously noted, communities go to war for political reasons.[108] Regardless of whether it is a state, guerrilla organisation or transnational terrorist group, the entity uses its collective resources to compel an enemy to do its will.[109] Clausewitz originally discussed two levels of war: the tactical[110] and strategic.[111] However, the strategic level has subsequently been divided into higher (grand strategy) and lower (strategy) planes. '[T]he role for grand strategy – higher strategy – is to co-ordinate and direct all the resources of a nation, or band of nations, towards the attainment of the political object of the war... with the responsibility of its execution being at the government level'.[112] Strategy, which is the responsibility of military commanders, is 'the art of distributing and applying

---

103. Ibid., ('A military advantage can only consist in ground gained and in annihilating or weakening the enemy armed forces.').

104. For example Dinstein, *supra* n. 33, p. 86 ('Surely, military advantage is not restricted to tactical gains. The spectrum is necessarily wide, and it extends to the security of the attacking force.'). See also J. Burger, 'International humanitarian law and the Kosovo crisis: Lessons learned or to be learned', 82 *IRRC* (2000) p. 129 ('"Military advantage" is not restricted to tactical gains. One must take into account the full context of war strategy.').

105. See Henckaerts and Doswald-Beck, *supra* n. 18, p. 49 n. 27. Such countries include Canada, France, Germany, the United Kingdom, the Netherlands, Belgium, Australia, New Zealand and Spain.

106. Ibid., p. 50 [emphasis added], where it is noted the ICRC has stated that adding 'overall' to the definition of the crime does not change existing law. See also M.N. Schmitt, 'Fault lines in the law of attack', in S. Breau and A. Jachec-Neale, eds., *Testing the Boundaries of International Humanitarian Law* (London, British Institute of International and Comparative Law, 2006) pp. 277 at 295.

107. Dinstein, *supra* n. 33, p. 87.

108. Clausewitz, *supra* n. 7, p. 75.

109. See R.A. Pape, *Dying to Win: The Strategic Logic of Suicide Terrorism* (New York, Random House 2005) p. 20, contemporary suicide terrorism 'occurs mainly in campaigns of suicide attacks carried out by organized armed groups for specific political goals and extending over a considerable period of time'. See also D. Galula, *Counterinsurgency Warfare: Theory and Practice* (New York, Frederick A. Praeger 2005) p. 3 ('Paraphrasing Clausewitz, we might say that "Insurgency is the pursuit of the policy of a party, inside a country, by every means."').

110. See Clausewitz, *supra* n. 7, p. 128, tactics involve 'the use of armed forces in the engagement'.

111. Ibid., strategy is described as 'the use of engagements for the object of the war.'

112. B.H. Liddell Hart, *Strategy*, 2nd edn. (New York, Meridian Group 1991) p. 322.

military means to fulfill the ends of policy' and 'is concerned not merely with the movement of military forces – as its role is often defined – but also with the effect'.[113] Another level, the 'operational' level of war, has been added between the strategic and tactical levels in order to direct military resources to achieve military objectives.[114]

This outline of levels of war is important for two reasons. First, it highlights the interface between political objectives and military action. The goal in inter-state conflict is to change the 'mind' of another state in order 'to cause the other State to desist from the action or abandon the claim which is the cause of offence'.[115] In effect what this means is forcing those holding political power within one state to acquiesce to the state attempting to wield influence. While this can be carried out in part by diplomatic, financial and commercial means, the fact remains that military force can be used to affect an opponent's will.

The issue of whom or what may be targeted is complicated by the incorporation of significant portions of modern society into a nation's war effort. It has been suggested that a 'purely political [advantage] … "forcing a change in the negotiating attitudes" of the adverse Party cannot be deemed a proper military advantage'.[116] Yet compelling political change is the ultimate goal of warfare. The answer may lie in the types of targets chosen and not the fact that the destruction of those targets influences political decision makers. A change of negotiating attitudes may well result from an attack on valid military objects that has significant impact on the economy of a nation. It has long been recognised under IHL that striking an enemy involves not only attacking military forces but also includes economic warfare, such as blockades.[117]

An indication that influencing an enemy population is not prohibited as long as the attack is not itself illegal is reflected in the humanitarian law principle that civilians are not to be subjected to '[a]cts or threats or violence *the primary purpose of which* is to spread terror among the civilian population … .'[118] A 'shock and awe' campaign directed at military objectives is not illegal even if civilian morale is degraded.[119] However, this is an area that must be approached with cau-

---

113. Ibid., p. 321.

114. See *British Airpower*, *supra* n. 80, at 1.1.2.

115. See Spaight, *supra* n. 8, p. 2.

116. See Dinstein, *supra* n. 33, p. 86.

117. See *San Remo Manual on International Law Applicable to Armed Conflicts at Sea* (Cambridge, Cambridge University Press 1995) pp. 26-27, Rules 93 to 104 (hereinafter, *San Remo Manual*); and Art. 42 of the UN Charter which states that action that 'may be necessary to maintain or restore international peace and security … may include demonstrations, *blockade*, and other operations by air, sea or land forces …' [emphasis added].

118. Art. 51(2) AP I [emphasis added]. See Schmitt, *supra* n. 106, p. 285 ('There is nothing unlawful about seeking to affect civilian morale by striking otherwise lawful military objectives.').

119. See Dinstein, *supra* n. 33, p. 116; Fenrick, *supra* n. 78, p. 498; and M.N. Schmitt, 'Targeting and humanitarian law: Current issues', *Israel YB HR* (2004) pp. 59 at 71-74. For a contrary view, see Benvenuti, *supra* n. 26, p. 509, where he considers the effect on civilian morale as a proportionality damage issue.

tion. It has been noted that there is significant pressure to adopt an axiological type of doctrine which focuses on the targets that the enemy leadership values so that 'their destruction (or neutralization) is likely to affect decision-making'.[120] Such thinking could lead to a liberal interpretation of military objectives 'or, perhaps, even ignoring the principle of distinction'.[121]

The second point related to the different levels of war is that they are reflected in national security documents[122] and airpower doctrine;[123] in effect, how wars are planned and fought. This is an issue which is particularly relevant to the use of airpower since, from its earliest beginnings, air warfare has been focused on strategic as well as tactical impacts. While early twentieth century predictions by airpower theorists that wars can be won by airpower alone have yet to materialise, the strategic use of airpower and measuring the cumulative effects of attacks at that level remain an essential part of air warfare.[124] Changes to strategic airpower doctrine have been driven by American theorists, who have moved away from attacks designed to attrit the industrial capacity of states. Instead '[e]ffects based operations...have replaced attrition targeting in US doctrine.'[125] While there was a struggle throughout the twentieth century between proponents of strategic airpower and those seeking to employ air assets to the air/land battle, the strategic use of airpower still remains an important part of military planning and operations.[126]

---

120. See Schmitt, *supra* n. 48, p. 50.

121. Ibid.

122. See, e.g., 'The national security strategy of the United States of America' (September 2002) <www.whitehouse.gov/nsc/nss.pdf>; 'The national military strategy of the United States of America: A strategy for today; A vision for tomorrow' (2004) <www.defenselink.mil/news/Mar2005/d20050318nms.pdf>; 'Securing an open society: Canada's national security policy' (2004) <www.pco-bcp.gc.ca/docs/Publications/NatSecurnat/natsecurnat_e.pdf>; and 'A role of pride and influence in the world: Defence in Canada's international policy statement' (April 2005) p. 5 <www.forces.gc.ca/site/ Reports/dps/pdf/dps_e.pdf>.

123. For examples, see *Air Warfare, supra* n. 80, at 2-1; and *British Airpower, supra* n. 80, at 1.1.2.

124. See *British Airpower, supra* n. 80, at 3.12.3. These theorists were of the view 'that the offensive nature of air power, through the medium of bomber aircraft, would dominate future wars and alone could decide the outcome.'

125. See Schmitt, *supra* n. 48, p. 60. See Colonel J.A. Warden, *The Air Campaign: Planning for Combat* (National Defense University Press 1988) p. 3 <www.au.af.mil/au/awc/awcgate/warden/ward-toc.htm>; ibid., 'The enemy as a system', *Airpower J* (Spring 1995) p. 10; and I.B. Holley, Jr., 'Reflections on the search for airpower theory', in P.S. Meilinger, ed., *The Paths of Heaven: The Evolution of Airpower Theory* (Maxwell AFB, Air University Press 1997) p. 592 ('Colonel Boyd developed the approach that '[s]uccess favors the side that can observe, orient, decide, and act (OODA) sooner than the enemy.').

126. See Lewis, *supra* n. 80, p. 48, for an account of the conflict between an airpower theorist and the American joint air forces commander prior to the start of the 1991 Gulf Conflict air offensive. See also Murray and Scales, *supra* n. 46, p. 162. The use of airpower in that conflict must be assessed from the perspective that 'the Coalition had waged a twelve year air campaign against Iraq's air defense system before the first shot was fired'. However, see also R. Grant, 'The Redefinition of airpower', 86 *Air Force Magazine* (2003) pp. 33 at 35-36 (outlining that strategic attack during the 2003 Iraq War was not a separate part of the air campaign).

The link between the levels of war and how wars are conducted is evidenced in military airpower doctrine and the use of terms such as the 'strategy to task' process.[127] Political objectives for the conflict are identified at the grand strategy level and military objectives at the military strategic level. The operational level commander oversees the production of an operational plan, allocates resources, identifies targets and directs the execution of missions.[128] Operations at the tactical level are designed to produce results that have strategic, operational and tactical effects. Planning can include sophisticated target development involving critical node analysis of 'the interaction and interrelationships among multiple target systems'[129] and an assessment of 'what effects are likely to be achieved by attacking the system, where the system must be attacked, and how long the attack will disrupt enemy plans or operations'.[130]

The effects of an attack in legal terms are linked to the 'concrete and direct' nature of the military advantage. The targeting process is designed to produce direct or indirect effects. The former consist of 'the immediate, first order consequence of a military action' while the latter are 'the delayed and/or displaced second- and third- order consequences'.[131] Indirect effects include attacks on military defences designed to impact on 'the legitimacy of the regime portraying them as incapable of protecting the populace'.[132] Both direct and indirect target effects can have cumulative, cascading or collateral and additional effects.[133]

If, therefore, the effects of attacks can be measured, a strong argument can be made that the military advantage is 'concrete and direct'. Such effects are not limited to tactical level results. For example, it has been suggested that the effects of World War II bombing were ultimately measurable and degraded German capacity to sustain or expand the war 'though it did not force capitulation'.[134] The challenge remains, however, in quantifying and interpreting the results of attacks during the

---

127. See *Air Warfare*, *supra* n. 80, p. 3 ('*It cannot be overemphasized that there must be a clear linkage between the targets chosen and the objectives sought .... Failure to properly analyze the mechanism that ties tactical results to strategic effects has historically been the shortcoming of both airpower theorists and strategists.*').

128. Ibid.

129. *USAF Intelligence Targeting Guide*, Air Force Pamphlet 14-210 (February 1998) para. 5.2.1 at 42 <www.e-publishing.af.mil/pubfiles/af/14/afpam14-210/afpam14-210.pdf> (hereinafter, *USAF Targeting Guide*).

130. Ibid., para. 5.2.2.

131. See United States *Joint Doctrine for Targeting*, Joint Publication 3-60 (2002) p. I-6 <www.dtic.mil/ doctrine/jel/new_pubs/jp3_60.pdf>.

132. Ibid., p. I-6.

133. Ibid., p. I-7.

134. See R. Overy, 'Air Warfare', in C. Townsend, ed., *The Oxford History of Modern War* (Oxford, Oxford University Press 2005) pp. 341 at 361. However, see also C.S. Maier, 'Targeting the city: Debates and silences about the aerial bombing of World War II', 87 *IRRC* (2005) pp. 429 at 435, for reference to an earlier less positive review regarding the effects of the bombing campaign: 'The issue of efficacy was raised by the famous results of the United States Strategic Bombing Survey, whose members – especially John Kenneth Galbraith – argued that bombing had achieved far less of an impact than had been claimed.'

actual conduct of a military operation. It is here that the 'expected to cause' phrase in the proportionality test has particular application. The use of sophisticated modelling can provide significant assistance in determining any potential collateral damage,[135] although actually assessing the effects of an attack is not always easy since the results are not necessarily immediately recognisable or available.[136] Notwithstanding the sophisticated scientific tools and analysis available to some countries, the ultimate challenge of assessing the value of life against other criteria, such as physical damage or the ultimate objective of the war, is not removed. It is that analysis which is often the most difficult, both morally and legally.

2.2.5 *Precautions*

Perhaps one of the most significant provisions of Additional Protocol I is the requirement to take 'constant care' to spare civilians.[137] With respect to 'acts of violence against the adversary in offence or in defence',[138] there is an obligation on those who plan or decide upon an attack to take certain precautions, including assessing whether the attack will cause excessive civilian death, injury or damage.[139] In effect, this imposes the duty to exercise a form of 'due care'.[140]

One practical effect of this obligation has been the formal development of targeting doctrine which often sets out a detailed process for target development[141] and battle damage assessment.[142] Further, the Protocol precautions are unique in that they refer specifically to those who plan an attack. The emphasis placed on

135. *USAF Targeting Guide*, *supra* n. 129, para. A7.5.2 at 183 ('A number of other programs are available or can be modified to compute large scale collateral damage. Nonnuclear weaponeering programs provided by the JMEM for programmable calculators provide an "offset" capability to determine collateral damage. In these programs, the range offset and the deflection offset can be used to represent distances from aimpoint for facilities that may be subjected to collateral damage. These programs can be modified to provide numerous computations.').

136. See T.A. Keaney, 'Surveying Gulf War airpower', 2 *Joint Force Quarterly* (Autumn 1993) p. 36, who notes that 'you can never have information available during the war to know exactly how you are doing'; and Murray and Scales, *supra* n. 46, p. 175 (commenting on how hard it is to assess the second order effect of bombing attacks).

137. Art. 57(1) AP I.

138. Art. 49(1) AP I: the definition of attack. While the precautions are referred to in terms of an 'attack' the obligation applies in both offensive and defensive uses of violence.

139. AP I, Art. 57(2): 'The precautions require that those who plan or decide on an attack do everything feasible to verify targets are lawful; take all feasible precautions in the methods and means of attack to avoid or minimize loss of life or injury to civilians or damage to civilian objects; and, of course, apply the proportionality test. An attack must be cancelled or suspended if it becomes apparent that target is not a military objective or excessive collateral damage is expected. There is also a requirement where circumstances permit to give effective advance notice to the civilian population. Finally there is a requirement to choose the military objective that is expected to obtain the least danger to civilian lives and objects where more than one choice is possible that will obtain a similar military advantage.'

140. See Walzer, *supra* n. 9, p. 156.

141. See, e.g., *Joint Doctrine for Targeting*, *supra* n. 131.

142. See the United States *Commander's Handbook for Joint Battle Damage Assessment* (2004).

'command responsibility' in IHL and the importance of 'command' in both military law and ethos often masks the broader responsibility of those who serve on staffs and generate the targeting plans and recommendations for commanders. While the ICC Statute refers more generally to '[i]ntentionally launching an attack'[143] and outlines a specific test for command and superior responsibility,[144] that does not mean that personnel other than commanders would not be criminally responsible for their participation in the preparation of an unlawful attack. In effect, in referring to both planners and commanders, the Additional Protocol I provisions highlight this broader responsibility.

However, there is a danger that the precautions and even the development of detailed targeting doctrine will create an impression that those processes can be slavishly followed prior to every offensive or defensive attack. The manner of complying with legal obligations must be assessed in the context of how wars are fought. Many aspects of military operations lend themselves to a deliberate planning process where targets can be identified and prioritised. However, that is not always the case. Targeting doctrine itself reflects some of the complexity that arises regarding the time available to identify targets by categorising them as 'planned' or 'immediate'. Planned targets (those known to exist) are further subdivided into 'scheduled'[145] and 'on-call'[146] targets. Immediate targets (those identified too late to be added to the normal targeting process) are classified as 'unplanned immediate'[147] and 'unanticipated immediate'.[148]

While targeting doctrine provides for the development of attacks on 'time sensitive targets', at some point the acceleration of the target decision-making cycle may necessitate a greater degree of risk of collateral damage.[149] The engagement of time sensitive targets, such as enemy artillery batteries and leadership targets, during the 2003 Iraq conflict was the subject of critical analysis by Human Rights Watch.[150] However, clearly not all targeting decisions fall neatly within the 'targeting cycle' doctrine. For example, during two days of the 2003 Iraq War (23-24 and 24-25 March) the Coalition launched 1,500 to 2,000 sorties per day of which only 500 targets were pre-planned in each 24-hour period. The remainder 'were targets

143. Art. 8(2)(b)(iv) ICC Statute.

144. Ibid., Art 28.

145. *Joint Doctrine for Targeting*, *supra* n. 131, p. 3 ('Scheduled targets are planned targets upon which fires are to be delivered at a specific time.').

146. Ibid., ('On-call targets are those that do not have fires scheduled to be delivered at a specific time, are known to exist in an operational area, and are located in time for deliberate planning to meet emerging situations specific to campaign objectives.').

147. Ibid., ('Unplanned immediate targets are those that are known to exist in an operational area but are not detected, located, or selected for action in sufficient time to be included in the normal targeting process.').

148. Ibid., ('Unanticipated immediate targets are those that are unknown or unexpected to exist in an operational area but, when detected or located, meet criteria specific to campaign objectives.').

149. Ibid., B-1. See Schmitt, *supra* n. 106, pp. 296-298, for a discussion of force protection and proportionality.

150. See 'Off-Target', *supra* n. 25.

of opportunity (where aircraft received their strike missions in flight) or close air support missions (where teams on the ground called in strikes against enemy forces in close proximity to Coalition ground forces)'.[151] Further, regarding combat in Iraq and Afghanistan, there appears to have been discussion within the US forces as to whether self-defence and tactical level fires were exceptions to the requirement to obtain higher level permission prior to attack.[152] This requirement to react quickly to emerging threats, particularly when acting in self-defence, limits the ability of decision-makers and their staffs to apply more formal doctrinal processes.

As a related matter, it is also evident that, consistent with the principle of distinction, persons participating directly in hostilities must apply targeting principles whenever they use force. However, the question remains at what level of decision-making the 'formal' Additional Protocol I principles can or should be applied. Since the development of Additional Protocol I, there has been an element of unease regarding this issue, leading in some cases to reservations in prescribing their application at lower levels of command.[153]

The reality of combat must also be taken into consideration when assessing precautionary measures. As a result, the written word of the Protocols must be interpreted in the practical context within which the rules were designed to be applied. Those assessing the actions of those participating in targeting decisions must remember that '[d]etached reflection cannot be demanded in the presence of an upturned knife.'[154] As Michael Walzer noted regarding the application of the moral doctrine upon which the proportionality test is based, 'the degree of risk that is permissible is going to vary with the nature of the target, the urgency of the moment, the available technology, and so on.'[155] This comment concerning the application of the doctrine of 'double effect' suggests a context-driven approach to interpreting the principle of proportionality. The article will now turn to exploring the relationship between the doctrine of 'double effect' and the legal principle of 'proportionality', and other factors impacting on the determination of whether an attack is justified.

151. Murray and Scales, *supra* n. 46, pp. 170-171.

152. See *Legal Lessons Learned From Afghanistan and Iraq*, Vol. I: *Major Combat Operations (11 September 2001 to 1 May 2003)* (Center for Law and Military Operations 2004) pp. 103-106

153. Henckaerts and Doswald-Beck, *supra* n. 18, p. 54, for reference to reservations made by Switzerland and Austria. Upon ratification, the United Kingdom took the view that the obligation to cancel or suspend an attack when it became clear an objective was not military or was likely to cause excessive damage only applied to 'those who have the authority and practical possibility to cancel or suspend the attack'.

154. See *Brown* v. *United States* 256 *US* 335, 343 (1921) Athough this United States Supreme Court case dealt with the issue of self-defence in a domestic law context, the comments of the court appear equally applicable in an international law context.

155. See Walzer, *supra* n. 9, p. 156.

26 *K. Watkin*

2.3 The doctrine of 'double effect' and the law

As has been noted, the principle of proportionality has its roots in the medieval Christian doctrine of 'double effect', although humanitarian law is not uniquely linked to one religious or moral code.[156] It might be argued that the wide acceptance of the secularised proportionality test reflected in conventional and customary law negates the need to refer to a religious-based moral doctrine. However, the 'moral' roots of the proportionality principle provide valuable insight into the scope and limits of the legal test.

The doctrine of double effect was developed by Catholic casuists in the Middle Ages and provided 'a way of reconciling the absolute prohibition against attacking non-combatants with the legitimate conduct of military activity'[157] in circumstances where civilians might be injured. Originally, the doctrine was conceived as a justification for the use of force in individual self-defence where the natural reaction to protect oneself (the good) was not unlawful if the assailant was killed (the evil). This concept was subsequently expanded to 'the killing of civilians in war when civilians are killed as part of the attempted achievement of some military goal'.[158] Under this doctrine, it is permissible to perform an act that has 'evil' consequences if four conditions are met: the act is good in itself or at least indifferent; the direct effect is morally acceptable; the intention of the actor is a good one and the evil effect is not one of the ends or a means to an end; and the 'good effect' is sufficiently good to compensate for any evil outcome.[159]

Michael Walzer has indicated that the burden of the argument is in the third part of the doctrine where '[t]he "good" and "evil" effects come together'.[160] At that point there is a single intention directed at the 'good' effect and not at the 'evil' consequences; however, there remains the question of 'all those unintended but foreseeable deaths, for their number can be large; and subject only to the proportionality rule – a weak constraint ... .'[161] The idea of accepting foreseeable civilian deaths has been the subject of some criticism on the basis that 'deaths must be, not only unintended but also unforeseen and reasonably unforeseeable (accidental killing is both unintended and unforeseen; collateral killing is foreseen)'.[162]

156. See Ishay, *supra* n. 20, pp. 16-61, for an outline of the early ethical contributions from a number of religions to both human rights and humanitarian law, however, also noting that 'Judeo Christian morality was secularized, separated from politics, and strengthened in influence by the advent of capitalism and colonialism, at the expense of other notions of ethics.'; L. Green, 'The relations between human rights law and international humanitarian law: A historical overview', in S. Breau and A. Jachec-Neale, *supra* n. 106, p. 49; and McKeogh, *supra* n. 51, p. 2.

157. Walzer, *supra* n. 9, p. 153.

158. See McKeogh, *supra* n. 51, p. 65.

159. See Walzer, *supra* n. 9, pp. 151-154; and J. Turner Johnson, *Morality and Contemporary Warfare* (New Haven, Yale University Press 1999) pp. 131-132.

160. Walzer, *supra* n. 9, p. 153.

161. Ibid., p. 169.

162. McKeogh, *supra* n. 51, p. 170.

The search for means to reconcile these concepts of good and evil has led to suggestions that simply not to intend the deaths of civilians is too easy and that the 'foreseeable evil be reduced as far as possible'.[163] In effect this would mean minimising the cost to civilians and the acceptance of some of that cost by the soldiers themselves.[164] The principle of double effect has been further criticised on the basis that culpability extends not only to intended consequences, but also 'for our negligence and for the foreseeable avoidance of the consequences of our acts'.[165] With this approach the only excusable deaths would be accidental ones.[166] However, demanding only accidental deaths does not readily match the reality of warfare.

The extent of moral uncertainty regarding this aspect of non-combatant immunity is evident in the debate concerning the frequent classification of civilians as 'innocent'. One interpretation of combatant and civilian status includes an assessment that '[c]ombatants are treated in international law as instruments; civilians remain persons.'[167] However, it has also been noted that the classification of persons can be ethically ambiguous with some soldiers being 'good and peaceful people forced to fight against their will, and some civilians may bear a large measure of responsibility for the war ...'.[168] Therefore when conducting an attack 'it becomes highly likely that both innocent and guilty people – whether they are combatants or non-combatants will die as a result.'[169]

Attempts to reconcile the weighing of good and evil required in the application of the doctrine of double effect has included suggestions that 'for a military act to be just, it must be reasonably probable that no civilian be killed' and that 'war, if it cannot be fought justly, must not be fought at all'.[170] These comments appear to be a step back to the just war theory. Interestingly, their author, Colm McKeogh, suggests that '[a] strategy of destroying civilian property may be an effective and technologically feasible way of avoiding the unjust taking of human life.' He draws support from the position put forward by Charles Dunlap which argues for the deliberate targeting of objects not indispensable to the survival of the civilian population. Colm McKeogh suggests such a position is supportable as long as the 'attacks on civilian property … were accompanied by a genuine immunity for civilian life in war'.[171]

However, this approach of expanding attacks to objects presently considered to be civilian has been identified as 'a fundamental rejection of a major element of the

163. Walzer, *supra* n. 9, p. 155.
164. Ibid.
165. McKeogh, *supra* n. 51, pp. 169-170.
166. Ibid., p. 170.
167. Ibid., p. 169. See Walzer, *supra* n. 9, p. 146 ('We call them innocent people, a term of art which means they have done nothing, and are doing nothing, that entails the loss of their rights.').
168. Thomas, *supra* n. 28, p. 95.
169. Ibid., p. 96.
170. McKeogh, *supra* n. 51, p. 170.
171. Ibid., p. 172. See Colonel C. Dunlap, 'The end of innocence: Rethinking noncombatancy in the post-Kosovo era', 28 *Strategic Review* (Summer 2000) p. 9; and Major J.M. Meyer, 'Targeting the will of the enemy and Air Force doctrine', 51 *Air Force LR* (2001) p. 143.

principle of distinction ...'.[172] Further, while this approach is subjected to significant caveats,[173] the morally charged circumstances under which it would be used[174] must also contend with the 'unfortunate predicament' where 'those truly innocent such as children, the infirm and the insane' would be unintentionally distressed.[175] Such an attempt to force the end of conflict by attacking 'civilian' objects would require fundamental changes to humanitarian law.[176] Inevitably, expanding the concept of what constitutes a military objective would significantly increase the potential for collateral civilian casualties. Further, the ability to foresee and contain the effects of some attacks has not necessarily proven to be as scientific or as antiseptic as an 'attack civilian objects' approach would appear to require.[177] However, what this search for ways of limiting the death of humans from both outside and within the military does highlight is the moral complexity present in any analysis of the doctrine of 'double effect'.

The transformation of a moral doctrine into a legal rule raises the question whether the weighing of the relative value of life and objects takes on a different connotation when it is assessed as a legal rule. Here there is a difference since, while the rules of law apply to conscience as much as morality, 'the latter requires to be enforced by the internal power of conscience only, whereas the former requires to be enforced by some external power'.[178] Therefore, it is likely that the application of the doctrine of 'double effect' as a legal test will impact on the nature of the assessment of collateral damage. The law introduces a different notion of accountability, including the requirement of *mens rea*, or criminal intent. Not only does the legally entrenched 'proportionality' doctrine guide the conduct of military commanders and civilian leaders who make targeting decisions, it also endeavours to hold them criminally accountable for excessive collateral effects.

172. Schmitt, *supra* n. 48, p. 72.

173. See Dunlap, *supra* n. 171, p. 15, the attacks should only be conducted where undermining the will of the people has a reasonable likelihood of success; the attacks must not be for the purpose *per se* of punishment for punishment's sake; civilian safe areas and evacuation routes should be designated; and the scope of the attacks must bear a reasonable relationship to the egregiousness of the conduct to be prevented.

174. Ibid., p. 14 ('when facing a society whose moral compass is wildly askew, it may well behove democracies to consider a similarly sweeping campaign against property – despite its terrible destructiveness.').

175. Ibid.

176. Ibid., p. 17. The article notes that there would have to be a 'revolutionary re-interpretation of "military objective"' and 'to fully achieve the purpose of coercing societal change, the classic concept of belligerent reprisal may need expansion'. See Art. 51(2) AP I as there would also be a need to reconcile this approach with the prohibition on conducting attacks the primary purpose of which is to terrorize the civilian population.

177. See Lewis, *supra* n. 80, pp. 504-507, for a discussion of the controversy that followed the attacks on Iraqi electricity production capacity and the follow-on effects on the civilian population. In particular Lieutanent-General Horner, the air component commander is quoted as stating that the impact of the loss of electricity 'was not foreseen by us'. See ibid., p. 506.

178. L. Oppenheim, *International Law: A Treatise*, 7th ed., H. Lauterpacht, ed. (London, Longman Green and Co. 1948) p. 8. Law is defined as 'a body of rules for human conduct within a community which by common consent of this community shall be enforced by external power'. See ibid., p. 10.

Previously, the moral debate concerning 'proportionality' involved questions about whether the harm should be 'in the same ballpark' as the good,[179] or whether 'the harm done [could] collaterally be matched or exceeded by the good achieved'.[180] However, it was not clear that these moral questions had to be definitively resolved. It will be up to interpreters of the law, most likely during a criminal proceeding, to determine such issues.

If it can no longer be said that 'the laws of war are of little help; no officer is going to be charged for killing too many people if he does not actually massacre them,'[181] that does not mean that contemporary interpretations of humanitarian law provide all the answers. The difficult moral issues associated with proportionality are not resolved with the ratification of a treaty or concurrence on a customary law standard regarding the proportionality test. A key issue to be resolved is the importance of the 'concrete and direct military advantage' to be gained against which the expected casualties are weighed. This is evident when the challenge of determining what might constitute excessive or 'clearly' excessive death, injury or damage is considered. At one end of the spectrum is the approach already mentioned that rejects any civilian casualties. A somewhat broader perspective appears to have been adopted by Human Rights Watch in its analysis of the Kosovo air campaign where, relying on the ICRC Commentary, it suggested that 'the argument of proportionality can never justify very high civilian casualties whatever the military advantage envisioned: "Incidental losses and damages should never be extensive."'[182] However, terms such as 'very high' and 'extensive' do not appear to add significant clarity to the challenge of assessing what constitutes excessive collateral damage.

One of the challenges legal analysts have had is expressing what would constitute unacceptable collateral damage, with interpretations often relying on obvious extremes, such as the destruction of whole villages or the levelling of an urban area.[183] This is all the more evident when it is considered there are often political

179. See McKeogh, *supra* n. 51, p. 167 (quoting W.R.P. Kaufman, 'On a purported error about the doctrine of double effect: A reply to Sophie Botros', 75 *Philosophy* (2000) pp. 283 at 292).

180. Ibid., p. 168. McKeogh takes the view 'one seems callous in its attitude to innocent life, the other calculating'. Ibid., p. 169.

181. Walzer, *supra* n. 9, p. 317.

182. See Human Rights Watch Report, *supra* n. 25, p. 8.

183. Ibid., (refering to the destruction of villages or the leveling of a whole urban area); and Dinstein, *supra* n. 33, pp. 122-123. See also the ICTY Final Report, *supra* n. 23, para. 48 ('For example, bombing a refugee camp is obviously prohibited if its only military significance is that people in the camp are knitting socks for soldiers. Conversely, an air strike on an ammunition dump should not be prohibited merely because a farmer is plowing a field in the area.'). See in Human Rights Watch Report, *supra* n. 25, p. 8, where relying on the ICRC Commentary, AP I, Art 57, *supra* n. 100, paras. 2213-2214, reference is made to the levelling of a village to target a soldier, or levelling an urban area to destroy a bridge as being unacceptable. However, see also E. David, 'Respect for the principle of distinction in the Kosovo war', 3 *YIHL* (2001) pp. 81 at 91, where the 16 dead and 16 wounded civilians resulting from an 1999 attack on the Serb television station was viewed as defying common sense.

aspects regarding the use of force during armed conflict that can impact on what is considered to be an 'acceptable' level of collateral damage.

2.4 Law and politics

One of the challenges in assessing the legal test for proportionality is the separation of the influence of politics from the determination of a legal standard. For example, it was reported that during the Kosovo campaign there was active high level political participation in the selection of targets.[184] Further, the US Secretary of Defense is reported to have retained approval authority in respect of operations in Iraq where the collateral damage was expected to be the loss of life of more than 50 people.[185] Such political involvement does not alter the fact that persons making targeting decisions would be legally accountable for their decisions.[186] However, what it does highlight is the political sensitivity of targeting in many contemporary armed conflicts and the necessity to separate political restrictions from legal obligations when assessing proportionality.

For example, during the 1991 Gulf War the political and policy reaction to the large number of civilian casualties that resulted from the attack on the Al Firdos bunker effectively 'ended the strategic air war campaign',[187] although it has been stated that 'it is doubtful that the action constituted a violation of international humanitarian law'.[188] Similarly, the decision to remove the 15,000 foot ceiling on aerial attacks during the 1999 Kosovo air campaign was also driven more by political and policy realities than a strict legal requirement to do so.[189] In another context, as Martin Van Creveld has noted, the precision targeting of terrorists in the Palestinian Occupied Territories has resulted not only in quite a few misses but also 'the number of bystanders killed or injured often exceeds that of the terrorists'.[190] As a result, he concludes that '[t]he results may well have been counterproductive.'[191]

In the November 2004 assault on Fallujah the US Marine forces had at one point identified over 200 targets, '[b]ut the military coalition at the Baghdad level, fearing adverse press coverage and collateral damage, approved strikes on fewer than twenty targets.'[192] Such restrictions placed on targeting have to be assessed in the

184. See Lieutenant-General M. Short, 'Operation Allied Force from the perspective of the NATO Commander', 78 *Int. Law Studies* (2002) pp. 19 at 23.

185. See D. Jehl and E. Schmitt, 'Errors are seen in early attacks on Iraqi leaders', in *The New York Times*, 13 June 2004.

186. Art. 28 ICC Statute.

187. Thomas, *supra* n. 28, p. 88 (quoting from the Gulf War Air Power Study, p. 206).

188. Ibid.

189. See Fenrick, *supra* n. 26, p. 53.

190. M. Van Creveld, 'Technology and War II, from nuclear stalemate to terrorism', in Townsend, *supra* n. 134, p. 362.

191. Ibid.

192. B. West, *No True Glory: A Frontline Account of the Battle of Fallujah* (New York, Bantam Books 2005) p. 263.

context of political pressure to limit casualties or damage in addition to that required by law.

Similarly, it is possible legally to adopt the position that voluntary human shields are direct participants in hostilities and therefore not considered to be collateral casualties.[193] However, the decision to attack may be difficult to undertake because it may be subjected to public criticism. As a result, an attack may for some be morally and politically unacceptable but still be permitted at law.

2.5 The difficult challenge

William Fenrick's observations on the difficulty of conducting a proportionality assessment are supported by another contemporary analyst, Michael Schmitt, who states: 'It is impossible to relate objectively the value of military advantage to collateral damage and incidental injury; they are dissimilar values that cannot be compared meaningfully in extreme cases.'[194] The proportionality test has also been assessed as 'notoriously difficult to apply'.[195] Yet this is exactly what states and the international legal community are asking military personnel to do. A similar sense of challenge is reflected in the *Kupreškić*[196] decision, where the ICTY first referred to the Additional Protocol I provisions as leaving a wide margin of discretion to belligerents and then suggested that the 'elementary considerations of humanity' provisions emphasised in IHL decisions of the International Court of Justice and the Martens clause 'be fully used when interpreting and applying *loose* international rules ...'.[197] This then led to the determination that the customary and conventional law should be read so as to construe 'as narrowly as possible the discretionary power to attack belligerents, and by the same token, so as to expand the protection accorded to civilians'.[198]

However, this is only the beginning of the inquiry as the application of the proportionality test, even within this narrow approach, can be carried out from a number of different perspectives. The inquiry now turns to assessing possible analytical frameworks to see how they might offer guidance on how to apply the proportionality principle.

3. ANALYTICAL FRAMEWORKS

The broad range of perspectives from which the proportionality principle might be applied is perhaps best described in the context of the post-World War I debate over the application of air power as two 'opposite tendencies ... the ideology of

193. See Schmitt, *supra* n. 106, p. 299; and Dinstein, *supra* n. 33, p. 130.
194. Schmitt, *supra* n. 48, p. 51.
195. Kretzmer, *supra* n. 65, p. 200. See also the ICTY Final Report, *supra* n. 23, para. 48.
196. *Prosecutor* v. *Kupreškić*, *supra* n. 22.
197. Ibid., paras. 524-525 [emphasis added].
198. Ibid., para. 525.

extreme pacifists, well intentioned, good but utterly utopian and the thinking of hard and shrewd people … who wanted to keep their hands free as to the conduct of the next war'.[199] These two extremes appear to reflect the inevitable requirement to balance humanitarian and military goals which was fundamental to the creation of IHL. They continue to directly impact the contemporary discussion regarding the application of the proportionality principle. The following outline of potential analytical frameworks covers the full range of these conflicting ideologies. For the purposes of this article, the analysis is categorised as pacifism and pacificism, human rights, tactical level control and the strategic approach.

3.1 Pacifism and pacificism

The connection between pacifism, pacificism and 'humanitarianism' is an obvious and understandable one. The 'rejection of organized mass violence has been a feature of many religious systems and sects, including Buddhism ... [and] many of the smaller Christian sects have been pacifist….'[200] This movement can entail a wide range of ideas and groups which have been described as 'pacifism' ('an absolute belief that wars are always wrong')[201] and 'pacificism' ('exploring all possibilities of peace but not necessarily rejecting all uses of violence in all circumstances').[202] It should come as no surprise that the efforts to restrict the horror of war grew as the terrible reality of modern technology-driven warfare became increasingly evident with the result that 'the respectability of the antiwar position, whether pacifist or pacificist, grew with disgust over World War I …'.[203] Even though the human longing for peace has 'not triumphed over the powerful propensity for war', powerful religious-based ideas of humanity 'have inspired every movement for peace…making possible the Geneva Convention, the League of Nations, the United Nations, and so on'.[204]

The moral basis for arguments limiting the conduct of hostilities is reflected in the critical reference by James M. Spaight to pre-World War II attempts to restrict aerial bombing to 'combat zones' as appealing to 'some ecclesiastical minds'.[205] The use of 'obliteration' bombing during the war was argued to be immoral 'be-

199. See Kunz, *supra* n. 3, p. 39.

200. A. Roberts, 'Against war', in Townsend, *supra* n. 134, p. 330.

201. L. Braudy, *From Chivalry to Terrorism: War and the Changing Nature of Masculinity* (New York, Vintage Books, 2005) p. 417 ('"Pacifism" itself was a French-coined word first used in the 1890s and then in 1901 adopted by the Universal Peace Congress in Glasgow.').

202. See Roberts, *supra* n. 200, p. 331. See also Braudy, *supra* n. 201, p. 417 ('pacifists may not be anti-war and may not even be nonviolent').

203. See Braudy, *supra* n. 201, p. 418.

204. See A. Stevens, *The Roots of War & Terror* (London, Continuum 2004) pp. 8-9.

205. J.M. Spaight, *Air Power and War Rights*, 3rd ed. (1947) p. 250 ('"The real work of the Air Force is to support the troops in battle," Dr. A. C. Headlam, the Bishop of Gloucester, wrote in his diocesan magazine for December 1943; any thing else was "a barbaric war."' quoting from the *Daily Mail*, 7 December 1943). See also Lindqvist, *supra* n. 73, p. 99 (quoting Bishop George Bell in the House of Commons: 'this progressive devastation of cities is threatening civilization').

cause no proportionate cause could justify the evil done; and to make it legitimate would soon lead the world to the immoral barbarity of total war'.[206] However, it has also been noted that twentieth century pacifism differed from its religious roots in that it included 'a stronger element of rationalism, basing itself more on pragmatic arguments'. It has become the basis for political movements and has been associated with conscientious objection.[207] Pacifist movements, while emerging weakened from World War II because of the legitimacy attached to thwarting German 'aggression and inhumanity', had a re-emergence during the development of the nuclear age.[208]

As Adam Roberts has noted, while the various efforts to oppose or at least control war, including pacifism, may not have eliminated war, 'they have nevertheless had a real impact'.[209] Earlier expressions regarding the immorality of indiscriminate target area bombing have now been incorporated into IHL.[210] Attempts to restrict combat in respect of specific areas or zones, such as the use of certain weapons or methods of warfare in urban areas, continue to be made with varying degrees of success.[211]

Concepts such as pacifism continue to have relevance to contemporary interpretations of the law, as it has been suggested that opponents of the Afghanistan war adopted such an approach in seeking to strengthen the constraints on warfare with the result that: [212]

> '[T]he easiest way to resist is to make non-combatant immunity into a stronger and stronger rule, until it is something like an absolute rule: all killing of civilians is (something close to) murder; therefore any war that leads to the killing of civilians is unjust; therefore every war is unjust. So pacifism reemerges from the very heart of the theory that was originally meant to replace it.'[213]

Such an approach appears fundamentally inconsistent with the historical meaning of the doctrine of 'double effect' and the wording of the proportionality test in Additional Protocol I. The 'excessive' loss of life standard can potentially encompass more than one, ten, twenty or possibly even hundreds of lives. To suggest that

206. Ibid., p. 272.

207. See Roberts, *supra* n. 200, p. 331.

208. Ibid., pp. 332-333.

209. Ibid., p. 340. The author identifies the means of limiting war as legal restraints; systems of international organization and collective security; pacifism and unilateralism; measures of arms control and disarmament; and peaceful methods of pressure and struggle. Ibid., p. 317.

210. See Art. 51(5)(a) AP I.

211. See Protocol on Prohibitions or Restrictions on the Use of Incendiary Weapons (Protocol III) 1980, Arts. 1(2) and 2(2) and (3) (prohibiting attacks by air-delivered incendiary weapons on military objectives located within a concentration of civilians (which includes inhabited parts of cities) or the use of other incendiary weapons to make such an attack except when the military objective is clearly separated from the concentration of civilians.).

212. See M. Walzer, *Arguing About War* (New Haven, Yale University Press 2004) p. 13.

213. Ibid.

no civilian deaths can result effectively seeks to apply a *jus ad bellum* norm to a *jus in bello* rule. Contemporary humanitarian law is founded on a separation of these two principles even if *jus ad bellum* continues to influence *jus in bello* in areas such as the determination of combatant status.[214]

As was experienced by the early Christian Church in its development of the just war tradition, pacifism rarely survives an interface with the responsibilities of governing human affairs.[215] In the final analysis, '[p]acifism has been elevated as an ideal; the lawful bearing of arms … has been accepted as a practical necessity.'[216] This is not to suggest that ideals such as pacifism and pacificism do not have an important role to play in interpreting the proportionality principle and other aspects of humanitarian law. Even among those who view war as inevitable there is also often a belief it can and should be controlled.[217] However, it is an ideal that must be tempered by the practical reality of war and how conflict is waged in its attempt to influence the assessments of collateral damage that must be made in contemporary conflict.

3.2 Human rights

In many ways, human rights law stands in contrast to IHL regarding the type of normative framework it offers to control the use of force. While descended from common ethical and religious roots,[218] human rights and humanitarian law have largely developed independently from one another in terms of their history and philosophy.[219] This independence was perhaps most graphically demonstrated during the separate but almost simultaneous drafting of the 1948 Universal Declaration of Human Rights and the 1949 Geneva Conventions.[220] This has led to the conclusion that '[a] technical and cultural gap separated these branches of the

214. See A. Roberts, 'Counter-terrorism, armed force and the laws of war', 44 *Survival* (2002) pp. 7 at 9; and G.L. Neuman, 'Humanitarian law and counterterrorist force', 14 *EJIL* (2003) pp. 283 at 286. See also K. Watkin, 'Controlling the use of force: A role for human rights norms in contemporary armed conflict', 98 *AJIL* 13-16 (2004) pp. 13-16.

215. See Ishay, *supra* n. 20, p. 44 ('Until the Christian church became the creed of the Roman Empire, Christians were to maintain an unbending position toward fighting and military service.') See Walzer, *supra* n. 212, pp. 3-4.

216. See J. Keegan, *A History of Warfare* (New York, Vintage Books 1993) p. 5.

217. See Stevens, *supra* n. 204, p. 9 ('Conflict is endemic to the human condition, as it is indeed in the nature of our universe.') and ibid., p. 241('Perhaps horror [based on the possibility of nuclear extinction] will enable us to overcome the otherwise invincible attraction of war.'). See also Keegan, *supra* n. 216, p. 385 ('[O]ver the course of 4000 years of experiment and repetition, warmaking has become a habit' and 'unless we unlearn the habits we have taught ourselves, we shall not survive.').

218. See Ishay, *supra* n. 20, pp. 16-61, for a discussion of the early ethical contributions to human rights including limits on the waging of war.

219. See L. Doswald-Beck and S. Vité, 'International humanitarian law and human rights law', *IRRC* (1993) p. 94.

220. R. Kolb, 'The relationship between international humanitarian law and human rights law: A brief history of the 1948 Universal Declaration of Human Rights and the 1949 Geneva Conventions', *IRRC* (1998) p. 409.

law which the vicissitudes of two very different paths had happened to bring relatively close to each other within the body of international law.'[221] For example, it has been suggested that '[u]nlike human rights law, the law of war allows, or at least tolerates, the killing and wounding of innocent human beings not directly participating in an armed conflict, such as civilian victims of lawful collateral damage.'[222]

Notwithstanding this separate practical development, human rights law has had a significant impact on the development of post-World War II humanitarian law.[223] Even though some interpretations stress the separation of these two bodies of law,[224] the continuing application of human rights law during armed conflict makes a tidy division of the two normative regimes difficult in both theory and practice.[225] At a minimum, some types of armed conflict, including occupation, internal armed conflicts and the contemporary 'war on terror', inevitably require an assessment of the interface between humanitarian law governing armed conflict and human rights law which applies to law enforcement situations.[226] There is a significant movement to further erode the gap between human rights law and humanitarian law. Human rights advocates and human rights tribunals are taking an increasing interest in applying human rights law to situations of armed conflict. This new movement has taken two main forms: the incorporation of humanitarian law norms into human rights law analysis and, more recently, an 'exclusionary' approach that applies more traditional human rights norms almost as a form of *lex specialis* in situations of internal armed conflict.

The first approach is reflected in cases like *Juan Abella* v. *Argentina*,[227] where the Inter-American Commission on Human Rights applied IHL to resolve a complaint brought under the American Convention on Human Rights in respect of an

221. Ibid., p. 416.

222. See T. Meron, 'The humanization of humanitarian law', 94 *AJIL* (2000) pp. 239 at 240.

223. Ibid.

224. See B.A. Feinstein, The applicability of the regime of human rights in times of armed conflict and particularly to occupied territories: The case of Israel's security barrier', 4 *Northwestern JIHR* (2005) p. 238 at 243 ('[T]here is an inherent contradiction between international humanitarian law applicable in armed conflict situations and international human rights, and they are consequently two mutually exclusive regimes.').

225. *Legality of the Threat or Use of Nuclear Weapons*, Advisory Opinion of 8 July 1996, *ICJ Rep.* (1996) p. 226, para. 26 (hereinafter, *Nuclear Weapons* Opinion); and *Legal Consequences of The Construction of a Wall in the Occupied Palestinian Territory*, Advisory Opinion of 9 July 2004, *ICJ Rep.* (2004) p. 136, para. 106 ('[T]here are thus three possible situations: some rights may be exclusively matters of international humanitarian law; others may be exclusively matters of human rights law; yet others may be matters of both these branches of international law.').

226. See L. Moir, 'Law and the Inter-American human rights system', 25 *HRQ* (2003) p. 182, where it is noted to be especially true in respect of internal armed conflicts; and Watkin, *supra* n. 214, pp. 24-30.

227. *Juan Carlos Abella* v. *Argentina*, Case No. 11.137, 13 *I/A YBHR* (1997) p. 602.

internal armed conflict situation.[228] In *Ergi* v. *Turkey*,[229] the European Court of Human Rights determined that Turkish security forces had not taken sufficient precautions to protect the civilian population[230] in circumstances where a single civilian was killed in a town during a firefight with Kurdish insurgents (PKK). In that case the Court determined:

> '[E]ven though it had not been established beyond a reasonable doubt that the bullet which killed Havva Ergi had been fired by security forces, the Court must consider whether the security forces' operation had been planned and conducted in such a way as to avoid or minimise, *to the greatest extent possible*, *any risk* to the lives of the villagers, including from the fire-power of the PKK members caught in the ambush'.[231]

The wording of this test for proportionality reflects the restrictive human rights approach towards controlling use of force that is applied in domestic law enforcement. It is not simply an issue of applying a proportionality standard as traditionally understood under humanitarian law, but rather one of 'strict' proportionality.[232] Traditionally, the goal of a human rights normative framework is the strict control on force intended to kill and any other unintended deprivation of life.[233] The concern is over the development of a 'shoot to kill' policy, with the result that the use of force and, in particular, firearms is limited to situations of absolute necessity.[234] In contrast, IHL focuses on controlling how a shoot to kill policy is implemented.[235]

To the extent that the *Ergi* test reflects a possible trend in using human rights norms to analyse proportionality,[236] its application in conflict situations beyond isolated low-level encounters with small groups of enemy forces approximating a criminal gang is potentially problematic. That approach might be relevant to some limited confrontations between security forces and elements of an organised armed force that are operating independently. However, even here the level of violence, the nature of the opposing non-state armed group and the inability of government forces to physically control the territory in which the engagement may be taking place would significantly limit the utility of adopting law enforcement standards.

---

228. For a discussion of the *Abella* case and other Inter-American human rights based cases, see Moir, *supra* n. 226.

229. 31 *EHRR* (1998) p. 388.

230. Ibid., p. 432.

231. Ibid., p. 431 [emhasis added].

232. See *McCann and Others* v. *United Kingdom*, 21 *EHRR* (1996) p. 97, para. 149. See also Kretzmer, *supra* n. 65, p. 178; and W Abresch, 'A human rights law of internal armed conflict: The European Court of Human Rights in Chechnya', 16 *EJIL* (2005) pp. 740 at 764.

233. See Watkin, *supra* n. 214, pp. 17-18.

234. See ibid., p. 18. See also J. Pejic, 'Terrorist acts and groups: A role for international law', 75 *BYIL* (2005) pp. 71 at 90 (linking a 'shoot to kill' policy to the conduct of hostilities).

235. See Watkin, *supra* n. 214, pp. 32-33.

236. See Abresch, *supra* n. 232, pp. 752-757; and Henckaerts & Doswald-Beck, *supra* n. 18, p. 314 n. 78.

For example, internal armed conflict and fighting during occupation can be exceedingly violent, as has been evidenced in the post-2003 conflict in Iraq. During the November 2004 struggle to take control of Fallujah there were '540 air strikes and 14,000 artillery shells and mortar shells fired, as well as 2,500 tank main gun rounds'.[237] This was not a 'law enforcement' operation easily subjected to a human rights-based normative regime.

The adoption of the *Ergi* type approach would, in effect, result in the addition of limiting phrases to the Additional Protocol I standard. The humanitarian law test for proportionality is not limited by words such as 'to the greatest extent possible' and there is no obligation to avoid or minimise 'any risk' to civilians. The obligation to minimise the impact of targeting on civilians is essential under humanitarian law; however, it does not extend to requiring the use of precision munitions, employing particular weapons systems,[238] or having to visually acquire a target.[239] Traditionally, it has neither been extended to attempting to capture rather than destroy a military objective.[240]

The question of the minimisation of risk to civilians also provides a context within which to discuss whether military forces have to be placed at increased risk in order to ensure that civilian casualties are minimised. The issue under humanitarian law is whether the civilian damage is 'excessive' or 'clearly excessive' and not whether 'any risk' remains. As Michael Walzer has noted, while due care must be taken to protect civilians there are limits to the risks that can be demanded of soldiers and '[w]e can only ask soldiers to minimize the dangers they impose.'[241] Humanitarian law is at one with morality in this respect. Contrary to suggestions that combatants are 'treated as instruments'[242] or 'the combatant trades his right to life for the right to kill',[243] the universal right to life continues to apply to all humans regardless of status, including combatants.[244] For a combatant, what has been lost is the right to be protected like a civilian, thereby allowing the enemy to target him or her.

It must also be remembered that the right to life is not absolute under human rights law.[245] This weighing of the relative value of military versus civilian life is

---

237. See West, *supra* n. 192, pp. 315-316.

238. See Dinstein, *supra* n. 33, p. 126.

239. Murray and Scales, *supra* n. 46, p. 161 ('Precision weapons also allowed Coalition fighters to fly at altitudes above enemy flak or shoulder-fired heat-seeking missiles and still hit their targets within several meters' accuracy, even when they could not see the target.').

240. See Parks, *supra* n. 59, p. 7 n. 6.

241. See Walzer, *supra* n. 9, p. 156.

242. See McKeogh, *supra* n. 51, p. 164.

243. See Abresch, *supra* n. 232, p. 757.

244. See Dinstein, *supra* n. 71, p. 63. See also I/A Comm HR, 'Report on terrorism and human rights', OAS Doc. OEA/Ser.L/V/II.116, doc. 5, rev. 1 corr. (2002) para. 81.

245. See Art. 2 European Convention on the Protection of Human Rights and Fundamental Freedoms 1950, 213 *UNTS* p. 221, where it is indicated that deadly force can be used in the defence of any person from unlawful violence; to effect a lawful arrest; prevent the escape of a lawfully detained person; and for the purpose of quelling a riot or insurrection.

inherent in the interpretation that the 'ECHR only permits the use of lethal force when capture is too risky'.[246] Such risk cannot just include that posed to civilians. The assessment of the value of a combatant's life is a much more complex one than interpreting the law in a manner that effectively objectifies that person. A combatant has the right to kill under specifically prescribed circumstances and may be killed; however, his or her life remains of value to his or her family and fellow combatants. Further, an opposing force that captures participants in hostilities must comply with humanitarian law standards. In this respect, rather than attempting to determine the relative value of the human lives of both soldiers and civilians, efforts may be more profitably spent on requiring military commanders seeking to protect their soldiers to place no greater value on their lives than the lives of the civilians who do not take an active or direct part in hostilities.

Finally, there is the question of how the reasonableness of the targeting decision is to be assessed. While the *Ergi*[247] decision does refer in passing to it not having been determined 'beyond a reasonable doubt' that the victim was killed by government security forces, it should be clarified that the standard applicable to targeting decisions is that set out in the *Prosecutor* v. *Galić* case as one of a 'reasonable belief' that the person or object being targeted is not 'civilian'.[248] This latter test is consistent with criminal law standards regarding the use of force.[249]

The reliance on human rights standards is most evident in two cases, *Isayeva I*[250] and *Isayeva II*,[251] which assessed the conduct of Russian security forces during hostilities in Chechnya. It has been considered by one commentator as 'a promising strategy'.[252] However, the approach taken by the European Court of Human Rights is in many respects controversial. The Court decided that, since the Russian government had not declared martial law or a state of emergency or made any derogation pursuant to Article 15 of the Convention (i.e., time of war or other public emergency threatening the life of the nation), a human rights normative framework was to be applied to the incident under investigation. This normative framework was used even though the Court accepted that justifiable exceptional measures to be taken by the state could include 'the deployment of army units equipped with combat weapons, including military aviation and artillery'.[253]

---

246. See Abresch, *supra* n. 232, p. 758. See also Pejic, *supra* n. 234, p. 89 ('law enforcement standards demand that, before force or firearms are used, other measures, including attempts to apprehend criminal suspects, be employed if possible.').

247. 31 *EHRR* (1998) p. 388.

248. *Prosecutor* v. *Galić*, *supra* n. 22, paras. 50-51, 55. See Schmitt, *supra* n. 106, p. 304, where a reasonableness test is used.

249. See *McCann* v. *The United Kingdom*, *supra* n. 232, para. 200.

250. *Isayeva, Usupova and Bazayeva* v. *Russia*, *supra* n. 24.

251. *Isayeva* v. *Russia*, *supra* n. 24.

252. Abresch, *supra* n. 232, p. 750.

253. Ibid., p. 41, para. 180.

Beyond the issue of whether a court should question the characterisation of hostilities by a state,[254] the decision applied a 'strict' proportionality standard to what has been identified by one commentator as an Additional Protocol II type conflict.[255] Even if that categorisation is not accepted, there remains the question of whether the violence was more than an internal disturbance and riot such that it could be considered a conflict not of an international character pursuant to common Article 3 of the 1949 Geneva Conventions. It has been suggested that the European Court of Human Rights has 'now done what the Inter-American Commission avoided [in the *Abella* case], by directly applying human rights law rather than turning to humanitarian law'.[256] In effect, the *lex specialis* of humanitarian law was not applied.[257]

However, what is missing is an explanation of what test the court would have used if the state had taken the view that an armed conflict was in existence. Would that have meant that there was little room for the restrictive application of human rights standards, with the result that the same situation would have been assessed on the basis of the humanitarian law standard of proportionality, free of those limitations? The *Isayeva* approach. supporting an exclusive use of human rights norms, also has to be reconciled with the *Prosecutor* v. *Tadić*[258] decision of the ICTY Appeals Chamber regarding the application of customary international law applicable to non-international armed conflict. Until such questions are answered, the impact of the *Isayeva* cases will likely remain limited to incidents falling within the jurisdiction of the European human rights process.

Further, it has been noted in respect of the *Isayeva* approach that '[h]uman rights law must be realistic in the sense of not categorically forbidding killing in the context of armed conflict or otherwise making compliance with the law and victory in battle impossible to achieve at once.'[259] This point is equally applicable if human rights-based standards are used to interpret humanitarian law in respect of international armed conflict. The levels of violence for either internal or external conflict are rarely those associated with isolated criminal acts. For example, during the 1999 Kosovo conflict NATO flew 38,004 sorties, including 10,484 strike sorties, with more than 23,000 bombs and missiles being used during the conflict.[260] Even the single act of shooting down a hijacked civilian airliner, the type of 'armed

254. See N. Quenivet, The applicability of international humanitarian law to situations of a (counter-) terrorist nature', in Arnold and Hildebrand, *supra* n. 63, p. 31 n. 19.

255. Abresch, *supra* n. 232, p. 754.

256. Ibid., p. 751.

257. Ibid., p. 749 ('[I]f there were a substantial body of customary humanitarian law that applied to internal conflicts, the case for applying humanitarian law as *lex specialis* to human rights law would be stronger.'). See also generally ibid., pp. 749-750, where the applicability of ICRC Customary Law Study Rules are questioned on the basis that states have traditionally been reluctant to accept such rules in the form of treaty law.

258. *Prosecutor* v. *Tadić*, Case No. IT-94-I, Decision on the Defence Motion for Interlocutory Appeal on Jurisdiction, Appeals Chamber, 2 October 1995, paras. 65-142.

259. Abresch, *supra* n. 232, p. 750.

260. See Fenrick, *supra* n. 78, p. 489.

attack' that started the 2001 armed conflict against Al Qaeda, would require the assessment of collateral damage on a scale not normally associated with law enforcement. Here, the issue is not whether a human rights normative regime could be used in isolated cases in an attempt to avoid using violence, but rather that such a regime would have to accept that hundreds of civilians may be 'collateral' damage as a result of a shoot down order.[261]

This does not mean that human rights law does not provide an important analytical framework by which to analyse proportionality. For example, the extension of human rights' emphasis on accountability to the use of force in armed conflict holds significant promise.[262] However, even here, such a process, due to its extensive procedural, time and resource requirements, lends itself more readily to the assessment of isolated acts of violence rather than the traditional scope of hostilities in either internal or international armed conflict. The danger lies in suggesting that such an accountability process has to be put in place for each attack during which an uninvolved civilian is killed, when there are potentially hundreds of such attacks in the course of a major conflict. It is easy to conceive of a situation in armed conflict beyond that paralleling a 'law enforcement' tempo of operations where this obligation would collapse under its own procedural weight. Developing criteria that invoke basic human rights-based accountability norms for use in situations approximating law enforcement operations (i.e., capturing rather than killing an opponent) under circumstances where violence is isolated and the territory in which the operations takes place is controlled by the state may minimise that danger.

Thus, there remains the question whether human rights norms should be applied out of context to 'control' warfare or if they would be better used incrementally to influence the use of force in armed conflict situations where there are parallels to law enforcement situations. The traditional human rights requirement of capturing 'criminals' might be used in complex security situations, such as occupation and internal conflict, to detain individuals or small groups of insurgents where security forces exercise sufficient control over the territory and the anticipated levels of violence do not present unacceptable risks to either security forces or the surrounding population.[263] However, for a human rights normative structure to have broad application to armed conflict it must account for the 'shoot to kill' paradigm within which humanitarian law is applied. In doing so, that normative framework would

261. For example, the Airbus A300-500 typically carries 267 passengers. See current Air Canada fleet, A300-500 <www.aircanada.com/en/about/fleet/a340-500.html>. For a discussion of this issue, see Pejic, *supra* n. 234, pp. 88-89 and Watkin, *supra* n. 214, p. 22.

262. See Kretzmer, *supra* note 65, pp. 201-204.

263. See M.N. Schmitt, *supra* n. 48, p. 80 n. 72, for reference to an Israeli newspaper (*Ha'aretz* of 4 February 2002) report indicating that as part of a targeting assessment of leaders of opposing armed groups the Israeli Defence Force Judge Advocate General requires well-supported information of the planning or conduct of an attack in the near future; appeals to Palestinian authorities to effect an arrest have been ignored; attempts to arrest the individuals by IDF forces have failed; and the attack is not to be carried out in retribution but rather to prevent future multiple casualty attacks. See also Abresch, *supra* n. 232, p. 759.

likely have to be fundamentally altered to be applied in a context in which it was not designed to operate.

3.3 Tactical level control

The assessment of the proportionality principle is further impacted by different approaches to the interpretation of humanitarian law. One such approach that concentrates on the tactical impact of an attack is perhaps best articulated in the ICRC Commentary which indicates that '[a] military advantage can only consist in ground gained and in annihilating or weakening the enemy armed forces.'[264] Further, '[Article 57] ... is not concerned with strategic objectives but with the means to be used in a specific tactical operation.'[265] This approach appears to focus on the tactical impact attacks have on armed forces and discounts the broader strategic nature of warfare.

Concentrating on tactical level operations does have the potential to limit collateral civilian casualties and damage. It has been suggested by Judith Gardam that Article 51(5)(b) 'requires that proportionality be assessed in relation to each individual attack, rather than on a cumulative basis'.[266] However, it is noted that this is not how campaigns are waged and proportionality assessed when she indicates that, during the 1991 Gulf conflict, 'it appears that the military advantage was calculated on a cumulative rather than a case-by-case basis as required by the Protocol'.[267] This occurs because military campaigns are planned and conducted to meet strategic objectives (both political and military).

It has been suggested that 'a case-by-case approach appears, however, to be too narrow and unrealistic in practice', as is evidenced by declarations by a number of states that an attack must be considered as a whole.[268] Further, there has been some acceptance of a broader interpretation in 'an example in which six military targets are considered as one attack when weighing military advantage and the principle of proportionality'.[269] The ICRC Commentary itself notes that 'it goes without saying that an attack carried out in a concerted manner in numerous places can only be judged in its entirety'.[270]

264. ICRC Commentaries, AP I, Art. 57, *supra* n. 100, para. 2218.

265. Ibid., para. 2207. The ICRC Commentary also notes that 'it goes without saying that an attack carried out in a concerted manner in numerous places can only be judged in its entirety'. Ibid., para. 2018. However, this wording does not appear to take away from the tactical focus of the Commentary. See Laursen, *supra* n. 26, p. 795.

266. See Gardam, *supra* n. 4, p. 407.

267. Ibid., p. 409.

268. See Laursen, *supra* n. 26, p. 795.

269. Ibid., p. 796 (referring to W. Fenrick, 'Attacking the enemy civilian as a punishable offense', 7 *Duke JCIL* (1997) pp. 539 at 548 (quoting from L. Doswald-Beck, 'The value of the 1977 Geneva Protocol: Was it a waste of time?', in A.J.M. Delissen and G.J. Tanja, eds., *Humanitarian Law of Armed Conflict: Challenges Ahead* (Boston, NIA, Martinus Nijhoff, 1991) p. 82)).

270. See ICRC Commentary AP I, Art 57, *supra* n. 100, para. 2018.

However, the broad approach found in the ICTY Final Report,[271] based on an assessment of the *Kupreškić*[272] case, has been criticised as concluding that the Trial Chamber 'meant to compare the total number of casualties when accumulated'.[273] The ICTY Prosecutor's committee had interpreted that case 'to refer to an *overall* assessment of the totality of civilian victims as against the goals of the military campaign'.[274] In fact, the *Kupreškić* judgement accepted that 'regard might be had to considerations such as the cumulative effects of attacks'. It was 'in the case of repeated attacks, all or most of them falling within the grey area between indisputable legality and unlawfulness' that a conclusion that the cumulative effect 'may not be in keeping with international law'[275] might be warranted.

Further, it should be noted that the use of the term 'grey areas' in the *Kupreškić* judgement reflects the considerable challenge that any analysis will face in attempting to assess the effects of attacks. To the extent that this case moves the discussion beyond the limits of the tactical effect of individual attacks it is, as was indicated in the ICTY Final Report, a progressive development.[276]

However, the debate is not resolved. A narrow interpretation is not unique to the assessment of proportionality. It has also been attempted with respect to the identification of military objects as valid objectives. For example, the ICRC Commentary defines the 'nature' test for a military objective as 'all objects *directly* used by the armed forces: weapons, equipment, transports, fortifications, depots, buildings occupied by armed forces, staff headquarters, communications centres etc.'[277] This approach would appear to limit 'military objectives' to objects that are functionally and temporarily tied to the actual conduct of operations.

Following the 1999 Kosovo campaign this narrower interpretative approach attracted some support as the legality of targeting strategic objects, such as bridges, communication facilities and oil storage depots, was assessed.[278] Arguments have been made that bridges were only valid targets while being used as military objectives in order to limit the overall scope of that target set.[279] Logically, the broader targeting of transportation systems can lead to greater casualties. It has been noted that, at the end of World War II, the extensive efforts by Allied forces to disrupt rail communication appeared to be impacted by 'the prevailing emotion that seems to have been no target should remain unspared' on the basis 'that the more destruction there was, the sooner the collapse would come … .'[280] However, the narrower interpretative approach can be contrasted with more traditional assessments based

271. See ICTY Final Report, *supra* n. 23.
272. *Prosecutor* v. *Kupreškić*, *supra* n. 22.
273. See Laursen, *supra* n. 26, p. 793.
274. See ICTY Final Report, *supra* n. 23, para. 52.
275. *Prosecutor v. Kupreškić*, *supra* n. 22, para. 526.
276. See ICTY Final Report, *supra* n. 23, para. 52.
277. ICRC Commentary, AP I, Art. 52, *supra* n. 79, para. 2020.
278. See David, *supra* n. 183; Human Rights Watch Report, *supra* n. 25; 'Collateral Damage or Unlawful Killing', *supra* n. 25.
279. See Benvenuti, *supra* n. 26, p. 516; and Bothe, *supra* n. 26, pp. 531, 534.
280. See Maier, *supra* n. 134, p. 435.

on the view that bridges remain valid targets because, by nature, they are integrated into the overall road network.[281]

Despite attempts to reconcile divergent interpretations of the use, nature, purpose and location criteria,[282] it remains that warfare, and in particular aerial warfare, can at law involve attacks on a broader range of target sets than military forces and objects. In this respect, determining the appropriate scope of many target sets depends upon a critical assessment of the true effect being sought. Ultimately, interpretations of target criteria and obligations such as the proportionality test must address the strategic aspects of warfare, including the indirect effects of attacking military objects targeted as part of the strategic prosecution of an economic warfare campaign.[283]

It has been suggested in an analysis supporting a narrow interpretation of the proportionality test that 'if the requirements of Article 51(5)(b) are to be complied with, military necessity will require considerable reappraisal'.[284] However, it is unlikely that the nature of warfare, and with it the application of military necessity, can be easily altered. Ultimately, the answer to this dilemma may be found in identifying the limits that a broader cumulative strategic approach would require if it is to support an acceptable weighing of humanitarian goals and military necessity. The analysis now turns towards consideration of such a strategic approach.

3.4 A strategic approach

The use of a strategic approach for assessing proportionality requires consideration of many of the same issues present in the other analytical frameworks. The complex issues of morality and the weighing of the relative value of life and objects is not made easier by adopting an approach which considers the strategic importance of a target or a series of targets. However, an additional challenge is presented because of the potential for large-scale death and destruction associated with strategic attacks.

In particular, the strategic analytical framework may raise concerns over an erosion of the principle of distinction, such as occurred during extensive bombing campaigns of World War II. The culmination of that campaign with the use of nuclear weapons represented the extreme extension of Clausewitzian thinking and introduced the threat of a previously unimaginable scale of death and destruc-

281. See Dinstein, *supra* n. 33, p. 92.

282. See Sassoli, *supra* n. 26, pp. 205-206, where he suggests attacks would be permissible 'on objects of a military nature even before they have an impact on military operations, while objects that are military because of their location, purpose or use could only be attacked at the moment they provide an effective contribution …'.

283. See, e.g., L.C. Green, *The Contemporary Law of Armed Conflict*, 2nd ed. (Yonkers, NY, Juris Publishing 2000) p. 191, for a wide range of military objectives including 'economic targets that directly but effectively support enemy operations'. See also the *San Remo Manual*, *supra* n. 117, p. 117.

284. Gardam, *supra* n. 4, p. 409.

tion.[285] Although the doctrine regarding the use of airpower has changed significantly since World War II and nuclear weapons have not been used for over 60 years, the spectre of such 'total' war remains with us. Therefore, in analysing the strategic approach it will be useful to look first at the guidance provided under humanitarian law regarding the use of nuclear weapons to see how well it deals with this level of warfare.

It might have been thought relatively easy for the ICJ in its *Nuclear Weapons* Opinion[286] to deal with the question of collateral damage. This, in turn, may have helped a better understanding of the limits of warfare at this extreme end of the conflict spectrum. However, although the Court affirmed that customary IHL applied to nuclear weapons, it did not 'reach a definitive conclusion as to the legality or illegality of the use of nuclear weapons by a state in an extreme circumstance of self-defence, in which its very survival would be at stake'.[287] Arguments suggesting a permissible use of tactical nuclear weapons presented to counter those arguing for the outright ban of nuclear weapons were left largely unresolved, although such limited use attracted the comment of some judges.[288]

It has been argued that '[a] persistent and serious flaw in much of the analysis of nuclear opponents is the apparent assumption that all uses of nuclear weapons would necessarily involve the destruction of population centers and the infliction of hundreds of thousands of civilian casualties … .'[289] In contrast, other issues, such as the potential for unnecessary suffering to be inflicted on combatants, have led to suggestions that even 'tactical weapons were probably illegal',[290] although that viewpoint is not universally shared by all.[291] Ultimately, the difficulty the ICJ had in dealing with this issue is reflective of the broader challenges facing those who seek to limit warfare. Perhaps the legacy of the *Nuclear Weapons* Opinion[292] is that it highlights the uncomfortable and continuing interface between the law and the political reality of warfare.

---

285. See Keegan, *supra* n. 216, p. 381 ('Nuclear weapons preyed upon the mind of man, and the fears they aroused exposed the hollowness of the Clausewitzian analysis once and for all. How could war be an extension of politics, when the ultimate object of rational politics is to further the well-being of political entities?').

286. *Nuclear Weapons* Opinion, *supra* n. 225.

287. Ibid., para. 97.

288. See L. Doswald-Beck, 'International humanitarian law and the Advisory Opinion of the International Court of Justice on the legality of the threat or use of nuclear weapons', 37 *IRRC* (1997) p. 35. For a discussion generally regarding the *Nuclear Weapons* Opinion, see D. Stephens, 'Human rights and armed conflict: The Advisory Opinion of the International Court of Justice in the *Nuclear Weapons* case', 4 *Yale HR & DLJ* (2001) pp. 1 at 3. See also Schmitt, *supra* n. 48, p. 46 n. 123, where possible lawful uses of nuclear weapons are identified as 'nuclear mines in remote areas of the high seas against enemy ballistic missile submarines or low-yield battlefield nuclear weapons employed against armor forces in remote parts of the desert …'.

289. See M. Matheson, 'The opinions of the International Court of Justice on the threat or use of nuclear weapons', 91 *AJIL* (1997) pp. 417 at 428.

290. See Green, *supra* n. 283, p. 132.

291. See Dinstein, *supra* n. 33, p. 79.

292. *Nuclear Weapons* Opinion, *supra* n. 225, para. 26.

This difficult interface between politics and law is most evident at the strategic (or, more accurately, the grand strategic) level of war. Warfare is conducted and must be assessed at the strategic level. A primary challenge for humanitarian law must be to clarify how conflict can be better regulated at that level. If clarity cannot be provided regarding the application of the proportionality test at a strategic level, it is difficult to see how it can be fully assessed at the lower levels of operations.

A key issue that has to be addressed in considering a strategic approach is the potential introduction of *jus ad bellum*[293] principles when assessing proportionality. This challenge is not unique to nuclear weapons, as it is also reflected in the theory advocating attacks only on military objects[294] and has been identified as a potential problem for human rights courts seeking to apply human rights norms in order to regulate armed conflict.[295] It is also an inherent part of an approach which suggests that intervention for humanitarian reasons should have the result that more restraints would be placed on the choice of targets and the proportionality balancing test.[296] The introduction of *jus ad bellum* factors in the interpretation of *jus in bello* rules is fraught with danger. Even if done for the best of intentions, it opens up the door to alternate interpretations of the rule of proportionality and can undermine the objective application of rules designed to protect all those touched by armed conflict.

Ultimately, coming to grips with a strategic approach for assessing proportionality requires acceptance of the link between tactical level action and strategic results. Suggestions that an attack must be considered 'a finite event'[297] and proportionality cannot be assessed 'at the end of the war or a lengthy campaign'[298] are the starting points of such an analysis. However, like the assessment of the limits of excessive damage, to date, significant guidance on how damage is to be assessed regarding attacks considered as a whole has not been provided. This issue may not be as complicated or as ominous as it may first appear, if the historical examples of World War II and the fear engendered by the potential use of nuclear weapons are set aside. As has been noted, warfare is conducted for strategic reasons pursuant to a 'plan'. The strategy to task process potentially provides a structured framework by which to consider a number of the factors relevant to the assessment of proportionality.

293. See Dinstein, *supra* n. 33, p. 78 ('[I]t appears to be utterly inconsistent with the basic tenet that LOIAC (the *jus in bello*) applies equally to all belligerent States, irrespective of the merits of their cause pursuant to the *jus ad bellum*.).

294. See Dunlap, *supra* n. 171.

295. See Abresch, *supra* n. 232, pp. 764-767.

296. See Laursen, *supra* n. 26, p. 811; and Bothe, *supra* n. 26, p. 535.

297. Dinstein, *supra* n. 33, p. 87 (quoting F.J. Hampson, 'Means and methods of warfare in the conflict in the Gulf', in P. Rowe, ed., *The Gulf War 1990-91 in International and English Law* (New York, Routledge 1993) pp. 89 at 94). See also Fenrick, *supra* n. 6, p. 107.

298. See Fenrick, *supra* n. 269, p. 548.

For example, one of the target sets identified during the 1991 Gulf conflict was oil refining and distribution facilities.[299] With a strategic goal of reducing the long-term availability of petroleum, oil and lubricants (hereinafter, POL) to Iraqi air and land forces while seeking to 'minimize long-term damage to Iraq's economic infrastructure', planners initially targeted Iraq's 'refining capacity, rather than production sites, to deter the replenishment of depleted POL stocks'.[300] Strikes were also planned against POL storage facilities, with many facilities being able to be attacked with 'non-precision' ordnance due to target 'size and separation from the civilian population'.[301] In the final analysis, '[c]oalition air strikes rendered 90 percent of Iraqi petroleum refining capability inoperative, based mainly on precision strikes against distillation towers.'[302] These attacks on 'Iraqi oil supplies were effective not because of their impact on the actual combat, but in limiting Iraq's ability to conduct a protracted ground campaign'.[303] The strategic goal of reducing POL available to opposing armed forces was a legally valid one. The effects of such an attack were potentially measurable, and a number of different options for reducing the POL available to the opposing military forces presented themselves.

What is missing from the public analysis is the number of civilian casualties or other collateral damage that would be considered 'excessive', either in respect of individual targets or from the neutralisation of the target set as a whole. It is here that greater accountability might be demanded of the strategic approach. In using such an approach, planners and commanders might be required to assess what constitutes 'excessive' death, injury and damage cumulatively on a strategic level. Such strategic level assessment cannot be limited to the simple cumulative assessment of lives lost or damage inflicted in the immediate tactical area of the target. The assessment of strategic level damage requires that those conducting attacks consider the potential reverberating effects on the civilian population. When the debate enters into areas such as the targeting of the electrical grid during the 1991 Gulf Campaign and its effect on the Iraqi civilian population, it has entered the strategic arena.[304] Making these assessments presents problems that are not unique to humanitarian law, since the use of sanctions raises similar issues regarding the effect of the denial of goods and services.[305] In this respect, the inherent contro-

---

299. See 'Conduct of the Persian Gulf War: Final report to Congress' (April 1992), p. 152 ('Fuel and lubricants are the lifeblood of a major industrial and military power. Iraq had a modern petroleum extraction, cracking, and distillation system, befitting its position as one of the world's major oil producing and refining nations. Coalition planners targeted Iraq's ability to produce refined oil products (such as gasoline) that had immediate military use, instead of its long-term crude oil production capability.') <www.ndu.edu/library/epubs/cpgw.pdf>.

300. See Lewis, *supra* n. 80, p. 495. The author relies on the Gulf War Air Power Survey: Operations and Effects and Effectiveness.

301. Ibid.

302. See Keaney, *supra* n. 136, p. 29.

303. Ibid.

304. See *supra* n. 80.

305. See K. Bennoune, '"Sovereignty vs. suffering"? Re-examining sovereignty and human rights through the lens of Iraq', 13 *EJIL* (2002) pp. 243 at 252-254, for a discussion of the negative effect of

versy with such assessments and the difficulty in assessing effects of such action in non-conflict situations should be remembered when assessing the proportional effect of strategic attacks during armed conflicts.

The use of a strategic approach in considering proportionality need not be viewed as a means by which conflict will get out of control as long as the analytical framework incorporates an assessment of the effects of attacks at tactical, operational and strategic levels. Further, this approach appears to offer a means by which decision makers at all levels can be held accountable.

4. A POSSIBLE WAY AHEAD

Having reviewed four possible analytical approaches for assessing proportionality, it is not clear if any of them provides the sole means by which proportionality can or should be assessed. Each has its own strengths and potential weaknesses, although the strategic level approach most realistically reflects how military campaigns are planned and executed.

One of the challenges for humanitarian law in coming to grips with the 'proportionality' test is its close link to the doctrine of 'double effect' and the context within which this limitation on the conduct of hostilities has to be applied. If it is accepted that '[w]ar is an evil ... but there are lesser and greater evils ...',[306] then 'evil' effects during war are inevitable. The proportionality principle is based on the acceptance that uninvolved civilians may be killed and civilian objects damaged or destroyed. The scale of violence during armed conflict and the fact that relatively little warfare takes place in areas isolated from the civilian population means that civilian casualties are a likely consequence of warfare. Further, any accountability process that seeks to review every use of force or investigate each loss of civilian life is probably going to be overwhelmed by the scope of a conflict itself.

As has been noted, the *Kupreškić*[307] decision seeks to narrowly interpret the proportionality test while expanding the protection of civilians. That goal may be best attained if the principle of distinction is reinforced by more clearly identifying who can be targeted; greater accountability is demanded regarding the approach of considering attacks as part of a whole in addition to the attention often paid to tactical level effects; the importance of the right to life is emphasised; and those principles are applied rigorously at all levels of warfare. The attainment of this goal would be helped by requiring an enhanced accountability framework and by establishing or reinforcing a culture of 'due diligence' among those who decide upon and plan attacks.

United Nations sanctions against Iraq in human rights terms. See also Reynolds, *supra* n. 73, p. 72 ('[A]n economic embargo or sanctions can have similar effects to collateral damage.').

306. See Maier, *supra* n. 134, p. 430.

307. *Prosecutor* v. *Kupreškić*, *supra* n. 22.

4.1 The principle of distinction: people

The principle of distinction can be reinforced by clarifying that it is the functions performed by persons that make them valid targets and not simply their status at law. Combatants and 'unlawful combatants' who provide visual cues by wearing uniforms, carrying weapons and manning military equipment assist in the application of the principle of distinction. However, not all combat in either international or internal armed conflict is conducted by persons who visually separate themselves from the civilian population. Similarly, the decision to employ civilians in roles ordinarily performed by combatants blurs the line as to when they should receive the protection associated with civilian status.

Civilians must be protected from attack. There can be no return to the concept of 'quasi-combatant' that became evident during World War II. However, literal interpretations of the law that see civilians retain their status but not their protection mean that some people who are technically 'civilians' (i.e., those who take a direct or active part in hostilities) can be intentionally targeted. Regardless of whether that group of participants is called 'civilians', 'unprivileged belligerents' or 'unlawful combatants', the activities which cause the loss of protection associated with uninvolved civilians must be carefully, but realistically, identified. There is a very real threat to the significantly larger group of uninvolved civilians if attempts are made to overextend the protective umbrella of their status to the members of armed groups who are active participants in hostilities.

As a result, criteria such as the exercise of a command function within an armed group; carrying out staff duties, such as logistics, intelligence, operational planning and communications designed to facilitate the conduct of hostilities; and acting pursuant to orders in order to carry out those activities should be used as indicia of the performance of a combatant-like function. A realistic assessment of what constitutes direct or active participation, whether it is by combatants or civilians, may offer the best protection to uninvolved civilians, particularly in the complex factual situations of contemporary armed conflict.[308] Such an approach should reflect the fact that participation in hostilities is primarily a group activity.

However, mere membership in a political group that may have a military wing would not suffice to make someone a target. This is particularly important with respect to insurgent-related political movements. While guerrilla operations are dependent upon the general support of a population, such support does not make those civilians members of an armed group.[309] Further, simply being a financier of insurgent activities may make someone subject to arrest or prosecution but not a direct participant in hostilities.

---

308. The reports of an ICRC/Asser Institute initiative seeking to outline what constitutes direct participation can be found at <www.icrc.org/Web/eng/siteeng0.nsf/htmlall/5TALL8/$File/ Direct_participation_in_ hostilities_2004_eng.pdf and <www.wihl.nl>.

309. See Maier, *supra* n. 134, p. 433. See also Galula, *supra* n. 109, p. 50 ('What makes it possible for the guerrillas to survive and to expand? The complicity of the population.').

4.2 Human life

An important impact human rights can have on any proportionality assessment is the emphasis that its normative regime places on the value of human life. This does not mean that a fundamental reality of warfare will be changed, since it has proven impossible to wage warfare with any guarantee there will be no loss of civilian life. Further, it is the nature of the proportionality test that an attack on, or defence of, an objective may result in collateral loss of life or injury, with civilian casualties being assessed against the concrete and direct military advantage to be gained from the use of such violence.

As has been noted, a narrow interpretation of the test for targeting 'people', based on their direct participation, places a higher value on 'life' than the traditionally much broader interpretation of objects as military objects. This separate approach to people and things must be maintained. Further, since the wording in the legal test for proportionality does not make a qualitative distinction between collateral losses of life and damage to objects, an interpretive approach could be adopted that seeks to do just that. That being said, this unequal weighting of life over objects may not be possible in all circumstances. For example, it is possible to conceive of circumstances where avoiding damage to protected objects, such as those constituting 'the cultural or spiritual heritage of peoples',[310] could result in commanders having to consider placing both military personnel and uninvolved civilians at greater risk.

There could also be a clarification of how all human life is to be valued. In that respect, the lives of all civilians, combatants and unlawful combatants should be respected, except in respect of their being targeted for direct or active participation in hostilities. Such an approach also results in a re-orientation of the assessment of the risk that members of armed forces might be exposed to when seeking to minimise civilian casualties and damage to civilian objects. There are limits to the risks that can be asked of soldiers.

4.3 Attacks as a whole: objects and people

It appears that the tension between a tactical level analytical approach and one which more fully recognises the strategic level of warfare may be based on a perception that considering attacks 'as a whole' could create widespread, if not uncontrolled, collateral damage. Yet there must be a solution to this dilemma, particularly since wars are planned and conducted at a strategic level. The answer may come from requiring strategic 'target sets' to be justified by establishing not only the military advantage to be gained but also by analysing expected civilian casualties at the tactical, operational and strategic levels.

In this respect, the close scrutiny of attacks on strategic targets, such as 'war supporting' industry and other economic targets, would appear to be consistent

310. See Art. 53(a) AP I.

with contemporary air warfare doctrine which favours attacking more narrowly identified command and control targets. The accountability process could require a clear articulation of the advantage to be gained, including the relative importance of such targets at all levels of war and how the effects are linked from the tactical to the strategic levels. Further, the tactical level's effects, both direct and indirect, could also be assessed as a 'whole' in an attempt to identify the true cost of prosecuting the campaign.[311] Such an approach would not apply to all offensive or defensive uses of force. Some attacks would continue to be assessed solely at the tactical level. However, where a strategic use of violence is advocated, an accounting of the overall damage and loss of life expected could also be considered.

In the final analysis, the test at law is one of 'excessive' loss of life, injury or collateral damage. It is here that the *Kupreškić*[312] approach to assessing the proportionality test must be considered, since the threat to uninvolved civilians can likely only be narrowed, not eliminated. The underlying moral issues of relating 'good' objectives to 'evil' effects and assessing the value of life against broader strategic objectives remain difficult to assess under the legal test of proportionality. Although the legal process requires a line to be drawn in order to provide clarity for those required to make such difficult decisions, there must remain a broad scope for the interpretation of significantly different concepts. Therefore, the law must address the extremes and, in the wording of the *Kupreškić* decision, accept that there will be significant grey areas between indisputable legality and unlawfulness.[313]

The credibility of both the decision and the accountability processes may be dependant upon how well the total effects of the targeting decision are articulated and analysed. The question of what constitutes excessive collateral damage will ultimately have to be considered on the basis of the reasonableness of the decisions made to launch an attack.[314] Further, in order to establish *mens rea* it would appear to be necessary to establish 'that the attack was launched wilfully and in knowledge of circumstances giving rise to the expectation of excessive casualties'.[315] As the ICTY Final Report indicates, the answers to the questions that should be asked in assessing proportionality may 'differ depending on the background and values

311. See the ICTY Final Report, *supra* n. 23, para. 41 (quoting F.J. Hampson, 'Means and methods of warfare in the conflict in the Gulf', in P. Rowe ed., *The Gulf War 1990-91 in International and English Law* (New York, Routledge 1993) pp. 89 at 100, where she indicates, in discussing amendments to the AP I definition of proportionality to account for effects on civilian infrastructure, '[e]ither it should require the likely cumulative effect on the civilian population of attacks against such targets to be taken into account, or the same result might be achieved by requiring that the destruction of the object offer a definite military advantage in the context of the war aim.').

312. *Prosecutor* v. *Kupreškić*, *supra* n. 22.

313. Ibid., para. 526.

314. See *Prosecutor* v. *Galić*, *supra* n. 22, para. 58 ('[I]n determining whether an attack was proportionate it is necessary to examine whether a reasonably well-informed person in the circumstances of the actual perpetrator, making reasonable use of the information available to him or her, could have expected civilian casualties to result from the attack.').

315. Ibid., para. 59.

of the decision maker'.[316] This has prompted the comment that '[t]his simple truth underlies the debates between human-rights-oriented NGOs and military circles.'[317] However, assessing reasonableness is not a foreign concept to most courts and tribunals and, ultimately, a review body must put itself in the place of the military or civilian decision maker in order to consider collateral damage.

4.4 A culture of accountability

Finally, efforts should continue to establish an effective and efficient accountability process for assessing the application of the proportionality test. This can be done either by creating a unique humanitarian law process for reviewing attacks[318] or by adapting existing judicial and human rights processes to consider humanitarian law problems. Courts and tribunals are already demonstrating a willingness to fill a perceived void under humanitarian law. This reality cannot be ignored by either civilian or military humanitarian law advocates. Such a process need not involve international review bodies and does not have to be conducted solely by civilian authorities. Demanding the level of transparency associated with some human rights tribunals is likely not realistic in the context of an armed conflict.[319] What should occur is that the accountability process applies the law appropriate to the environment in which operations are being conducted. In this respect, an operation involving the use of aircraft to drop bombs or shoot down other aircraft or the employment of military units to engage opposing armed groups should cause a review body to pause and question whether human rights norms designed for peacetime law enforcement offer the most realistic means by which to deal with levels of violence associated with armed conflict.

Finally, the development of a reporting process should be encouraged to address allegations of the misuse of force. Such a process can respond not only to legal inquiries but also the public and world community at large.[320] These suggestions for assessing proportionality may not reflect the level of accountability sought by some. However, in armed conflict violence is a regular occurrence. Trying to establish an accountability framework that would exhaustively review every use of force is neither practical nor likely desirable. Ultimately, for the law to be effective in this area it must reflect the practical realities and levels of violence associated with armed conflict.

---

316. See ICTY Final Report, *supra* n. 23, para. 50.

317. See Bothe, *supra* n. 26, p. 535, for a comment that if the assessment of reasonableness is to be based on the judgement of the reasonable commander it should be a commander defined more in civilian terms.

318. See Green, *supra* n. 283, ch. 17, for an outline of means available to prevent breaches of humanitarian law. See also Art. 90 AP I (the International Fact Finding Commission).

319. See Watkin, *supra* n. 214, pp. 32-34.

320. See S. Sewall, 'An empty pledge to civilians?', in *The New York Times*, 21 March 2003, p. A19; and Reynolds, *supra* n. 73, pp. 104-106 (arguing for the development of a 'collateral damage response team' to 'expose adversary disinformation, as well as to responsibly report collateral damage'). Ibid., p. 104.

5. CONCLUSIONS

As this article has outlined, the term 'proportionality' masks a complex assessment of morally charged issues. Rather than presenting a scientific balancing of opposing interests the test is a secularised version of a medieval moral doctrine requiring a nuanced interpretation of the principle of discrimination, one of the foundational principles upon which humanitarian law is based. While there is wide acceptance that the proportionality test is a part of conventional and customary humanitarian law, there has been less agreement on how it is to be applied.

The credibility of the proportionality test will be based on the degree to which realistic and clear distinctions can be made between those who participate in combat and civilians who do not. Further, a requirement for the group using violence to explain both the strategic and tactical importance and effects of an attack could align the proportionality assessment with how wars are fought. A significant advance in humanitarian law has been the outline of precautionary measures in Additional Protocol I. The integration of this process within military planning and decision making offers one of the most important ways to ensure application of the proportionality standard. With the common goal of limiting the effects of unrestricted conflict, the four approaches set out in the article: pacifism and pacificism, human rights, tactical level control and strategic assessment, all present potential advantages and disadvantages as analytical models. It has been suggested that reinforcing the principle of distinction, emphasising the value of life and assessing targeting at all levels of warfare provides a realistic way of limiting collateral damage.

Yet; whatever approach is adopted, two other factors may be of particular relevance. First, the doctrine of 'double effect', and the underlying principle of distinction upon which it is based, had already fallen victim to large scale armed conflict during World War II. The rule against 'excessive' collateral damage must be applied across the broad range of contemporary armed conflict, ranging from small scale but violent insurgencies to interstate conflict approaching total war. It cannot be forgotten that the use of legal rules to restrict the conduct and effect of hostilities has its limits and is fragile[321] with the result that 'narrowly legal efforts to restrict the use of force have had only limited impact ...'.[322] There is significant danger of overreaching if humanitarian law and with it the principle of proportionality are asked to do too much in terms of limiting conflict.

Secondly, the protection of human life during armed conflict depends not only on the direct application of norms written in humanitarian law treaties but also on the culture and command climate developed within armed groups. If much depends on 'the heart of men',[323] the law can only provide one means by which to limit collateral injury and death. However, it has also been suggested there is a

321. See Gray, *supra* n. 51, p. 394.

322. See Roberts, *supra* n. 200, p. 323.

323. See the quotation at the beginning of this paper.

powerful resistance to killing which 'gives us cause to believe there may just be hope for mankind after all'.[324] That hope may rest to a large degree on the commitment to limiting excessive collateral casualties pursuant to the legal obligations set out in humanitarian law.

324. D. Grossman, *On Killing* (Boston, Little, Brown & Co. 1996) p. 39.

Part II
Maritime Warfare

[5]

SUBMARINE WARFARE

By PROFESSOR A. PEARCE HIGGINS, C.B.E., LL.D.

Whewell Professor of International Law in the University of Cambridge, and Professor of International Law in the University of London

A DISTINGUISHED British Naval Officer who had unrivalled sources of information in regard to the submarine campaign of the Germans during the late war has recently stated that it " provided perhaps the finest vindication of International Law in history." [1] This apparently paradoxical statement requires explanation, since almost from the beginning of the war writers were constantly referring to " problems " raised by submarine warfare. Submarine warfare does raise certain problems; but, in my opinion, these problems can be dealt with and solutions provided by applying principles which, until the late war, were of general acceptance. Neutrals in the long run were, or ought to have been, the guardians of the Law of Nations; in the future such guardianship and enforcement must lie with the League of Nations. In the past the duty has not been fulfilled as it ought to have been; sometimes because of the difficulties in stating what the law was, sometimes by reason of the violations not being of a sufficiently flagrant character to call forth the strong moral reprobation of mankind. Property and life do not stand on the same plane, technical rules relating to the former have been violated, on occasion, by belligerents with comparative impunity. Human beings are, of course, agents through whom States conduct their warlike operations; but the taking of life in war has been regulated by customary and conventional rules, and so long as these were observed in principle, the neutral could say or do nothing. But when the

[1] Rear-Admiral S. S. Hall, C.B., in Vol. V. of the *Transactions of the Grotius Society* (1919), p. 84.

humane principles which underlie the gradual evolution of the laws of war were violated in a wholesale manner and in such a way as to jeopardise friend and foe alike, neutrals have come forward in defence of the law against the law-breaking State.

The view which will be put forward in the following pages is that the advent of the submarine does not require the making of new laws, that the old rules are sufficient, but need rigid enforcement. It is proposed therefore to discuss the rules of naval warfare as they had been received by the customary Law of Nations regarding the functions and duties of surface warships; to consider their application to submarines, and to examine some of the contentions advanced by the German apologists for the unrestricted use of submarines.

I

The submarine had for some time before the outbreak of the late war formed an integral part of the naval forces of many States, it is one of the vessels used for military offensive purposes and comes under the general term of a " ship of war." The functions and duties of ships of war in belligerent operations had been settled by the customary Law of Nations, and it will be well, therefore, to state concisely what those were before considering the particular problems which submersible warships raise.

All enemy warships may be at once attacked without any preliminary visit or demand for surrender; they may, of course, defend themselves. Submarines may therefore attack warships and be themselves attacked by them without preliminary warning.

Enemy merchant ships, with certain exceptions, are liable to capture and condemnation, but a belligerent is under a duty recognised by International Law, before attacking her, to visit or to attempt to visit a merchant ship in order to ascertain her character and whether she is in fact liable to capture. Merchant vessels may attempt flight or resist visit, as visit is the first act of capture; if they do so they may be compelled by force to surrender. They may be armed in self-defence. When resistance has ceased or the vessel has hauled down her colours she is captured as a prize. It is the duty of the captor to make all reasonable efforts to save all on board. The crew on surrendering become prisoners of war and must be treated with humanity. By the 11th Hague Convention, 1907, they are entitled to be released if they give a written promise not to engage in any service connected with the operations of war while hostilities last. Captured merchant ships should be taken into a port of the captor and proceedings in prize taken for their condemnation. It is a point not free from doubt as to the moment when the property in the captured merchant ship passes to the captor. In my opinion the property of the original owner is not fully divested until there has been a condemnation by a regular prize tribunal having jurisdiction of the case. Condemnation acts retrospectively to the moment of capture.[1]

The subject of the resistance of enemy merchant ships may be elaborated rather more fully. The master of a belligerent merchant ship seeing a suspicious vessel might either decide to attempt escape by flight or continue his voyage and wait till summoned to surrender, or he might decide to resist. The latter decision would be conditioned by the type of enemy warship whose approach he was awaiting; if the merchant captain considered his chances favourable he would wait till some offensive act was done by the enemy, and an attempt by the latter to visit was the first step towards capture.[2] The possibility that a merchant ship might carry guns and resist was always present in the old wars to the minds of captains of warships and privateers, but it was never suggested that the latter were entitled without warning to open fire with heavy guns, or in modern times with torpedoes, merely because of the possibility of finding on closer approach that the enemy merchant ship was armed. The warship was not allowed to make the

[1] For authorities see W. E. Hall, *International Law*, 7th ed., p. 491.

[2] Dr. Hans Wehberg, *Das Seekriegsrecht* (1915), p. 285.

merchantman's possible strength the excuse for a surprise attack, or for sinking at sight.

Captured enemy merchant ships may, however, be destroyed under certain conditions—the unseaworthiness of the prize or the commander's inability to spare a prize crew are given as the examples of justification in Article 303 of the British Naval Prize Manual (Holland's ed. 1888). The Institute of International Law in 1882 gave the following as good grounds for allowing such destruction : (1) When it is not possible to keep the vessel afloat owing to her bad condition and the rough state of the weather; (2) When the vessel cannot keep up with the warship and might easily be recaptured by the enemy; (3) When the approach of a superior enemy force creates fear of recapture; (4) When the captor cannot put on board an adequate prize crew without reducing his own beyond what is essential for his own safety; (5) When the port to which it would be possible to take the captured vessel is too distant.[1]

Systematic destruction of enemy's vessels has been rare in the past, but it was ordered by the American Government during the war of 1812–1814,[2] and Dr. Lushington during the Crimean War said that it may be justifiable or even praiseworthy in the captors to destroy an enemy's vessel, and that the bringing to adjudication of an enemy's vessel is not called for by any respect to the right of the enemy proprietor where there is no neutral property on board.[3] Russia, during the war with Japan, sank twenty-one Japanese vessels captured as prizes, and during the early stages of the late war the German cruisers, *Emden*, *Karlsruhe* and *Kronprinz Wilhelm*, finding themselves unable to spare prize crews, sank numerous captured British vessels after first removing crews and passengers, as also did the *Moewe* later on.

In order that discipline may be maintained and reasons for destruction reduced, many States require that proceedings for condemnation in their Prize Courts shall be taken in respect of destroyed enemy ships, but as regards the legitimacy of

[1] *Ann. de l'Institut de Droit International*, VI. 221.

[2] Hall, *International Law*, § 150.

[3] *The Leucade* (1855), Spinks, 217.

destruction of enemy merchant ships, under certain conditions, there can be no dispute.

The British Prize Rules provide that on a decree of condemnation of a ship that has been destroyed the Order of the Court declares that the destruction of the ship was necessary and the grounds on which the Court held the destruction to have been justified. Several cases occurred in British Prize Courts during the war, *e. g.* the German steamships *Baden* and *Santa Isabella* which were sunk in the course of the operations off the Falkland Islands.

Destruction of enemy vessels under certain conditions being recognised as legitimate, it is also a rule of International Law that the crew, passengers, and, if possible, the cargo together with relevant papers and documents must be first removed and placed in safety.

This rule has been introduced and observed by the traditions of all seafaring people until the present War. It is for the protection of the lives of all on board merchant vessels, whether enemies or neutrals. It was expressly laid down in the Rules for Naval Warfare adopted by the Institute of International Law at its meeting in 1913 that, "before destruction, persons on board are to be placed in safety."[1] The British Naval Prize Manual (1888) Article 304, the French Instructions of 1912,[2] the German Naval Prize Regulations, 1914,[3] the Italian Naval Prize Regulations, to mention only a few, are equally specific. But more important than these is the provision in Article 3 of the 6th Hague Convention, 1907, which gives permission to a belligerent to destroy, subject to an indemnity, enemy merchant ships met at sea which are ignorant of the outbreak of war; in case of destruction it is expressly stated that it is "under the obligation of providing for the safety of the persons as well as the preservation of the papers on board." The official report of the Comité d'Examen at the Hague discloses the fact, also mentioned in the Report of M. Fromageot to the Plenary Meeting of the Conference on September 27, 1907, that Baron Charles de Macchio, the Second Delegate Plenipo-

[1] *Annuaire,* XXVI. p. 669. [2] Art. 28, §§ 153, 154. [3] Art. 116.

tentiary of Austria-Hungary insisted on the insertion in the Article of a provision for the security of passengers and crew and the preservation of the papers.[1]

When, during the American War of Independence, Paul Jones sank captured ships he removed all persons on board before destroying them; and Captain Semmes of the *Alabama*, during the American Civil War, either placed in safety persons on board ships he was about to destroy or released the ship when he found it impossible to accommodate them. Mr. J. A. Bollas, the Solicitor to the United States Navy, examined all the charges of cruelty brought against Captain Semmes, and in no case did he find any evidence that he had inflicted unavoidable hardship on those he captured.[2]

Whether attempted visit of an enemy vessel is necessary before attack may not be so easily capable of proof from Naval Instructions, as is the rule of preservation of the lives of those on board; also, the taking in for adjudication of enemy merchant ships may not be required by the regulations of all countries; but visit or summons to surrender has been hitherto universally regarded as necessary prior to attack as a means of avoiding bloodshed of non-combatants and in order to give effect to certain recognised exemptions from capture. To put the matter in another way, to attack a merchant ship, without warning, by gunfire—*a fortiori* by a torpedo, has hitherto been recognised as illegitimate. In this connection the following observations of Lord Stowell on the use of false colours by a privateer may be cited. He said : "To sail and chase under false colours may be an allowable stratagem of war, but firing under false colours is what the maritime law of this country does not permit; for it may be attended with very unjust consequences; it may occasion the loss of the lives of persons who, if they were apprised of the real character of the cruiser, might, instead of resisting, implore protection." [3] Ample warning is essential before destruction of the ship is resorted to, and sufficient time

[1] *Actes et Documents*, I. 255; III. 955.

[2] See J. W. Garner, *American Journal of International Law*, IX. p. 614.

[3] *The Peacock*, 4 C. Rob., 185.

allowed for the purpose of transshipment. A captor cannot be relieved of this obligation even though his position would be seriously endangered through the sudden approach of superior enemy forces.

Neutral merchant ships are liable to visit and search in time of war by belligerent warships and they are under a duty to submit. No attack on a neutral ship is lawful except where the vessel attempts to avoid visit and search or forcibly resists, and such attack must only be proportionate to what is requisite for obtaining the exercise of this right, and must cease when the vessel stops or ceases to resist. Forcible resistance to visit and search entails capture and condemnation of the neutral ship.[1]

A neutral merchant ship is also liable to capture if engaged in the carriage of contraband, or analogues of contraband, attempting to break blockade or in performing acts of unneutral service.

Until the Russo-Japanese War instances of the destruction of neutral merchant ships are rare. According to the practice of the English Prize Courts the destruction of neutral vessels entailed a liability to compensation on the part of the destroyer.[2] Compensation is, however, possibly not due if the vessel is clearly liable to condemnation, but this point is not free from doubt. The British Naval Prize Manual (1888 ed.) provides that if the captured vessel is not in a condition to be sent into any port for adjudication, or if the commander is unable to spare a prize crew, he should release the vessel and cargo without ransom, unless there is clear proof that she belongs to the enemy (Article 303). The Russian practice during the Russo-Japanese War called forth effective protests from Great Britain. The doctrine of many States, however, as evidenced by the Memoranda prepared for and by discussions at the Hague and London Naval Conferences, showed that the British view was not generally accepted. The compromise embodied in Chapter IV of the Declaration of London laid down the rule that a neutral vessel which has been captured may not be destroyed by the captor, but must be sent into a port for adjudication. It

[1] *The Maria*, 1 C. Rob., 369.

[2] *The Actæon*, 2 Dod., 48; *The Felicity*, 2 Dod., 381.

provides, however, that, as an exception, a captured neutral vessel may be destroyed : (1) if she would be liable to condemnation, and (2) if the taking in of the vessel would involve danger to the safety of the warship or the success of the operation in which she was engaged (Article 48). This does not appear to be a very satisfactory compromise, as the captor is judge both of the liability to condemnation and of the military necessity. It may be going too far to say that under no circumstances is it ever lawful to destroy a neutral vessel, but the view may be maintained that in every case where a neutral ship is destroyed before adjudication by a Prize Court the owner should be entitled to compensation, except possibly where such vessel was liable to condemnation as being in effect an enemy ship.

As the lives of persons on board captured enemy ships must be saved before the vessel is destroyed, *a fortiori* must they be in the case of destruction of neutral ships. Article 50 of the Declaration of London recognised this and provided that before destruction all persons on board must be placed in safety, and all the ship's papers and other documents must be taken on board the warship. It will be seen that a distinction appears to be made between persons and papers; the former are to be placed "in safety" while the ship's papers are to be taken on board the warship.

II

In a Declaration presented to the Governments of a number of neutral countries by Sir Edward Grey on March 1, 1915, after enumerating the duties of a warship in attacks on commercial vessels, it was stated that "A German Submarine, however, fulfils none of these obligations. She enjoys no local command of the waters in which she operates. She does not take her captures within the jurisdiction of a Prize Court. She carries no prize crew which she can put on board a prize. She uses no effective means of discriminating between a neutral and an enemy vessel. She does not receive on board for safety the crew of the vessel she sinks. Her methods of warfare are therefore entirely outside the scope of any of the international instruments regulating operations against commerce in time of war." [1]

These views were re-echoed by Mr. Bryan, the United States Secretary of State, in a dispatch to the American Ambassador in Berlin, dated May 13, 1915 : " The Government of the United States, therefore, desires to call the attention of the Imperial German Government with the utmost earnestness to the fact that the objection to their present method of attack against the trade of their enemies lies in the practical impossibility of employing submarines in the destruction of commerce without disregarding those rules of fairness, reason, justice and humanity which all modern opinion regards as imperative. It is practically impossible for the officers of a submarine to visit a merchantman at sea and examine her papers or cargo. It is practically impossible for them to make a prize of her without leaving her crew and all on board of her to the mercy of the sea in her small boats. These facts, it is understood, the Imperial German Government frankly admit. We are informed that in the instances of which we have spoken time enough for even that poor measure of safety was not given, and in at least two of the cases cited not so much as a warning was received. Manifestly submarines cannot be used against merchantmen, as the last few weeks have shown, without an inevitable violation of many sacred principles of justice and humanity." [2]

Most of the foregoing defects are inherent in the submarine torpedo-boat in attacks against commerce, but they are not all of equal legal importance. The chief defect is due to the non-provision for the safety of persons removed from destroyed ships, and the fact that a submarine cannot take a captured ship in for adjudication, but must in all, and not merely in exceptional cases, resort to destruction. The destruction of captured enemy merchant ships, as has already been pointed out, is not in all cases an illegitimate act of war.

[1] *Parliamentary Papers*, No. 6 (1915), p. 23.

[2] Special Supplement to *American Journal of International Law*, Vol. IX. July 1915, p. 131.

The assurances given by Germany to the United States on May 4, 1916 (the withdrawal of which on January 31, 1917, led to the severing of diplomatic relations by the United States on February 3, 1917), contained the following statement of the orders which had been issued to the German naval forces. It showed that Germany recognised that by International Law enemy merchantmen are entitled to receive the hitherto accepted rights in relation to visit and search both from submarines as well as from surface warships : " In accordance with the general principles of visit and search and destruction of merchant vessels recognised by International Law, such vessels, both within and without the area declared as naval war zones shall not be sunk without warning and without saving human lives, unless such ships attempt to escape or offer resistance." [1]

The United States, in reply to this communication, having had experience of the duplicity of the German Foreign Office, felt " it necessary to state that it takes it for granted that the Imperial German Government does not intend to imply that the maintenance of its newly announced policy is in any way contingent upon the course or result of diplomatic negotiations between the Government of the United States and any other belligerent Government, notwithstanding the fact that certain passages in the Imperial Government's Note of the 4th instant might appear to be susceptible of that construction. In order, however, to avoid any possible misunderstanding, the Government of the United States notifies the Imperial Government that it cannot for a moment entertain, much less discuss, a suggestion that respect by German naval authorities for the rights of citizens of the United States upon the high seas, should in any way or in the slightest degree be made contingent upon the conduct of any other Government affecting the rights of neutrals and combatants. Responsibility in such matters is single, not joint, absolute, nor relative."

No reply was made to this Note by Germany.[2]

[1] Special Supplement to the *American Journal of International Law*, Vol. XI. October 1917, p. 336.

[2] *Ibid.*, cited *supra*, pp. 336–7.

III

It may be as well now to turn to some of the arguments advanced by or on behalf of the German methods.

It was contended by Germany (*a*) that the introduction of new weapons and new conditions of warfare demands the modification or alteration of the old rules.[1] During the war the Allies made use of the argument of altered conditions of warfare as justification for certain of their methods of dealing with enemy commerce, but they also contended, with good reason, that there was no change in the principles involved. Whatever may be the objections raised by enemies or neutrals to British and Allied practices, whether in relation to visit and search, blockade or contraband, none of them violated the rules of justice and humanity hitherto regarded as universally obligatory. The claim of the Germans on this head cannot be substantiated; the rules of naval warfare above stated have stood the test of other important alterations in the modes of naval warfare. The introduction of steam and other means of propulsion did not modify these rules. When torpedoes came into general use and fast torpedo-boats were built, it was feared in some quarters that their speed and the nature of their armament would induce a practice similar to the German practice of sinking at sight. On this point Admiral Bourgeois of the French Navy wrote in 1886 : " The advent of the torpedo, whatever its influence on naval *matériel*, has in no way changed international treaties, the Law of Nations or the moral laws which govern the world. It has not given the belligerent the right of life and death over the peaceable citizens of the enemy or neutral state." [2] This observation applies equally to the submarine torpedo-boat as to the surface warship.

(*b*) Furthermore, the claim that the comparatively fragile character of the submarine renders the exercise of the right of visit and search or of the summons to surrender dangerous

[1] I have dealt with some of the arguments here discussed in my *Defensively-armed Merchant Ships and Submarine Warfare* (1917).

[2] *Nouvelle revue* (1886), II. 499.

and is a reason for their non-compliance with the rule in this respect is contrary to the hitherto accepted principles of war. If a belligerent uses force against his adversary's commerce it is his duty to see that it is strong enough for the purpose, and capable of conforming to the humane rules adopted in naval warfare; it is not for him to complain if his weapon turns out to be too feeble for the purpose for which it was employed. The attempt to change existing rules to the advantage of the party that is not in command of the surface of the sea, is an attempt to avoid the consequence of naval weakness. War is not conducted on the analogy of handicapping rules at race meetings. The limitations which are inherent to the submarine cannot be appealed to in order to justify its success. New weapons are illegitimate if their use necessarily entails violation of fundamental principles.

(*c*) It was also urged that the prohibition of the arming of merchant ships would enable a submarine to operate against commerce without violating the laws of war. The legitimacy of defensively arming merchant ships is not disputed by any Power, so far as I am aware, except Germany, and to give up the practice would deprive a merchant vessel of a means of protecting the lives of the passengers and crew, and would also increase the effectiveness of the submarine. In short, all that a State would require in war against commerce would be a fleet of fast vessels armed with signalling guns if defensive armament of merchant ships were abandoned.[1]

(*d*) With a view to render rarer, or to prevent the destruction of prizes, Article 23 of the 13th Hague Convention, 1907, provides that a neutral Power may allow prizes to enter its ports and roadsteads when they are brought there to be sequestrated pending the decision of a Prize Court. Great Britain has not ratified this Convention, and in signing the Convention excluded this Article; the United States, Japan and Siam on ratifying the Convention also excluded it. The Article does not impose on neutral States a duty of reception of prizes into their ports. Since Great Britain and the other Powers mentioned refused

[1] See my *Defensively-armed Merchant Ships and Submarine Warfare*, p. 26.

to agree to this principle for warships generally, an exception on behalf of the submarine should not be entertained.

(*e*) The policy of unrestricted submarine warfare introduced by Germany in February, 1917, purported to be by way of reprisals for British illegalities; but even if the latter were admitted, German practices went beyond anything hitherto known under the head of reprisals, and for the purpose of this paper in relation to submarine warfare in general they need not be discussed in detail. It is enough to say that no reprisals directed against enemy and neutral ships alike can be permitted which violate fundamental laws of humanity involving the certainty of death or mutilation to non-combatants, neutral as well as enemy. This was the view taken by the United States in the Dispatch of February 3, 1917, severing diplomatic relations with Germany.[1]

(*f*) One of the arguments used by Germany in controversy with the United States, who protested against attacks on merchant vessels flying a neutral flag, was that in consequence of the " misuse " of neutral flags by the British merchant ships there was no certainty that a vessel showing the flag of a neutral was not a defensively-armed enemy merchant ship, and that any attempt to visit such a ship would render the submarine liable to destruction.

This was an attempt to cast doubts upon a *ruse de guerre* of long standing in naval warfare. Arising from a certain anxiety that the policy of a general use of the flag of the United States by British merchant ships might imperil the lives and property of their citizens, the United States Government expressed a hope that the use of their flag in the German war zone might be checked,[2] but Sir Edward Grey replied that this ruse of employing false colours had always hitherto been permitted and that United States vessels had availed themselves of this facility during the American Civil War,[3] and that the British Government had no intention of advising their merchant shipping to use foreign

[1] Supplement to *American Journal of International Law*, cited *supra*, p. 337.
[2] *Parliamentary Papers*, Misc. No. 6 (1915), p. 16.
[3] *Ibid.*, p. 21.

flags as a general practice or to resort to them otherwise than for escaping capture or destruction. A distinguished German Jurist, Dr. Perels, admits the legitimacy of this *ruse de guerre*,[1] and though the abolition of the rule has been advocated,[2] the customary Law of Nations permitted it both to warships and merchant ships.

This argument was an attempt to excuse the submarines from complying with the duty of ascertaining the nationality and character of the ship before capturing or destroying it. " If that obligation is fulfilled," said Sir Edward Grey in the dispatch above referred to, " hoisting a neutral flag on board a British vessel cannot possibly endanger neutral shipping." Prof. Dupuis had some years ago pointed out that the indiscriminate destruction of enemy ships without visit and search must inevitably involve, on occasion, the destruction of neutrals; flags, he said, are no necessary criteria of nationality, and the usages of the sea admit of enemy merchant ships flying neutral flags: visit and search are necessary to ascertain the nationality of a merchant ship.[3]

Attacks without warning by submarines have shown, even on the most favourable assumption, that the imperfect and limited vision from the vessel have led to mistakes being made and neutral vessels being sunk. In the case of the (neutral) American vessel, the *Gulflight*, " the American flag was first observed at the moment of firing the shot "; in the case of another (neutral) American, the *Nebraskan*, " in the twilight which had already set in, the name of the steamer was not visible from the submarine," and the excuse made by the German Government for an attack without warning on the Cunard steamer *Orduna* was the difficulty of observation, caused by the unfavourable weather.[4] These difficulties appear to be inherent to the nature of the submarine, so that even in the case of a belligerent whose good faith is irreproachable, mistakes would certainly be made

[1] *Das internationale öffentliche Seerecht*, § 35.

[2] *U.S. Naval War College, International Law Discussions*, 1903, pp. 37–42.

[3] *Le droit de la guerre maritime* (1899), p. 350.

[4] See my *Defensively-armed Merchant Ships*, p. 32.

if sinking at sight were permissible. The treacherous belligerent can also by means of the torpedo and submarine adopt the policy of sinking "without leaving a trace," a policy which, though not impossible in the case of surface vessels, is less likely to be adopted by them.

IV

As regards the future of submarines, it is certainly possible to construct submarines sufficiently large and strong to act as surface warships have acted and to conform to the traditional practice of commerce destroyers. Cruiser warfare by submarines armed with guns, and large enough to carry spare men for prize crews, can be built and are capable of a wide range of action.[1]

Whether the abolition of the right of capture of private property at sea would tend to produce a mitigation of the difficulties occasioned by the use of submarines against merchant ships is not in my opinion at all certain, since captures for the carriage of contraband, breach of blockade and unneutral service, etc., would presumably still remain. This question, again, is too wide for discussion in this connection.

It has been suggested that the practice of Ransom or Bonding captured vessels might reduce to a minimum the danger to merchant vessels captured by submarines. Ransom was effected by an agreement made between the commander of the captured vessel or cargo, and the captor, by which the latter permits the former to depart with his vessel and gives him a safe conduct in consideration of a sum of money which the former, in his own name and in the name of the owners of the vessel and cargo, promises to pay at a future time named. The contract was in writing in duplicate, one copy being kept by the captor which was the Ransom-Bill proper, the other copy being kept by the master of the captured vessel which acted as a safe-conduct. The practice of ransom has not been viewed with favour by Great Britain, owing probably to her naval superiority in the past which

[1] See Rear-Admiral S. S. Hall's paper in *Transactions of the Grotius Society* (1919), p. 86.

generally enabled her fleets to protect her commerce, and owing to the fact that it was considered that the permission to ransom a ship tended to relax the energy of war, so that merchant vessels would not be so diligent in seeking to escape or resist capture. Statutes of the reign of George III prohibited to British subjects the privilege of ransom unless in cases of extreme necessity to be decided by the Court of Admiralty; and to-day Section 45 of the Naval Prize Act, 1864, while allowing the King in Council to make Orders prohibiting or allowing ransom, provides that Ransom Bills or Bonds given in contravention of any Order in Council shall be deemed to have been given on an illegal consideration, and persons so giving them are liable to a fine of £500. Practice varies in other States, ransom being allowed in some and forbidden in others. The United States has not prohibited their use, and ranks them among the *commercia belli*.[1] Each State decides for itself as a matter of policy the expediency of allowing its merchant vessels to enter into ransom contracts, and the question is not peculiar to submarines except in so far as the submarine is less likely than a surface warship to be able to spare the necessary prize crew to navigate the prize into port. The threat to sink under penalty of an exorbitant ransom would not necessarily be operative in compelling a submarine to conform to the laws of civilised warfare.

The conclusions suggested after the foregoing examination may be summed up shortly by the statement that the introduction of the submarine does not call for the making of new laws for naval warfare, but demands the rigid application of those hitherto accepted. Submarines, whether armed with torpedoes or guns, are legitimate means of attacking warships. The attack on a merchant ship without previous warning is illegal and officers guilty of violating the rule are guilty of a war-crime. Submarines are legitimate means of attacking enemy commerce only if they conform to the laws of naval warfare hitherto observed by surface warships.

The use of torpedoes against merchant ships, on which there

[1] Hall, *International Law*, § 151; Halleck, II. p. 365; Moore's *Digest*, VII. § 1214.

is little or no authority either from Conventions or national prize manuals, though there is no evidence of their use for this purpose until the late war, must be considered in the light of the accepted principle that instruments of war are illegal if they cause superfluous injury.[1] There is a considerable body of opinion against the legality of the employment of torpedoes against merchant ships.[2]

The questions of *ruses de guerre* in naval warfare, such as the use of false flags, decoy ships and disguises must be considered as part of the general laws of naval warfare, as also must the general subject of the taking of prizes by captors into neutral ports.

If the submarine is to receive full recognition as a ship of war for all purposes, the rules applicable to it must be the same as for surface ships. There was a divergence of opinion as to the expediency of continuing to recognise the legitimacy of the use of false flags before the advent of the submarine, and a clear-cut division of opinion between States which recognised or declined to recognise the legitimacy of the taking of prizes into neutral ports to await prize proceedings. It may be that further exploration of these points will result in an agreement.

The German methods of submarine warfare failed partly by reason of the courage, tenacity and ingenuity of the British and Allied seamen of their navies and mercantile marines, partly by the assertion of neutrals of the violated majesty of the Law of Nations. No State can ultimately hope to triumph over the combined world-consciousness of "fairness, reason, justice and humanity." All is not fair in war; in sea warfare as in land warfare, "belligerents have not an unlimited right as to the choice of means for injuring the enemy." [3] *Kriegsräson geht nicht vor Kriegsrecht.*

[1] See *Declaration of St. Petersburg* (1868), *Hague Regulations for Land Warfare* (1907), Art. 23 (e).

[2] See authorities cited by J. W. Garner, *op. cit.*, p. 625.

[3] *Hague Regulations for Land Warfare*, 1907, Art. 22.

[6]

THE INTERNATIONAL LAW OF MINE WARFARE AT SEA*

*By Wolff Heintschel von Heinegg***

INTRODUCTION

Minelaying has long been an integral part of both strategic and operative naval planning. Naval mines are comparatively cheap and can be laid from all platforms, including submarines and aircraft. Besides their employment against the enemy's surface and subsurface forces they are particularly effective for cutting off sea lanes, coastal defence and the enforcement of a naval blockade.[1] Minefields on the high seas reshape nature, thus enabling belligerents to channelize and control shipping. A further effect is the tying down of enemy forces in time-consuming countermeasures.[2] For example, North Korea succeeded in delaying the operations of US/UN amphibious forces for more than one week by mining the coastal waters of *Wosang*.[3] In the Iraqi-Kuwaiti conflict of 1990–91, Iraq's naval forces had been neutralized very

* This a modified version of a German article on the same subject published in *Beiträge zum humanitären Völkerrecht, zur völkerrechtlichen Friedenssicherung und zum völkerrechtlichen Individualschutz*, (Institut für Friedenssicherungsrecht ed., 1993).

** Dr. iur., Ruhr-Universität Bochum, Federal Republic of Germany.

1 *Cf.* R.F. Hoffman, "Offensive Mine Warfare: A Forgotten Strategy?", 103 *U.S. Naval Institute Proceedings* 143–55 (1977); C.F. Horne III, "New Role for Mine Warfare", 108 *U.S. Naval Institute Proceedings* 34–40 (1982); T. Hooton, "Naval Mines: The Hidden Menace", 8 *Military Technology* 27–33 (1984); W. McDonald, "Mine Warfare: A Pillar of Maritime Strategy", 111 *U.S. Naval Institute Proceedings* 46–58 (1985); S.C. Truver, "Weapons That Wait . . . and Wait . . .", 114 *U.S. Naval Institute Proceedings* 32–46 (1988).

2 For the technical effort on mine countermeasures, *see* L. Gerken, *Mine Warfare Technology*, at 135 ff., 161 ff. (1989).

3 *See* M.W. Cagle & F.A. Manson, *The Sea War in Korea* 121 ff. (1957); L.E. Prina, "Deep Threat: The Navy is Flunking Higher on Mine Warfare", 26 *Sea Power* 41–48, 41 (1983). It may be added that this effect can also be achieved by merely feigning the laying of mines.

early on.[4] Still, the mines laid by Iraq formed a severe threat to the coalition's forces. On 18 February 1991, two US warships, the *USS Tripoli* and the *USS Princeton*, were damaged by Iraqi mines.[5]

Notwithstanding the military advantages, naval mines constitute a severe danger to third State shipping and the lives of innocent seamen. During and after the Russo-Japanese War of 1904–1905 – the first war in which naval mines were offensively employed[6] – numerous neutral merchant vessels were hit by mines that had broken loose from their moorings.[7] The history of the two World Wars provides countless examples of neutral merchant vessels sunk by mines.[8] Neutral merchant shipping has also been interfered with since 1945.[9] Although the Indo-Pakistani war (1971) lasted only two weeks, at least five neutral merchant vessels were sunk by mines.[10] In 1984, approximately nineteen ships struck mines in the Suez Canal and the Red Sea.[11] Eight merchant vessels not registered in Nicaragua were damaged by mines laid off the coast and ports of that State.[12] During the Iranian-Iraqi war (1980–1988), most of the damage inflicted by the belligerents on international merchant shipping was by aircraft attacks.[13] However, between

4 *Cf.* US Dept. of Defense, *Conduct of the Persian Gulf War (Final Report to Congress)* 268, 274 ff. (1992).

5 *Ibid.*, 284 ff.; *Int'l Herald Tribune* 19 February 1991 at 1.

6 *See* Hoffmann, *supra* note 1, at 145.

7 *See* G.K. Hartmann, *Weapons that Wait* 40 (1979); L. Rieß, "*Die Störungen der neutralen Schiffahrt im Russisch-Japanischen Kriege*", 3 *Marine-Rundschau* 1313–36, at 1319 ff. (1906).

8 *Cf.* J.S. Cowie, *Mines, Minelayers and Minelaying* 43 ff., 119 ff. (1949); H.S. Levie, *Mine Warfare at Sea* 65 ff., 77 ff. (1992); C.C. Hyde, 3 *International Law* 1936 ff. (2nd rev. ed., 1951); Hoffmann, *supra* note 1, at 145 ff.

9 The mining of *Haiphong* resulted in a most effective blockade. However, neutral merchant shipping did not suffer damages. *See* Levie, *supra* note 8, at 141 ff., 144 ff.; Prina, *supra* note 3, at 42.

10 *See* J. Rohwer, "*Der indisch-pakistanische Konflikt* 1971", 71 *Marine-Rundschau* 7–26, 24 ff. (1974).

11 *See* S.C. Truver, "Mines of August: An International Whodunit", 111 *U.S. Naval Institute Proceedings* 95–117, 116 ff. (1985); Levie, *supra* note 8, at 159 ff.

12 *See* J.M. Martin, "Sea Mines in Nicaragua", 116 *U.S. Naval Institute Proceedings* 111–16, 114 (1990); Levie, *supra* note 8, at 163.

13 *See* report by D.L. Peace, "Major Maritime Events in the Persian Gulf War", 82 *ASIL Proceedings* 146–54, 147 (1988): "Since 1984, more than 400 commercial ships have been attacked by the two belligerents, killing more than 200 seamen. Eighty-three percent of those ships were registered in neutral countries. Last year alone, 177 ships were hit by Iran and Iraq. . . . Between 1984 and 1987, Iran attacked 163 ships of more than 32 nationalities. . . . During the same period Iraq attacked 234 ships, almost all belonging to or chartered by Iran." *See also* statement by Vice Admiral J.R. Hogg before the Seapower and Strategic and Critical Materials Committee of the Committee on Armed Services, H.A.S.C. No. 100-150 at 13 ff.

1984 and 1987 more than eleven tankers and other ships were also damaged by Iraqi and Iranian mines.[14] Still, until today the only international instrument governing mine warfare at sea is the 1907 Hague Convention VIII relative to the Laying of Automatic Submarine Contact Mines (hereinafter: Hague Convention VIII).[15] In view of the technical developments that have taken place since 1907 it is, however, doubtful whether this treaty may still be considered adequate for securing the principle that the right of the parties to the conflict to choose methods and means of warfare is limited.[16]

I. THE 1907 HAGUE CONVENTION NO. VIII

The extensive use of mines during the Russo-Japanese War and the damage caused to innocent shipping, even after the end of hostilities, induced the delegates to the Second Hague Peace Conference to include the subject of naval mines in the agenda.[17] Already in 1907, the result of the Conference's deliberations, Hague Convention VIII, was considered a meagre compromise between the interests of the great and minor sea-powers.[18] Great Britain had urged outlawing the use of

---

(17 September 1987); E. Magnusson, "Caught in the Act", *Time Magazine* 10–13 (5 October 1987); R. Watson, "The Mines of August", *Newsweek* 8–11 (24 August 1987).

14 *See* R. Danziger, "The Persian Gulf Tanker War", 111 *U.S. Naval Institute Proceedings* 160–67, 162 (1985); Levie, *supra* note 8, at 167 ff.

15 For the English text, *see The Hague Conventions and Declarations of 1899 and 1907*, at 151–54 (J.B. Scott ed., 1915). In 1990, Sweden proposed to amend Protocol II of the 1980 Conventional Weapons Convention by a Protocol on naval mines; UN Doc. A/CN.10/141 of 8 May 1990. At the 1993 Review Conference, Sweden again proposed the adoption of a Protocol on naval mines.

16 For the applicability of this principle in the naval context, *see* US Dept. of the Navy, *The Commander's Handbook on the Law of Naval Operations* (hereinafter: NWP 9), paras. 8.1(1) and 9.1 (1989); Canadian Forces, *Law of Armed Conflict Manual (Second Draft)*, para. 707 (1) (1989); Federal Ministry of Defence of the Federal Republic of Germany, *Humanitarian Law in Armed Conflicts – Manual* (ZDv 15/2), para. 1017 (1992); E. Castrén, *The Present Law of War and Neutrality* 185 (1954); R.W. Tucker, *The Law of War and Neutrality at Sea* 45 ff. (1957); G.J.F. van Hegelsom, "Introductory Report", in *The Military Objective and the Principle of Distinction in the Law of Naval Warfare* 1–44, 3 (W. Heintschel von Heinegg ed., 1991).

17 *See* 9 J.H.W. Verzijl, *International Law in Historical Perspective* 297 (1978).

18 Hence, in the preamble, the contracting parties deplore that "the existing position of affairs makes it impossible to forbid the employment of automatic submarine contact mines". They also express their hope that, in the future, it will be possible "to formulate rules on the subject which shall ensure to the interests involved all the guarantees desirable".

automatic contact mines in open sea areas beyond the belligerents' territorial waters,[19] their reason being that it considered their use on the high seas prejudicial to its naval supremacy. The majority of States represented at the Hague, however, was unwilling to refrain from the use of this most effective means of naval warfare.[20]

Hence, Hague Convention VIII contains neither a general prohibition nor specific area limitations on the use of automatic contact mines. In particular, it lacks a rule on the mining of international straits which overlap the territorial waters of belligerents. Despite several proposals on the prohibition of mining in such straits submitted by the Netherlands,[21] the majority held that questions relating to straits were not covered by the mandate of the General Assembly's Third Committee or of the Conference, respectively.[22] The existing treaty regime on

[19] Article 4 of the British proposal that served as a basis for discussion (Annexe 9) provided: "*Les belligérants ne pourront se servir de mines sous-marines automatiques de contact que dans leurs eaux territoriales ou celles de leurs ennemis.*"

[20] The United States and Germany in particular were in favour of an explicit rule regarding the use of mines on the high seas. Hence, Germany proposed the following amendment to Article 4 of the British proposal: "*La pose des mines automatiques de contact sera aussi permise sur le théâtre de la guerre; sera considéré comme théâtre de la guerre l'espace de mer sur lequel se fait ou vient de se faire une opération de guerre ou sur lequel une pareille opération pourra avoir lieu par suite de la présence ou de l'approche des forces armées des deux belligérants.*" At first, the *Comité d'examen*, in Article 2 of its draft, had been in favour of the British proposal. After the US delegate Sperry had made clear the US standpoint, the Third Committee dispensed with any spatial limitation of the use of mines. In its report of 9 October 1907, the Third Committee explained this as follows: "*Cette solution n'a pas obtenu, devant la Commission, la majorité absolue des suffrages. L'alinéa 2 de l'article 4, qui établissait la différence mentionnée entre l'attaque et la défense, fut même rejeté, n'ayant obtenu que 10 voix contre 12 et 10 abstentions.*"

[21] The proposals by the Netherlands (Annexe 12 and 22) provided: "*En tous cas les détroits qui unissent deux mers libres ne peuvent pas être barrés.*" "*Dans aucun cas la communication entre deux mers libres ne peut être barrée entièrement et le passage ne sera permis qu'aux conditions qui seront indiquées par les autorités compétentes.*"

[22] Thus, the Third Committee, in its report to the plenary, stated: "*Après discussion, il fut jugé préférable de ne rien ajouter au texte du Règlement, mais de modifier le passage du Rapport qui parle de la résolution prise sur cette question par le Comité d'Examen.; on établirait dans le Rapport que les détroits sont restés en dehors les délibérations de la présente Conférence et, tout en réservant expressément les déclarations faites au sein du Comité par les Délégations des Etats-Unis d'Amérique, du Japon, de la Russie et de la Turquie, on indiquerait la conviction de voir appliquer sur les mines dont on pourrait se servir dans les détroits les conditions techniques adoptées par le présent Règlement.*"

certain straits was not to be jeopardized by general rules on mining. Hence, the Netherlands' proposals were rejected.[23] The only provision referring to the area of minelaying is Article 2, which prohibits the laying of automatic contact mines "off the coasts and ports of the enemy, with the sole object of intercepting commercial shipping".[24] The material scope of Hague Convention VIII is limited to automatic submarine contact mines (and to torpedoes[25]). To this effect, the Hague Convention differentiates between anchored and unanchored mines. According to Article 1 paragraph 1, the latter may not be laid, "except when they

[23] In the report of the *Comité d'examen*, these statements are summarized as follows: ". . . *la Délégation du Japon . . . qui, tout en déclarant qu'il n'aavait pas d'objection, si la règle s'appliquait seulement aux pays neutres, avait fait observer . . . que l'amendement néerlandais . . . lui paraissait pouvoirs' adapter peut-être aux conditions géographiques des Etats continentaux mais pas toujours à celles des Puissances insulaires. En raison de la configuration particulière du Japon . . . détroits qui sont partie intégrante de son territoire, mais qui tomberaient néanmois sous le coup de la définition inscrite dans le dit amendement, la Délégation japonaise ne pourrait adhérer à cette disposition. . . . le Contre-Admiral Sperry déclara, au nom de la Délégation des Etats-Unis d'Amérique, que 'prenant en considération le grand nombre d'îles qui composent le groupe des Philippines, et l'incertitude des rèsultats que pourrait avoir la stipulation en question, envisageant en outre les stipulations de traités comprises dans l'alinéa ajouté, il ne pourrait pas prendre part à la discussion comme, à son avis, la matière sort des limites de ses instructions . . . la Délégation ottomane . . . exposa que: 'La Délégation Impériale Ottomane croit de son devoir de déclarer qu'étant donné la situation exceptionnelle crée par les traités en vigeur aux détroits des Dardanelles et du Bosphore, détroits qui sont partie intégrante du territoire, le Gouvernement Impérial ne saurait, d'aucune façon, prendre un engagement quelconque tendant à limiter les moyens de défense qu'il pourrait juger nécessaire d'employer pour ces détroits, en cas de guerre ou dans le but de faire respecter sa neutralité'. . . . La Délégation de Russie estime que le régime de certains détroits étant réglé par des traités spéciaux, basés sur des considérations politiques, les stipulations concernant ces détroits ne peuvent faire l'objet d'une discussion. Quant à créer un régime spécial pour une partie des détroits en exceptant les autres, ce procédé lui paraîtrait inconséquent et très dangereux. La diversité de régime qui en résulterait tant pour les neutres que pour les belligérants, serait inévitablement une nouvelle source de conflits entre eux.*"

[24] With regard to the difficulties in establishing the subjective element, *see* Y. Dinstein, "The Laws of War at Sea", 10 *Israel Yearbook on Human Rights* 38–69, 45 (1980). J. Stone, *Legal Controls of International Conflict* 584 ff. (1954) states: "The escape from this prohibition provided by the reference to the *object* of the operation largely frustrated it from the start."

[25] The use of torpedoes is regulated in Art. 1 para. 3. Originally, the Conference's agenda was restricted to torpedoes. "Torpedo" used to be the general designation that also covered mines. However, in view of the existence of self-propelling destructive devices, the Conference in 1907 had already agreed on the notion of "mines".

are so constructed as to become harmless one hour at most after the person who laid them ceases to control them". The one hour limit is designed to enable warships to escape from pursuing enemy units by sowing mines.[26] According to Article 1 paragraph 2, anchored mines must "become harmless as soon as they have broken loose from their moorings". Furthermore, the belligerents must take "every possible precaution . . . for the security of peaceful, [*i.e.*, neutral], shipping"[27] (Article 3 para. 1). Finally, they should "undertake to do their utmost to render these mines harmless within a limited time, and, should they cease to be under surveillance, to notify the danger zones as soon as military exigencies permit, by a notice addressed to ship owners, which must also be communicated to the Governments through the diplomatic channel" (Article 3 para. 2).

In view of the unrestricted mine warfare during the two World Wars and technical developments in the field of naval mines[28] the continued legal relevance of Hague Convention VIII has become a matter of dispute.[29] Indeed, it is open to some doubt whether its provisions are applicable to bottom mines, modern anchored mines[30] or to remote-controlled minefields that are activated, *e.g.*, by means of VLF-transmissions. These sophisticated and highly discriminating mines are not covered by the wording of the Convention because they react on magnetic and acoustic signatures, or on changes in water pressure, rather than on mere physical contact.[31] However, it should be noted that the old automatic contact mine is still in use in most of the world's navies.[32]

26 *See* Dinstein, *supra* note 24, at 44; Cowie, *supra* note 8, at 170.

27 *See* Dinstein, *supra* note 24, at 45; Cowie, *supra* note 8, at 175.

28 *See* Levie, *supra* note 8, at 97 ff. With regard to the current technological state *see Jane's Underwater Warfare Systems* 43 (B. Blake ed., 1990); Hartmann, *supra* note 7, at 106 ff.; M. Griffiths, *The Hidden Menace* 60 ff., 144 ff. (1981).

29 Baxter in particular considers Hague Convention VIII to have become obsolete by *desuetude*; R.R. Baxter, "Treaties and Custom", 129 *Recueil des Cours* 25–104, 97 (1970-I). *See also* Stone, *supra* note 24, at 584 ff.

30 Since modern anchored mines may be employed in greater depths than bottom mines, they are a highly effective means of naval warfare.

31 According to a minority opinion, Hague Convention VIII may be applied to modern mines by analogy. *See* E. Rauch, *The Protocol Additional to the Geneva Conventions for the Protection of Victims of International Armed Conflicts and the United Nations Convention on the Law of the Sea: Repercussions on the Law of Naval Warfare* 116 (1984). However, according to the view taken here, it is not possible to apply an international treaty by way of analogy to subjects not expressly regulated therein.

32 Allegedly, the former Soviet Union still disposes of a vast number of automatic contact mines of the World War II type. Other States, such as Iraq, were supplied with these mines.

During armed conflicts since 1945, belligerents have employed modern sophisticated mines only in rare cases.[33] Hence, apart from the problem of whether Hague Convention VIII is of significance to modern mines, it seems proper to view that Convention *qua* customary law as far as the use of automatic contact mines is concerned.[34]

II. INTERNATIONAL LAW RESTRICTIONS ON MINELAYING AND THE USE OF MODERN MINES

Hague Convention VIII has thus acquired the status of customary international law governing the use of automatic contact mines. However, its provisions are not as such applicable to modern technology and other sophisticated mines. These are, it is submitted, governed by rules and principles of customary international law that also provide norms regarding the area where naval mines – antiquated or sophisticated – may be employed. It must be added that international law still lacks a general agreed definition of naval mines. Within NATO, a naval mine is defined as "an explosive device laid in the water, on the seabed or in the subsoil thereof, with the intention of damaging or sinking ships or of deterring shipping from entering an area."[35]

Since that definition is also employed in Article 2 of the Swedish proposal for amending the 1980 Conventional Weapons Convention,[36] it will also be used as a basis for the present article. Hence, the following means of naval warfare will not be dealt with:

- anti-aircraft systems launched from submarines, such as the French *SM Polyphem*;
- devices attached to the bottom of ships or to harbour installations by personnel operating underwater; and
- devices such as the "encapsulated torpedo" (CAPTOR) that are usually designated mines, but in fact are torpedoes.

[33] *See* Levie, *supra* note 8, at 135 ff.

[34] *E.g.*, during the Iraq-Kuwait conflict, the US expressly referred to Hague Convention VIII. *See* US Dept. of Defense, *supra* note 4, Appendix O. With regard to the customary status of the Convention, *see also* Levie, *supra* note 8, at 177 ff.; I. Bock, *Die Entwicklung des Minenrechts von 1900–1960* 75 ff. (1963); NWP 9, paras. 9.2 and 9.2.3; Canadian Draft Manual, para. 710 (1).

[35] *See* van Hegelsom, *supra* note 16, at 27.

[36] *See supra* note 15.

1. *Special Treaty Provisions*

Before elaborating on the rules and principles of international law governing modern conventional mines and the area of minelaying, a short reference to two important treaties is necessary. The use of nuclear mines is subject to the 1971 Seabed Treaty.[37] Although it is an arms control treaty, its provisions are binding not only in peacetime but also in times of armed conflict.[38] Accordingly, in sea areas beyond its own 12 nautical miles of territorial sea,[39] a belligerent may not "emplant or emplace on the sea-bed and the ocean floor and in the subsoil thereof . . . any nuclear weapons", including nuclear mines.[40] This prohibition also covers tethered[41] tactical nuclear mines of low yield that are used for anti-submarine purposes.[42] The contrary view, taken by Professor O'Connell,[43] is incompatible with the wording ("nuclear weapons") as well as with the object and purpose of the Seabed Treaty.[44]

The second treaty relevant in this respect is Protocol II of the 1980 Conventional Weapons Convention.[45] Article 1 refers, inter alia, to "mines laid to interdict beaches". In some cases such mines are laid in waters that are not deeper than five metres. Still, Protocol II does

[37] Treaty on the Prohibition of the Emplacement of Nuclear Weapons and Other Weapons of Mass Destruction on the Seabed and the Ocean Floor and in the Subsoil Thereof, London, Moscow, Washington, 11 February 1971. For the text, *see* [1970] *UN Juridical Y.B.* 121–24.

[38] *See* NWP 9, para. 10.2.2; L. Migliorino, "Commentary on the 1971 Seabed Treaty", in *The Law of Naval Warfare* 615–22, 620 (N. Ronzitti ed., 1988).

[39] According to Article II the 12 nautical mile limit applies even when the breadth of the territorial sea is less than 12 nm.

[40] On 7 October 1969, *e.g.*, the US delegate declared: "The Treaty would therefore prohibit, inter alia, mines that were anchored to or emplaced on the sea-bed."; Documents on Disarmament 479 (1969). *See also* A.G.Y. Thorpe, "Mine Warfare at Sea – Some Legal Aspects of the Future", 18 *Ocean Development and International Law* 255–78, 262 (1987).

[41] Drifting or floating mines are neither "emplanted" nor "emplaced" in the sense of Article I. *See* E. Rauch, *supra* note 31, at 131; A.G.Y. Thorpe, *supra* note 40, at 262.

[42] *Ibid.*

[43] D.P. O'Connell, *The Influence of Law on Seapower* 157 (1975).

[44] *See* T.A. Clingan, Jr., "Submarine Mines in International Law", in *Law of Naval Operations* 351–61, 354 ff. (H.B. Robertson ed., 1991); Thorpe, *supra* note 40.

[45] Convention on Prohibitions or Restrictions on the Use of Certain Conventional Weapons which May Be Deemed to Be Excessively Injurious or to Have Indiscriminate Effects, Geneva, 10 October 1980; Protocol on Prohibitions or Restrictions on the Use of Mines, Booby Traps and Other Devices (Protocol II). For text, *see*, *The Laws of Armed Conflicts*, 179 ff. (D. Schindler & J. Toman eds., 3rd. ed., 1988).

not apply to naval warfare, but rather to anti-personnel mines and land warfare.[46]

2. *Area of Minelaying*

Mines may be laid only within the general area of naval operations.[47] Accordingly, they may not be laid in the territorial seas[48] and internal waters of States not parties to the conflict. This also holds true with regard to archipelagic waters[49] since they are subject to the sovereignty of the archipelagic State. In addition, mining shall not have the practical effect of preventing passage between neutral and international waters. In principle, the Exclusive Economic Zones (EEZ) and continental shelf areas of neutral States are part of the general area of naval operations.[50] However, the belligerents shall have due regard for the rights of the coastal State concerning the exploration and exploitation of the natural resources in such sea areas. In particular, there should be no interference with artificial islands, installations, structures and safety zones. In any event, if mines are laid within the EEZ or on the continental shelf of a neutral State, the belligerent is obliged to notify that State.[51]

In regard to mining of the high seas, there seem to exist few restrictions. Article 3 of Hague Convention VIII, in particular, obviously accepts the implication that "belligerents may sow anchored automatic contact mines anywhere upon the high seas."[52] It should, however, be

[46] *See* Levie, *supra* note 8, at 138.

[47] For the "general area of naval operations", *see* H.B. Robertson, Jr., "Theatre of Operations in Naval Warfare – Different Maritime Areas", paper presented at the Round Table of Experts on International Humanitarian Law Applicable to Armed Conflicts at Sea, Ottawa, 29 September–1 October 1992 (forthcoming [hereinafter: Round Table of Experts]); C.J. Colombos, *The International Law of the Sea* 486 ff. (5th ed., 1962).

[48] It may be added that according to military manuals, the 12 nautical mile territorial sea is generally accepted as in accordance with international law and must be respected in times of armed conflict. *See* NWP 9, para. 7.3.4.2; Canadian Draft Manual, para. 706; ZDv 15/2, para. 1010, 1118.

[49] *See* NWP 9, para. 7.3.6; Canadian Draft Manual, para. 1509; ZDv 15/2, para. 1011.

[50] Canadian Draft Manual, para. 1509; ZDv 15/2, para. 1012 ff.

[51] Canadian Draft Manual, para. 1509 (1); ZDv 15/2, para. 1012 ff. The Round Table of Experts (*supra* note 47) arrived at similar conclusions to be published in 1994.

[52] Tucker, *supra* note 16, at 303.

noted that according to the preamble, the contracting States were "[i]nspired by the principle of the freedom of sea routes, the common highway of all nations". The generally accepted rules on treaty interpretation, as laid down in Article 31 of the 1969 Vienna Convention on the Law of Treaties, would allow taking the preamble into consideration.[53] It would thus be possible to deduce a prohibition of unrestricted mining in the high seas. On the other hand, this conclusion may be doubted in view of the practice of States during the two World Wars.[54] If, however, recent statements on the law of naval warfare are taken into account, it becomes quite obvious that even though international law still lacks a general and comprehensive prohibition, the right of belligerents to lay mines in the high seas is not unlimited.[55] For example, the US Navy *Commander's Handbook on the Law of Naval Operations* (hereinafter: NWP 9) expressly states that "mining of areas of indefinite extent in international waters is prohibited. Reasonably limited barred areas may be established by naval mines, provided neutral shipping retains an alternate route around or through such an area with reasonable assurance of safety."[56]

The provisions of the German manual provide that "all feasible precautions shall be observed for the safety of peaceful shipping" and that "the shipping lanes of neutral and non-belligerent states shall be kept open to an appropriate extent".[57] Hence, unless free and safe passage for peaceful shipping is provided for, the mining of the high seas is contrary to international law.[58] Of course, during an international

53 1155 *U.N.T.S.* 331 ff.

54 Tucker states: "Indeed, the severe condemnation of war zones from which neutral shipping is barred under threat of destruction from submarines and aircraft has not infrequently been accompanied by the acquiescence to zones from which neutral shipping is barred by means almost equally destructive"; R.W. Tucker, *supra* note 16, at 303.

55 *See* Thorpe, *supra* note 40, at 264.

56 NWP 9, para. 9.2.3 (8).

57 ZDv 15/2, paras. 1040, 1042.

58 *See* Levie, *supra* note 8, at 41 ff., 177; G. Hoog, "Mines", in 3 *Encyclopedia of Public International Law* 283–85, 284 (R. Bernhardt, ed., 1982). The corresponding *opinio juris* can also be deduced from the practice of States during the Iranian-Iraqi war. States not parties to that conflict, by deploying naval units in the Persian Gulf, made abundantly clear that they were not willing to acquiesce to a restriction of the freedom of navigation by unrestricted mine warfare. The Round Table of Experts in its Draft Harmonised Text [hereinafter: Draft Harmonised Text] (para. 88), has agreed as follows: "The minelaying States shall respect the high seas freedoms in all areas where such freedoms are applicable and pay due regard to legitimate uses of the seas by, *inter alia*, providing safe alternative routes for shipping of neutral States."

armed conflict at sea, freedom of navigation is not absolute.[59] Still, the parties to the conflict are not entitled to nullify it.

Furthermore, another issue that had remained unsettled at the Hague now seems to have been clarified: the mining of international straits. In view of the provisions of the 1982 UN Convention on the Law of the Sea (hereinafter: UNCLOS III) guaranteeing a non-suspendable right of transit passage, such mining constitutes a violation of international law if the belligerents do not provide for safe alternative routes of similar convenience.[60] It may be added in this context that at least in the first months of World War II free passage through international straits, as well as piloting services, were provided for by the belligerents.[61] The conditions under which the right of transit passage may be exercised will depend on the prevailing circumstances at the time. It is probable that vital security interests will entitle a belligerent to close an international strait temporarily. Such closure, however, will be legitimate only in exceptional cases and may not last indefinitely.

59 *See* Thorpe, *supra* note 40, at 257. Schwarzenberger holds: "On the high seas, fields of anchored automatic contact mines, even if announced and supervised, amount to a purported occupation of a portion of the high seas of indefinite duration. It appears impossible to square pretensions of this character with the rules underlying the principles of the freedom of the seas; for they deny the free use of the mined area of the high seas not only to the enemy, but also to neutral shipping at large"; 2 G. Schwarzenberger, *International Law as Applied by International Courts and Tribunals* 417 (1968). However, this position finds no foundation in State practice.

60 NWP 9, para. 9.2.3 (6) provides: "Naval mines may be employed to channelize neutral shipping, but not in a manner to impede the transit passage of international straits or archipelagic sea lanes passage of archipelagic waters by such shipping." Para. 89 of the Draft Harmonised Text reads as follows: "Transit passage through international straits and passage through waters subject to the right of archipelagic sea lanes passage shall not be impeded unless safe and convenient alternative routes are provided." *See also* ZDv 15/2, para. 1042; Hoog, *supra* note 58; L.M. Alexander, "International Straits", in *The Law of Naval Operations*, *supra* note 44, at 91–108, 94 ff.

61 According to a compilation of secret documents prepared by the German Naval High Command, free passages and piloting services were provided by the belligerents in the following straits: Skagerrak, the Sound and the Great Belt, the Kattegat, the Dover Strait, and the Firth of Forth. *See* Oberkommando der Kriegsmarine, *Urkundenbuch zum Seekriegsrecht* (Record of the Law of Sea Warfare) (1 September 1939 until 31 August 1940), documents Nos. 340, 345, 346, 348, 354, 361 (1941). *See also* Levie, *supra* note 8, at 77 ff.

3. *Rules on Naval Minelaying*

The provisions of Hague Convention VIII are neither applicable as such, nor by analogy, to mines other than automatic contact mines. Nevertheless, there is general consensus in State practice, as well as in the literature, that the customary principles that can be derived from Articles 1, 2, 3, and 5 of the above Convention must be taken into account when laying modern naval mines.[62] To this effect, the German manual provides as follows: "Any mode of mine laying . . . shall be subject to the principles of effective surveillance, risk control and warning. In particular, all feasible measures of precaution shall be observed for the safety of peaceful navigation."[63]

This may not be considered an exhaustive enumeration of the duties incumbent upon a State engaged in mine-laying. Rather, the general principles of the (maritime) *jus in bello* equally apply,[64] in particular the principle of distinction.[65] Any indiscriminate use of mines, *i.e.*, those that are not or cannot be directed against a military objective, is contrary to international law.

A. *The Principle of Effective Surveillance*

The principle of effective surveillance is designed to ensure the principle of warning and the duty of clearing mined areas after the cessation of hostilities. This can be deduced from Articles 3 and 5 of Hague Convention VIII. In particular, it implies that the mine-laying belligerent is obliged to carefully record the location of minefields.[66] Otherwise,

[62] Thus, NWP 9, para. 9.2, provides: "the general principles of law embodied in the 1907 Convention continue to serve as a guide to lawful employment of naval mines." *See also* Canadian Draft Manual, para. 710 (2); Dinstein, *supra* note 24, at 46; Thorpe, *supra* note 40, at 259 f.; P. Rowe, *Defence – The Legal Implications* 128 (1987); Clingan, Jr., *supra* note 44, at 353; O. Bring, "Regulating Conventional Weapons in the Future – Humanitarian Law or Arms Control?", 24 *J. Peace Research* 275–86, 283 (1987); O'Connell, *supra* note 43, at 157.

[63] ZDv 15/2, para. 1040.

[64] *See* NWP 9, para. 9.2; ZDv 15/2, para. 1017; Rauch, *supra* note 31, at 130.

[65] Art. 3 of the Swedish proposal provides: "The indiscriminate use of mines is prohibited. Indiscriminate use is (a) any use of mines which is not or cannot be directed against a military objective; (b) any laying of mines which may be expected to cause incidental loss of civilian life, injury to civilians, or a combination thereof which would be excessive in relation to the concrete and direct military advantage anticipated."

[66] NWP 9, para. 9.2.3 provides: "The location of minefields must be carefully recorded to ensure accurate notification and to facilitate subsequent removal and/or deactivation." *See also* para. 84 of the Draft Harmonised Text: "Belligerents shall record

the responsibilities for warning and mine clearance would be nullified. Moreover, belligerents are obliged to ensure, *e.g.*, by random tests, that its mines are programmed correctly and will not be activated by others than the envisaged signatures.

B. *Risk Control*

Closely related to the foregoing is the principle of risk control. It can be deduced from Articles 1 and 3 of Hague Convention VIII. Risk control does not mean that the mine-layer would be obliged to exercise permanent surveillance over a minefield. It is sufficient if he be able to effectively manage the dangers that minefields constitute for peaceful shipping. The concrete duties resulting from the principle of risk control may, therefore, vary according to the type of mine used. Controlled mines, in particular remotely controlled minefields that are designed for ASW purposes, do not generally pose a serious threat to peaceful surface shipping.[67] Therefore, the mine-laying State will normally comply with the principle of risk control by equipping the minefield with a remote control device. It must be stressed that, in practice, remote-controlled minefields will be laid only if the control system is nearly infallible. Otherwise, the envisaged military advantage of long duration and flexibility cannot be achieved. Control systems dependent on VLF transmissions from land, require a considerable amount of energy and will probably not be absolutely fool-proof against failure.[68] Hence, the mines must also be equipped with a deactivation device. If the control system breaks down, the belligerent is, of course, obliged to issue an appropriate warning. If other than (remote) controlled mines are used, anchored mines that are not remote-controlled must become deactivated as soon as they have broken loose from their moorings,[69] which means

---

the locations where they have laid mines." *See also* Article 7 para. 1 of the Swedish proposal: "The parties to a conflict shall record all zones where they have laid mines."

[67] In NWP 9, para. 9.2.1, the differences between controlled and armed mines are explained as follows: "Armed mines are either emplaced with all safety devices withdrawn or are armed following emplacement, so as to detonate when preset parameters (if any) are satisfied. Controlled mines (including mines possessing remote control activation devices) have no destructive capability until affirmatively activated by some form of controlled arming order (whereupon they become armed mines)." *See also* Dinstein, *supra* note 24, at 46.

[68] *See Jane's Underwater Warfare Systems*, *supra* note 28, at 43.

[69] Art. 1 para. 2 Hague Convention VIII; NWP 9, para. 9.2.3. Art. 4 of the Swedish proposal states: "It is prohibited to lay anchored mines which do not become harmless as soon as they have broken loose from their moorings."

they must be equipped with a self-destruction or some deactivation device.[70] If Article 1 paragraph 7 of the Hague Convention VIII were applied to bottom mines that are designed to explode upon contact by magnetic or acoustic impulses and/or changes in the water pressure they would have to become harmless "one hour at most after the person who laid them ceases to control them".[71] Customary international law, however, has not developed in that direction. Modern bottom mines are highly sophisticated weapons systems that can be programmed to react on specific types of ships and even on a single ship if sufficient data are available.[72] Hence, it is unnecessary for such mines to become harmless within one hour after their positioning on the ocean floor. When it is impossible to ensure by programming that a mine will be directed strictly at military objectives it will have to be equipped with some kind of deactivation device.[73] Due to the sometimes overestimated[74] dangers

70 While the mines used for the blockade of *Haiphong* were equipped with such devices, the mines laid by Iran in the Gulf war (1980–88) were not deactivated after they had broken loose from their moorings.

71 Professor Dinstein seems to be in favour of a rule to that effect: "The rule must be that the use of any mine – antiquated or sophisticated – is permissible only if they are anchored (even though the anchor may enable them to home in on a ship within a given range), and on condition that they become harmless as soon as they are disconnected from their moorings"; Dinstein, *supra* note 24, at 46. For the contrary view, *see* H.S. Levie, "Means and Methods of Combat at Sea", 14 *Syracuse J. Int'l L. & Com.* 727–39, 732 ff. (1988); Thorpe, *supra* note 40, at 260 ff.

72 See *Jane's Underwater Warfare Systems*, *supra* note 28, at 43.

73 NWP 9, para. 9.2.3. (4): "Unanchored mines otherwise affixed or imbedded in the bottom must become harmless within an hour after loss of control over them." Art. 4 para. 3 of the Swedish proposal provides: "It is prohibited to lay mines, unless an effective neutralizing mechanism is used on each mine, that is to say, a self-actuating or remote controlled mechanism which is designed to render a mine harmless or cause it to destroy itself when it is anticipated that the mine will no longer serve that military purpose for which it was placed in position, or at the latest 2 years after such emplacement."

74 In the course of the proceedings of the *Corfu Channel* case it became evident that drifting automatic contact mines were less dangerous than generally believed. Cowie states: "Incidentally, the legend has grown that all drifting mines are dangerous to shipping, but this is by no means the case. When moored, mines are normally kept dangerous due to the tension in the mooring rope, and if they break adrift the tension is relaxed and a strong spring takes charge, so opening a switch in the circuit between the firing battery and the detonator. If a mine breaks adrift with a length of mooring trailing from it, that mooring may get caught up on rocks, pier structures, and so forth; the mine in effect becomes moored once more and so liable to detonate if one of the horns is struck. . . . Finally, it is extremely difficult to ram a mine or any small object floating freely on the surface

they pose to peaceful shipping, drifting or floating mines still have to become harmless within one hour.[75]

C. *Warning*

The necessity for warning becomes operative as soon as effective control of the risk involved is not feasible. The obligation to issue warnings regarding armed or dangerous minefields is, however, not absolute. The belligerent is obligated to indicate danger zones or the position of a minefield only if "military exigencies permit".[76] This does not mean that the belligerent may refrain from issuing effective warnings because he may still possibly have a military advantage. Rather, according to the general principles of maritime *jus in bello*, the military advantage anticipated under the prevailing circumstances must be definite.[77] In case of doubt, the limits of the mined areas must be notified at least roughly. Judge Schwebel, in his dissenting opinion to the *Nicaragua* Judgment, has summarized these obligations in a manner that may be applicable for times of armed conflict as well:

> However, as against third States whose shipping was damaged or whose nationals were injured by mines laid by or on behalf of the United States, the international responsibility of the United States

---

of the sea. The chances of a ship being sunk or damaged by a mine which has broken adrift from its moorings are in fact remote, but none the less the prudent seaman will give them a clear berth."; Cowie, *supra* note 8, at 188 ff.

75 The Draft Harmonised Text provides in para. 82: "It is forbidden to use free-floating mines unless: (a) they are directed against a military objective; *and* (b) they become harmless within an hour after loss of control over them." *See also* Art. 4 para. 4 of the Swedish proposal: "It is prohibited to use drifting mines."

76 Art. 3 para. 2, Hague Convention No. VIII; NWP 9, para. 9.2.3 (1). Art. 6 para. 1 of the Swedish proposal provides: "Effective warning, through notification of danger zones, of any use of activated mines which may affect neutral or non-belligerent shipping or vessels protected under Art. 4, shall be given as soon as military considerations permit." Para. 83 of the Draft Harmonised Text reads: "The laying of armed mines or the arming of prelaid mines must be notified unless the mines can only be exploded by ships which are military objectives." This implies that warning need not be given in respect of such sophisticated and discriminating mines.

77 This formulation stems from Art. 52 para. 2 of the 1977 Additional Protocol to the Geneva Conventions of 12 August 1949. For text, *see* 16 *I.L.M.* 1391 ff. (1977). The definition of military objectives contained in that provision is now generally accepted as customary international law and thus applicable in naval warfare. *See* NWP 9, para. 8.1.1; Canadian Draft Manual, para. 714 (1); ZDv 15/2, para. 1017.

> may arise. Third States were and are entitled to carry on commerce with Nicaragua and their ships are entitled to make use of Nicaraguan ports. If the United States were to be justified in taking blockade-like measures against Nicaraguan ports, as by mining, it could only be so if its mining of Nicaraguan ports were publicly and officially announced by it and if international shipping were duly warned by it about the fact that mines would be or had been laid in specified waters; . . . international shipping was not duly warned by it in a timely, official manner.[78]

The form in which these warnings must be issued will depend upon the circumstances of each case. In general, it will suffice to inform international shipping by the usual means, as *e.g.*, the "Notices to Mariners". If, however, a vessel that may not legitimately be considered a military objective is about to enter a mined sea area, the belligerent responsible for the mining will have to do its utmost to prevent that ship from proceeding, inter alia, by making use of internationally recognized emergency frequencies. Article 3 paragraph 2 Hague Convention VIII also obliges the belligerents to communicate details on danger zones to the "Governments through the diplomatic channel". In view of the advanced state of modern communications it is, however, doubtful whether such formal notification is still necessary.[79]

D. *Precautionary Measures*

In principle, a belligerent is required to allow peaceful shipping to leave the sea area that is, or is about to be, mined.[80] Since it is not an absolute obligation, the belligerent may refrain from granting such a period of grace if his otherwise anticipated military advantage will be jeopardized. If the safety of peaceful shipping cannot be ensured by any of the means described above, the belligerent is obliged to take additional

[78] [1986] *I.C.J. Rep.* 379 ff.

[79] According to the judgment of the ICJ in the *Nicaragua* case, obviously any form of information is to be considered sufficient as long as it is effective; *see* [1986], *I.C.J. Rep.*, *ibid.*, para. 292.

[80] The US, when mining Haiphong, employed mines that were activated three days after they had been laid. Thus, innocent shipping was able to leave Haiphong unmolested; *see* Levie, *supra* note 8, at 147. Para. 85 of the Draft Harmonised Text provides: "Mining operations in [internal waters, territorial sea or archipelagic waters] of a belligerent State should provide, when the mining is first executed, for free exit of shipping of neutral States."

precautionary measures.[81] This may imply the responsibility to designate safe sea lanes or to provide piloting.

E. *The Prohibition of Mine Laying with the Sole Object of Intercepting Commercial Shipping*

According to a widely held view, the prohibition of Article 2 Hague Convention VIII also applies to modern mines.[82] Thus, it is forbidden to lay mines "off the coast and ports of the enemy, with the sole object of intercepting commercial shipping". In practice, a violation of this prohibition rarely occurs. In any event, only in exceptional cases will mining activities be exclusively motivated by considerations of economic warfare.[83] Still, even under conditions of modern naval warfare, this prohibition is not meaningless. It implies that the offensive use of mines for the sole object of conducting economic warfare at sea is strictly forbidden.[84] Of course, while mines may be employed for establishing and enforcing a naval blockade they may not, however, be the only means for so doing. If mines are used with the intent of blockading, the belligerent is obliged to deploy warships or other units of his armed forces near the blockaded area.[85] The rationale behind that obligation is to ensure a place of safety within reach of ships in distress.

4. *Removal of Mines*

At the close of the armed conflict, the former belligerents must do their utmost to remove the mines they have laid.[86] This responsibility

81 To this effect Art. 6 para. 2 of the Swedish proposal provides: "When mines are employed, all feasible precautions shall be taken for the safety of vessels and shipping protected under Art. 4. Feasible precautions are those precautions which are practicable or practically possible taking into account all circumstances ruling at the time, including humanitarian and military considerations."

82 *See* NWP 9, para. 9.2.3 (7); Canadian Draft Manual, para. 710; ZDv 15/2, para. 1042; Dinstein, *supra* note 24, at 45.

83 *See* Levie, *supra* note 8, at 32 ff.; Dinstein, *supra* note 24, at 45; Stone, *supra* note 24, at 583 ff. For an evaluation of Art. 2 from a purely military point of view, *see* W. Heintschel v. Heinegg, "Exclusion Zones, Mines, Abuse of Neutral Flags and Insignia, Booty in Naval Warfare", in *The Gladisch Committee on the Law of Naval Warfare* 39–59, 46 ff. (D. Fleck ed., 1990).

84 *See* NWP 9, paras. 7.7.5 and 9.2.3; Dinstein, *supra* note 24, at 45.

85 *See* ZDv 15/2, para. 1053.

86 Art. 5 para. 1 Hague Convention No. VIII; NWP 9, para. 9.2.3; Canadian Draft Manual, para. 710; ZDv 15/2, para. 1043.

is a generally accepted practice in customary international law.[87] Accordingly, each belligerent is obliged to remove the mines it laid in its own territorial waters and on the high seas. Regarding those mines laid in a belligerent's own territorial waters, it is sufficient to merely render them harmless. Minefields under remote control have only to be switched off. Those mines laid in the territorial waters of the former adversary may be removed only with the latter's express consent. Mine clearing operations in a State's territorial sea without permission by the coastal State is a violation of its territorial sovereignty.[88] If the coastal State is unwilling to permit mine clearing operations by the other State, the latter is, in principle, obliged to notify the former of the locations of the mines.[89] In practice, the performance of this obligation may lead to considerable problems. The mine-laying State may, for security reasons, be unwilling to provide its former adversary with information on the construction of the mines it uses. International law provides no rules for such cases, beyond the general liability to resolve international disputes by peaceful means. Finally, if a State is unable to remove the mines it has laid because it lacks the necessary technical means, it shall ask other States for assistance.[90]

[87] In one of the Protocols of the US-North Vietnamese Agreement of 27 January 1973, the US accepted international responsibility for the removal of approximately 8,000 mines it had laid in North Vietnamese coastal waters. *Operation End Sweep* started in February 1973 and was completed in July 1973. Egypt, after the end of the Yom Kippur war (1973), also accepted its responsibility for the removal of mines it had laid in the Suez Canal and in the Red Sea. During the Gulf War (1980–88) Iran, on 13 August 1987, announced it would sweep mines in international waters of the Persian Gulf; *The Times* (London), 1 September 1987, at 6. For further references, *see* Levie, *supra* note 8, at 49 ff., 75, 88, 122, 149 ff.

[88] This follows from the Judgment of the ICJ in the Corfu Channel Case, [1949] *I.C.J. Rep.*, 4 ff.

[89] *See* Art. 7 para. 2 of the Swedish proposal:
"All such records shall be retained by the parties who shall
(a) as soon as possible, by mutual agreement, provide for the release of information concerning the location of activated mines, particularly in agreements governing the cessation of hostilities;
(b) immediately after the cessation of active hostilities take all necessary and appropriate measures including the use of such records, to protect civilians from the effects of mines; and make available to each other and to the Secretary-General of the United Nations all information in their possession concerning the location of activated mines."

[90] *E.g.*, after the end of the Yom Kippur War, Egypt asked the US for assistance. Within three months (April to June 1973) the waters were cleared of the mines. *See* Levie, *supra* note 8, at 157 ff; H. Kowark & S.M. Taylor, "*Die Räumung des Suezkanals*", 71 *Marine-Rundschau* 724–36 (1974).

India, after the close of the 1971 conflict with Pakistan, removed the mines it

III. REMOVAL OF MINES BY NEUTRALS

Of course, the parties to an ongoing international armed conflict at sea do not always fulfil the above obligations. Drifting mines are laid in sea areas with a high traffic density. In many cases, the mines used can neither be directed at military objectives nor are they equipped with effective deactivation devices. In such instances, the question arises whether neutral States are entitled to protect their shipping by removing the illegally laid mines. The practice of States during the Iran-Iraq War has, it is submitted, contributed to the emergence of a rule of international law to this effect.

On 24 July 1987, the reflagged tanker *Bridgeton* hit a mine 18 nautical miles off the Iranian island *Farsi*. Almost immediately the US sent mine experts to assist Saudi Arabia and Kuwait in removing the mines sowed off their respective coasts and ports. It soon became clear, however, that the mines could be removed only if the necessary equipment were available. Therefore, the US started deploying its "airborne mine countermeasure units (AMCM)" in the area.[91] On a request by the US, Great Britain and France also deployed naval units in the Gulf region to protect peaceful shipping and to remove mines in international sea lanes.[92] On 21 September 1987, two US helicopters detected an Iranian landing craft, the *Iran Ajr*, approximately 50 nautical miles northeast of Bahrain. After verifying that the *Iran Ajr* was engaged in mining activities they opened fire. Five members of the Iranian crew were killed, the other 26 were captured.[93] While the Iranian government accused the US of having killed innocent seamen, the Legal Adviser of the Department of State, Judge A. Sofaer, justified the attack on the *Iran Ajr* as follows:

---

had laid with the assistance of the former Soviet Union. *See* Ch.H. Petersen, "Die Operationen der sowjetischen Marine für die Wiedereröffnung der Häfen in Bangladesch. März 1972–Juni 1974", 72 *Marine-Rundschau* 665–76 (1975).

Art. 8 of the Swedish proposal provides: "After the cessation of active hostilities, the parties shall endeavour to reach agreement both among themselves and, where appropriate, with other States and with international organizations, on the provision of information and technical and material assistance – including, in appropriate circumstances, joint operations – necessary to remove or otherwise render ineffective mines placed in position during the conflict."

91 *See* Levie, *supra* note 8, at 167 ff.

92 *See* A. Gioia & N. Ronzitti, "The Law of Neutrality: Third States' Commercial Rights and Duties", in *The Gulf War of 1980–1988* 221–42, 223 ff., 237 ff. (I.F. Dekker & H.H.G. Post eds., 1992);Levie, *supra* note 8, at 168.

93 *See* D.L. Peace, *supra* note 13, at 151; E. Magnusson, "Caught in the Act", *Time Magazine* 10 (5 October 1987).

> Where, as here, a government engages in manifestly illegal use of armed force, international law entitles the victim to act in self-defense. The response must be necessary and proportionate. The United States' action plainly comported with these requirements. The United States acted to stop the unlawful act itself, and an imminent threat to U.S. shipping was thereby avoided. The U.S. immediately reported this action to the Security Council pursuant to Article 51 of the U.N. Charter and stated its hope and intention that the incident not be followed by additional hostilities.[94]

Regarding the removal of mines in areas beyond the territorial waters of the belligerents, there is unanimous agreement in the literature that the above activities were in compliance with international law.[95] State practice supports this view, since even the parties to the conflict in the Gulf War acquiesced in the removal of mines by neutral States.[96] Possible justifications are either the inherent right of self-defence[97] or the right to enforce the freedom of navigation against illegal interference by belligerent mining.[98]

A far more difficult question is whether neutral States would be entitled to remove mines illegally laid in international straits. So far the only precedent is the *Corfu Channel* case.[99] The facts are well-known. On 13 November 1946, Great Britain removed 22 mines in the Corfu Channel because Albania had refused to clear the mines itself or give permission to Great Britain to do so. The ICJ held Albania responsible for damages caused to two British warships that had struck mines when passing through the Corfu Channel.[100] The British action, however, was also considered illegal because it constituted a violation of Albania's sovereignty. The Court was not prepared to accept any

94 Quoted *in* Th. Meron, "Neutrality, the Right of Shipping and the Use of Force in the Persian Gulf – Remarks", 82 *ASIL Proceedings* 164–69, 164 (1988).

95 *See* N. Ronzitti, "La guerre du Golfe, le déminage et la circulation des navires", 33 *Annuaire Français de Droit International* 647–62, 651 (1987); M.H. Nordquist & M.G. Wachenfeld, "Legal Aspects of Reflagging Kuwaiti Tankers and Laying of Mines in the Persian Gulf", 31 *German Y.B. Int'l L.* 138–64, 162 ff. (1988); Gioia & Ronzitti, *supra* note 92, at 237; Meron, *supra* note 94, at 168.

96 Originally, Iran had denied having laid mines for purposes other than coastal defence against US (!) attacks. When mines were detected in Omani waters, however, Iran proposed to remove them from Omani territorial waters. *See* Levie, *supra* note 8, at 168.

97 Nordquist & Wachenfeld, *supra* note 95, at 162 ff.; Meron, *supra* note 94, at 167 ff.

98 Ronzitti, *supra* note 95, at 651.

99 [1949] *I.C.J. Rep.* 4 ff.

100 *Ibid.*, 22.

justification for the British action. If the *Corfu Channel* decision were still to be considered a valid legal yardstick, the removal of mines in international straits overlapping the territorial sea of the riparian State would be contrary to international law, whether or not the mines were laid in accordance with the maritime *jus in bello*. In view of the new rules on non-suspendable transit passage and of the importance of international straits for international commerce, it is open to doubt whether the mere reference to the sovereignty of the belligerent riparian State is sufficient to consider the removal of illegally laid mines by neutral States a violation of international law. The right of transit passage may be infringed upon only by measures that comply with the maritime *jus in bello*. Therefore, if the belligerents are not willing to observe these rules and if there exist no alternative routes of similar convenience, third States are entitled to remove mines in international straits in order to enforce their right of transit passage.[101]

IV. EXCURSUS: MINELAYING PRIOR TO THE OUTBREAK OF AN INTERNATIONAL ARMED CONFLICT

The rules and principles elaborated upon above relate to the employment of naval mines during an international armed conflict. Since, however, the laying of mines consumes a considerable amount of time, it may become necessary to start mining the sea prior to the actual outbreak of armed conflict. In the process of naval planning in times of crisis, the armed forces will mine sensitive areas of their own territorial waters in order to be able to effectively protect them as soon as armed hostilities commence. For military reasons, it may even be deemed necessary to mine parts of the seas beyond the coastal State's sovereignty. This holds especially true for anti-submarine mines. Both the US and German manuals contain rules on minelaying prior to the outbreak of an international armed conflict.[102]

1. *Minelaying in One's Own Territorial Waters*

According to these two manuals, the laying of mines is permissible in the territorial sea, in the internal waters and in the archipelagic waters

[101] Accordingly, para. 91 of the Draft Harmonised Text provides: "Neutral States do not commit an act inconsistent with the laws of neutrality by clearing mines laid in violation of the rules of this document."

[102] NWP 9, para. 9.2.2; ZDv 15/2, para. 1041.

of the mine-laying State. The question arises as to whether and to what extent these rules are compatible with the international law of the sea, where the territorial sea is concerned. While a coastal State's sovereignty extends over its territorial sea, it is not free to suspend the right of innocent passage.[103] Innocent passage may be temporarily suspended, but only in exceptional cases.[104] The ICJ in the *Nicaragua* case emphasized that

> if a State lays mines in any waters whatever in which the vessels of another State have rights of access or passage, and fails to give any warning or notification whatsoever, in disregard of the security of peaceful shipping, it commits a breach of the principles of humanitarian law underlying the specific provisions of Convention No. VIII of 1907.[105]

Hence, if a State mines its own territorial sea, it must warn peaceful shipping. The rules laid down in the two manuals do, however, comply with these principles. Mining of one's own territorial waters is said to be permissible only when either peaceful shipping remains unaffected or when such activity is warranted by fundamental security considerations.[106] If States, such as Sweden, in times of peace already lay controlled minefields in their own territorial waters, they are not obliged to reveal the minefield, nor are they obliged to issue warnings.[107] Only when a minefield is activated, the right to temporarily suspend innocent passage presupposes a prior warning.[108]

Prior to the outbreak of an international armed conflict, a coastal State is not entitled to suspend the right of transit passage through international straits.[109] In the *Corfu Channel* case, the ICJ held that "unless

103 *See* Clingan, *supra* note 44, at 355 ff.

104 *See* 1982 UN Convention on the Law of the Sea, Art. 25. Text *in* 21 *I.L.M.* 1261 ff. (1982).

105 [1986] *I.C.J. Rep.* 112.

106 NWP 9, para. 9.2.2; ZDv 15/2, para. 1041.

107 NWP 9, para. 9.2.2 provides: "Emplacement of controlled mines in a nation's own archipelagic waters or territorial sea is not subject to such notification or removal requirements."

108 NWP 9, para. 9.2.2 states: "If armed mines are emplaced in archipelagic waters or the territorial sea, appropriate international notification of the existence and location of such mines is required." ZDv 15/2, para. 1041 states: "If it is indispensable for the protection of its security and if the ships have been appropriately warned, the coastal state may temporarily prohibit innocent passage through specific parts of its territorial waters."

109 *See* ZDv 15/2, para. 1041.

otherwise prescribed in an international convention, there is no right for a coastal State to prohibit such passage through straits in time of peace".[110] Since controlled minefields do not interfere with transit passage there is no reason for denying the riparian State the right to employ them within international straits.

2. *Mining of International Waters*

It goes without saying that prior to the outbreak of an international armed conflict, mine-laying in the territorial waters of a foreign State is prohibited.[111] The question remains whether it is also prohibited to lay mines in sea areas beyond the outer limit of one's own territorial sea. According to the German manual, the laying of mines – armed or controlled – in international waters is contrary to international law.[112] According to the US manual, mining of international waters is considered legitimate under the following conditions:

> Controlled mines, however, may be emplaced in international waters beyond the territorial sea subject only to the requirement that they do not unreasonably interfere with other lawful uses of the oceans. The determination of what constitutes an 'unreasonable interference' involves a balancing of a number of factors including the rationale for their emplacement (i.e., the self-defense requirements of the emplacing nation), the extent of the area to be mined, the hazard (if any) to other lawful ocean uses, and the duration of their emplacement. Because controlled mines do not constitute a hazard to navigation, international notice of their emplacement is not required. Armed mines may not be emplaced in international waters prior to the outbreak of armed conflict, except under the most demanding requirements of individual or collective self-defense. Should armed mines be emplaced in international waters under such circumstances, prior notification of their location must be provided and the anticipated date of their complete removal must be clearly stated. The nation emplacing armed mines in international waters during peacetime also assumes the responsibility to maintain an on-scene presence

110 [1949] *I.C.J. Rep.* 28. *See also* R.R. Baxter, "Passage of Ships through International Waterways in Time of War", 31 *Brit. Y.B. Int'l L.* 187–216 (1954).

111 *See* NWP 9, para. 9.2.2; ZDv 15/2, para. 1041. In the *Nicaragua* case, the ICJ held: "In peacetime for one State to lay mines in the internal or territorial waters of another is an unlawful act"; [1986] *I.C.J. Rep.* 112.

112 ZDv 15/2, para. 1041.

> in the area sufficient to ensure that appropriate warning is provided to ships approaching the danger area. All armed mines must be expeditiously removed or rendered harmless when the imminent danger that prompted their emplacement has passed.[113]

Even though there is some support in the literature for the US position, especially by those who acknowledge a right of preventive self-defence,[114] and according to the view taken here, the rules laid down in NWP 9 are not covered by existing international law. Prior to the outbreak of an international armed conflict, the rights and duties of States are exclusively governed by the law of peace, *i.e.*, in the present context, by the international law of the sea. Hence, the freedom of navigation as well as the duty of peaceful uses of the high seas must be observed. An infringement of these rules and principles is only justified if an armed attack occurs. It may be that according to NWP 9 the scope of the right of self-defence is broader. But even then it is open to some doubt whether a case of "most demanding requirements of individual or collective self-defense" is still governed by the law of peace.[115]

V. CONCLUDING REMARK

The customary rules of the maritime *jus in bello* are an appropriate means for restricting the employment of mines in naval armed conflicts. Still, the present legal situation is not satisfactory. In view of the modern *jus ad bellum*, it is indispensable that the rules designed to apply in situations where States are unwilling or unable to refrain from the use of force are as specific as possible. The only promising means of achieving this aim is an international codification of the laws of naval warfare.

113 NWP 9, para. 9.2.2.

114 *See, inter alia*, Thorpe, *supra* note 40, at 267 ff.; Rowe, *supra* note 62, at 128. Bowett states: "It can scarcely be contemplated that a state must remain passive whilst a serious menace to its security mounts on the high seas beyond its territorial sea. It is accordingly maintained that it is still permissible for a state to assume a protective jurisdiction, within the limits circumscribing every exercise of the right of self defence on the high seas in order to protect its ships, its aircraft and its right to territorial integrity and political independence from an imminent danger or actual attack"; D.W. Bowett, *Self Defense in International Law* 71 (1958).

115 *See* Clingan, Jr., *supra* note 44, at 356.

[7]

SOME ASPECTS IF MODERN CONTRABAND CONTROL AND THE LAW OF PRIZE

By G. G. FITZMAURICE

I

THE term contraband control is here employed to denote the aggregate of the techniques whereby a belligerent in a position to enforce such control by naval action seeks to prevent supplies from overseas reaching his enemy.[1] Of these techniques there are a number and it will only be possible to treat of the three principal ones, and of these only in part, i.e. in so far as they present questions of law which are either novel or as yet unresolved, or alternatively depend on legal considerations the importance of which may not have been fully realized.

The main technique of contraband control is and always must be the interception of ships at sea, their diversion into port,[2] the examination of their cargoes, and the seizure and placing in Prize (either immediately or after further inquiries) of any consignments suspected on reasonable grounds of having an enemy destination—to be eventually followed either by their final condemnation as prize by the Prize Court, or by their release if the case against them cannot be sustained. It is not, however, proposed here, except incidentally, to treat of the various grounds on which a ship or consignments carried by her can properly be seized as Prize. This is a vast and many branched subject,[3] any single part of which would require a paper to itself, even to be dealt with in outline. So far as seizures go, therefore, it is proposed to treat only of the legal aspects of certain matters which, though in a sense of a procedural character, nevertheless have a very great, even a paramount, practical importance for the efficiency of contraband control. With regard to the other two main techniques of contraband control, namely, "navicerting" and "rationing" it will be possible to give their legal aspects fairly full treatment.

II

The points which it is proposed to deal with under the head of the interception and diversion of ships and the examination and seizure of their cargoes can conveniently be introduced by noticing the fact that the naval or blockade aspect of economic warfare has attracted comparatively little

[1] No attempt is made here to deal with the general "blockade" of the enemy, e.g., such matters as the seizure of enemy exports, the denial of financial resources to the enemy, &c. Still less is it possible to deal with the wider aspects of "economic warfare" such as the bombing of enemy industry, the organization of sabotage in enemy territory, &c.

[2] The legitimacy of diversion into port for examination was established in the last war and it is not proposed to discuss it here, although the present war has raised a number of questions of considerable legal interest in connexion with this practice. In many cases actual diversion is not necessary, because vessels prefer to call voluntarily at a contraband control base and arrangements are made with shipping companies accordingly.

[3] Even if, as will be the case in this paper, the matter be confined to the seizure of goods only, not ships, a full treatment would require discussion of such topics as "continuous voyage", "produits similaires", "conditional contraband", "enemy character", "infection" and many others.

attention in this war as compared with the last, and by suggesting the probable reasons for this. The last war occurred at the end of an interval during which, apart from the limited number of cases that arose during the Crimean War, this country had not been involved in major naval operations against commerce for about a century. The law of Prize stood therefore virtually where it was left by Lord Stowell at the end of the Napoleonic wars. In the meantime, enormous changes had occurred both in the field of international commerce and in methods of warfare, changes not merely of scale and degree, but of kind. With a few exceptions, the cases decided in such contests as the Crimean War, the American Civil War, and the Russo-Japanese War, &c., afforded but little guidance as to how these developments should be met. The consequence was that a great number of cases came up for decision by the Prize Court in the last war. The Crown was obliged to have frequent recourse to the Court, not merely to obtain the actual condemnation as Prize of ships and goods that had been seized, but also in order to test, directly or indirectly, its right to effect any seizure at all in novel cases (i.e. even an initial seizure in Prize) irrespective of whether final condemnation ensued or not.[1] The great number and range of the Prize decisions of the last war, went very far to establishing what amounts to a sort of code of the grounds on which the seizure of goods in Prize can properly be effected, and although this code may stand in need of considerable expansion in the light of factors revealed by the present war, its existence, coupled with certain considerations to be noticed directly, has much reduced the necessity of recourse to the Prize Court.[2] In addition, physical factors peculiar to the present war have greatly diminished the scope, or rendered unnecessary the enforcement, of contraband control by naval action.[3]

III

A further important factor, in reducing the number of cases heard and decided in Prize during the present war has been the shift in emphasis

[1] It will be appreciated that a simple "seizure" in Prize is justified if there appears to be an adequate prima facie case of enemy ownership, destination or (in certain circumstances) origin. Final condemnation only follows if the enemy ownership, destination or origin is in due course held by the Court to be established. Even if, however, the case against the ship or goods ultimately fails and they are ordered to be released, the Crown will not be liable in damages if the original grounds of suspicion on which the initial seizure was based were adequately strong. The difficulties which have arisen have turned largely on the meaning to be given under modern conditions to the notions of enemy ownership, destination, and origin.

[2] It is of course always necessary to have recourse to the Court where it is desired to obtain the final condemnation of any goods and it is then necessary to establish the required case to that end. But, as will be seen, it is not now always essential, from a purely "blockade" standpoint, that actual condemnation should be obtained at all.

[3] Speaking generally, if the enemy effects imports directly through his own ports, or ports in territories occupied by him, their destination is obvious and few if any legal questions arise. Germany, not having command of the sea, could not do this and always sought to obtain overseas supplies through neighbouring neutral countries. Such imports are always more or less "disguised" and their control raises many legal problems. In the last war Germany was throughout fringed by neutral states such as Holland and the Scandinavian countries. In this war Germany soon came to occupy most of Europe, and the limited number of the unoccupied neutrals left greatly reduced the naval and control problem. So also did operational factors, for in consequence of the type of air and submarine warfare waged by the enemy, the Allies were obliged to declare as operational zones large areas of the waters off Europe and in the Mediterranean, and in these zones many ships were sunk which would normally have been captured or diverted.

as between the condemnation of goods and their initial seizure. Formerly it was all important not merely to seize goods but to obtain their actual condemnation. Apart from such considerations as the award of Prize money to the individual captor,[1] there was no other way of ensuring that the goods would not ultimately find their way to the enemy, for, unless condemned, seized goods must eventually be released to the owner, and under the system prevailing during the wars of the last century, there was, on release, little or nothing to prevent the owner from re-shipping his goods to any destination he pleased, other than an obviously enemy one; thus they might easily find their way to the enemy unless a further interception could be effected. The decision rendered in 1921 by the Judicial Committee of the Privy Council in the case of *The Falk*,[2] however, established[3] the principle that an order for the release of goods seized in Prize only operates to place the owner of the goods in possession of them in this country and does not of itself entitle him to remove them out of the realm. Whether he can do this or not will depend on extraneous factors such as whether shipping space can be found for them, or whether the goods themselves and their destination are amongst those for which the licensing authorities will grant the necessary export and transhipment licence. In fact, the position which appears to result from this decision is that goods seized in Prize (as opposed to those merely detained pending investigation) are deemed to have actually entered the country and, on release from Prize, automatically fall under the general legislation governing the export or removal of goods from the country and can therefore only be exported or removed by complying with the requirements of this legislation.[4] This position appears to be clearly established in the following extracts from the judgment of the Privy Council[5] (the cargo involved consisted of tanning materials):

"At this time neither quebracho extract nor chestnut extract could be exported from the United Kingdom except by special licence, by virtue of a proclamation dated February 3, 1915, and of an Order in Council dated March 18, 1915, issued under the Customs and Inland Revenue Acts of 1879 (42 and 43 Vict. c. 21), the Customs (Exportation Prohibition) Act, of 1914 (4 and 5 Geo. V, c. 64), and other statutes. . . .

"No doubt the effect of sending the vessels in for further inquiry was to bring this cargo within the ambit of the prohibition of export of tanning materials, but it does not follow that all the claimants' loss thereby can be thrown on the captors. The same misfortune would have fallen on them if the vessels had come into a British port of refuge and had there discharged the goods. . . .

"A decree for release does not warrant actual ability to remove the goods from the realm. This might be impossible for want of bunker coals, or of labour, or of repairs, and yet it could not be said that the redress given by the Prize Court was

[1] A right to this could of course only arise on actual condemnation, for only then did the ship or cargo become, in the final sense, good and lawful Prize. During the last war the old Prize money system was replaced by one under which all the personnel of the navy became entitled to share in a sum set aside for the purpose out of the proceeds of condemned captures, i respective of whether the individual recipient had actually been concerned in any capture or not.

[2] 3 British and Colonial Prize Cases, 955.

[3] Though, as it was not rendered until 1921, its practical consequences have only come to the fore in the present war.

[4] These are of course applicable generally to all persons in the country, and to goods whether originating here or imported.

[5] *Ubi supra*, pp. 957–8, 959, and 966–7.

made inefficacious by reason of something of which that Court ought to take notice. As is assumed in *The Dusseldorf*, release means release out of the custody of the Marshal in this country, where the goods are, and it is for the owner of them to arrange to remove or dispose of them as he can. The Court of Prize cannot give itself a more extensive jurisdiction in cases where the neutral is unable to remove his property out of the realm, or award damages against the Procurator-General for consequences arising from matters to which he is a stranger, merely because he and the officers of the Customs are alike in the service of the Crown. As a matter of fact, in this case the prohibition on export was duly made under statutory authority, and the question of granting a licence to export was not raised, but had it been otherwise the claimants should have sought their remedy, if any, against the officials actually concerned, in the ordinary Courts of the country. An imaginary case was put of sovereign power being used to thwart neutral claimants, to stultify the Prize Court, and to defeat the benefit of adjudication in prize, by an executive prohibition of the export of any and every subject matter released. Their Lordships cannot entertain so far-fetched a case. Should it ever arise, the Courts of the country concerned will be most fitted to pass upon it. The jurisdiction of the Court of Prize is to condemn or to release, not to override the executive after release has taken place. It is bound by the statutes of this country, in which it sits, and cannot interfere with acts done under Proclamations or Orders in Council validly issued by virtue of those statutes. If this is so, it cannot do indirectly what it has no power to do directly, and give damages against the Crown in prize because it has no power to give to the successful claimants permission to export."

The first of the foregoing passages is of interest as implying that the Court deemed seized goods to rank as imports for purposes of export licensing, but the point is only of incidental importance since even if the goods did not rank as imports the question of their leaving the country would be one of transhipment and they would be subject to the regulations governing that matter. The second passage indicates that goods are not immune from the export or transhipment regulations by reason of the fact that they were discharged and seized only in the exercise of contraband control and would not otherwise have left the ship or entered the country.[1] The third passage shows that the Prize Court is only concerned with the question of release or no release, and that a claimant to whom goods have been released could not make the refusal to him of a licence to send the goods out of the country, or to a given destination, the subject of a claim for damages in the Prize Court. Nor could it, as such, be the subject of a claim in the ordinary courts, which are bound by the licensing regulations.[2]

[1] It is of interest to compare this with the view taken by the Privy Council in *The Zamora* (see p. 81 below) that goods brought in purely for contraband control ought not to be regarded as liable to be requisitioned under the municipal regulations governing the requisitioning of property in the country—although if seized as Prize they could be requisitioned by order of the Prize Court acting under international law principles. There is, however, an obvious difference between goods still subject to contraband examination at a control base by an extension of the right of visit and search at sea, and which have never technically entered the country at all, and goods seized as Prize, placed in the custody of the Court and subsequently released.

[2] The possibility of such a claim, indicated in the third of the above citations from *The Falk*, would only arise if a licence were refused, or rather shipment prohibited for lack of a licence, in circumstances not warranted by the regulations themselves, in which case proceedings might lie in the ordinary Courts against the individual officer responsible. But this possibility is in no way peculiar to the case of released goods: it exists every time a licence is refused for the export of, e.g., goods produced or manufactured in this country, or for the transhipment of goods not seized as Prize and passing in transit through the country.

It does not, of course, follow from the inability of the owner of released goods to take action in the courts in the event of a refusal of leave to remove them or to license their departure to a given destination, that his Government or the Government of the country to which the goods were originally consigned cannot make the refusal the subject of a diplomatic complaint. The argument would doubtless be that a belligerent can stop goods consigned to a neutral country only on the ground of ultimate enemy destination, and that once the existence of any such destination has been negatived by the release of the goods there is no valid reason for not letting them proceed. The reply would be that absence of enemy destination certainly entitles the claimant to the release of his goods out of the custody of the Prize Court, but that it does not operate to free them from restrictions due to other causes; that all goods in the country are subject without distinction to the licensing regulations irrespective of where they originated or of how they came there; that although goods still undergoing their initial contraband examination would not be deemed to have entered the country, this cannot be the case with goods actually seized as Prize, the right to interim possession of (though not the property in) which is vested in the captors, i.e. the Crown, and the care and custody of which lies with the Admiralty Marshal, who could not discharge his functions if the goods were not deemed to be in the country; that a State at war has, subject perhaps to the provisions of particular treaties, an absolute right to prevent or control, without assigning reasons, the egress from or transhipment in its territories of all goods which are in or have entered them; and that, in consequence, release restores the goods to the owner, but does not entitle him to deal with them except in accordance with the local regulations. The case may be arguable either way, but in any event the matter would be between the two Governments as a diplomatic issue and could not be made the subject of proceedings in any Prize or municipal court.

It is important to notice that the principle established by the decision in the case of *The Falk* applies not only where the condemnation of the goods has actually been sought and not obtained, but also where it has not been sought at all, the court ordering release with the consent of the Crown[1] or on the application of the owner where the Crown, having seized the goods, has not proceeded with the matter. It is evident therefore that, purely from the standpoint of the authorities responsible for the conduct of the blockade, the principle in question has greatly diminished the importance of and need for obtaining actual condemnation.[2] Since the goods can in any event be prevented from reaching any suspect or undesirable destination, it is often a matter of relative indifference to the Crown, in its belligerent capacity,[3] whether actual condemnation is obtained or not. This would foster a tendency to confine the process of seeking condemnation to cases where the enemy destination, origin, or ownership of the goods was clear beyond any peradventure, and to release in all other cases.[4] Needless to say the decision

[1] Cf. footnote 2 on p. 78 below.

[2] The main *practical* effect of condemnation may often now be only a financial one, i.e. a matter of revenue, or of Prize money.

[3] If the Crown requires the actual goods they can in any event be requisitioned out of Prize in a proper case, irrespective of eventual condemnation (see below, p. 79). The revenue aspect remains, of course, for if requisitioned goods are eventually condemned the Crown will not have to pay for them.

[4] As to release, see footnotes on p. 78 below.

in the case of *The Falk* in no way relieves the Crown from a liability for *damages* in cases where the *initial* seizure of the goods was not justified (i.e. not based on adequate grounds of suspicion[1]): consequently it affords no encouragement for effecting light-hearted seizures in the belief that any inadequacy in the case for seizure can be cured by a subsequent release. Similarly the decision affords no immunity from any liability that might arise if goods were seized or simply retained indefinitely in Prize without the case being either prosecuted to condemnation or the goods being released voluntarily.[2]

IV

The power of the Prize Court to make an order for the sale of goods seized in Prize, or for their requisitioning on behalf of the Crown, is another factor which has greatly reduced the importance from a blockade standpoint of actual condemnation. Where such an order is made the goods are at once disposed of to a private buyer or to a government department, and their price or appraised value stands in the Prize Court in lieu of them. Any eventual order for release or condemnation operates not on the goods themselves but on the money representing them. If there is a release, what the owner gets is not his goods but a sum of money. If there is condemnation, this sum accrues to the Crown or to the Exchequer.[3] In any case the goods can never reach their original suspect[4] destination. As a result of new factors created by modern warfare and of certain decisions of the Prize Court in the last war, a very considerable extension has been given to the process of ordering the sale or requisition of seized goods. In view of the practical importance of the matter and of certain obscurities formerly connected with it, some account of the law on the subject will be desirable. It should, however, be noticed that the decisions of the last war, on which the law is very largely based, do proceed on the assumption (then quite valid) that if the owner received the fair market value of his goods it was a matter of relative indifference to him if what was released to him was money and not the goods themselves. Consequently his position was in no way prejudiced by an interim sale or requisition of the goods. For reasons to be indicated, it is far from certain that this assumption is, under present-day conditions, still warranted. Nevertheless it seems unlikely that there will be any major change in the law and practice of sale and requisitioning, since the process is one which really arises from the necessities of the case.

So far as the sale of seized goods is concerned, there is no inherent *general* power in the Prize Court[5] to order this, but on the other hand there is power

[1] See below, p. 80, 81, 94.

[2] Despite the duty in principle of the captor to proceed with the case or consent to a release, there are under modern conditions various circumstances in which inaction would, over a considerable period at any rate, be justified; but the matter cannot be discussed here.

[3] According to whether it ranks as Droits of the Crown or Droits of Admiralty.

[4] It must, of course, have been suspect and for sufficient cause, or the initial seizure would not have been justified.

[5] It will be appreciated that once goods have been seized and placed in Prize no further dealings with them can take place except by order of the Prize Court, although its orders may in certain respects be purely formal. Thus it is often convenient to speak of the Crown (or rather the proper officer of the Crown; in the United Kingdom the Procurator-General) releasing goods, when what actually occurs is that the Crown consents to an order for release. The order issues out of the Registry of the Prize Court (Prize Court Rules, 1939, Order XIII,

to do so in given cases, and claimants have no absolute right to receive their goods back *in specie* if released (see *per* Sir Samuel Evans in *The Zamora*, 1 B. and C.P.C. 309, at p. 321). Although the "Primary duty of the Prize Court . . . is to preserve the *res* for delivery to the persons who ultimately establish their title" (the Privy Council in *The Zamora*, 2 B. and C.P.C. 1, at p. 19), yet sale can properly be effected in certain cases, namely, "either because the *res* is perishable in its nature or because there is some other circumstance which renders its preservation impossible or difficult" (*ibid.*).

There are obviously various circumstances besides perishability which will justify an early sale. The difficulties and expense of warehousing are a case in point, especially where there is congestion or lack of accommodation. The expenses of warehousing if prolonged, as is often the case where proceedings are pending or negotiations going on, may eat heavily into the value of the goods and make a cargo not physically perishable one of dwindling or perishable value. In this connexion it is important to notice that unless an order for release otherwise directs, the Admiralty Marshal is only bound to release goods "upon payment to him of all fees due to and charges incurred by him or on his behalf in respect of the property" (Prize Court Rules, 1939, Order XIII, rule 7). It would, in fact, be unusual for a release order to provide otherwise (see *The Leonor*, 29 July 1922, unreported, and *The Dusseldorf*, 3 B. and C.P.C. 664, at p. 672). In such cases sale is as much in the owner's interest as if the goods were physically perishable. In areas exposed to the risks of bombing, moreover, it may be that certain types of goods ought not to be stored at all, or not in certain buildings, and if alternative accommodation cannot be found they must be disposed of.

Turning now to requisitioning, although the right to requisition seized goods was extensively practised by American courts in the Civil War, the only known[1] case of it in any British Prize Court, previous to the last war, was that of *The Curlew* in 1812 (Stewart's Vice-Admiralty Reports, Nova Scotia, p. 312) in which it was held that "although as a rule the Court has no power of selling or bartering vessels or goods in its custody, prior to adjudication, to any Departments of His Majesty's Service, nevertheless there may be cases of necessity in which the right of self-defence supersedes and dispenses with the usual modes of procedure".[2]

In the last war the matter was finally and authoritatively settled by the

---

[*Note continued from previous page.*]

rule 4 (a)) and is necessarily formal in that if the Crown is ready to see the goods released no one else has any motive for opposing. Similarly, when it is stated that the Admiralty Marshal sells goods or that the Crown requisitions them, what has happened is that an application for a sale or requisitioning has been made to, and granted by, the Court. The application is normally made to the Registrar and, if unopposed, would as a rule be granted, unless this would be clearly at variance with the recognized rules governing the subject. But there is an appeal from the Registrar to the Judge of the Prize Court, and any contentious proceedings would be likely to come before the latter.

[1] See Colombos, *Law of Prize*, p. 277, and the Privy Council in *The Zamora* (2 B. and C.P.C. 1, at p. 22).

[2] Although in this case the matter was put upon the possibly rather limited ground of immediate self-defence, it is interesting to note that the actual goods requisitioned appear for the most part to have been taken for general war purposes. Apart from the case of some small arms "very much and immediately needed for the defence of the province" there was some timber for use in the naval yard at Halifax, and the ship itself was taken for use as a prison ship.

judgment of the Privy Council in *The Zamora* (2 B. and C.P.C. 1), where it was laid down (at p. 26) that

"A belligerent power has by international law the right of requisitioning vessels or goods in the custody of its Prize Court pending a decision on the question whether they should be condemned or released, but such right is subject to certain limitations."

The limitations were then stated as follows:

First "the vessel or goods in question must be urgently required for use in connexion with the defence of the realm, the prosecution of the war, or other motives involving national security";

Secondly "there must be a real question to be tried, so that it would be improper to order an immediate release";

Thirdly "the right must be enforced by application to the Prize Court,[1] which must determine judicially whether, under the particular circumstances of the case, the right is exercisable".

The first of these conditions gives rise to no difficulty since the Privy Council itself went on to state that

"the Judge ought, as a rule, to treat the statement on oath[2] of the proper officer of the Crown . . . as conclusive. . . . This is so in the case of property being requistioned under . . . municipal law . . . and there is every reason why it should be so also in the case of property requisitioned under . . . international law. Those who are responsible for the national security must be the sole judges of what the national security requires. It would be obviously undesirable that such matters should be made the subject of evidence in a Court of Law, or otherwise discussed in public".

It follows that the only substantial ground on which an application for a requisitioning order could be contested would be failure to comply with the second of the foregoing conditions. As to this the Privy Council, elaborating its view, said (*ibid.*, at p. 27) that

"the judge should, before allowing a vessel or goods to be requisitioned, satisfy himself—having regard, of course, to modern conditions—that there is a real case for investigation and trial, and that the circumstances are not such as would justify the immediate release of the vessel or goods."

(In an earlier case, *The Antares* (1 B. and C.P.C. 261, at p. 268), Sir Samuel Evans had put it much more widely and thought it sufficed if "there was . . . reason . . . to believe that the cargo might not be entitled to be released".) In actual practice, since seizure is directed only in cases where there are appreciable circumstances of suspicion calling for investigation and explanation, this matter should not, and normally does not, give rise to any difficulty. Generally speaking it may be said that unless the seizure has taken place in spite of such an absence of any reasonable grounds for it as would give rise to a claim for damages, there will be no reason why a requisitioning order should not be made. In this connexion it will be appreciated that English Prize Courts have repeatedly expressed the view that the existence of any reasonable circumstances of suspicion, or of facts calling for explanation, will suffice to throw the onus of proving innocence on to

[1] Normally to the Registrar—see footnote 5 on p. 78.

[2] Usually in the form of a written affidavit by an officer of the Department requiring the goods.

the claimant and to avoid any liability in the Crown for damages (see, for instance, *The Ostsee* (Spink, at p. 178); *The Louisiana* (3 B. and C.P.C. at p. 61); *The Falk* (*ibid.* at pp. 959, 962, and 964); *The Baron Stjernblad* (*ibid.*, pp. 18–19); *The Antares* (1 B. and C.P.C. at p. 271.)

The significance of the third of the foregoing conditions, namely, that there must be an application to the Prize Court, before a ship or cargo is requisitioned, will be apparent from the following explanation given by the Privy Council in *The Zamora* (*ubi supra* at p. 28) in which this condition was stated to be

"based on the principle that the jurisdiction of the Prize Court commences as soon as there is a seizure in prize. . . . From the moment of seizure the rights of all parties are governed by international law. It was suggested . . . that a vessel brought into harbour for search might, before seizure, be requisitioned under the municipal law. This point, if it ever arises, would fall to be decided by a Court administering municipal law, but from the point of view of international law it would be a misfortune if the practice of bringing a vessel into harbour for the purpose of search—a practice which is justifiable, because search at sea is impossible under the conditions of modern warfare—were held to give rise to rights which could not arise if the search took place at sea".[1]

It is clear from this passage that the reason for the rule obliging application to be made to the Court is to prevent the seizure of goods against which no real suspicion of enemy destination exists, merely because the Crown would like the use of them, the proceeds being subsequently released to the owner. It is equally clear on the other hand that if an adequate case for seizure does exist there is no reason why the goods should not be requisitioned if wanted in the national interest.

The theory underlying the sale or requisitioning of seized goods is (*a*) that it would be unreasonable that goods the preservation of which was difficult or impossible, or which were urgently required for national use, should have to be kept *in specie* to await the outcome of the proceedings, and (*b*) that the rights of the claimant are not prejudiced since, if an order for release is made in his favour, he will obtain, if not the goods themselves, their value. In *The Zamora* (2 B. and C.P.C. 1) the Privy Council stated (at p. 19) in regard to cases where special circumstances affected the preservation of a shipment that "it is in the interests of all parties that it should be sold or realized" and as regards the requisitioning of goods (*ibid.*, p. 23) that "there are special reasons which render it reasonable that a belligerent should in a proper case have power to requisition them". In *The Pellworm* (3 B. and C.P.C. 1053) the Privy Council pointed out (p. 1067) that a claimant "pending adjudication . . . has no benefit from the use of the ship, and she remains at his risk in the Marshal's custody. Accordingly . . . a practice [requisitioning] has been established which is beneficial alike to the captors, to the Court, and to the claimant". They went on to say that "If ultimately a decree [of release] is made in his favour, the claimant could desire nothing better than the appraised value . . ." This last point was also dealt with by Sir Samuel Evans in *The Zamora* (1 B. and C.P.C. 309 at p. 320): "Any

[1] It is implicit in this passage that the Prize Court would regard it as contrary to international law for the Crown to requisition goods brought or coming in purely for contraband control and still in process of examination and inquiry. Any other view would clearly be entirely destructive of neutral rights.

order made upon the interlocutory application will not prejudice the case for the claimants upon the final hearing. It may be that their cargo will then be decided to be confiscable. . . . Or it may happen . . . that the decision will be the other way; in which case the claimants will have the value of the cargo decreed to be paid to them, and possibly, in addition, they may be awarded sums for damages and costs". In the same case Sir Samuel Evans rejected the view that claimants have any absolute right in all circumstances that their goods should "be preserved to be delivered up in the same character if release is ordered; and that they cannot, except with the consent of the claimants, be sold or converted into a fund . . ." This view was (so far as this point goes) upheld on appeal to the Privy Council.

There is an assumption implicit in the foregoing citations that a claimant, while *prima facie* entitled to the return of his goods if released, is yet to be regarded as having received full satisfaction if he gets their value, so that a sale or requisitioning effected on proper grounds is not to be regarded as prejudicial to his rights. This is of particular interest from the standpoint of contraband control where the real aim is not to mulct the owner but to prevent the goods reaching any dangerous destination.[1]

The sale and requisitioning of seized goods is not of course a mere matter of procedure peculiar to British courts. It is a right recognized by international law. In *The Pellworm* (*ubi supra* at p. 1067) it was stated to be "no mere matter of municipal law which does not bind a foreign Government . . . it is part of the practice of a Court which administers the law of nations . . ." A leading foreign authority on Prize Law, Verzijl, states indeed (*Le Droit des Prises de la Grande Guerre*, p. 1275), that it is only in the English courts that the legality of requisitioning has ever been questioned, the courts of other countries accepting it as a matter of course, and he cites decisions of the French, Italian and German Prize Courts to that effect. As to French practice he says, "les administrations de la guerre et de la marine ont souvent réquisitionné ou vendu des chargements saisis à bord de navires neutres ou alliés, même de nature non périssable". Colombos (*Law of Prize*, p. 279) equally draws a contrast between the limitations placed by English practice on the right to requisition which provide "a serious guarantee to neutrals", the determination of the question not depending "on the executive orders of the belligerent's Government", and the practice of other countries where the "legality of the step was not questioned by their respective Prize Courts, and no special conditions were raised on its application, other than the payment of indemnity to the neutral owners". As regards American practice, a long list of decisions of the United States Prize Courts was cited in *The Zamora* indicative of an inherent power to order sale for any reason that seemed good to the court, and of an absolute right in the belligerent Government to requisition. It will thus be seen that English practice on these points is more favourable to neutrals than that of most countries.

[1] In actual fact, as opposed to law, goods may in particular circumstances have an intrinsic value not appraisable in terms of money. The reason for the attitude of the Prize Courts is that they have tended to regard transactions largely as matters of buying and selling, goods and money being interchangeable, and also because they necessarily treat Prize causes as matters between the Crown and an individual claimant, to the exclusion of the desire of some Government that the actual goods should be imported into its territory. In the case of a requisitioned vessel the point often does not arise since, if there is an eventual order for her release, and she still exists, she will in due course be returned to her owner.

V

The second main technique of contraband control is the so-called "navicert" system. Its mechanics can be studied elsewhere, but, as is presumably generally known, a navicert is a document issued by the competent belligerent authority in respect of a given consignment stating that, so far as is known at the time of issue, there is no objection to the consignment. A "ship navicert" is a certificate issued to and carried by the master of the vessel when her entire cargo consists of navicerted goods. Neither document is a guarantee against interception or seizure. Fresh facts may have come to light since the document was issued (particularly when, as not infrequently happens, there is a considerable interval between issue and actual shipment). Or the situation may have changed, e.g., the destination of the ship or goods may have become an enemy or enemy occupied one since the journey started. Subject to such considerations as these, however, and to the right which all belligerents must reserve to effect occasional interceptions and diversions as a deterrent against the clandestine carriage of unnavicerted or "smuggled" goods, the possession of a navicert will normally protect the vessel from interception, and the goods from interference or delay.

In essence, therefore, and subject to certain considerations which will be noticed presently, a navicert is a facility, voluntarily provided by the belligerent, of which neutral traders can (but are in no way bound) to avail themselves. If they do, they will normally save themselves, their goods and their ships much trouble, expense, and delay. The absence of a navicert will not however in any way entail of itself the forfeiture of ship or goods.

Although this seems a simple position, there has been a good deal of misconception as to the nature and legal aspects of the system, and to these some consideration must now be given. It is sometimes asked on what legal foundations the system rests. To this the answer must be that the system as described above rests, so far as legal foundation goes, on the ordinary and acknowledged right of a belligerent to intercept any vessel at sea, to divert her into port for examination, to seize any items of cargo suspected on reasonable grounds of being enemy-owned or of having an enemy destination, and in certain circumstances to seize the ship also. In instituting a navicert system a belligerent in effect announces that, subject to a general reservation of his rights, he will not in practice exercise them if certain specified requirements are fulfilled by ship and cargo, and if certificates to that effect are issued by his competent authorities. Traders can then please themselves; but so far as the belligerent is concerned he clearly requires no special legal warrant either for issuing his navicert, or for refusing it if the necessary conditions are not, in his opinion, fulfilled; or for exercising his ordinary belligerent rights in cases where a navicert has not been applied for, or has been refused. Equally, under the system as originally instituted,[1] the absence of a navicert is not in itself a ground for seizure, still less for condemnation. If unnavicerted goods are seized it is because of the circumstances of suspicion attaching to them which caused a navicert to be refused for them, or would have caused this had one been applied for.

[1] I.e. in the last war and during the early part of the present one.

Such was the legal position up to, at any rate, the issue of the Reprisals Order in Council of 31 July 1940. It must now be considered how far, if at all, the provisions of that Order modified the position. Before doing this, however, it will be well to notice certain practical results of the navicert system. The inconveniences, delays and expenses entailed by the diversion of vessels in the exercise of contraband control and the subsequent examination and consideration of their cargoes, are apt to be so serious that as soon as a navicert system is instituted there is a widespread tendency on the part of shippers to make use of it.[1] This in turn soon causes shipowners to refuse to carry unnavicerted goods, because the presence of even a single such consignment on board will disentitle the ship to a ship navicert and render her liable to diversion. This attitude on the part of shipowners is reinforced by that of the shippers themselves who, for similar reasons, do not care to ship their goods on a vessel that does not qualify for a ship navicert. These factors act and re-act on one another until, presently, a situation is reached in which it is virtually impossible to ship unnavicerted goods.[2] There is still, of course, no *legal* bar to such shipments, but there is a very definite practical bar; and although it is not imposed by the belligerent and arises out of the surrounding circumstances, it is a consequence, even if an indirect one, of the fact that a navicert has not been issued.

Under such conditions, it is easy to understand a tendency in neutral quarters to question the legality of the navicert system and to raise various queries, as for instance on what legal grounds can a belligerent assume to "compel" a shipper to obtain a navicert as a condition of being able to ship his goods, or how can he justify refusing a navicert for consignments of an apparently innocent character. As regards the first question, and subject to any considerations arising out of the Order in Council of 31 July 1940, the answer, as has been seen, is that the belligerent does not in fact compel the shipper to obtain a navicert or prevent him from shipping his goods without one (if he can).

As regards the second question, it is clear that *in its origin* a navicert is simply a facility which the belligerent is not in any way obliged to afford and the grant or refusal of which in any given case he cannot be legally obliged to justify. Since the absence of a navicert is not in itself a ground for seizure or condemnation, and only entails the exercise of a contraband control which the belligerent in any case has an absolute legal right to exercise, the grant or refusal of any certificate on the basis of which the belligerent is prepared to forgo or modify his strict rights, must legally be within his absolute discretion.

Naturally, the navicert system is capable of grave abuse at the hands of an unscrupulous belligerent, as for instance if navicerts were refused arbitrarily or capriciously or allocated with a view to the belligerent's own commercial advantage, or as a means of bringing political pressure to bear. It would seem however that such abuses would be of a political and not a legal

[1] Indeed, there may well be a demand from shippers for the institution of a system of this kind, even where the belligerent does not initiate it.

[2] In practice (save in exceptional cases such as those instanced in footnote 1 on p. 88) such a thing can only occur if the shipment is clandestine or effected with the connivance of the Master, or if it is on a definite blockade runner intending to attempt a direct passage to an enemy-controlled port.

character, that they could be made the subject of diplomatic complaint on general and political grounds by the neutral government concerned, but that it would be difficult to allege a breach of any rule of international law. The refusal of a navicert could in any case certainly not, as such, be made the subject of any claim or proceeding in the Prize Court, which is not concerned with the grant or refusal of these documents but solely with the physical dealings by way of seizure or detention which a belligerent may have with the actual ship or goods. The propriety or otherwise of refusing a navicert can only arise in the Prize Court, and then only in incidental fashion, in the event of a belligerent proceeding to seize goods which have been shipped despite the refusal. The belligerent is however entitled, in answer to any complaint against the refusal based on any supposed *legal* ground, to point out that seizure or even detention is by no means a necessary consequence of shipment without a navicert; that if either does in fact take place and the circumstances do not justify it, the neutral has his remedy in the Prize Court; and that it is not until the belligerent takes some overt action of this kind against ship or goods that any legal question can arise: up to that point the belligerent has merely been asked to issue what amounts to a pass through his legitimate contraband controls and, as a matter of law, he can neither be bound to issue it nor to justify its non-issue.

Even if the above view should call for modification in the light of the particular provisions of the Order in Council of 31 July 1940, it has seemed desirable to stress the basic position, since there has been much misconception about it. Moreover it must be frankly recognized that belligerents often do (and with perfect justification) refuse to issue a pass for goods, on grounds which might well not justify an actual seizure if the goods came forward without a pass. If a belligerent has a definite objection to a given shipment, not based on arbitrary or capricious grounds but connected in some form with the conduct of the war, it would obviously place him in an entirely false position if he were bound to issue a pass for it merely because there was doubt whether any eventual seizure in Prize could be justified. The belligerent is entitled to say that he will not *facilitate* any shipment he objects to, that the shipper can then decide whether to try and ship it notwithstanding, and that should be succeed in doing so the belligerent must then decide whether he can seize the goods or not, the shipper having his legal remedy if an unjustified seizure in fact occurs.

VI

The position must now be considered in the light of the Reprisals Order in Council of 31 July 1940. The situation out of which this Order arose was the following. The navicert system had originally been introduced in November 1939, and gradually extended until, by the summer of 1940, its use was general for all shipments to European destinations. The process of intercepting vessels and diverting them into port for contraband control had nevertheless, though in diminishing degree, continued. Owing to the supervening German occupation of all that part of the western European coastline stretching from Northern Norway to Bayonne, this process had now become highly perilous to all shipping, and in the interests of traders it was desirable to discontinue it so far as possible and to rely on some form of control "at the source" (i.e. exercised previous to or on shipment). The navicert system, now in general use, afforded the obvious means of doing this, but, in the circumstances, it seemed desirable to place it on a more definite foundation. Although the strict legal position still was that the absence of a navicert was not, as such, a ground for seizure, two factors had created a situation in which unnavicerted goods were necessarily extremely suspect. The first of these was the almost universal use of the system by all bona fide shippers. The second was the enemy occupation or control, as from the summer of 1940, of so great a part of the European continent as to create an overwhelming presumption that some considerable percentage of the goods consigned to European neutral destinations (the only channels of entry) must be intended for the enemy or, if not so intended originally, would nevertheless find their way into enemy hands. That any unnavicerted goods were highly likely to form part of this percentage was obvious.

Even so, it may be doubtful whether these factors, taken by themselves, would have afforded legal justification for pursuing a policy of making the absence of a navicert a formal ground *per se* for a seizure in Prize; though the authorities might well have decided to adopt such a policy and pursue it unless and until challenged in, and declared to be unwarranted by, the Prize Court. It so happened however that fresh and recent illegalities on the part of the enemy occurred, not only adding to but differing in kind from those which had led to the issue of the original Reprisals Order of November 1939. These were held clearly to justify further Reprisals against the enemy's commerce; and the resulting Order of 31 July 1940, therefore, (*inter alia*) formally declared a liability to seizure on the mere ground that the goods, being of the class specified in the Order, were not covered by a valid navicert. After reciting the enemy illegalities on which the Order was based the Preamble concluded with the following recital:

"AND WHEREAS, for the convenience of traders and for the avoidance of the risks and delays inseparable from the diversion of ships into port in the exercise of belligerent rights against commerce at sea, a system has been instituted whereby passes can be obtained for approved cargoes and for ships which carry none but approved cargoes:"

Next there came definitions of (*inter alia*) the term "navicert":

"the term 'Cargo Navicert' means a pass issuable by the appropriate British or Allied authority in the neutral country of shipment in respect of goods consigned to any port or place from which they might reach the enemy, to the effect that, so far as is known at the date of issue, there is no objection to the consignment;

"the term 'Ship Navicert' means a pass issuable to a vessel in respect of a given voyage by the appropriate British or Allied authority at all principal British, Allied or neutral ports, if that authority is satisfied that the vessel is duly qualified to receive it".

Finally the relevant operative provisions on this subject read as follows:

"2. Any vessel on her way to or from a port through which goods might reach or come from enemy territory or the enemy armed forces, not being provided with a Ship Navicert valid for the voyage on which she is engaged, shall, until the contrary is established, be deemed to be carrying contraband or goods of enemy origin or ownership, and shall be liable to seizure as Prize; provided that a vessel, other than a vessel which sailed from or has called at an enemy port, shall not be liable to seizure under the provisions of this Article unless she sailed from or could have called at a port at which she would, if duly qualified, have obtained a Ship Navicert.

"3. (1) Goods consigned to any port or place from which they might reach enemy territory or the enemy armed forces, and not covered by a valid Cargo Navicert or, in the case of goods shipped from a British or Allied port, by a valid Export or Transhipment Licence, where such Licence is required, shall, until the contrary is established, be deemed to have an enemy destination."

This Order has sometimes, loosely, been called the "compulsory" navicert Order, with a view to distinguishing the régime set up by it from the previous "voluntary" system. The use of these terms has an element of convenience if their purport is confined to the distinction between a system under which the absence of a navicert is *per se* a ground for seizure and one under which it is not.[1] Unless carefully so confined, however, the term "compulsory" navicert is apt to be misleading. This Order did not (and clearly could not), any more than was previously the case, *compel* shippers to take out navicerts as a pre-condition of effecting shipment. There was still no *legal* bar to shipment without a navicert. The Order did not even purport to make the absence of a navicert an automatic or inevitable ground of seizure, still less of condemnation. Indeed, beyond materially increasing the likelihood of seizure and the prospects of condemnation, the Order made little difference in these respects.[2] The real changes effected by it were, it would seem, that for the first time a legal *liability* to seizure was created, arising from the mere fact of the absence of a navicert, coupled with a legal presumption (unless and until rebutted) that unnavicerted goods had an enemy destination. The effect of this was twofold. In the first place it would seem that the absence of a navicert must necessarily be a complete answer to a claim for damages based on the allegation that there never was any reasonable or probable cause for the seizure; for the legal presumption of enemy destination or ownership arising from the absence of a navicert would itself constitute reasonable and probable cause for the seizure. Secondly, the presumption prevailed until rebutted. Consequently, unless the owner came forward and established the innocence of the goods, the Crown could, it would seem, in theory at any rate,[3] obtain their condemnation on the simple ground that there was no navicert and without alleging any more material fact than that, or disclosing the grounds on which a navicert was or would have been refused. Neither of these consequences has, so far as is known, been tested in the Prize Court, partly because of the small number of unnavicerted goods that are shipped (other than those of a deliberately blockade running

[1] I.e. under which the absence of a navicert is merely a factor of greater or lesser suspicion calling for further inquiry and possibly leading to seizure, according to the circumstances, but not in itself constituting the formal ground of the seizure.

[2] Less even than might be supposed, for by that time it could be taken as a virtual certainty that unnavicerted goods were not innocent unless a manifestly convincing explanation of the absence of a navicert was forthcoming.

[3] In practice, it is most improbable that no other ground would exist and perhaps unlikely that, if it did not, the Crown would regard it as necessary to seek condemnation. The alternative in this case would be to consent to a release of the goods to the owner on his giving an undertaking in suitable terms as to their future disposal.

character whose enemy character is in any case obvious), and partly because the Crown has doubtless refrained from exercising its technical rights under the Order where it has appeared that the goods were in fact innocent and there was a reasonable explanation for the absence of a navicert.[1]

Despite the fact that, for the reasons already given, the Order did not make navicerts "compulsory" the results just noticed do raise the following serious point. It may be argued that the definition of a navicert given in the Order, coupled with the presumption of enemy destination or ownership which it attaches to unnavicerted goods, implies and carries with it an obligation that the competent authorities will normally grant a navicert in all cases where there is no adequate reason for suspecting an enemy interest; and similarly that it would be improper for the authorities to refuse a navicert except in cases where the goods would, if they came forward, be liable to seizure on the merits of the case, so to speak. The Crown cannot have it both ways, it might be said; if it takes power to seize, and even in certain events to obtain the condemnation of goods, on the simple ground of the absence of a navicert, then, since the Crown is also itself the navicerting authority, this must carry with it an obligation not to refuse a navicert except on adequate grounds of suspicion of an enemy character or interest of some kind in the goods.

It is submitted however that, whatever cogency this view may possess, it lies in the political and diplomatic, rather than in the strictly legal sphere. If there is any such implication or obligation as has been suggested, it is of a political or moral, not of a legal, character. For reasons which will be indicated, the Order certainly does not involve any obligation to refuse navicerts only on evidence which would have warranted a seizure.

In the first place it is clear that the object of the Order must have been, as an act of legitimate reprisals, to enlarge the normal legal powers of the Crown in the matter of effecting seizures and obtaining condemnations, for otherwise there would have been no point in it. Now it is obvious that this object must be defeated if one of the effects of the Order is that the Crown is obliged to confine refusals of navicerts to cases where the circumstances are such as would in any event make the goods legally liable to seizure if shipped and intercepted, for if the goods are of that kind they could lawfully be seized anyhow, as a normal exercise of ordinary belligerent rights, and no special or additional powers by way of reprisals would be necessary to produce this result. So interpreted, the Order would simplify procedure but would add little or nothing to the Crown's existing rights and powers. Such an interpretation would take away with the one hand what had been given with the other and would render the Order, as a means of bringing increased pressure to bear on the enemy, which was one of its declared objects, largely nugatory. It would apparently have the result that a seizure effected on the ground of the absence of a navicert could be challenged in the Prize Court by challenging the refusal of the navicert and establishing that this was unjustified. It seems however abundantly clear on the face of the Order that its intention was to create an absolute liability to *seizure* (though not

[1] For instance, it might be necessary to ship goods immediately in order to catch a particular vessel, the application for a navicert being made after shipment and being possibly still pending at the time of the vessel's examination for contraband.

necessarily to eventual condemnation) on the mere ground that there was no navicert, and to render the seizure as such, effected on these grounds, immune from challenge or from any claim for damages. If this view is correct, it follows that the Prize Court must necessarily (unless the Crown volunteers information or possibly on an application for condemnation) refuse to go into, or even consider, the reasons why a navicert was refused. From this it follows that, except by challenging the whole basis of the Order as a legitimate act of reprisals, neither a seizure based on the absence of a navicert nor the refusal of the navicert itself, could be made the subject of any diplomatic claim based on legal grounds nor the subject of any claim in the Prize Court.

In fine, the object of the Order was, precisely, as a legitimate act of reprisals, to simplify the conduct of the blockade and to put increased pressure on the enemy by broadening the basis on which seizures could be effected—in fact to create a right to seize in cases where it would not necessarily have existed under the basic rules of Prize law. The exercise of this right would not necessarily entail the final loss of the goods to the owner, for it remains open to him to establish their innocence, in which case they or their proceeds would be released to him; but he would not be able to claim damages in respect of the seizure even if he could shew that there never had been any adequate case against the goods in point of substance. No doubt the same general implication underlay the régime set up by the Order as had always underlain the navicert system, i.e. that there would not be any deliberate abuse of belligerent rights and that navicerts would not be arbitrarily refused. No doubt any serious abuse could be made the subject of stringent diplomatic representations by the neutral government concerned, and even of political or economic counter-measures: but not, it would seem, of any legal claim.

The conclusion seems to be that, although on general grounds it may be less easy in consequence of the Order in Council to regard a navicert as a mere facility which it is within the absolute discretion of the belligerents to grant or withhold, yet from a formal and legal point of view the Order does not, in this respect, effect any substantial alteration in the pre-existing situation.

VII

The third main technique of contraband control is the so-called "rationing" of neutral countries. The idea underlying this process, expressed in a non-legal manner, is that it is only by limiting neutrals who have land communications with enemy territory to their own strict necessities in the matter of overseas imports that it is possible to ensure that no substantial proportion of these will reach the enemy. Failing that, however innocent many shipments may appear, or indeed be, in themselves at the time, it is certain that some considerable part of them, or of goods processed or manufactured from them, will find its way to the enemy. Put in legal terms, the foundation of a rationing system is that, where a neutral country is found to be importing greater quantities of any commodity on the contraband list than can be accounted for by its reasonable domestic needs, having regard to all the circumstances, including manufacture for export to innocent destinations, a presumption arises that the surplus is going to the enemy. This will justify seizure, it being open to the owner to obtain the release of his goods (or their proceeds if there has been a sale or requisitioning in Prize) upon rebutting the presumption and establishing their innocence.

Further consideration must be given to the legal position, but first a word as to the mechanics of rationing. The system may either be agreed with the neutral country or imposed on it by the belligerent. In almost every case it is done by agreement, and there is usually little difficulty about this because the shortages of almost every kind of vital commodity which speedily make their appearance in any major modern war create a paramount necessity for neutrals dependent on overseas imports to make such agreements with the belligerent having command of the sea as will ensure the safe and regular arrival of their essential imports.[1] The agreement will fix the total annual amount of each rationed commodity to be imported, its distribution over the year (i.e. the monthly or quarterly "quotas") and the procedure for licensing the agreed shipments (e.g. by a combination of import licensing on the part of the neutral and the issue by the belligerent of navicerts for shipments within the quota, so long as such shipments are also unobjectionable in other respects[2]).

If a ration has to be "imposed", the belligerent will himself have to decide on the amounts up to which the neutral is to be allowed to import, seizing or detaining shipments in excess of these amounts. The fixing of these figures will be both an important and a difficult matter. It will be important because, unless the figures are reasonable having regard to all the circumstances and taking account of the neutral's position, it is clear that the necessary presumption (justifying seizure) that excess shipments are intended for the enemy, will not exist. It is difficult because, in war time, all sorts of factors may operate to justify a neutral in importing *more* than its normal peace-time requirements of a given commodity.[3] For instance, general war difficulties will probably justify the creation and holding of stocks over and above actual consumption. Again, a neutral will often be perfectly justified from its own standpoint in effecting greatly increased imports of vital war materials, and it may be quite clear that such imports are genuinely intended for the neutral. Yet they may be very objectionable from the standpoint of the belligerent. In one class of case the belligerent may have the strongest ground for thinking that the neutral intends in due course to enter the war on the enemy's side and is piling up armaments with that end in view.[4] Yet

[1] During both this and the last war the surface command of the sea on the part of the Allies, as regards all traffic going to Europe, has been so nearly absolute that they could have brought about a virtually complete stoppage of such traffic.

[2] The mere fact that the proposed shipment is within the current quota will not of course procure it a navicert if the consignor or consignee is listed as an enemy or has known enemy connexions; and there are of course other possible grounds of objection.

[3] It is perhaps worth noticing the converse, i.e. that a neutral country's imports may be statistically suspect even though not in excess of normal peace-time quantities. For instance, it is not inconceivable that the war might actually have reduced the neutral country's need for certain commodities, or at any rate for *overseas* imports of those commodities. Another possible case is that a neutral sympathetic to the enemy might have rationed or curtailed its own use of some essential war material, but continued to import as much as before, with a view to re-exporting the surplus to the enemy.

[4] An example is afforded by the policy and actions of Mussolini and the then Italian Fascist Government in the period September 1939 to June 1940.

the destination of the armaments is, at the time, unquestionably neutral. Or the belligerent may have every justification for the view that the neutral is likely sooner or later to be attacked by the enemy and to be unable to make effective resistance, whereupon its accumulated stocks of war materials will fall into enemy hands. Yet again the imports have, according to existing concepts of Prize law, a neutral, not an enemy, destination. These are matters which raise most difficult questions of contraband control, involving the question whether some revision of the concept of what constitutes enemy destination is not called for under modern conditions. However, the matter is one which in reality goes much beyond the topic of "rationing" alone, and various considerations, including those of space, prevent its further discussion here.

Assuming that, in imposing a rationing system, the belligerent has in fact fixed a ration excess over which will, in all the circumstances, raise a presumption of enemy destination, the next question is, what is the exact legal position if and when some consignment is seized in Prize as exceeding the ration?[1] This question has never been fully answered, but decisions of the last war afford considerable guidance. It appears to be settled, for instance (see further below), that an adequate "statistical" case[2] will *per se* (i.e. even in the absence of any suspicion attaching to the consignment on grounds specially connected with it as such) justify seizure and place upon the owner the burden of proving innocence, so that no damages can be recovered against the Crown in respect of the seizure. On the other hand, no case has yet occurred where goods have been *condemned* on statistical evidence alone. Despite this, there is ground for thinking (this view is the writer's: the matter is decidedly controversial) that the possibility of such condemnation, in an appropriate case, is by no means ruled out, and that the decisions even contain warrant for the view that it would be ordered in certain circumstances on a statistical basis only.

The purely legal difficulty inherent in the condemnation of goods on statistical grounds alone can be very shortly stated. It may be quite true that if a neutral country having land or short sea communications with enemy territory is found to be importing goods from overseas in clear excess of its normal domestic requirements even allowing for the maintenance and building up of legitimate stocks, a strong presumption may arise that all or part of the excess consists of imports which the enemy is seeking to effect, directly or indirectly, through the neutral territory. But it does not follow from this alone that the particular consignment which is the subject of the seizure is itself one of those destined for the enemy. For instance, it is quite possible (and in some cases even likely) that it was previous consignments within the figure of the neutral's normal imports that in fact went on to the enemy, the subsequent "excess" consignments being intended to remain

[1] It does not, of course, follow that every consignment that comes forward in excess of the ration will be seized in Prize. For one thing, it is not impossible in certain cases for such a consignment to come forward duly navicerted. Where relatively slight excesses, not over the annual ration as a whole but only over the current quota, are concerned, the usual practice would be, by arrangement with the parties, to detain the consignment until the start of the next quota period.

[2] A "statistical" case might perhaps be defined as one based on such evidence, mainly quantitative, as to the state of the neutral country's commerce, as will indicate trade by it with the enemy in the commodity concerned and create a presumption, on quantitative grounds alone, that the particular consignment is part of or intended for such trade.

in the neutral country; and although *vis-à-vis* the neutral state, considered as a whole so to speak, it might be legitimate to condemn goods on the ground that they were destined to replace goods the neutral had chosen to re-export to the enemy, the difficulty is that the Prize Court is not as a rule dealing with the neutral state or government, but with the individual shipper or consignee of the goods, who is in most cases a private individual or firm or a company. The individual owner of the goods can disclaim all responsibility for any general excess of imports effected into the country as a whole, and claim that there is no proof that his particular goods have an enemy destination. In consequence, while excessive imports may raise a presumption of enemy destination, Prize Courts are liable to hesitate about proceeding to condemnation, unless, over and above the purely statistical evidence, there are grounds for thinking that the particular consignment itself is intended for the enemy. Furthermore, where there are in fact other circumstances of suspicion attaching to the shipment[1] the Court will prefer to rest condemnations largely on those grounds, or at any rate to include them as a prominent factor in the case, however strong it may already be on a statistical basis. This position is well illustrated by the case of *The Kim* (1 B and C.P.C. 405). There, the statistical case was overwhelming. Cargoes of lard on four ships bound for Copenhagen were in question and, in the words of Sir Samuel Evans (at p. 439)

"these vessels were carrying towards Copenhagen within less than a month more than thirteen times the quantity of lard which had been imported annually into Denmark for each of the three years before the war".

There was also evidence to shew that the imports of lard into the Scandinavian countries generally during the period concerned were no less than sixty times those for the corresponding pre-war period. This was coupled with evidence of an enormous drop in the shipments of lard from overseas to Germany direct (i.e. to German ports). Sir Samuel Evans, however, went on (*ibid.*):

"These facts give practical certainty to the inference that an overwhelming portion (so overwhelming as to amount to almost the whole) of the consignments of lard in the four vessels we are dealing with was intended for, or would find its way into, Germany. These, however, are general considerations, important to bear in mind in their appropriate place, but not in any sense conclusive upon the serious questions of consecutive voyages, of hostile quality, and of hostile destination, which are involved before it can be determined whether the goods seized are confiscable as prize."

Sir Samuel Evans then went on to review the particular facts and circumstances of suspicion relating to each individual consignment and finally concluded (*ibid.* at p. 483):

"Upon this branch of the case, for reasons which have been given when dealing with the consignments generally *and when stating the circumstances with respect to each claim* [italics added], I have no hesitation in stating my conclusion that the cargoes . . . were on their way at the time of capture to German territory as their actual and real destination".

[1] This, of course, is often the case, particularly where the statistical evidence is really strong: a fact which both endorses the soundness of the presumption of enemy destination based on statistical evidence alone, and at the same time tends to mask the statistical element in the case.

Despite the implied rejection of statistical evidence as a ground in itself for condemnation which appears to result from the decision in *The Kim*, later decisions of the Privy Council place the matter in a different light. It will be well however to begin by discussing statistical evidence as a ground *per se* for an initial *seizure*. Here there seems to be no doubt that statistical evidence alone will suffice, irrespective of any specific suspicion attaching to the individual consignment on other grounds. The difference between the position in this respect as regards seizure and as regards condemnation is well illustrated by the case of *The Baron Stjernblad* (3 B. and C.P.C. 17) in which the Prize Court refused to *condemn* a shipment of cocoa going to Sweden despite evidence that Swedish imports of cocoa had increased tenfold since the war and that a previously non-existent re-export trade with Germany in this commodity had developed. The grounds of the refusal were that a director of the Swedish importing firm had appeared and given oral evidence before the Court which satisfied it that the particular shipment would in fact be consumed in Sweden. But the Court refused to award the claimant any damages or costs. The claimant appealed against this refusal, but it was upheld by the Privy Council on the ground that "there were circumstances of suspicion calling for further inquiry, and amply sufficient to justify the seizure" (at p. 22). As there does not appear to have been any specific evidence against the goods themselves, but only a general state of affairs in which Sweden was known to be importing abnormal quantities of cocoa and to have developed a re-export trade in it to Germany, this decision appears to be an authority for the view that an adequate statistical case will by itself justify seizure. The claimants tried, in regard to the seizure, to make the same point that has been noticed above as constituting a strong argument against *condemnation* on statistical evidence only. To quote the Privy Council (*ibid.* at p. 19), they contended that:

"in considering whether there were circumstances of suspicion which justified the seizure, the Court must confine its attention to those circumstances for which the owner of the property seized is in some way responsible, and cannot take into consideration circumstances the existence of which is not due to any act or omission on the part of such owner or his agents or employees".

This view the Privy Council (*ibid.* at p. 22) roundly refused to accept, stating that their Lordships

"are of the opinion that this contention is wholly untenable. The question in every case is whether circumstances of suspicion exist and not who is responsible for their existence".

As regards the statistical case the Privy Council, after reviewing the facts, put the point as follows (p. 21):

"The position is therefore this. If the shipments of cocoa beans to Sweden be considered collectively, a considerable portion thereof must be destined for or find its way to Germany either by the re-export to Germany of the beans themselves or by the export to Germany of the various products of the beans. . . . The appellants then belong to a class of importers, some of whom must be engaged in a contraband trade, while others may not. It is impossible in any particular case to avoid suspicion, or to predicate with regard to any particular importer that his intention is innocent."

From this it will be seen that, given the statistical case, seizure will be justified in the purely negative circumstance that there is no evidence indicating the *innocence* of the particular consignment. As has been noticed, it is much less easy to apply the same principle in order to secure the final *condemnation* of the goods. Nor has it yet been done. *The Baron Stjernblad* does, however, suggest that it might be. It clearly implies that a general statistical case, unaccompanied by any circumstances tending to establish the innocence of the particular consignment, creates a prima facie presumption that the consignment is intended for the enemy. In *The Baron Stjernblad* this presumption was rebutted by oral evidence given by the importer which satisfied the Court that the consignment was in fact innocent. But if this evidence had not been forthcoming, it would seem that the presumption must have stood and that condemnation must have followed on the statistical evidence alone. This appears to result from what has now become a fundamental principle of Prize Law, at any rate as applied in English Prize Courts, that once adequate prima facie grounds of suspicion are shown by the captors to exist, the onus of clearing away this suspicion and establishing innocence lies on the claimant, and if he cannot discharge it the goods are liable to condemnation.[1]

The deductions thus drawn from *The Baron Stjernblad* are strongly supported by another decision of the Privy Council in the later case of *The Urna* (IX Lloyd's Reports of Prize Cases, 104). The facts and the principle involved are stated in the following passage from the judgment in that case (p. 114):

> "A statistical table was put in evidence, which proved that in 1915 the imports into Denmark of dried fruits were 18,651 tons, whereas the annual average of imports before the war (1911–13) were 6,300 tons. The President has found that the statistical evidence established a case which throws upon the appellants the onus of showing that the goods were not going to Germany. Their Lordships concur in this opinion. There is ample statistical evidence to place an obligation on the appellants to show that the destination of the goods is innocent. The President further finds that it is impossible for him to say that the appellants have discharged the onus thrown upon them, and Their Lordships concur in this finding."

Actually there were certain independent grounds of suspicion attaching to the goods in *The Urna*, and therefore the condemnation, though resting mainly, did not rest exclusively, on a statistical basis. In consequence *The Urna* cannot be cited as a definite authority for condemnation on statistical evidence alone, and the above *dictum* is in some sense *obiter*. Nevertheless it seems virtually to establish that statistical evidence can by itself create a presumption of enemy destination, that the onus will then be on the claimant to show that the destination is innocent, and that if he cannot do this the goods will be liable to condemnation on the statistical evidence without any more.

The conclusion seems to be, therefore, that, although the Prize Court in the case of *The Kim* appeared to reject the possibility of a condemnation

[1] For the main cases establishing this principle (which, however, emerges inferentially from a great number of decisions) see p. 81 above. For a discussion of the principle see Garner's *Prize Law During the World War*, Section 396 *et seq.*; Colombos, *Law of Prize*, Section 172; also Erle Richards in *B.Y.* 1920–1 ("British Prize Courts and the War", pp. 25 *et seq.*).

on statistical grounds alone, the later cases of *The Baron Stjernblad* and *The Urna*, which were decisions of the Privy Council, seem to leave the way open for it, in an appropriate case. This does not of course mean, on the present run of the decisions, that a statistical case could ever be an *absolute* ground for condemnation. However abnormal the imports of the neutral country or clear the evidence that a large part of this trade was on enemy account, and though the particular consignment formed part of the excess imports over normal, these considerations would not overrule positive evidence that the particular consignment was in fact innocent, though they might make innocence much more difficult to establish.

[8]
Naval Blockade

Wolff Heintschel von Heinegg

THE VARIETY AND QUANTITY of Professor Leslie Green's work on the law of armed conflict make it nearly impossible to choose a subject that has not already been covered by him. This also holds true for the law of naval warfare. Suffice it to mention that Professor Green was one of the most important members of the Round Table of Experts that drafted the San Remo Manual on International Law applicable to Armed Conflicts at Sea.[1] It was on that occasion that the author first met Professor Green and since then he has continuously profited from Professor Green's deep knowledge of the law and of the practical issues involved. The discussions with him, especially on controversial questions, have always been a delight. The present contribution on the law of naval blockade is therefore but a modest expression of the author's gratitude to a practitioner, teacher and academician who will certainly continue to influence strongly the progressive development of the law of armed conflict.

Introduction

According to a widely accepted definition, blockade is "a belligerent operation to prevent vessels and/or aircraft of all nations, enemy as well as neutral, from entering or exiting specified ports, airfields, or coastal areas belonging to, occupied by, or under the control of an enemy nation."[2] The purpose of establishing a blockade is "to deny the enemy the use of enemy and neutral vessels or aircraft to transport personnel and goods to or from enemy territory."[3] If solely aimed against the enemy's economy, the legality of a blockade has to be judged in the light of the law of economic warfare and of the law of neutrality. However, in contrast to the practice of the 19th century and of the two World Wars, in modern State practice such economic blockades have been the exception. Today the establishment of a blockade is very often an integral part of a military operation that is not directed against the enemy's economy but against its armed forces. For example, a blockade may be declared and enforced in preparation of a landing operation. It may also help in surrounding enemy armed forces or in cutting off their lines of supply. But even if an economic blockade in the strict sense were established, there would always be a strategic element: cutting off the enemy's trade links and weakening its economy will also weaken its military power of resistance.[4] No matter which purpose is pursued by the establishment of a blockade, it always involves the use of military force directed against the enemy's coastline or ports. Accordingly, a blockade is a method of naval warfare to which the general principles and rules of the law of naval warfare—the maritime *jus in bello*—also apply.[5]

While naval blockades still have to be distinguished from other, although related, concepts (e.g., operations designed to interdict contraband, unilateral embargoes, defensive measure zones, and exclusion zones),[6] there is no longer any need to deal separately with so-called "pacific blockades."[7] Since the establishment of a "pacific blockade" involves the use of military force by one State against another State, there is an international armed conflict in the sense of common Article 2 of the 1949 Geneva Conventions. The (maritime) *jus in bello* applies to all belligerent measures taken in such conflicts. The existence of a state of war is not a precondition for the legality of certain methods and means of warfare anymore. If they are taken, they have to be in accordance with the applicable *jus in bello*. Hence, the same rules will apply in either case.

Whether and to what extent the *jus ad bellum* also serves as a legal yardstick for naval blockades is a highly disputed issue. Leslie Green has always taken the position that the *jus in bello* and the *jus ad bellum* are distinct from one another[8] and it has always been an ambitious task to take the opposing view. However, this is not the proper place to reenter that discussion and to repeat arguments put forward elsewhere.[9] An interesting issue that is also far from settled, but that does need to be addressed here is the question of whether and to what extent the rules governing naval blockades also apply to blockades established in accordance with Article 42 of the UN Charter.

Before entering into that question the present article will first offer an overview of the development of the law of naval blockade in State practice and in international treaties and drafts. An assessment of the current state of the law of blockade by special reference to the legal literature will follow.

Development of Blockade Law in State Practice and International Instruments

As blockades were originally restricted to coastal fortifications, they differed only slightly from sieges in land warfare.[10] With the increasing importance of sea trade at the end of the 16th century, it became necessary to also cut off the enemy's sea links without taking possession of the respective part of the coastline or port.[11] Presumably, the first naval blockade was declared by the Dutch in 1584. The Flemish ports that then were under Spanish control were declared barred in order to cut off the Spanish troops from supplies.[12] In fact, this blockade, as well as subsequent blockades, was declared for the sole purpose of enabling the Dutch to seize neutral merchant vessels even if they were not carrying enemy or contraband goods.[13] In the early 17th century, Hugo Grotius took the view that regardless of their contraband character all goods destined to a blockaded location were subject to capture and seizure provided their delivery jeopardized the success of the closure of the respective enemy port. That, according to Grotius, was the case if surrender or peace were imminent.[14] State practice at the close of the 16th and during the 17th centuries, however, fails to evidence general acceptance of such a restriction. Hence, one hundred years later, Cornelius van Bynkershoek could easily establish that Grotius' opinion was not in accordance with existing treaties and edicts or even reason.[15]

Although a blockade affected all ships and goods regardless of their enemy or contraband character,[16] in those days belligerents were not obliged to maintain and enforce a blockade by a sufficient number of warships. Regularly, they were "fictitious" or, to use the more popular expression, "paper blockades" (also called "blocus de Cabinet" or "blocus per notificationem")[17] that were not enforced by capture in case of breach. Rather, as laid down in the Dutch decree of June 26, 1630,[18] or in the Anglo-Dutch Treaty of Whitehall (1689),[19] ships could be captured at far distance from the blockaded area if it was established that they clearly intended to breach the blockade ("droit de prévention").[20] Thus, the basis was laid for the doctrine of "continuous voyage," according to which ships destined to a neutral port are subject to capture if their ultimate destination is a blockaded port. According to the "droit de suite," ships were subject to capture not only during a breach of blockade and subsequent pursuit, but also until they reached their port of destination.

Despite Danish and Swedish resistance that was in part successful in the last decade of the 17th century, England and Holland did not give up their practice of "fictitious blockades."[21] Moreover, England, especially in the 18th century, maintained that the French and Spanish ports were blockaded by the mere geographical situation of the English islands.[22] That practice, as well as the stern application of the law of contraband, resulted in grave restrictions on neutral merchant shipping. Therefore, affected States reacted by means of the first armed neutrality.[23] In her famous declaration of February 28, 1780,[24] the Russian Czarina Katharine II claimed that blockades, in order to be legal, needed to be effective:

> Que pour déterminer ce qui caractérise un port bloqué, on n'accorde cette dénomination qu'à celui où il y a, par la disposition de la puissance qui l'attaque avec des vaisseaux arrêtés et suffisamment proches, un danger évident d'entrer.

While a considerable number of European States acknowledged the principle of effectiveness in their treaties,[25] England continued its practice of fictitious blockades.[26] After neutral merchant shipping had again been severely affected by Anglo-French hostilities, some European powers reacted by a second armed neutrality.[27] Russia, Denmark, Sweden and Prussia, in their treaties of December 14 and 16, 1800, confirmed the principles of the first armed neutrality, especially the requirement that a blockade needed to be effective.[28] This requires a blockade, in order to be binding, to be maintained by a force sufficient actually to prevent access to the coast of the enemy. The blockading power, according to those treaties, was obliged to inform neutral shipping of the blockade.

The principle of effectiveness was later expressly confirmed in Article III, paragraph 4, of the Anglo-Russian Treaty of June 17, 1801, to which Denmark (October 23, 1801) and Sweden (March 30, 1802) acceded.[29] Still, the blockade of England effected by the Decree of Berlin of November 21, 1806,[30] and by the Decree of Milan of December 17, 1807,[31] as well as the blockade of France and its allies by Orders-in-Council of January 7 and November 11, 1807,[32]were hardly in conformity with that principle, for neutral trade was interfered with by all means at hand. The time of the continental blockade has, therefore, correctly been characterized as a decisive step backwards in the development of international law governing the belligerent rights in naval warfare.[33]

Despite the aspirations of some south-American States,[34] it was not until the Crimean War (1854–1856) that the English and continental European positions on the law of blockade could be reconciled. In view of the Anglo-French alliance against Russia, it had become imperative to adjust the rules for the respective naval forces. This explains why France, England, Austria, Prussia, Russia, Sardinia and Turkey were able to agree in the Paris Declaration of April 16, 1856,[35] upon the principle, among others, of effectiveness:

> Blockades, in order to be binding, must be effective, that is to say, maintained by a force sufficient really to prevent access to the coast of the enemy.

Thus, fictitious or paper blockades had become illegal. It must be stressed, however, that the Paris Declaration fell behind the rules agreed upon during the armed neutralities. In particular, it lacks a clear definition of what is to be understood by "effective." On the other hand, an obligation similar to that of the armed neutralities according to which the blockading warships must be "arrêtés et suffisamment proches," in view of the introduction of torpedo boats and the improvement of coastal artilleries, would not have been feasible anyway.[36] Altogether, the requirement of effectiveness was not interpreted restrictively. It was not necessary for the blockading warships to be stationed at visual range from the coast. There existed no clear rule on the number of warships necessary.[37] Rather, the effectiveness of a blockade was to be judged in the light of the circumstances of each single case.[38] Hence, even blockades whose effectiveness could only be ascertained after a lapse of time were generally accepted as binding.[39] The application of the doctrine of continuous voyage to blockades led to a further erosion of the principle of effectiveness.[40]

The Second Peace Conference at the Hague (1907) did not succeed in reaching agreement upon the international law governing naval blockades. At the beginning of the conference Great Britain had proposed the following article:

> L'emploi de mines sous-marines automatiques de contact pour établir ou maintenir un blocus de commerce est interdit.[41]

In the course of the conference, that proposal was not discussed further in the Third Commission.[42] In its report and draft convention, the Comité d'examen merely included the following paragraph 3 in Article 4:

> Il est interdit de placer des mines automatiques de contact devant les côtes et les ports de l'adversaire dans le seul but d'intercepter la navigation de commerce.[43]

With regard to that rule the Comité d'examen held that

> il s'agirait seulement de déterminer, en examinant les mines, comme moyen de nuire à l'ennemi, si l'on peut s'en servir dans le but de barrer la navigation commerciale de l'adversaire—question à laquelle, paraît-il, on devrait répondre négativement. Cela établi, on pourrait confier au Comité le soin de bien faire ressortir cette pensée commune, tout en laissant hors de discussion l'application, au sujet de l'emploi des mines, des principes de la Déclaration de Paris concernant l'effectivité du blocus.[44]

Although the Third Commission did not intend to agree on rules applicable to blockades, some of the participants drew the conclusion that Article 4, paragraph 3, prohibited the establishment of a blockade by the laying of mines only.[45] Be that as it may, the vague formulation in Article 2 of Hague Convention VIII (which is identical with Article 4, paragraph 3, of the draft) gave—and still gives—rise to dispute. But even if the provision applied to an enforcement of a blockade by naval mines, it would be quite difficult to establish whether its sole purpose was, indeed, to intercept commercial navigation.[46]

Hence, it was left to the 1909 London Conference to codify the law applicable to naval blockades. The 21 articles devoted to that subject in the 1909 London Declaration can be summarized as follows:[47] A blockade, in order to be binding, must be effective, that is to say, it must be maintained by a force sufficient really to prevent access to the enemy coastline (Article 2). Whether that precondition is met is, however, a question of fact (Article 3). The delegates to the 1909 Conference were unable to agree upon a more specific rule. They expected that the determination of effectiveness was in any case reserved to the competent (international or national) prize court.[48] According to Article 4, a blockade is not regarded as raised, and thus remains effective, if the blockading force is temporarily withdrawn on account of stress of weather. It must be applied impartially to the ships of all nations (Article 5), and warships (Article 6) and merchant vessels in distress (Article 7) may be allowed to enter and leave a blockaded port or place. The declaration and notification are constitutive for a blockade's legality (Articles 8, 10, and 11).[49] A declaration of blockade is made either by the blockading power or by the naval authorities acting in its name. It must specify (1) the date when the blockade begins, (2) the geographical limits of the coastline under blockade, and (3) the period within which neutral vessels may come out (Article 9). Additionally, it must be notified to both neutral powers and the local authorities (Article 11). The provisions on declaration and notification also apply to cases where the limits of a blockade are extended or where a blockade is re-established after having been raised (Article 12). Notice is similarly required upon the voluntary raising or any restriction in the limits of a blockade (Article 13). If no declaration of blockade has been notified to the local authorities, or if no period of grace has been provided, neutral vessels must be allowed to leave the blockaded area (Article 16, paragraph 2). Vessels that in actual or presumptive knowledge of the blockade[50] attempt to leave or enter the closed port may be captured as long as they are being pursued by a warship of the blockading force and are subject to condemnation (Articles 14, 17, 20, and 21). The limitation of the right of capture to the area of operation of the warships detailed to render the blockade effective is the result of a compromise between the English and the continental European position. In any event, according to Articles 17, 19, and 20, neither the doctrine of continuous voyage nor the "droit de suite" that had been practiced excessively during the 18th century survived.[51] In case of a vessel approaching a blockaded port, without (actual or presumptive) knowledge of the blockade, notification must be made to the vessel itself (Article 16 paragraph 1). Finally, a blockade must be confined to ports and coasts belonging to or occupied by the enemy (Article 1) and may not bar access to neutral ports or coasts (Article 18).

Although the 1909 London Declaration never entered into force because of resistance by the House of Lords to ratification, its provisions on blockade were observed during the Balkan Wars and were included in a number of national prize regulations.[52] Apart from the applicability of the doctrine of continuous voyage, at the beginning of the First World War they were generally regarded as customary in character.[53] However, in view of the rapid development of weapons technologies (long distance artillery, submarines, military aircraft) and the necessary modification of naval strategies and tactics it soon became impossible to observe Articles 1 ff. of the London Declaration. The traditional blockade was replaced by the long-distance blockade that—by a simultaneous excessive application of the doctrine of continuous voyage—in fact led to the barring of neutral ports and coasts.[54] Neutral trade was subjected to far-reaching control measures, some even taken in their respective home ports. For instance, merchant vessels that did not possess a navicert were either diverted or captured, even if they had not approached blockaded coasts or ports. Moreover, the belligerents established huge minefields and exclusion zones ("Sperrgebiete") within which all vessels, regardless of the flag they were flying, were attacked without prior warning.[55] During the Second World War that practice was repeated and led to even further restrictions of neutral trade.[56] To give but one example of the excessive use of the right of blockade, it suffices to quote the British Order-in-Council of November 27, 1939:

> 1. Every merchant vessel which sailed from any enemy port, including any port in territory under enemy occupation or control, after the 4th day of December,

1939, may be required to discharge in a British or Allied port any goods on board laden in such enemy port.

2. Every merchant vessel which sailed from a port other than an enemy port after the 4th day of December, 1939, having on board goods which are of enemy origin or are enemy property may be required to discharge such goods in a British or Allied port.

3. Goods discharged in a British port under either of the preceding Articles shall be placed in the custody of the Marshal of the Prize Court, and, unless the Court orders them to be requisitioned for the use of His Majesty, shall be detained or sold under the direction of the Court. The proceeds of goods so sold shall be paid into the Court.

> On the conclusion of peace such proceeds and any goods detained but not sold shall be dealt with in such manner as the Court may in the circumstances deem just, provided that nothing herein shall prevent the payment out of Court of any such proceeds or the release of any goods at any time (a) if it be shown to the satisfaction of the Court that the goods had become neutral property before the date of this Order, or (b) with the consent of the proper officer of the Crown.

4. The law and practice in Prize shall, so far as applicable, be followed in all cases arising under this Order.

5. Nothing in this Order shall affect the liability of any vessel or goods to seizure or condemnation independently of this Order.

6. For the purposes of this Order the words "goods which are of enemy origin" shall include goods having their origin in any territory under enemy occupation or control, and the words "goods which [. . .] are enemy property" shall include goods belonging to any person in any such territory.

7. Proceeding under this Order may be taken in any Prize Court having jurisdiction to which the Prize Court Rules, 1939, apply.

8. For the purposes of this Order the words "British port" mean any port within the jurisdiction of any Prize Court to which the Prize Court Rules, 1939, apply.[57]

In view of that practice, Frits Kalshoven has concluded that

[. . .] developments in the techniques of naval and aerial warfare have turned the establishment and maintenance of a naval blockade in the traditional sense into a virtual impossibility. It would seem, therefore, that the rules in the Declaration on blockade in time of war are now mainly of historical interest. [58]

Some consider the British practice a contribution to the progressive development of the international law on blockades.[59] Still others stress the fact that the United Kingdom had justified its practice by reference to reprisals. Hence, they maintain, the London Declaration has not been substantively derogated by that practice. They merely concede that the requirement of effectiveness today has to be interpreted in the light of the development of weapons technologies, such that the blockading forces may be deployed at some distance from enemy coasts and ports.[60]

In fact, the limitations of the traditional blockade law have, to a considerable extent, been observed in the practice of States since 1945. Of course, the principle of effectiveness as well as the requirement of maintaining and enforcing a blockade by solely surface warships have been modified. Moreover, it seems that today aircraft may also be subjected to blockade measures. Still, the law as laid down in the 1909 London Declaration has not become obsolete.

The closure of the areas and ports under the control of communist China declared by the national Chinese government on June 26, 1949, although not justified as blockade, widely conformed with the traditional rules. Both the measures to be taken and the geographical limits were declared and notified in advance. The national Chinese armed forces were able to effectively enforce the closure/blockade because, by deploying reconnaissance aircraft, they were fully and constantly aware of all movements within the Chinese territorial sea.[61]

During the Korean War the U.S./UN naval armed forces, because of their superiority, were able to maintain and enforce the blockade declared on July 4, 1950, in nearly full accordance with the provisions of the London Declaration.[62] Warships—except of the North Korean navy—were excluded, as was the port of Rashin that served as a naval base of the former Soviet navy.[63]

During its 1971 conflict, the Indian navy closed the entire coast of Bangladesh. The superior Indian navy was supported by military aircraft deployed on the carrier *Vikrant*. Thus, all vessels were successfully prevented from entering or leaving the blockaded area. Altogether, six merchant ships and numerous small boats were captured. Those small boats that did not comply with the orders given by the warships' commanders were attacked and sunk.[64]

The blockade of Haiphong in May 1972 also widely corresponded with the requirements of a classical blockade, although, again, the notion "blockade" was not used. Prior to the closure becoming effective, it was publicly announced and all States presumably affected were informed.[65] However, it was not maintained and enforced by surface units but by mines laid by aircraft. Those mines became automatically armed after a predetermined period of time had elapsed.[66]

The Egyptian blockades of Eilat and of the Gulf of Aqaba in 1967 and of the Bab el-Mandeb in 1973[67] were similar to the British blockades of World War II insofar as the forces entrusted with their enforcement were deployed at a considerable distance from the areas in question. Still, the Egyptian measures were effective because no vessel could enter or leave the areas without running the risk of being attacked.

At the beginning of the Iran-Iraq conflict (1980–1988), Iran, on September 22, 1980, declared the transport of all goods and cargoes to Iraq prohibited.[68] The Iranian naval forces were in a position to enforce that prohibition, as well as the closure of the Shat-al-Arab, which was declared on October 1, 1980,[69] during the course of the entire armed conflict. Altogether 71 neutral merchant ships were affected by the closure of the Shat-al-Arab. Iran offered to allow them to leave the area under the condition that they flew the UN flag. However, Iraq required those ships to fly the Iraqi flag as long as they were within the Shat-al-Arab.[70]

In most of these cases, neutral States, in view of the lack of protests, obviously accepted the blockades.[71] If at all, they merely doubted their legality under the *jus ad bellum* not the *jus in bello*. For example, the British government protested against the blockade of the Shat-al-Arab[72] because, in its view, the right of self-defense did not allow its establishment. However, the British government did not consider the Iranian measures illegal under the maritime *jus in bello*.

The customary character of the principles of the 1909 London Declaration is also widely acknowledged in the military manuals of the U.S. Navy,[73] and of the Canadian[74] and German[75] armed forces. According to those manuals, blockades must be restricted to ports or coastal areas belonging to, occupied by, or under the control of the enemy. They must not bar access to or departure from neutral ports and coasts.[76] The declaration, either by the government or by the commander of the blockading force, must include the details laid down in Article 9 of the London Declaration and must be notified to affected neutral States and to the local authorities.[77] Because knowledge of the existence of a blockade is an essential element of the offenses of breach and attempted breach of blockade, neutral vessels are always entitled to notification.[78] Moreover, according to the three manuals, a blockade, in order to be valid, must be effective. That means that it must be maintained by a force or other mechanism[79] that is sufficient to render ingress or egress of the blockaded area dangerous. The temporary absence of the blockading force is without prejudice to the blockade's effectiveness, if such absence is due to stress of weather or to some other reason connected with the blockade.[80] The blockade need not be restricted to vessels; it may also be applied and enforced against aircraft.[81] In any event, a blockade must be applied impartially to the vessels of all States, including merchant ships flying the flag of the blockading power.[82] However, although neutral warships and military aircraft enjoy no positive right of access to blockaded areas, the belligerent imposing the blockade may authorize their entry and exit.[83] Neutral vessels in distress should not be prevented from entering and subsequently leaving a blockaded area.[84] According to the U.S. and the German manuals, a further exception applies to neutral vessels (and aircraft) engaged in the carriage of qualifying relief supplies for the civilian population and the sick and wounded. Those vessels should be authorized to pass through the blockade cordon (safe passage).[85] The German manual and Canadian draft manual contain provisions according to which starvation of the civilian population as a method of warfare is prohibited.[86] Neutral vessels and aircraft that, in knowledge of a notified and effective blockade, breach or attempt to breach a blockade are subject to capture.[87] If they resist an attempt to establish identity, including visit and search, they may be attacked.[88]

The Contemporary Law of Blockade

As already mentioned, some authors consider traditional blockades to have become obsolete because, in their view, developments in weapons technologies have made it impossible for belligerents to comply with the strict requirements of blockade law.[89] The short overview of modern State practice has shown, however, that States will continue to make use of this method of naval warfare at least in cases in which they possess superior naval forces and aerial reconnaissance capabilities. Blockade remains an especially efficient method for subduing the enemy in limited armed conflicts.[90] Moreover, it is the only way by which a belligerent is entitled to prevent the enemy from not only the import but also the export of goods that would otherwise enable it to continue the armed conflict. Neutral commercial sea and air traffic can be subjected to far-reaching restrictions, even if they carry goods that do not qualify as contraband.[91] Hence, as in the beginning of the 20th century, identifying the legal restrictions that apply if a belligerent decides to establish and enforce a naval blockade is indispensable. It may be added that according to the position taken here, a special theoretical justification[92] is no longer necessary because the maritime *jus in bello* is appropriately considered a legal order of necessity that prescribes the minimum standards that have to be observed by States, even if they are unwilling or unable to refrain from the use of armed force.[93]

Declaration, Notification, Impartiality and Effectiveness. In general, States are willing to accept the customary character of the principles laid down in the 1909 London Declaration. When it comes to the specification of the rights and duties, however, no general agreement exists. Of course, it is undisputed[94] that

- a blockade must be declared and that the declaration must contain the details laid down in Article 9 of the London Declaration;
- it must be notified to those affected; and
- impartial application is required.

According to the prevailing position in legal literature, neutral vessels are to be granted a period of grace to leave the blockaded port or roadstead.[95]

The reason for this wide agreement is that these requirements do not pose any considerable problems. The belligerent establishing a blockade will, of course, be interested in informing all those possibly affected, since it is the object and purpose of a blockade to close certain enemy areas and to cut them off. In addition, today such information will not take long to reach its addressees. Rather, it can be disseminated universally within a couple of hours.[96] Finally, any discrimination, in view of the practical problems of identification, would not be practicable.

Problems and disagreement exist, however, with regard to the principle of effectiveness. The authors only agree that when judging the effectiveness of a blockade the development of modern weapons systems have to be taken into consideration—a stipulation that was first raised prior to World War I and which obviously is generally recognized now.[97] Accordingly, it is no longer necessary for the blockading force to be deployed in close vicinity to the coast, it may also be stationed at some distance seaward as long as ingress or egress continues to be dangerous.[98] Whether that is the case cannot be determined *in abstracto* but, as in Article 3 of the London Declaration, remains a question of fact.[99] There exists, however, an ultimate legal limitation with regard to the area affected. A blockade must be restricted to coastal areas and ports belonging to, occupied by, or under the control of the enemy. It may not be established outside the general area of naval warfare.[100]

For the purpose of maintaining and enforcing a blockade, belligerents are not restricted to the use of surface warships. This means that they may choose a combination of legitimate methods and means of warfare provided this combination does not result in acts inconsistent with the other rules and principles of the maritime *jus in bello.*[101] In view of the overall importance of aerial reconnaissance and of the legitimate incorporation of the airspace into the regime of blockades,[102] a blockade may be maintained by military aircraft, submarines or even by naval mines.[103] However, a blockade may not be maintained and enforced by naval mines alone. This prohibition does not follow from Article 2 of Hague Convention VIII of 1907, for it is nearly impossible to prove that the mines have been laid "for the sole purpose of intercepting commercial navigation."[104] Rather, it has to be observed in this context that certain categories of vessels and aircraft may not be denied ingress or egress. Hence, generally, it is necessary that manned units (or "at least one man-o-war")[105] are present in the vicinity of the blockaded area in order to make sure that such vehicles remain unharmed.[106] The mining of Haiphong is merely a single incident that fails to establish the contrary, even though only the former USSR raised protests against it.[107] Despite the obvious perils submarines and missiles pose to surface warships, in most cases the presence of at least one surface unit, for humanitarian reasons, remains an indispensable requirement for the legality of a naval blockade. And it makes no difference whether the blockade serves strictly military or economic purposes.[108] Only if controlled mines are laid may their sole use for maintaining and enforcing a blockade be legitimate. Of course, apart from naval mines, other obstacles, such as wrecks, can be used to close a port or a part of the enemy's coast.[109]

Consequences of Breach and Attempted Breach of Blockade. It is generally acknowledged that vessels (and aircraft) breaking or attempting to break blockade are liable to capture.[110] If, after prior warning, they clearly resist capture, they may be attacked.[111] However, it remains unclear which behavior may be characterized as attempted (inward[112]) breach of blockade. While the German Manual is silent on this issue, the U.S. Manual[113] defines attempted breach of blockade as follows:

> Attempted breach of blockade occurs from the time a vessel or aircraft leaves a port or airfield with the intention of evading the blockade, and for vessels exiting the blockaded area, continues until the voyage is completed. [. . .] It is immaterial that the vessel or aircraft is at the time of interception bound for neutral territory, if its ultimate destination is the blockaded area. There is a presumption of attempted breach of blockade where vessels or aircraft are bound for a neutral port or airfield serving as a point of transit to the blockaded area.

This implies that the doctrine of continuous voyage may be applied to the legal regime of naval blockades. As in the beginning of the 20th century, this question is a matter of dispute in the legal literature.[114] There are good reasons to maintain that the doctrine of continuous voyage may not be applied to blockades. First, neutrals have only in rare cases been willing to tolerate interference with their merchant shipping in areas distant from blockaded coasts or ports.[115] Second, the doctrine has not played a significant role in the practice of States since 1945. It has only been recognized in the military manuals of some Anglo-American States. Most continental European authors have always rejected the doctrine's applicability to blockade.[116] The arguments put forward do not have to be repeated. If blockade law is perceived as part of an order of necessity that, by its nature, has to be interpreted restrictively and that merely modifies but does not abrogate the peacetime rules of international law applicable between belligerents and neutrals, an obligation of States not participating in an international armed conflict to tolerate belligerent measures can be justified only under strict conditions. In the context of blockade, one of these conditions is the principle of effectiveness. That principle would be rendered meaningless if belligerents were entitled to enforce a blockade at a far distance from the area in question. As long as neutral merchant vessels are situated outside the range of operations of the forces maintaining the blockade, and as long as they do not carry contraband or act in a way that makes them liable to attack, the freedoms of navigation and overflight supersede the belligerents' interest in a comprehensive prohibition of imports to their respective enemies. Of course, the practical consequences of this position are of a solely secondary nature. If a neutral merchant vessel is captured outside the range of operation of the blockade forces because it—in fact or presumably—was destined to a blockaded port, that violation of the law of neutrality results in a duty to return the vessel and its cargo and to compensate any damage.

Relief for the Civilian Population and the Wounded and Sick. A blockade preventing all ingress to or egress from the blockaded area by vessels and aircraft, in general, negatively affects the civilian population's supply of food and other objects essential for survival. For that reason it was—at least to a certain extent—justified to characterize the British long-distance blockades as "hunger blockades."[117] Still, that notion should not be used too easily. In World War II, the United Kingdom maintained that naval blockades did not differ from sieges in land warfare in which the responsible commander was under no duty to allow food and other goods to pass into the town.[118]

Today, according to Article 54, paragraph 1, Additional Protocol I, "starvation of civilians as a method of warfare is prohibited." Contrary to an assertion by the Australian delegation to the Geneva Diplomatic Conference,[119] as well as some authors,[120] the position of that provision in Part IV of the Additional Protocol I does not prevent its application to naval blockades. Blockade is, in the sense of Article 49, paragraph 3, Additional Protocol I, a method of "sea warfare which may affect the civilian population [. . .] on land." Therefore, States parties to Additional Protocol I may not establish and maintain a blockade that serves the specific purpose of denying them essential foodstuffs, "whatever the motive, whether in order to starve out civilians, to cause them to move away, or for any other motive."[121] As part of customary international law, the prohibition of starving the civilian population by the establishment of a naval blockade is also binding on States not party to Additional Protocol I, since it follows from the generally accepted principles of humanity and proportionality.[122] Methods and means of naval warfare are illegal "if the damage to the civilian population is, or may be expected to be, excessive in relation to the concrete and direct military advantage anticipated."[123] In that context, it makes no difference whether the blockade serves genuine military or economic purposes. Moreover, even States not bound by Additional Protocol I recognize that belligerents are under an obligation not to prohibit relief consignments in case of a naval blockade.[124] That obligation, which is also recognized in the literature,[125] would be meaningless absent prohibition of a so-called "hunger blockade." The military and strategic interests involved are met by the fact that relief consignments must be granted free passage subject to

- the right to prescribe the technical arrangements, including search, under which such passage is permitted; and
- the condition that the distribution of such supplies shall be made under the local supervision of a Protecting Power or a humanitarian organization which offers guarantees of impartiality, such as the International Committee of the Red Cross.[126]

Blockades under Chapter VII of the UN Charter

The final question that remains is whether the rules just described also apply if a blockade is ordered by the Security Council pursuant to Article 42 of the UN Charter.[127] In an annotation to paragraph 7.7.2.1, NWP1-14M, the authors hold that "it is not possible to say whether, or to what extent, a UN blockade would be governed by the traditional rules."[128] This statement is certainly correct insofar as the Security Council, when taking action under Chapter VII, has a wide range of discretion and that it—as an organ of the UN—is not directly bound by rules of international law that are primarily designed to regulate the conduct of States in situations of armed conflict. On the other hand, a blockade ordered by the Security Council will, of course, have to be declared. The respective resolution will at least contain all the elements that are prescribed for a belligerent blockade (geographical limits, duration). The practice of the Security Council also demonstrates that, for humanitarian reasons, certain goods essential for the survival of the civilian population may be transported to a blockaded area.[129] If feasible and if not counterproductive to the aim pursued (restoration of international peace and security), the Security Council will also ensure that access to ports and coasts of third States is not barred. However, an important exception applies. Despite allegations to the contrary,[130] in the case of enforcement measures under Chapter VII, there is no room for neutrality. Therefore, third States may well be affected by a blockade ordered pursuant to Article 42. Affected States, according to Article 50, have the right to "consult the Security Council with regard to a solution of those (= economic) problems." A second exception concerns the applicability of the doctrine of continuous voyage. Situations are conceivable in which the Security Council is forced to order the capture of vessels (and aircraft) at great distance from the blockade area if international peace and security cannot otherwise be restored. Finally, in view of the binding force of the decisions taken under Chapter VII and of the ultimate goal of maintaining international peace and security, a blockade pursuant to Article 42 will not have to fully comply with the principle of effectiveness.[131]

It must, however, be realized that, in view of the lack of UN armed forces proper, a blockade ordered by the Security Council will always be maintained and enforced by the members of the United Nations and their (national) armed forces. Those forces are bound by the rules and principles of the maritime *jus in bello* that, according to the position taken here, has to be considered an "order of necessity." That legal order has to be conceived of as primarily formulating duties which, as a minimum, have to be observed if States resort to the use of armed force.[132] In other words, the restrictions contained in the rules of war are, in principle, the most that international law is ready to accept when States are unwilling or unable to refrain from the use of armed force. This means that, when ordered to maintain and enforce a blockade pursuant to Article 42, they may only deviate from the rules of blockade law described above if there is an express decision by the Security Council to that effect. Whether and to what extent the Security Council is entitled to exempt member States from the restrictions of the maritime *jus in bello* will depend on the circumstances of each case. In that regard, the Security Councils discretion is wide but—especially with regard to the elementary considerations of humanity—not unlimited.

Wolff Heintschel von Heinegg

Notes

1. L. Doswald-Beck (ed.), SAN REMO MANUAL ON INTERNATIONAL LAW APPLICABLE TO ARMED CONFLICTS AT SEA, Cambridge 1995.

2. DEPARTMENT OF THE NAVY (Office of the Chief of Naval Operations), THE COMMANDER'S HANDBOOK ON THE LAW OF NAVAL OPERATIONS, NWP 1-14M, para. 7.7.1.

3. *Ibid.*

4. For a discussion of the differences and similarities between economic (commercial) and strategic blockades, see C.J. COLOMBOS, INTERNATIONAL LAW OF THE SEA, 6th rev. ed., London 1967, § 818; L. OPPENHEIM, INTERNATIONAL LAW (ed. by H. Lauterpacht), Vol. II, 7th ed., London 1963, p. 769 f.

5. In textbooks, the law of blockade is dealt with in the context of the law of neutrality because a blockade always implies interference with neutral trade. The authors acknowledge, however, that blockade is a "means of warfare against the enemy" (e.g., Oppenheim, *supra* note 4, p. 768). Blockades are not directly aimed against neutral shipping. If neutral shipping is affected by a blockade, this is an indirect consequence resulting from the very nature of this concept. Accordingly, the law of blockade is not an integral part of the law of neutrality. It is being dealt with in that context for practical reasons only. For a characterization of blockades as acts of war, see the references in M.M. WHITEMAN, DIGEST OF INTERNATIONAL LAW, Vol. 10, Washington D.C. 1968, p. 868 ff.

6. For a distinction, see M.N. SCHMITT, BLOCKADE LAW: RESEARCH DESIGN and SOURCES, Legal Research Guides, Vol. 12, Buffalo 1991, p. 3 ff.

7. "Pacific blockades" were established quite often. Still, in view of the lack of a (formal) state of war, their legality was disputed. See W. SCHUMANN, DIE FRIEDENSBLOCKADE, Hamburg 1974, *passim*; A.H. Washburn, *The Legality of the Pacific Blockade*, COLUMBIA LAW REVIEW 1921, pp. 55–69, 227–241, 442–459; Institut de Droit International, *Droit de blocus en temps de paix*, AIDI 9 (1887-88), pp. 275–301. See also the references in M.M. WHITEMAN, DIGEST 10, *supra* note 5, p. 870 f. For early State practice, see the references in H.J.W. VERZIJL/W.P. HEERE/J.P.S. OFFERHAUS, INTERNATIONAL LAW IN HISTORICAL PERSPECTIVE, Part IX-C, Dordrecht 1992, p. 419 ff.

8. In his commentary on a report presented during the Round Table in Bergen (Norway), Leslie Green stated:

> It should be pointed out at the very beginning that my own view is based on the premise that the Charter is an instrument concerned with peace and only becomes involved in questions relating to armed conflict when the Security Council decides in accordance with Chapter VII to take action directed to the prevention or termination of hostilities. It is essentially an instrument concerned with the preservation of peace and there is no article therein to suggest that its provisions operate once a conflict has commenced, other than as indicated above. L.C. Green, Comment No. 5 on Mr. Greenwood's Report, in: W. Heintschel v. Heinegg (ed.), VISIT, SEARCH, DIVERSION AND CAPTURE/THE EFFECT OF THE UNITED NATIONS CHARTER ON THE LAW OF NAVAL WARFARE, Bochum 1995, p. 191.

9. See, *inter alia*, Ch. Greenwood, *The Effects of the United Nations Charter on the Law of Naval Warfare*, *ibid.*, p. 133 ff.; and the commentaries on that report, *ibid.*, p. 177 ff. (by A.W. Dahl); p. 181 ff. (by L. Doswald-Beck); p. 185 f. (by W.J. Fenrick/K.S. Carter); p. 187 ff. (by D. Fleck); p. 201 ff. (by J.A. Roach); p. 205 f. (by H.B. Robertson, Jr.).

Naval Blockade

10. See H. Wehberg, *Das Seekriegsrecht*, in: F. Stier-Somlo (ed.), HANDBUCH DES VÖLKERRECHTS V, Berlin 1915, p. 26; R.W. TUCKER, THE LAW OF WAR AND NEUTRALITY AT SEA, Washington D.C. 1957, p. 283. According to PH.C. JESSUP/F. DEÁK, NEUTRALITY. ITS HISTORY, ECONOMICS AND LAW, Vol. I: THE ORIGINS, New York 1935, pp. 105, 112 f., 114 ff., naval blockade was distinguished from siege with the Anglo-Swedish Treaty of 1656. For further references see H.J.W. VERZIJL, *supra* note 7, p. 415 ff.

11. See also R. KLEEN, LA NEUTRALITÉ D'APRÈS LE DROIT INTERNATIONAL CONVENTIONNEL ET COUTUMIER DES ÉTATS CIVILISÉS, Tome I: PRINCIPES FONDAMENTAUX - DEVOIRS DES NEUTRES, Paris 1898, p. 542 ff., who explains the emergence of naval blockade with the increase of naval forces.

12. Edict of July 27, 1584. *Cp.* C. VAN BYNKERSHOEK, QUAESTIONUM JURIS PUBLICI, Liber I, Cap. XI, p. 89; C.J. COLOMBOS, *supra* note 4, § 814.

13. In addition to the proclamations of 1586, 1622 and 1694, the Decree of the General States of June 26, 1630, is especially worth mentioning. See C. VAN BYNKERSHOEK, QUAESTIONUM JURIS PUBLICI, *supra* note 12, p. 89; H. Wehberg, *Seekriegsrecht*, *supra* note 10, p. 26 f. For the practice of other States/entities, see PH.C. JESSUP/F. DEÁK, NEUTRALITY, *supra* note 10, p. 111 ff.

14. HUGO GROTIUS, DE JURE BELLI AC PACIS, Liber III, Cap. I, Para. V.

15. C. VAN BYNKERSHOEK, QUAESTIONUM, *supra* note 12, p. 87 ff., with references to the Dutch practice. For the 17th century practice of other States/entities, see PH.C. JESSUP/F. DEÁK, NEUTRALITY, *supra* note 10, p. 107 ff.; H.J.W. VERZIJL, *supra* note 7, p. 424 ff. See also E. DE VATTEL, LE DROIT DES GENS OU PRINCIPES DE LA LOI NATURELLE, Book III, § 117, who maintains that in case of blockade and siege the respective belligerent is entitled to prevent anybody from entering the respective area and to consider that person an enemy if he endeavors to enter the area or to transport something into that area.

16. It should be noted that according to Chapter 276 of the *Consolato del Mare* only enemy goods on board neutral merchant vessels were subject to capture. If, however, the captain refused to transport those goods to an ordered destination, the commander (the "Admiral") of the privateer was entitled to use armed force. According to the consolato del mare, as well as according to the "*Breve curiae maris*" of Pisa (1298) and the Statutes of Genoa (1316), neutral goods, in principle, were exempt from capture. See F. JORDÁ, DAS "CONSULAT DES MEERES" ALS URSPRUNG UND GRUNDLAGE DES NEUTRALITÄTSRECHTS IM SEEKRIEGE BIS ZUM JAHRE 1856, Hamburg 1932, p. 25 f.

17. See H.J.W. VERZIJL, *supra* note 7, p. 421 f.

18. According to the second clause of that decree, all ships and goods were to be confiscated even if encountered at a certain distance from the blockaded area if the ship's documents gave sufficient proof that they were destined to a Flemish port. An exception was provided for the case in which the vessel in question, prior to visit or pursuit, deliberately changed course. See C. VAN BYNKERSHOEK, QUAESTIONUM, *supra* note 12, p. 87 f.

19. C.J. COLOMBOS, *supra* note 4, § 816.

20. H. Wehberg, *Seekriegsrecht*, *supra* note 10, p. 26 f., with further references.

21. PH.C. JESSUP/F. DEÁK, NEUTRALITY, *supra* note 10, p. 117 ff., with further references.

22. H. Wehberg, *Seekriegsrecht*, *supra* note 10, p. 30.

23. P. FAUCHILLE, LA DIPLOMATIE FRANÇAISE ET LA LIGUE DES NEUTRES DE 1780, Paris 1893, pp. 20, 68 ff.; R. KLEEN, NEUTRALITÉ I, *supra* note 11, p. 576 ff.; U. Scheuner, *Neutralität, bewaffnete*, in: Strupp/Schlochauer (eds.), WÖRTERBUCH DES VÖLKERRECHTS, Vol. II, pp. 596–597.

Wolff Heintschel von Heinegg

24. That declaration can be found in: TH. NIEMEYER, URKUNDENBUCH ZUM SEEKRIEGSRECHT, Berlin 1913, p. 1 f.

25. See the references in H. WEHBERG, SEEKRIEGSRECHT, *supra* note 10, p. 33; TH. NIEMEYER, URKUNDENBUCH, *supra* note 24, p. 6 ff.

26. H. Wehberg, *Seekriegsrecht*, *supra* note 10, p. 34 ff.

27. R. KLEEN, NEUTRALITÉ I, *supra* note 11, p. 28 ff.; M.C. DE BOECK, LA PROPRIÉTÉ PRIVÉE ENNEMIE SOUS PAVILLION ENNEMI, Paris 1882, p. 70 ff.

28. Those treaties are printed in: TH. NIEMEYER, URKUNDENBUCH, *supra* note 24, p. 13 ff.

29. Printed in: TH. NIEMEYER, URKUNDENBUCH, *supra* note 24, p. 17 ff.

30. Printed in: TH. NIEMEYER, URKUNDENBUCH, *supra* note 24, p. 47 f.

31. Printed in: TH. NIEMEYER, URKUNDENBUCH, *supra* note 24, p. 48 f.

32. Printed in: TH. NIEMEYER, URKUNDENBUCH, *supra* note 24, p. 39 ff.

33. H. Wehberg, *Seekriegsrecht*, *supra* note 10, p. 40. Still, there are some examples of blockades in the traditional sense; see H.J.W. VERZIJL, *supra* note 7, p. 421 f.

34. See the references in: H. Wehberg, *Seekriegsrecht*, *supra* note 10, p. 41 f

35. Printed in: TH. NIEMEYER, URKUNDENBUCH, *supra* note 24, p. 53 ff.; J. HINZ/E. RAUCH, KRIEGSVÖLKERRECHT, 3rd ed., Cologne 1984, no. 1525

36. CH. DUPUIS, LE DROIT DE LA GUERRE MARITIME D'APRÈS LES DOCTRINES ANGLAISES CONTEMPORAINES, Paris 1899, p. 201:

> Les manoeuvres navales de l'Angleterre, en 1888, paraissent avoir démontré la nécessité, pour l'escadre de blocus, de modifier fréquement la position de ses navires, de les éloigner de temps à autre, pour donner aux équipages un repos indispensable. [...] Les attaques de nuit sont les plus périlleuses; il faut, pour les prévenir ou les déjouer, changer souvent de place, tromper par la mobilité du but les calculs de l'aggresseur projeter parfois en un point inattendu la lumière qui permettra de le surprendre, au besoin disparaître et le laisser s'épuiser à son tour des recherches vaines.

See also R. KLEEN, NEUTRALITÉ I, *supra* note 11, p. 572; H. Wehberg, *Seekriegsrecht*, *supra* note 10, p. 42 ff.

37. Already in the case of the *Nancy* [(1809) Roscoe II, 106 and 108], Lushington had held that "if a blockade was effective, the Court must not appreciate the number and the disposition of the ships of the blockading force," and that "even a single warship might maintain it."

38. During the Crimean War it was sufficient for the effective blockade of Riga to station one warship at a distance of 120 NM because it was indeed able to really prevent access via the only approach. See CH. DUPUIS, LE DROIT DE LA GUERRE MARITIME, *supra* note 36, p. 203.

39. S.V. Mallison/W.T. Mallison Jr., *A Survey of the International Law of Naval Blockade*, U.S. Naval Institute PROCEEDINGS 102 (Feb. 1976), pp. 43–53, 46.

40. See the judgements of the U.S. Supreme Court in the cases of The *Bermuda* [3 Wall. 514 (1865)], The *Springboek* [5 Wall. 1 (1866)] and The *Peterhoff* [5 Wall. 1 (1866)]. See also H.W. Malkin, *Blockade in Modern Conditions*, BRITISH YEARBOOK OF INTERNATIONAL LAW III (1922–23), pp. 87–98, 92 ff.; H. Wehberg, *Seekriegsrecht*, *supra* note 10, p. 158 ff.; G. SCHRAMM, DAS PRISENRECHT IN SEINER NEUESTEN GESTALT, Berlin 1913, p. 172 ff.

41. Printed in: TH. NIEMEYER, URKUNDENBUCH, *supra* note 24, p. 736.

42. In its report, the Comité d'examen stated that

> on dut se demander, si la discussion de la proposition britannique n'outrepassait pas les limites de la compétence de la Troisième Commission. On fit observer que la question de

savoir quand et comment un blocus peut être établi, est du ressort de la Quartième Commission, qui aurait à s'occuper de la matière du blocus de guerre; c'est notamment à la Quatrième Commission qu'il devrait appartenir de se prononcer sur toute question concernant l'effectivité du blocus

printed in: TH. NIEMEYER, URKUNDENBUCH, *supra* note 24, p. 772.

43. Printed in: TH. NIEMEYER, URKUNDENBUCH, *supra* note 24, p. 772.

44. Printed in: TH. NIEMEYER, URKUNDENBUCH, *supra* note 24, p. 773.

45. For example, Rear Admiral Siegel during the fifth session on September 17, 1907.

46. Hence, Rear Admiral Siegel was right when he stated: "C'est là une clause qui laisse au belligérant une échappatoire bien dangereuse"; printed in: TH. NIEMEYER, URKUNDENBUCH, *supra* note 24, p. 805.

47. For a more detailed discussion, see N. BENTWICH, THE DECLARATION OF LONDON, London 1911, p. 44 ff.; F. Kalshoven, *Commentary on the 1909 London Declaration*, in: N. Ronzitti (ed.), THE LAW OF NAVAL WARFARE, Dordrecht et al. 1988, pp. 257–275; NAVAL WAR COLLEGE, THE DECLARATION OF LONDON OF FEBRUARY 26, 1909, Washington, D.C. 1910, p. 25 ff.

48. See the Rapport général présenté à la Conférence Navale au nom du Comité de Rédaction; printed in: TH. NIEMEYER, URKUNDENBUCH, *supra* note 24, p. 1604 ff., 1608.

49. While, according to the French position, the notification was regarded as constitutive, by the Anglo-American position knowledge of the establishment of a blockade was considered sufficient. See C.J. COLOMBOS, *supra* note 4, §§ 826 ff.; H. Wehberg, *Seekriegsrecht*, *supra* note 10, p. 164 f.; G. SCHRAMM, PRISENRECHT, *supra* note 40, p. 202 f. See also the different proposals submitted to the 1907 Hague and to the 1909 London Conferences and the Rapport général; printed in: TH. NIEMEYER, URKUNDENBUCH, *supra* note 24, pp. 1247 ff. and 1610.

50. According to Article 15, knowledge is presumed, failing proof to the contrary, "if the vessel left a neutral port subsequently to the notification of the blockade to the Power to which such port belongs, provided that such notification was made in sufficient time."

51. W.E. HALL, INTERNATIONAL LAW, Oxford 1880, p. 846 ff.; H. Wehberg, *Seekriegsrecht*, *supra* note 10, p. 170. In the Rapport général (printed in: TH. NIEMEYER, URKUNDENBUCH, *supra* note 24, p. 1616) it is made clear that:

> Le rayon d'action d'une force navale bloquante pourra s'étendre assez loin, mais, comme il dépend du nombre des bâtiments concourant à l'effectivité du blocus, et comme il reste toujours limité par la condition d'effectivité, il n'atteindra jamais des mers éloignées sur lesquelles naviguent des navires de commerce, peut-être destinés aux ports bloqués, mais dont la destination est subordonnée aux modifications que les circonstances sont susceptibles d'apporter au blocus au cours du voyage. En résumé, l'idée de rayon d'action liée à celle d'effectivité telle que nous avons essayé de la définir c'est-à-dire, comprenant la zone d'opérations des forces bloquantes, permet au belligérant d'exercer d'une matière efficace le droit de blocus qui lui est reconnu, et, d'un autre côté, elle évite aux neutres d'être exposés à grande distance aux inconvénients du blocus, tout en leur laissant courir les dangers auxquels ils s'exposent, sciemment en s'approchant des points dont l'accès est interdit par le belligérant.

52. See the references in G. SCHRAMM, PRISENRECHT, *supra* note 40, p. 203. Many of those national prize regulations can be found in: H. HECKER/E. TOMSON, VÖLKERRECHT UND PRISENRECHT, Frankfurt a.M./Berlin 1965, p. 29 ff.

53. H. Wehberg, *Seekriegsrecht*, *supra* note 10, p. 166; H.W. Malkin, *supra* note 40, BYIL III (1922-23), p. 93; R.W. TUCKER, *supra* note 10, p. 285.

54. The British long-distance blockade, even though the notion "blockade" was not used, was proclaimed by Order-in-Council of March 11, 1915 (printed in: REICHS-MARINE-AMT, SEEKRIEGSRECHT IM WELTKRIEGE, SAMMLUNG DIPLOMATISCHER NOTEN UND ANDERER URKUNDEN, Berlin 1916, No. 150). In its note to the American Ambassador (*ibid.*, No. 155), the British government expressly stated that the blockade had been established "to prevent vessels from carrying goods for or coming from Germany." For the practice of blockade during the First World War, see J.W. GARNER, PRIZE LAW DURING THE WORLD WAR, New York 1927, p. 621 ff.; L. GUICHARD, THE NAVAL BLOCKADE, 1914–1918, New York 1930, *passim*; OPPENHEIM, *supra* note 4, p. 791 ff.; R.W. TUCKER, *supra* note 10, p. 305 ff.; CH. ROUSSEAU, LE DROIT DES CONFLITS ARMÉS, Paris 1983, p. 272 ff.; E. RAUCH, THE PROTOCOL ADDITIONAL TO THE GENEVA CONVENTIONS FOR THE PROTECTION OF VICTIMS OF INTERNATIONAL ARMED CONFLICTS AND THE UNITED NATIONS CONVENTION ON THE LAW OF THE SEA: REPERCUSSIONS ON THE LAW OF NAVAL WARFARE, Berlin 1984, p. 83 ff.

55. Such exclusion zones have to be distinguished from blockades. See W.J. Fenrick, *The Exclusion Zone Device in the Law of Naval Warfare*, CANADIAN YEARBOOK OF INTERNATIONAL LAW XXIV (1986), p. 91 ff. See also the references in M.M. WHITEMAN, DIGEST 10, *supra* note 5, p. 872 ff.; L.F.E. Goldie, *Maritime War Zones & Exclusion Zones*, in: H.B. Robertson, Jr. (ed.), THE LAW OF NAVAL OPERATIONS, Newport 1991, p. 156 ff.; J. SCHMITT, DIE ZULÄSSIGKEIT VON SPERRGEBIETEN IM SEEKRIEG, Hamburg 1966, *passim*.

56. OPPENHEIM, *supra* note 4, p. 795 ff.; R.W. TUCKER, *supra* note 10, p. 312 ff.; S.W.D. Rowson, *Prize Law During the Second World War*, BRITISH YEARBOOK OF INTERNATIONAL LAW XXIV (1947), pp. 160–215, 193 ff.; E. RAUCH, PROTOCOL ADDITIONAL, *supra* note 54, p. 87 ff. For reflections within the German Navy during World War II, see the references in: W. Heintschel v. Heinegg, *Exclusion Zones, Mines, Abuse of Neutral Flags and Insignia, Booty in Naval Warfare*, in: D. Fleck (ed.), THE GLADISCH COMMITTEE ON THE LAW OF NAVAL WARFARE, Bochum 1990, p. 39 ff.

57. Stat. Rules and Orders 1939, No. 1709; printed in: OBERKOMMANDO DER KRIEGSMARINE, URKUNDEN ZUM SEEKRIEGSRECHT, Berlin 1941, No. 398.

58. F. KALSHOVEN, COMMENTARY, *supra* note 47, p. 274.

59. Especially J. STONE, LEGAL CONTROLS OF INTERNATIONAL CONFLICT. A TREATISE ON THE DYNAMICS OF DISPUTES – AND WAR – LAW, New York 1959, p. 508: "The realities of the present century require the British long distance blockade to be viewed as a long term transformation of the traditional law of blockade, rather than as mere reprisals, or mere breach of the traditional law." See also H.W. Malkin, *supra* note 40, BYIL III (1922–23), p. 87 f.; OPPENHEIM, *supra* note 4, p. 796 f.; C.J. COLOMBOS, *supra* note 4, §§ 839 ff.

60. That view is taken by R.W. TUCKER, *supra* note 10, p. 285 f.; and E. CASTRÉN, THE PRESENT LAW OF WAR AND NEUTRALITY, Helsinki 1954, p. 314 ff.

61. L.H. Woolsey, *Closure of Ports by the Chinese Nationalist Government*, AM. J. INT'L L. 44 (1950), pp. 350–356; R. OTTMÜLLER, DIE ANWENDUNG VON SEEKRIEGSRECHT IN MILITÄRISCHEN KONFLIKTEN SEIT 1945, Hamburg 1978, p. 74 f.; E. BECKERT/G. BREUER, ÖFFENTLICHES SEERECHT, Berlin/New York 1991, no. 1126 ff.

62. S.V. Mallison/W.T. Mallison Jr., *supra* note 39, U.S. Naval Institute PROCEEDINGS 102 (Feb. 1976), p. 49; R. OTTMÜLLER, ANWENDUNG VON SEEKRIEGSRECHT, *supra* note 61, p. 106 f.; J.G. Verplaetse, *The Ius in Bello and Military Operations in Korea 1950–1953*, ZEITSCHRIFT FÜR AUSLÄNDISCHES ÖFFENTLICHES RECHT UND VÖLKERRECHT 23 (1963), pp. 679–738, 698 ff.

Naval Blockade

63. M.W. CAGLE/F.A. MANSON, THE SEA WAR IN KOREA, Annapolis 1957, p. 281 ff. See also M.M. WHITEMAN, DIGEST 10, *supra* note 5, p. 866 f.

64. J. ROHWER, *Naval Warfare Since 1945*, U.S. Naval Institute PROCEEDINGS 104 (May 1978), p. 66 ff.; J. Rohwer, MARINE-RUNDSCHAU 71 (1974), pp. 7–26, 19; R. OTTMÜLLER, ANWENDUNG VON SEEKRIEGSRECHT, *supra* note 61, pp. 274, 285 f.; D.K. PALIT, THE LIGHTNING CAMPAIGN, Salisbury 1972, p. 145.

65. The speech by President Nixon ("Denying Hanoi the Means to Continue Aggression,") was delivered on May 8, 1972, U.S. DEPT. OF STATE BULL., Vol. 66 (May 29, 1972), pp. 747–751. See also D.P. O'CONNELL, THE INFLUENCE OF LAW ON SEAPOWER, Manchester 1975, pp. 64 f., 93 ff.; F.B. Swayze, *Traditional Principles of Blockade in Modern Practice: United States Mining of Internal and Territorial Waters of North Vietnam*, JAG JOURNAL XXIX (1977), pp. 143–173.

66. S.V. Mallison/W.T. Mallison Jr., *supra* note 39, U.S. Naval Institute PROCEEDINGS 102 (Feb. 1976), p. 51; R. OTTMÜLLER, ANWENDUNG VON SEEKRIEGSRECHT, *supra* note 61, p. 231 ff.

67. D.P. O'CONNELL, INFLUENCE, *supra* note 65, p. 101 ff.; S.V. Mallison/W.T. Mallison Jr., *supra* note 39, p. 51; R. OTTMÜLLER, ANWENDUNG VON SEEKRIEGSRECHT, *supra* note 61, pp. 293 f., 301; R.R. Baxter, *The Law of War in the Arab-Israeli Conflict: On Water and on Land*, TOWSON STATE JOURNAL OF INTERNATIONAL AFFAIRS 5 (1971), pp. 1–17, 8.

68. Notice to Mariners No. 17/59.

69. Notice to Mariners No. 18/59.

70. See the references in: A. Gioia/N. Ronzitti, *The Law of Neutrality: Third States' Commercial Rights and Duties*, in: I.F. Dekker/H.H.G. Post (eds.), THE GULF WAR OF 1980–1988, Dordrecht *et al.* 1992, p. 234

71. For the reactions of neutral States in the aforementioned conflicts, see the references in: R. OTTMÜLLER, ANWENDUNG VON SEEKRIEGSRECHT, *supra* note 61, pp. 71 f., 96 f., 235 f., 282, 298.

72. Printed in: BYIL LIX (1988), 581.

73. THE COMMANDER'S HANDBOOK ON THE LAW OF NAVAL OPERATIONS, NWP 1-14M/MCWP 5-2.1/COMDTPUB P5800.1 (hereinafter NWP 1-14M).

74. While NWP 1-14M applies to the Canadian armed forces, there also exists a draft manual that is not yet completed. Since there are some differences, that draft will be cited in the following notes.

75. HUMANITARIAN LAW IN ARMED CONFLICTS Manual, edited by the Federal Ministry of Defence of the Federal Republic of Germany, Bonn, August 1992 (hereinafter GERMAN MANUAL).

76. NWP 1-14M, paras. 7.7.1 and 7.7.2.5; GERMAN MANUAL, para. 1051; Canadian Draft, para. 722 (1)(5).

77. NWP 1-14M, paras. 7.7.2.1 and 7.7.2.2; GERMAN MANUAL, para. 1052; Canadian Draft, para. 722.

78. NWP 1-14M, para. 7.7.2.2; GERMAN MANUAL, para. 1052; Canadian Draft, para. 722 (3).

79. As to the question whether and to what extent a blockade may be maintained only by naval mines, see the section on Declaration, Notification, Impartiality and Effectiveness *infra*.

80. NWP 1-14M, para. 7.7.2.3; GERMAN MANUAL, para. 1053; Canadian Draft, para. 722 (4).

81. NWP 1-14M, para. 7.7.1; GERMAN MANUAL, para. 1051 (1); Canadian Draft, para. 722 (1).

82. NWP 1-14M, para. 7.7.2.4; Canadian Draft, para. 722 (6).
83. NWP 1-14M, para. 7.7.3; Canadian Draft, para. 722 (10).
84. NWP 1-14M, para. 7.7.3; Canadian Draft, para. 722 (11).
85. NWP 1-14M, para. 7.7.3; GERMAN MANUAL, para. 1051 (2).
86. GERMAN MANUAL, para. 1051. However, in an annotation to paragraph 722 (1) of the Canadian Draft, a more cautious approach is taken:

> In so far as the purpose of a blockade is to deprive the enemy population of foodstuffs, so as to starve them in the hope that they would apply pressure to their government to seek peace, it would now appear to be illegal in accordance with AP I Art. 54 (1), which prohibits starvation of civilians as a method of warfare and which, as part of Section II concerning the general protection of the civilian population against the effects of hostilities, applies to all attacks from the sea against objectives on land Art. 49 (3) [...].

87. NWP 1-14M, para. 7.10; Canadian Draft, para. 722 (9).
88. NWP 1-14M, para. 7.5.2, according to which in those cases they acquire the character of an enemy merchant vessel or civil aircraft and may be treated in accordance with paragraph 8.2.2.
89. F. KALSHOVEN, COMMENTARY, *supra* note 47, p. 272; G.J.F. van Hegelsom, *Introductory Report*, in: W. Heintschel v. Heinegg (ed.), METHODS AND MEANS OF COMBAT IN NAVAL WARFARE, Bochum 1992, pp. 1 ff., 46; R.W. TUCKER, *supra* note 10, p. 285; CH. ROUSSEAU, *supra* note 54, p. 272.
90. A similar position is taken in NWP 1-14M, para. 7.7.5: "Notwithstanding this trend in belligerent practices (during general war) away from the establishment of blockades that conform to the traditional rules, blockade continues to be a useful means to regulate the competing interests of belligerents and neutrals in more limited armed conflict."
91. According to the well-established principles of prize law, capture and seizure of neutral goods are allowed only if they qualify as contraband, i.e., if they are destined to the enemy armed forces. Goods being exported from enemy ports may therefore not be considered contraband. The same position is taken by the ILA. According to the Helsinki Principles (5.2.3), "contraband are goods ultimately destined to the enemy of a belligerent which are designed for the use of war fighting and other goods useful for the war effort of the enemy." In the commentary it is made clear that, since the goods in question must be destined to the enemy, "the doctrine of contraband is not applicable to exports from enemy territory."
92. For the different theoretical approaches to blockade, see H. Wehberg, *Seekriegsrecht*, *supra* note 10, p. 138 ff.; G. SCHRAMM, PRISENRECHT, *supra* note 40, p. 163 ff.
93. Hence, the applicability of the legal limitations merely depends on the establishment of a blockade. According to Oppenheim (*supra* note 4, p. 774), a special justification is not necessary for the following reasons:

> The fact is that the detrimental consequences of blockade to neutrals stand in the same category as the many other detrimental consequences of war to neutrals. [...] A blockade interferes indeed with the recognised principle of the freedom of the sea, and, further, with the recognised freedom of neutral commerce. But all three have developed together, and when the freedom of the sea in time of peace and war, and, further, the freedom of neutral commerce, became generally recognised, the exceptional restrictions of blockade became at the same time recognised as legitimate.

Naval Blockade

94. R.W. TUCKER, *supra* note 10, pp. 287 f., 291; CH. ROUSSEAU, *supra* note 54, p. 267 f.; OPPENHEIM, *supra* note 4, p. 775 f.; C.J. COLOMBOS, *supra* note 4, §§ 822, 824, 826; E. CASTRÉN, *supra* note 60, p. 296 ff.; Y. Dinstein, *The Laws of War at Sea*, ISR. YBHR 10 (1980), pp. 38 ff., 50 ff., and *Sea Warfare*, in: R. Bernhardt (ed.), ENCYCLOPEDIA OF PUBLIC INTERNATIONAL LAW, Installment 4, North Holland 1981 ff., pp. 201–212, 205 f.; F. BERBER, LEHRBUCH DES VÖLKERRECHTS, Vol. II, 2nd ed., Munich 1969, p. 189. See also the SAN REMO MANUAL, paras. 93 ff., 99; and Articles 74, 77–79 of the 1939 Harvard Draft. According to the ILA Helsinki Principles (5.2.10), "in order to be valid, the blockade must be declared, notified to belligerent and neutral States, effective and applied impartially to ships of all States."

95. E. CASTRÉN, *supra* note 60, p. 297; C.J. COLOMBOS, *supra* note 4, § 825; OPPENHEIM, *supra* note 4, p. 777; R.W. TUCKER, *supra* note 10, p. 287; Article 78 para. 1 lit. (c) of the 1939 Harvard Draft.

96. For example, the Iranian declaration of October 1, 1980, was made known to international shipping within a few hours.

97. OPPENHEIM, *supra* note 4, p. 778 ff.; C.J. COLOMBOS, *supra* note 4, §§ 819 f.; 840 f.; J. STONE, *supra* note 59, p. 493; CH. ROUSSEAU, *supra* note 54, p. 263 ff.; R.W. TUCKER, *supra* note 10, p. 288 f.; E. CASTRÉN, *supra* note 60, p. 299 ff.; L. Weber, *Blockade*, in: EPIL 3, *supra* note 94, p. 48 ff.; E. RAUCH, PROTOCOL ADDITIONAL, *supra* note 54, p. 81; D.P. O'CONNELL, THE INTERNATIONAL LAW OF THE SEA (ed. by I.A. Shearer), Vol. II, Oxford 1984, p. 1151 ff.; Y. Dinstein, *supra* note 94, ISR. YBHR 10 (1980), p. 49 f.; P.A. MARTINI, BLOCKADE IM WELTKRIEG, Berlin/Bonn 1932, p. 84 ff. According to the commentary on Principle 5.2.10 of the Helsinki Principles "the force maintaining the blockade may be stationed at a distance determined by military requirements." For a position according to which a close cordon remains necessary, see F. BERBER, *supra* note 94, p. 190.

98. In that context, R.W. Tucker (*supra* note 10, p. 289) explains: "The element of danger associated with an effective blockade is therefore to be understood in terms of liability to seizure and eventual condemnation, though not in terms of a liability to destruction upon entrance into the forbidden area." See also the foregoing references and para. 96 of the SAN REMO MANUAL ("The force maintaining the blockade may be stationed at a distance determined by military requirements.).

99. In addition to the foregoing references, see para. 95 of the SAN REMO MANUAL; Article 72 of the 1939 Harvard Draft.

100. For the general area of naval warfare ("regions of operations"), see paras. 10 ff., 14 ff. of the SAN REMO MANUAL. For the legal status of international straits in naval warfare, see W. Heintschel v. Heinegg, *Straits and the Law of Naval Warfare*, in: L.C. Green/M.N. Schmitt (eds.), THE LAW OF ARMED CONFLICT: INTO THE NEXT MILLENIUM, U.S. Naval War College, International Law Studies Vol. 71, Newport, 1998, p. 263 ff.

101. The same position is taken in the commentary on Helsinki Principle 5.2.10 and, *inter alia*, in NWP 1-14M, para. 7.7.2.3.

102. For an in-depth analysis of the legality of aerial blockades, see M.N. Schmitt, *Aerial Blockades in Historical, Legal, and Practical Perspective*, USAFA JOURNAL OF LEGAL STUDIES, Vol. 2 (1991), pp. 21–86. See also OPPENHEIM, *supra* note 4, p. 781; E. CASTRÉN, *supra* note 60, p. 301. R.W. TUCKER, *supra* note 10, p. 283, footnote 1, maintains: "The extension of blockades to include the air space over the high seas remains a development for the future. It is next to impossible to declare with any degree of assurance what procedures may govern blockade by air. Certainly, there are grave difficulties in assuming that the practices of naval blockade can be applied readily, by analogy, to aerial blockade." Still, he does not doubt the principal legality of the incorporation of the airspace. Of course, in view of the dangers involved, belligerents are

obliged to observe certain rules of conduct, as, for example, proposed by the ICAO in its Safety Recommendations, ICAO Doc. C-WP/8803, AM. J. INT'L L.83 (1989), p. 335.

103. OPPENHEIM, *supra* note 4, p. 780 f.; C.J. COLOMBOS, *supra* note 4, § 842; E. CASTRÉN, *supra* note 60, p. 300 f.; R.D. Powers Jr., *International Law and Open-Ocean Mining*, JAG JOURNAL XV (1961), pp. 55–58, 71; M.S. MCDOUGAL/F.P. FELICIANO, MINIMUM WORLD PUBLIC ORDER, New Haven 1961, p. 495; H. Wehberg, *Seekriegsrecht*, *supra* note 10, p. 152; Art. 73 of the 1939 Harvard Draft. See also SAN REMO MANUAL, para. 97: "A blockade may be enforced and maintained by a combination of legitimate methods and means of warfare provided this combination does not result in acts inconsistent with the rules set out in this document."

104. See *infra* notes 45 f.

105. J. STONE, *supra* note 59, p. 496.

106. Obviously, the same position is taken by H. Wehberg, *Seekriegsrecht*, *supra* note 10, p. 152; E. CASTRÉN, *supra* note 60, p. 300 f.; OPPENHEIM, *supra* note 4, p. 781; Article 73 of the 1939 Harvard Draft ("For the purpose of establishment and maintenance of a blockade, a belligerent must use surface or submarine vessels or aircraft, and may also used fixed obstacles and anchored automatic contact mines which become harmless on becoming unanchored."). The commentary to paragraph 97 of the San Remo Manual makes clear that "this paragraph . . . does, however, prohibit the enforcement solely by weapon systems, such as mines, unless they are employed in such a manner as not to endanger legitimate sea-going commerce." In an annotation to paragraph 7.7.2.3, NWP 1–14M, the authors maintain that "the presence of at least one surface warship is no longer an absolute requirement to make a blockade legally effective, as long as other sufficient means are employed."

107. The former USSR opposed the mining of Haiphong by referring to the freedom of navigation. It did not claim a violation of the maritime *jus in bello*.

108. The position taken by O'Connell, according to which the mining of Haiphong was a "strategic blockade" and could, thus, be maintained and enforced solely by mines, is untenable. The maritime *jus in bello* does not distinguish between "strategic" and "economic" blockades. D.P. O'CONNELL, LAW OF THE SEA II, *supra* note 97, p. 1139.

109. J. STONE, *supra* note 59, p. 496; E. CASTRÉN, *supra* note 60, p. 301; H. Wehberg, *Seekriegsrecht*, *supra* note 10, p. 152; Article 73 of the 1939 Harvard Draft.

110. NWP 1-14M, para. 7.10; Principle 5.2.10 of the Helsinki Principles ("Neutral vessels believed on reasonable and probable grounds to be breaching a blockade may be stopped and captured"); SAN REMO MANUAL, para. 98; R.W. TUCKER, *supra* note 10, p. 292 ff.; C.J. COLOMBOS, *supra* note 4, § 832; E. CASTRÉN, *supra* note 60, p. 304 ff.; D.P. O'CONNELL, LAW OF THE SEA II, *supra* note 97, p. 1156 f.; OPPENHEIM, *supra* note 4, p. 782 ff.; Articles 81 f. of the 1939 Harvard Draft.

111. Besides the foregoing references, see NWP 1-14M, paras. 7.5.2 and 8.2.2.

112. For the differentiation between inward and outward breach of blockade, see C.J. COLOMBOS, *supra* note 4, §§ 829, 831.

113. NWP 1-14M, para. 7.7.4. See also Canadian Draft, para. 722 (8).

114. In favor: C.J. COLOMBOS, *supra* note 4, § 835; J. STONE, *supra* note 59, p. 498; E. CASTRÉN, *supra* note 60, p. 306 f.

Against: R.W. TUCKER, *supra* note 10, pp. 310, 316, footnote 80; H. Wehberg, *Seekriegsrecht*, *supra* note 10, p. 161; P.A. MARTINI, BLOCKADE, *supra* note 97, p. 72 ff.; CH. ROUSSEAU, *supra* note 54, p. 271. See also TH. NIEMEYER, DAS SEEKRIEGSRECHT NACH DER LONDONER DEKLARATION, Berlin 1910, p. 21.

115. See the protests by neutral States printed in: OBERKOMMANDO DER KRIEGSMARINE, *supra* note 57, p. 18 ff., 329 ff.

Naval Blockade

116. See the references in H. Wehberg, *Seekriegsrecht, supra* note 10, p. 156 ff.; F. BERBER, *supra* note 94, p. 190 f.; F.D. v.Hansemann, *Die Lehre von der einheitlichen Reise im Rechte der Blockade und Kriegskonterbande*, ZEITSCHRIFT FÜR VÖLKERRECHT UND BUNDESSTAATSRECHT, Beiheft zum IV. Bande, Breslau 1910, p. 6 ff.

117. That expression was used in a German bulletin of September 13, 1939, printed in: OBERKOMMANDO DER KRIEGSMARINE, *supra* note 57, No. 40. See also P.A. MARTINI, BLOCKADE, *supra* note 97, p. 94 ff.; A.C. BELL, DIE ENGLISCHE HUNGERBLOCKADE IM WELTKRIEG 1914–15, Essen 1943, *passim*.

118. In his statement of September 26, 1939, the British Prime Minister said:

> There have been many proposals founded in the highest motives that food should be allowed to pass the blockade for the relief of these populations. I regret that we must refuse these requests. Many of these valuable foods are essential to the manufacture of vital war materials. Fats are used to make explosives. Potatoes make the alcohol for motor spirit. The plastic materials now so largely used in the construction of aircraft are made of milk. If the Germans use these commodities to help them to bomb our women and children rather than to feed the populations who produce them, we may be sure imported foods would go the same way, directly or indirectly, or be employed to relieve the enemy of the responsibilities he has so wantonly assumed;

Parl. Deb. House of Commons Bd. 351, 1237, cited in: W.N. MEDLICOTT, THE ECONOMIC BLOCKADE, Vol. I, London 1952, p. 666. See also P.A. MARTINI, BLOCKADE, *supra* note 97, p. 115.

119. The Australian delegate stated that "Article 48 [= Art. 54] does not prevent military operations intended to control and regulate the production and distribution of foodstuffs to the civilian population, and that it does not affect existing legal rules concerning the right of military forces to requisition foodstuffs. Moreover, in the view of my delegation, nothing in Article 48 directly or indirectly affects existing rules concerning naval blockade." CDDH Off. Rec. VI, 220. The same position was taken by the Third Committee in its 1975 Report, CDDH Off. Rec. XV, 279.

120. H. Meyrowitz, *Le protocole additionel I aux conventions de Genève de 1949 et le droit de la guerre maritime*, REVUE GÉNÉRALE DE DROIT INTERNATIONAL PUBLIC 89 (1985), pp. 243–298, 270 ff., 276 ff.; G.J.F. van Hegelsom, *Introductory Report, supra* note 89, p. 46. It is unclear whether Levie shares that view. H.S. Levie, *Means and Methods of Combat at Sea*, SYRACUSE JOURNAL OF INTERNATIONAL LAW AND COMMERCE 14 (1988), pp. 727 ff., 732. See also C. Pilloud/J. Pictet, in: ICRC, COMMENTARY ON THE ADDITIONAL PROTOCOLS OF 8 JUNE 1977 TO THE GENEVA CONVENTIONS OF 12 AUGUST 1949, GENEVA 1987, no. 2092. These authors, while rejecting the applicability of Article 54 to naval blockades, apply Article 70 on relief actions. There is, however, some contradiction, if these authors also hold (*ibid.*, no. 2095) that "it should be emphasized that the object of a blockade is to deprive the adversary of supplies needed to conduct hostilities, and not to starve civilians." Obviously, they were eager to avoid any contradiction to the Report of the Third Committee.

121. M. Bothe, *Commentary on the 1977 Geneva Protocol I*, in: N. Ronzitti, *supra* note 47, p. 764; E. RAUCH, PROTOCOL ADDITIONAL, *supra* note 54, p. 93 f. A more cautious approach is taken by W.A. Solf, in: M. BOTHE/K.J. PARTSCH/W.A. SOLF, NEW RULES FOR VICTIMS OF ARMED CONFLICTS, The Hague *et al.*, 1982, p. 338: "The Committee III report disclaims any intention to change the law of naval blockade, citing the provisions of Art. 49(3), although,

indirectly, it may have had some effect on that law through the provisions dealing with relief actions."

122. W.A. SOLF, *supra* note 121, p. 336. See also SAN REMO MANUAL, para. 102: "The declaration or establishment of a blockade is prohibited if: (a) it has the sole purpose of starving the civilian population or to deny it other objects essential for its survival [. . .]." Article 54 Additional Protocol I is to be considered a "new rule" that, as such, is not yet part of customary international law. In an annotation to NWP 1–14M, para. 8.1.2, the authors state that "Article 54(1) of Additional Protocol I would create a new prohibition on the starvation of civilians as a method of warfare [. . .] which the United States believes should be observed and in due course recognized as customary law [. . .]. Starvation of civilians as a method of warfare has potential implications on the law of blockade [. . .]."

123. SAN REMO MANUAL, para. 102 lit. (b). This is also accepted by those authors who reject an application of Article 54 of Additional Protocol I to naval blockades. See G.J.F. van Hegelsom, *Introductory Report*, *supra* note 89, p. 46: "[. . .] if the sole purpose of the blockade is to starve the civilian population, the blockade should be deemed illegal on the grounds that it is not directed at a military objective [. . .]. Termination of the blockade might be prompted if the collateral damage would be excessive in the light of the military advantage anticipated."

124. According to Article 23, paragraph 1, of the Fourth Geneva Convention (1949), "each High Contracting Party shall allow the free passage of all consignments of medical and hospital stores and objects necessary for religious worship intended only for civilians of another High Contracting Party, even if the latter is the adversary. It shall likewise permit the free passage of all consignments of essential foodstuffs, clothing and tonics intended for children under fifteen, expectant mothers and maternity cases." Relief consignments for the civilian population are regulated in Article 70, Additional Protocol I. The customary character of that provision is, *inter alia*, recognized in NWP 1–14M, paragraph 7.7.3: "Similarly, neutral vessels and aircraft engaged in the carriage of qualifying relief supplies for the civilian population and the sick and wounded should be authorized to pass through the blockade cordon."

125. M. Bothe, *Commentary*, *supra* note 121, p. 763 f.; G.J.F. van Hegelsom, *Introductory Report*, *supra* note 89, p. 46 f.; Y. Dinstein, *supra* note 94, 47 ff.; Y. Sandoz, in: ICRC, COMMENTARY, *supra* note 120, no. 2805; SAN REMO MANUAL, paras. 103 and 104. According to Principle 5.3 of the Helsinki Principles, "a blockade may not be used to prevent the passage of relief consignments which has to be free according to the applicable rules of international humanitarian law, in particular those contained in Articles 23, 59 and 61 of the Fourth Geneva Convention or Articles 69 and 70 of Protocol I Additional to the Geneva Conventions." See also the commentary thereon: "The provisions of the Geneva Conventions and the Additional Protocol referred to in this principle constitute an exception to the general rules of blockade. It is also submitted that these rules are part of customary law. Thus, they also bind those States which have not ratified the treaties mentioned in this principle."

126. SAN REMO MANUAL, para. 103. See also Article 23, para. 2, of the Fourth Geneva Convention and Principle 5.3 of the Helsinki Principles. In the commentary to the latter provision, the ILA states: "This obligation is, however, subject to the right to prescribe the technical arrangements, including search, under which such passage is permitted, and the condition that the distribution of such supplies shall be made under the local supervision of a Protecting Power or a humanitarian organisation which offers guarantees of impartiality."

127. Also covered are embargoes ordered by the Security Council pursuant to Article 41 if the member States are entitled to enforce the respective embargo "by all necessary means", i.e., the use of armed force. For example, by UN Security Council Resolution 217 of November 20, 1965, the United Kingdom was entitled to enforce the oil embargo against Rhodesia. The

economic sanctions imposed on Iraq by UNSC Resolution 661 of August 6, 1990, were, according to UNSC Resolution 665 of August 25, 1990, enforced by the States cooperating with Kuwait. In both cases, the Security Council did not decide according to Article 42, but according to Article 41 UN Charter.

128. ANNOTATED SUPPLEMENT TO THE COMMANDER'S HANDBOOK ON THE LAW OF NAVAL OPERATIONS, Newport 1997, para. 7.7.2.1, footnote 131.

129. For example, in UNSC Resolution 661 of August 6, 1990.

130. During the second Gulf War Iran, in particular, tried to assume a neutral status. This position, however, was rejected by the vast majority of States and international lawyers.

131. In its commentary on Principle 5.2.10 on blockade of the Helsinki Principles on the Law of Maritime Neutrality, the ILA maintains that "the Security Council, when acting by virtue of Chapter VII of the Charter, may adopt decisions deviating from this Principle (see Principle 1.2)." Principle 1.2 in part reads as follows:

> Nothing in the present Principles shall be construed as implying any limitation upon the powers of the Security Council under Chapters VII and VIII of the United Nations Charter. In particular, no State may rely upon the Principles stated herein in order to evade obligations laid upon it in pursuance of a binding decision of the Security Council.

In the commentary it is made clear that "the provision serves as a reminder that the principles do not preclude a modification of the rules of neutrality due to the law of the United Nations Charter ...."

132. W. Heintschel v. Heinegg, *The Current State of International Prize Law*, in: H.H.G. Post (ed.), INTERNATIONAL ECONOMIC LAW AND ARMED CONFLICT, Dordrecht *et al.* 1994, pp. 5 ff., 27.

[9]

The Exclusion Zone Device in the Law of Naval Warfare

W. J. FENRICK*

THE LAW OF NAVAL WARFARE has been a relatively unexplored field of law since the end of the Second World War, perhaps because of the depressing impact of state practice during the two world wars on the presumed content of the law as it existed prior to the First World War and because of the increasing complexity of the naval art.[1] A certain amount of scepticism concerning the relevance and effectiveness of law in time of armed conflict is quite justified. In the words of the late D. P. O'Connell,

> The only prediction that can be made with assurance is that the lower the level of conflict, the more localised the situation and the more restricted the objectives, the more predominant will be the element of law in the governing of naval conduct; and that the law will assume a diminished role — as it did in the Second World War — when the conflict becomes global, when the neutrals have been mostly drawn into it or their sympathies engaged, and when an element of desperation has entered into operational planning.[2]

The attempt to articulate legal standards for wartime conduct is a useful pursuit, as one of the major objectives of the law of armed conflict in general is to mitigate human suffering; in the pursuit of that objective, even marginal advances are worth attempting. The legal standards applied to wartime conduct must, however, be pre-

* Lieutenant-Colonel W. J. Fenrick, Director of International Law, Department of National Defence, Ottawa. The views expressed herein are those of the writer and do not necessarily reflect either the policy or the opinion of the Canadian government.

1 D. P. O'Connell, "International Law and Contemporary Naval Operations," (1970) 44 B.Y.I.L. 18-85.

2 D. P. O'Connell, *The Influence of Law on Sea Power* 3 (Manchester, 1975).

pared with full awareness of the realities of combat, and of technological constraints and possibilities. Standards that could be applied with ease to the activities of warships under sail might be technologically impossible to apply to warships and combat aircraft operating off the Falklands or in the Persian Gulf today. The purposes of naval forces in armed conflicts should also be borne in mind. These purposes include controlling sea areas so that one's own state can use them while denying control and use to the enemy. Armed conflict at sea has always had an economic element and has almost involved some interference by the naval forces of parties to the conflict with the shipping of non-parties.

In the twentieth-century conflicts, the ships and, more recently, the aircraft of non-participants have been most endangered in the two World Wars, the Spanish Civil War, and the Iran/Iraq Conflict. Exclusion zones were used in all these conflicts except in the Spanish Civil War. Further, with the exception of the Falklands conflict, major losses of non-participant lives and property occurred at sea in all conflicts in which exclusion zones have been used. An exclusion zone, also referred to as a military area, barred area, war zone, or operational zone, is an area of water and superjacent air space in which a party to an armed conflict purports to exercise control and to which it denies access to ships and aircraft without permission. It thus interferes with the normal rights of passage and overflight of ships and aircraft of non-parties. Unauthorized ships or aircraft entering the zone do so at the risk of facing sanctions, often including being attacked by missiles, aircraft, submarines, or surface warships, or of running into minefields. Exclusion zones are different from the more traditional blockade zones because in blockade zones the primary risk is that of capture, while in exclusion zones it is, frequently, the risk of attack on sight; they are also different from more recent devices such as the cordon sanitaire, which is intended to be used primarily in a period of tension prior to the commencement of hostilities.[3] A review of the history of the use of exclusion zones necessitates brief consideration of the areas in which naval warfare may lawfully be conducted and a more extensive consideration of what actions warships and aircraft engaged in a naval conflict may lawfully take against other ships or aircraft.

[3] M. E. Bowman, *Cordon Sanitaire: The Interaction of Law and Sea Power* (unpublished L.L.M. thesis, George Washington University, 1983) and S. F. Gilchrist, "The Cordon Sanitaire: Is It Useful? Is It Practical," (1982) 35 Naval War College Review (N.W.C.R.) 60-72.

The general area in which the naval forces of parties to an international armed conflict (hereinafter referred to as belligerents)[4] are permitted to conduct operations include: the high seas (including exclusive economic zones),[5] the territorial seas and internal waters of belligerents, the territory of belligerents, and the air space over these waters and territories. Although vessels and aircraft of non-parties to the conflict (hereinafter referred to as neutral vessels and aircraft),[6] which are not assisting an opposing belligerent in any way, have a right to proceed within the general area of naval operations because this area includes all of the high seas, their movements may be restricted or prohibited by a belligerent within the immediate area or vicinity of naval operations. The immediate area of naval operations is normally considered to be a relatively limited area within which naval hostilities are taking place or belligerent naval vessels are operating at the time.[7] If neutral vessels or aircraft refuse to comply with belligerent orders within this restricted area, they expose themselves to the risk of being fired upon. Belligerents are forbidden to use neutral territory, territorial waters, or air space as a base for hostile operations, or to conduct hostilities in such areas.[8]

Certain enemy vessels and aircraft, when innocently employed, are exempt from destruction or capture: cartel vessels and aircraft,

[4] In theory, a belligerent is a party to an armed conflict which has indicated it is in a state of war. In the past, nations often went to war without making a declaration of war. Formal declarations of war are now rare because of the restrictions on the use of force in the U.N. Charter. Parties to an international armed conflict may exercise belligerent rights even though they have not declared war: R. R. Baxter, "The Legal Consequences of the Unlawful Use of Force under the Charter," (1968) 62 Amer. Soc. Int'l. L. Proc. 68-75.

[5] The exact status of the exclusive economic zone defined in the 1982 Law of the Sea Convention is somewhat unclear. As it is an area where high seas freedoms apply, it is considered to be an area where warlike operations may occur. E. Rauch, *The Protocol Additional to the Geneva Conventions for the Protection of Victims of International Armed Conflicts and the United Nations Convention on the Law of the Sea: Repercussions on the Law of Naval Warfare* 33-38 (Berlin, 1984).

[6] The existence and content of the concept of neutrality is also unclear in the post-Charter era: P. M. Norton, "Between the Ideology and the Reality: The Shadow of the Law of Neutrality," (1976) 17 Harv. Int'l L. J. 249-311.

[7] *Law of Naval Warfare*, N.W.I.P. 10-2 at 4-6 (Washington, 1955 as amended).

[8] Art. 5, Hague Convention XIII of 1907 Concerning the Rights and Duties of Neutral Powers in Naval War, in D. Schindler and J. Toman, *The Laws of Armed Conflict* 855, 856 (2nd ed., Geneva, 1981).

that is, vessels or aircraft engaged in the exchange of prisoners of war, hospital ships, medical transports and medical aircraft, vessels charged with religious, scientific, or philanthropic missions, and small coastal fishing vessels and small boats engaged in local coastal trade.[9]

Enemy warships and military aircraft, including auxiliary vessels, may be attacked and destroyed or captured outside of neutral jurisdiction. The central question related to the legality of the use of exclusion zones is when, and to what extent, does a merchant vessel constitute a legitimate military objective that may be treated as an enemy warship or naval auxiliary vessel, that is, attacked on sight. If all merchant vessels constitute legitimate military objectives, then quite clearly the exclusion zone is purely a conflict control device to limit the scope of a conflict. If, however, all merchant vessels are not lawful military objectives, the zone may also be used as a means of increasing the intensity of a conflict by taking extraordinary measures within the zone.

Prior to the First World War, the law of naval warfare permitted the capture of enemy merchant vessels anywhere outside of neutral waters and the capture of neutral merchant vessels when these vessels breached a blockade, were engaged in the carriage of contraband, or were engaged in unneutral service. Under certain circumstances, warships could open fire on merchant vessels, normally when they resisted visit and search or when they were deemed to be resisting visit and search because they were being convoyed by warships. Generally speaking, however, warships were not permitted to open fire on merchant vessels without first warning them and giving them an opportunity to submit. The normal practice would be for the warship to capture the offending merchant vessel and to send it and its crew into port for adjudication by a prize court. Under limited, and contentious, circumstances a warship could destroy a captured merchant vessel but only after all persons on board were placed in a position of safety.[10] As an additional complicating factor, for his-

[9] Arts. 3 and 4, Hague Convention XI of 1907 Relative to Certain Restrictions with regard to the Exercise of the Right of Capture in Naval War, *ibid.*, 731, 732-33, and Art. 22, 24, 25, 28, and 39, Geneva Convention (II) for the Amelioration of the Wounded, Sick and Shipwrecked Members of Armed Forces at Sea, *ibid.*, 333-54.

[10] J. W. Garner, "War Zones and Submarine Warfare," (1915) 9 Am. J. Int'l L. 594, 612-26, and "Destruction of Neutral Merchant Vessels," (1916) 10 Am. J. Int'l L. 12-41.

torical reasons, merchant vessels were permitted to carry weapons for "defensive" purposes.[11]

Although Japan made the first minor effort in this century to establish an exclusion zone during the Russo-Japanese war,[12] the warring powers during the First World War made the first major attempts to make use of the concept. Allegedly in retaliation for indiscriminate mine-laying in the open seas by Germany, the British government in November 1914 issued an order declaring the North Sea an exclusion zone or military area. The order emphasized that entry into the area by any vessels without permission would be dangerous because mines had been laid there and because warships were searching for the enemy in the area. The threat to merchant vessels and fishing vessels was oblique; they were not directly threatened but "warned of the dangers they encounter by entering this area except in strict accordance with Admiralty directions."[13] Certain safe passage routes were provided, however, for ships trading to or from European neutral states. The British measure was further justified as an "exceptional measure, appropriate to the novel conditions under which this war is being carried on."[14] The area of the zone was extended in 1916 and on a number of occasions in 1917.

In retaliation for various British measures in the naval war, the German Admiralty published the following decree on February 4, 1915:

> The waters around Great Britain, including the whole of the English Channel, are declared hereby to be included within the zone of war, and after the 18th inst. all enemy merchant vessels encountered in these waters will be destroyed, even if it may not be possible always to save their crews and passengers.
>
> Within this war zone neutral vessels are exposed to danger, since, in view of the misuse of the neutral flags ordered by the Government of Great Britain on the 31st ult. and of the hazards of naval warfare, neutral vessels cannot always be prevented from suffering from the attacks intended for enemy ships.
>
> The route of navigation around the north of the Shetland Islands, in the eastern part of the North Sea, and in a strip thirty miles wide along the Dutch Coast are not open to the danger zone.[15]

11 A. Pearce Higgins, *Studies in International Law and Relations* 239-304 (Cambridge, 1928).

12 J. W. Garner, *International Law and the World War*, Vol. I, at 351-52 (London, 1920).

13 *Ibid.*, 333.

14 *Ibid.*, 334.

15 Garner, *op. cit. supra* note 10, "War Zones," at 594.

From 1915 until 1917, Germany made various extensions and alterations to its exclusion (war) zone and adopted various policies within it. Finally, in January 1917, Germany announced that it intended to adopt a policy of unrestricted warfare. Within the zone, effective February 1, 1917, "all sea traffic was to be forthwith opposed by means of mines and submarines."[16] This final German action, coming after several disputes with the United States concerning German actions at sea, provided a catalyst for the American entry into the war in April.

A few comments concerning the nature of the conflict and the means available to the contending belligerents are necessary before appraising the use of exclusion zones in the First World War. Throughout the conflict, Great Britain maintained control of the surface of the seas. As the conflict degenerated into a war of attrition, it commenced an increasingly rigorous war against the German economy in an attempt to starve the population and to weaken the economy so that Germany would be compelled to surrender. The general effect of British actions was to sweep enemy merchant vessels from the seas, and to render liable to seizure all cargoes proceeding, directly or indirectly, to or from Germany. The British economic warfare campaign was both extremely successful[17] and of debatable legality, more because of its reliance on a so-called "long distance blockade"[18] than because of its use of an exclusion zone in the North Sea. As a general statement, however, British actions did not involve direct attacks on neutral shipping.

Germany also considered itself compelled to take drastic measures in the war at sea. As the weaker surface naval power, it was not in a position effectively to contest command of the sea with the British fleet or to protect merchant shipping en route to Germany. It did, however, discover that the mine and, in particular, the submarine could be employed extremely effectively in commerce warfare. As the submarine was a small vessel and, with the exception of torpedoes, weakly armed, it was not able to perform the traditional tasks of visit and search of merchant vessels once the opposing belligerent began to arm merchant vessels and ordered them to act

[16] Garner, *op. cit. supra* note 12, at 337.

[17] L. Guichard, *The Naval Blockade, 1914-1918* (New York, 1930).

[18] H. W. Malkin, "Blockade in Modern Conditions," (1922-23) 3 B.Y.I.L. 86-98.

aggressively in self-defence by ramming.[19] In order to exert economic pressure on Britain similar to that exercised through other means by Britain on Germany, Germany began to use its submarines to attack merchant shipping en route to and from Britain. The German economic warfare campaign against Britain, waged with submarines and mines, was effective but not as effective as the British economic warfare campaign against Germany, enforced primarily by surface warships and through a variety of self-help measures. The German campaign did, however, involve direct attacks on allied and neutral merchant shipping which resulted in substantial loss of lives and property. Although British actions did not result in direct loss of life, German writers at the time and since have argued that the British campaign caused substantial indirect loss of life to the German civilian population through starvation and malnutrition.[20]

Although exclusion zones were used by both sides during the First World War, they were not approved of by legal writers who, generally speaking, viewed them as an illegitimate interference with the rights of neutrals to exercise the freedom of the seas.[21] Criticism of the British North Sea exclusion zone was somewhat muted because of British measures to provide alternative routes for neutral ships and because it did not appear that any neutral ship ever ran into a British mine. In the words of a pro-British, American writer, J. W. Garner, "[B]elligerents have no right to appropriate any portion of the high seas and close them to the navigation of neutral vessels, and it is very doubtful whether they may lawfully plant mines in them in such a way as to expose neutral ships to the danger of destruction while peacefully navigating the waters thereof."[22] Garner's opinion of German actions from 1917 onward was concise: "As for the German war zone decree of January, 1917, it was so flagrantly contrary to the laws of maritime warfare that nothing can

[19] Captain Fryatt, the captain of an unarmed British merchant vessel, was condemned as an unlawful combatant for attempting to ram a German submarine and was executed by Germany in 1916. The view that Captain Fryatt was an unlawful combatant was not accepted outside Germany. Garner, *op. cit. supra* note 12, at 407-14.

[20] Garner, *op. cit. supra* note 12, Vol. II, at 336-39, and Rauch, *op. cit. supra* note 5, at 86-87.

[21] J. A. Hall, *The Law of Naval Warfare* 246-47 (2nd ed., London, 1921); C. C. Hyde, *International Law Chiefly as Interpreted and Applied by the United States* 1948-52 (2nd rev. ed., Boston, 1951).

[22] Garner, *op. cit. supra* note 12, at 352-53.

be said in defence of it."[23] Some German writers argued that, in a sense, "new weapons make new law," and that in a war that tended towards totality, merchant vessels carrying goods to and from a belligerent constituted military objectives that could be attacked in the same way as warships.[24] As defenders of the losing side in the war, their views went unheeded.

During the interwar period, a number of attempts were made by Britain to abolish submarines, notably at the Washington Conference of 1921-22 and the London Conference of 1930, but on all such occasions Britain was blocked by France, which argued that submarines were useful vessels of war, particularly for weaker powers, although they should be required to follow the same rules as surface vessels.[25] A set of rules for submarine warfare was developed at the London Naval Conference and inserted as Part IV, Article 22, in the 1930 London Treaty for the Limitation and Reduction of Naval Armaments[26] and reaffirmed in a 1936 Procès-Verbal (the London Protocol of 1936).[27] The rules are as follows:

(1) In their action with regard to merchant ships, submarines must conform to the rules of international law to which surface vessels are subject.

(2) In particular, except in the case of persistent refusal to stop on being duly summoned, or of active resistance to visit or search, a warship, whether surface vessel or submarine, may not sink or render incapable of navigation a merchant vessel without having first placed passengers, crew and ship's papers in a place of safety. For this purpose the ship's boats are not regarded as a place of safety unless the safety of the passengers and crew is assured, in the existing sea and weather conditions, by the proximity of land, or the presence of another vessel which is in a position to take them on board.

The proper interpretation of the above rules is by no means clear, but some assistance can be derived from the Report of the Committee of Jurists which prepared the text of the 1930 London Treaty. The report stated in part: "The Committee wish to place it on record that the expression 'merchant vessel,' where it is em-

[23] *Ibid.*, 354.

[24] Authorities are cited in R. W. Tucker, *The Law of War and Neutrality at Sea* 301-2 (Washington, 1957).

[25] W. T. Mallison, *Studies in the Law of Naval Warfare: Submarines in General and Limited Wars* 36-47 (Washington, 1968).

[26] Schindler and Toman, *op. cit. supra* note 8, at 793-94.

[27] *Ibid.*, 795-97.

ployed in the declaration, is not to be understood as including a merchant vessel which is at the moment participating in hostilities in such a manner as to cause her to lose her right to the immunities of a merchant vessel."[28] Unfortunately, the Committee did not go on to explain the meaning of "participating in hostilities." A review of the documents of the 1930 London Conference does not indicate there was any discussion of exclusion zones or related concepts.[29]

The Spanish Civil War of 1936-39 was the one conflict between the two World Wars in which there was a large number of attacks on merchant vessels of non-parties to the conflict.[30] The major legal controversy during the conflict concerned whether or not parties to the civil war could exercise belligerent rights on the high seas.[31] As the major naval powers denied such rights to the parties, the Nationalists, with the covert assistance of Italy, began to attack ships without warning on the high seas en route to and from Republican Spain and without the proclamation of exclusion zones. To discourage such attacks, several states met at Nyon in 1937 and agreed to direct their navies to take action against any aircraft, surface vessels, or submarines that attacked merchant vessels outside Spanish territorial waters in contravention of the London Protocol rules.[32] Article 3 of the Nyon Agreement created a type of reverse exclusion zone, as it directed the navies of the parties to the arrangement to counterattack and destroy submarines "in the vicinity" of merchant vessels that had been attacked even if the submarine was not known to have been the initial attacker.

During the Second World War, Great Britain waged economic warfare on the seas and elsewhere against Germany in a manner essentially similar to that used in the earlier conflict. The economic warfare campaign at sea was much less effective than its First World War equivalent because, until the final period of the war, Germany was able to draw resources as needed from the countries it occupied. As in the First World War, Great Britain sought to legitimize many of its actions on the basis of reprisals.[33] Britain also established a

28 *Documents of the London Naval Conference 1930* 443 (London, 1930).

29 *Ibid.*, in entirety.

30 W. C. Frank, "Naval Operations in the Spanish Civil War, 1936-39" (1984) 37 Naval War College Review 24-55.

31 O'Connell, *op. cit. supra* note 2, at 115-22.

32 Schindler and Toman, *op. cit. supra* note 8, at 799-802.

33 F. Kalshoven, *Belligerent Reprisals* 115-60 (Leyden, 1971).

small exclusion zone in the Skaggerak for a portion of the war. Within this zone, all German ships were to be sunk by day and all ships by night.[34] At the time when this zone was in effect, it was most unlikely that neutral ships would be in the area.

Germany initially attempted to conduct sea warfare not only in compliance with the London Protocol Rules on submarine warfare but also in compliance with the 1909 Declaration of London.[35] For reasons essentially similar to those in the First World War, however, it soon relied upon unrestricted submarine warfare and upon an equally unrestricted anti-shipping campaign conducted by aircraft within ever wider exclusion zones.[36]

Prior to its entry into the war, the United States, in order to minimize the possibility of its involvement, took two actions involving zones similar to exclusion zones. First, as a unilateral act, under the 1939 Neutrality Act it set up European danger zones extending far out to sea from the waters of the belligerents and ordered its merchant ships not to sail in these zones.[37] The purpose of the danger zones was to minimize the risk of American ships being attacked by German submarines as had occurred in the First World War. Germany paid considerable heed to the limits of declared United States danger zones in declaring its own exclusion zones.[38] Neither Germany nor the United States wanted the latter to be dragged into the war as a result of German submarine warfare practices as in 1917. Second, the foreign ministers of all the American republics approved the Declaration of Panama on October 3, 1939 which established a security zone, also referred to as a chastity belt, around the Americas south of Canada, ranging from 300 to 1000 miles out to sea depending on the coastline.[39] Belligerents were warned to re-

[34] Mallison, *op. cit. supra* note 25, at 86-87.

[35] *The German Prize Ordinance of 1939, with a Commentary and Introductory Note by Professor H. A. Smith* (1939) Cdn. D Hist. File 81/520/1540. The *Athenia,* an unarmed British passenger liner, was sunk by a German submarine on September 3, 1939, but it appears that this action was the responsibility of an inexperienced submarine commander who believed the *Athenia* was an armed merchant cruiser.

[36] Exclusion zone declarations are contained in *U.S. Naval War College, International Law Documents 1943* 51-67 (Washington, 1945) and U.S. Naval War College, *International Law Documents 1940* 44-52 (Washington, 1942).

[37] T. A. Bailey and P. B. Ryan, *Hitler vs. Roosevelt: The Undeclared Naval War* 35-38 (New York, 1979).

[38] *Trials of the Major War Criminals before the International Military Tribunal,* Vol. XVIII, at 328 (Nuremberg, 1948).

[39] Bailey and Ryan, *op. cit. supra* note 37, at 38-40.

frain from naval action within the zone. Its creation did interfere with belligerent rights on the high seas but the belligerents did not protest over-loudly, as Britain knew it depended on American support and as Germany did not wish to antagonize the Americans.[40]

During the Second World War, the United States Navy also waged an extremely successful unrestricted anti-shipping campaign against Japanese sea communications in the Pacific.[41] Following Pearl Harbor, the United States declared the whole Pacific Ocean an exclusion zone and attacked all non-allied shipping in the area with submarines, aircraft, and mines,[42] with the exception of a limited amount of shipping to and from the USSR, which was a neutral in the Pacific war until August 1945. Although the area of the United States exclusion zone was enormous, it must be conceded that, except for traffic to and from the USSR, it is most unlikely that there would have been merchant vessels in the Pacific for reasons unconnected to the conflict while the zone was in effect.

Law of naval warfare issues were raised in a number of war crimes trials following the war. Admirals Doenitz and Raeder were tried, together with the other German major war criminals, before the International Military Tribunal at Nuremberg for, among other things, war crimes on the high seas. The decision concerning Admiral Doenitz is the only international judicial decision to address the exclusion zone issue explicitly. Doenitz, charged with waging unrestricted submarine warfare contrary to the London Protocol of 1936, argued in defence that the German Navy remained within the confines of international law and of the Protocol. Initially, German submarines were ordered to attack all merchant ships in convoy and all that refused to stop or used their radio upon sighting a submarine, as such ships were deemed to be resisting visit and search and therefore, under the traditional law, were subject to attack. By October 17, 1939, when German reports indicated British merchant ships were being used to give information by wireless, were being armed, and were attacking submarines on sight, Doenitz ordered his submarines to attack all enemy merchant ships on sight. The Tribunal found:

40 O'Connell, *op. cit. supra* note 2, at 162-64.

41 C. Blair, *Silent Victory: The U.S. Submarine War against Japan* (New York, 1975).

42 Testimony of Admiral Nimitz, Document Donitz — 100 in Trials, *op. cit. supra* note 40, Vol. XL, at 109-11.

Shortly after the outbreak of war the British Admiralty, in accordance with its Handbook of Instructions of 1938 to the Merchant Navy, armed its merchant vessels, in many cases convoyed them with armed escort, gave orders to send position reports upon sighting submarines, thus integrating merchant vessels into the warning network of naval intelligence. On 1st October, 1939, the British Admiralty announced British merchant ships had been ordered to ram U-boats if possible.

In the actual circumstances of this case, the Tribunal is not prepared to hold Doenitz guilty for his conduct of submarine warfare against British armed merchant ships.[43]

Although the wording of this portion of the judgment is by no means clear, in its context it exonerated Doenitz from responsibility for attacks on all belligerent merchant vessels because of the general belligerent practice of incorporating all such vessels into the war effort.

Presumably when belligerents make a general practice of arming and convoying their merchant vessels, integrating them into their intelligence networks, and ordering them to ram U-boats if possible, the vessels are considered to be participating in hostilities to such an extent as to disentitle them to the benefits of the London Protocol. This portion of the judgment indicates that the London Protocol is a document that, because of the very nature of submarine warfare and of modern general war, is likely to be of very little significance in a general war. Any argument as to which came first, British submarine countermeasures or German submarine warfare practices, is of the chicken and egg variety. If the Germans were going to use submarines, the British had to adopt such countermeasures. If the British adopted such countermeasures, the Germans had to adopt unrestricted submarine warfare or to abandon use of submarines against enemy commerce. Unfortunately, although the tribunal indirectly faced the issue of the compatibility of the London Protocol Rules with the demonstrated conduct of belligerent merchant shipping, it avoided addressing the substantially similar issue of the compatibility of the London Protocol Rules with the demonstrated conduct of neutral merchant shipping when such shipping was used in a manner functionally indistinguishable from the use of belligerent merchant shipping.

A partial explanation for the muddiness of the Tribunal's judgment on submarine warfare is that that portion of the judgment was drafted by Francis Biddle, the American member of the Tribunal

[43] *Judgement of the International Military Tribunal for the Trial of German Major War Criminals* 108-9 (London CMD 6946, 1946).

who was opposed to the conviction of Doenitz on submarine warfare charges and threatened to file a public dissent. The other judges agreed to let him write this portion of the judgment to forestall his dissent.[44]

The Tribunal then considered a charge that Doenitz deliberately ordered the killing of shipwrecked survivors, but found the evidence of this charge insufficient, although it did censure him for ordering that rescue operations not be carried out, saying:

> The evidence further shows that the rescue provisions were not carried out and that the defendant ordered that they should not be carried out. The argument of the defence is that the security of the submarine is, as the first rule of the sea, paramount to rescue and that the development of aircraft made rescue impossible. This may be so, but the Protocol is explicit. If the commander cannot rescue, then under its terms he cannot sink a merchant vessel and should allow it to pass harmless before his periscope. These orders then, prove Doenitz is guilty of a violation of the Protocol.[45]

This charge arose as a result of the *Laconia* order issued by Doenitz following an attack by an American aircraft on German submarines attempting to rescue survivors from the *Laconia*, which one of their number had torpedoed.[46] Following the incident, Doenitz ordered that no attempts be made to rescue survivors. This particular finding is inconsistent with the earlier finding exonerating him on a charge concerning the conduct of submarine warfare against belligerent merchant vessels. H. B. Robertson has suggested that this finding applies exclusively to neutral merchant vessels.[47] It is, however, difficult to understand why neutral merchant vessels should be treated in a different manner from belligerent merchant vessels if they are in fact incorporated in the belligerent war effort.

On a number of occasions, the German government established exclusion zones around the British Isles and announced that all ships, including neutral merchant ships, would be sunk without warning in these areas. Concerning exclusion zones, the Tribunal held:

44 B. F. Smith, *Reaching Judgment at Nuremberg* 247-65, particularly 262 (London, 1977).

45 Judgment, *op. cit. supra* note 43, at 109.

46 L. Peillard, *The Laconia Affair* (New York, 1963) and Mallison, *op. cit. supra* note 25, at 137-39.

47 H. B. Robertson, "Submarine Warfare," (1956) JAG Journal 3, 7.

However, the proclamation of operational zones and the sinking of neutral merchant vessels which enter those zones present a different question. This practice was employed in the War of 1914-18 by Germany and adopted in retaliation by Great Britain. The Washington Conference of 1922, the London Naval Agreement of 1930, and the Protocol of 1936, were entered into with full knowledge that such zones had been employed in the First World War. Yet the Protocol made no exception for operational zones. The order of Doenitz to sink neutral ships without warning when found within these zones was, therefore, in the opinion of the Tribunal violation of the Protocol. . . .

In view of all the facts proved and in particular of an order of the British Admiralty announced on the 8th May, 1940, according to which all vessels should be sunk at night in the Skagerrak, and the answers to interrogatories by Admiral Nimitz stating that unrestricted submarine warfare was carried on in the Pacific Ocean by the United States from the first day that nation entered the war, the sentence of Doenitz is not assessed on the ground of his breaches of the international law of submarine warfare.[48]

This portion of the judgment appears to accept the legitimacy of exclusion zones for belligerent merchant vessels under certain circumstances but to prohibit such zones when they affect neutral merchant vessels. In so doing it ignores the fact that in a general war many neutral vessels will be engaged in transporting cargoes in support of one belligerent's war effort and will, therefore, be functionally indistinguishable from belligerent merchant vessels. The rationale for the decision concerning exclusion zones is not as clear as might be desired. Presumably, as the London Protocol did not explicitly address the issue, and as both sides used exclusion zones, it would have been quite possible for the Tribunal to decide that these zones were permissible under certain circumstances. A colloquy between Kranzbuhler, Doenitz's counsel, and the Tribunal during the proceedings indicates that the Tribunal was concerned about the possibility that legitimizing exclusion zones might result in shipping being endangered by navally "weak" states solely on the basis of a declaration. The Tribunal apparently considered that the right to declare an exclusion zone should depend upon the power to enforce the zone or to make it effective. It appears to have concluded that, as with traditional blockades, exclusion zones must be enforced by surface warships rather than by submarines alone. It was not persuaded by Kranzbuhler's argument that all that was necessary for a legitimate zone was a declaration plus the probability of danger to neutral shipping from any form of attack to-

[48] Judgment, *op. cit. supra* note 43, at 109.

gether with the impossibility for operational reasons of the belligerent declaring the zone to protect neutral shipping in the zone.[49] The Tribunal's decision notwithstanding, the submarine appears to be a terribly effective weapon in the commerce destruction role and the use of submarines in exclusion zones does not appear to be a confession of true naval weakness.

The Tribunal made the same finding against Raeder as it did against Doenitz on the charge of waging unrestricted submarine warfare, that is, guilty of waging unrestricted submarine warfare against neutrals but no sentence imposed because of similar Allied practices.[50] The acceptance of a *tu quoque* argument in mitigation is unprecedented in the Tribunal's proceedings themselves although, at a preliminary stage, the United Nations War Crimes Commission declined to address the issue of offences resulting from air warfare, including aerial attacks on shipping, probably because the Allies were the major practitioners of the art.[51]

Assessing the impact of the Tribunal's judgment on the scope and applicability of the London Protocol is not a simple task. D. P. O'Connell has attempted to cut the Gordian knot by arguing:

> The truth is that the requirements of the London Protocol are to be observed only in the situation where the submarine can act with minimal risk on the surface. Since that situation is now an ideal hardly ever in practice to be realized, one is compelled to draw from the Doenitz trial the conclusion that submarine operations in time of war are today governed by no legal text, and that no more than lip-service is being paid in naval documents to the London Protocol.[52]

There is some basis for arguing that the London Protocol was drafted in favour of surface naval powers, particularly Great Britain, as a fall-back position after efforts to outlaw the employment of submarines had failed and as an attempt to neutralize the effectiveness of the submarine in the commerce destruction role. The Protocol is virtually unworkable in a general war between naval powers where one side has a substantial preponderance in surface naval strength, because it does not confer substantially equal benefits on both sides. The practical effectiveness of the law of war in a particular conflict

[49] Trials, *op. cit. supra* note 38, Vol. XVIII, at 332-34.

[50] Judgment, *op. cit. supra* note 43, at 112.

[51] *History of the United Nations War Crimes Commission* 492 (London, 1948).

[52] O'Connell, *op. cit. supra* note 1, at 52.

is conditional upon, among other factors, a crude reciprocity and a rough equivalence of benefits.

The key to a workable interpretation of the London Protocol lies in determining the proper meaning of the undefined term "merchant vessel" in that document. In a general war, the true merchant vessel is rarely to be found because the belligerent states normally assume such a degree of control over their own vessels and neutral vessels engaged in trading with them as to convert them into de facto naval auxiliaries. As such, they should be subject to the same treatment as *de jure* naval auxiliaries, that is, they may be sunk on sight outside neutral waters. Even in a general war, however, there may be genuine neutral traffic which is entitled to proceed unmolested and in a war more limited than that of the Second World War, many merchant vessels, even those of the contending parties, will be engaged in normal trade quite unconnected with the war effort. Being clearly not de facto naval auxiliaries, they are entitled to all the benefits of the London Protocol.[53]

With the exception of Doenitz and Raeder, no one charged with war crimes following the two World Wars was convicted for sinking ships in exclusion zones or for sinking merchant ships without warning. The few relevant convictions registered in reported decisions were for massacring survivors (*Llandovery Castle*, *Peleus*),[54] ordering that survivors be killed (*Moehle*),[55] and for both continuing to fire after the enemy surrendered and for sinking merchant vessels without making any provision for the safety of the survivors (*Von Ruchteschell*).[56] Von Ruchteschell was the commander of a German surface raider and he was operating in circumstances in which it would have been quite possible for him to take survivors aboard, in

[53] Mallison, *op. cit. supra* note 25, at 117-23.

[54] There were two war crimes trials concerning submarine warfare held before German courts at Liepzig following the First World War. In the *Dover Castle* case, (1922) 16 Am. J. Int'l L. 704-8, the accused, a German submarine commander, was acquitted on a charge of sinking a British hospital ship on the basis of superior orders and a belief that his actions were a legitimate reprisal. In the *Llandovery Castle* case, (1922) 16 Am. J. Int'l L. 708-23, two German submarine officers were convicted for massacring the survivors of a torpedoed hospital ship. Their plea of superior orders was not accepted because "The killing of defenceless shipwrecked people is an act in the highest degree contrary to ethical principles." J. Cameron, ed., *The Peleus Trial* (London, 1948).

[55] *Moehle Trial*, 9 *Law Reports of Trials of War Criminals* (L.R.T.W.C.) 75-81.

[56] *Von Ruchteschell Trial*, 9 L.R.T.W.C. 82-90.

contrast to the circumstances in which submarines usually operated. It is significant that although merchant ships were attacked without warning in both the *Peleus* and *Von Ruchteschell* cases, in neither case did these actions form the basis of a charge. Unless a deliberate effort is made to massacre survivors, it appears that individual unit commanders are unlikely to expose themselves to war crimes charges if they attack merchant ships without warning in exclusion zones in compliance with superior orders. As the law is not entirely clear, it appears appropriate that if individuals are to be penalized for such actions, it should only, at most, be those in the most senior command positions, such as Doenitz and Raeder. Indeed, it might be more appropriate to consider actions occurring in exclusion zones, other than breaches of explicit and generally accepted treaty law, as perhaps giving rise to state responsibility but not forming the basis of war crimes charges.[57]

Assessments of the legitimacy of the exclusion zones since the Second World War have been much more cautious than those made in the aftermath of the First World War. Some writers continued to argue that exclusion zones that pose the risk of attack on sighting are illegal per se, both when applied against neutrals and in the relations between belligerents.[58] Others adopt a slightly more qualified approach. Colombos is typical of these: "any declaration of war zones by a belligerent is unlawful unless supported by naval forces sufficient to ensure the effective control of his regulations within the declared area of belligerent operations and unless it is of such a character as not to imperil the lives of neutral and non-combatant persons."[59] This approach appears to accept exclusion zones but only if they are not enforced by a sink-on-sight policy. As such, it is more restrictive than the Doenitz decision, which appears to

[57] The Second World War *Awa Maru* incident and aftermath may be a more accurate indication of future trends than the war crimes trials. The *Awa Maru* was a Japanese ship torpedoed by a U.S. submarine after it was given safe passage by American authorities. The submarine commander was court-martialed by American authorities and convicted of negligent performance of duties: R. Spear, "Let Pass Safely the *Awa Maru*," (1974) 100 U.S. N.I.P. 69. The approach taken in the *Corfu Channel* case may also be relevant: *The Corfu Channel Case (Merits)*, in R. Churchill, K. R. Simmons, and J. Welch, eds., *New Directions in the Law of the Sea*, Vol. IV, at 286-319 (London, 1973).

[58] Castren and Guggenheim as referred to in M. M. Whiteman, *Digest of International Law*, Vol. X, at 607-8 (Washington, 1968).

[59] C. J. Colombos, *The International Law of the Sea* 466 (4th rev. ed., London, 1961).

accept exclusion zones enforced by a sink-on-sight policy directed against belligerent merchant shipping incorporated into the enemy war effort. Tucker accepted the Doenitz decision as setting the basic criterion, although he observed, "while a legal analysis cannot be unmindful of current — and persistent — realities it cannot make so easy an identification of legal right with belligerent practices."[60] Other writers have argued that exclusion zones enforceable by sink-on-sight policies directed against both neutral and belligerent shipping are permissible in general war provided that the shipping involved is incorporated in the belligerent war effort.[61] It is clear that post-war writers did not have a common view concerning the legitimacy of the use of exclusion zones in future general wars, but that almost all expected them to be used in such conflicts. A number of writers expressed the hope, however, that more restrained approaches might be possible in limited or small wars.[62]

For the purposes of the law of naval warfare, general war can be considered as a war similar to the Second World War, that is, a war fought in large part on the high seas to achieve the overthrow of the enemy's social system by major naval powers with all the resources at each belligerent's command. Limited wars include wars involving lesser naval powers and wars involving major powers but limited in areas of operations, weapons used, and targets attacked. It is desirable that a more restrictive *lex specialis* for limited conflicts be developed, but the concept of a law of naval warfare for limited conflicts presents intellectual difficulties because of the broad range of conflicts that can be classified as limited.[63] It is also important that the law of naval warfare for a particular conflict be readily ascertainable by the parties to a conflict and have the same content for all such parties. If one party, for political reasons, considers it a relatively limited conflict and an opposing party for its own reasons considers it to be much less limited, the contending parties should not be held to differing legal standards. This is not an artificial problem. During the Vietnam conflict, many opponents of the American cause subjected American actions to much more stringent criticism than that applied to North Vietnamese actions.

[60] R. W. Tucker, *The Law of War and Neutrality at Sea* 302 (Washington, 1957).

[61] Mallison, *op. cit. supra* note 25, at 91-93, and Sohler as referred to in Whiteman, *op. cit. supra* note 59, Vol. X, at 609.

[62] H. A. Smith, *The Crisis in the Law of Nations* 57-58, 64-66 (London, 1947), and Mallison, *op. cit. supra* note 25, at 93-96.

Limited wars are the typical wars of our time. Relatively few of the armed conflicts occurring since 1945 have involved combat on the high seas or interference with neutral shipping outside of the territorial waters of the participants. With the exception of the Iran/Iraq conflict, there has been no post-1945 conflict that has involved sustained attacks on neutral shipping, although a few such attacks have occurred in the various Arab/Israeli conflicts and in the short-lived Indo-Pakistan War of 1971. In the Korea and Vietnam conflicts, blockades were established for portions of the conflicts but there is no indication ships attempted to breach these blockades or were captured or attacked for so doing.[64] The use of exclusion zones has been most pronounced in the Falklands conflict and in the Iran/Iraq conflict.

One unusual aspect of the 1982 Falklands naval conflict was the proliferation of exclusion zones utilized by Britain and Argentina. The rationale for these zones is difficult to determine;[65] presumably they were intended to provide a visible manifestation of both sides' conscious efforts to limit the scope of the conflict. In all, there were seven zones, four British: (a) April 12 Maritime Exclusion Zone (MEZ), (b) April 23 Defensive Bubble, (c) April 30 Total Exclusion Zone (TEZ), and (d) May 7 Policy Statement; and three Argentinian: (a) April 8 Maritime Zone, (b) April 29 strengthened Maritime Zone, and (c) May 11 South Atlantic War Zone. In addition, when the Total Exclusion Zone was lifted by Britain on July 22, 1982, after the conflict was over, Britain asked Argentina to ensure that its warships and military aircraft did not enter a

[63] The late D. P. O'Connell was a prime exponent of the idea of a *lex specialis* for limited naval warfare although his position altered over time. A discussion of his varying positions is contained in J. Crawford, "The Contributions of Professor D. P. O'Connell to the Discipline of International Law," (1980) 51 B.Y.I.L. 1, at 62-66.

[64] W. J. Fenrick, *Developments in the Law of Naval Warfare since World War II: The Potential Emergence of a Law of Naval Warfare for Limited Conflicts* 53-91 (unpublished L.L.M. thesis, George Washington University, 1983).

[65] In a letter to the London *Times* (April 7, 1982, at 5) Col. G. I. A. D. Draper observed, with reference to a suggestion in Parliament that a 200-mile zone be created: "This is a rather curious proposal. In time of armed conflict at sea, such a limit would restrict action by the Royal Navy to an extent not required by international law. In time of normality a 200-mile limit will be difficult to justify because such a claim for a territorial sea is not yet accepted in international law."

zone 150 miles around the islands where they would pose a potential threat to British forces.[66]

On April 7, Britain informed Argentina that, as of April 12, "a maritime exclusion zone will be established around the Falkland Islands." The zone would extend for 200 miles from the centre of the islands. "Any Argentine warships and Argentine naval auxiliaries found within this zone will be treated as hostile and are liable to be attacked by British forces."[67] Britain also reserved its right to take further action in self-defence under Article 51 of the U.N. Charter. Argentina responded by attacking the British communication concerning the MEZ as "a notification of blockade — an act expressly defined as aggression in UNGA Res. 3314 (XXIX) of 14 December 1974, Article 3(c) of which specifies that, regardless of a declaration of war, the blockade of the ports or coasts of a State by the armed forces of another state is an action of aggression."[68] Since the MEZ declaration was preceded by the Argentinian invasion of the Falkland Islands, this argument appears to be based on a misreading of the aggression definition.

On April 23, Britain established a "Defensive Area" or "bubble" around its task force as an additional measure for self-defence and so informed the Argentine government and the United Nations.

> Her Majesty's Government wishes to make clear that any approach on [the] part of Argentine warships including submarines, naval auxiliaries or military aircraft which could amount to a threat to interfere with [the] mission of British forces in [the] South Atlantic will encounter appropriate responses. All Argentine aircraft, including civil aircraft engaging in surveillance of these British forces will be regarded as hostile and are liable to be dealt with accordingly.[69]

On April 28, Britain announced it was establishing a Total Exclusion Zone (TEZ) effective April 30. The announcement stated the TEZ would apply to the same zone as the MEZ and went on to state:

> [T]he exclusion zone will apply not only to Argentine warships and naval auxiliaries but also to any other ship, whether naval or merchant vessel, which is operating in support of the illegal occupation of the Falkland Islands by Argentine forces.

66 "United Kingdom Materials on International Law 1982," (1982) 53 B.Y.I.L. 556.

67 London *Times*, April 7, 1982, at 6.

68 Congressional Record, May 3, 1982, at S4431.

69 London *Times*, April 26, 1982, at 5.

The zone will also apply to any aircraft, whether military or civil, which is operating in support of the Argentine occupation. Any ship and any aircraft, whether military or civil, which is found within the zone without authority from the Ministry of Defence in London will be regarded as operating in support of the illegal occupation and will therefore be regarded as hostile and will be liable to be attacked by British forces.[70]

Britain continued to reserve its right to take additional measures in self-defence. In a clarifying statement, a British spokesman emphasized that the TEZ applied to all ships and all aircraft, including any Soviet spy ships that might be trailing British forces inside the Zone.[71] The USSR condemned the TEZ, stating: "The British Government continues expanding the zone of combat operations in the Atlantic Ocean, arbitrarily proclaiming vast expanses of high seas closed to ships and aircraft of other countries. These actions clearly contradict the 1958 Convention on the High Seas and, consequently, are regarded by the Soviet side as unlawful."[72]

On May 7, Britain issued a new policy statement concerning additional measures it would take in self-defence: "Because of the proximity of Argentine bases and the distances that hostile forces can cover undetected, particularly at night and in bad weather, Her Majesty's Government warns that any Argentine warship or military aircraft which is found more than 12 nautical miles from the Argentine coast will be regarded as hostile and is liable to be dealt with accordingly."[73] This measure has been referred to as an extension of the TEZ,[74] but such a classification is inaccurate as it refers solely to Argentine warships or military aircraft and does not include Argentine civil aircraft or vessels, let alone the aircraft or vessels of non-participants. Argentina condemned this action as "a belligerent action, which can only escalate the conflict and the dangers of renewed hostilities."[75]

The Argentine exclusion zones appear to have been created as reactions to the British zones. Following British notification of the MEZ, on April 8 Argentina declared a 200-mile maritime zone

70 *Ibid.*, April 29, 1982, at 1.

71 *Ibid.*

72 *Ibid.*, May 15, 1982, at 14.

73 *Ibid.*, May 8, 1982, at 1.

74 R. P. Barston and P. W. Birnie, "The Falkland Islands/Malvinas Conflict: A Question of Zones," (1983) Marine Policy 14-24.

75 London *Times*, May 8, 1982, at 1.

around the Falklands, South Georgia, and the Argentine coast as a theatre of operations in which military action could be taken if necessary for self-defence.[76] Following British notification of the TEZ, on April 29 Argentina declared that all of the waters in the maritime zone were Argentine waters and declared that all British vessels, naval or commercial, and all British aircraft entering the zone would be subject to attack.[77] Following British notification that all Argentine warships or military aircraft found more than twelve nautical miles from the Argentine coast would be subject to attack, on May 11 Argentina declared the entire South Atlantic to be a war zone and threatened to attack any British vessel found therein.[78] It appears that the only neutral vessel attacked during the entire conflict was the Liberian tanker *Hercules*, which was bombed and slightly damaged by an Argentine C-130 aircraft in the South Atlantic War Zone 450 miles south of the Falklands while engaged in a passage unrelated to the conflict.[79]

Assuming the Doenitz decision sets the criteria for the law of naval warfare for general wars, the only zone that on its face appears to present substantial legal problems from a general war perspective is the British Total Exclusion Zone of 200 miles around the Falklands created on April 30. The TEZ announcement subjected all vessels within the zone without British approval to risk of attack and, in so doing, contravened the Doenitz judgment prohibition of exclusion zones affecting neutral shipping. The British MEZ, defensive bubble, and policy statement of May 7 were directed at Argentine warships, naval auxiliaries, military aircraft, and civil aircraft that had the British task force under surveillance. All these were clearly valid military objectives by any normal definition and, under the law for general wars, automatically would have been subject to attack anywhere outside neutral territory or neutral waters. The three Argentine zone declarations could also be valid on the basis of the Doenitz judgment, on the assumption that British merchant vessels found within the zones were in fact incorporated in the British effort. It is probable that any British merchant vessel or civil aircraft approaching within 200 miles of the Falklands, South

[76] *Ibid.*, April 10, 1982, at 1.

[77] *Ibid.*, April 30, 1982, at 1.

[78] *Ibid.*, May 12, 1982, at 1.

[79] S. L. Morison, "Falklands (Malvinas) Campaign: A Chronology," (1983) 109 United States Naval Institute Proceedings (U.S.N.I.P.) 119, at 124.

Georgia, or Argentina following the Argentine proclamation of April 29 would be engaged in supporting the British task force and, as such, a legitimate military objective and subject to attack on sight. On the other hand, as a factual matter, the May 11 Argentine declaration of the entire South Atlantic (undefined) as a war zone within which any British vessel could be attacked on sight probably would contravene the principles of the Doenitz judgment because of the possibility that British merchant vessels engaged in normal passage completely unconnected with the conflict could be found in the zone.

Since the British TEZ of April 30 might be considered to present some problems under the principles of the Doenitz judgment, it merits further consideration. The main Law of Naval Warfare publication of the United States Navy, NWIP 10-2, states in paragraph 430(b): "Within the immediate area or vicinity of naval operations, a belligerent may establish special restrictions upon the activities of neutral vessels and aircraft and may prohibit altogether such vessels and aircraft from entering the area. Neutral vessels and aircraft which fail to comply with a belligerent's orders expose themselves to the risk of being fired upon."[80] This paragraph is amplified in part by paragraph 520(a): "within the immediate vicinity of his forces, a belligerent commanding officer may exercise control over the communications of any neutral merchant vessel or aircraft whose presence might otherwise endanger the success of his operations.... A neutral vessel or aircraft which does not conform to a belligerent's control exposes itself to the risk of being fired upon...."[81] The immediate area of naval operations is normally considered to be a relatively restricted area around naval forces, that is, a much smaller area than the TEZ.

80 Law of Naval Warfare, *op. cit. supra* note 7, at 4-6. In the course of the war crimes trials conducted after the Second World War, the question of the status of such official publications as the British and United States military manuals arose on various occasions. Although the courts recognized these publications as "persuasive statements of the law" and noted that insofar as the provisions of military manuals are acted upon they mould state practice, itself a source of international law, it was nevertheless stated that since these publications were not legislative instruments they possessed no formal binding power. Hence, the provisions of military manuals which clearly attempted to interpret the existing law were accepted or rejected by the courts in accordance with their opinion of the accuracy with which the law was set forth.

81 *Ibid.*, 5-8.

Both Tucker[82] and Mallison[83] support the view that neutral vessels may be legitimately subjected to attack if they are engaged in non-neutral service and that one example of that service is providing intelligence to the enemy. Britain implemented the TEZ to assist in target identification and because of concerns that neutral, particularly Russian, vessels were providing intelligence concerning the British task force to Argentina, and apparently it had legitimate reasons for so doing. The TEZ, however, represented a threat to other neutral vessels in the area, not merely to those engaged in intelligence-gathering. In the absence of more explicit criteria, the legitimacy of the TEZ ultimately must be determined on the basis of reasonableness. The area of the TEZ was substantial, a circle with a 200-mile radius, but it was not located close to major shipping routes or fishing areas and it was substantially smaller than the exclusion zones of the Second World War. Two days' notice was given of establishment of the TEZ. In any event, no neutral ships were attacked by British forces in the TEZ. Further, the only complaints made about the TEZ were those of Argentina and the USSR. The very absence of complaint is a strong indication that most interested states acquiesced in it as reasonable.

Analysis of the legitimacy of the various exclusion zones in a limited war context — and the Falklands conflict was clearly a limited struggle — raises additional issues. There has been a trend of sorts, exemplified particularly by the Korea and Vietnam conflicts but also by the controversy over the sinking of the Israeli destroyer *Eilat* in the Arab-Israeli conflicts,[84] to restrict naval operations to the territorial seas and contiguous zones of the disputing parties. Further, both the 1958 High Seas Convention (Article 2) and the 1982 Law of the Sea Convention (Article 87) specify that freedom of navigation and freedom of overflight are included among the freedoms of the high seas. Both these documents also indicate, however, that these freedoms are subject to other applicable rules of international law. Traditionally these other applicable rules have included belligerent rights in wartime. Belligerent rights have certainly included visit, search, and seizure of merchant shipping and, on the basis of the Doenitz judgment, they appear to include the

[82] Tucker, *op. cit. supra* note 24, at 319-21.

[83] Mallison, *op. cit. supra* note 25, at 129-32.

[84] R. D. Colvin, "Aftermath of the Elath," (1969) 95 U.S.N.I.P. 61, and D. P. O'Connell, "International Law and Contemporary Naval Operations," (1970) 44 B.Y.I.L. 28-29.

invocation of exclusion zones directed against enemy merchant shipping in a general war in certain circumstances.

Although an argument might be made that one party to a conflict can only attack another party's warships, naval auxiliaries, and military aircraft within certain circumscribed areas in a limited conflict, there is certainly no treaty obligation to such effect, and it is considered that the evidence of such an obligation in customary law is insufficient. Any restrictions concerning attacks on an opponent's warships, naval auxiliaries, and military aircraft outside neutral waters or territory which are observed by a party to a limited conflict, are voluntary self-limitations.The British MEZ of April 12, Defensive Bubble of April 23, and Policy Statement of May 7 are considered to be such voluntary self-limitations and as such compatible with the law of naval warfare for general war and with limited warfare trends.[85] The Argentine Maritime Zone declaration

[85] One incident which generated a considerable amount of controversy during and after the conflict was the sinking of the ancient Argentine cruiser *General Belgrano* on May 2, 1982 by the British submarine *Conqueror* with the loss of more than 300 Argentine sailors. The *General Belgrano* and two destroyers were sighted several miles south of the TEZ on May 1 by the nuclear submarine HMS *Conqueror*. According to an Argentine account (R. L. Scheina, "The Malvinas Campaign," (1983) 109 U.S.N.I.P. 104, at 106), the mission of the Argentine force was to provide an early warning for the southern mainland and to be in a position to intercept any British reinforcements that might come from the Pacific. Its operating area was entirely outside the TEZ. At the time of sighting, Britain had indicated that it would attack Argentine warships in the TEZ and Argentine warships that threatened the British task force by penetrating its defensive bubble. It is clear that the Argentine force did not enter the TEZ and it is most unlikely it presented an immediate threat to the British task force as it would, presumably, have been attacked on sight if it had presented such a threat. The *Conqueror*'s commanding officer reported the sighting to his superiors, a request for permission to sink the *General Belgrano* was considered by the British war cabinet on May 2, and such permission was granted.

At the time of sinking, according to Argentine accounts, the *General Belgrano* was about 360 miles from the British task force and steaming away from it. The sinking may or may not have been politically unwise; the question here is whether or not it was legally objectionable. Britain did indicate it would attack Argentine warships in the TEZ and in the Defensive Bubble. It is unlikely the *General Belgrano* was in either of these areas. On the other hand, perhaps out of a justifiable abundance of caution, Britain reserved its right to take other unspecified measures in self-defence. There is no question that under the general law of naval warfare the *General Belgrano* was a legitimate object of attack and the fact that members of the crew would die in the attack would be unfortunate but irrelevant because they were combatants and getting sunk is a normal occupational hazard in wartime. It is unlikely that the situation is different for warships in a limited conflict. Viewed from a narrow perspective, the *General Belgrano* prob-

of April 8 and, on the reasonable assumption that British merchant ships and civil aircraft would only be in the zone to support the task force, the strengthened Argentine Zone declaration of April 29 are similarly compatible.

The British TEZ of April 30 is on its face an arbitrary interference with the freedom of navigation and overflight of aircraft and ships of non-parties to the conflict. Similarly, the Argentinian South Atlantic War Zone of May 11 appears to be an arbitrary interference with the freedom of navigation of British merchant ships unconnected with the conflict. In the particular circumstances of the Falklands conflict, however, the British TEZ was a reasonable temporary appropriation of a limited area of the high seas away from major shipping routes for self-defence purposes to prevent non-party clandestine participation in the conflict. The appropriation was accompanied by adequate notice, did not result in any casualties to the ships or aircraft of non-parties, and was terminated after a brief period on July 22, once the British consolidated their position in the Falklands. The British TEZ was, in the circumstances, compatible with the law of naval warfare for general wars and with limited warfare trends. The Argentine South Atlantic War Zone declaration does not, however, appear to have been so compatible because the area of application was undefined, being apparently much larger than the British TEZ, because no notice was given, and because it was not related to the self-defence of Argentina, which was already adequately provided for by the Maritime Zone Declaration of April 29.

The Iran/Iraq conflict, which began in September 1980 and shows no signs of ending, provides a contrast with the brief and conspicuously limited Falklands conflict. The fighting in the case of the Falklands occurred in an isolated area of the South Atlantic which was away from heavily travelled shipping lanes. The anti-shipping campaigns in the Iran/Iraq conflict occur in the restricted

---

ably did not constitute a direct threat to the British task force when it was torpedoed. Viewed from a broader perspective, it may have constituted such a threat at a later point in the conflict and that alone would justify an attack upon it. On the same day as the attack on the *General Belgrano* by HMS *Conqueror*, the Argentine carrier *25 de Mayo* attempted to launch an air strike against the British task force. Following the sinking, the Argentine surface navy essentially withdrew from the conflict. To the extent that the sinking caused the withdrawal, it may be that more lives were saved by it than caused by it. See D. Rice and A. Gavshon, *The Sinking of the Belgrano* (London, 1984).

area of the Persian Gulf, in one of the world's most important shipping lanes. The Persian Gulf, the arm of the Indian Ocean lying between the Arabian peninsula and Iran, has an area of some 241,000 square kilometres — slightly larger than the Gulf of St. Lawrence. From its head at the mouth of the Shatt al-Arab River system to its entrance at the Strait of Hormuz, its length is about 430 nautical miles and its maximum width about 160 nautical miles. The Strait of Hormuz connects the Persian Gulf with the Gulf of Oman, an open sea. The strait is about 104 nautical miles long measured along the median line and, at its narrowest point, it has a width of about 21 miles.[86] The Persian Gulf is bordered by seven states — Iran (635 nautical miles), the United Arab Emirates (420), Saudi Arabia (296), Qatar (204), Kuwait (115), Bahrain (68), and Iraq, which has a mere ten nautical miles at the mouth of the Shatt al-Arab. Iran is the only state located on the entire length of the eastern coast of the Gulf.[87] In 1975, it was estimated that the states bordering the Gulf contained over 50 per cent of the world's oil reserves.[88] The Strait of Hormuz is an international oil highway and, even as late as 1984, about eight million barrels of oil per day were exported through the Strait, including about 56 per cent of Japan's total consumption and 36 per cent of France's.[89] Neither Iran nor Iraq are major naval powers but both, as a result of oil profits, were well equipped with modern combat aircraft at the beginning of their conflict and were able to use these resources to attack shipping.

On September 22, 1980, Iran commenced the use of exclusion zones in the conflict by declaring that all waterways near Iranian shores were war zones, that Iran would not allow any merchant ship to carry cargo to Iraqi ports and that, for the sake of the safety of shipping in the Persian Gulf, certain routes should be followed.[90] Iran also indicated that it would not take any responsibility for damage caused to those who did not comply with its rules. Except for minor variations in the locations of the safe shipping routes and in the wording of the prohibition on the carriage of goods to Iraqi

[86] R. Young, "The Persian Gulf," in R. Churchill, K. R. Simmonds, and J. Welch, eds., *New Directions in the Law of the Sea*, Vol. III, at 231 (London, 1973).

[87] R. K. Ramazani, *The Persian Gulf and the Strait of Hormuz* 7 (Alphen aan den Rijn, 1979).

[88] *Ibid.*, 9.

[89] T. M. Daly, "The Enduring Gulf War," (1985) 111 U.S.N.I.P. 148, 150.

ports, Iran has not varied its declared policy concerning exclusion zones since the beginning of the conflict.

On October 7, 1980, Iraq declared that the area of the Persian Gulf north of 29° 03′ N was a prohibited war zone.[91] This declared zone applied only to the northern part of the Iranian coast in the Gulf. On August 16, 1982, the Iraqi government expanded its zone and indicated that it would attack all shipping in the zone and all tankers docking at Kharg Island.[92] Iraq made minor modifications to its zone in 1984.[93] In February 1984 the Iraqis declared a blockade in a fifty-mile radius around Kharg Island and warned that they would hit any ship in that region.[94]

In May 1984, as a measure to protect the interests of neutrals, Saudi Arabia and its Gulf Cooperation Council partners declared an exclusion zone of sorts of their own by asking tanker traffic to follow a route within their territorial waters forming a strip twelve miles wide along the edge of the Gulf.[95] As the purpose of this zone was to protect neutral shipping within neutral waters against attack by belligerents, it raised no significant legal issues.

The Iraqi anti-shipping campaign can be broken into two phases, from May 1981 until March 1984, and from March 1984 until the present. During the first phase, the Iraqis, with three exceptions for ships damaged during air raids on Kharg Island and on the more southern port of Bushire, restricted their attacks on ships at sea to vessels sailing in the northern zone of the Persian Gulf to or from the Iranian ports of Bandar Khomeini and Bandar Mahshahr.[96] All attacks were delivered by shore-based aircraft. Since March 1984, most attacks have been aimed at tankers sailing to or from Kharg

[90] U.S. Defense Mapping Agency and Hydrographic Center (DMAHTC) Special Warning No. 48, September 22, 1980.

[91] DMAHTC Special Warning No. 50, October 7, 1980.

[92] DMAHTC Special Warning No. 62, August 16, 1982.

[93] R16 *Persian Gulf Pilot* (12th ed.), Supplement #1 corrected to June 23, 1984.

[94] New York *Times*, May 20, 1984, at 1.

[95] Daley, *supra* note 89, at 157. In January 1984 the United States established a 5-nautical mile defensive bubble around its naval forces in the Persian Gulf and indicated that it might take defensive measures against ships or aircraft penetrating the bubble without permission: M. N. Leich, "Contemporary Practice of the United States Relating to International Law," (1984) 78 Am. J. Int'l L. 884-85.

[96] R. Danziger, "The Persian Gulf Tanker War," (1985) 111 U.S.N.I.P. 160, 161.

Island, the very heavily defended main Iranian oil terminal, located towards the northern end of the Persian Gulf.[97] Iran's ability to continue conducting the war is dependent in large part on the revenue generated from oil exports. The Gulf tanker traffic is the most vital yet weakest link of Iran's war economy. According to one set of statistics, Iraq attacked sixty commercial vessels in the Gulf during 1980-84 and 90 per cent of these attacks were carried out by air-launched missiles. Sixty per cent of the attacks occurred in 1984, after Iraq switched the focus of its Gulf offensive to the tanker traffic around Kharg Island.[98] Almost all the tankers attacked belonged to neutrals. Fortunately, because large tankers are difficult to sink, very few vessels were sunk and the number of persons killed was somewhat limited, probably less than 200 to date. United Nations statistics indicate that Iraq has continued to attack neutral shipping around Kharg Island since the end of 1984.[99] It appears that Iraq has two purposes for waging its tanker war — damaging the Iranian economy and arousing world interest in the conflict, presumably in the hope that other powers will take effective action to resolve the conflict.

Iranian bomb attacks closed down the two Iraqi oil terminals in the Persian Gulf and blocked access to all three of Iraq's commercial ports at the start of the conflict. No commercial vessels of any kind have sailed to Iraq since 1980.[100] Iran did not attack commercial shipping at sea until after Iraq began attacking the tanker traffic with Kharg Island in March 1984. Since there was no sea traffic with Iraq, Iran's only possible response in the Gulf itself was to attack other shipping, presumably in an effort to persuade Iraq's financial backers, the other Gulf states, to dissuade Iraq from its campaign against the Kharg Island tankers. Iran's attacks on shipping have been much less numerous than those of Iraq and, in general, much less costly in lives and property damage because they have been conducted with rockets instead of missiles. In 1984, for example, Iran carried out seventeen attacks while Iraq carried out thirty-seven.[101] On the other hand, the Iranian attacks have been directed against neutral ships travelling to and from neutral ter-

97 *Ibid.*, 163.

98 *Ibid.*, 162.

99 U.N. Doc. S/16877, December 31, 1984, S/106877/Add. 1, January 22, 1985, and S/16877/Add. 2, December 31, 1985.

100 Danziger, *supra* note 96, at 163.

101 *Ibid.*, 162.

ritory. Iran does not appear to have been conducting its attacks in a declared exclusion zone and, indeed, some of its attacks have been carried out in neutral territorial waters.[102]

Navigational rights in the Persian Gulf have been discussed by the Security Council of the United Nations on two occasions. In 1983, the Council passed a resolution affirming the right to free navigation and commerce and calling upon the belligerents to cease all hostilities in the region of the Gulf.[103] On June 1, 1984, the Council met at the request of the Persian Gulf states other than Iran and Iraq to consider a complaint concerning recent attacks by Iran on commercial ships en route to and from the ports of Kuwait and Saudi Arabia. Iran did not deny that it had attacked the ships in question but it argued that Iraq has escalated the conflict into attacks on international shipping in the Gulf, that Iraq had attacked many more ships than had Iran, and that the other Gulf states, because of their financial support for Iraq, could not be considered innocent third parties. Iran summed up its position: "If the security of the Persian Gulf is violated, then it is violated for all. We will not permit the Persian Gulf, on which we have more than a thousand kilometres of littoral, to be closed to us and to be used by others against us."[104] Notwithstanding the Iranian arguments, the Security Council passed a resolution condemning the Iranian attacks, calling upon all states to respect the right of free navigation, and demanding that there should be no interference with ships en route to and from neutral states.[105] Although the resolution itself has an anti-Iranian tilt, a review of the verbatim record indicates that a more even-handed approach was taken by almost all the speakers. This statement by the United Kingdom representative gives the general tenor of the debate:

> The draft resolution concentrates for understandable reasons on one particular act of escalation, but clearly this does not mean that it condones other attacks on merchant shipping in the Gulf. We are therefore particularly pleased that the draft resolution in its revised form contains a clear and general reaffirmation of the right of free navigation. This right is laid down in international law, and we look to all States of the region to respect it. In our view neither side has the right to attack neutral shipping indiscriminately, whatever its destination. The breach

[102] *Ibid.*, 166.

[103] U.N. Doc. S/RES/540 (1983).

[104] U.N. Doc. S/6585, May 25, 1984.

[105] U.N. Doc. S/RES/552 (1984) June 1, 1984.

of international law is flagrant if the shipping attacked is in transit to the ports of third countries and compounded if the attacks take place in the territorial waters of the third countries. Such attacks violate the sovereignty of the coastal States as well as the rights of the flag State.[106]

An attempt to appraise legal aspects of the use of exclusion zones in the Iran/Iraq conflict must take cognizance of the fact that neither belligerent appears to be paying particular heed to legal issues in determining their courses of action. It is futile to discuss exclusion zones used in this conflict utilizing presumed limited war standards, as both belligerents probably have gone beyond the standards hitherto considered permissible in general war. The Doenitz decision accepted the legitimacy of exclusion zones directed against enemy merchant shipping incorporated into the enemy war effort. As seen above, neutral merchant ships incorporated into the enemy war effort can also be considered legitimate military objectives and, as such, acceptable targets in an exclusion zone. The primary Iraqi targets in the declared Iraqi exclusion zone are neutral tankers proceeding to and from Kharg Island. Some of these tankers are convoyed by Iranian warships. It is debatable whether or not unconvoyed neutral tankers can be considered as incorporated into the Iranian war effort. The tankers are unarmed and are not integrated into the Iranian intelligence system. It is, however, possible to argue that the tankers are essential to the Iranian war economy and, just as oil refineries and trains may be attacked in war on land, so may tankers be legitimately attacked at sea. One is reluctant to be dogmatic when appraising conduct in naval warfare, but it is considered that Iraqi practice in using exclusion zones touches the outer limits of legal acceptability and may well overstep the boundary. About Iranian conduct, one can quote J. W. Garner again concerning German war zones and simply observe, "it was so flagrantly contrary to the laws of maritime warfare that nothing can be said in defence of it." Iran is attacking neutral ships proceeding to and from neutral ports outside of declared exclusion zones and, on occasion, in neutral waters. Even if one concedes that the other Gulf states are providing financial support to Iraq, it does not appear possible to consider the neutral ships engaged in traffic with these states to be incorporated into the Iraqi war effort. Iran's desire to take action to force Iraq to refrain from attacking the Kharg Island tanker traffic does not legitimize its actions. It is somewhat surpris-

106 U.N. Doc. S/PV 2546, June 1, 1984, at 33.

ing that the actions of Iran and Iraq in the Persian Gulf have not generated a stronger, or at least more vociferous, response on the part of other states. It is presumed the relative lack of response is owing to the desire of the superpowers to avoid conflict with each other in a sensitive area, and to the facts that there is a tanker surplus and an oil glut, that the tankers attacked usually belong to flag of convenience states, and that the loss of life has been relatively limited.

On the basis of the history of the use of exclusion zones, it is reasonable to conclude that such zones will be used in some future conflicts. One can, of course, list post-Second World War conflicts in which exclusion zones have not been used, such as Korea, Vietnam, and the various Arab-Israeli conflicts. In Korea and Vietnam, however, one party had overwhelming naval superiority and the Arab-Israeli conflicts have been too short to require the parties to make the maximum effective use of sea power. Exclusion zones are most likely to be used in future conflicts which are a few months or more in duration, which are fought in part on or over the high seas, and in which sea control is disputed because both parties are able to deploy signficant air or naval resources to the disputed area. These zones have been used for a variety of purposes: as an economic warfare device in the two World Wars and in the Iran/Iraq conflict, as a conflict limitation device, as a means to assist in identifying hostile forces in the Falklands conflict, and as a means of arousing neutral interest in the Iran/Iraq conflict.

As new technologies have become available, they have been used in exclusion zones. In the First World War, the zones were enforced by surface ships, submarines, and mines. In subsequent conflicts, aircraft were added, and short-range missiles from ships or aircraft, such as the Exocet, used in the Falklands and the Iran/Iraq conflicts. It is probable that missiles with a range beyond the radar range of controlling ships or aircraft will be used in future conflicts. These longer-range missiles are particularly relevant to the exclusion zone issue because of the problem of target identification. They may be programmed to search an area and to attack any object within that area possessing certain characteristics. If the first such object located by a missile is a neutral ship uninvolved in the conflict, that ship may be attacked.[107]

[107] D. P. O'Connell, "The Legality of Naval Cruise Missiles," (1972) 66 Am. J. Int'l L. 785 and S. C. Truver, "The Legal Status of Submarine Launched Cruise Missiles," (1977) 103 U.S.N.I.P. 82, have both suggested that these missiles should be prohibited, at least in limited conflicts, because

One might argue that the law of naval warfare as it existed prior to the First World War remains valid and that all that has occurred since then is illegal or, at best, justified solely on the basis of reprisals. It cannot be disputed that the pre-1914 law is, superficially, considerably more humane, than a law that takes account of state practice since 1914. It does not, however, accord with present realities. A legal approach that takes account of what has happened, and almost certainly will happen, is more likely to be observed and to provide marginal humanitarian benefit.

An assessment of legal aspects of the use of exclusion zones depends upon an assessment of the current validity and meaning of the London Protocol concerning submarine warfare. Canada, and most major naval powers, are parties to this treaty, which prohibits attacking merchant vessels on sight. State practice has either caused this treaty to fall into desuetude[108] or, at a minimum, to be broadly interpreted.[109] If "merchant vessel" in the London Protocol includes all vessels that are not warships or naval auxiliaries, then the London Protocol will be ignored in any future conflict in which a belligerent considers that it will be disadvantaged by compliance. As an historical example, the United States made a deliberate, albeit covert, decision to ignore the London Protocol in its war-planning several months before it entered the Second World War.[110] If one wishes to retain some practical humanitarian value from the London Protocol, the expression "merchant vessel" must be interpreted as excluding all belligerent and neutral vessels that are incorporated in the belligerent war effort. Some criteria for incorporation are set forth in the Doenitz judgment. The Doenitz decision, however, insofar as it ignores the possibility of incorporation of neutral vessels in the belligerent war effort, adopts too narrow an approach concern-

---

of the possibility they might strike innocent targets. W. Hays Parks, "Submarine Launched Cruise Missiles and International Law: A Response," (1977) 103 U.S.N.I.P. 120, argues that the missiles are not illegal per se but must be employed with due regard to the rule of proportionality. The writer favours a rule of proportionality approach.

108 A. Vanvoukos, *Termination of Treaties in International Law* 271-73 (Oxford, 1985), contends that the London Protocol is no longer binding, but his only authorities are the Doenitz decision and the views of O'Connell expressed earlier in this text.

109 Mallison, *op. cit. supra* note 25, at 117-23.

110 J. E. Talbott, "Weapons Development, War Planning and Policy: The U.S. Navy and the Submarine," (1984) 37 N.W.C.R. 53-71.

ing the exclusion of vessels from the "merchant vessel" category in the London Protocol.

If one accepts the arguments that exclusion zones are likely to be used in future conflicts and that exclusion zones in which a sink-at-sight policy is enforced are not illegal per se because warships, naval auxiliaries, and ships incorporated into the belligerent war effort may be so targeted, then it is desirable to attempt to develop legal standards for the use of these zones. The standards must comply with existing law, be militarily practicable, and encourage the minimization of net human suffering. They must also be somewhat open-ended because the law is in a state of flux and because the perceived legitimacy or illegitimacy of particular uses of exclusion zones will depend to a considerable extent on the context of the conflict in which they are used.[111] It is unlikely that generally agreed standards would vary from conflict to conflict or between general and limited wars. The application of the standards to the facts would, however, produce differing assessments of the legitimacy of similar types of zones in different conflicts. If merchant ships trading with belligerents are incorporated into the belligerent war effort, more stringent exclusion zones would be acceptable than if they were not so incorporated.

If belligerents use exclusion zones, they should publicly declare the existence, location, and duration of the zones, what is excluded from the zone, and the sanctions likely to be imposed on ships or aircraft entering the zone without permission, and also provide enough lead time before the zone comes into effect to allow ships to clear the area. As with blockades, "paper" zones are insufficient. Belligerents declaring zones should deploy sufficient forces to the zone to make it "effective," that is, to expose ships or aircraft entering the zone to a significant probability of encountering submarines, ships, or aircraft engaged in enforcing the zone. All militarily practicable efforts should be made to employ minimum sanctions, such as seizure instead of attack on sight. Similarly, all militarily practicable measures should be taken to ensure proper target identification and to ensure that only legitimate military objectives, such as military aircraft,

[111] M. S. McDougal and N. A. Schlei, "The Hydrogen Bomb Tests in Perspective: Lawful Measures for Security," (1955) 64 Yale L.J. 648-710, adopt a similar approach in assessing the legitimacy of temporary appropriation of a portion of the high seas. Also see M. McDougal, "The Hydrogen Bomb Tests and the International Law of the Sea," (1955) 49 Am. J. Int'l L. 356.

warships, and ships incorporated into the belligerent war effort, are attacked. The emphasis on what is militarily practicable is important. Sometimes the minimum practicable sanction will be attack on sight; sometimes ships or aircraft that are not legitimate military objectives will be attacked because of errors in target identification. There must be a proportional and demonstrable nexus between the zone and the self-defence requirements of the state establishing the zone. For example, it was suggested in the discussion of the Falklands conflict above that Argentina's 200-mile zone around the Falklands was probably adequate and that its declaration that the entire South Atlantic was a war zone was disproportionate to its defence requirements and would affect shipping unconnected with the conflict. The size, location, and duration of zones are also relevant factors in determining their acceptability. Zones located in isolated areas far from normal shipping routes, such as those used in the Falklands, are less likely to raise objections than zones on major shipping routes such as the Persian Gulf. Zones occupying relatively small areas or established for relatively brief periods are more likely than the converse to be considered acceptable. If there is a significant possibility that ships not involved in the conflict will have to pass through the zone, special routes should be provided for them and special measures should be taken to minimize the risk of attack upon them. Finally, the purpose of the zone is particularly relevant. If the purpose of the zone is to limit a conflict to a confined geographic area, it is probable that it will be considered acceptable. If use of the zone is an essential part of a campaign directed against the enemy's war economy, it is more likely that unacceptable acts will occur than if the primary purpose of the zone is to assist in identification of hostile targets.

In this area of law, history compels agreement with the remarks of Julius Stone:

> It is idle to seek to reduce this matter to a cri de coeur of humanity. War law, even at its most merciful, is no expression of sheer humanity, save as adjusted to the exigencies of military success, a truth as bitter (but no less true) about attacks on merchant ships, as about target area saturation bombing. And it is also quite idle for Powers whose naval supremacy in surface craft enable them to pursue the aim of annihilating the enemy's seaborne commerce without "sink at sight" warfare, to expect that States which cannot aspire to such supremacy will refrain from seeking to annihilate that commerce by such naval means available to them as submarines, aircraft and mines. To refuse

to face this will save neither life nor ship in any future war; and it will also forestall the growth of real rules for the mitigation of suffering under modern conditions.[112]

[112] J. Stone, *Legal Controls of International Conflict* 606-7 (New York, 1954).

Sommaire

Le système de la zone d'exclusion dans le droit de la guerre navale

Les zones d'exclusion sont constituées d'espaces maritimes et aériens sur lesquels un participant à un conflit armé prétend exercer le contrôle et auxquels il interdit l'accès aux navires et aéronefs non autorisés. De telles zones ont été établies entre les deux guerres mondiales ainsi que durant les conflits Iran-Irak et des Malouines (Falklands). À l'exception de celui des Malouines, ces conflits ont occasionné des pertes nombreuses chez les non-combattants, qu'il s'agisse de personnes ou de navires.

L'établissement de zones d'exclusion n'a aucun fondement en droit conventionnel. Il n'est cependant pas impossible que d'éventuelles guerres prolongées, livrées en partie en haute mer ou dans son espace aérien, donnent lieu à des luttes pour le contrôle de la mer. L'auteur présente un historique du recours aux zones d'exclusion et tente d'identifier les fondements juridiques d'un acte tendant à instituer de telles zones lors de futurs conflits. L'auteur laisse entendre que l'un des traités se rapportant à la question, le Protocole de Londres concernant la guerre sous-marine, *conclu en 1936, doit être interprété de façon à ne pas s'appliquer aux navires marchands mis à contribution dans l'effort de guerre d'un belligérant et ce même, même s'ils sont neutres.*

L'auteur envisage par ailleurs la possibilité que soit promulguée une loi spéciale concernant les guerres navales d'envergure limitée. En ce qui a trait aux zones d'exclusion cependant, l'auteur énonce l'opinion que les règles en la matière ne sont guère définies et que leur application donne lieu à des évaluations divergentes de légitimité, selon la nature du conflit. L'auteur cite, à ce propos, l'exemple des zones d'exclusions établies pour mener une guerre économique et dans lesquelles tous les navires marchands s'exposent à être attaqués "à vue."

L'établissement de telles zones pourrait être acceptable dans le contexte d'une guerre généralisée, comme ce fut le cas durant la deuxième guerre mondiale, puisqu'il est probable que tous les navires marchands soient appelés à contribuer à l'effort de guerre du belligérant. En revanche, leur établissement pourrait être considéré comme inacceptable durant une guerre restreinte, comme le conflit des Malouines, dans la mesure où il serait peu probable que la marine marchande soit mise à contribution dans un tel effort de guerre.

Part III
Air Warfare

[10]

AREA BOMBARDMENT: RULES AND REASONS*

By HANS BLIX[1]

WHILE a main ambition behind the law of armed conflict which has evolved since the middle of the nineteenth century has been to save civilian lives, practice has seen an increasing toll of civilians during the last fifty years. Estimates indicate that out of those who died as a result of war events civilians formed around 5 per cent in the First World War, 50 per cent in the Second World War, perhaps 60 per cent in the Korean War and even more in the Vietnam War.[2] Although the exactness of such figures may be discussed, the trend is not subject to doubt. Nor is it in doubt that modern practices of air warfare form one of the principal reasons for this trend.[3] While civilian populations may often have a chance to seek refuge from the effects of ground combat through evacuation or otherwise, the suddenness of attacks from the air and the circumstance that such attacks can be launched virtually against any point in the hinterland make the civilian population much more exposed to their effects. The precision in air attacks has also generally speaking been much less than in ground attacks, with consequent effects upon civilians and civilian objects.

Although it is a speculation, it seems plausible to suggest that the absence of international rules specifically regulating air warfare may have contributed to the relative absence of restraints which the world has witnessed. With the development toward total air warfare the demands for rules of restraint have grown stronger. The diplomatic conference convened by the Swiss government for the reaffirmation and development of international humanitarian law applicable in armed conflicts took up this question among others. This conference will be referred to below as the 'Diplomatic Conference'. At its fourth, and last, session, in 1977, it adopted two protocols, one relating to international armed conflicts, the other relating to non-international armed conflicts.[4] The first protocol—referred to below as Protocol I—contains a number of articles relevant to air warfare. The basic proposals were submitted by the International Committee of the Red Cross but the texts finally adopted differ greatly from the original drafts.

The main purpose of this article is to focus upon one matter covered by these new rules, that of area bombardment. It may be useful, however, first to review

[1] Ph.D. (Cantab.), LL.D. (Stockholm); Minister for Foreign Affairs, Stockholm.

[2] Statement by Minister Carl Lidbom in the general debate of the first session of the Conference on Humanitarian Law in Armed Conflicts, 7 March 1974. See press release of the same day by the Swedish Ministry for Foreign Affairs.

[3] But see J. M. Spaight, *Air Power and War Rights* (London, 3rd edn., 1947), p. 28.

[4] First session 20 February–29 March 1974; second session 3 February–18 April 1975; third session 20 April–11 June 1976; fourth, and last, session 13 April–10 June 1977; the Final Act was signed on 10 June 1977. The term 'diplomatic' has been used to distinguish the conference from the two conferences of government experts, which preceded it.

existing general principles as well as earlier attempts at specific regulation and the military practices which form the background of the present efforts.

Pre-Second World War rules and proposals

The two pillars upon which the law of armed conflict rests have hardly been better described than in the preamble of the *St. Petersburg Declaration of 1868*, which refers to the 'technical limits at which the necessities of war ought to yield to the requirements of humanity' and to the weakening of the military forces of the enemy as 'the only legitimate object which States should endeavour to accomplish during war'.[1] The passages quoted reflect firstly the legal relevance of humanitarian concerns to the conduct of war; and secondly the basic tenet that the licence of the belligerents does not go any further than the 'necessities of war'. Only that which is rationally required for the pursuit of the aim to subdue the enemy is permissible.[2] This was interpreted to be only actions to 'weaken the *military forces* of the enemy'. Civilians and civilian objects were evidently deemed to be only of marginal importance to the contest. Hence there was no rational need to attack them. And without a rational need it was not legitimate.

Air warfare did not exist at the time when the St. Petersburg Declaration was adopted, but the declaration has been cited at the outset because it expresses the fundamental philosophy which underlies most of the law of armed conflict and because there is hardly any other instrument which more clearly establishes the principle of the immunity of the civilian population.[3] If modern belligerents were not to accept the basic premiss upon which this principle is established, namely the view that, for the armed battle, only marginal importance can be attributed to the civilian population and civilian objects, the immunity would be in question. Yet there can be no doubt that, especially in non-international conflicts of ideological colouring and in any guerrilla-type warfare, the support and allegiance of the civilian population may be significant; and that this fact has tended to subject the rule on the immunity of the civilian population to strain.

Even in large-scale international conflicts, bombardment affecting the civilian population has taken place with the purpose of destroying its morale and its allegiance to the opponent. Such 'terror' bombardment does not appear to be defended on legal grounds by anyone and where it has taken place it has been presented as having another alleged justification. Thus, although the morale and allegiance of the civilian population may have some relevance to the armed contest, no one seems ready to argue that it is legally justifiable to bombard the population for this reason. There are, moreover, serious doubts as to whether

1 For the text see Schindler and Toman, *The Laws of Armed Conflicts* (1973), p. 95.

2 Cf. G. J. Adler, 'Targets in War; Legal Considerations', *Houston Law Review*, 8 (1970), at p. 15.

3 Article 48 of Protocol I adopted by the Diplomatic Conference is somewhat less categorical: 'In order to ensure respect for and protection of the civilian population and civilian objects, the Parties to the conflict shall at all times distinguish between the civilian population and combatants and between civilian objects and military objectives and accordingly shall direct their operations only against military objectives.'

morale and allegiance can be pulverized by bombs. If these doubts should be well-founded, there would be no rational reason for such bombardment and, hence, in any case no justification under the basic principle.

Most air warfare affecting civilian populations does not, however, have morale, but rather lines of communication, industries, radio stations, etc. as targets. That some such targets, e.g. certain lines of communication and war industries, are of direct relevance to the armed contest is not doubted by anyone.[1] If the view is taken, however, that practically the whole productive force of the belligerent is sufficiently relevant to justify attacks, the basic immunity of the civilian population is immediately placed in jeopardy. The vital question of what constitute military objectives and protected objects is not focused upon in this paper. Suffice it to say that targets of the kind mentioned have probably always been of some significance for the armed contest. If the question of the permissibility of their destruction has become a central question only from the Second World War and thereafter, it is certainly because the means—heavy bombers, missiles—did not exist earlier to bring about such destruction. With growing facilities for achieving destruction in far away hinterlands the temptations to do so increase. Even very marginal gains may appear attractive if the costs are not too high or the resources for air war are abundant.

The Hague Conventions of 1899 and 1907 reflect the beginning of concern about attacks from the air. The Declaration prohibiting 'the discharge of projectiles and explosives from balloons or by other new methods of a similar nature' was presumably prompted *inter alia* by fear that such launchings might have indiscriminate effects. While this Declaration—theoretically still in force[2]—is no longer attributed any significance, Article 25 of the Hague Regulations, contained in the Fourth Convention of 1907, is still cited as relevant:

> The attack or bombardment, by any means whatever, of undefended towns, villages, dwellings, or buildings, is forbidden.

There is no doubt that this provision was intended to cover the case of bombardment from the air,[3] but there is equally no doubt that this aim of the article, formulated at a time when there was little practical experience of air warfare, could not be realized, unless 'defended' were given a very artificial and extensive meaning.[4] The military value of air attacks against military supplies or troops in

[1] Article 8 (1) a of the Hague Convention of 1954 for the protection of cultural property is sometimes referred to on this matter. It gives as 'examples' of an 'important military objective constituting a vulnerable point', 'an aerodrome, broadcasting station, establishment engaged upon work of national defence, a port or railway station of relative importance or a main line of communication'. See Schindler and Toman, op. cit. (above, p. 32 n. 1), p. 534. The question of a definition is now directly answered by Article 52 (2) of Protocol I: 'Attacks shall be strictly limited to military objectives. In so far as objects are concerned, military objectives are limited to those objects which by their nature, location, purpose or use make an effective contribution to military action and whose total or partial destruction, capture or neutralization, in the circumstances ruling at the time, offers a definite military advantage.'

[2] See Schindler and Toman, op. cit. (above, p. 32 n. 1), p. 133. See also the interesting account in D. H. N. Johnson, *Rights in Air Space* (Manchester, 1965), pp. 7 et seqq.

[3] K. A. Raby, *Bombardment of Land Targets—Military Necessity and Proportionality Interpellated* (Washington, 1968), p. 16; Cf. Johnson, op. cit. (previous note), p. 18.

[4] See Adler, loc. cit. (above, p. 32 n. 2), p. 26. Cf. Raby, op. cit. (previous note), p. 255.

transit in a town was understandably too great to be disregarded by belligerents. A more realistic line of guidance, which took account of this military value, was adopted for naval warfare, when Article 2 of Hague Convention IX provided an exception to the general prohibition of bombardments by naval forces of undefended ports, towns, villages, dwellings or buildings:

Military works, military or naval establishments, depots of arms or war material, workshops or plant which could be utilized for the needs of the hostile fleet or army, and the ships of war in the harbour, are not . . . included. . . .

This article ties the right of attack to the military value of the target. The same approach was taken in Articles 22 and 24 of the *1923 Hague Rules of Air Warfare*. Article 22 provides:

Aerial bombardment for the purpose of terrorizing the civilian population, of destroying or damaging private property not of a military character, or of injuring non-combatants, is prohibited.

Article 24 provides:

(1) Aerial bombardment is legitimate only when directed at a military objective, that is to say, an object of which the destruction or injury would constitute a distinct military advantage to the belligerent.

(2) Such bombardment is legitimate only when directed exclusively at the following objectives: military forces; military works; military establishments or depots; factories constituting important and well-known centres engaged in the manufacture of arms, ammunition, or distinctively military supplies; lines of communication or transportation used for military purposes.

(3) The bombardment of cities, towns, villages, dwellings, or buildings not in the immediate neighbourhood of the operations of land forces is prohibited. In cases where the objectives specified in paragraph 2 are so situated that they cannot be bombarded without the indiscriminate bombardment of the civilian population, the aircraft must abstain from bombardment.

(4) In the immediate neighbourhood of the operations of land forces, the bombardment of cities, towns, villages, dwellings or buildings is legitimate provided that there exists a reasonable presumption that the military concentration is sufficiently important to justify such bombardment, having regard to the danger thus caused to the civilian population.

(5) A belligerent State is liable to pay compensation for injuries to person or to property caused by the violation by any of its officers or forces of the provisions of this article.[1]

Although the Hague Rules were drafted against the background of considerable experience of air warfare, they were not adopted by governments. Assessments of their value vary. One writer states that they hover 'like an unwanted ghost in the home of aerial warfare law', but nevertheless agrees with Lauterpacht's conclusion that they embody some 'general principles of a customary or conventional character' and provide a convenient starting-point for any future attempt at air law codification.[2]

[1] For the full text of the 1923 draft see Schindler and Toman, op. cit. (above, p. 32 n. 1), p. 139.

[2] Raby, op. cit. (above, p. 33 n. 3), p. 12; Oppenheim, *International Law*, vol. 2 (7th edn. by

Events and efforts in the thirties

Neither the Hague Conventions of 1907 nor the draft Hague Rules of 1923 had any significant restraining effect in the armed conflicts of the thirties. The Japanese air raid on Chapei in Shanghai of 29 January 1932 has been described as the first terror bombing of a civilian population.[1]

A variety of far-reaching proposals designed to prevent or restrict bombing from the air were advanced during the Disarmament Conference of 1932–4. Under a French proposal bombing aircraft were to be abolished and all bombardment from the air prohibited.[2] Under one of the schemes advanced by the British Government there would be an agreement to confine air attacks to military objectives and a complete prohibition of attacks upon civilian populations. After the failure of the Disarmament Conference, further proposals for the curbing of air warfare were advanced in the face of fears of the effects of such warfare. Even Germany, whose development in the thirties was a main cause of the collapse of the Disarmament Conference, made proposals in 1935 for agreements prohibiting the dropping of gas, incendiary and explosive bombs outside the real battle zone.[3]

The actual military practice of the period pointed, however, to an increasing lack of restraint in the use of aircraft in armed conflicts. This is true of the Italian campaign in Abyssinia, of bombardments during the Spanish Civil War (including that of Guernica), and of the Japanese bombings of Nanking, Canton and Hankow in 1937. Condemnation by the League of Nations, individual governments and public opinion had no effect. Upon notification from the Japanese side about the bombing of Nanking, the United States, through its ambassador to Japan, responded in part as follows on 22 September 1937:

> This Government has the view that any general bombing of an extensive area wherein resides a large populace engaged in peaceful pursuits is unwarranted and contrary to principles of law and humanity . . .[4]

A British-sponsored resolution, which was adopted without dissenting vote by the Assembly of the League of Nations in 1938, was even more explicit. It appears to have been prompted not only by the bombings which had taken place in China and in Spain but also by the awareness of the inadequacy of British air defence in case of German attacks by air on British cities.[5] The resolution of the

Lauterpacht, London, 1952), pp. 520 and 519. Johnson agrees with the judgment that the rules were demanded more by public opinion than by governments: op. cit. (above, p. 33 n. 2), pp. 39 et seqq. See also his account of bombing in the First World War, which was the background of the 1923 Rules: ibid., p. 27. For the historical background in general, see B. M. Carnahan, 'The Law of Air Bombardment in Historical Context', *The Air Force Review*, 17 (1975), pp. 39–60.

[1] B. W. Tuchman, *Stilwell and the American Experience in China 1911–1945* (Bantam, 1972), p. 172.

[2] For a brief account of the proposals see Spaight, op. cit. (above, p. 31 n. 3), pp. 245 et seqq.

[3] See ibid., p. 249.

[4] Hackworth, *Digest of International Law*, vol. 6 (1943), pp. 265–6.

[5] See Spaight, op. cit. (above, p. 31 n. 3), pp. 257–8; cf. Rosenblad, 'Area Bombing and International Law', *The Military Law and Law of War Review*, 15 (1976), p. 77.

Assembly recognized the following principles as a necessary basis for any subsequent regulations:

(1) The intentional bombing of civilian populations is illegal;

(2) Objectives aimed at from the air must be legitimate military objectives and must be identifiable;

(3) Any attack on legitimate military objectives must be carried out in such a way that civilian populations in the neighbourhood are not bombed through negligence.[1]

Second World War and subsequently

The outbreak of the Second World War saw a similar attempt to contain the horrors which could be foreseen in case of unrestricted air warfare. On 1 September 1939 President Roosevelt appealed to the United Kingdom, France, Italy, Germany and Poland to affirm that their

> armed forces shall in no event and under no circumstances undertake bombardment from the air of civilian populations or unfortified cities, upon the understanding that the same rules of warfare shall be scrupulously observed by all their opponents.

The United Kingdom and France welcomed the appeal and replied that they had instructed their armed forces 'prohibiting the bombardment, whether from the air or the sea, or by artillery on land, of any except strictly military objectives in the narrowest sense of the word'. Hitler replied that 'The German Air Force has received the command to confine itself to military objectives'.[2] There was apparently a brief moment at the beginning of the war when at least the public British pledge was coupled with orders to give practical effect to the pledge. It is reported that at the outbreak of the war the Royal Air Force was not permitted to attack German warships in docks or at quay sides because of the risk of civilian casualties.[3]

The escalation into unrestricted air warfare was swift, however. For the purposes of this article it is not necessary to examine what prompted what.[4] It is enough to note some of the stations in the spiral. In the early phases there were the German bombardments of Warsaw in September 1939, of Kristiansand and Elverum (Norway) in April 1940, of Rotterdam in May 1940, British strategic bombing of Germany, beginning in May 1940, the German 'Blitz' from August 1940, including the raids upon London, Coventry and many other cities in the United Kingdom. Already this early phase of the air war caused sizeable losses among the civilian populations and departed from the professed determination to attack only military objectives.

[1] *League of Nations Official Journal*, Special Supplement No. 186, *Records of the Nineteenth Ordinary Session of the Assembly*.

[2] Cited from Spaight, op. cit. (above, p. 31 n. 3), pp. 259–60; cf. Hackworth, *Digest of International Law*, vol. 6 (1943), p. 269.

[3] See Saundby, 'The Ethics of Bombing', *Air Force and Space Digest*, June 1967, p. 51. Cf. Spaight, op. cit. (above, p. 31 n. 3), p. 268; see also Johnson, op. cit. (above, p. 33 n. 2), p. 47. On pre-Second World War British military divergencies regarding such restrictions see also Johnson, pp. 39 et seqq.

[4] See the divergent views of Spaight and of E. Spetzler, *Luftkrieg und Menschlichkeit. Die völkerrechtliche Stellung der Zivilpersonen im Luftkrieg* (Göttingen, 1956).

In the succeeding phases these civilian losses were multiplied many times and reached their peaks in the Allied raids upon Hamburg in July 1943, which left some 40,000 civilians dead, and upon Dresden in February 1945, which killed perhaps as many as 135,000 civilians including a great number of refugees.[1] In the Asian sphere, raids upon Tokyo in March 1945 rendered about 1 million people homeless and left some 85,000 dead and 40,000 wounded.

As is well known, the Nuremberg trials contained no judgment of indiscriminate air warfare. Telford Taylor explains that

> Aerial bombardment had been used so extensively and ruthlessly on the Allied as well as the Axis side that neither at Nuremberg nor Tokyo was the issue made a part of the trials.[2]

Before certain features in the air warfare are discussed from the legal viewpoint it should be noted that practices which caused very great civilian losses did not end with the Second World War. In the Korean War two large air raids early in 1951 caused the destruction of 35 per cent of the North Korean capital Pyongyang. The extensive air war in Indo-China was also considered the main cause of the high rate of civilian casualties in that war.

What rules should there be?

One might, of course, try to distil the existing rules on air warfare from conventions and custom. A court of law would be required to do so, if concrete questions were put to it in which this law was relevant. The Nuremberg tribunal refrained from passing any judgment whatever upon practices of unrestricted bombardment during the Second World War. As Schwarzenberger points out, the tribunal stamped neither legal nor illegal upon these practices.[3] It is not doubted, however, that such rules can be found, even though a recent United Nations survey reports that 'throughout the literature runs a concern that the large-scale bombardments of the Second World War, technological developments, especially the invention of nuclear weapons, and the mobilization of the total economy of a country in support of its war efforts have called in question what fragile legal restraints there are'.[4]

[1] *The New Encyclopedia Britannica*, vol. 19, 'World Wars', p. 1011; cf. Irving, *The Destruction of Dresden* (London, 1963). In a recent work on Dresden earlier estimates of losses are criticized as exaggerated and a figure of 35,000 killed is given: G. Bergander, *Dresden im Luftkrieg* (Köln, 1977), p. 166.

[2] *Nuremberg and Viet Nam, an American Tragedy* (1970), p. 89. Johnson cites with approval Schwarzenberger's view that the only way for the future to protect civilians against air warfare would be to herd them into sanctuaries: op. cit. (above, p. 33 n. 2), p. 56. I.C.R.C. proposals in this direction were, however, disapproved by many at the conferences of government experts, and were never tabled in final form. See I.C.R.C., *Report on the Work of the Conference of Government Experts*, 24 May–12 June 1971, § 469 at p. 82.

[3] 'The Law of Air Warfare and the Trend towards Total War', *Mélanges en l'honneur de Gilbert Gidel* (Paris, 1961), p. 535.

[4] United Nations, *Report on Human Rights in Armed Conflicts. Existing Rules of International Law concerning the Prohibition or Restriction of Use of Specific Weapons, Survey prepared by the Secretariat* (hereafter cited as *United Nations Survey*): A/9215 (7 November 1973), vol. 1, p. 171; cf. Johnson, op. cit. (above, p. 33 n. 2), pp. 54 et seqq. But Johnson seems critical of the statesmen and air chiefs who were inclined to the view that there existed no rules on air warfare simply because explicit conventions were missing.

Friedmann may be quoted as an exponent of the pessimistic school. He discusses the laws of war in the context of the concept of desuetude and comments that

> . . . the Second World War showed the practical obliteration of the basic distinction between combatants and non-combatants, between military and non-military objectives, as war became more and more the organized attempt to destroy the enemies' total war-making capacity and will to resist. . . . The various attempts to establish rules of air warfare which had not gone beyond draft conventions were overtaken by the total air war strategy of the Second World War.[1]

Lauterpacht is, likewise, pessimistic in his assessment of what rules of restraint may remain for air warfare. He seems to limit them to the prohibition of 'bombing of the civilian population for the mere purpose of terrorization'.[2]

The continued existence of rules is most emphatically affirmed, on the other hand, by the Institut de Droit International, holding that the rules have 'kept their full validity notwithstanding the infringements suffered'.[3] Even a writer like Spaight, who offers a blanket justification for Allied bombing practices during the Second World War, holds that 'indiscriminate bombing' and bombing 'for a moral effect only' remain unlawful and that 'it is the special, not the general war potential of the enemy that is still the objective'.[4]

It is not the purpose of this paper to argue that any particular rule is *lex lata*, but rather to discuss what rule should be accepted today—whether it constitutes codification or progressive development—keeping in mind both humanitarian needs and rational military necessity. Such a discussion must, however, take place against the background of the known practices of States and what may be existing rules. Lastly, it must focus upon rules on air warfare which the Diplomatic Conference on Humanitarian Law has recently adopted and analyse and assess them.

The need for new rules

As to the need for authoritative rules of guidance in air warfare there is no doubt. Spetzler concludes his thorough study *Luftkrieg und Menschlichkeit* (1956) by stating that although existing customary law gives a basic protection to the civilian population, there is a pressing need to dispel doubts through codification.[5] Spaight states almost at the outset of his monograph *Air Power and War Rights* that 'unless air power is regulated and controlled it will destroy civilization'. Those who have pointed to the need for clear rules have often done so against the background of the Second World War.[6]

[1] *The Changing Structure of International Law* (London, 1964), pp. 132–3.

[2] Lauterpacht, 'The Problem of the Revision of the Law of War', this *Year Book*, 29 (1952), p. 368. Johnson agrees with Lauterpacht: op. cit. (above, p. 33 n. 2), pp. 56–7.

[3] *Annuaire de l'Institut de Droit International*, 53–II (1969), p. 375. See also Spetzler, op. cit. (above, p. 36 n. 4), p. 375.

[4] Spaight, op. cit. (above, p. 31 n. 3), p. 277.

[5] See p. 390.

[6] Spaight, who regrets that the Hague Rules of 1923 were not in force in the Second World War, states that 'the lack of some international agreement on the subject of bombing was especially

Fresh impetus for working out such rules came, however, from the long conflict in Indo-China in which bombardment from the air was a dominant element causing heavy civilian losses. It was against that background that the so-called Cornell study, entitled *The Air War in Indochina*, stated in conclusion:

Clearly air warfare has been left almost totally unregulated, and air commanders and crews have been left with only general customary rules of land warfare as sources or guidance. The need for new and precise law is evident . . .[1]

This concern was also voiced in political organs of the United States. The subcommittee on international organizations and movements of the Committee on Foreign Affairs in the House of Representatives adopted a report containing, *inter alia*, the following recommendation:

The Department of State and the Department of Defense, and the Diplomatic Conference on the Reaffirmation and Development of International Humanitarian Law Applicable in Armed Conflicts, should support:

. . .

(c) Greater protection of civilians in armed conflicts including—

(1) standards and restrictions governing methods or means of combat which strike or affect indiscriminately the civilian population and combatants, or civilian objects and military objectives;

(2) restriction or prohibition of attacks on objects designed for civilian use, objects indispensable to the survival of the civilian population, and works and installations containing dangerous forces—dams, dikes, and nuclear generating stations; . . .[2]

Even more explicit is a statement prepared for the Diplomatic Conference by Senator Edward Kennedy, calling for rules protecting 'objects indispensable to the survival of the civilian population' like 'food, water and livestock' and rules to restrain 'zonal bombardment'.[3]

The prospects of achieving new rules—as contrasted with the desirability of rules—were assessed variously. In hearings which preceded the adoption of the resolution quoted above, the Acting Legal Adviser of the Department of State, Mr. George H. Aldrich, stated as regards possible restrictions on air warfare:

This is a much more difficult area. In essence, the question is whether it will be possible to put back into the bottle the genie of strategic bombing of urban-industrial areas that was let out with such tragic consequences during the Second World War. Given the nature and goals of contemporary warfare, we cannot be optimistic. One thing certain is that quick and easy answers will not solve the problems of protecting civilians.[4]

felt': op. cit. (above, p. 31 n. 3), pp. 42–3. See also Kunz, 'The Chaotic Status of the Laws of War and the Urgent Necessity for their Revision', *American Journal of International Law*, 45 (1951), pp. 37–61.

1 Ed. by Littauer and Uphoff (revised edn., Boston, 1972).

2 93rd Congress, 2nd Session: Committee Print, 27 March 1974, at p. 38.

3 Speech released 10 March 1974, printed in the *Congressional Record—Senate*, 11 March 1974.

4 International Protection of Human Rights, Hearings before the subcommittee on international organizations and movements of the Committee on Foreign Affairs of the House of Representatives, 93rd Congress, 1st Session, 1 August; 13, 19, 20, 27 September; 3, 4, 10, 11, 16, 18, 24, 25 October; 1 November; 7 December 1973: U.S. Government Printing Office, 1974. See p. 98. Cited below as *Hearing 1973*.

It is evident that rules on air warfare which are to be acceptable today must squarely face the question of military necessity and take it into account. They would otherwise risk remaining a dead letter.[1] 'Military necessity' is not simply to be equated with every past military practice, however, but must be assessed as objectively as possible. Nor should it be assumed that capacity for air warfare can remain the possession of a few countries. As Spaight states, 'air power . . . can never be the monopoly of any single nation'.[2] Accordingly, the rules to be worked out must be based on the premiss that even nations which traditionally have strong air forces have a long-term interest in rules of restraint which are not excessively lax. This would be for all to act in their own enlightened long-term interest.[3] Even Stone, whose attitude on air warfare is well reflected in the statement that 'it is far easier to moralise about air attacks on civilians, and to offer soothing verbal statements . . . than to frame rules for mitigation of human suffering with some hope of belligerent observance amid the realities of modern war', nevertheless, in his discussion of possible future rules, concedes that 'it should not be assumed that the smallest tittle of military advantage warrants a total denial of humanity'.[4]

What then are the 'military necessities' which cannot be disregarded, and what rules of restraint will they allow? This will now be discussed and in the course of the discussion the rules adopted by the Diplomatic Conference on International Humanitarian Law in 1977 will be examined.[5] The draft rules submitted by the International Committee of the Red Cross, and the rules adopted in 1975, constitute a package, the central elements of which can be summed up as follows:

1. The civilian population 'as such' shall not be the object of attack (Article 46 (1)).

2. Methods to spread 'terror' among civilians are prohibited (Article 46 (1)).

3. Methods which strike or affect indiscriminately the civilian population and combatants, or civilian objects and military objectives, are prohibited (Article 46 (3)).

4. Zonal bombardment is prohibited in populated areas (Article 46 (3) (a)).

5. Attacks shall be limited to military objectives (Article 47).

6. The military objectives must be duly identified before attack (Article 50).

7. Military objectives are defined in abstract terms. No exhaustive list is attached to the definition (Article 47).

8. Certain objects indispensable for the survival of the civilian population are given special immunity from attack (Article 48).

[1] Spaight, op. cit. (above, p. 31 n. 3), p. 43, holds that the Hague Rules of 1923 have influenced belligerents, while Stone, *Legal Controls of International Conflict* (London, 1959), p. 609, maintains the opposite.

[2] Spaight, op. cit. (above, p. 31 n. 3), pp. 15–16.

[3] Senator Edward Kennedy, speech of 10 March 1974, in *Congressional Record—Senate*, 11 March 1974, at p. S 33.

[4] Stone, op. cit. (above, n. 1), pp. 627 and 616.

[5] For the draft text submitted by the I.C.R.C. see I.C.R.C., *Draft Additional Protocols to the Geneva Conventions of August 12, 1949* (Geneva, June 1973). For the text of the rules adopted in 1977 see Protocol I (and II) 'Additional to the Geneva Conventions of 12 August 1949, and relating to the Protection of Victims of International Armed Conflicts (Non-International Armed Conflicts)' (Geneva, July 1977).

9. Certain objects containing dangerous installations are also granted special immunity (Article 49 (1)).

10. Attacks upon military objectives may be undertaken even though incidental losses among the civilian population or destruction of civilian objects can be expected, as long as such losses and destruction are not disproportionate to the anticipated military advantage of the attack (Articles 46 and 50).

11. Attacks by way of reprisals upon the civilian population are prohibited (Article 46 (4)).

'Undefended places'

It is somewhat paradoxical that almost the only thing that can be said with certainty about the law of air warfare is that the one conventional rule which has been clearly adopted to cover it is capable only of very limited application. This is Article 25 of the 1907 Hague Regulations which lays down:

> The attack or bombardment, by any means whatever, of undefended towns, villages, dwellings, or buildings, is forbidden.

The rule, in which the expression 'by any means whatever' was inserted in 1907 to cover attacks from the air, was devised with the thought of traditional land war in mind. Bombardment by artillery or from the air was—and remains—clearly unnecessary to assist ground troops in *occupying* places which are undefended. The conference adopting the rule did not contemplate the case of bombardment for the sake of *destruction* of objects of direct military use in the hinterland, which became possible through air war. It is not necessary to elaborate upon this point, which is well discussed by many authorities.[1]

Guidance has been sought rather in Article 2 of the Ninth Hague Convention concerning bombardment by naval forces. This article qualifies the general ban on bombardment of undefended places as follows:

> Military works, military or naval establishments, depots of arms or war material, workshops or plant which could be utilized for the needs of the hostile fleet or army, and the ships of war in the harbour . . .[2]

It is rightly commented by authorities that the case of bombing missions into

[1] Most ably by Spetzler, op. cit. (above, p. 36 n. 4), pp. 41, 129, 302; *United Nations Survey*, loc. cit. (above, p. 37 n. 4), pp. 167–8; Stone, op. cit. (above, p. 40 n. 1), pp. 621 et seqq.; Raby, op. cit. (above, p. 33 n. 3), pp. 16 et seqq; Schwarzenberger, loc. cit. (above, p. 37 n. 3), pp. 530, 537. Sir Arthur Harris, Marshal of the Royal Air Force, does not appreciate the difference between hinterland bombardment and front-line bombardment. He writes: 'What city in what war has ever failed to receive the maximum bombardment from all enemy artillery within range so long as it has continued resistance?': *Bomber Offensive* (London, 1945), p. 177. Is any hinterland city equipped with anti-aircraft artillery resisting? If it had no such artillery, would it be immune? The argument advanced by Sir A. Harris was also invoked by the British Government in a reply in Parliament on 9 February 1944: '. . . I am sure your Lordships would not refuse to accept the idea of shelling cities and towns in the front line . . . The German cities which I have mentioned are in the front line and they must be bombarded': *Hansard*, H.L. Deb., vol. 130, cols. 737–55.

[2] Text in Schindler and Toman, op. cit. (above, p. 32 n. 1), p. 592.

enemy hinterland is akin to ships bombarding and then withdrawing from enemy coastal towns. The aim in both instances is destruction of certain objects rather than immediate occupation. This reasoning has led, in turn, to the tenet, which is universally admitted, that bombardment of *military objectives* is permissible, whether from the air or from the sea.[1] What constitutes a 'military objective' is, however, a major question which is outside the scope of this paper.[2]

The civilian population 'as such'

A draft I.C.R.C. rule, which was adopted without any change of substance in Article 51 (2) of Protocol I, lays down that 'The civilian population as such, as well as individual civilians, shall not be the object of attack'. This formulation echoes Resolution 2444 (XXIII), adopted unanimously by the General Assembly of the United Nations on 19 December 1968,[3] and it is similar to the League of Nations' condemnation of 'the intentional bombing of civilian populations'.[4]

It is evidently possible that a belligerent—and individual combatants—may strike at non-combatants simply out of hatred or revenge, or coldly for the purpose of decimating an enemy population. Strafing of civilians is a case not unheard of.[5] A clear-cut ban on such war acts may, accordingly, be of use. Such acts cannot possibly have any rational military purpose, unless the spreading of terror is seen as a legitimate military purpose. This point is discussed below.[6]

The expression 'as such' may be redundant but is no doubt inserted as a reminder that civilians may be hit by attacks upon military objectives in which they find themselves, e.g. factories for war *matériel* and broadcasting stations. In these cases the civilians are not attacked 'as such', but the attacks upon the objectives take place in full awareness that they will also hit civilians.[7]

It should be noted that a rule of this kind must be read in conjunction with a definition of who is a 'civilian'. Under the Protocol I rules—Article 50—only persons belonging to the armed forces are excluded from falling under the concept of 'civilian'. Thereby a discussion might be ended which has often been heard to the effect that some 'civilians', notably those who work in munition or armament factories, ought to be regarded as 'quasi-combatants' and hence susceptible 'as such' to attack on their way to or from work and at their homes.

[1] See the quotations from the Austrian and Swiss military manuals in *United Nations Survey*, loc. cit. (above, p. 37 n. 4), p. 168.

[2] See below, however (p. 57), and see above, p. 37 n. 4.

[3] See also a resolution adopted by the XXth International Conference of the Red Cross. Cf. a statement by General Prugh before a United States House of Representatives subcommittee: 'The United States has consistently maintained the position that attacks against civilians as such . . . must not be carried out': *Hearing 1973*, p. 104.

[4] Resolution of 30 September 1938: *League of Nations Official Journal*, Special Supplement No. 186.

[5] See Spetzler, op. cit. (above, p. 36 n. 4), p. 314.

[6] See p. 44.

[7] Under the rule of proportionality a military objective may be rendered immune from attack, if the military value of its destruction stands in no proportion to the losses which would be expected in civilian lives and objects. Cf. Raby. op. cit. (above, p. 33 n. 3), p. 58. The Diplomatic Conference on Humanitarian Law adopted explicit rules—Articles 51 (5) (b) and 57 (2) (a) (iii)—on this matter. See below, p. 51.

This has been argued by Spaight[1] and Stone,[2] whereas Mme Bindschedler has termed quasi-combatants 'an entirely new concept and one which must be fought energetically'. In her view it would be impossible to draw distinctions between different groups of civilians. The result would be that the immunity of the civilian population 'as such' would be brought into question. She continues:

It creates a class of non-privileged combatants . . . and it fails to account for the fact that workers are engaged in activities useful to the war only as long as war installations to that end exist. The lawful objectives to be destroyed are those installations rather than an elusive and easily replaceable labour force.[3]

Under the rules of Protocol I—Article 51 (3)—the civilians only lose their 'personal' immunity if and for such time as 'they take a direct part in hostilities'.

'Deliberate' attacks on the civilian population

Use is sometimes made of the term 'deliberate' in discussions of attacks upon civilians.[4] It serves to distinguish this case from the case where such attacks occur by mistake or negligence.

Evidently the element of deliberateness is of relevance in determining the question of *responsibility* for an action, but the circumstance that there might be *no criminal* responsibility for attacks upon civilians occurring by mistake or negligence—which is not gross—does not make such acts *permitted*, nor does it exclude the possibility that liability for damage might arise for the State ultimately responsible. Stone is sceptical about the value of rules prohibiting 'deliberate' or 'careless' attacks. He doubts whether they provide more than 'verbal protection of civilians', since proof of 'deliberate' or 'careless' attack against civilians as such would rarely be possible.[5] A weightier argument, it is submitted, is that a formulation of a prohibition couched in terms of 'deliberation' would seem *e contrario* to make attacks by mistake or negligence permitted. This effect can only be avoided if the element of intent is dealt with separately in rules regarding responsibility.

[1] Spaight, op. cit. (above, p. 31 n. 3), pp. 44, 261. In 1928 Lord Trenchard, Chief of Air Staff of the Royal Air Force, maintained more modestly in a controversy concerning the role of the air force that while 'indiscriminate bombing of a city for the sole purpose of terrorizing the civilian population' would be illegitimate, it was 'an entirely different matter to terrorize munition workers (men and women) into *absenting themselves* from work . . . through fear of an air attack *upon the factory* . . . concerned': recorded in Webster and Frankland, *The Strategic Air Offensive against Germany 1939–1945*, vol. 4 (1961), p. 73. Italics added.

[2] Stone, op. cit. (above, p. 40 n. 1), p. 630.

[3] Bindschedler-Robert, *The Law of Armed Conflicts* (1971), p. 26; cf. Spetzler, op. cit. (above, p. 36 n. 4), p. 187.

[4] General Prugh stated that '. . . we would prohibit a deliberate aerial bombardment of a city containing no military targets and we would equally oppose deliberate rocket attacks on urban population centers': *Hearing 1973*, p. 105; cf. an amendment which was tabled at the 1972 expert conference, and which would have prohibited 'attacks which are intentionally launched indiscriminately against civilians and military objectives': see below, p. 62.

[5] Stone, op. cit. (above, p. 40 n. 1), p. 625 and n. 118 therein.

'Terror' bombardment

The draft rules proposed by the I.C.R.C. had the following provision—Article 46 (1) second sentence, of Protocol I—on international conflicts: '. . . methods intended to spread terror among the civilian population are prohibited'.[1] Such a rule would seem to have strong support if applied to the case of aerial bombardment. The 'morale' of the civilian population is not deemed a military objective by most authorities and bombing for the purpose of spreading terror is not deemed permitted. Stone, who advocates the distinction between 'genuine civilians' and 'quasi-combatants' who work in armament industries, seems isolated in holding that once this distinction is accepted 'the hard fact that belligerents do regard the morale of the enemy's quasi-combatant work force as a military objective can be faced . . .'.[2] To hold that the morale of the 'quasi-combatants' constituted a military objective would, indeed, be even worse than holding that they, themselves, were such an objective. Adler comments with reason that

> If it is permissible to violently attack the morale of war workers, it may be that the best way to do so is to kill his family, who are genuine civilians.[3]

The United Nations Survey reports that several military manuals and authorities state that bombardment carried out for the purpose of terror is unlawful.[4] Lauterpacht writes that

> There is one principle bearing on the subject under discussion which was embodied in the Hague Rules of 1923 and the essential correctness of which seems unimpeachable, namely, that it is unlawful to resort to bombarding of the civilian population for the mere purpose of terrorization. For in this case the civilian population becomes the direct object of attack regardless of any connexion with a military objective.[5]

Spaight writes that 'bombing for a moral effect only remains unlawful. In that sense, attack on the civilian population is contrary to international law.' He denies that any of the Allied bombing during the Second World War had the purpose of spreading terror. Had that been the case, heavily defended industrial centres would not have been selected as targets, but unprotected towns would have been preferred.[6] The United States Strategic Bombing Survey states, however, that the term 'area raids' came to be used to denote raids having four chief characteristics: one being that 'they were *intended primarily to destroy morale*, particularly that of the industrial worker'.[7]

[1] I.C.R.C., *Draft Additional Protocols to the Geneva Conventions of August 12, 1949* (1973).

[2] Stone, op. cit. (above, p. 40 n. 1), p. 631.

[3] Adler, loc. cit. (above, p. 32 n. 2), p. 41.

[4] See p. 170 and p. 177 of the *United Nations Survey*, loc. cit. (above, p. 37 n. 4).

[5] Lauterpacht, loc. cit. (above, p. 38 n. 2), p. 368.

[6] Spaight, op. cit. (above, p. 31 n. 3), pp. 277 and 279. Cf. reply by British Government in Parliament on 9 February 1944: '. . . we have never concentrated upon sleepy country towns and villages. That would not only have been unnecessarily brutal; it would have been utterly futile from our point of view . . .': *Hansard*, H.L. Deb., vol. 130, cols. 737–55, quoted from Johnson, op. cit. (above, p. 33 n. 2), p. 51.

[7] *Over-all Report, European War* (1945), p. 71. The various British directives under which

The view that much of the Allied bombing was primarily intended to destroy morale is widespread. Raby states that the Allied practice of target area bombardment during the Second World War unfortunately 'at times' degenerated into terror attacks. And he holds that 'it is generally accepted that terror bombing violates the law of war'.[1]

Adler cites the United States Bombing Survey in support of the following observation:

> By the end of the Second World War, however, morale had become by practice a permissible target. . . .
>
> The area bombing of World War II was used to attack the collective will to fight, perhaps even more so than it was used to hit military and industrial complexes.[2]

There seems to be broad agreement that bombing for the purpose of spreading terror or—amounting to the same thing—of undermining the morale of the industrial worker was not rational and might even have been counter-productive from a purely military viewpoint. More will be said on this subject in the subsequent section about area bombardment. This discussion is well summed up by Adler as follows:

> The impermissible line is reached in terror bombing of the civilian community with the aim of pressuring the political elite to accept the attacker's political demands. It is impermissible, because it is inhumane and ineffective . . .[3]

It seems fully justified to conclude that bombing for the purpose of spreading terror among the civilian population is illegal and that this ban is based not only on the inhumanity of such practices, but also on the rationale that there is no military necessity for them and that they might even be counter-productive for the purpose of subduing an enemy.

While the general conclusion comes easily, the exact formulation of the ban raises difficulties. Immediate questions as to the efficacy of the ban arise, if it is confined to 'methods *intended* to spread terror' or to 'attacks for the *purpose* of spreading terror'. As Stone points out, it will be very difficult to prove the intention of a belligerent.[4] As we have seen, Spaight denies that Allied bombings

morale gradually became a main object of attack are interestingly recorded in Johnson, op. cit. (above, p. 33 n. 2), pp. 48–9. Under the Casablanca Directive, issued 21 January 1943 by the combined chiefs of staff, the bomber commands in the United Kingdom were instructed that 'your primary object will be the progressive destruction and dislocation of the German military, industrial and economic system, and the undermining of the morale of the German people to a point where their capacity for armed resistance is fatally weakened': Webster and Frankland, op. cit. (above, p. 43 n. 1), vol. 4, p. 153.

[1] Raby, op. cit. (above, p. 33 n. 3), pp. 68 and 65.

[2] Adler, loc. cit. (above, p. 32 n. 2), p. 41; cf. R. Bindschedler, 'Die Unterscheidung zwischen Civilbevölkerung und Bewaffneten Kräfter', *Internationale Festschrift für Alfred Verdross* (Munich, 1971), p. 58.

[3] Adler, loc. cit. (above, p. 32 n. 2), p. 42; cf. Castrén, *The Present Law of War and Neutrality* (Helsinki, 1954), p. 200.

[4] Stone, op. cit. (above, p. 40 n. 1), p. 625. The same concern is presumably behind the following statement in a Report of the Subcommittee on International Organizations and Movements of the Foreign Affairs Committee of the United States House of Representatives: 'General Prugh [who had testified before the Committee], reflecting the unwillingness of the Department

during the Second World War aimed at 'morale' or at 'spreading terror', while most others conclude that they did. On the other hand, a formulation which banned 'methods which *are likely* to spread terror', and which would build upon an objective test rather than a subjective one, might raise the difficulty that methods can have terror as a likely incidental effect, and yet have other effects which are deemed vital from a military viewpoint.

At the Diplomatic Conference on Humanitarian Law in Armed Conflicts a formula was found after much informal discussion. Article 51 (2) lays down:

> . . . Acts or threats of violence the primary purpose of which is to spread terror among the civilian population are prohibited.[1]

The Committee Rapporteur's interpretation—which is not authoritative—is that the article is

> directed to intentional conduct specifically directed toward the spreading of terror and excludes terror which was not intended by a belligerent and terror that is merely an incidental effect of acts of warfare which have another primary object and are in all other respects lawful.[2]

It is no doubt correct that the adopted ban is directed to the case where terror is an 'objective', i.e. intended. This intention will have to be deduced from the circumstances—which may be difficult. It is an odd result of the text that it would seem permissible to carry out acts which have 'terror' as a secondary purpose. This was hardly intended by the authors. Intentional terror was never thought permissible, but incidental terror effects were thought quite likely and inevitable. Perhaps a happier formulation would have been to speak of 'acts . . . the primary effect of which could be expected to be that of spreading terror . . .'.

It may lastly be noted that in a sense the ban on terror bombing and other methods of bringing about terror among the civilian population is a duplication: the civilian population must not be subjected to direct attacks at all. This general ban evidently covers the case also where the 'objective' or 'purpose' is to terrorize. This is not to say that a separate ban on 'terror attacks' or 'terror methods' is redundant. In view of past practices of belligerents such a ban may be a useful reminder.

Indiscriminate warfare

The draft I.C.R.C. rules provided—in Article 46 (3)—that

> The employment of means of combat, and any methods which strike or affect indiscriminately the civilian population and combatants, or civilian objects and military objectives, are prohibited.

of Defense to restrict its capabilities, stated that only the following acts should be prohibited: "attacks against civilians *as such*", "intentionally terrorizing civilian noncombatants", "aerial bombardment of a city containing *no* military targets" and "*deliberate* rocket attacks on urban population centers": Report of 27 March 1974, 93rd Congress, 2nd Session.

[1] Only stylistic changes were made in the draft rule—Article 46 (1)—adopted by Committee III. See CDDH/III/286 Add. 1. Regarding the bans on terror attacks and on area bombardment, see also Rosenblad, *International Humanitarian Law of Armed Conflict—Some Aspects of the Principle of Distinction and Related Problems* (Dissertation, Stockholm, 1977), pp. 125–43.

[2] CDDH/III/286, p. 13.

There is little disagreement on the generalization that 'indiscriminate' means and methods of warfare are prohibited. There may, however, be less than a common understanding of what the prohibition means.

Spaight writes:

It is necessary to state, or re-state, the fact that nothing that has happened in the Second World War has shaken the legal objection to ***indiscriminate*** bombing[1] . . . There is still no warrant whatever for the deliberate bombing of a town which is neither a centre of war industry nor otherwise immediately related to the enemy's war effort . . . , or of those parts of such centres which, being purely residential or given up to retail trade or other non-warlike business, cannot be regarded as an essential part of the enemy's war machine . . .[2]

These statements must be read in the awareness, however, that Spaight considers area bombardment fully justified.

Another writer, Raby, defines the concept as follows:

[Indiscriminate bombardment] occurs when a legitimate military target is attacked in such an intentional or negligent manner that wanton destruction, rather than permissible, incidental damage, results. . . . However, the prohibition against negligent, indiscriminate bombardment is not absolute. ***Incidental damage resulting from military objective bombardment is lawful.*** A thin line often exists between incidental damage and negligent, indiscriminate bombardment . . .[3]

While it would seem that Spaight actually discusses the case of attacks upon the civilian population and civilian objects as such, Raby's analysis seems more pertinent in pointing to the circumstance that the attack does not distinguish—or does not adequately distinguish—between the legitimate military objectives and civilians or civilian objects. When the latter are protected from attack and the former are not, it is obvious that the attacker must take this fundamental distinction into account in his planning and performance. If he does not, he will bring death and destruction to civilians and civilian objects. He will, moreover, waste his explosives. The general rule does not, however, explain *to what extent* the distinction must be taken into account. Without interpretations in this regard and supplementary rules on this matter general formulations such as that drafted by the I.C.R.C. and quoted above or that adopted by the United Nations General Assembly unanimously in 1968[4] remain somewhat pointless.

The Hague Rules of 1923 required that where military objectives which are not near the operations of land forces cannot be bombarded 'without the indiscriminate bombardment of the civilian population, the aircraft must abstain from bombardment'.[5] In the early phases of the Second World War these precepts appear to have been of some influence.[6] The restraints quickly

[1] Italics added.

[2] Spaight, op. cit. (above, p. 31 n. 3), p. 277.

[3] Raby, op. cit. (above, p. 33 n. 3), p. 66.

[4] 'A distinction must be made at all times between persons taking part in the hostilities and members of the civilian population to the effect that the latter be spared as much as possible': G.A. Res. 2444 (XVIII).

[5] See above, p. 34.

[6] See above, p. 36 and n. 3. See also Spetzler, op. cit. (above, p. 36 n. 4), p. 255.

disappeared, however, and no one would dream of asserting that they were expressive of today's rule against indiscriminate attacks. The escalation was swift during the Second World War and most authorities have been shown above to be critical both on humanitarian and utilitarian grounds of what they consider to have been 'terror attacks' against the labour force. It would seem, accordingly, that the standard required of belligerent parties under the rule against indiscriminate attacks and methods should lie somewhere between these extremes. This spectrum is broad.

Three elements that are parts of this standard can easily be perceived:

(a) that targets must be *identified* with some certainty as military objectives,
(b) that attacks must be *directed* to such identified targets, and
(c) that the weapons and methods must be such that the target may be hit with some degree of likelihood.

These three elements are reflected in the rules which have been adopted by the Diplomatic Conference on Humanitarian Law. Article 57 (2) (a) of Protocol I provides that

> (a) Those who plan or decide upon an attack shall:
>
> (1) do everything feasible to verify that the objectives to be attacked are neither civilians nor civilian objects and are not subject to special protection but are military objectives within the meaning of paragraph 2 of Article 52 and that it is not prohibited under the provisions of this Protocol to attack them . . .

Identification with full *certainty* may, indeed, be an unattainable standard and one that would not be accepted by governments. The expression 'everything feasible' does not point to such a rigid standard. While the Committee which adopted the text deliberately avoided the term 'reasonable', which was seen as susceptible of too flexible an interpretation, the word 'feasible' can hardly be taken to mean everything that is 'physically possible'. The Rapporteur of the Committee suggested that the intention was to require everything that was 'practicable or practically possible'.[1] The expression chosen is thus not free from difficulty and questions of interpretation arise.

It is clear, as Castrén points out, that bombardment *at random* is unlawful.[2] Such bombardment evidently risks hitting civilians and civilian objects. Moreover, from the military viewpoint, it must be largely a waste of ammunition. Serious queries can be raised whether certain modern methods of identification of targets—e.g. sensors registering noise or smell or heat—are adequate. Without digressing into the discussion of the so-called 'electronic battlefield' it may be suggested that a decisive consideration in this matter is *where* the methods are used. It is evident that most mobile *matériel* and personnel in the battlefield will be military objectives, while this is not so in most parts of the hinterland.

In the Plenary's discussion of Article 51 (earlier 46) the United Kingdom delegate, Mr. Freeland, welcomed the restraints placed in Article 51 upon mili-

[1] CDDH/III/286, p. 25.
[2] Castrén, op. cit. (above, p. 45 n. 3), p. 202.

tary action with a view to protecting civilians. He added, however, on the problem of identification

> that military commanders and others responsible for planning, initiating or executing attacks had to reach decisions on the basis of their assessment of the information available to them from all sources at the relevant time.[1]

There is evidently nothing in any of the new articles to contradict this view. To 'do everything feasible' to identify military objectives must include the use of all kinds of observations and intelligence. The expression does not limit the means to be used, but rather sets an—admittedly vague—requirement of intensity of effort. The rumoured presence in a village of some guerrilla soldiers cannot be enough to identify the village as a military objective.

The second and third elements of importance to prevent indiscriminate warfare, namely, that attacks must be directed to the identified targets and that the means and methods employed must be such that the targets may be hit with some degree of likelihood, are also reflected in the rules adopted by the Diplomatic Conference. The fundamental rule adopted is the following in Article 51 (4):

> Indiscriminate attacks are prohibited. Indiscriminate attacks are:
> (a) those which are not directed at a specific military objective;
> (b) those which employ a method or means of combat which cannot be directed at a specific military objective; or
> (c) those which employ a method or means of combat the effects of which cannot be limited as required by this Protocol; and consequently, in each such case, are of a nature to strike military objectives and civilians or civilian objects without distinction . . .

This article is supplemented by the injunction—in Article 57 (2) (a) (ii)—to those who plan or decide upon an attack to

> take all feasible precautions in the choice of means and methods of attack with a view to avoiding, and in any event to minimizing, incidental loss of civilian life, injury to civilians and damage to civilian objects . . .[2]

The articles adopted call for some comments. It was the submission of the present writer at the conference—particularly in the discussions in the informal working group that did the drafting work under the chairmanship of the Rapporteur—that some weapons are by their construction or necessary or normal use so imprecise that the degree of likelihood of their hitting the identified military objective aimed at must be deemed too low. The V-1 bombs developed by

[1] See CDDH/SR. 41, 26 May 1977, p. 30.

[2] It may be noted that Article 51 (4) (figuring as Article 46 (3)) was adopted by the Committee III by consensus. Article 57 (figuring as Article 50) was adopted at the Committee stage by a vote of 66 to 0, with 3 abstentions. See the Rapporteur's Report, CDDH/III/286, §§ 60 and 100.

In the Plenary, Article 51 (figuring as Article 46) was adopted by 77 votes in favour, 1 against (France) and 16 abstentions. Many explanations of vote were given. See CDDH/SR. 41 of 26 May 1977 at p. 29. Article 57 (2) (figuring as Article 50) was adopted by the Plenary by 90 votes to none, with 4 abstentions. See also below.

Germany during the Second World War were given as one example and biological weapons were mentioned as other examples of 'blind weapons'. It was noted that the military manual of the Federal Republic of Germany stipulates that the use of flying bombs would be illegal, if their inaccuracy makes it likely for the civilian to be hit with full power.[1] Other participants in the discussion would not admit that any weapons existed which could not be directed to a military objective. It may be surmised that this attitude was taken to foreclose any discussion of the question whether nuclear weapons are inevitably indiscriminate. Their view was reflected in the language of the Rapporteur, as follows:

> ... Many but not all of those who commented were of the view that this definition was not intended to mean that there are means or methods of combat the use of which would involve an indiscriminate attack in all circumstances. Rather, it was intended to take account of the fact that means and methods of combat which can be used perfectly legitimately in some situations could, in other circumstances, have effects that would be contrary to some limitations contained in the Protocol, in which event their use in those circumstances would involve an indiscriminate attack.[2]

In the Plenary the United Kingdom delegate explained his delegation's affirmative vote on Article 51 (4) (now figuring as Article 46 (4)) by saying that

> His delegation considered that the definition of indiscriminate attacks given in that paragraph was not intended to mean that there were means of combat the use of which would constitute an indiscriminate attack in all circumstances. The paragraph did not itself prohibit the use of any specific weapon, but it took account of the fact that the lawful use of any means of combat depended on the circumstances.

Similar statements were made by the representatives of the Federal Republic of Germany and Italy. By contrast, the delegate of the German Democratic Republic expressed himself as follows:

> The prohibition of indiscriminate attacks or of attacks which employed methods of combat that could not be directed at a specific military objective was of the utmost importance, since it re-established the priority of humanitarian principles over the uncontrolled development of barbarous use of highly sophisticated weapons and means of warfare, which from the outset disregarded the fundamental rights of the human being.

The Mexican delegation declared—in a written statement—that Articles 51 and 52 (figuring as 46 and 47) were essential and that they could not

> be the subject of any reservations whatsoever since these would be inconsistent with the aim and purpose of Protocol I and undermine its basis.[3]

The persistent controversy as to whether any weapon exists that would, by its very nature, be indiscriminate was perhaps somewhat artificial. All agree that in

[1] See I.C.R.C., *Report on Weapons that may cause unnecessary suffering or have indiscriminate effects* (Geneva, 1973), p. 17 and see *Kriegsvölkerrecht—Leitfaden für den Unterricht* (Teil 7) (Bonn, 1961), §§ 73 and 90.

[2] CDDH/III/286 and correction in CDDH/III/215, § 55.

[3] The quotations from the Plenary are from CDDH/SR. 41 at pp. 29, 30, 33, and Annex, pp. 1 and 10.

the case of most arms indiscriminate effects will be the result of indiscriminate *use* rather than of the nature of the weapon. Arms which are incapable of being directed to or limited in their effects to a military target are unlikely to be projected by the arms manufacturers, because they would often be militarily uneconomical. It is not hard, on the other hand, to imagine 'means' of warfare which would inevitably be indiscriminate. The various devices mentioned in the discussion of environmental warfare may be referred to.[1] It is satisfactory, therefore, that Article 51 (4), as it was adopted, does refer to 'a method or means of combat which cannot be directed at a specific military objective'.

It is clear that both Article 51 (4) and Article 57 (2) (a) (ii) quoted above implicitly admit that means and methods of warfare have incidental effects upon civilians and civilian objects. The extent to which this is tolerated—'limited as required by this Protocol', in the words of Article 51 (4) (c)—is described in Article 57 (2) (a) (iii), under which those who plan or decide upon an attack shall

> refrain from deciding to launch any attack which may be expected to cause incidental loss of civilian life, injury to civilians, damage to civilian objects, or a combination thereof, which would be excessive in relation to the concrete and direct military advantage anticipated.

This rule—of proportionality—was incorporated after much discussion, during which its protagonists emphasized the restraining effect which could be served by it and its opponents voiced the concern they felt for the misuse which could be made of it.[2] In this context it is enough to note that a method or means of warfare would be deemed indiscriminate, under the general rule on this subject, if the incidental effects expected to be caused by it to civilians or civilian objects would be disproportionate to the direct military advantage of hitting the military objective. While, as we have seen, it is still argued that no means of warfare exist that are by their nature incapable of direction, it can hardly be doubted that any means—weapons or other devices—or method the *normal or typical employment* of which results in military objectives and civilians and civilian objects being hit without distinction and in disregard of the rule of proportionality would stand condemned.

[1] See the Soviet draft treaty submitted to the 1974 session of the United Nations' General Assembly, U.N. Doc. A/C. 1/L. 675, and Convention on the Prohibition of Military or Any Other Hostile Use of Environmental Modification Techniques in U.N. Doc. A/31/382.

[2] A letter of 22 September 1972 from the General Counsel of the Defense Department, J. F. Buzhardt, to Senator E. Kennedy refers to the rule of proportionality and states that 'a review of the operating authorities and rules of engagement for all our forces in Southeast Asia, in air as well as ground and sea operations, by my office, reveals that not only are such operations in conformity with this basic rule, but that in addition, extensive constraints are imposed to avoid if at all possible the infliction of casualties on non-combatants and the destruction of property other than that related to the military operations in carrying out military objectives': *Congressional Record—Senate*, 2 October 1972, at p. S 16522.

If it were even after the Indo-China War to be a considered United States opinion that the rule of proportionality was observed by United States forces throughout the war in that region, the value of the rule to induce restraint could, indeed, be queried. At p. 54 n. 5, below, Raby's view is recorded to the effect that the atomic bombing of Hiroshima and Nagasaki did not violate the rule of proportionality.

Area bombardment—the notion

The preceding section of this paper has discussed the general principles against indiscriminate warfare.

The legal rule which should be applied to the method of *area bombardment*—sometimes termed 'zonal bombardment' or 'saturation bombing'—will now be in focus.

The I.C.R.C. draft rules—Article 46 (3)—contained under the general rule against indiscriminate means and methods of warfare a specific rule on area bombardment. Under this draft rule it was prohibited

> to attack without distinction, as one single objective by bombardment or any other method, a zone containing several military objectives, which are situated in populated areas and are at some distance from each other.[1]

This draft rule contemplated cases more general in scope than the type of area bombardment that is described in the United States Bombing Survey typical during the Second World War:

> The term 'area raids' came to be used to denote raids having four chief characteristics: they were directed against large cities; they were designed to spread destruction over a large area rather than to knock out any specific plant or installation, and they were intended primarily to destroy morale, particularly that of the industrial worker.[2]

Spaight—who denies that the chief purpose of these attacks was to destroy morale[3]—has explained how the practice of area bombardment arose, when German anti-aircraft action made daylight precision bombing too costly and camouflage made the identification of military objectives difficult. The alternative method of attack then became night bombing with big forces over whole areas *within which* there were military objectives—armament industries etc. as well as residential areas.[4] Spaight quotes an author explaining that since the German workers tend to live near their factories and the German defence prevents precision bombing of the latter, 'the German authorities, by trying to spare their factories, divert much of the attack on their own civilian population'.[5]

It may suffice at this point in the discussion of Second World War area bombardment to note that it is not doubted that in many cases the area attacked contained certain military objectives. The main legal question the attacks have raised, however, is whether they fell short of the standard required in distinguishing between military objectives and civilians and civilian objects. Relevant in this regard is the fact that within the target area evidently no attempt was made at all to achieve any distinction between objects attacked.

Bombardment of a whole area within which various military objectives are found[6] can be used for other purposes than those which were common in Allied

[1] I.C.R.C., *Draft Additional Protocols to the Geneva Conventions of August 12, 1949* (1973).
[2] *Over-all Report, European War* (1945), p. 71.
[3] See above, p. 44.
[4] See Spaight, op. cit. (above, p. 31 n. 3), pp. 264 and 269 et seqq.
[5] Ibid.—citing Hector Hawton—at p. 273.
[6] Cf. the description of area bombing by Raby, op. cit. (above, p. 33 n. 3), p. 67.

bombings of German cities during the Second World War. A whole area might be bombarded—by air or artillery—in preparation for an attack by land forces. The aim in such cases is to destroy not productive capacity, but military personnel, arms and vehicles. Although in such cases, too, civilians and civilian objects might be much affected, this kind of area pounding or saturation bombing has hardly been criticized by modern authorities. The military need for it is evident and the humanitarian case against it is not so strong. The areas that might be affected by such attacks are likely to be less numerous than the areas in the hinterland which might be chosen for attack, e.g. because they contain productive capacity that is deemed militarily relevant. Moreover, civilians are likely to have moved from areas which are on the verge of becoming battlefields. If, in exceptional cases, the civilian population is still present, e.g. in a city, the rules on siege would apply. Castrén writes that

> State practice permits so-called psychological bombing to induce the surrender of a *besieged* town, and such bombing may probably be carried out also by aircraft.

Castrén puts this case apart, however, from hinterland bombing. He continues:

> It is not possible, however, to extend this rule by treating the whole enemy country as a kind of besieged and fortified area where even civilian targets may be bombed.[1]

Bombardment of a whole area has also been practised when there was certainty—or strong suspicion—that an area harboured guerrilla forces and/or bases. Where such 'strike zones' or 'free fire zones' are defined in land which is not populated, the humanitarian case against them is not so strong. There may be ecological arguments against such practices, however.[2] And their military utility has been doubted.

While the I.C.R.C. draft rule would have prohibited area attacks only in 'populated areas', it was not confined to the case of night bombing or bombing for psychological purposes. It rather prohibited—as indiscriminate—the technique of trying to hit individual legitimate military objectives by hitting a whole area in which these were found together with a civilian population. Indirectly it proclaimed that in such areas at any rate, only individual objectives could be attacked.

The Diplomatic Conference on Humanitarian Law adopted a text that is slightly different. That text, and the discussions that preceded and followed it, will be analysed below. Current doctrine and *ratio legis* will first be examined.

[1] Castrén, op. cit. (above, p. 45 n. 3), p. 404. Sir Arthur Harris seeks precisely to invoke the case of siege to defend the practice of area bombardment of cities: see Harris, *Bomber Offensive* (1945), p. 177. See also p. 41 n. 1 above.

[2] The Diplomatic Conference on Humanitarian Law in Armed Conflicts adopted two articles on the protection of the environment. The more general of these two—Article 35 (3) (earlier Article 33 (3))—provides that 'It is forbidden to employ methods or means of warfare which are intended, or may be expected, to cause widespread, long-term and severe damage to the natural environment'. The other provision in Protocol I is found in Article 55. Among the articles on 'ecological warfare' see, for instance, A. Westing, 'Proscription of Ecocide', *Bulletin of the Atomic Scientists*, vol. 30, No. 1 (January 1974).

Area bombardment—current doctrine

A United Nations survey rightly reports that there is a conflict of views on the permissibility of target area bombardment.[1] It would seem, indeed, that the preponderant view among authorities is to hold this practice illegal when applied to populated areas. Even writers who come out in support of the legality of area bombardment during the Second World War do so hesitantly or hold it to be on the border of illegality. Thus although Spaight, the most elaborate and articulate defender, writes:

> ... one of the practices of the war which must be regarded now as established usage is that of the bombardment of *target areas* rather than of specific military objectives therein ...

he nevertheless concludes:

> ... International law cannot trim its sails so quickly to the winds of expediency as that [i.e. to permit atom bombing]. It should hold to the view that, while target area bombing comes close to the border-line of permissibility, atom bombing definitely oversteps it.[2]

The arguments which Spaight adduces for the distinction he thus makes are not very convincing:

> ... The area included in the assault [in target area bombing] is not out of proportion to that which the actual objectives occupy. In atom bombing the disproportion is immense ... A whole city is engulfed ...[3]

This is a curious argument coming from an author who can describe a raid upon Berlin as follows:

> ... it was one of the most devastating attacks ever made by Bomber Command. It left not a single shop intact in Unter den Linden, and it practically razed Leipzigerstrasse, Potsdamerstrasse and Wilhelmstrasse to the ground. Significant testimony to the effect of this and the other November raids was the closing of no less than 31 out of Berlin's 35 theatres ... And worse was to follow.[4]

And apart from Spaight's description of Berlin dying from conventional bomb explosions, it is hard to close one's eyes to the fact that huge areas of the cities of Hamburg, Dresden and Tokyo were practically razed to the ground by explosive and incendiary bombs. If the areas of assault were out of proportion to the actual objectives in the cases of Hiroshima and Nagasaki, they were no less so in the cases of, for example, Hamburg, Dresden and Tokyo.[5]

Stone, who states that the starting point must be that target area bombing is not 'a mere barbarous whim, but a policy adopted under certain pressures', nevertheless admits that 'the legality of British "target area bombing" would call for anxious inquiry, involving as it did the destruction on a great scale not

[1] *United Nations Survey*, loc. cit. (above, p. 37 n. 4), p. 176.

[2] Ibid., p. 276.

[3] Ibid., p. 274.

[4] Ibid., p. 36.

[5] Raby, who also defends area bombardment under 'proper conditions', subjects atomic bombing to the same tests and concludes that the attacks upon Hiroshima and Nagasaki met those tests and were thus legitimate: op. cit. (above, p. 33 n. 3), p. 70.

only of factories and the lives of the quasi-combatant force, but also as in the case of Hamburg in July 1943, the obliteration of a whole city'.[1]

What then are the legal arguments adduced in support of area bombardment? Spaight offers several. One is that the massive Allied air-offensive 'was an evil which . . . must be held to have been justified by the "proportionate cause" which was at stake'.[2] Arguments of this kind are akin to doctrines of just war, providing different rules for the just and the unjust. It is generally believed that no viable system of laws of war can rest upon such a doctrine.[3]

Another argument advanced by Spaight is that if target area bombing was the *only* method which could achieve the desired military result, then it was legal:

> If in no other way than by target-area bombing can a belligerent destroy his enemy's armament centres and interrupt his enemy's process of munitionment, then target-area bombing cannot be considered to offend against the principles of the international law of war.[4]

This, too, would seem a line of reasoning that is dangerous. For Raby, a condition for area bombardment is that 'no other equally effective means of mission accomplishment exists, which would inflict *less* injury and damage to the enemy'. But this is only *one* of several conditions which Raby considers must be satisfied in order legally to justify area bombardment.[5] Mme Bindschedler writes that Spaight's conception 'seems to extend unduly, the notion of the measure "imperatively demanded by the necessities of war" '.[6]

It may be asked whether, if a belligerent saw 'no other way' of achieving victory than by obliterating the whole civilian population, this would make the method legal. As a factual matter doubts are advanced that area bombardment was needed in the later phases of the Second World War in order to hit armament industries and communication centres. Spetzler states that from the autumn of 1943 new mechanisms had been invented which made pin-point night bombing possible.[7] Stone, dealing with the same point, states that by 1945 night bombing was more accurate than day bombing.[8] This circumstance points to the conclusion that during this later phase of the war the principal aim of area bombardment was psychological. The following passage by Spaight would seem to reflect full awareness of this:

> Germany had to be taught beyond all possibility of doubt that war does not pay. It is true that by the spring of 1944 she had had a lesson inculcating that truth. Her ruined cities were the memorials of the folly of 1939 . . .[9]

[1] Stone, op. cit. (above, p. 40 n. 1), pp. 627–8.

[2] Spaight, op. cit. (above, p. 31 n. 3), pp. 272 and 47.

[3] Raby terms Spaight's argument quasi-emotional: Raby, op. cit. (above, p. 33 n. 3), pp. 68 and 179; cf. the following line by Adler: 'Appraisals of a quantum of evil to justify a given stratagem are too subjective and emotive to be the basis for definitive legal criteria': loc. cit. (above, p. 32 n. 2), p. 36.

[4] Spaight, op. cit. (above, p. 31 n. 3), p. 271; cf. ibid., p. 47.

[5] See Raby, op. cit. (above, p. 33 n. 3), p. 70.

[6] Bindschedler-Robert, op. cit. (above, p. 43 n. 3), p. 15 n. 10.

[7] Spetzler, op. cit. (above, p. 36 n. 4), p. 300.

[8] Stone, op. cit. (above, p. 40 n. 1), p. 628 n. 131.

[9] Spaight, op. cit. (above, p. 31 n. 3), p. 38.

Another argument advanced by Spaight seems more serious from a legal viewpoint. Target area bombing, he writes,

> could reasonably be claimed to be justified where the target, even though in a hinterland, had become, in effect, a *place d'armes*. It would not be reasonable, on the other hand, to apply the principle of the target area to other towns in the hinterland, e.g. to one which contained perhaps one or two military objectives of no great consequence and was otherwise innocent of warlike activity. In such an instance it could properly be demanded that the precise objectives, and these only, should be attacked.[1]

What is meant by this concept becomes clearer in the following pages of Spaight's discussion. He terms the towns with armament industries 'battle-towns'. And the powerful anti-aircraft artillery around them make 'the centres in question . . . in a double sense *places d'armes*'.[2] While the example of 'fortress of the Ruhr' still seems to point to '*places d'armes*' being a reasonably limited category, the statement that 'the great urban agglomerations are in fact the areas in which the armament factories that really matter are located'[3] seems to widen the concept so drastically that few would accept it. Several writers have, indeed, been sceptical about its introduction.[4]

Adler, who finds much of the Allied area bombing aimed at morale and considers such 'terror bombing' illegal, is ready to accept target area bombing in the case of the Ruhr Valley:

> German industry was in a small area, especially in the Ruhr Valley, heavily defended, concealed, and camouflaged. The bombs fell generally in the location of the objectives: armament and associated factories in the widest sense, oil production, and transportation. There was no real attempt to separate military targets from more general targets. In a nation geared for war, with military factories interspersed and unidentifiable, such targeting and bombing cannot be called illegal.[5]

Although Adler is not quite clear, it would seem that to him—as to Raby[6]—a critical measuring rod for the permissibility of area bombardment is that of proportionality, in this context meaning that area bombardment becomes permissible if the damage thereby inflicted in the area upon civilians and civilian objects is proportionate to the military value of the destruction of the military objective:

> Saturation bombing, which will certainly hit non-military targets, is by definition not indiscriminate because the target is confined to a particular area and the purpose is to destroy the military objectives; all other destruction is thus incidental and, *if not disproportionate*, is legal.[7]

The idea that an attack cannot be indiscriminate as soon as the attacked area is *defined* is strange. The emphasis seems, however, to lie in the requirement of proportionality.

1 Spaight, op. cit. (above, p. 31 n. 3), p. 254. 2 Ibid., p. 263. 3 Ibid., p. 262.

4 See Stone, op. cit. (above, p. 40 n. 1), p. 620 n. 87, and Spetzler, op. cit. (above, p. 36 n. 4), p. 288.

5 Adler, loc. cit. (above, p. 32 n. 2), p. 36.

6 Raby, op. cit. (above, p. 33 n. 3), p. 70.

7 Adler, loc. cit. (above, p. 32 n. 2), pp. 30–1; italics added.

There runs through the writings of the various authorities one line which is in common. This is the idea that legitimate military objectives may be so *concentrated* in a single area that the whole area can be regarded as a military objective. Greenspan expresses it as follows:

> . . . that the area is so preponderantly used for war industry as to impress that character on the whole of the neighbourhood, making it essentially an indivisible whole . . .[1]

Stone writes that the doctrine and practice of target area bombing 'assume that a "target area" contains a concentration or spread of military objectives . . .'.[2] Spaight's references to 'battle-towns' are in the same vein, although he extends the notion to cover almost all urban agglomerations, thereby losing the reasonable element which is introduced by the notion of concentration in this context. An argument might, indeed, be made to the effect that in cases where pin-point bombing of all military objectives in a hinterland area, because of the concentration and importance of such objectives would, in fact, through its direct and incidental effects, yield the same result as a systematic target area bombardment of the whole area, such target area bombardment ought to be permitted. This seems to be the conclusion reached by Mme Bindschedler when she admits the legality of bombardment of 'zones where military objectives are contiguous and cover a considerable part of the relevant territory'.[3] The danger of such a rule would be the vagueness of the concepts of 'concentration' and 'contiguity' and the clear-cut departure from the principle that only military objectives may be attacked. In target area bombing of populated areas civilians and civilian objects are hit not only incidentally—or accidentally—together with the military objective and in the vicinity of it, but also by bombs which are neither aimed at nor hit any military objectives. The extensive use of area bombardment on big cities during the Second World War would seem to demonstrate amply how the elasticity of the doctrine allowed it to turn into what most writers now would regard as terror bombing of civilians.

In addition to the quotations offered above in the discussion of terror bombardment a few more may be included at this point. Castrén, speaking of area bombardment during the Second World War, writes:

> The evident intention was to destroy military objects, although the effects of this type of bombing did not differ greatly from those of so-called psychological or terror bombardment. It also seems probable that the military advantages which were sought bore no relation to the suffering and damage inflicted upon the civilian population.[4]

Lauterpacht writes about the bombing of civilian populations for the purpose of terrorization as emanations of the doctrine of total war. He adds that

> they may not be altogether alien to the practice—though not the avowed principle—of

[1] Greenspan, *The Modern Law of Land Warfare* (1959), p. 336.
[2] Stone, op. cit. (above, p. 40 n. 1), p. 628.
[3] Bindschedler-Robert, op. cit. (above, p. 43 n. 3), p. 26.
[4] Castrén, op. cit. (above, p. 45 n. 3), p. 404.

strategic bombing which is, at least in theory, directed against military objectives, however widely conceived.[1]

Lastly, Raby writes: 'A thin line often exists between incidental damage and negligent, indiscriminate bombardment'.[2]

It may be concluded on the basis of the above survey that the draft I.C.R.C. proposals prohibiting area bombardment in populated areas were advanced against a background of legal writings which either reject such practices as being illegal or point to illegal abuses to which such practices have led, or, at the very least, admit that the practices during the Second World War were on the border of legality.

Area bombardment—the military case against it

It is an often-repeated truism that the rules regulating warfare must take 'military necessity' into account, lest that notion be advanced in attempts to justify departures from the rules. Accordingly, the views of authorities must be examined as to the need for area bombardment. Already in the preceding section some authorities have been quoted who have stated that area bombardment is a militarily indispensable method, even in populated areas. Thus Raby considered it 'very essential under proper conditions' and he did not limit it to cases where there was a concentration of military objectives but considered the method equally essential in case of a single target of sufficient importance, e.g. a nuclear weapons facility.[3] The view of Spaight has also been cited to the effect that it was the *only* method by which Nazi Germany could be hit.[4] At the 1972 I.C.R.C. Conference of government experts one military authority stated that

> . . . we cannot expect governments easily to undertake commitments to eschew attacks on the urban, industrial sinews of its enemies, *to refrain from area bombardment*, or to spare essential lines of communication . . .[5]

Despite these scattered statements, it would seem that if the existing legal principles were deemed to prohibit area bombardment of populated areas, such prohibition would not contradict needs for military effectiveness. On the contrary it would seem to conform with what has been referred to in a United States Congressional hearing as 'one of the classic principles of war: Economy of force'.[6]

Perhaps it is in the analysis of the effectiveness of area bombardment that the most serious indictment of the practice lies. Spaight states that

> An air arm, apart from its purely tactical work, has open to it two ways of achieving the results which its capacity for direct action should make possible. It can break the

[1] Lauterpacht, loc. cit. (above, p. 38 n. 2), p. 369. Cf. quotations from Lauterpacht above at pp. 38 and 44. Lauterpacht's conclusion that 'strategic' and 'tactical' bombing is permitted, while 'terror-bombing' is prohibited, is shared by Johnson, op. cit. (above, p. 33 n. 2), pp.56–7.

[2] Raby, op. cit. (above, p. 33 n. 3), p. 66.

[3] Ibid., pp. 71 and 72.

[4] Spaight, op. cit. (above, p. 31 n. 3), p. 47.

[5] Cited from Blix, 'Human Rights and Armed Conflicts: conflicting views', *Proceedings of the American Society of International Law*, 1973, p. 153.

[6] *Hearing 1973*, p. 102.

will to war of the enemy nation, or it can break that nation's material capacity to continue to wage war . . .[1]

Although, as we have seen, these two methods were used in the Second World War and in the Indo-China War, the results would seem to refute the idea that it is at all feasible to crush the morale of a civilian population and bombard an enemy's will into submission, whether by pulverizing his cities or seeking to push him back to the stone age, or, at any rate, to indicate that it is a method that is not economic in military terms.

Facts would also seem to point to the conclusion that breaking a nation's material capacity to continue waging a war by bombardment is a problematic endeavour and that far from being a military necessity, methods that bring about general devastation simply constitute a waste of resources which could have been put to better military use. If this is so—and a number of quotations are offered below to prove the point—it should be possible to codify with general acceptance a rule of international law built upon the premiss that there is no military necessity for psychological bombing of civilians and for general devastation by area bombardment of populated areas.

Describing the effects upon Berlin of area bombardment Spaight cites a British newspaper report from 5 June 1945:

> The heart has been blown out of the largest city on the Continent, and the standards which apply when measuring the destruction of other cities cannot be applied to Berlin. For one thing, in many sections it is not a question of craters or shattered houses; it is merely one of height of hills of rubble . . . There is a peculiar feeling that one is seeing the world in its twilight when you drive through the worst damaged parts of Berlin.[2]

The rationale of such destruction is quoted by Spaight from Churchill—speaking in the United States Congress on 19 May 1942—as follows:

> Opinions are divided as to whether the use of air power could by itself bring about a collapse in Germany or Italy. Well, there is certainly no harm in trying.[3]

The preponderant post-Second World War view is that general destruction by air is not effective in military terms. The United States Strategic Bombing Survey has this to say:

> What effect the area raids—as distinguished from precision raids on specific plants and installations—had in the final collapse of Germany cannot be measured with any accuracy.

And this:

> Throughout the period the losses inflicted by area raids fell mostly on industries relatively unessential to the war effort.

[1] Spaight, op. cit. (above, p. 31 n. 3), p. 34.

[2] Ibid., p. 37.

[3] Ibid. According to Webster and Frankland, op. cit. (above, p. 43 n. 1), vol. 1, p. 162, there emerged under the impact of German raids on English cities an 'increasing insistence of the Prime Minister and members of his government on a more ruthless bombing policy'.

And this:

War production is the critical measuring rod of the effects of lowered morale in the German war effort . . . As has been seen, armaments production continued to mount till mid-1944, in spite of declining civilian morale, but from that point on, arms production began to decline and dropped every month thereafter at an increasing rate. A minor, but not negligible, portion of this drop was the result of the cumulative effects of lowered morale.[1]

And among the conclusions the Bombing Survey brings out the following:

The importance of careful selection of targets for air attack is emphasized by the German experience. The Germans were far more concerned over attacks on one or more of their basic industries and services—their oil, chemical, or steel industries, or their power, or transportation networks—than they were over attacks on their armament industry and city areas.[2]

Other authorities have reached the same conclusion. A quotation from Churchill, who authorized the general onslaughts on the German cities, may be offered first:

The destruction of Dresden remains a serious query against the conduct of allied bombing. I am of the opinion that military objectives must henceforth be more strictly studied in our own interests rather than that of the enemy . . .

I feel the need for more precise concentration upon military objectives, such as oil and communications behind the immediate battle-zone, rather than on mere acts of terror and wanton destruction, however impressive.[3]

In Allen's book *The Legacy of Lord Trenchard* the following is found:

It is also apparent that American precision attacks caused the breakdown of German industry and that area bombing of the cities was to a large extent a waste of effort.[4]

In Higham's work *Air Power—A Concise History* (London, 1972) the following comment on area attacks is found:

The whole grand strategy was wrong. Area attacks, while perhaps justifiable as retaliation, were a complete violation of the principles of war strategically. They vitiated forces rather than concentrating them against the decisive point, they were uneconomical of force, and they strengthened the enemy will to resist . . .[5]

A similar judgment is passed by Blackett in his book *Military and Political Consequences of Atomic Energy* (London, 1948):

. . . The area bombing, which was originally adopted just because of the inability to do

[1] *Over-all Report, European War* (1945), pp. 73, 74 and 97–8.

[2] Ibid., p. 108. An interesting article on the subject is John A. Lauder's 'Lessons of the Strategic Bombing for Contemporary Defense Policy', *Orbis*, vol. 18, pp. 770–90.

[3] Cited from Webster and Frankland, op. cit. (above, p. 43 n. 1), vol. 3, p. 112. This minute was toned down in its final version (Webster and Frankland, vol. 3, p. 117). The two historians write that 'the Prime Minister and others in authority seemed to turn away from the subject (the strategic air offensive) as though they had forgotten their own recent efforts to initiate and maintain the offensive' (vol. 3, p. 284). They defend the area bombing offensive and compare it favourably with naval blockade (vol. 3, pp. 116–17).

[4] See p. 185.

[5] See p. 132.

precision bombing, did little to help win the war and greatly increased our difficulties afterwards.[1]

The views quoted above are in the majority. In her report *The Law of Armed Conflicts* Madame Bindschedler-Robert states:

Military experts today admit that the results of Allied bombing in Germany fell very much short of expectations, that they did not become effective until they concentrated on sources of energy and transport, and that the brutality of that form of warfare, far from shattering the enemy's morale, may even have encouraged a spirit of resistance which prolonged the war.[2]

From the Indo-China War similar conclusions seem to emerge from studies of some aspects of the air warfare, although less definitive judgments are available for this war. One might compare the famous—or infamous—statement about bombing the enemy in Vietnam back to the stone age with the critical assessment of the results achieved through a discharge of bomb quantities that were several times those dropped during the whole of the Second World War. A study, based on the Pentagon Papers, and prepared for the United States Senate Committee on Foreign Relations, entitled *Bombing as a policy tool in Viet Nam: Effectiveness*,

calls into serious question the efficacy of strategic and interdiction bombing against a highly motivated guerilla enemy in an underdeveloped country.[3]

The Diplomatic Conference on Humanitarian Law in Armed Conflicts

At its second session, in 1975, the Diplomatic Conference adopted by consensus, in a first reading, a rule on area bombardment (Article 46). It was confirmed in 1977 and included as Article 51 (5) (a) in Protocol I. This rule will be analysed below. However, it might be useful to trace the legislative history of this article.

At the first conference of government experts convoked by the I.C.R.C.—in 1971—no draft rule was advanced by the I.C.R.C. on the question of area bombardment. The matter was only discussed in one of the I.C.R.C. documents before the conference.[4] A concrete proposal was tabled, however, by the experts of Egypt, Mexico, Netherlands, Sweden (the present writer) and Switzerland. This proposal, which was contained in a comprehensive working paper entitled 'Outline of an Instrument for the Protection of the Civilian Population against

[1] See p. 26. For a contrary view see 'The Ethics of Bombing' by R.A.F. Air Marshal Sir Robert Saundby, *Air Force Magazine*, June 1967, p. 53. It is amazing to see the statement made in the late twenties by Sir C. Madden, Chief of the British Naval Staff, to the effect that the role advocated for the Royal Air Force as an independent attacker of *inter alia* vital centres of communication would lead to a 'dispersion of bombing operations which will have little military effect on the conduct of the war'. See Webster and Frankland, op. cit. (above, p. 43 n. 1), vol. 4, p. 82.

[2] See p. 24; cf. Mirimanoff-Chilikine, 'Protection de la population et de personnes civiles contre les dangers résultant des opérations militaires', *Revue belge de droit international*, 8 (1972–I), p. 128; Spetzler, *Luftkrieg und Menschlichkeit* (1956), pp. 302, 379; Schnez 'Luftkrieg ohne Terrorangriffe' in *Wehrwissenschaftliche Rundschau*, 1952 (6), p. 279.

[3] Study No. 5 (Washington, 1972).

[4] I.C.R.C., Conference of Government Experts, Geneva, 24 May–12 June 1971, vol. 3, *Protection of the Civilian Population against Dangers of Hostilities*, p. 108.

the Dangers of Hostilities',[1] was incorporated from a text which the I.C.R.C. had submitted to the Red Cross Conference in New Delhi in 1956 and read as follows:

> It is forbidden to attack without distinction, as a single objective, an area including several military objectives at a distance from one another where elements of the civilian population or dwellings are situated in between the said military objectives.[2]

At the second conference of government experts convoked by the I.C.R.C.—in 1972—a concrete proposal was tabled by the I.C.R.C. Under this proposal it would have been prohibited to attack

> as one sole objective, by means of bombardments or any other methods, an area comprising several military objectives which are at some distance from each other and situated in populated regions.[3]

This proposal, which was linked to the rule on proportionality, differed slightly from the 1956 I.C.R.C. draft which had been resuscitated by the experts of Egypt, Mexico, Netherlands, Sweden and Switzerland in 1971. It extended the ban to cover area attacks not only by bombardment, but by 'any other method', e.g. rockets. This new formulation led to difficulties and reformulation in 1975. These will be discussed later. The new reference to 'populated regions', on the other hand, was probably a limitation as compared to 'an area . . . where elements of the civilian population or dwellings are situated'.

As pointed out by the present writer at the 1973 annual meeting of the American Society of International Law[4] the draft rule was not much debated. One expert from a big Western power expressed his scepticism.[5] Amendments tabled by important Western powers significantly omitted any rule which would have prohibited area bombardment.[6] An amendment tabled by the experts of Australia, Belgium, Canada, the Federal Republic of Germany, the United Kingdom and the United States dealt with indiscriminate warfare as follows:

> Attacks which are intentionally launched indiscriminately against civilians and military objectives shall be prohibited.[7]

In a proposal by experts of the United States, 'indiscriminate attacks' were explained to be those 'which have no specific military objective'.[8]

The proposal submitted by the I.C.R.C. to the Diplomatic Conference which convened in 1974 contained—with slight rephrasings—the same rule on area bombardment as had been laid before the second expert conference, but the rule was now placed in the context of a prohibition of indiscriminate methods

[1] I.C.R.C., *Report on the Work of the Conference* (Geneva, 1972), pp. 97–9 and 83–6.

[2] See I.C.R.C., Conference of Government Experts, Geneva, 24 May–12 June 1971, vol. 3, *Protection of the Civilian Population against Dangers of Hostilities*, pp. 049–057. The text incorporated comes from Article 10 of the 1956 I.C.R.C. draft.

[3] I.C.R.C., *Basic Texts* (Geneva, 1972), Protocol I, Article 50 (2).

[4] Blix, in *Proceedings of the American Society of International Law*, 1973, p. 153.

[5] Quoted above, p. 58.

[6] See I.C.R.C., *Report on the Work of the Conference*, vol. 2 (Geneva, 1972), CE/COM III/PC. 11 (U.S.); PC. 29 (U.K.); PC. 74 (France).

[7] Ibid., CE/COM III/PC. 106. See also above, p. 43 and n. 4.

[8] Ibid., CE/COM III/PC. 110.

rather than in the context of the principle of proportionality.[1] This new draft rule was subjected to a number of comments and draft amendments at the 1974 session of the Diplomatic Conference. During the 1975 session there were hardly any comments, but informal negotiations took place which led to a consensus compromise.

In the general debate which opened the first session the Swedish Minister of State, Carl Lidbom, on 7 March 1974, had this to say as regards air warfare:

> . . . The production of food, clothes and other things which are needed by civilians and soldiers alike has hardly become of greater importance to modern belligerents than it was to those of the 19th century. The large-scale modern attacks affecting civilians and civilian production are probably better explained by the availability of greater destructive capacities in modern big powers. Our era is wasteful not least in its use of bombs. There are, however, several indications that the military gains from large-scale bombardments of populated areas upon analysis, have been found marginal. . . .
>
> . . .
>
> . . . These views point to the conclusion that such methods of attack, not founded upon military necessity, can and should be prohibited. The rapid technical evolution of means of directing weapons to specific targets should make it even less defensible to maintain a license for belligerents to use means and methods which are indiscriminate in their effects, in particular those which affect large populated areas.
>
> It is against the background I have described that my Government strongly supports the draft rules submitted by the I.C.R.C. explicitly prohibiting terror attacks and indiscriminate attacks, particularly area bombardment . . .[2]

In the Third Committee of the conference the present writer, as representative of Sweden, developed the theme advanced by the Minister in a statement on 19 March 1974:

> . . . I want . . . to express the support of my delegation for draft article 46 as submitted by the I.C.R.C. . . .
>
> It would seem that the development of smart bombs guided to their targets by laser or TV should facilitate the acceptance of the proposed ban upon area bombardment. Although these bombs may yet be a weapon only for the technologically advanced states, the same is actually true of the capacity to engage in the costly practice of area bombardment.
>
> My delegation is very conscious of the need in our treatment of draft article 46 to combine what is desirable with what is feasible. The absence of written rules on the matters treated in article 46 is probably part of the reason for terrible practices which the world has witnessed. Hence, explicit rules of restraints are urgently called for. If these rules were to go too far to be broadly acceptable the progress would be limited. On the other hand, it would serve no humanitarian purpose to adopt rules which leniently permitted that for which at present no authority exists. . . .

The draft rule on area bombardment was not commented upon by most of those who discussed draft Article 46 (finally adopted as Article 51). The tendency was to direct remarks only to points on which representatives were

[1] See above, p. 62.

[2] The quotation comes from the press release of the Swedish Ministry for Foreign Affairs 1974-03-07. The summary records of the conference, both of plenary and of committees, are so compressed that most arguments advanced are lost. For this reason original texts will be cited here to the extent they are available to the present writer.

critical. A fairly large number of delegates from Communist States and from developing countries, accordingly, made remarks on the draft ban on terror attacks and on the rule of proportionality. Most—critical—remarks on the draft rule on area bombardment came from representatives of Western States. Only two amendments were tabled on this point. One of these was submitted by Brazil, Canada, the Federal Republic of Germany and Nicaragua and read as follows:

> . . . it is forbidden:
> (a) to attack by bombardment as a single military objective a zone comprising a populated area containing several military objectives if such objectives are so distant from one another that it is reasonably possible to attack them individually; . . .[1]

The other was tabled by Australia:

> . . . it is forbidden:
> (a) to attack without distinction, as one single objective by bombardment or any other method, a zone containing several military objectives, which are situated in populated areas and are at such distance from each other that they are capable of being attacked individually; . . .[2]

The representative of the Federal Republic of Germany introduced the first amendment and explained that the expression 'bombardment' comprised both bombardment from the air and artillery bombardment; further, that the phrase 'are so distant from one another that it is reasonably possible to attack them individually' had been advanced in order to be more explicit than the I.C.R.C. expression 'some distance'.[3] Some other delegates supported this view. Thus, the delegate of Canada—a co-sponsor with the Federal Republic of Germany—said that the amendment greatly clarified the I.C.R.C. text. He added that 'the question of what constituted an area bombardment could be subjective and his delegation therefore supported a more precise explanation'.[4] The delegates of Denmark, the United Kingdom, the Netherlands and the United States supported the amendment introduced by the Federal Republic of Germany.[5] The United Kingdom delegate joined in the criticism of the expression 'at some distance from each other' and felt that the point was clarified by the amendment. By contrast, the Swedish representative—the present writer—criticized the expression 'reasonably possible to attack them individually' and noted that a qualifying phrase of this kind did not exist in the corresponding rule of the military manual of the Federal Republic of Germany. He was answered by the representative of that State that he

> might have overlooked the fact that the German military manuals are fully responsive to the demands of practicality and even military necessity.[6]

[1] CDDH/III/27.
[2] CDDH/III/43/Rev. 1.
[3] Statement 19 March 1974 in Committee III.
[4] Quoted from summary record in CDDH/III/SR. 7.
[5] See summary records for the eighth meeting of the Third Committee, on 19 March 1974, in CDDH/III/SR. 8.
[6] Quoted from the original text, delivered on 20 March 1974 in Committee III.

The relevant passage in the manual—ZDv 15/10, paragraph 68—was quoted as follows:

It is forbidden to treat several military objectives and populated areas between them as a single objective and to attack or bombard this area indiscriminately in its entire extension.

During the second session of the Diplomatic Conference—in 1975—extensive informal discussion took place, which eventually resulted in the following text, which was adopted by consensus in the Third Committee:

. . . Among others, the following types of attacks are to be considered as indiscriminate:

(a) An attack by bombardment by any methods or means which treats as a single military objective a number of clearly separated and distinct military objectives located in a city, town, village, or other area containing a concentration of civilians or civilian objects; . . .[1]

The provision finally adopted by the Conference and included as Article 51 (5) (a) in Protocol I is identical with the text adopted by Committee III, except for the addition of the word 'similar' before the word 'concentration'. The discussions which preceded the text adopted by the Committee are, accordingly, fully relevant to the final provision. They were, naturally, much more extensive than those in the Plenary.

The discussions which took place in the Informal Working Group chaired by the Rapporteur are not recorded. In the view of the present writer, who took an active part in these discussions, the Rapporteur's Report accurately reflects a few of the essential points of those discussions:

56. In subparagraph 3 (a), 'bombardment by any methods or means' refers to all attacks by fire and the use of any type of projectile, except for direct fire by small arms. The subparagraph prohibits all types of bombardment which treat as a single military objective a number of objectives separated by some distance which are located in an area where there is a concentration of civilians. Thus, after much deliberation, the Working Group considered it unnecessary to refer to 'massive' bombardment, 'target area' bombardment, or 'carpet bombing' since all are covered by this prohibition and the use of such expressions might be construed to restrict the protection of civilians from other types of bombardment.[2]

The article adopted represents a compromise. Some would have preferred a limitation to 'urban areas', others an extension to any areas. Representatives of some underdeveloped areas pointed out that most of their people lived in villages, not in urban areas, and it was agreed to limit the ban to areas with a concentration of civilians or civilian objects.

The original I.C.R.C. phrase 'by bombardment or any other method', which had been criticized as perhaps covering even an infantry assault with small arms, was replaced by the expression 'by bombardment by any methods or means'. As noted by the Rapporteur, this expression could not cover attack by small arms. But it was meant to cover, e.g., bombardment by artillery or rockets.

[1] CDDH/III/286 and 286 Add. 1/Corr. 1.

[2] CDDH/III/286 and 215.

Several delegates from Eastern European States would have wished to refer explicitly to 'massive bombardment'. With the understanding, recorded by the Rapporteur, that neither this notion nor some others were excluded, it was agreed only to define in abstract terms a particular kind of attack, rather than to introduce the various labels in current use, e.g. 'massive bombardment', 'target area bombing', 'carpet bombing', 'zonal bombardment'. Such notions, if used explicitly, would anyway have required a definition.

The greatest difficulty was presented by the phrase 'objectives . . . at some distance from each other' in the I.C.R.C. text. It had been criticized for vagueness by several Western representatives. The alternative suggested by the critics, 'objectives . . . so distant from one another that it is reasonably possible to attack them individually', seemed to other representatives to give too much latitude in application. The Australian formulation, 'objectives . . . at such distances from each other that they are *capable* of being attacked individually', seemed too rigid to some, who felt that it implied only 'physically possible'. The solution eventually found was to avoid relating the distance between the targets directly to the means of attack and to replace 'at some distance' by the more articulate expression 'clearly separated and distinct military objectives'. Even this notion, regrettably, cannot be applied in complete disregard of the means of attack which exist. Objectives which are a hundred metres apart may be 'clearly separated', but they are hardly 'distinct', if the bombs required to destroy them have effects which extend a hundred metres or more. By contrast, with the development of 'smart bombs' guided by laser or other devices, which allow precision attacks, perhaps more targets become 'distinct'. Thus even the seemingly absolute description employed is not free from difficulty in interpretation.

After the adoption by the Third Committee of this text, the representative of the United States explained his vote in a way which seemed to point to this problem:

> We voted in favour of the article and support it. In Art. 46 (3) (a) the term 'clearly separated and distinct military objectives' is used. It is the position of the United States delegation that the words 'clearly separated' refers not only to a separation of two or more military objectives which can be observed or which are visually separated, but also includes the element of a significant distance. Further, that that distance must be at least of such a distance that will permit the individual military objectives to be attacked separately.

As can be seen from the statement quoted, the United States delegation tied its reservation to the expression 'clearly separated' rather than to the term 'distinct'. This is immaterial. The important feature lies in the construction that visual separateness is not enough and that the distance between the military objectives '*will permit*' separate attacks. This notion is evidently connected with the means of attack that exist at any given period.

Some points should be noted from the Plenary treatment of the provision. Article 51 (figuring as Article 46) was adopted in the Plenary by a roll-call vote of seventy-seven votes in favour, one against (France) and sixteen abstentions (Turkey, Zaïre, Afghanistan, Algeria, Federal Republic of Germany, United

Republic of Cameroon, Colombia, Italy, Kenya, Madagascar, Mali, Morocco, Monaco, Republic of Korea, Senegal, Trinidad). Voting paragraph by paragraph was not allowed. Most of the abstentions were unrelated to sub-paragraph 5 (a). Hesitation among the Western States was due mostly to the concern that sub-paragraph 4 (c) implied the possible existence of weapons which are indiscriminate by their very nature. Only the representatives of France and Turkey mentioned sub-paragraph 5 (a) specifically. The French delegate stated that sub-paragraphs 4, 5 and 6 'were too complex and likely to hamper defensive operations in any country'. The Turkish delegate said that 'paragraphs 4 and 5 were open to different interpretations'.[1]

The criticism that the text is complex is certainly justified. But it is a criticism that can be directed against many of the provisions of the Protocols. Indeed, it may be queried whether that feature is not to some extent inevitable when international legislation seeks to embrace complex and controversial matters. Agreement has to take into account a great many concerns. When the alternative to complexity is absence of explicit regulation, complexity may seem more bearable. But it admittedly carries within itself risks of self-destruction. To avoid those risks it is evidently important that military manuals explain the new rules more fully than is done in treaty articles.

It is certainly easier to describe past practices, especially from the Second World War, which would stand condemned under the formulation now adopted than to suggest for the future how far apart objectives must be in metres to call for separate attacks under the rule. Even so the new rule and the consensus by which it was adopted in the Committee and the near-consensus by which it was adopted in the Plenary should be of significance. The rule is in line with the idea—noted above[2]—that area bombing could be legitimate only where there is a concentration of military objectives.

Article 51 (figuring as Article 46) was welcomed by several delegates. The delegate of Byelorussia was the only one who mentioned the Second World War. Referring to 'mass bombings, which cause the loss of countless lives among civilian population' he said:

> This too we know well from our experience of the Second World War, when many of our towns, among them Minsk, the capital of the Republic, were reduced to ruins and tens of thousands of peaceful citizens were killed as a result of barbarous bombing by the fascist air forces.
>
> The Byelorussian S.S.R. considers that by banning such attacks Article 46 of Protocol I makes a substantial contribution to the development of humanitarian law and we welcome it.[3]

The Swedish delegation stated that Article 51 (figuring as Article 46) was of fundamental value for the whole Protocol and of importance for the protection of the civilian population against the effects of attacks.[4]

With a prohibition of area bombardment as defined and in circumstances defined in the new rule, some other rules acquire even greater significance than

[1] CDDH/SR. 41 (26 May 1977), p. 28.
[2] See above, p. 57.
[3] CDDH/SR. 41 (26 May 1977), p. 15.
[4] Ibid., p. 21.

before. This is true of the definitions of military objectives and protected objects and of the point at which incidental damage to civilians and civilian objects becomes too serious to permit attack even upon a military objective (rule of proportionality). It is evident that if nearly everything were deemed to constitute military objectives permissible for attack, or if almost unlimited incidental damage were tolerated to civilians or civilian objects in connection with attacks upon military objectives, the ban upon area bombardment could lose all meaning.[1]

The vitally important questions of what constitute military objectives and protected objects and of what is permissible incidental damage have been subjected to much discussion at the Diplomatic Conference on Humanitarian Law in Armed Conflicts and new rules have been adopted by consensus or near consensus.[2] These matters and the new rules on them deserve detailed analysis. In this article, which has been confined to the specific question of area bombardment, it must suffice to mention only some interpretations advanced in the Plenary of the provision defining military objectives. Article 52 (2) (earlier Article 47 (2)) as finally adopted reads:

> Attacks shall be limited strictly to military objectives. In so far as objects are concerned, military objectives are limited to those which by their nature, location, purpose or use make an effective contribution to military action and whose total or partial destruction, capture or neutralization, in the circumstances ruling at the time, offers a definite military advantage.

Article 47 as a whole was adopted by the Plenary by seventy-nine to none, with seven abstentions.[3] No one seems to have objected to the definition of 'military objectives', but the French delegate criticized the first sentence. Explaining his abstention he said that

> there were many situations in armed conflicts in which it was difficult or even impossible to determine precisely the limits of a military objective, particularly in large towns and in forest areas, in either of which enemy armed forces and groups of civilians might be intermingled.[4]

Another point which was raised by several N.A.T.O. countries must be noted here. The United Kingdom delegate, Mr. Freeland, said that

> his delegation, which had voted in favour of Article 47, was glad to have in paragraph 2 a partial definition of the term 'military objective', which appeared to provide a necessary clarification of the law. It had noted in particular that *a specific area of land might be a military objective* if, because of its location or for other reasons specified in the article, its total or partial destruction, capture or neutralization, in the circumstances ruling at the time, offered a definite military advantage.[5]

[1] See the views of Buzhardt and Raby, quoted above at p. 51 n. 2 and p. 54 n. 4.

[2] The definition adopted on 'military objectives' has been quoted above at p. 33 n. 1. The formulation adopted on the rule of proportionality was quoted above, p. 51.

[3] CDDH/SR. 41 (26 May 1977), p. 35.

[4] Ibid., p. 35.

[5] Ibid., p. 36 (italics added). Similar statements by the Federal Republic of Germany in ibid., annex, p. 2; Canada, annex, p. 4; United States of America, annex, p. 6; Netherlands, annex, p. 13.

These points, made under the definition of 'military objectives', do not seem to have been advanced to neutralize the acceptance of the prohibition of area bombardment as defined in Article 51 (5) (a), which is the subject of this article. Rather than dealing with the technique of covering several military objectives with one blanket attack, they point to the case where a specific area—the whole of it—is a genuine military objective. This point is germane to the consideration advanced above that there might be a legitimate military need to pound an area—rather than any objects—in advance of ground attack or to pound an area to deny it to the enemy.[1] The statements made in the Plenary may thus be said to have pointed to some problems of application but not to have eroded the broad agreement that was reached at the Diplomatic Conference on the matter of area bombardment.

[1] See above, p. 53.

[11]

Air War and the Law of War

W. HAYS PARKS

I. INTRODUCTION

For many it must seem incongruous to speak of "law of war" in light of the degree of destruction wrought during World War II. It appears a contradiction in terms when one considers the number of civilian dead,[1] recalls British Prime Minis-

---

Mr. Parks (B.A., J.D., Baylor University) is Chief, International Law Team, International Affairs Division, Office of The Judge Advocate General of the Army; Professorial Lecturer on International Law, The George Washington University School of Law, Washington, D.C.

---

1. Estimates of German deaths vary. The United States Strategic Bombing Survey, Summary Report (European War) 15 (1945) estimated that 250,253 civilians were killed by Allied bombing between January 1, 1943, and January 31, 1945. Hans Rumpf in THE BOMBING OF GERMANY 164 (1962), places the figure at 600,000. David Irving in THE DESTRUCTION OF DRESDEN 41 (1963) sets the number of civilian deaths at 635,000. However, Irving originally estimated civilian deaths resulting from the February 1945 Allied air raids on Dresden at "more than 135,000." *Id.* at 11. Subsequently, in a letter to The Times, London, July 7, 1966, at 13c, he reduced the total to 25,000. But later historians continue to cite Irving's original figure in arriving at their own conclusions as to total civilian deaths. *See, e.g.*, L. BIDINIAN, THE COMBINED ALLIED BOMBING OFFENSIVE AGAINST THE GERMAN CIVILIAN 1942–1945 37, 51, 242 (1976); and G. QUESTER, DETERRENCE BEFORE HIROSHIMA 150 (1966) (the error remained, uncorrected, in a 1986 edition).

Civilians killed in Great Britain have been accounted for as follows:

Bombing	51,509
Flying bombs	6,184
Rockets	2,754
Cross-channel guns	148
Total	60,595

B. COLLIER, THE DEFENCE OF THE UNITED KINGDOM 528 (1957).

From a law of war standpoint, there is a potential for discrepancy in these figures. Civilian workers killed within a legitimate target, such as a military base, munitions plant, or aircraft engine manufacturing plant, are not regarded as "civilian casualties." While this should not be construed so broadly as to include all civilians in an industrial city, as occurred during World War II, reasonable persons could arrive at different numbers, but disagreement would have only a fractional impact on the total numbers. The United States Strategic Bombing Survey, The Effects of Bombing on Health and Medical Services in Japan 5 (1947) notes that the majority of civilian casualties in Germany and Japan were women and children, while placing German civilian casualties at 500,000 and Japanese civilian deaths at 338,000, the latter all occurring in one year. *See, e.g.*, F. IKLE, THE SOCIAL IMPACT OF BOMB DESTRUCTION 205 (1958). The DEUTSCHLAND HEUTE 156 (1958), official statistical publication of the Federal Republic of Germany, provides the following figures:

Losses among German civilians through hostile action:	500,000 dead
Losses among German civilians from the eastern provinces:	1,550,000 dead

See also M. SORGE, THE OTHER PRICE OF HITLER'S WAR 67 (1986).

Obviously not all civilian casualties can be attributed to bombing. The devastation of Berlin by Russian artillery bombardment was so great that the United States Strategic Bombing Survey could not perform an evaluation of the damage done to that city by the Allied strategic air offensive. *A Brief Study of the Effects of Area Bombing on Berlin, Augsurg, Bochum, Leipzig, Hagen, Dortmund, Oberhausen, Schweinfurt, and Bremen*, 39 THE UNITED STATES STRATEGIC BOMBING SURVEY (2d ed. 8, Jan. 1947).

ter Winston Churchill walking amidst the rubble of Coventry,[2] or views the photographs of the massive cathedral of Cologne surrounded by an utterly devastated city.[3] Having directed much of one nation's strategic air offensive and daily witnessed its deadly effects, it is not surprising that Sir Arthur Harris,[4] Marshal of the Royal Air Force (RAF), concluded after the war that, "International law can always be argued pro and con, but in this matter of the use of aircraft in war there is, it so happens, no international law at all."[5] The wartime commander of RAF Bomber Command regrettably was more right in his comment than he was wrong. Rather than a reflection of lawlessness on the part of any or all parties to the conflict, it is more a recognition of the limits of the law in total war. It is an acknowledgement of the failure of nations to come to agreement on practical limitations on the employment of arms during the four decades preceding that conflict, despite reasonable warnings regarding the potential level of destruction.

There has been criticism of the bombing campaigns of World War II, and particularly the Allied strategic air offensive and the United States' bombing campaign against Japan (including the use of atomic bombs against Hiroshima and Nagasaki). This is an inevitable outcome of postwar debate in democracies. The questions posed and answered, in the first part of this article, to the extent possible, are the following:

(1) What was the law of war with regard to aerial bombardment (hereinafter "bombing," for brevity's sake) prior to, and during, World War II?

(2) To what extent did national leaders and/or air forces observe it?

The latter portion of the article will address the legislative endeavors of the 1970s, which produced the 1977 Protocols Additional to the Geneva Conventions of August

---

Total German civilian casualties have been placed at 1.5 million [E. ZIEMKE, STALINGRAD TO BERLIN: THE GERMAN DEFEAT IN THE EAST 500 (1968)] in close agreement with the DEUTSCHLAND HEUTE figure cited above. Hence, the Allied strategic air offensive accounted for 20% to 40% of the civilian losses in Germany. It is important to note that it was not the major cause of death, in Germany or elsewhere. In Russia, where strategic (rather than tactical) airpower played an insignificant role, Russian civilian and military losses have been listed as 22 million, of which 10.15 million were civilians. While the very high military losses can be attributed to a number of factors, including inefficient military medical services, high civilian and military losses are directly attributable to Soviet tactics, which throughout the war tended to be extravagant in terms of Soviet lives. ZIEMKI, *id.* at 500.

2. N. LONGMATE, AIR RAID: THE BOMBING OF COVENTRY facing 238 (1976).

3. The attacks on Cologne are described in R. BARKER, THE THOUSAND PLAN (London, 1965); E. TAYLOR, 1000 BOMBER AUF KOLN (Dusseldorf, 1979); W. RANKE, AUGUST SANDER: DIE ZERSTORUNG KOLNS (Mosel, 1945); and E. TAYLOR, OPERATIONS MILLENIUM (London, 1987). Again, a certain perspective is appropriate. During the Allied strategic air offensive, the Cologne Cathedral was struck by fourteen bombs. It is estimated that postwar damage by air pollution, principally automobile exhaust emissions, has caused substantially greater damage. German tourguide to author during visit to Cologne Cathedral, October 1986.

4. Sir Arthur T. Harris, British, 1892–1984; joined the 1st Rhodesian Regiment, 1914–1915; joined the Royal Flying Corps, 1915; Feb. 1942 assumed the position of Commander-in-Chief, Bomber Command, Royal Air Force; retired as Air Chief Marshal, Sept. 1945; promoted to Marshal of The Royal Air Force, Jan. 1946; awarded Baronetcy, 1953. During World War II, he executed Britain's strategic air offense against Germany, including saturation bombing actions, alone carried the bombing offensive into Germany from Sept. 1939 to Jan. 1944; joined by the United States Eighth Bomber Command in the middle of 1943. *See generally* A. HARRIS, BOMBER OFFENSIVE (1947); D. SAWARD, "BOMBER" HARRIS (1984); The Times, London, Apr. 7, 1984, 1c, 10g, 10f, 14; May 25, 1984, 14d; and *cf.* C. MESSENGER, "BOMBER" HARRIS AND THE STRATEGIC BOMBING OFFENSIVE, 1939–1945 (1984).

5. A. HARRIS, *supra* note 4, at 177. Lest this be dismissed as the cynicism of a nonlawyer, it should be noted that Sir Hersch Lauterpacht, one of the preeminent international lawyers of this century (and author of the postwar British manual on the law of war), once opined: "If international law is the weakest point of all law, then the law of war is virtually its vanishing point." For a general historical survey of the law of war relating to aerial bombardment, *see* Parks, *Conventional Aerial Bombing and the Law of War*, 108 U.S. NAVAL INST. PROC. 98–115 (May 1982).

12, 1949, and the 1980 Conventional Weapons Convention, and the United States' military review of certain articles in those treaties that relate to aerial bombardment.

II. BACKGROUND

A. Rendulic Decision

In answering the former questions, the author has endeavored to follow the judgment of the court in one of the postwar war crimes trials. In *United States v. List*,[6] Generaloberst Lothar Rendulic was charged with carrying out a "scorched earth" policy in the Norwegian province of Finnmark. General Rendulic acknowledged his actions, but argued that they were taken in the belief that Russian forces were in hot pursuit of his retreating units. The court, in acquitting General Rendulic of the charge, concluded:

> There is evidence . . . that there was no military necessity for this destruction and devastation. An examination of the facts in retrospect can well sustain this conclusion. But we are obliged to judge the situation as it appeared to the defendant at the time. . . .
>
> The course of a military operation by the enemy is loaded with uncertainties. . . . It is our considered opinion that the conditions, as they appeared to the defendant at the time were sufficient upon which he could honestly conclude that urgent military necessity warranted the decision made. . . . [T]he defendant may have erred . . . but he was guilty of no criminal act.[7]

The Rendulic decision is an important guideline, and one not always followed by historians, some of whom, with hindsight and lacking the pressures of command, may have leaped to conclusions unduly critical of bombing during World War II,[8] prompting responses by some participants.[9] The issue is joined once again in two recent books, each of which makes reference to the corollary issues of legality and morality of bombing in World War II. In Michael S. Sherry's *The Rise of American Air Power*,[10] the author intimates that more might have been accomplished between the wars to regulate warfare, while Ronald Schaffer, in *Wings of Judgment*,[11] raises questions about the "moral issue" of American bombing policies during World War II. Both books are well-researched and thought-provoking. While Schaffer's book is more balanced, his very imprecise definition of the moral issue, "a phrase that usually meant . . . the bombing of cities and civilians, though it also referred to air attacks on artifacts of civilization, such as libraries, cathedrals, monasteries, and famous works of art," illustrates the difficulty of defining the subject of law and/or morality, or of determining the bomber's intent. More than reaching judgment, this article will endeavor to identify the legal parameters available to World War II military and civilian leaders, and their moral bases.

---

6. XI TRIALS OF WAR CRIMINALS BEFORE THE NUERNBERG MILITARY TRIBUNALS 1296–1297 (1947–48); *See* Mitchell v. Harmony, 54 U.S. (Howard) 115 (1851).

7. *Id.* at 1296–297. Or, as R. Overy says in his preface to THE AIR WAR 1939–1945 xi–xii (London, 1980): "I have concentrated . . . on trying to establish the historical context within which such decisions were made. This account is not about the history of post-war recrimination. It is about the war as it was understood, however imperfectly or unethically, at the time."

8. *See, e.g.*, HASTINGS, BOMBER COMMAND (London, 1979); and BEST, HUMANITY IN WARFARE 279–84 (London, 1980). With regard to the latter, this is a small flaw in a book that otherwise offers a superb treatment of the history of the modern law of war. It is also a point about which the author readily acknowledges that reasonable people can disagree.

9. D. SAWARD, *supra* note 4; and *cf.* C. MESSENGER, *supra* note 4.

10. M SHERRY, THE RISE OFAMERICAN AIR POWER 33–38 (1987).

11. R. SCHAFFER, WINGS OF JUDGMENT (1985). *See also* PASKINS AND DOCKRILL, THE ETHICS OF WAR 1–57 (1979); W. O'BRIEN, THE CONDUCT OF JUST ANDLIMITED WAR 121 (1981); and Anderson, *Air Warfare and Morality*, 3 AIR U. Q. REV. 5–14 (Winter 1949).

B. Just War Tradition

What is legal is not necessarily moral and what is moral is not always legal; but, particularly with regard to the law of war, the two are inextricably intertwined. Historically, civilians seldom have fared well in wars,[12] and it was primarily with their protection in mind that the modern law of war evolved. There is a certain irony in the realization that the twentieth century law of war traces its origins to the Just War Tradition developed by clergy, international lawyers, and philosophers from Western Europe, the principal strategic air battleground in World War II.[13] But with the limitations of the Just War Tradition remain the shortcomings of the modern law of war: while there was general agreement on the propriety of resort to arms (*jus ad bellum*)[14] and limited protection for the innocent (noncombatants) in the hands of a belligerent (a portion of *jus in bello*),[15] the Just War Tradition and the modern law of war generally are silent, or at least reluctantly acquiescent, regarding the actual use of force on the battlefield.[16]

Discrimination. At the heart of the Just War Tradition and the modern law of war lies the principle of discrimination which, in simple terms, means noncombatant immunity. But noncombatant immunity is not without exceptions. Within both the Just War Tradition and the law of war, it has always been permissible to attack combatants even though some noncombatants may be injured or killed; so long as injury to noncombatants is ancillary (indirect and unintentional) to the attack of an otherwise lawful target, the principle of noncombatant immunity is met. There were two other conditions that are important:

a. Noncombatants forfeit their right of protection from intentional injury if they carry out actions in favor of one belligerent over another; and

b. In the siege of a city, injury or death to noncombatants within the besieged city was regarded as permissible in that it created a burden on the besieged commander, or because it was his responsibility as a result of his refusal to surrender. If an offer of surrender were refused, the besieging commander was justified in putting to the sword all within the besieged city, including noncombatant women and children, for their refusal to surrender. While the latter practice had diminished by the nineteenth century, the law of war continued to place responsibility for civilian casualties in the hands of the besieged commander and permitted the besieger to look upon their injury as not only permissible but an effective means of war on the morale of the besieged. As an ancillary of this rule, any action taken by the besieged that placed noncombatants at risk was the responsibility of the besieged commander.[17]

In more recent times the four Geneva Conventions for the Protection of War Victims of August 12, 1949, renounce any dependency on reciprocity in the treatment of prisoners of war, enemy wounded, sick, or shipwrecked, or enemy civilians

12. *See* R. HARTIGAN, THE FORGOTTEN VICTIM: A HISTORY OF THE CIVILIAN (1982): SMALL, CRUSADING WARFARE, 1097–1193 (1956); B. TUCHMAN, A DISTANT MIRROR (1978); and P. CONTAMINE, WAR IN THE MIDDLE AGES (Oxford, 1984).

13. *See* J. JOHNSON, JUST WAR TRADITION AND THE RESTRAINT OF WAR (1981).

14. *Jus ad bellum* is a Latin term meaning "up to the commencement of war." Basically, the proper circumstances to resort to force or war.

15. *Jus in bello* is a Latin term meaning "the law of war during hostilities" once the war has commenced.

16. *See* M. HOWARD, WAR IN EUROPEAN HISTORY (1976); Howard, *Temperamenta Belli: Can War Be Controlled?*, in RESTRAINTS ON WAR 1–16 (M. HOWARD, London, 1979); BEST, *supra* note 8; O'BRIEN, *supra* note 11; and JOHNSON, *supra* note 13.

17. JOHNSON, *supra* note 13, at 196–98, 200–03, 222–23.

in the hands of an occupying power. This renunciation of a portion of the Just War Tradition was not extended to the conduct of hostilities.

One of the great ethical dilemmas that remains unresolved by the law of war is the Just War Tradition that, where a war is clearly just, the general immunity of enemy noncombatants may be overridden in order to protect the very values that ultimately guarantee the safety of such persons.[18] This argument formed the basis for justifications in bombing by both sides during World War II. Objectionable as that argument is by what is perceived to be today's moral standards, the matter remains unresolved. It continues to be an active element in Socialist military doctrine; has been cited by leaders of terrorist organizations, most of whom have been trained in Socialist nations; and has been relied upon by both sides in the Iran-Iraq War of the 1980s as justification for particular military actions, such as the war on each other's cities.

The Just War Tradition condemns indiscriminate bombing; the dilemma over the past century has been in identifying the line where military actions cease being permissible and become indiscriminate. As a leading moralist has noted, under the Just War Tradition "[t]his distinction is not determined by the amount of the devastation or the number of deaths, but by the direction of the action itself, i.e., by what is deliberately intended and directly done."[19]

Nation-State System of War. The Just War Tradition and law of war concepts were confronted with yet another dilemma with the arrival of the Industrial Revolution. Previously battles were open, pitched struggles, or involved an attempt to capture (usually through siege) a heavily defended city. A city or village might remain undefended because it contained nothing of military value, in which case it was open to physical occupation by the enemy. So long as the citizens of the village or city offered no resistance to an enemy force marching through or occupying the area, they were left alone, with one important exception: a naval force could approach an undefended coastal town for provisions and, if refused the supplies requested, could bombard the town to a degree proportionate to the severity of the refusal.

---

18. M. Walzer, Just and Unjust Wars: A Moral Argument with Historical Illustrations 251–55 (1977); Johnson, *supra* note 13, at 223; and Saundby, *The Ethics of Bombing*, Air Force Magazine June 1967, at 48–53. *Cf.* Lammers, *Area Bombing in World War II: The Argument of Michael Walzer*, J. of Religious Ethics 96–113 (Spring 1983). Some confusion exists today with respect to *discrimination* because of the attempted injection of the concept of *proportionality* into the law of war. Historically, proportionality in its *jus in bello* sense of matching force against force, is defined in relative terms. Discrimination was of a higher moral priority than proportionality. Johnson, *supra* note 13, at 196, in his examination of the arguments of Paul Ramsey. While the concept of proportionality has been urged by some international lawyers, it also has been adopted by some contemporary utilitarian moral philosophers connecting it, in Johnson's words, "to that of the greatest good for the greatest number." Johnson, *supra* note 13, at 228. While proponents offer the classic example of disproportionate use of force as evidenced by the destruction of a village of 500 in order to kill a single sniper, they falter in further explanation of the concept. Western nations and the International Committee of the Red Cross sought to codify the concept of proportionality at the Diplomatic Conference on the Reaffirmation and Development of International Humanitarian Law Applicable in Armed Conflicts, held in Geneva from 1974 to 1977. The concept was categorically rejected by the Socialist bloc. Ultimately language was drafted in article 51(5)(b) of Protocol I that enables the Western nations to claim the concept is codified therein, while permitting the Socialist nations to deny the same; yet its violation is made a war crime in article 85. The language is so general and subject to contradictory views that under U.S. domestic law it would be constitutionally void for vagueness. As one pundit noted, "Only international lawyers would make something a crime they couldn't define." For this and a number of other reasons, the United States has decided not to become a party to Additional Protocol I.

The important point in the concept of proportionality is consideration of the potential for collateral civilian casualties in the vicinity of a target, which will be discussed later in this article. As Dr. James Turner Johnson has correctly noted, however, "the idea of collateral damage in contemporary limited war thought is a pregnant one." Johnson, *supra* note 13, at 221. What is important is that the concept was not even a gleam in its parents' eyes prior to and during World War II.

19. Ramsey, The Just War: Force and Political Responsibility 154 (1968).

Until the eighteenth century, wars generally were private conflicts, fought between relatively small units. By that time, however, the modern nation-state system was emerging; full-time professional armies were representing those states; and a civilian bureaucracy was supporting the insatiable appetite of an army on the march. The Industrial Revolution was developing components that would link a nation together for reasons that would be as important to commerce in peace as it would be to the defense of the nation when it was threatened. Railroads are one example. The railroads were important to the movement of units from one point to another at speeds greater than allowed by road march. Also, for the first time they enabled a government to organize and mobilize a nation for war. A nation's leaders, in contemplating military operations against another nation, no longer thought of war solely in terms of a confrontation between uniformed battalions on a battlefield largely devoid of civilians; now ways were considered to destroy or capture an enemy nation's economic or industrial capacity to wage war.

These types of operations first were waged during the American Civil War, as Union General William Tecumseh Sherman carried out his famous march to the sea, cutting the Confederacy in half while destroying its industrial resources and denying it the ability to grow cotton for export in order to finance the war.[20] The naval blockade conducted by the U.S. Navy served similar purposes, preventing the import of war materials and denying the Confederacy the ability to export cotton—an action similar to the "tanker war" during the present-day Iran-Iraq War.[21] Economic and industrial targets had become an important element in modern war. Railroads and other lines of communication also had taken on significance, and foreign military observers of the Civil War learned their lessons well.[22]

There was another development as a result of the nation-state system. Nations continued to maintain small standing armies, but relied upon mobilization of the population to provide for their defense. The minutemen who fought the British at Concord, Massachusetts, on April 19, 1775, can trace the basis for their origin to

---

20. General Sherman's march to the sea started at Atlanta, Georgia, in November 1864 and ended at Savannah, Georgia, in December 1864. *See generally* B. DAVIS, SHERMAN'S MARCH (1980); R. WHEELER, SHERMAN'S MARCH (1978); J. GLATTHAAR, THE MARCH TO THE SEA AND BEYOND (1985). Or, similarly, the 1865 Union raid by Major General James H. Wilson to Columbus, Georgia, and Selma, Alabama, to attack two of the South's most productive industrial communities. *See* JONES, YANKEE BLITZKRIEG (1976); B. DAVIS, SHERMAN'S MARCH (1980); J. MCDONOUGH and J. JONES, WAR SO TERRIBLE: SHERMAN AND ATLANTA (1987); and E. HAGERMAN, THE AMERICAN CIVIL WAR AND THE ORIGINS OF MODERN WARFARE (1988). Sherman's attack of Confederate railroads was a model for the allied air offensive against German rail lines eighty years later. *See* A. MIERZEHEWSKI, THE COLLAPSE OF THE GERMAN WAR ECONOMY, 1944–1945: ALLIED AIR POWER AND THE GERMAN NATIONAL RAILWAY (London, 1988); *cf.* O. HOEFFDING, GERMAN AIR ATTACKS AGAINST INDUSTRY AND RAILROADS IN RUSSIA, 1941–1945, RAND RM-6206-PR (Santa Monica, 1970).

21. OFFICIAL RECORDS OF THE UNION AND CONFEDERATE NAVIES IN THE WAR OF THE REBELLION (1894–1922), Series I, Vol. 1–27, Series II, Vol. 1–3; V. JONES, THE CIVIL WAR AT SEA Vol. I at 60–122, 165–176, 332–348, Vol. II at 239, 246, 247, 249, 250, 255; H. NASH, A NAVAL HISTORY OF THE CIVIL WAR (1972); 2 C. BOYNTON, THE HISTORY OF THE NAVY DURING THE REBELLION 72–107 (1868).

22. Railroads were employed with great success by the Prussian military during the Franco-Prussian War. M. HOWARD, THE FRANCO-PRUSSION WAR 2–4, 22, 43, 61–2, 230 (London, 1961). *See* M. VAN CREVELD, SUPPLYING WAR 75–108 (Cambridge, 1977); and M. PEARTON, DIPLOMACY, WAR AND TECHNOLOGY SINCE 1830 (1984). Pearton concludes that in the period between 1830 and 1870, railroads "emerged as *the* decisive factor in modern war" at 75 (emphasis in original). The use of railroads was important in one of the conflicts cited by many international lawyers as the point of conception of the modern law of war. At the outbreak of the war between France and Austria that led to the Battle of Solferino, Napoleon III was able to move his forces to Turin by rail in ten days. By foot and horseback, the move would have required two months. PEARTON, *id.* at 67. On Solferino, *see* H. DUNANT, A MEMORY OF SOLFERINO (Geneva, 1862); C. ROTHKOPF, JEAN HENRI DUNANT: FATHER OF THE RED CROSS (1969); and P. TURNBULL, SOLFERINO (1985).

the English Muster Law of 1572, and to the articles of New England confederation published in 1643. But the French Revolution of 1789 generally is credited with taking this concept to its logical conclusion, tying political rights to civic responsibilities in mobilizing the entire population for defense of the nation. Nations provided a sense of identity to its citizens, and an invading army frequently found itself faced with guerrillas—civilians of the invaded nation who would offer armed resistance. From this time came such terms as *francs-tireurs* and *levee en masse*. As Michael Howard notes in commenting on the developments of the nineteenth century, "War was beginning to become total—a conflict not of armies but of populations."[23] Units of civilian guerrillas were used to great effect during the American Civil War, particularly against Union Army supply lines,[24] and France organized its *francs-tireurs* into an Auxiliary Army during the Franco-Prussian War.

The problems of guerrilla warfare are not a part of this article. But the national use of *francs-tireurs*, coupled with the industrial mobilization of a nation for war, illustrates the degree to which warfare had expanded in a nation's utilization of its entire resources to advance its war aims. No longer was warfare merely a matter of a contest pitting soldier against soldier; it had become a national effort. Able-bodied men were conscripted for military service, while all others, men, women, and children, assumed other responsibilities to support the war effort. And it was into this changing environment of war that international lawyers stepped to devise the modern law of war.

C. Lieber's Code: Foundation of Modern Law of War

The first effort began in the United States during its Civil War. Faced with the problems of guerrilla warfare, President Abraham Lincoln, acting through Henry Wager Halleck, General-in-Chief of the Union Armies, tasked Dr. Francis Lieber with the preparation of a code of law for the Union forces. Lieber wrote two documents, one of which addressed the issue of guerrillas and the law of war; the second, adopted by the Union Army as General Orders No. 100, became the first modern statement of the law of war and the foundation for much of the law of war as it was to exist over the next century, including World War II.[25] Several of its provisions relate to the questions posed earlier:

> 14. Military necessity, as understood by modern civilized nations, consists in the necessity of those measures which are indispensable for securing the ends of the war, and which are lawful according to the modern law and usages of war.
>
> 15. Military necessity admits of all direct destruction of life or limb of armed enemies, and of other persons whose destruction is incidentally unavoidable in the armed contests of war; it allows of the capturing of every armed enemy, and every enemy of importance to the hostile government, or of peculiar danger to the captor; it allows of all destruction of property, and obstruction of the ways and channels of traffic, travel, or communication, and of all withholding of sustenance or means of life from the enemy. . . .

---

23. *See* J. GALVIN, THE MINUTE MEN (2d ed. 1989); W. MILLIS, ARMS AND MEN 13–71 (1981); Strachen, *The Nation in Arms*, in G. BEST, THE PERMANENT REVOLUTION 49–74 (London, 1988); G. BEST, WAR AND SOCIETY IN REVOLUTIONARY EUROPE, 1770–1870 (London, 1982); and HOWARD, *supra* note 16, at 93.

24. SPIES, SCOUTS AND RAIDERS: IRREGULAR OPERATIONS 106–61 (1985); P. STERN, SECRET MISSIONS OF THE CIVIL WAR (1959); W. TIDWELL, COME RETRIBUTION 132–54 (1988). France was to organize its *francs-tireurs* into an Auxiliary Army during the Franco-Prussian War. M. HOWARD, *supra* note 16 at 245, 249–56, 374–75, 377–81, 407, 409, 412.

25. R. HARTIGAN, LIEBER'S CODE AND THE LAW OF WAR (1983); Davis, *Doctor Francis Lieber's Instructions for the Government of Armies in the Field*, 1 AM. J. INT'L LAW 13–25 (1907).

20. Public war is a state of armed hostility between sovereign nations or governments. It is a law and requisite of civilized existence that men live in political, continuous societies, forming organized units, called states or nations, whose constituents bear, enjoy, and suffer, advance and retrograde together, in peace and war.

21. The citizen or native of a hostile country is thus an enemy, as one of the constituents of the hostile state or nation, and as such is subjected to the hardships of war.

22. Nevertheless, as civilization has advanced during the last centuries, so has likewise steadily advanced, especially in war on land, the distinction between the private individual belonging to a hostile country and the hostile country itself, with its men in arms. The principle has been more and more acknowledged that the unarmed citizen is to be spared in person, property, and honor as much as the exigencies of war will admit.

29. Modern times are distinguished from earlier ages by the existence at one and the same time of many nations and great governments related to one another in close intercourse.

Peace is their normal condition; war is the exception. The ultimate object of all modern war is a renewed state of peace. The more vigorously wars are pursued the better it is for humanity. Sharp wars are brief [26]

General Orders No. 100 remained the principal law of war reference for the balance of the nineteenth century. Although efforts were made to develop the law of war relating to the conduct of hostilities into a treaty, including a conference held in Brussels in 1874,[27] none met with success. With the exception of a brief treaty for protection of the wounded, the first real multilateral law of war negotiations did not take place until the closing years of the century.

III. THE FIRST HAGUE PEACE CONFERENCE OF 1899

A. Background

On August 24, 1898,[28] acting on behalf of Tsar Nicholas II, Russian Foreign Minister Count Mikhail Muraviev[29] proposed the convening of an international disarmament conference to address issues relating to disarmament, the proscription or regulation of certain modern weapons of war, and establishment of a mechanism for arbitration of international disputes.[30] In a letter dated January 11, 1899,[31] Count Muraviev listed eight proposals, two of which marked the beginning of efforts to regulate aerial bombardment with the latter proposal also calling for a revision of the law of war: 3. . . . prohibition of the discharge of any kind of projectile or explosive from balloons or by similar means. . . . 7. Revision of the declaration concerning the

26. R. HARTIGAN, *supra* note 25, at 48-50. General Orders No. 100, War Dep't, Adjt. General's Office, Washington, D.C., April 24, 1863, section I, ¶ 14–29.

27. D. SCHINDLER & J. TOMAN, THE LAWS OF ARMED CONFLICT 25–34 (1981); THE LAW OF WAR 194–203 (L. FRIEDMAN, Vol. 1, 1972); P. BORDWELL, LAW OF WAR 101–16 (1908).

28. Russia used the Julian calendar until shortly after the October (actually November) Revolution in 1917 when the Gregorian calendar was adopted. It is the Gregorian calendar that is used today for international purposes. The letter was dated August 12, 1898, (Julian calendar) but the date used in this article and by others is August 24, 1898, (Gregorian calendar).

29. Count Mikhail Muraviev's last name was also spelled Mouravieff in English.

30. INSTRUCTIONS TO THE AMERICAN DELEGATES TO THE HAGUE PEACE CONFERENCES AND THEIR OFFICIAL REPORTS 1–2 (J. Scott, ed. 1916), [hereinafter INSTRUCTIONS]; F. HOLLS, THE PEACE CONFERENCE AT THE HAGUE 8–10 (1900); THE HAGUE CONVENTIONS AND DECLARATIONS OF 1899 AND 1907 xiv–xv (J. Scott, ed. 1915) [hereinafter HAGUE CONVENTIONS].

31. INSTRUCTIONS, *supra* note 30, at 3–5; HOLLS, *supra* note 30, at 24–27; HAGUE CONVENTIONS, *supra* note 30, at xv–xvii. The letter was dated Dec. 30, 1898, by the Julian calendar and Jan. 11, 1899, by the Gregorian calendar.

laws and customs of war elaborated in 1874 by the Conference of Brussels, and not yet ratified.[32]

While disarmament and peace groups were enthusiastic in their support of the Russian call for an international conference, the reaction of governments was underwhelming. Each of the invited nations accepted the invitation with suspicion, and without great expectations. The Russian invitation correctly was seen as lacking in altruism. The Russian Minister of War had determined that Austria, its principal rival, was about to procure an improved field gun capable of firing six rounds per minute, six times the rate of comparable Russian field pieces. The newer gun already was standard in the armies of Germany and France. Faced with the prospect of embarking on a major, costly arms procurement program, the Russian Ministers of War, Finance, and Foreign Affairs considered alternatives. Rather than seek bilateral accommodation with the Austrians, whom the Russians did not trust, a solution was framed in terms of the multilateral negotiations proposed by Count Muraviev.[33] The First Peace Conference was convened in The Hague on May 18, 1899, with delegations present from twenty-six nations.[34]

The work of the conference was divided among three commissions. Commission I addressed disarmament issues and the issues concerning new weapons, and was divided into two subcommissions, one for land warfare and one for naval warfare. The proposal calling for a prohibition on discharge of explosives from airborne vehicles was assigned to the subcommission on land warfare. Commission II addressed the revision and codification of the law of war problems. Commission III reviewed international arbitration, which is not addressed in this article.

B. Commission I

Russian attempts in Commission I to limit force levels and budgets died in subcommission sessions. Proposals by Russia to limit fleets, armor plate, and naval gun sizes also were defeated, as were moves to ban submarines, torpedo boats, and naval mines. Three proposals met with moderate success: a limitation on the use of chemical weapons;[35] a prohibition on expanding (also called dum-dum) bullets;[36] and a five-year moratorium on the launching of projectiles and/or explosives from the air,[37] the latter being within the focus of this article.

32. INSTRUCTIONS, *supra* note 30, at 4; HOLLS, *supra* note 30, at 26; HAGUE CONVENTIONS, *supra* note 30, at xvii.

33. B. TUCHMAN, THE PROUD TOWER 251–67 (1966); and Hawkins, *Captain Mahan, Admiral Fisher and Arms Control at the Hague, 1899*, 39 NAVAL WAR C. REV. 77–91 (No. 1, January–February 1986). Nations sending delegations were Austria-Hungary, Belgium, Bulgaria, China, Denmark, France, Germany, Great Britain, Greece, Italy, Japan, Luxemburg, Mexico, Montenegro, Netherlands, Persia, Portugal, Romania, Russia, Serbia, Siam, Spain, Sweden and Norway, Switzerland, Turkey, and the United States.

34. F. HOLLS, *supra* note 30, at 36.

35. Hague Declaration (IV, 2) concerning asphyxiating gases (July 29, 1899); SCHINDLER & TOMAN, *supra* note 27, at 50, 99–100; F. HOLLS, *supra* note 30, at 118–20, 377; HAGUE CONVENTIONS, *supra* note 30, at 225–26.

36. Hague Declaration (IV, 3) concerning expanding bullets (July 29, 1899); SCHINDLER & TOMAN, *supra* note 27, at 50, 95; F. HOLLS, *supra* note 30, at 98–117, 377; HAGUE CONVENTIONS, *supra* note 30, at 227–28. For an interesting account of the politics of this treaty, *see* Greenwood, *The Political Factors*, GUN DIGEST 161–68 (34th ed. 1980); *see also*, Spiers, *The Use of the Dum Dum Bullet in Colonial Warfare*, 4 THE J. IMPERIAL AND COMMONWEALTH HIST. 3–14 (1975).

37. Hague Declaration (IV, 1) concerning launching projectiles from the air (July 29, 1899); SCHINDLER & TOMAN, *supra* note 27, at 50, 103–05; F. HOLLS, *supra* note 30, at 95, 377; HAGUE CONVENTIONS, *supra* note 30, at 220–22.

Limitation of Balloon Projectiles Resolution. Balloons had been used for limited military purposes for some time.[38] The use of dirigible airships had been discussed in international conferences in Chicago in 1893 and Paris in 1899,[39] and most delegates undoubtedly had some idea of where their respective national efforts were headed.[40] Many of the smaller or less-developed nations were quick to embrace the proposed prohibition as a way of disarming nations that were either more developed, or possessed a greater capacity for development.[41] Although slow in expressing their respective opposition, the delegates from France, Germany, Great Britain, and the United States were under instructions to oppose the prohibition.[42]

---

38. L. KENNETT, A. HISTORY OF STRATEGIC BOMBING 1–9 (1982). *See* C. GIBBS-SMITH, THE INVENTION OF THE AEROPLANE 1793-1909 (London, 1966). The first bombing raid took place in 1849, when the Austrians launched unmanned bomb-carrying balloons against Venice. Gibbs-Smith, *Commentary*, in A. HURLEY & R. EHRHART, AIR POWER AND WARFARE 50 (1979). The attacks were not unlike those conducted by the Japanese against the United States during World War II. Penfold, *Japan's Rambling Balloon Barrage*, 73 U.S. NAVAL INST. PROC. 963–65 (August 1947); Frankoski, *The Silent Bombers*, AIR DEF. MAG. 34–36 (April–June 1976). *See* Hidagi, *Attacks Against the U.S. Heartland*, 27 AEROSPACE HISTORIAN 87–93 (Summer 1981); and R. MIKESH, JAPAN'S WORLD WAR II BALLOON BOMB ATTACKS ON NORTH AMERICA (1973). Tethered balloons were employed for observation purposes during the American Civil War, while the French employed untethered manned balloons during the Prussian siege of Paris (September 1870–January 1871). J. FISHER, AIRLIFT 1870 (London, 1965). As early as 1893, British Major J. D. Fullerton of the Royal Engineers presented a paper at a meeting of military engineers in Chicago predicting that aeronautics would create "as great a revolution in the art of war as the discovery of gunpowder," and that "the arrival of the aerial fleet over the enemy capital would probably conclude the campaign." Mason, *Air Power and Warfare, 1903–1941: The British Dimension*, in HURLEY & EHRHART, 22 AIR POWER AND WARFARE. *See* R. BRETT, HISTORY OF BRITISH AVIATION, 1908–1914 (London, 1933).

39. Watt, *Restraints on War in the Air Before 1945*, in M. HOWARD, RESTRAINTS ON WAR 60 (London, 1970).

40. Parkinson, *Aeronautics at the Hague Conference of 1899*, 7 THE AIRPOWER HIST. 106–11, at 108 (Apr. 1960); Watt, *Restraints on War in the Air Before 1945*, in RESTRAINTS ON WAR, *supra* note 39, at 60.

41. Thus General den Beer Poortugael, in the first consideration of the proposed ban, advised the subcommission that the Government of the Netherlands supported the Russian proposal. THE PROCEEDINGS OF THE HAGUE PEACE CONFERENCES, THE CONFERENCE OF 1899 341 (J. Scott, ed., 1920) [hereinafter PROCEEDINGS].

42. For example, the British delegation was under instructions not to agree with any restrictions on the employment of weapons. Memorandum, War Office to Foreign Office (May 17, 1899), contained in BRITISH DOCUMENTS ON THE ORIGINS OF THE WAR 1898–1914 226 (Gooch and Temperley, eds., London, 1927) [hereinafter BRITISH DOCUMENTS]. Instructions from the Secretary of State to the U.S. delegation provided in part:

> The second, third, and fourth articles [being the proposals in Court Muraviev's memorandum, supra n. 31], relating to the non-employment of firearms, explosives, and other destructive agents, the restricted use of existing instruments of destruction, and the prohibition of certain contrivances employed in naval warfare, seem lacking in practicability, and the discussion of these propositions would probably prove provocative of divergence rather than unanimity of view. It is doubtful if wars are to be diminished by rendering them less destructive, for it is the plain lesson of history that the periods of peace have been longer protracted as the cost and destructiveness of war have increased. The expediency of restraining the inventive genius of our people in the direction of devising means of defense is by no means clear, and considering the temptations to which men and nations may be exposed in a time of conflict, it is doubtful if an international agreement to this end would prove effective. The dissent of a single powerful nation might render it altogether nugatory. The delegates are, therefore, enjoined not to give the weight of their influence to the promotion of projects the realization of which is so uncertain.

INSTRUCTIONS, *supra* note 30, at 7–8.

British military reaction following the conference paralleled the American delegation instructions. Lord Wolseley, Commander-in-Chief of the British Army, wrote to the British Secretary of State on Oct. 7, 1899, with the following comments:

> Restrictions on scientific inventions deprive a nation of the advantages which accrue from its scientific men and from the productive capacity of its manufacturing establishments.

The Commission I subcommission on land warfare considered the Russian proposal for a prohibition on the discharge of explosives or projectiles from balloons or by "similar methods" with little formal discussion, adding the word "new" between "similar" and "methods" to clarify the proposal's intent. The proposal was adopted without consideration of a recommendation by the German delegate to limit the prohibition to a term of five years. With the exception of the delegate from Rumania, who reserved his vote in preference for a limitation on the prohibition to a term of five years, and British abstention, the subcommission vote was unanimous in adoption of the resolution.[43]

Crozier's Amendment. Nine days later, however, apparently following consultations with other members of his delegation and reconsideration of the Secretary of State's instructions to the U.S. delegation, the U.S. delegate to the subcommission, Captain William Crozier, an Army artillery officer, attempted to reopen discussion of the prohibition within the subcommission.[44] Crozier noted that:

> [I]t seems to me difficult to justify by a humanitarian motive the prohibition of the use of balloons for the hurling of projectiles or other explosive materials. We are without experience in the use of arms whose employment we propose to prohibit forever. Granting that practical means of using balloons can be invented, who can say that such an invention will not be of a kind to make its use possible at a critical point on the field of battle, at a critical moment of the conflict, under conditions so defined and concentrated that it would decide the victory and thus partake of the quality possessed by all perfected arms of localizing at important points the destruction of life and property and of sparing the sufferings of all who are not at the precise spot where the result is decided. Such use tends to diminish the evils of war and to support the humanitarian considerations which we have in view.
>
> I do not know of machines thus efficient and thus humanitarian, in the incomplete stage of development in which aerostation now is; but is it desirable to shut the door to their possible introduction among the permitted arms? In doing so, would we not be acting entirely in the dark, and would we not run the risk of error inherent in such a manner of procedure? The balloon, as we know it now, is not dirigible; it can carry but little; it is capable of hurling, only on points exactly determined and over which it may pass by chance, indecisive quantities of explosives, which would fall, like useless hailstones, on both combatants and non-combatants alike. Under such conditions it is entirely suitable to forbid its use, but the prohibition should be temporary and not permanent. At a later stage of its development, if it be seen that its less desirable qualities still predominate, there will still be time to extend the prohibition; at present let us confine our action within the limits of our knowledge.
>
> That is why I have the honor to propose the substitution of the following text for the text already voted:
>
> For a period of five years from the date of the signature of this act it is forbidden to employ balloons or other similar means not yet known for the purpose of discharging projectiles or explosives.[45]

> It can be proved to the hilt that scientific development of engines of destruction had tended
> (a) to make nations hesitate before going to war;
> (b) to reduce the percentages of losses in war;
> (c) to shorten the lengths of campaigns, and thus to reduce to a minimum the sufferings endured by the inhabitants.

Watt, in RESTRAINTS ON WAR, *supra* note 39, at 60–61.

43. PROCEEDINGS, *supra* note 41, at 342.

44. Captain Alfred Thayer Mahan, USN, was a member of the U.S. delegation and Crozier's co-delegate on Commission I. Mahan represented the United States before the subcommission addressing naval warfare matters, while Crozier was the U.S. representative before the subcommission on land warfare. Mahan was of rather firm opinion on these matters and, there appears no doubt, that Crozier was "counseled" on his responsibilities by Mahan, who was his senior in rank, experience, and knowledge of international affairs. B. TUCHMAN, *supra* note 33, at 262; and Hawkins, *supra* note 33, at 84.

45. PROCEEDINGS, *supra* note 41, at 353–54.

The President of the subcommission declined Captain Crozier's amendment because the proposal had been voted on, and suggested that he raise the matter in the next plenary session of Commission I, to be held two weeks later.

Captain Crozier's presentation at that subsequent meeting was briefer, but to the point: it was correct to limit aerial bombardment at this time,

> Since it is impossible to foresee the place where the projectiles or other substances discharged from a balloon will fall and since they may just as easily hit inoffensive inhabitants as combatants, or destroy a church as easily as a [artillery] battery. However, if it were possible to perfect aerial navigation in such a way as to do away with these defects, the use of balloons might decrease the length of combat and consequently the evils of war as well as the expenses entailed thereby.[46]

Crozier's amendment proposing a five-year moratorium enabled the delegates to take a wait and see attitude toward aeronautical developments and postpone any decision until the Second Hague Peace Conference, while gaining unanimity for the proposal under consideration. Crozier's amendment was accepted by Commission I. Ultimately the Conference changed the original language of the subcommission's resolution "similar new methods" and adopted a Declaration (IV, I) that prohibited: "for a term of five years, the launching of projectiles and explosives from balloons, or by other new methods of a similar nature."[47]

Crozier's action has been credited with saving the prohibition, at least at the first conference.[48] In all likelihood this analysis is correct, for with several major powers unwilling to accept an unlimited prohibition—and it seems certain that it would not have been accepted by France, Germany, Great Britain, or the United States—it is unlikely that other nations would have accepted the prohibition unilaterally. Captain Crozier's amendment also changed the focus of the debate from prohibition of aerial bombardment, a disarmament issue, to regulation of aerial bombing, a law of war area.

C. Disarmament or Deterrence?

Disarmament advocates anticipating the First Hague Peace Conference were dismayed by Count Muraviev's latter proposal set out earlier in this article: "7. Revision of the declaration concerning the laws and customs of war . . . ,"[49] because the law of war constituted an acceptance of the inevitability of war, rather than striving for general disarmament and world peace. The law of war also was viewed with pessimism by some military delegates to the conference, but for different reasons. For these men it seemed impractical to speak of moderation in war.[50]

---

46. PROCEEDINGS, *supra* note 41, at 280.

47. Hague Declaration (IV, 1) To prohibit for the term of five years the launching of projectiles and explosives from balloons, and other new methods of a similar nature (July 29, 1988), SCHINDLER & TOMAN, *supra* note 27, at 50, 141–45; F. HOLLS, *supra* note 30, at 377; HAGUE CONVENTIONS, *supra* note 30, at 220–22. The treaty ultimately was ratified by all nations party to the negotiations except Great Britain.

48. Kuhn, *The Beginnings of an Aerial Law*, 4 AM. J. INT'L LAW 118 (1910).

49. F. HOLLS, *supra* note 30, at 26; INSTRUCTIONS, *supra* note 30, at 4; HAGUE CONVENTIONS, *supra* note 30, at xvii.

50. For example, the senior British naval representative to the conference was Vice Admiral Sir John A. Fisher, RN, whose philosophy toward the law of war has been described as follows:

> Fisher's ideas as to war, and especially as to naval war, were all based upon those current in Nelson's time. He was a bit of a barbarian who talked like a savage at times, to the no small scandal of his colleagues at The Hague.
>
> "The humanizing of War!" he declared. "You might as well talk of humanizing Hell! When a silly ass at The Hague got up and talked about the amenities of civilized warfare and putting your

The pessimism had two bases. The first was the philosophy expressed in article 29 of the Lieber Code, that the more vigorously wars are pursued, the briefer they will be, and the less humanity will suffer.[51] This philosophy has never been rejected by any nation, and, in fact, was a part of the basis for U.S. employment of atomic weapons against Hiroshima and Nagasaki in 1945.[52] A corollary is manifested by the theory that a promise of prosecution of a war without moderation may deter aggression by others. This theory of deterrence was adopted by air power advocates and pursued with vigor by a number of nations, commencing with the writings of Giulio Douhet.[53a] It is not the intention of this article to join the debate over the degree to which the between-the-wars airpower planners were influenced by Douhet, or the degree to which airpower contributed to the allied victory in World War II, but rather to illustrate that there existed a philosophy that militated against regulation of warfighting as such.

The second argument against regulations moderating war is more practical. It comes from the degree of control a nation or its military forces has over implementation of the law of war. Where a nation has total control over law of war implementation, the law of war has been moderately successful. But where the law of war largely is dependent upon the good faith of other nations, both promulgation and implementation of the law have been substantially less successful.

---

prisoners' feet in hot water and giving them gruel, my reply, I regret to say, was considered totally unfit for publication. As if war could be civilized! If I'm in command when war breaks out I shall issue my orders":

> "The essence of war is violence."
>
> "Moderation in war is imbecility."
>
> "Hit first, hit hard, and hit anywhere." [Footnote omitted.]

He [continued Stead] had the not uncommon notion . . . that nations are deterred from going to war by fear of the atrocities which accompany conflict. He exclaimed impatiently . . . "What you call my truculence is all for peace. If you rub it in, both at home and abroad, that you are ready for instant war with every unit of your strength in the first line, and intend to be first in, and hit your enemy in the belly, and kick him when he is down, and boil your prisoners in oil (if you take any!), and torture his women and children, then people will keep clear of you." [Footnote omitted.]

A. MARDER, THE ANATOMY OF BRITISH SEA POWER 347 (1976), quoting from BACON, FISHER, (I), 75–76, 120–22, 171 (London, 1929). The pessimistic philosophy expressed by Fisher is mirrored in the official instructions to the British and American delegations, BRITISH DOCUMENTS, *supra* note 42, at 226; INSTRUCTIONS, *supra* note 30, at 7–8. Fisher had his predecessors in the U.S. Army. In a letter dated Sept. 4, 1864, to Chief of Staff of the Army General Henry Wager Halleck from General William Tecumseh Sherman, Sherman observed: "If the people raise a howl against my barbarity and cruelty, I will answer that war is war, and not popularity-seeking. If they want peace, they and their relatives must stop the war." W. SHERMAN, MEMOIRS OF W. T. SHERMAN II 111 (1891).

51. HARTIGAN, *supra* note 25, at 50.

52. This article examines the political, diplomatic, military, and legal history of the development of the law of war as it relates to conventional bombing only. Nuclear weapons are *lex specialis*, and the law of war relating to them is substantially less developed. However, their use against Hiroshima and Nagasaki in August 1945 centers on the argument that their employment saved far more lives (by hastening the Japanese decision to surrender) than they cost. For an analysis of this point, *see* S. HARPER, MIRACLE OF DELIVERANCE: THE CASE FOR THE BOMBING OF HIROSHIMA AND NAGASAKI (1985). *See* CLAUSEWITZ, ON WAR 75 (Howard and Paret, eds. and trans. [1976]):"Kind-hearted people might of course think there is some ingenious way to disarm or defeat an enemy without too much bloodshed, and might imagine this is the true goal of the art of war. Pleasant as it sounds, it is a fallacy that must be exposed: war is such a dangerous business that the mistakes which come from kindness are the very worst." For an excellent discussion that places Clausewitz in perspective with the modern law of war, *see* HOWARD, *supra* note 16. *See also* MARDER, *supra* note 50, at 76.

53a. G. DOUHET, THE COMMAND OF THE AIR 203–07 (R. Kohn & J. Harahan, eds. 1983).

For example, regulations related to the care for and protection of enemy prisoners of war have proved successful because the captor has complete control of the situation. If an enemy soldier resists after capture, or attempts escape, the captor has the ability to resolve the matter to his favor. But this is not the case with rules that affect the employment of force. A rule proposing moderation in the use of weapons systems, ostensibly for the protection of the civilian population of an enemy nation, or the civilians of a friendly nation occupied by an enemy, is dependent upon respect for the law by both the attacker and the defender. But international law has no effective enforcement mechanism, and a malevolent belligerent, whether attacker or defender, stands to gain potentially significant tactical advantages over a law-abiding opponent. It was this concern that made military men reluctant to support the regulation of hostilities. As international law scholar Julius Stone concluded years later, "It is far easier to moralize about air attacks on civilians, and to offer soothing verbal solutions, and to dismiss target area bombing as probably unlawful, than to frame rules for mitigation of human suffering with some hope of belligerent observance amid the realities of modern war."[53b] This problem plagued law of war negotiators at the First Hague Peace Conference, and all succeeding conferences to the present day.

D. Commission II

Commission II was assigned the responsibility for codification of the law of war, which it did with moderate success. The Hague Conference adopted Convention II with Respect to the Laws and Customs of War on Land. Article 23(g) of the Annex to Convention II provided that "it is especially prohibited . . . to destroy or seize the enemy's property, unless such destruction or seizure be imperatively demanded by the necessities of war."[54]

In applying this principle, a fundamental corollary has been the principle of discrimination; that is, that military violence will be directed toward military targets. The two articles in the Annex of Convention II applicable to aerial bombardment state:

> 25. The attack or bombardment of towns, villages, habitations or buildings which are not defended, is prohibited.
>
> 27. In sieges and bombardments all necessary steps should be taken to spare as far as possible edifices devoted to religion, art, science, and charity, hospitals, and places where the sick and wounded are collected, provided they are not used at the same time for military purposes.[55]

The intent of these articles was to codify existing practice, rather than create new law.[56] But there are matters of significance associated with articles 25 and 27.

"Undefended" town. The term was well defined in practice, but remained undefined in article 25 of the Annex of Convention II of the treaty, perhaps because

53b. J. STONE, LEGAL CONTROLS OF INTERNATIONAL CONFLICT 627 (1954).

54. SCHINDLER & TOMAN, *supra* note 27, at 76–77; F. HOLLS, *supra* note 30, at 437. Of note is that articles 14 and 15 of the Lieber Code state the same principle. HARTIGAN, *supra* note 25, at 48. What the Lieber Code authorizes, however, Convention II prohibits. This is a manifestation of the fundamental distrust international lawyers have for things military, and a reluctance to permit battlefield commanders any latitude in situations that require a judgment call. This affects the credibility of the law of war in its implementation by the military.

55. SCHINDLER & TOMAN, *supra* note 27, at 77–78; F. HOLLS, *supra* note 30, at 439.

56. J. SCOTT, I THE HAGUE PEACE CONFERENCES OF 1899 and 1907 537 (1939) [hereinafter HAGUE PEACE CONFERENCES].

it was assumed the term was commonly understood. Because the treaty did not define the term, however, it caused a great deal of confusion in the years that followed. One scholar noted the background of the term: "Unfortified cities were not attacked because they were not of sufficient military importance, and all that was necessary to take them was to march in without the necessity of resorting to bombardment."[57] The term had but one meaning, as previously stated: it was a town or city lacking military defenses and open to physical occupation by the enemy. And yet it created problems. When during World War I the zeppelin raids commenced, British defense authorities hesitated in placing antiaircraft guns in and about London for fear that such gun placement would make the city "defended," and, therefore, subject to attack—or, conversely, that the city would be legally immune from attack so long as it contained no gun emplacements.[58]

Either interpretation would have been incorrect. As a German delegate observed, article 25 was not intended to prohibit the intentional destruction of any buildings, when military operations rendered it necessary. His observation met with no objection in the subcommission and was noted in the subcommission's report of July 5, 1899.[59] Yet a misunderstanding of "undefended towns" plagued politicians, military planners, international lawyers, and historians for many years.[60]

The reciprocal nature of the law of war. The law of war succeeds only insofar as it does not provide, or appear to provide, an opportunity for one party to gain a tactical advantage over another. The delegates to the First Hague Peace Conference recognized this in the language of article 27 of the Annex of Convention II, which provides limited protection for certain civilian objects, such as hospitals, museums, and schools, so long as each is not being used for military purposes. Although article 27 essentially addresses minimization of collateral damage, it has a kinship to the prohibition contained in article 23(g) on intentional attack of all civilian property. In retrospect, it would have been wiser for the delegates to have made a clearer connection between the concepts expressed in these two articles.

Issue avoidance. The delegates to the First Hague Peace Conference attempted to codify the law of war only to the extent consensus could be reached. Controversial

57. Quindry, 2 *Aerial Bombardment of Civilian and Military Objectives*, 2 J. AIR L. & COM. 474–509, at 484 (Oct. 1931). The term "unfortified" was used in the Brussels Rules of 1874, Article 15; it was changed to the broader "undefended" in Article 25 of the Annex of Convention II of 1899. *See* SCHINDLER & TOMAN, *supra* note 27, at 29, 77–78.

58. C. COLE & E. CHEESMAN, THE AIR DEFENCE OF BRITAIN 1914–1918 6 (London, 1984).

59. PROCEEDINGS, *supra* note 41, at 424.

60. In many cases this confusion was the product of inadequate research, usually as a result of reading the language of the treaty only. The intent was clear: "It is to be noticed that this article speaks of undefended, not of unfortified, towns. Only where there are no fortifications, no troops, and no open resistance by the population, does this article apply." BORDWELL, THE LAW OF WAR BETWEEN BELLIGERENTS 287 (1908). The U.S. Army's law of war manual, which would have provided guidance to Army Air Corps planners through World War II, offered clarification in each of its editions (1914, 1917, 1940, 1944, and 1956). The language was further clarified in 1976 in change 1 to FIELD MANUAL 27–10, The Law of Land Warfare (1976) by addition of the following to paragraph 39:

> b. Interpretation. An undefended place, within the meaning of Article 25, HR, is any inhabited place near or in a zone where opposing armed forces are in contact which is open for occupation by an adverse party without resistance. In order to be considered as undefended, the following conditions should be fulfilled:
>
> (1) Armed forces and all other combatants, as well as mobile weapons and mobile military equipment, must have been evacuated, or otherwise neutralized;
> (2) no hostile use shall be made of fixed military installations or establishments;
> (3) no acts of warfare shall be committed by the authorities or by the population; and,
> (4) no activities in support of military operations shall be undertaken.

areas, such as reprisal, were avoided, as was any acknowledgement of the inevitability of collateral or incidental civilian casualties in modern war. The delegates addressed (obliquely) the subject of collateral damage to civilian objects in the admonitory language of article 27; but the issue of collateral civilian casualties was ignored—or avoided. Perhaps this was due in part to the fact that extension of a conflict beyond the immediate battlefield was not contemplated. Yet more could have been said and was said thirty-six years earlier by the Lieber Code: "Art. 15. Military necessity admits of all direct destruction of life or limb of armed enemies, and of other persons whose destruction is incidentally unavoidable in the armed contests of war."[61]

The First Hague Peace Conference passed into history. After five years, the prohibition on discharge of explosives from balloons or by other new methods lapsed.[62] Moves were afoot for a second conference, but the formal call for a conference had to be delayed for a number of reasons, not the least of which was the conclusion on September 5, 1905, of the Russo-Japanese War. Although President Theodore Roosevelt earlier had been approached to propose a second conference, and actually had begun steps in that direction in 1904, he relinquished that privilege to Tsar Nicholas II following receipt of a request to that effect delivered by the Russian Ambassador to Washington.[63]

IV. THE SECOND HAGUE PEACE CONFERENCE OF 1907

A. Background

A great deal had occurred since the First Hague Peace Conference that would affect the second conference, which convened at The Hague on June 15, 1907. The Wright Brothers had accomplished man's conquest of the air; their efforts, along with those of Alberto Santos-Dumont, were watched carefully in both the public and private sectors. France, Germany, Russia, and Italy had commenced programs for the production of military dirigibles; the threat of attack from the air loomed larger. But domestic politics also had come into play; the Liberal Government of Great Britain was committed to a reduction of its military and naval budgets.

The Tsar's call for a second conference eschewed limitation of armaments issues,[64] as Russia, with recent military defeat behind it, was more interested in undertaking an arms buildup than it had been at the time of the First Hague Peace Conference. While Britain was anxious to add disarmament to the conference agenda, Germany made it clear that its delegates would walk out of the conference if the subject of disarmament were raised. All of these matters have been discussed in greater detail elsewhere,[65] but they set the tone for the conference.

B. Convention II of 1899 and Convention IV of 1907

As with the First Hague Peace Conference of 1899, the work of the Second Hague Peace Conference of 1907 was divided among various commissions. The First Com-

61. HARTIGAN, *supra* note 25, at 48.

62. Hague Declaration (IV, 1) SCHINDLER & TOMAN, *supra* note 27, at 50, 141–45; F. HOLLS, *supra* note 30, at 95, 377; HAGUE CONVENTIONS, *supra* note 30, at 220–22.

63. HAGUE CONVENTIONS, *supra* note 30, at xix–xxix.

64. I THE PROCEEDINGS OF THE HAGUE PEACE CONFERENCES: THE CONFERENCE OF 1907 1 (J. Scott ed. (1920)) [hereinafter I PROCEEDINGS OF 1907].

65. B. TUCHMAN, *supra* note 33, at 277–88; GELLIN, NO LONGER AN ISLAND (London, 1984), particularly chapter IX; and C. GIBBS-SMITH, THE REBIRTH OF EUROPEAN AVIATION (London, 1974).

mission examined the topics of an international prize court, pacific settlement of international disputes, obligatory arbitration, court of arbitral justice, and limitation of the employment of force for the recovery of ordinary public debt. The Second Commission dealt with land warfare. The Third Commission handled warfare on the sea. The Fourth Commission reviewed juridicial relations incident to the latter. The 1907 Hague Conference adopted thirteen Conventions and one Declaration. The issues assigned to the Second Commission are germane to this article.

The prohibition on delivery of munitions from aerial platforms was considered for renewal. Some opposition to the renewal was expressed, in part because of the restriction on bombardment contained in article 25 of the Annex to Convention II of 1899. Ultimately the prohibition was renewed, but rather than for another set term of five years as it was originally in Declaration (IV, I) of 1899, it was left in effect until the Third Hague Peace Conference. That conference never took place and the prohibition in its subsequent form known as Declaration XIV of 1907,[66] generally is regarded as having no legal significance.[67] Of historical interest (but not significance) is that while France, Germany, Italy, Japan, Russia, and the United States ratified the 1899 prohibition, Great Britain did not; only Great Britain and the United States committed themselves to the 1907 treaty. Because the treaty was only binding in case of war between parties to it, the treaty had no effect in World War I or II.

The prohibition essentially had been supplanted by language amending article 25 of the Annex to Convention II of 1899. In its subsequent form as article 25 of the Annex to Convention IV of 1907, article 25 reads: "The attack or bombardment, *by whatever means*, of towns, villages, dwellings, or buildings which are undefended is prohibited. (Emphasis notes the amending language.)"[68]

C. Convention IX of 1907

Attempts to bring naval forces under the rubric of Convention II of 1899 had proved unsuccessful at the First Hague Peace Conference, and became part of the Tsar's agenda for the second conference. This endeavor proved successful, but not without adding to the confusion in the process. Convention IX of 1907 *Concerning Bombardment by Naval Forces in Time of War* provided clearer rules—and authority—than did either Convention II of 1899 or its successor, the 1907 Convention IV, both of which pertain to the *Laws and Customs of War on Land*.[69] While repeating the restrictions on bombardment contained in the 1907 Convention IV (as well as the prohibition on attack of undefended towns, again without definition of the term), article 2 identified particular military objects that could be attacked, and recognized the inevitability of collateral damage in the execution of such attacks. While this created further confusion in interpretation of the law of war, some people believing (erroneously) that naval forces had greater latitude in execution of attacks than ground forces, a review of the negotiating record indicates that the drafters of 1907 Convention IX simply were more equal to the task. With the exception of naval authority to engage in punitive bombardment of an undefended

66. SCHINDLER & TOMAN, *supra* note 27, at 141–46.
67. J. STONE, *supra* note 53, at 623.
68. SCHINDLER & TOMAN, *supra* note 27, at 77–78. Article 27 also was amended to add historic monuments to the list of specially-protected property.
69. SCHINDLER & TOMAN, *supra* note 27, at 54, 723–30.

city if its requisition of supplies were declined, the obligations and authority regarding bombardment essentially were the same—and were intended to be.[70]

Military significance of a target. The 1907 Convention IX was significant for other reasons. It was the first treaty codification, or acknowledgment, that bombardment (or bombing) was related to the military significance of the target rather than whether the city, town, or village in which the target was located was defended.[71] It also served to confirm the permissibility of attacking targets wherever located. It provided the only list of lawful targets contained in any law of war treaty which, while incomplete by World War I, World War II, and modern standards, nonetheless, was an improvement over past and future treaties.[72] Article 2 listed as lawful targets "military works, military or naval establishments, depots of arms or war materiel, workshops or plant(s) which could be utilized for the needs of the hostile fleet or army, and the ships of war in the harbor." Thus lawful targets were not limited to objects purely military in nature, but included industrial targets of value to the enemy war effort. The list was regarded by the head of the U.S. delegation as declaratory of customary international law as it existed in 1907.[73]

Unavoidable collateral damage. Of equal importance was that the treaty absolved the attacker of responsibility for "unavoidable" collateral damage. This was not new law; this, again, was a codification of the customary practice of nations. What must be realized is that collateral civilian casualties were regarded as the cost of war to a nation rather than the responsibility of the attacker. As one international law scholar of the time noted:

> *Bombardment of the resident portions of towns.*—It has been questioned whether towns separated somewhat from the fortifications which defend them are liable to bombardment. This is a part of the larger question as to whether the portions of towns not used for military purposes are exempt from bombardment. It must be admitted, however, that this is one of the rigors of war which belligerents have held to be so useful as not to be given up. Of its hardship there can be no question, though it cannot compare with that of a siege.[74]

---

70. Committee II was responsible for the redraft of the 1989 Hague Convention II (with respect to the laws and customs of war on land) into the 1907 Hague Convention IV (respecting the laws and customs of war on land), while Committee III drafted Hague Convention IX (concerning bombardment by naval forces in time of war). That there was little or no coordination between the two committees is illustrated by the prefatory language in the naval bombardment treaty (Hague Convention IX of 1907), which refers to the Hague Convention II Regulations of 1899, rather than its successor (Hague Convention IV of 1907), then being drafted with only slight change. SCHINDLER & TOMAN, *supra* note 27, at 63–92, 723–29. For additional detail on the confusion created, *see* Carnahan, *The Law of Air Bombardment in Its Historical Context*, 17 A. F. L. REV. 39–49 (1985). The intent to meld land and naval rules dated from efforts of the Institute of International Law at Oxford in 1881. HAGUE PEACE CONFERENCES, *supra* note 56, at 587–98. The U.S. delegation to the Second Hague Peace Conference of 1907 regarded Hague Convention IX as bringing the rules of land and naval warfare into "exact harmony." The Institute of International Law, meeting at Madrid in 1911, concluded that "aerial war is permitted, but on the condition of not presenting greater dangers than land or sea war for the persons or properties of the peaceful population." J. WESTLAKE, II INTERNATIONAL LAW, WAR (Cambridge, 1913). While each of these statements seems to indicate the clear intent of the 1907 conferees to establish one legal regime for bombardment by land and naval forces, the conferees exacerbated the problem with the statement in the Final Act of the 1907 conference expressing the hope that "in the program of the next conference, and that in any case the powers may apply, as far as possible, to war by sea the principles of the convention relative to the laws and customs of war on land." I PROCEEDINGS OF 1907, *supra* note 64, at 289.

71. Williams, *Legitimate Targets in Aerial Bombardment*, 23 AM. J. INT'L LAW 570–81 at 572 (1929).

72. SCHINDLER & TOMAN, *supra* note 27, at 147–57. The Hague Rules of Air Warfare of 1923, though containing a list of lawful targets, were never adopted by any nation.

73. INSTRUCTIONS, *supra* note 30, at 112; report to the Secretary of State of the U.S. Delegation to the Second Hague Conference.

74. BORDWELL, *supra* note 60, at 287.

As previously noted, collateral civilian casualties during a siege were regarded as a burden upon the besieged commander—an inducement to end the siege. Bombardment not connected to a siege but resulting in collateral civilian casualties was not illegal; it was merely a cost of doing the business of war.

D. Technological Changes

From an academician's standpoint, the Second Hague Peace Conference might be regarded as a disaster. Lawyers on the United States delegations to the 1899 and 1907 conferences sought to regulate (if not prohibit) "uncontrollable forces dangerous to neutrals or noncombatants."[75] There had been partial success in that article 1 of Convention VIII of 1907 *Relative to the Laying of Automatic Submarine Contact Mines* required self-neutralization mechanisms on unanchored naval contact mines, on anchored naval contact mines that broke loose from their moorings, or for torpedoes that missed their target. This was not a great international law achievement, however, inasmuch as such a proscription was consistent with prudent military practice; the free-floating mine or torpedo posed a threat to its own forces as much as to enemy or neutral shipping.

An increasing capability for controlled flight had destroyed forever any chance of prohibiting bombing in future conflicts. One international lawyer viewed the outcome of the 1907 Hague Peace Conference as a "direct retrogression from the humanitarian viewpoint" in that the conferees were unable to "restrict the means of warfare to those heretofore employed."[76] This position manifests a fundamental problem with codification of the law of war: some international lawyers want to roll the clock back to the "good old days" of warfare while concluding that any progress in technology must be less humane. Each premise is erroneous. But rather than work with change, there has been—and continues to be—a resistance to change, and codification has suffered accordingly.[77] The result is basic to this article and the questions it raises; the rules codified in 1907 at The Hague were the rules in effect when war broke out thirty-two years later, unchanged by any subsequent treaty. The Hague Peace Conferences of 1899 and 1907 were the first—and last—successful effort at codification of regulations affecting combat operations.[78] There were subse-

---

75. KUHN, *supra* note 48, at 119.

76. *Id. See also* HAGUE PEACE CONFERENCES, *supra* note 56, at 653–54.

77. In part, this may be because most international lawyers have little knowledge of military operations, doctrine, and technology. For example, at the 1974–1977 Geneva Diplomatic Conference, the international lawyers who were delegates went to extraordinary lengths to establish a legal regime for protection for medical aircraft operating in a combat environment, finally arriving at provisions that they hailed as a great advance in the law of war. *See*, Solf, *Protection of Medical Aircraft*, 24 U.S. ARMY AVIATION DIG. 15–17 (Apr. 1978); 33–36 (May 1978); 26–29 (June 1978); and 12–19 (July 1978). However, the provisions are highly dependent on agreement between the parties to the conflict in the area in which an aircraft would be flying its mission, which would be virtually impossible on the modern electronic battlefield. When the principal negotiator of these provisions was asked by the author about this dilemma, he confessed that neither he nor any other Geneva negotiator ever considered the potential impact of electronic warfare on their work. He acknowledged that he knew nothing about electronic warfare.

78. Save and except for the 1923 Hague Air Rules, SCHINDLER & TOMAN, *supra* note 27, no attempt was made to amend or update the 1907 Hague law of war treaties until 1974. If one considers the technological advances made in aviation, bombing, and air defenses during the sixty-seven year span between the 1907 Hague Peace Conference and the Geneva Diplomatic Conference that met from 1974 to 1977 to produce the 1977 Additional Protocols I and II, or the advances that occurred from 1907 to 1945, one can appreciate how far behind technology the law of war lagged. The treaty that was to update Hague Conventions IV and IX of 1907, the 1977 Protocol I, was not successful in that endeavor. The United States and France have decided not to become a party to it. By 1988, of the principal participants in World War II, only Italy had ratified Protocol I.

quent treaties dealing with military wounded and sick, hospital ships, prisoners of war, and chemical and bacteriological warfare, but the rules formulated in 1899 and 1907 provided the only law of war guidance available to the military men who planned and executed the air campaigns of World War II.

Efforts to continue codification of the law of war began at the Second Hague Peace Conference. In the *Final Act* of that conference, the conferees recommended that a preparatory committee appointed by governments should begin planning for the Third Hague Peace Conference, which they recommended be held in 1914, two years in advance of the conference.[79] Arrangements for a third conference had begun, but were overcome by the commencement of World War I. This may have been propitious. As Lee Kennett has noted, "In the years leading up to 1914, the major powers had given little attention to the legal and moral implications of the weapons they were developing. Most of them were preoccupied with the technical aspects of bombing."[80]

Had a Third Hague Peace Conference been held on the eve of World War I, there is a strong possibility that the progress in codification of the law relating to aerial bombardment that was accomplished at the first two conferences might have been lost altogether. Conventions IV and IX of 1907 were intended to be no more than a codification of the customary practice of nations and, properly read, relieved an attacker of any responsibility for collateral damage or collateral injury short of indiscriminate bombing. But nations are reticent to regulate a new means of war with rules that might have the potential of hampering its effective employment, or limit its use against an opponent who has no concern for the law of war. At a meeting of the Institute of International Law in 1911, some members continued to press for abolishment of the airplane as a weapon of war, while others urged special rules for its employment. But rules are made by nations, and any such attempt to slow the advance of aviation in the years immediately preceding World War I would have been much the same as the proverbial broom sweeping to hold back the tide.

E. Observations of Early Aerial Campaigns

The aerial bombing campaigns of World War I, the Zeppelin and Gotha offensives, the Allied counteroffensives (executed or planned), and other bombing operations, have been described in other works.[81] It is obvious that law of war considerations

79. II THE HAGUE PEACE CONFERENCES OF 1899 AND 1907, 289–90 (J. Scott ed. 1909) [hereinafter II HAGUE PEACE CONFERENCES].

80. KENNETT, *supra* note 38, 19–20. *See also* MORROW, BUILDING GERMAN AIRPOWER (1976), and HIGHAM, THE BRITISH RIGID AIRSHIP 1908–1931 (London, 1961).

81. *See* W. RALEIGH & H. JONES, THE WAR IN THE AIR (Oxford, 1922–1927); THE U.S. AIR SERVICE IN WORLD WAR I (Maurer, 1979); C. WISE, CANADIAN AIRMEN AND THE FIRST WORLD WAR (Toronto, 1980); J. MORRIS, THE GERMAN AIR RAIDS ON GREAT BRITAIN 1914–1918 (London, 1920–1969); G. NEUMANN, THE GERMAN AIR FORCE IN THE GREAT WAR (London 1921, 1969); J. CUNEO, WINGED MARS (1942); J. CUNEO, THE AIR WEAPON (1947); Fredette, *Bombers of the Black Cross: German Bombardment Aviation in World War I*, 7 THE AIRPOWER HIST. 165–77 & 205–15 (1960); C. WEBSTER & N. FRANKLAND, I THE STRATEGIC AIR OFFENSIVE AGAINST GERMANY 1939–1945, 34–51 (London, 1961); K. POOLMAN, ZEPPELINS AGAINST LONDON (1961); G. HADDOW & P. GROSZ, THE GERMAN GIANTS (London, 1962); D. ROBINSON, THE ZEPPELIN IN COMBAT (1962); R. FREDETTE, THE SKY ON FIRE (1966); F. MASON, BATTLE OVER BRITAIN 17–40 (London, 1969); H. PENROSE, BRITISH AVIATION: THE GREAT WAR AND ARMISTICE, 1914–1918 (London, 1969); R. HIGHAM, AIR POWER: A CONCISE HISTORY (1972); N. JONES, THE ORIGINS OF STRATEGIC BOMBING (London, 1973); B. POWERS, STRATEGY WITHOUT SLIDE-RULE 11–106 (London, 1976); H. CASTLE, FIRE OVER ENGLAND (London, 1982); C. COLE & E. CHEESMAN, THE AIR DEFENCE OF BRITAIN, 1914–1918 (London, 1984); M. COOPER, THE BIRTH OF INDEPENDENT AIR POWER (London, 1986); and C. WHITE, THE GOTHA SUMMER (London, 1986).

received little (if any) attention, except as a tool for propaganda alleging indiscriminate attacks by the enemy. Several observations can be made about the campaigns conducted by the warring parties, however:

1. The practice of the various nations provided a fairly clear indication of the types of objects regarded as lawful targets: military and naval bases; warehouses, airfields, and docks; lines of communication; and industrial targets that offered a contribution to the enemy's war effort. (The degree of contribution established the priority of attack, not the legality of the target.)

2. While industrialization of the modern European societies and mobilization of their citizenry for "total war" further clouded the distinction between combatant and civilian, bombing operations were regarded as analogous to naval blockade or siege, in which the blockader or besieger saw collateral injury as a natural, inevitable, and lawful consequence of such operations. In the very best case, collateral civilian casualties resulting from the attack of a legitimate target were not regarded as the responsibility of an attacker, as the ability to limit such casualties lay more with the defender or, for that matter, with the civilian population itself. This was the case with regard to civilians in the vicinity of ground combat operations, and no special legal regime to the contrary had been proposed, much less established, for aerial bombardment.[82]

3. Whether a particular operation was regarded as "illegal" or "immoral" depended entirely upon whether the person was the bomber or the "bombee," that is, the recipient of the bombs.

4. Bombing did have an effect upon morale on both sides. German steel manufacturers reported a thirty percent decrease in worker efficiency during the period of air attacks on the Saar and Lorraine Luxembourg in 1916,[83] while British Minister of Munitions, Winston Churchill, in a meeting of the War Cabinet on October 1, 1917, established that German air raids on preceding nights had had a pronounced effect on employee attendance and production at Woolwich Arsenal. As the official British history noted, "the loss of output was out of all proportion to the percentage of employees who stayed away from work."[84] This effect is mentioned not to enter into the debate as to the efficacy of attacks on morale,[85] but to suggest that both sides

---

82. For example, following the second Gotha raid on London (7 July 1917), the British War Cabinet, under heavy public pressure to undertake retaliatory actions, sought legal advice regarding the bombing of cities. The responding memorandum of law stated: "No legal duty has been imposed on attacking forces to restrict bombardment to actual fortifications, and the destruction of its public and private buildings has always been regarded as a legitimate means of inducing a town to surrender." Mills, *Bomber Command of the Royal Air Force*, 7 AIR U. Q. REV. 40 (Spring, 1955).

83. WILLIAMS, *supra* note 71, at 581, n.36.

84. 5 RALEIGH & JONES, *supra* note 81 at 86–88. *See* POWERS, *supra* note 81, at 22.

85. Post-World War II critics of the strategic air offensive against Germany have argued that the attack on the morale of the German people was unsuccessful, *see* HASTINGS, *supra* note 8, at 323 and BEST, *supra* note 8, at 283 quoting WRIGHT, ORDEAL OF TOTAL WAR 181 (1968), for the most part relying upon a single paragraph in the *Summary Report (European War)*, THE UNITED STATES STRATEGIC BOMBING SURVEY 16 (1945). However, the assessment by the Morale Division of the U.S. Strategic Bombing Survey (USSBS) was quite specific in concluding that "Bombing seriously depressed the morale of German civilians." *The Effects of Strategic Bombing on German Morale*, THE UNITED STATES STRATEGIC BOMBING SURVEY 1 (1947). Any discrepancy between the two reports may be explained by the fact that John Kenneth Galbraith, a civilian with the USSBS who held strongly antibombing prejudices, was highly influential in the contents of the Summary report and actively sought to downplay the effect of strategic bombing. Galbraith, *After the Air Raids*, 32 AM. HERITAGE 65–80 (Apr./May 1981). *See also* M. ISAAC, STRATEGIC BOMBING IN WORLD WAR TWO: THE STORY OF THE UNITED STATES STRATEGIC BOMBING SURVEY (1976). "The 'area' bombing attacks did have a direct and palpable effect on the morale of the German population, and the German leadership, in response to that impact, seriously skewed Germany's strategy." W. MURRAY, LUFTWAUFFE 283 (1985). Murray's finding is supported by R. Overy in GOERING 77–108, 156–57, 94–97, 226 & 228 (London,

from World War I had experience to indicate there was value in such attacks. Certainly the theory of demoralizing the enemy in this way was consistent with the theory of collateral casualties as a burden on the commander of a besieged area.

5. Suffering visited upon the civilian population occurred more through errors in target identification and/or bombing accuracy than malice aforethought, and were compounded as air defenses improved. Strengthening defenses forced each side to resort to the cover of darkness in carrying out its attacks, which had a concomitant effect on target identification and bombing accuracy. It was a vicious circle of cause and effect that was to repeat itself in World War II and, more recently, in the U.S. air strike against Libya in April 1986.[86]

6. Airpower did not cause the greatest civilian suffering during World War I; the British naval blockade of Germany during the war resulted in the deaths of a far greater number of civilians, especially women, children, and the elderly, than did the strategic bombing offensives of World Wars I and II combined.[87]

7. However inaccurate, bombing was not the least discriminate weapon of World War I. That distinction lay with the German Paris Gun which, firing from distances up to seventy-five miles, could be aimed only at the center of Paris. Used in conjunction with the German offensive of March 1918, it had but one purpose: an attack upon the morale of the citizens of Paris.[88] As its use generally was regarded as lawful by international law scholars, statesmen, and military men of the time, it would be difficult to conclude that the more discriminate bomber was not legal, or that collateral civilian casualties were regarded as something other than an inevitable consequence of war.

Yet postwar periods inevitably bring efforts at modernization of the law of war, as was seen with the two Hague conferences, and the years following "The War to End

1984). While the effect on morale cannot be disregarded completely as critics suggest, from the standpoint of military efficiency it appears to be an ancillary consideration in the attack of other targets rather than an effect that can be sought independently. *See also* Spaight, *Morale as Objective*, 3 THE ROYAL A. F. Q. 287 (Oct. 1951).

86. For a detailed description of the planning and execution of this attack, *see* Parks, *Crossing the Line*, 112 U.S. NAVAL INST. PROC. 40–52 (Nov. 1986).

87. It is estimated that almost 800,000 German civilians died of starvation as a result of the British naval blockade of Germany during World War I. D. SAWARD, *supra* note 4, at 299. Historian Michael Glover, using German sources, states that the British blockade was responsible for 726,766 deaths between 1915–1918. M. GLOVER, THE VELVET GLOVE 125 (London, 1982). On the blockade in general, *see* L. GUICHARD, THE NAVAL BLOCKADE (1930); A. BELL, A HISTORY OF THE BLOCKADE OF GERMANY (London, 1937); M. SINEY, THE ALLIED BLOCKADE OF GERMANY, 1914–1916 (1957); and R. HOUGH, THE GREAT WAR AT SEA 1914–1918 (London, 1983). As one Royal Air Force officer noted, "No woman or child can escape from the entirely indiscriminate effects of a naval blockade. But every woman and child, and indeed every man, in Germany [during World War II] could have escaped from the area bombing of German cities by decamping to the towns and villages and woods." G. Garrod, *The Ethics of Area Bombing: Correspondence*, CVII J. ROYAL UNITED SERVICE INST. 242 (Aug. 1962).

Curiously, while delegates to the 1974–1977 Diplomatic Conference strove so hard to formulate rules that would prohibit bombing beyond the immediate battlefront, nothing in Protocol I of 1977 would prevent a recurrence of the deaths caused by naval blockade. Article 49(3) provides that the rules stated in Protocol I relating to hostilities do apply to naval warfare to the extent that naval warfare actions may affect the civilian population, and article 54 prohibits starvation as a weapon of warfare, but only to the extent that the attack, destruction, removal, etc. (but not denial) of food is for the *specific purpose* of starvation of the civilian population. Starvation incidental to a total blockade is not prohibited. The relief provisions contained in articles 68–71 of Protocol I and articles 14 and 18(2) of Protocol II are permissive, as events in the 1980s in Ethiopia and the Sudan have shown. An estimated 250,000 people died of hunger and hunger-related diseases in southern Sudan in 1988 because of, in principal measure, delays by the Government of Sadik Mahdi in granting international relief organizations access to that area. Harden, *Life in Sudan Worsened Under Mahdi*, Washington Post, July 1, 1989, at A12. Mahdi was deposed by a *coup d'etat* on June 30, 1989.

88. H. MILLER, THE PARIS GUN (1930).

All Wars'' were no exception. While aerial bombardment may have been regarded as lawful, a bombing phobia had begun that would build until the beginning of World War II. This fear of being bombed would have an effect disproportionate to its military effectiveness.[89] This obsession had a four-fold, contradictory effect on interwar disarmament discussions and military planning that nullified the former while deceiving the latter. Fear of being bombed (a) led to public pressure for a prohibition or regulation of bombing; (b) which could not be accomplished unilaterally or in any way that was dependent upon trust in a ''piece of paper''; (c) this same fear produced a counterargument for bombing as a war deterrent; (d) should deterrence fail, it provided justification for the use of bombing to attack the will (morale) of the nation in order to exploit the obvious fear, the fear of being bombed. This thinking was an enlargement of the conventional acceptance of collateral casualties in a siege as a burden placed upon a defender. Strategic bombing was vertical envelopment of an enemy's military forces to attack a nation's means for waging war.

Coupled with this thinking was the determination by many nations, particularly Great Britain, to avoid a repetition of the battlefield carnage that cost many nations almost a generation of young men; airpower offered a substitute for land battles, which meant that a nation was prepared to substitute the loss of enemy civilian lives for the loss of enemy military and, of course, (in theory) losses among its own military. During the ''no more war'' years of postwar isolationism, it also offered an excuse for nonintervention in European crises; a nation with a small peacetime army has no means with which to intervene on land.[90] But the dependency of each nation on foreign commerce made isolationism virtually impossible. Increasingly that commerce relied upon aviation, which reinforced the potential threat. The hope lay with (in today's vernacular) ''mutual and verifiable'' disarmament or, failing that, an updated law of war treaty to regulate bombing. The moment of opportunity came in the years immediately following World War I. As will be seen, it came—and went.

V. THE TREATY OF VERSAILLES

The conclusion of World War I brought an attempt at unilateral disarmament. Under the Treaty of Versailles, Germany was to dispose of all aviation-related equipment; its military was to be disbanded. Although Germany submitted to the Versailles Treaty, it did not acquiesce totally. Germany stated it was prepared to submit to any limitation of aerial capabilities to which all members of the League of Nations were subjected, a proposal that was rejected by the victorious nations. A game of legal and diplomatic intrigue followed, continuing for almost two years, as (in the words of one historian), ''the Allies attempted to contain Germany's air potential through legal restraints that Germany assiduously tried to avoid.''[91] Other parts of the Treaty of Versailles also suffered from the inability to enforce them. A desire to bring to trial certain former German military officers for war crimes related

89. C. Webster & N. Frankland, *supra* note 81, at 46, which notes that

> [The] exaggeration of the number of casualties which strategic bombing was likely to produce was a major factor in all strategic thinking before the Second World War and exercised a profound influence on the minds of the services, the political chiefs, and being translated into even more sensational language by journalists and publicists, on public opinion at large.

90. M. Howard, The Continental Commitment (London, 1972).
91. E. Homze, Arming the Luftwaffe 3 (London, 1976).

to Germany's aerial attacks on Great Britain brought this cautionary advice from the British Air Council:

> [T]he present situation makes it necessary to emphasize the peculiar reverberation of such contemplated prosecutions upon the RAF. These German officers and men are to be tried in time of peace before a court exclusively composed of their ex-enemies for acts which do not differ from those ordered to be carried out by the Royal Air Force upon German towns. The orders given included directions to bomb German towns (where any military objective was situated), to destroy the industrial activities there by bombings during the day, and to weaken the morale of the civilian inhabitants (and thereby their 'will to win') by persistent bomb attacks which would both destroy life (civilian and otherwise) and should, if possible, originate a conflagration which would reduce to ashes the whole town and thereby delete a whole centre of industrial activity.[92]

This highly-legalistic Allied approach to maintaining the peace—or keeping Germany disarmed—failed in virtually every respect, and should have served as a clear indication of the difficulty of arms control or regulation of hostilities through legal documents lacking an effective means of enforcement.

VI. THE WASHINGTON CONFERENCE ON THE LIMITATION OF ARMAMENT OF 1922

Greater, multilateral disarmament steps were envisaged. At the Washington Conference on the Limitation of Armament[93] (popularly known as the Washington Naval Conference) held in Washington, D.C., in 1921, representatives from the United Kingdom, France, Italy, Japan and the United States initially considered a total prohibition on new methods of warfare such as submarines, poisonous gas, and aircraft. But there was distrust among nations who were allies only three years earlier,[94] which ultimately led to a conference conclusion that it was "not at present practicable to impose any effective limitations upon the numbers or characteristics of aircraft, either commercial or military."[95] When it became apparent that prohibitions were unlikely, the delegates turned to the possibility of "rules for control of new agencies of warfare,"[96] suggesting regulation rather than limitation. It was obvious the issue could not receive adequate consideration in the limited time remaining at the conference. The delegates unanimously accepted a recommendation that aircraft should operate only within rules established by a subsequent

92. As quoted in Maier, *The Relationship Between Air Doctrine and Total War*, presentation before the Air War College, Maxwell Air Force Base, Montgomery, Alabama, September 11, 1980. In fact, the call for war crimes trials met with virtual rejection. *See* WILLIS, PROLOGUE TO NUERNBERG: THE POLITICS AND DIPLOMACY OF PUNISHING WAR CRIMINALS OF THE FIRST WORLD WAR (1982).

93. CONFERENCE ON THE LIMITATION OF ARMAMENT (1922); SCHINDLER & TOMAN, *supra* note 27, at 789–91. The treaty was not ratified by France and thus it did not enter into force. Limitation of Naval Armament (Five-Power Treaty or Washington Treaty), signed Feb. 6, 1922; ratified Aug. 17, 1923; 43 Stat. 1655.

94. Thus in official correspondence to the head of the British delegation (Nov. 23, 1921), it was noted that

> Although good relations between [Great Britain and France] will no doubt continue, the [Committee of Imperial Defence] cannot but view the situation which may arise in a few years' time if the French military proposals are carried out whilest Great Britain is reducing her fleet. The committee regards the comparative air strengths of France and Great Britain as even more serious. . . . The danger to England to attack by a French air force is very great.

DOCUMENTS ON BRITISH FOREIGN POLICY, 1919–1939 498 (First series, Vol. XIV, London, 1966).

95. A. TOYNBEE, SURVEY OF INTERNATIONAL AFFAIRS, 1920–1923 498 (London, 1925).

96. CONFERENCE ON THE LIMITATION OF ARMAMENT, *supra* note 93, at 10. Tentative suggestions by the Secretary of State of the United States with respect to the agenda.

conference.[97] That subsequent conference was to consider a number of issues, including the following:

> (a) Do existing rules of international law adequately cover new methods of attack or defense resulting from the introduction or development, since the Hague Conference of 1907, of new agencies of warfare?
>
> (b) If not so, what changes in existing rules ought to be adopted in consequence thereof as a part of the law of nations?[98]

Thus the first postwar consideration of aerial bombardment ended inconclusively, with the issue passed to a separate conference.[99] The latter conference, desired less by governments than by public opinion, convened in The Hague on December 11, 1922.[100] But if the actions of United States officials were an indication of the approach each nation was to take towards the conference, it was doomed before it began.

VII. THE HAGUE COMMISSION OF JURISTS OF 1923

A. Background

The United States sought to send a strong delegation, headed by Ambassador John Bassett Moore, a member of the Permanent Court of International Justice at The Hague. Military representation was equally impressive and included Rear Admiral W. L. Rodgers, USN, former President of the prestigious Naval War College. But at the outset the U.S. delegation guidance had to be prepared and there was a clear divergence of views between the Army and the Navy. Draft rules relating to aerial bombardment proposed by the Secretary of the Navy were more restrictive than those proffered by the Secretary of War.

Although both sets of draft rules were passed to the U.S. delegation by the Secretary of State, the Navy rules very early became the basis for U.S. delegation negotiation. There were several reasons for this: the Navy rules closely paralleled those proposed by the British delegation. Ambassador Moore's decision appears to have been influenced considerably by Admiral Rodgers, the senior military member of the delegation.[101] The guidance to Ambassador Moore from the Secretary of State

---

97. *Id.* at 800.

98. *Id.* at 356.

99. *See* R. BUELL, THE WASHINGTON CONFERENCE 201–39, 417–18 (1922); T. BUCKLEY, THE UNITED STATES AND THE WASHINGTON CONFERENCE 1921–1922, 40, 121–26 (1970); CONFERENCE ON THE LIMITATION OF ARMAMENT, *supra* note 93; and 1 FOREIGN RELATIONS OF THE UNITED STATES, 1922, 228 (1938). For a discussion of international attempts to abolish or limit submarines as combatants, *see* W. MALLISON, JR., STUDIES IN THE LAW OF NAVAL WARFARE: SUBMARINES IN GENERAL AND LIMITED WARS 31–50 (1968). *See also* Roxburgh, *Submarines at the Washington Conference*, 3 BRITISH YEAR BOOK INT'L L. 150–58 (1922–1923); Douglas, *The Submarine and Washington Conference of 1921*, 26 NAVAL WAR C. REV. 86–97 (Mar.–Apr. 1974); and J. TERRAINE, THE U-BOAT WARS 1916–1945 (1989). Regulation of the machine-gun was equally unsuccessful. *See* J. ELLIS, THE SOCIAL HISTORY OF THE MACHINE GUN (1975).

100. The Washington Conference adopted a resolution for the appointment of a Commission of Jurists. The Commission met at The Hague from December 11, 1922 to February 19, 1923. The charge to the Commission was to prepare rules relating to aerial warfare (part II) and rules concerning the use of radio in time of war (part I). The rules were never legally adopted. *See* SCHINDLER & TOMAN, *supra* note 27, at 147–57.

101. As with all aspects of law and politics, personal relationships often play a key role. As a professor of law at Columbia in 1900, Ambassador Moore began the Naval War College's International Law Studies series that continues to this day. As President of the Naval War College nine years later, Admiral Rodgers became close friends with Ambassador Moore. Acceptance of the Navy draft rules

left it to Moore as delegation head to decide between the Navy and War Department drafts. Admiral Rodgers proved more persuasive than his Army counterpart, Brigadier General William H. Johnston, despite the fact that Major William C. Sherman, an early proponent of long-range aerial bombardment and protege of U.S. Army Brigadier General Billy Mitchell, was General Johnston's aviation advisor on the U.S. delegation.

The point of view of the U.S. Navy and the British was influenced more by the internecine fighting over postwar defense budgets within each nation than by humanitarianism. Both navies had been experimenting with and developing aircraft carriers for more than a decade.[102] While the Royal Naval Air Service had conducted bombing raids during World War I and Brigadier General Mitchell had raised international interest when Martin bombers under his command sank the "unsinkable" German battleship *Ostfriesland*, on July 21, 1921, sixty miles off the Virginia coast,[103] the aircraft-versus-battleship controversy was far from over in either nation or, for that matter, within their respective navies.

Aircraft carrier development in the immediate postwar era was prompted by several events. The Royal Air Force had been established on April 1, 1918, and Marshal of the Royal Air Force Trenchard's strong voice in favor of strategic bombing was beginning to be heard, as was Brigadier General Mitchell's in arguing for an independent air service in the United States. The Washington Naval Conference that had proposed the forthcoming Hague Commission of Jurists of 1923 to regulate aerial warfare, adopted capital ship limitations that ultimately led to the completion of the U.S. battle cruisers *Lexington* and *Saratoga* as aircraft carriers;[104] the decision was greeted with enthusiasm by naval aviators, and was viewed by battleship sailors as a counter to the move for an independent air service. The Royal Navy took similar steps, converting the light battle cruisers *Courageous* and *Glorious*

was inevitable, too, as they most closely approximated the philosophy of rules developed by the International Law Association in August 1922. Colby, *Aerial Law and War Targets*, 19 AM. J. INT'L L. 713 (1929).

102. Roskill, *The Period of Anglo-American Antagonism, 1919–1929* I NAVAL POLICY BETWEEN THE WARS, 234–68, 356–99, 467–97 (London, 1968); N. POLMAR, AIRCRAFT CARRIERS 1–53 (1969); C. MELHORN, TWO-BLOCK FOX: THE RISE OF THE AIRCRAFT CARRIER, 1911–1929 (1974); and G. TILL, AIR POWER AND THE ROYAL NAVY Chapter 2 (London, 1979). By 1921 the President of the Naval War College, Admiral W. S. Sims, had turned against the battleship and was in favor of the aircraft carrier as the capital ship of the future and so advised Brigadier General Billy Mitchell by letter on April 8, 1921. R. O'CONNELL, OF ARMS AND MEN 271 (1989). The opinion of the President of the Naval War College carried some weight. Along with the Chief of Naval Operations, Commandant of the Marine Corps, and head of the Office of Naval Intelligence, he served as an ex-officio member of the General Board of the United States Navy, which served as an advisory board to the Secretary of the Navy for program planning and the formulation of ship characteristics. S. ROSKILL, *supra*, at 20, 26–27.

103. N. POLMAR, *id.* at 44–45; and A. HURLEY, BILLY MITCHELL: CRUSADER FOR AIR POWER 58–70 (1964). United States Navy opposition to strategic bombing concepts cannot be overstated. This opposition was mission- and budget-related, and would continue until the Japanese attack on Pearl Harbor destroyed the myth of battleship invulnerability, (but would return in the post-World War II interservice debates over aviation roles and missions of the Navy and Air Force). One example will be offered to illustrate the intensity of the debate. On May 12, 1938, Army Air Force B–17 aircraft intercepted the Italian liner *Rex* 776 miles off the East Coast of the United States; the photograph of the B–17 overflight appeared in more than 1,800 newspapers, magazines, and other periodicals. The following day, apparently following Navy protests, Army Chief of Staff Malin Craig directed that thereafter all over-water flights by Air Force aircraft were not to exceed a distance of one hundred miles from the shore—the logic being that attacks at a greater distance were a Navy mission. D. COPP, A FEW GREAT CAPTAINS 418–24 (1980).

104. N. POLMAR, *supra* note 102, at 50. The United States was building two large battle cruisers (*Lexington* and *Saratoga*) when the treaty was signed. The two ships were redesignated as aircraft carriers and assigned to the yet unfilled treaty category for aircraft carrier tonnage. Both were still formidable ships when World War II started.

to aircraft carriers. Both navies essentially regarded the carriers and their aircraft complement as scouting rather than offensive forces. Even if used for bombing operations against land targets, the range of the aircraft was not significantly greater than that of naval gunfire and the weight of the attack was considerably less. Hence, naval "humanitarianism" in the upcoming Hague meetings was fundamental self-protection. There also was a tinge of national security interest. Japan completed its first aircraft carrier, the *Hosho*, in December 1922, and a British test pilot made the first landing on her deck, February 22, 1923, three days after the conclusion of the Hague Commission of Jurists.[105]

But Britain's greatest threat remained France, in that French airpower capabilities were on the rise. Having learned the painful lesson during World War I that Great Britain no longer was an island, the British were quite anxious to place limitations on the ability of any potential enemy to attack the British Isles. For Britain, development of limitations on strategic bombing would serve economic as well as national security purposes, while U.S. interests were limited to the former.

The consideration within the U.S. and British delegations up to this point was with the legality of targets and the depth of the extended battlefield. Another question was the issue of collateral damage to civilian objects or injury or death to civilians. The draft U.S. Army rules provided in part: "In conducting a bombardment [by air], the obligation of a belligerent is discharged if due care is exercised not to injure objects which happen to be in the vicinity of the permitted target. . . ." The U.S. Navy rules stated: "Injuries to non-combatants and to places excluded [by the rules] which is incidental to legitimate bombardment can not be regarded as unlawful, but it shall be the duty of the belligerent conducting a bombardment to exercise due care to confine the injury as much as possible to the objectives not prohibited."

Two noteworthy matters were contained in these drafts. The Navy provision was the first to address the issue of collateral injury to noncombatants, while both the Army and Navy proposals established ordinary care as the standard for an attacker in carrying out an aerial attack.

B. Proposed Rules for Wartime Aviation

The Commission of Jurists and its Military and Naval Advisors convened at The Hague on December 11, 1922, with delegations in attendance from the United Kingdom, United States, France, Italy, Japan, and the Netherlands. Germany, still ostracized by her former enemies, was not invited. The charter enjoined negotiators to consider the regulation of aviation in time of war, to include regulations for aerial bombardment. During the first ten days of meetings, discussion focused on the British and American drafts. Following adjournment for the Christmas and New Year's holidays, a subcommittee was formed to address separately the issues related to aviation. The Subcommittee on Aviation met from January 8 through the balance of the month, at which time plenary sessions of the Commission resumed.

C. Aerial Bombardment

John Bassett Moore, writing after the conference, observed that "From the begin-

105. N. POLMAR, *supra* note 102, 35–37; COX, *The Rise and Fall of the Imperial Japanese Air Forces, reprinted in* 27 AEROSPACE HIST. 74–86 (June 1980); H. JENTSCHURA, D. JUNG, & P. MICKEL, WARSHIPS OF THE IMPERIAL JAPANESE FLEET 1969–1945, 40–42 (1977); R. LAYMAN, BEFORE THE AIRCRAFT CARRIER 83–90 (1989). Layman details early aircraft carrier developments throughout the world in this treatise.

ning of the sessions, . . . it was generally felt that perhaps the severest test of the possibility of a general agreement would be found in the efforts of the Commission to regulate the subject of bombardment from the air."[106] Although similar in effect, the British and American drafts differed in their approach to the issue. The British proposal phrased its draft in terms of attacks upon "military objectives," without defining the term, while the U.S. draft designated specific objects which might be bombed while avoiding the use of "military objective" or "military target." As Ambassador Moore observed, "The British delegation set great store by the phrase 'military objective' as having a limitative effect, while the delegation of the United States thought the phrase left too much to the discretion of the individual commander."[107]

While all subcommittee members favored adopting rules that would protect the civilian population, there was disagreement as to the best way in which to reach this objective and as to the terms by which these rules should be expressed. Japan and the Netherlands were in favor of the greatest restriction on bombing, including a total prohibition on bombing outside the immediate area of military operations. Subcommittee members were unanimous in accepting the principle that enemy forces, military works, lines of military communication, military or naval bases, and depots of arms, ammunition, or war materiel could be attacked. But no draft formula gained a majority of votes; the fundamental difficulty was "the determination of the conditions under which the bombardment of objects, intrinsically liable to attack, was to be forbidden, when they were found in centers of population."[108]

D. Analysis of the Arguments

The issue as described begs the question in two respects. First, it assumes that a lawful target situated in a populated area should be protected from attack. Such a rule would invite mischief on the part of a defender, who could resolve target vulnerability problems simply by constructing high-value targets in populated areas, or encouraging urban growth around preexisting targets. The United States learned this to its regret—and at the cost of many aircraft and the loss of many American lives—in the Rolling Thunder bombing campaign conducted against North Vietnam from 1965 to 1968. At the outset of that campaign Secretary of Defense Robert McNamara placed off-limits targets located in populated areas, and personally selected all fixed targets authorized for attack. In response, the North Vietnamese stored war materiel, parked military convoys, and located air defense sites (fighter aircraft, antiaircraft guns, and surface-to-air missile sites) in populated areas, making them immune from attack under the restrictions established and openly publicized by Secretary McNamara.[109]

The second error was the assumption that responsibility for avoidance of collateral civilian casualties or damage to civilian objects should be shifted to the attacker. It is

---

106. J. Moore, International Law and Some Current Illusions 182, 194 (1924).

107. *Id.* at 194. In this regard the Ambassador's philosophy suffered from a philosophical deficiency. Commanders generally work in a "target-rich" environment, and targeting doctrine over the years has emphasized attack on those targets posing the greatest threat, or which would result in the greatest damage to the enemies' war effort. The doctrinal philosophy encourages efficiency in the selection of targets and employment of the commander's military assets, while arguing against attack on nonmilitary targets or indiscriminate attack on the civilian population.

108. *Id.* at 197.

109. Parks, *Rolling Thunder and the Law of War*, 33 Air U. Rev. 2–23 (Jan.–Feb. 1982). For a pilot's view of the devastating effect of these restrictions, *see* J. Broughton, Thud Ridge (1969); J. Broughton, Going Downtown (1988); and J. Nicholas & B. Tillman, On Yankee Station (1986).

a shared obligation of the attacker, defender, and the civilian population. The objective of a defender's antiair forces is to protect military targets from attack through defenses that either destroy attacking aircraft or cause those aircraft to miss the target; the bomb that misses its intended target (or the crashing aircraft) may cause damage to civilian objects or injury to civilians in the vicinity of the target. Thus, if a defender has succeeded in forcing the attacker to miss the target, in so doing he knowingly has placed his civilian population at greater risk.

In this sense, a collateral error exists because there is an assumption that responsibility for incidental damage or injury always can be attributed to someone; yet when an attacking force is carrying out a lawful attack on a legitimate target, and the defender is using its antiair capabilities lawfully to defend targets, responsibility for collateral damage, injury, or death usually will be shared, or may be attributable only to the fog of war. In many cases the actions of the attacker may be consistent with the law of war, yet actions of the defender will cause the attack to result in collateral civilian casualties. The actions of the defender are an intervening cause for which the attacker is not responsible.

This concept, though unstated as such, has been recognized in naval and land warfare for centuries. Thus, a naval blockade may prevent food from reaching an enemy, though the modern law of war admonishes that a blockade should not be intended to starve the civilian population. The nation executing the blockade agrees to permit sufficient food for the civilian population, which the defender promptly gives to his military; and the civilian population starves. The nation executing the blockade, when faulted for starving innocent civilians, would counter that it was the intervening action of the defender that caused the civilians to starve. That defense would be appropriate. Yet for inexplicable reasons the general public, diplomats, and international lawyers have had difficulty in applying this same concept to the actions of a defender in an aerial attack.[110]

Finally, the civilian population and individual civilians must assume some common sense responsibility for the risks of war. The individual civilian who continues to live adjacent to a factory or other facility that clearly would be a lawful target must assume a certain degree of risk for his or her decision. Both Germany and Great Britain recognized this during World War II by evacuating nonessential personnel from cities or areas containing military targets, or by requiring those who remained to construct individual air raid protection or move to air raid shelters during an attack.[111]

---

110. The difficulty has been caused in large measure by the necessity for secrecy of nations at war in the struggle for measures, countermeasures, counter-countermeasures, etc., particularly in highly sensitive areas such as electronic warfare. It has been only over the past decade that much of the electronic warfare battle of World War II has been revealed. *See* Jones, *Scientific Intelligence*, 567 J. ROYAL UNITED SER. INST. 352–69 (Aug. 1947); R. JONES, MOST SECRET WAR: BRITISH SCIENTIFIC INTELLIGENCE 1939–1945 (London, 1978); A. PRICE, INSTRUMENTS OF DARKNESS (London, 1978); M. STREETLY, CONFOUND AND DESTROY (London, 1978); and A. PRICE, I THE HISTORY OF U.S. ELECTRONIC WARFARE (1984).

An example from the World War II electronic battlefield suggests the difficulty of accountability. On May 31, 1941, 90 Luftwaffe aircraft set out to conduct a night attack on Bristol and Liverpool, depending upon ground-based radio beams (*Knickebein*) for guidance to their target areas. But British countermeasures jammed the radio beams, possibly causing one attacker to bomb Dublin in neutral Ireland, killing 34 civilians. Winston Churchill attributed this attack to British countermeasures based upon a suggestion made to him in 1946 by R. V. Jones. W. CHURCHILL, THEIR FINEST HOUR 389 (London, 1949). The evidence of a causal relationship is inconclusive, further illustrating the problems of accountability in the fog of war. *Cf.* A. PRICE, *supra*, at 37; and R. FISK, IN TIME OF WAR 435 (1983).

111. *See* T. O'BRIEN, CIVIL DEFENCE (London, 1955); *Civil Defense Division—Final Report*, THE UNITED STATES STRATEGIC BOMBING SURVEY (1945); and STANFORD RESEARCH INSTITUTE, APPENDIXES

E. The Hague Aerial Bombardment Rules

The delegates at The Hague in February 1923 had difficulty reconciling these problems with a desire to improve protection for the civilian population. The Aviation Subcommittee turned the matter over to the overall committee, which reduced the issue to two drafts, one Italian, one American, in which there was substantial difference.[112] Following a plea to all conferees by Ambassador Moore, the elected chairman of the Commission, the delegates worked for the next five hours to draft the following, which were adopted unanimously.[113]

> Art. 22. Aerial bombardment for the purpose of terrorizing the civilian population, of destroying or damaging private property not of military character, or of injuring non-combatants is prohibited.
>
> Art. 23. Aerial bombardment for the purpose of enforcing compliance with requisitions in kind or payment of contributions in money is prohibited.
>
> Art. 24. (1) Aerial bombardment is legitimate only when directed at a military objective, that is to say, an object of which the destruction or injury would constitute a distinct military advantage to the belligerent.
>
> (2) Such bombardment is legitimate only when directed exclusively at the following objectives: military forces; military works; military establishments or depots; factories constituting important and well-known centres engaged in the manufacture of arms, ammunition or distinctively military supplies; lines of communication or transportation used for military purposes.
>
> (3) The bombardment of cities, towns, villages, dwellings or buildings not in the immediate neighbourhood of the operations of land forces is prohibited. In cases where the objectives specified in paragraph (2) are so situated, that they cannot be bombarded without the indiscriminate bombardment of the civilian population, the aircraft must abstain from bombardment.
>
> (4) In the immediate neighbourhood of the operations of land forces, the bombardment of cities, towns, villages, dwellings or buildings is legitimate provided that there exists a reasonable presumption that the military concentration is sufficiently important to justify such bombardment having regard to the danger thus caused to the civilian population.[114]

F. Analysis of the Rules

Problems of Codification. The problem of aerial bombardment was the most important and the most difficult with which the Commission had to deal. Nations generally agree with the principle of discrimination, from the standpoints of military efficiency and humanitarianism. But there were in 1923, and remain today, fundamental problems with codification of appropriate language that would be equally applicable to all nations, under all circumstances, and that would not provide a tactical or strategic advantage to one nation over another, nor establish rules for aerial bombardment that are fundamentally different from those applicable to land-based artillery or naval gunfire. The Hague Air Rules, adopted by the Commission upon conclusion of its meetings on February 19, 1923, were unsuccessful in accomplishing this. While espousing humanitarian rules, in the words of Admiral Rodgers,

1 THROUGH 7 TO THE HAMBURG POLICE PRESIDENT'S REPORT ON THE LARGE SCALE AIR ATTACKS ON HAMBURG, GERMANY 39–271 (1968), which contains civil defense materials for one German city. *See also* R. INGLIS, THE CHILDREN'S WAR: EVACUATION 1939–1945 (London, 1989).

112. J. MOORE, *supra* note 106, at 197–99.

113. J. MOORE, *supra* note 106, at 199–201.

114. SCHINDLER & TOMAN, *supra* note 27, at 142.

"each nation seemed chiefly guided by the principle of promoting its own national policies, and its position in the world. . . . Each national delegation was a unit in standing for a code which should favor its national situation."[115]

Differing Viewpoints. The formulation of balanced, practical rules also suffered from a fundamental gap between the international lawyers who constituted the Commission and their technical (military) advisors. As Admiral Rodgers observed,

> The majority of commissioners had little or no technical acquaintance with the art and practice of war. Some seemed inclined to believe that the course of war, even when great national emotions were aroused, might be guided by the phrases of a code of rules previously agreed upon. They did not appear always to realize that at any time the code of accepted rules of warfare is based almost entirely on past experience and that when a new war arises, new social, economic, and belligerent conditions will make the existing code more or less unsuitable to meet the exigencies of the situation as developed in the course of the current war.[116]

As the 1923 Hague Air Rules[117] never were adopted by any nation, they were an immediate and total failure. This occurred in part because of a skepticism towards the law of war that existed during the interwar period,[118] but in the main because international lawyers endeavored to draft a set of rules that were totally at odds with state practice, technological advances, and military thinking.[119]

Aerial Law of War, 1923. If it is possible to summarize the law of war as it existed at that time, it could be reduced to two principles: (a) that the indiscriminate (that is, intentional) attack of the civilian population as such was prohibited, but that (b) a legitimate military objective could be attacked wherever located so long as ordinary care was exercised in its attack; that is, that collateral civilian casualties were not the concern of the attacker but, by state practice, were regarded as an inevitable consequence of bombardment and a legitimate way to destroy an enemy's will to resist. The historic distinction of noncombatant immunity had been tied to the range of artillery; anything within artillery range was regarded as part of the battle-

115. Rodgers, *The Laws of War Concerning Aviation and Radio*, 17 AM. J. INT'L L. 629–40, at 633 (1923).

116. *Id.* at 633.

117. SCHINDLER & TOMAN, *supra* note 27, at 147–57.

118. *See* J. Spaight, *The Doctrine of Air Force Necessity*, 6 BRITISH YEAR BOOK INT'L L. 4 (1925): "To imagine that, because of any paper rule, this foundation [attack of a military target, wherever located without concern for collateral civilian casualties] will not be attacked is to dwell in a fool's paradise. . . . No restrictive covenant can avail to prevent that which is the nature of things."

Similarly, international lawyer J. W. Garner, addressing the Grotius Society in London on January 15, 1936, observed:

> Since the World War . . . there has been a disposition to neglect the law of war and to abandon, in the main, further effort to rehabilitate and strengthen it. As everyone knows, the law of war was very much discredited by the events of the World War. Mankind generally lost faith in its utility. Many persons spoke of it more or less contemptuously as the "so-called" law of war, as if a rule of conduct embodied in a convention dealing with war is any less a rule of law than one embodied in a convention dealing with matters of peace. University professors dropped the subject from their courses, and even text writers omitted it from their books, or at least passed it over lightly. As you know, the curatorium of The Hague Academy of International Law has not permitted the law of war to be discussed at any sessions of the Academy.

Garner, *The Outlook for the Law of War and of Neutrality*, 22 TRANSACTIONS OF THE GROTIUS SOCIETY 1 (1936).

119. Colby, *supra* note 101, at 713: "In August, 1922, the International Law Association at its meeting in Buenos Aires, declared that the radius of operations of military aircraft ought to be restricted, and thus attempted to take from armies all the advantage which an aircraft . . . permits. These were vain and fruitless efforts to send the science of war backward in its steps." The work of the International Law Association undoubtedly formed a part of the basis for Ambassador Moore's support for the Navy draft, and in fact may have been a basis for the Navy draft.

field and at risk. The battlefield was extended by the industrialization of nation-states and by a capacity for attack of military objects beyond artillery range. The Hague Air Rules of 1923 attempted to stem this tide in the following ways.

Prohibiting Terrorization. In the practice of land and naval warfare, destruction of civilian objects was regarded as lawful as a psychological means for impressing upon an enemy nation the prudence of surrender. While a line between the attack on morale and terrorization existed—the former being ancillary, the latter intentional—the principal distinction lay in military efficiency. It would be inefficient to shell or bomb merely to terrorize, but an attack on morale ancillary to the bombardment of military targets was efficient, lawful, and an accepted practice. Article 22 was perceived as limiting this practice with respect to airplanes, but not for land artillery or naval bombardment. Such a proposal doubtless was viewed at the time as not only a constraint on air operations, but by land and naval warfare authorities as a dangerous precedent for their operations.

Limiting the Range of Attack. While article 24(4) applied to aerial bombing the same degree of permissibility for widespread destruction given land bombardment, effective use of aircraft was limited by this article to the range of artillery, or certainly was perceived that way.[120]

Military Objective. There is no dispute that the purpose of all bombardment, whether ground, naval, or air, was and remains to attack military objectives. Articles 24(1) and (2) were potentially troubling for several reasons:

(1) For the first time, article 24(1) impressed upon an attacker an obligation for concern for collateral civilian casualties in the attack of individual targets. However praiseworthy this may appear in today's peacetime environment, this was a 180-degree change of course in then-existing bombardment philosophy. Again, while it applied only to aerial bombardment, it could not have escaped notice as a precedent by land and naval authorities.

(2) The term military objective used in article 24(1) was undefined. As Webster and Frankland correctly noted,

> Part of the argument centered upon the difference between 'military' and 'civilian' targets and developed somewhat along the lines of the conventions which had been attached to military and naval warfare. There was a school of thought which demanded that bombing should be restricted to 'military targets' which could be destroyed without undue risk to 'civilian' life or property. This argument turned upon what was meant by the term 'military target.' Clearly, a tank on the battlefield was a military target, but was a tank on the assembly line in a factory a civilian target? Clearly a soldier in the front line was a military target, but was a worker engaged in the manufacture of his rifle a civilian target? There was also the question of what constituted 'undue risk' to civilian life and property. A battleship at sea, it might be assumed, would be manned only by naval personnel and a badly aimed bomb would be unlikely to fall anywhere other than in the water. But the same battleship in port might have civilian workers on board and a badly aimed bomb might destroy anything from a warehouse to a church.
>
> Obviously a strict interpretation of these obscure questions meant the absolute prohibition of strategic bombing and the confinement of all operations to the actual area of land fighting or to war ships at sea. . . . In modern war between major powers there is, after all, practically nothing worth attacking which does not have some bearing upon the national war effort.[121]

This attempt at limitation on the attack of military objectives (or targets, a term regarded as synonymous) must be viewed through the eyes of airpower planners of

120. *See* Chambliss, *Air Bombardment Regulation*, 60 U.S. NAVAL INST. PROC. 1577–81 (Nov. 1934).

121. 1 C. WEBSTER & N. FRANKLAND, *supra* note 81, at 14–15.

the time. Writing five years after the 1923 Hague conference, Air Marshal Trenchard commented:

> To attack the armed forces is . . . to attack the enemy at his strongest point. On the other hand, by attacking the sources from which these armed forces are maintained infinitely more effect is obtained. In the course of a day's attack upon the aerodromes of the enemy perhaps 50 aeroplanes could be destroyed; whereas a modern industrial state will produce 100 in a day—production will far more than replace any destruction we can hope to do in the forward zone. On the other hand, by attacking the enemy's factories, then output is reduced by a much greater proportion.[122]

Writing in the same vein, also in 1928, G. F. Milne, Chief of the Imperial General Staff said:

> [Military] objectives will, naturally, differ from time to time, and their relative importance can only be measured by the influence they happen to be exerting at any given moment. For instance, when an enemy is concentrating for an attack, the dislocation of his railways and other means of communication may produce results which will influence the course of the war far more than will the bombardment of some of his munition factories.[123]

Air Marshal Trenchard's and Sir Milne's statements were consistent with the law of war as it existed, in that they emphasized the efficient use of military force. They also illustrated the dynamic nature of targeting, as the value of a potential military objective may vary depending upon the circumstances ruling at the time. But Trenchard accomplished what the negotiators at The Hague failed to do; he defined military objective as:

> any objectives which will contribute effectively towards the destruction of the enemy's means of resistance and the lowering of his determination to fight.[124]

Trenchard and others, whether military officers or international lawyers, understood these deficiencies in the Hague Air Rules, and for that reason condemnation of the rules was virtually unanimous.[125]

(3) The limited nature of the list of military objectives contained in article 23(2) was inconsistent with the practice of nations as well as military thinking. James Maloney Spaight, a member of the British delegation to the 1922–23 Hague conferences and employee of the Air Ministry, illustrated the deficiency of the list in his 1924 book, *Air Power and War Rights.*[126] He provided a three-page list of targets attacked during World War I, such as an aqueduct; blast furnaces; electric works; gas works; iron works and foundries; magneto works; motor works; steel works; and petroleum, oil, and lubricant production, manufacturing, storage facilities, that would be excluded from attack by article 23(2).[127] One need only carry out a quick mental review of targets attacked by all parties during World War II (or regarded as lawful today) to see the shortcomings of the list contained in article 23(2).

---

122. IV C. WEBSTER & N. FRANKLAND, *supra* note 81, at 74.
123. *Id.* at 78.
124. *Id.* at 74. The term "military objective" remained undefined in the law of war for another half century. Ultimately it was defined in article 52(2) of Additional Protocol I of 1977 to the Geneva Conventions of 1949 as "those objects which by their nature, location, purpose or use make an effective contribution to military action and whose total or partial destruction, capture or neutralization, in the circumstances ruling at the time, offers a definite military advantage." *See* SCHINDLER & TOMAN, *supra* note 27, at 305–523, 551–618.
125. *See* Colby, *supra* note 101; Quindry, *supra* note 57, at 474–509; and particularly J. SPAIGHT, AIR POWER AND WAR RIGHTS 226–59 (London, 1924).
126. J. SPAIGHT, *supra* note 125.
127. *Id.* at 233–35.

(4) Article 24(2) further limited attack to military forces, thereby turning a blind eye to the important role played by civilians directly supporting a nation's war effort. This insistence upon maintenance of an obsolete distinction did not escape criticism by international lawyers of that era, and further contributed to the demise of the 1923 Hague Air Rules.[128]

Risk of Collateral Civilian Casualties. Article 22(3), in prohibiting the attack of the targets listed in article 22(2) if indiscriminate bombardment (another undefined term) could not be avoided, was a substantial shift in responsibility for avoidance of collateral civilian casualties from the defender and the civilian (however that term may be defined) to the attacker. Thus, bombing of military objectives beyond the tactical battlefield became dependent upon effect or result rather than intent. Two historical examples illustrate the difficulty of such a rule:

(1) During the 1864 Union siege of Atlanta, General J. B. Hood, commanding general of the Confederate forces defending Atlanta, wrote to Union General W. T. Sherman to condemn shelling that resulted in civilian casualties. Sherman replied, criticizing Hood for his failure to evacuate the civilians from Atlanta while placing his defenses "on a line so close to town that every cannon-shot and many musket-shots from our line of investment, that overshot its mark, went into the habitations of women and children."[129]

(2) As noted by one critic, during World War I "Two British [airplanes] were out to raid Brussels. . . . They came in sight of a Zeppelin and brought it down. The debris fell upon a convent near Ghent, and killed three nuns. Such are the consequences of war."[130]

There are at least two difficulties with the rule set forth in article 22(3). The first is that it placed a burden to avoid indiscriminate attack upon an attacker, even though the means that might lead to an "indiscriminate" attack were not within his exclusive control. The second concerns the potential for assessment of an attack based upon results rather than intent, a concept seriously flawed, as one critic observed at that time:

> The question is a question of accuracy and not a question of intent. No belligerent should be required to forfeit the normal percentage of hits which might be expected on his target, simply because there will be a percentage of 'misses.' The percentage of 'hits' is a military calculation. By his effective five per cent he may destroy his 'military objective' wherever the other ninety-five per cent may go. By it he may be able to win the war. It is not a question of an intention to hit civilians instead of military depots, or of an intention to terrorize generally. Like the actuary figuring expectant mortality for a life insurance company, he cannot foretell what will happen in any individual case, [footnote omitted] but he can tell what his average will be. His intent is to place 'the maximum number of hits' on his target according to his average accuracy.[131]

---

128. *See* Garner, *International Regulation of Air Warfare*, 3 AIR L. REV. 103–26, at 117 (Apr. 1932). *See also* J. STONE, *supra* note 53, at 338, where he observes:

> The bounds between the legitimate pursuit of victory, and the infliction of suffering unnecessary to victory, may in words seem clear and settled. Concretely, however, they have been revolutionized in the last half century. When air supremacy becomes a critical factor in victory, and when sixty civilians and masses of industrial equipment must stand behind each plane in the air, the humane principle of civilian immunity retreats before the search of victory by the cheapest and quickest means.

129. W. SHERMAN, *supra* note 50, at 112–29, contains the entire exchange of correspondence.

130. Colby, *supra* note 101, at 705.

131. Colby, *supra* note 101, at 710; and Quindry, *supra* note 57, at 500–01, which noted that in a 1927 United States Air Corps peacetime test by aircraft against a bridge four hundred feet wide (approximately 120 meters), it was estimated that only 11% of the bombs would strike the target. In the

But the potential difficulty of this concept was perhaps best explained by Air Marshal Trenchard:

> As regards the question of legality, no authority would contend it is unlawful to bomb military objectives, wherever situated. . . . Such objectives may be situated in centres of population in which their destruction from the Air will result in casualties also to the neighboring civilian population, in the same way as the long-range bombardment of a defended coastal town by a naval force results also in the incidental destruction of civilian life and property. The fact that air attack may have that result is no reason for regarding the bombing as illegitimate provided all reasonable care is taken to confine the scope of the bombing to the military objective. Otherwise a belligerent would be able to secure complete immunity for his war manufactures and depots merely by locating them in a large city, which would, in effect, become *neutral* territory—a position which the opposing belligerent would never accept.[132]

G. The Result

The 1923 Hague Air Rules suffered an ignominious death, doomed from the outset by language that established rules for black-and-white situations in a combat environment permeated by shades of gray. While Japan and the United States expressed some support for their adoption, the European nations were more cautious owing to their distrust of and proximity to one another. As aircraft capabilities grew, national security concerns increased. The launching of the U.S. aircraft carrier *Lexington* in 1925 changed the marginal support for the 1923 Hague Air Rules by the United States to nonsupport, as the big ship caught the public's fancy and, with it, increased interest in the importance of aviation to national security.[133] Rapidly the 1923 Hague Air Rules drifted into obscurity, adopted by no nation, and completely ignored by most aviation historians.[134]

The 1923 Hague Air Rules were the first, last, and only effort at regulation of aerial bombardment before World War II. Nations expressed interest in forms of restraint on other occasions, most associated with the Geneva Disarmament Conference, and all were illusory if not contrived. The details of this busy but legislatively unproductive period are provided elsewhere, and will not be elaborated here.[135] Writing on the eve of World War II and sixteen years after his participation in the conference that produced the 1923 Hague Air Rules, Vice Admiral W. L. Rodgers concluded:

> The extensive use of airplanes in bombing cities and noncombatants is not likely to be controlled by pre-war agreements. In former times centers of industry and accumulations of supplies were small, and being scattered in many places, most of them were inaccessible to the enemy. Now

---

actual bombing tests, 27% of the bombs struck the target. Quindry commented: "Even under these conditions, where the bombs are dropped from a relatively low altitude [6,000 feet, or 1,800 meters] and by especially trained personnel, a great majority of them will hit only in the vicinity of the objective."

132. IV C. Webster & N. Frankland, *supra* note 81, at 73.

133. R. Bilstein, Flight Patterns 25 (Athens, 1983).

134. The records of the Commission are contained in Commission of Jurists to Consider and Report Upon the Revision of the Rules of Warfare (The Hague, 1923). *See also* Brune, *An Effort to Regulate Aerial Bombing: The Hague Commission of Jurists, 1922–23*, 29 Aerospace Hist. 183–85 (Sept. 1982); and Wyman, *The First Air Rules of Warfare*, 35 Air U. Rev. 94–102 (Mar.–Apr. 1984).

135. H. Hyde, British Air Policy Between the Wars (London, 1976); B. Powers, *supra* note 81, at 107–207; U. Bialer, The Shadow of the Bomber: The Fear of Air Attack and British Politics 1932–1939 (London, 1980); L. Kennett, *supra* note 38, at 58–71; M. Smith, British Air Strategy Between the Wars (London, 1984); W. Murray, Strategy for Defeat: The Luftwaffe, 1933–1945 (Maxwell Air Force Base, Ala., 1983); W. Murray, Luftwaffe, *supra* note 85; R. Overy, Goering 37 (London, 1984). But *cf.* N. Jones, The Beginnings of Strategic Air Power (London, 1987).

> they are larger and more concentrated and everywhere accessible to airplane attack. In many cases they will be worth attacking and will suffer because their destruction will tend to end the war. The incidental presence of property and noncombatants will confer no immunity on property capable of aiding the national resistance.[136]

VIII. LAST-DITCH EFFORTS

As the war clouds over Europe darkened, and with the experience of the wars in China, Spain, and Ethiopia in mind, several last-ditch efforts were made to establish bombing standards. During debate in the House of Commons on June 21, 1938, British Prime Minister Neville Chamberlain suggested three basic rules for bombing.

> 1. It is against international law to bomb civilians as such and to make deliberate attacks upon civilian populations.
>
> 2. Targets which are aimed at from the air must be legitimate military objectives and must be capable of identification.
>
> 3. Reasonable care must be taken in attacking those military objectives so that by carelessness a civilian population in the neighborhood is not bombed.[137]

Although these rules contain a number of flaws,[138] they were adopted by a nonbinding League of Nations resolution on September 30, 1938.[139] On the commencement of general hostilities on September 1, 1939, President Franklin D. Roosevelt sent the following message to the warring nations: "I am . . . addressing this urgent brief to every government which may be engaged in hostilities publicly to affirm its determination that its armed forces shall in no event, and under no

---

136. Rodgers, *Future International Laws of War*, 33 AM. J. INT'L L. 441–51, at 450 (1939). Admiral Rodgers was not alone in his views. International lawyer J. W. Garner observed in 1936:

> The fact of the matter is the law of war . . . is . . . in a some what chaotic state, and when the next great war comes, if unhappily it does come—it will have to be carried on in large measure without rules that have been agreed upon, or with rules which have not been settled and as to the meaning of which there has been no argument. As to air warfare I think we can say there is practically no conventional International Law dealing with it.

Garner, *supra* note 118, at 5. In fact, the British Air Raid Precautions Committee expressed no confidence in the unadopted 1923 Hague Air Rules or in the law of war for protection of the civilian population against air attack. T. O'BRIEN, *supra* note 111, at 18. For further temper of the times, *see also* H. HYDE & G. NUTTALL, AIR DEFENSE AND THE CIVIL POPULATION (London, 1937); J. SPAIGHT, AIR POWER IN THE NEXT WAR (London, 1938); H. THUILLIER, GAS IN THE NEXT WAR (London, 1939); and L. HART, THE DEFENCE OF BRITAIN (London, 1939). As Williamson Murray notes, "British alarms over the 'growing air threat' and hopes of realizing an air limitation agreement between the European powers were a useful diplomatic tool that allowed Hitler to manipulate the island power." W. MURRAY LUFTWAFFE, *supra* note 85, at 16. *See also* W. MURRAY, THE CHANGE IN THE EUROPEAN BALANCE OF POWER, 1938–1939 (Princeton, 1984), for further description of this period. *See also* J. Spaight, *The Chaotic State of the International Law Governing Bombardment*, 9 THE A.F.Q. 24–32 1938.

137. J. SPAIGHT, AIR POWER AND WAR RIGHTS 257–58 (3d ed., London, 1947).

138. While the first rule is an accurate reflection of the law as it existed at the time as well as today, the difficulty with the last two rules lay in their favoring a defender (who would endeavor to camouflage and defend targets) over an attacker (who was required to identify that which the defender was concealing, dispersing, and defending). Although "reasonable care" may be an appropriate standard suggesting good-faith intent or effort on the part of an attacker, "carelessness" (or "negligence," as the League of Nations resolution was worded) is a less-than-perfect legal standard so long as an attacker is not in control of all elements affecting his degree of care.

139. LEAGUE OF NATIONS OFFICIAL JOURNAL Document A.69, 1938 IX, 15–16 (Special Supplement 182 [1938]). SCHINDLER & TOMAN, *supra* note 27, at 221–22.

circumstances, undertake the bombardment from the air of civilian populations or of unfortified cities.''[140]

Although most nations responded favorably, an affirmative response to such a plea is not a legally binding act; neither the Chamberlain/League of Nations rules nor the Roosevelt pledge were to have any effect on the conduct of the aerial bombing campaigns of World War II.[141] Klaus Maier provides a succinct summary for the interwar legislative process: ''Attempts to limit air war by international agreement failed, because the conflicting national interests and divergent concepts for the use of air power could not be reconciled.''[142]

IX. DETERMINING THE LAW: OTHER SOURCES

There are other ways of determining what the law of war relating to aerial bombardment was during World War II. Each will be addressed briefly.

A. Court Decisions

In 1927, a Greco-German Mixed Arbitral Tribunal constituted in accordance with the Versailles Peace Treaty considered a claim against Germany for compensation on account of damage suffered as the result of the aerial bombing of Salonica by German aircraft in January 1916. As a result of the bombing, nonmilitary goods belonging to the plaintiff were destroyed. Judgment was rendered in favor of the plaintiff on the basis that German authorities failed to provide warning of the impending attack, as required by article 26 of Hague Convention IV of 1907. But for the failure to warn, the German attack would have been lawful, and the collateral damage to plaintiff's goods would have been a consequence of war for which the plaintiff could not have recovered damages. The case is of little value in determination of the issue before us.[143]

Although Professor Telford Taylor has intimated that the 1940 Luftwaffe attacks on Britain were illegal,[144] this was not the position he took as the Chief Counsel for War Crimes at the Nuernberg War Crimes Trials. In his final report, then-Brigadier General Taylor observed:

> In the course of preparing the indictment for the first Nuernberg trial, it became apparent that . . . 'combat crimes' would prove of considerably less importance. . . . Many of the provisions of the Hague Conventions [of 1907] regarding unlawful means of combat . . . were antiquarian. Others had been observed only partially during the First World War and almost completely disregarded during the Second World War. . . . If the first badly bombed cities—Warsaw, Rotterdam, Belgrade, and London—suffered at the hands of the Germans and not the Allies, nonetheless the ruins of German and Japanese cities were the results not of reprisal but of deliberate policy, and bore witness that aerial bombardment of cities and factories has become a recognized part of modern warfare as carried on by all nations.

140. I FOREIGN RELATIONS OF THE U.S., 1939, 541–42 (1956).

141. *Id.* at 542–57. *See* J. SPAIGHT, *supra* note 137, 259–63 for a critical analysis.

142. Maier, *Total War and German Air Doctrine Before the Second World War*, in THE GERMAN MILITARY IN THE AGE OF TOTAL WAR 211 (W. Deist, ed. 1985).

143. *Coenca Brothers v. Germany* (1927), in ANNUAL DIGEST OF PUBLIC INTERNATIONAL LAW CASES 570–72 (McNair and Lauterpacht, eds. London, 1931) [hereinafter ANNUAL DIGEST]. The warning requirement in article 26 of the Annex to Hague IV of 1907 states that ''the officer in command of an attacking force must, before commencing a bombardment, except in cases of an assault, do all in his power to warn the authorities.'' At the time of the German attack, Greece was neutral. Once hostilities have begun, in actual practice the warning requirement is less of an issue due to the exception for assaults. *See also Kereadolu v. Germany* 516 ANNUAL DIGEST (1930).

144. T. TAYLOR, THE BREAKING WAVE 112–18 (1967).

The indictment in the first Nuernberg trial, accordingly, contained no charges against the defendants arising out of their conduct of the war in the air.[145]

The Charter of the Nuernberg International Military Tribunal listed "indiscriminate bombing" as a crime recognizable by the Tribunal, but in practice the United Nations War Crimes Commission routinely rejected cases alleging indiscriminate bombing if the bombarded towns or cities contained military objectives.[146]

B. Law of War Manuals

Another way of determining the law of war at a particular period of time—such as in the decade immediately preceding World War II—is to look at the law of war manuals of the military services of the nations involved in that conflict. While military law of war manuals are not regarded as policy statements binding upon a nation and its military forces, they are at least an indication of a nation's probable interpretation of the law of war. Were an air staff planner to wonder if the plans he was writing were consistent with the law of war, in all likelihood he would go to the law of war manual. A review of available materials for the period provides the following information:

United States. The principal law of war manual for operations on or over land was *U.S. Army Field Manual* 27–10, "Rules of Land Warfare." There were two editions available to planners: the 1914 edition (updated to 1917) and the 1940 edition. Other than defining what constituted a "defended place," neither manual provided much information beyond that actually contained in Hague Convention IV of 1907. Guidance to members of the U.S. Army Air Corps preparing the various war plans, then, would have been minimal at best.[147]

In May of 1941, the U.S. Navy issued "Tentative Instructions for the Navy of the United States Governing Maritime and Aerial Warfare." Two paragraphs provided guidance to the reader who consulted the manual:

> 229. Aerial bombardment for the purpose of terrorizing the civilian population, of destroying or damaging private property not of a military character, or of injuring noncombatants is prohibited. In any bombardment every practicable precaution should be taken to avoid injury to civilians.
>
> 230. The bombardment of enemy troop concentrations, communication centers, lines of communications, military or naval establishments, depots of arms or war material, workshops,

---

145. T. Taylor, Final Report to the Secretary of the Army on the Nuernberg War Crimes Trials Under Control Council Law No. 10 65 (1949).

146. Brand, *The War Crimes Trials and the Laws of War*, 26 The British Year Book Int'l L. 414–27, at 419 (1949). The issue of legality of bombing was raised in other ways in some trials, as in the charge against former Luftwaffe chief Hermann Goering of devastation of towns, not justified by military necessity, in violation of the law of war. Indictment (Count Three), in I Trial of the Major War Criminals Before the International Military Tribunal 42–43 & 61–62 (1947). The issue was considered in volume IX at 175–78, 214–19, and is summarized in R. Conot, Justice of Nuremberg 334–35 (1983).

147. The United States Air Force was not formed as a separate service until September 18, 1947. U.S. Army Air Corps planners would have looked to the Army law of war manual for guidance. A separate U.S. Air Force manual on the law of war was not completed until November 19, 1976, more than three decades following the conclusion of the war, and then only after considerable resistance by the Air Staff. There were lone crusaders. *See* DeSaussure, *International Law and Aerial Bombing*, 3 Air U. Q. Rev. 23–34 (Fall 1962); DeSaussure, *The Laws of Air Warfare: Are There Any?*, 12 A. F. L. Rev. 242–51 (Fall 1970); DeSaussure, *The Laws of Air Warfare: Are There Any?*, 23 Naval War C. Rev. 35–47 (Feb. 1971); DeSaussure, *The Laws of Air Warfare: Are There Any?*, 5 Int'l Law 527–48 (July 1971). Colonel DeSaussure was an original moving force behind an Air Force law of war manual.

plants, and factories actually used for the manufacture of war material wherever situated is not prohibited.[148]

United Kingdom. The British *Manual of Military Law* was revised in 1929, with amendments to January 1936. There are no separate paragraphs addressing aerial bombardment. However, in the paragraphs regarding bombardments, assaults, and sieges, paragraph 122 states:

> No legal duty exists for the attacking force to limit bombardment to the fortifications or defended border only. On the contrary, destruction of private and public buildings by bombardment has always been, and still is, considered lawful, as it is one of the means to impress upon the local authorities the advisability of surrender.[149]

The Royal Air Force was a separate service, with its own separate law manual, and employed one of the leading experts on the law of war.[150] Yet the preface to the second (1933) edition of the British *Manual of Air Force Law* (reprinted without change in 1939) stated: "It has not yet been found possible to include in this volume a chapter relating to air warfare corresponding to the chapter on the law and usages of war on land in the Manual of Military Law."[151]

Germany. Although there was no separate Luftwaffe law of war manual, in 1936 the Luftwaffe issued service directive L. Dv. 16 entitled *The Conduct of the Air War* (Die Luftkriegfuhrung). While paragraph 186 stated unequivocally that "Attacks on cities for the purpose of terrorizing the civilian population are absolutely forbidden," the directive acknowledged that the single most important task of the Luftwaffe was an offensive against (a) the combat strength of the enemy, and (b) its population's will to resist. In order to accomplish this, the Luftwaffe should carry out offensive operations against the enemy's population and country at its most sensitive points, including economic targets. Although the directive was reissued with minor changes in 1940, these statements remained without change.[152]

148. "Tentative Instructions for the Navy of the United States Governing Maritime and Aerial Warfare," at 229–30.

149. MANUAL OF MILITARY LAW 1929, Amendment No. 12 (Jan. 1936) at 31. An Australian legal scholar of the time concluded:

> The law of war is to-day under a cloud. It is highly doubtful whether it can any longer be called 'law.' The 1929 Edition of the British Manual of Military Law recognizes this and is not able to do more than repeat the rules as they existed in 1914.

LEWIS, AUSTRALIAN MILITARY LAW 214 (1936).

The 1958 BRITISH MANUAL OF MILITARY LAW, which is the current manual, contains the following:

> The title of this Part of the Manual, 'The Law of War on Land,' makes it clear that it is not concerned with the law of warfare at sea or with aerial warfare. Nevertheless, the rules governing land combat will apply to members of naval and air forces when employed in combat duties on land.

By 1988, forty-nine years after the start of World War II, the Royal Air Force still does not have a law of war manual, despite the fact that Hague Convention IV (to which the United Kingdom has been a party since November 27, 1909) requires that each party "issue instructions to their armed forces which shall be in conformity with the Regulations respecting the laws and customs of war on land." (article 1).

150. James Maloney Spaight was the author of *Air Power and War Rights*. First published in 1924, a second edition was published in 1933. Each was far more comprehensive than any law of war manual used by any military service at that time.

151. MANUAL OF AIR FORCE LAW (2d ed. London, 1933).

152. D. IRVING, THE RISE AND FALL OF THE LUFTWAFFE 46–47 (1973); E. HOMZE, ARMING THE LUFTWAFFE 131–32 (London, 1976); W. DEIST, THE WERMACHT AND GERMAN REARMAMENT 64–65

Italy. On July 8, 1938, the Italian Government issued its first law of war manual. A report summarized its provisions of interest to the air planner of that time:

> On its face, the law repudiates the Douhet theory by defining the conditions of valid bombardment: bombardment of 'enemy objectives' is permitted when their total or partial destruction may benefit military operations . . .; bombardment of cities and other inhabited areas is permitted when there exists a 'reasonable presumption' that they harbor military preparations or supplies . . .; but bombardment 'for the sole purpose of punishing civil populations or of destroying or damaging properties of nonmilitary importance,' is in every case prohibited.[153]

There were dissenting voices to this language, and the report concludes: "The almost universal affection of Italian airmen for the theory of Douhet makes it unlikely that [these articles] will be observed in a strict sense. In this affection they have been joined by Il Duce."[154]

C. Experts on International Law

Another secondary source for determination of the law is the writing of recognized experts on international law. While the writings of a number of international lawyers (and nonlawyers as well) have been cited in these pages for specific points, only two individuals stand out as authorities in the period prior to World War II. Interestingly enough, neither was a lawyer.

Royse. One recognized authority is M. W. Royse,[155] whose *Aerial Bombardment and the International Regulation of Warfare* was published in 1928.[156] Royse was a pragmatist; while he relied upon the historical practice of nations for precedent, he also brought combat aviation experience into his analysis and writing. In examining the general history of bombardment, for example, Royse cuts to the central point: "The history of bombardment regulation shows a distinct utilitarian development, in which the idea of military effectiveness dominates, and in which the doctrines of permissible violence and social sanction are of secondary importance as checks or influences."[157]

(Toronto, 1981); M. Cooper, The German Air Force 1933–1945 39–42 (London, 1981); and W. Murray, The Change in the European Balance of Power 1938–39, 1939–40 (1984). It was not difficult to "split the difference" between bombing the civilian population of an enemy solely for the purpose of terrorizing it and bombing economic and industrial targets, incidentally terrorizing the civilian population. This apparently was given serious consideration by the Luftwaffe. In May, 1933, Dr. Robert Knauss completed a major study for Erhard Milch, the state secretary in the new German Air Ministry. Knauss argued that not only should modern industrial centers be attacked in order to destroy an enemy nation's economic capability to wage war, but that population centers offered the possibility of attacking morale directly. Knauss suggested that "the terrorizing of the enemy's chief cities and industrial regions through bombing would lead that much more quickly to a collapse of the social and political rifts that cleave his society." W. Murray, *supra*, at 38, 40. The 1936 service directive is not inconsistent with Knauss's proposals.

153. Steiner, *Italian War and Neutrality Legislation*, 33 Am. J. Int'l L. 151–57 (1939).

154. *Id.* at 153.

155. Dr. Royse served as a United States Marine Corps aviator in World War I, obtained his Ph.D. in international relations from Columbia following the war, and served with the Office of Strategic Services during World War II. Between the wars and following World War II, he enjoyed a distinguished university teaching career.

156. M. Royse, Aerial Bombardment and International Regulation of Warfare (1928). *See also* M. Royse, La Protection des Populations Civiles Contre les Bombardments 72–116 (Geneva, 1930).

157. M. Royse, La Protection des Populations Civiles Contre les Bombardments 147 (Geneva, 1930).

After examining the history of the modern law of war up to and including the Hague Air Rules of 1923, Royse concludes:

> There are thus no conventional rules in actual force which directly affect aerial bombardment.- At the present time the only restrictions bearing on such operations are those general and rather vague limitations known as the customary practices of war.
>
> It cannot reasonably be affirmed to-day that it is wrongful or illegal to bombard a military objective, fairly regarded as such, by all available means of attack; nor does a military objective lose that character merely because it is situated in the midst of a crowded city remote from the immediate zone of land operations. Military objectives are likely to be hunted down and attacked, and the fact that the incidental harm may fall upon non-combatants and that the incidental destruction of property may at times approximate devastation probably will be accepted, as heretofore, as an unavoidable incident of warfare.The problem of regulation and its discussion will, as heretofore, hinge upon the question of what may properly be regarded as a military objective, and the question of the military importance of its destruction, viewed in relation to its situation and the probable effects of an attack upon it. In other words, the test in the future, as in the past, will be purely utilitarian.[158]

Participating in a conference of experts held by the International Committee of the Red Cross in 1930,[159] Royse offered a number of points that summarize the law as it seems to have existed in the decade preceding World War II as well as during the period of that conflict:

- The civilian population is not totally immune from the effects of bombardment, whether land, naval or air; indeed, the rules and practices of warfare do not protect civil populations against incidental bombardment even when such bombardment means wholesale destruction of property and civilian life.
- The extent to which civil populations are legally protected against bombardment has never been precisely determined; there is no agreement among jurists as to the extent of violence on the plea of military necessity.
- The law of war is based upon the practice of nations. In that regard, during World War I demoralization of the enemy by means of widespread bombardment was accepted by the military services as part of the functions of the aviation bombardment groups, as it was for artillery.
- To base the legitimacy of a means of warfare upon the extent of its incidental damage to civil populations would be a distinct innovation in the regulation of warfare on land.
- To interpret indiscriminate bombardment on the basis of incidental damage to non-combatant populations would thus, in effect, illegitimize aerial bombardment, since the permissible objectives would almost invariably be found surrounded by civil populations.
- At no time has the effective operation of vital weapons been limited by international regulations. It is therefore hardly likely that air power will be so restricted.[160]

In every respect, Royse was proved right.

Spaight. James Maloney Spaight published his first law of war text, *War Rights on Land*,[161] in 1911; his last was the third edition of his *Air Power and War Rights*,[162] published in 1947. Like Royce, Spaight was a pragmatist. He excelled as

158. *Id.* at 238, 241.
159. *Id.*
160. *Id.* at 73–74, 79.
161. J. SPAIGHT, WAR RIGHTS ON LAND (London, 1911).
162. J. SPAIGHT, *supra* note 137.

a writer on the law of war as he paid close attention to the other primary source of international law: history, or the practice of nations. Each of his three editions of *Air Power and War Rights*[163] is worthy of close scrutiny. Consideration here is limited to the second edition, published in 1933, as it reflects Spaight's thinking closest in time to World War II; had air planners sought to consult a standard work, it would have been Spaight's second edition. Spaight broadens the list of military objectives contained in the unadopted Hague Air Rules of 1923, as he did in his first edition,[164] and acknowledges that a legitimate target may be attacked wherever located,[165] but concludes: "If a military objective is situated in such a densely populated neighborhood, or if the circumstances of the case are otherwise such that any attack upon it from the air is likely to involve a disastrous loss of non-combatant life, aircraft are bound to abstain from bombardment."[166]

Spaight qualifies this conclusion in two ways, first by noting the quasi-military nature of men and women in munitions factories. He cites other legal authorities who acknowledge these persons may be regarded as auxiliary services of the armies while at work, but notes a split of opinion as to whether they may be attacked at home.[167] As to bombing of civilian property, he recognizes the historical practice that permitted general devastation, and the limitation contained in Hague Convention IV of 1907 regarding a connection between intentional destruction and military necessity. Then he ties destruction of civilian property to military utility (that is, efficiency) and the degree of risk to innocent civilians—again, the concept of "disastrous loss of non-combatant life" noted above.[168] While recognizing the impact of antiaircraft fire and weather on bombing operations,[169] Spaight errs in assuming that night bombing would be more accurate.[170] Beyond the concept noted in this paragraph, Spaight reached no conclusions.

In June 1945, perhaps in response to the controversy that surrounded the destruction of Dresden,[171] Spaight prepared an extraordinary document that until recently remained classified. Entitled *International Law of the Air, 1939–1945*,[172] it was intended as a confidential supplement to the second edition of his *Air Power and War Rights*.[173] Although Spaight published a substantially-rewritten third and final edition of *Air Power and War Rights*[174] in 1947, it lacks the comprehensiveness of

163. J. SPAIGHT, AIR POWER AND WAR RIGHTS (London, 1924); J. SPAIGHT, AIR POWER AND WAR RIGHTS (2d ed. London, 1933); J. SPAIGHT, *supra* note 137.

164. J. SPAIGHT, AIR POWER AND WAR RIGHTS 233–35 (2d ed. London, 1933).

165. *Id.* at 195–210.

166. *Id.* at 210. While this may reflect emergent thinking of scholars of the time, it did not constitute an obligation accepted by nations. A single scenario suggests the impracticality of the rule. Assume a bomber force battles its way to its target deep in enemy territory, only to find the enemy has obscured the target—located in the midst of a populated area—with smoke. It would be foolhardy to think that the bombers would not bomb anyway, regardless of the consequences to the civilian population. Any other action would encourage a defender to continue his actions in order to frustrate any bombing.

167. *Id.* at 211.

168. *Id.* at 239–47.

169. *Id.* at 222–26, 253–54.

170. *Id.* at 247–52.

171. III C. WEBSTER & N. FRANKLAND, *supra* note 81, at 108–09, 112–13; E. RICHARDS, PORTAL 191–92 (London, 1977); M. Clodfeller, *Culmination Dresden: 1945*, 26 AEROSPACE HIST. 134–47 (Sept. 1979); J. TERRAIN, THE RIGHT OF THE LINE 677–78 (London, 1985); and M. GILBERT, ROAD TO VICTORY: WINSTON S. CHURCHILL 1941–45, 1257–58 (London, 1986). For a comprehensive analysis of the decision to bomb Dresden, *see* M. Smith, Jr., *The Bombing of Dresden Reconsidered: A Study in Wartime Decision-Making* (unpublished dissertation, Boston University, 1971).

172. J. SPAIGHT, INTERNATIONAL LAW OF THE AIR 1939–45, British Public Records Office [PRO] file AIR 41/5.

173. J. SPAIGHT, *supra* note 164.

174. J. SPAIGHT, *supra* note 137.

the confidential supplement. That supplement will be examined briefly, primarily to illustrate the chaotic state of the law of war as it related to aerial bombing in the opening phases of and, indeed, throughout the whole of World War II.

As early as 1937 British authorities began considering what Royal Air Force bombing policy should be if war with Germany were to begin. It is clear that British bombing policy was driven primarily by self interest and not by law of war or humanitarian concerns. In Spaight's words, "Our policy before the war and for the first nine months of the war was inspired by the consideration that the less bombing there was, the better for us. We were apprehensive about the effect of heavy attacks on London, and . . . we were not in a position to return blow for blow."[175]

Malkin Report. During the period of pre-war consideration, policies were proposed that were not always consistent with ongoing plans. Thus, a memorandum prepared by the Air Staff and circulated by the Secretary of State (Lord Swinton) to the Cabinet on March 1, 1938, supported a three-ton weight limitation on bomber aircraft. The limitation was consistent with the proposal made by the British Government to the ill-fated Geneva Disarmament Conference five years earlier in 1933. However, the weight limitation proposed in the 1938 Air Staff memorandum had been overcome by events in that the Air Council three years earlier, in 1935, had approved the construction of the Stirling, Halifax, and (via the Manchester) Lancaster bombers at weights substantially in excess of the three-ton weight limitation.[176]

On July 7, 1938, a call was issued by the Limitation of Armaments Sub-Committee of the Committee of Imperial Defence for a report on certain legal aspects of the issue of bombing, to be conducted under the chairmanship of Sir William Malkin, the Legal Adviser to the Foreign Office. After referring to the previously discussed three principles that had been laid down by Prime Minister Chamberlain in the House of Commons on June 21, 1938, the committee rejected a total prohibition on bombing and any restriction limiting bombing to the immediate area of military or naval operations. It then proposed the following rule:

> Air bombardment is only legitimate in the following circumstances:
> (1) Against warships, including transports and fleet auxiliaries, at sea;
> (2) On land, in accordance with the following rules:
>
> Any objective on land which may legitimately be bombarded under the rules applicable to land warfare, may be bombarded from the air if it is within the range of medium artillery, which for this purpose should be taken as ten miles from any of the forces of the belligerent who effects the bombardment or his allies.
>
> In addition, the following objectives on land may be bombarded, provided that they are either anywhere on territory occupied by an invader or within a radius of fifty miles of the nearest troops or air forces of the belligerent carrying out the bombardment or of his allies: —
>
> (a) Enemy troops and air forces;

175. J. SPAIGHT, *supra* note 172, at D–1. *See also* J. BUTLER, II GRAND STRATEGY, App. I(a) 567–68 (London, 1957); and I C. WEBSTER & N. FRANKLAND, *supra* note 81, at 134–35.

176. J. SPAIGHT, *supra* note 172, at D–1 to D–3. The prototype two-engine Avro Manchester, built in response to Air Ministry Specification had an empty weight of 25,959 pounds. B. ROBERTSON, LANCASTER – THE STORY OF A FAMOUS BOMBER 13/36, 124 (London, 1964). By 1937 Air Ministry officials were talking in terms of building bombers weighing between 50,000 and 90,000 pounds by spring 1941. M. POSTON, D. HAY, & J. SCOTT, DESIGN AND DEVELOPMENT OF WEAPONS 78–79, 92–93, 124–126 (London, 1964) [hereinafter M. POSTON]. In fact the Air Ministry in the opening months of 1938 developed a paper on the ideal bomber, the weight of which was substantially greater than that proposed by the British Secretary of State. J. SLESSOR, THE CENTRAL BLUE 174–78 (1957). By way of contrast, Boeing B–17 models in the prewar era had an empty weight between 21,000 and 29,000 pounds. E. JABLONSKI, FLYING FORTRESS 310–11 (1965). Hence it is unlikely that the proposal would have been greeted with any enthusiasm in the United States.

(b) Ammunition dumps, military supply depots, artillery parks and similar well defined aggregations of distinctly military equipment, stores or supplies;
(c) Supply columns and other means of transport which are engaged in transporting supplies to or from the depots etc. mentioned under (b).[177]

The Malkin Report went on to make several other recommendations, one of which was to prohibit bombing of military objectives between sunset and sunrise, except in the immediate vicinity of the operations of land forces or against warships at sea. At least two major problems existed with the Malkin Report. Offered as a quasi-legal opinion, the list of targets nonetheless was fully at odds with target lists then being developed by the Air Ministry as part of Bomber Command war plans. For example, the Air Ministry on October 1, 1937, sent to Bomber Command a series of thirteen plans, called W.A. (Western Air) plans, with instructions to concentrate their planning on the first three. Some W.A. plans were:

(1) W.A. 1: the attack on the German Air Striking Force and its maintenance organization, to which was later added the German aircraft industry, originally listed under W.A. 6;

(2) W.A. 4: the attack on German military rail, canal, and road communications (a) during the period of the concentration of the armies, and (b) to delay a German invasion of the Low Countries and France;

(3) W.A. 5: the attack on the German War Industry including the supply of oil with priority to that in the Ruhr, Rhineland and Saar.[178]

Spaight noted the second way in which the Malkin Report was in conflict with contemporary planning. The Air Staff's heavy bomber construction program at the time of the Malkin Report (Scheme L) called for a force of forty-seven heavy bomber squadrons which were to be used solely as night bombers. Shortly thereafter and undoubtedly because of these fundamental differences, the Malkin proposals were dropped in their entirety.

X. THE AIR WAR PLANNERS OF WORLD WAR II

A. Air Ministry Policy

On September 15, 1938, the Air Ministry issued instructions to Bomber Command which began by quoting the Prime Minister's three principles. Acknowledging that those principles might prejudice otherwise legitimate courses of action, the instructions nonetheless advised that bombing would be limited to objectives that

177. J. SPAIGHT, *supra* note 172, at D–4. Uri Bialer notes that the Subcommittee on Limitation of Armaments "was unanimous in its view that Britain's interests would best be served by a [new] legal convention, despite its equally unanimous opinion that the convention would not be observed for long after an outbreak of war . . . . For this purpose, [the Malkin Committee] . . . was specifically charged with determining the degree of immunity which Britain should aim for, and the manner in which she should attempt to improve the draft [1923] Hague [Air] Rules." U. BIALER, *supra* note 135, at 119–20. Thus the Malkin list was not one of lawful targets, but limitations Britain hoped Germany would agree to until Britain obtained bomber parity. One reason that the Malkin Report failed to attract support was the fear that Britain's request would be met by a German demand to accept a similar limitation on belligerent rights at sea, where Britain enjoyed superiority. U. BIALER, *supra* note 135, at 121. *See also* Bialer, *"Humanization" of Air Warfare in British Foreign Policy on the Eve of the Second World War*, 13. J. CONTEMP. HIST. 79–96 (Jan. 1978).

178. J. SPAIGHT, *supra* note 172, at D–5. *See also* I C. WEBSTER & N. FRANKLAND, *supra* note 81, at 94. The Western Air Plans continued to undergo revisions and refinement. Their form as of September 1, 1939, is contained in IV C. WEBSTER & N. FRANKLAND, ANNEXES AND APPENDICES, Appendix 6.

were manifestly and unmistakably military in the narrowest interpretation of the term; and that even such objectives should not be attacked "unless [they can be] attacked with a reasonable expectation of damage being confined to them." The Air Ministry considered it vital in the opening phases of a war to avoid any action which could be represented as an attack on the civil population, in view both of the effect on neutral opinion and of the importance of ensuring that the enemy is given no genuine pretext for retaliatory action.

The Chief of Air Staff, in forwarding the instructions to the Secretary of State, stated "I feel sure that this instruction will not last very long, but we obviously cannot be the first to 'take the gloves off.' "[179] These limitations clearly were taken for policy reasons and not because they were considered to represent the current state of the law of war.

Additional proposals were considered over the next year. All chose to forego the attack of any target which entailed the possible loss of civilian lives, regardless of the cause of the loss of life. All considered targets or target categories as they had been identified in Hague Convention IX of 1907 or the 1923 Hague Air Rules, though without any geographic restriction related to proximity to land operations. All were premised on the Prime Minister's three principles, with elaboration of the second principle ("Objectives . . . must be identifiable.") to the effect that "the governing principle is that it is illegal to bomb a populated area in the hope of hitting a legitimate target which is known to be in the area but which cannot be precisely located and identified." These became part of Air Council Instructions issued on August 22, 1939, less than two weeks before Germany's invasion of Poland.

Although much of the guidance contained in the Air Council Instructions was couched in terms of the law of war, on October 16, 1939, the Chief of the Air Staff sent a message that the Royal Air Force was "no longer bound by [the Air Council Instructions] nor . . . [President] Roosevelt's appeal," because of the Luftwaffe actions in Poland. Continuing, he advised that, "Our action is now governed by expediency, i.e., what it suits us to do having regard to (a) the need to conserve our resources, (b) possible enemy retaliatory action, and (c) our need still to take into account to some extent influential neutral opinion." In considering the Prime Minister's three principles, the third ("civilian populations in the neighborhood will not be bombarded through negligence") was moderated where air attacks were in proximity to land operations, undoubtedly in recognition of the likelihood of increased air defenses in those areas. The realities of war were beginning to have an effect on a subject that heretofore had been dealt with only in hypothetical terms.

Five days later, the British Chiefs of Staff formally adopted an air policy that continued to take a "wait and see" attitude. While recognizing that Germany's weakest spot was the Ruhr Valley and its vital industries, their memorandum concluded:

> We should not be the first to 'take the gloves off.' From that it follows that until and unless Germany, by killing large numbers of civilians, either by indiscriminate air attack on France or Great Britain, or in the course of a violation, gives the necessary justification, there could be no question of attacking the Ruhr, or anything other than strictly military objectives.[180]

B. Policy Revision

The bombing policy was revised on June 4, 1940, following Germany's invasion

179. J. SPAIGHT, *supra* note 172, at D–8.
180. *Id.* at D–18.

of Denmark and Norway on April 9 and the Low Countries on May 10. The third of the Prime Minister's principles was amended to "The attack must be made with reasonable care to avoid undue loss of civil life in the vicinity of the target." This standard is important, as while it seems to consider the concept of proportionality, previously discussed, at the same time it recognized that an attacker in the heat of battle should only be held to a standard of due care. The new instructions were, in part, as follows:

2. The action of armies is well established by practice. Commanders of land forces will use every reasonable precaution to avoid undue loss of civilian life by artillery bombardment.

3. Bombardment by naval and air forces is to be confined to military objectives and must be subject to the following general principles:

(a) The intentional bombardment of [the] civil population as such is illegal.

(b) It must be possible to identify the objective.

(c) The attack must be made with reasonable care to avoid undue loss of civil life in the vicinity of the target.

(d) The provisions of [the] Red Cross Conventions are to be observed.

In paragraph 4, a new list of authorized targets was provided, with the note that military was to be interpreted in the broadest sense of the word:

(a) Military forces, including naval auxiliaries of whatever description and whether or not attendant on the fleet; troop transports and military supply ships whether at sea or in port. This does not include merchant ships, whether defensively armed or not. *Note*: Areas in which all shipping can be treated as enemy transports or military supply ships will be specifically notified.

(b) Military works and fortifications.

(c) Military establishments and depots, including barracks, camps, billets and naval dockyards; aerodromes, whether designated military or civil; stores and dumps of military supplies.

(d) Shipyards, factories and other establishments engaged in the manufacture, assembly or repair of military material, equipment or supplies, [and] power stations ancillary thereto; fuel and oil producing plants, refineries and storage installations.

(e) Lines of communication and transportation and means of intercommunication serving military purposes.

(f) Provided that the principles set out in paragraph 3 above are observed, other objectives, the destruction of which is an immediate military necessity, may be attacked for particular purposes.

5. In the case of naval bombardment of objectives in a town, warning should be given if the safety of the attacking force or the success of the operation is not jeopardized by so doing.[181]

181. *Id.* at D–21. Significant in these instructions is the military's conclusion that the warning requirement contained in article 26 of the annex to Hague Convention IV of 1907 and article 6 of Hague Convention IX of 1907 did not apply to aerial bombardment of the targets listed in the memorandum. Article 26 of the annex to Hague Convention IV states: "The officer in command of an attacking force must, before commencing a bombardment, except in cases of assault, do all in his power to warn authorities." Article 6 of Hague Convention IX provides: "If the military situation permits, the commander of the attacking naval force, before commencing the bombardment, must do his utmost to warn the authorities."

The effectiveness of aerial attack of a target was (and remains) dependent upon myriad factors, not the least of which is surprise and a commensurate diminishment of enemy air defenses. No doubt this played significantly in the British decision against application of the warning requirement to aerial bombardment. The 1977 Protocol I relaxed the warning requirement while simultaneously aligning it with the customary practice of nations in this century. Article 57 (2)(c) provides: "Effective advance warning shall be given of attacks which may affect the civilian population, unless circumstances do not permit." This language actually *realigned* the law of war with customary international law before the codification of Hague Conventions IV and IX. In General Orders No. 100, *see supra* note 26, Francis Lieber had summarized the practice of nations in rule 19 of that regulation:

Commanders, whenever admissible, [must] inform the enemy of their intention to bombard a place, so that the noncombatants, and especially the women and children, may be removed before the bombardment commences. But it is no infraction of the common law of war to omit thus to inform the enemy. Surprise may be a necessity.

Thereafter, Bomber Command became the recipient of a series of messages identifying either target categories or specific targets authorized for attack. These included aircraft depots, aircraft assembly factories, oil plants, aluminum factories, power plants, particular warships at particular locations, aircraft factories, an optical instrument factory, aerodromes in occupied territory from which England was being attacked, anti-invasion objectives (barges, ships, etc.), and railway marshalling yards.

By September the city of Berlin had slipped onto the list, in response to Luftwaffe attacks on London. Although few specific targets were identified, Spaight observes that "as a result of experience afforded by the German raids on London, it was considered that gas and electrical plants in Berlin and its environs were the most profitable targets." Although a list of Berlin power stations and coal gas works were contained in an appendix, given the extremely limited capability of RAF crews for target identification at night, the value of their incorporation into the target authorization is questionable. The Prime Minister's second principle had to accommodate to the harsh realities of war.[182]

C. Spaight

Spaight's classified supplement continues at length through the rest of the war. Much of the subsequent information has been discussed in the myriad volumes on the strategic air offensive[183] and, as with World War I, it is not the purpose of this article to discuss that history at this time. The value of the Spaight supplement lies in its examination of the various documents produced by the British Government during the two years prior to commencement of hostilities and the initial phases of World War II. While British desires to limit bombing were not entirely altruistic, neither was the government of Great Britain possessed of any greater knowledge as to what the law of war related to aerial bombardment might be. The Malkin Report clearly shows the degree to which the thinking of international lawyers had failed to keep pace with changes in warfare and technology. Except for the limitation on the intentional attack of the civilian population, the Prime Minister's widely-trumpeted principles for the limitation of aerial bombardment, subsequently adopted by the

---

At the same time, the British were quite familiar with the early warning capabilities of radar, which they would put to good use only weeks later upon commencement of the Battle of Britain. It is entirely possible that they believed that radar obviated the necessity for advance warning. Significantly, they did not believe that protection for the civilian population of an enemy nation rested exclusively with the attacker; neither do article 26 of the annex to Hague Convention IV, article 6 of Hague Convention IX, nor article 57 (2)(c) suggest such.

182. J. SPAIGHT, *supra* note 172, at D–21 to D–25.

183. *See also* W. CRAVEN & J. CATE, Vol. 1–8 THE ARMY AIR FORCES IN WORLD WAR II, (1948–1954); J. ROSS, ROYAL NEW ZEALAND AIR FORCE, NEW ZEALAND IN THE SECOND WORLD WAR 1939–45 (Wellington, 1955); J. HERRINGTON, AIR WAR AGAINST GERMANY & ITALY, 1939–1943 (Canberra, 1954); J. HERRINGTON, AIR POWER OVER EUROPE, 1944–1945 (Canberra, 1963); G. ODGERS, AIR WAR AGAINST JAPAN, 1943–1945 (Canberra, 1957); D. GILLISON, ROYAL AUSTRALIAN AIR FORCE, 1939–1942 (Canberra, 1962); N. FRANKLAND, THE BOMBING OFFENSIVE AGAINST GERMANY (London, 1965); A. VERRIER, THE BOMBER OFFENSIVE (London, 1968); A. REVIE, THE LOST COMMAND (London, 1971); D. COPP, FORGED IN FIRE (1982); N. LONGMATE, THE BOMBERS: THE RAF OFFENSIVE AGAINST GERMANY, 1939–1945 (London, 1983); D. SAWARD, VICTORY DENIED (London, 1986); and C. SHORES, B. CULL & N. MALIZIA, AIR WAR FOR YUGOSLAVIA, GREECE, AND CRETE, 1940–41 (London, 1987). Examination of the practice of the principal parties to World War II—Germany, Italy, Japan, the Soviet Union, Great Britain, and the United States—reveals no distinction in their employment of airpower *vis-à-vis* concern for collateral damage or collateral civilian casualties; any distinction that existed was in capability rather than intent.

League of Nations, were forced to undergo substantial modification in the face of combat if they were to remain any sort of guidance.

D. Temper of the Times

One further indication of the state of the law of war existed prior to World War II. It is not one traditionally considered by international lawyers, but it certainly is critical to the questions addressed in this article. That factor is the temper of the times. The expectation in Great Britain and Europe was that, were war to break out, the initial phases would consist primarily of massive aerial attacks—in all likelihood with chemicals—upon cities and the civilian population as such. Private citizens fully expected it; governments planned for it through the development of air raid precaution plans, evacuation plans, and plans for the treatment of massive numbers of casualties that far exceeded the numbers experienced once war actually began. At the beginning of 1938, for example, Great Britain had manufactured and stored 19,500,000 gas mask canisters (filters) and 1,500,000 gas masks for the civilian population, and was assembling 150,000 gas masks per week. In April 1939, the British Ministry of Health prepared and issued to local authorities 1,000,000 burial forms in anticipation of civilian deaths from bombing. As one official history notes:

> During these [pre-war] years there was not, in essential outline, any substantial difference between the views held by the man in the street and by the officials in the social service departments as to the character of a future war. . . . . The general view which had emerged by 1938, . . . contained the following basic features. At the outset . . . London would be subjected to concentrated and intensive aerial air attack by bombers operating from Germany. In the first twenty-four hours the Germans might attempt to drop as much as 3,500 tons [of bombs]. Subsequently, and for a period of weeks, the daily weight of attack might average 700 tons . . . . It was thought that high explosive [bombs] would be employed to a greater extent than incendiary bombs, while the use of gas was considered possible.[184]

Beginning as early as 1924—a period when peace initiatives were much at hand, and fear of war very much distant—various British Government offices had begun planning for the eventuality that war might occur again. In that year official British estimates anticipated a casualty ratio of fifty civilian deaths per ton of bombs dropped on Great Britain. That figure increased steadily over the years prior to World War II, eventually reaching seventy-two civilian casualties per ton of bombs based upon Italian air raids upon Barcelona, Spain, in March 1938, when forty-two tons of bombs allegedly resulted in 3000 civilian casualties.[185]

In 1925 the nations of the world had negotiated the Geneva Protocol for the Prohibition of the Use in War of Asphyxiating, Poisonous, or Other Gases, and of

184. R. TITMUSS, PROBLEMS OF SOCIAL POLICY 8, 10 (London, 1950). *See also* U. BIALER, *supra* note 135, at 145. German air raid precautions are contained in the CIVIL DEFENSE DIVISION: FINAL REPORT, 48 UNITED STATES STRATEGIC BOMBING SURVEY, 2d ed., (1947). For a summary of British and European concerns and measures to alleviate them, *see* R. OVERY, *supra* note 7, at 25. British Prime Minister Chamberlain continued to press for some form of law of war restriction during this era, but expressed serious doubt that any agreed restrictions would survive the opening days of a conflict with Germany. U. BIALER, *supra* note 135, at 115. While Hitler feared any attack on German civilians because it might lead to a second "stab-in-the-back," in 1938 he was quite willing to use the threat of strategic bombing by the Luftwaffe as a diplomatic tool. R. OVERY, *supra* note 7, at 18, 24. This tended to confirm public and official fears that any war would commence with the bombing of cities.

185. R. OVERY, *supra* note 7, at 14. The actual casualty figures were lower, amounting to 1300 civilians killed, or 30.95 civilian deaths per ton of bombs. H. THOMAS, THE SPANISH CIVIL WAR 806–07 (rev. ed. 1977). Unlike Guernica, Barcelona was defended by antiaircraft guns. *See infra* note 188. But Mussolini was intent on causing as much devastation as possible, in part to impress Hitler.

Bacteriological Methods of Warfare.[186] In 1928 the League of Nations had produced the Kellogg-Briand Treaty outlawing resort to war.[187] Yet simultaneously Great Britain and the European nations were anticipating the worst; not merely war, but war in which civilian populations would be subjected to aerial attack, possibly with chemical munitions.

There existed a mood that affected both governments and individual citizens. It was exacerbated by the popular press, particularly in its reports on the Spanish Civil War, the Japanese bombing of Nanking, China, and Italian air force operations in Abysinnia, Ethiopia, (which included the employment of chemical weapons) and by books written by military "experts" (some less expert than others) forecasting the worst. One historian observed that "Concern that the civilian population would form a likely target in future war was both widespread and deeply felt."[188] As Winston Churchill commented, "We had entered a period when the weapon [the airplane] which had played a considerable part in the previous war had become obsessive in men's minds, and also a prime military factor. Ministers had to imagine the most frightful scenes of ruin and slaughter in London if we quarreled with the German dictator."[189]

The point to be made is a simple one: neither governments nor individual citizens placed much faith, if any, in the law of war (if the latter even knew of its existence) to prevent war or the aerial attacks upon the civilian population that were anticipated by all. No international lawyer stepped forward to say, "Don't worry—the law of

---

186. SCHINDLER & TOMAN, *supra* note 27, at 115. Although chemical weapons were used by Italy in Abyssinia and by Japan in China prior to World War II, their use between 1939 and 1945 was deterred by the danger of retaliation in kind, rather than by the existence of the 1925 Geneva Protocol. *See* Harris, *British Preparations for Offensive Chemical Warfare, 1935–1939*, 125. J. ROYAL UNITED SERVICES INST. 56–42 (June 1980); and van Courtland Moon, *Chemical Weapons and Deterrence: The World War II Experience*, 8 INT'L SECURITY 3–35, 36–54 (Spring 1984).

187. 46 Stat. 2343; T.S. 796. Contained in *U.S. Army Pamphlet 27–161–2*, II INT'L L. 300–01 (Washington, 1962).

188. U. BIALER, *supra* note 135, at 2. Few events captured the attention of the world and fueled the fear of bombing as much as the three-hour German Condor Legion aerial attack on the Basque town of Guernica on April 27, 1937. The air assault destroyed the center of the town, killing at least 100 civilians and perhaps as many as 1000. Initial German denials of responsibility did little for the credibility of subsequent statements that the destruction occurred because of errant bombing by inexperienced crews. The first admission of German responsibility did not come until eight years after World War II. A. GALLAND DIE ERSTEN UND DIE LETZEN 42–43 (Darmstadt, 1953). Galland came to Spain as part of the Condor Legion two weeks after the attack on Guernica. Curiously English-language editions of Galland's book inexplicably omitted this important chapter. A recent edition contains this chapter. *See* THE FIRST AND THE LAST 26 (Mesa, Arizona, 1986). As Telford Taylor has noted, "[Nationalist General Emilio] Mola's earlier threat to 'raze all Vizcaya [the province in which Guernica is located] to the ground,' the preceding attack on Durango [on March 31, in which 250 civilians were killed], the duration of the Guernica bombing, the false denials of German responsibility, and the later German raids on Barcelona do little to support the apologia." T. TAYLOR, MUNICH: THE PRICE OF PEACE 286–87 (1979). *See also* G. THOMAS & M. MORGAN-WATTS, GUERNICA (1976); and H. THOMAS, THE SPANISH CIVIL WAR, *supra* note 185, at 624–29. The point here is not the cause of the bombing of Guernica, but the significant impact that it had on private citizens and foreign governments as to the likely nature of any future war. The bombing had a substantial effect on public debate in the Western world, particularly in Great Britain and the United States. *See* H. SOUTHWORTH, GUERNICA! GUERNICA! A STUDY OF JOURNALISM, DIPLOMACY, PROPAGANDA, AND HISTORY 89 (1977). The United States issued a formal note of protest to Japan about the Japanese plan to bomb Nanking. *U.S. Note to Japan*, N. Y. Times, 19 (Sept. 23, 1937). The note did not prevent the attacks. *See Hull Backs League in Rebuking Japan*, N. Y. Times, 8 (Sept. 29, 1937). The League of Nations rules with regard to aerial bombardment were adopted as a direct result of the Japanese bombing of Nanking. *See supra* note 139. For a discussion of Italian air operations in Abyssinia, *see* Spencer, *Some Legal Aspects of Aircraft in Belligerent Operations*, PROC. AM. SOC'Y INT'L L. 95–135 (1937); A. DEL BOCA, THE ETHIOPIAN WAR 1935–1941 (1965); J. DUGAN & L. LAFORE, DAYS OF EMPEROR AND CLOWN: THE ITALO-ETHIOPIAN WAR 1935–1936 (1973); and A. MOCKLER, HAILE SELASSIE'S WAR: THE ITALIAN-ETHIOPIAN CAMPAIGN, 1935–1941 (1984).

189. W. CHURCHILL, I THE SECOND WORLD WAR, THE GATHERING STORM 115 (London, 1948).

war will protect you." In fact, as previously indicated, international lawyers of that era doubted the applicability of the law of war to modern warfare and particularly to aerial bombardment. As Churchill observed in an earlier debate, "The only direct measure of defence on a great scale was to possess the power to inflict simultaneously upon the enemy as much damage as he himself could inflict."[190]

It was within this framework that air planners conducted their preparations for the war that was to come—with little to no confidence in the ability of the law of war to ameliorate the suffering and damage anticipated, and a substantial vacuum in the law of war when it came to delineating what law actually applied to aerial bombardment. But air planners of that era were not alone in this regard; their views were shared by private citizens, international lawyers, and government leaders. In the years preceding World War II, the credibility of the law of war to protect the civilian population from aerial attack was, at best, substantially lacking.

XI. PROBLEMS OF THE AIR WAR PLANNERS OF WORLD WAR II

An air planner in any nation in the interwar era as well as during World War II would have had a difficult time determining the law governing aerial bombardment. He would have found it impossible to find clear, well-defined, express language prohibiting or permitting the actions he was contemplating; at best, he would have found considerable disagreement and confusion among scholars. He would have been unable to find a comprehensive list of objects that legitimately could be considered military objects; and, in particular, he would not have been able to find appropriate language explaining the distinction between combatants and noncombatants in contemporary terms. While these may be attributable to a failure of diplomacy, it is the opinion of the author that the last must be laid directly at the feet of international lawyers and moral philosophers who failed to adjust international law and moral thinking to major technological changes in society and warfare. International law Professor Philip C. Jessup warned in 1941 of the danger of such torpidity in the development of the law relating to bombing, noting presciently that the "law often lags behind facts, but if it does not correspond to facts it is eventually nullified or modified."[191] Such was the fate that befell the law of war relating to aerial bombardment during World War II.

---

190. M. GILBERT, WINSTON S. CHURCHILL: THE PROPHET OF TRUTH, 1922–1939 573 (London, 1976). *See also* Spaight, *The Chaotic State of the International Law Governing Bombardment*, 9 THE A.F.Q. 24–32 (1938).

Commenting on this period and the thinking of the average man on the street, British historian Noble Frankland noted that "[W]ar normally ensues when international regulation has failed. The scale of weapons and the ruthlessness of their application depends not upon international agreements reached before the outbreak of the war, but upon the will and determination of those employing the weapons." Letter to author, February 16, 1979.

191. Jessup, *International Law and Totalitarian War*, 35 AM. J. INT'L L. 329 (April 1941).

It is at this point that some international lawyers may turn to the famous Martens clause contained within the Preamble to Hague Convention II of 1899 and Hague Convention IV of 1907 which states:

> Until a more complete code of the laws of war has been issued, the High Contracting Parties deem it expedient to declare that, in cases not included in the Regulations adopted by them, the inhabitants and the belligerents remain under the protection and the rule of the principles of the law of nations, as they result from the usages established among civilized peoples, from the laws of humanity, and the dictates of the public conscience.

SCHINDLER & TOMAN, *supra* note 27, at 70.

Such an answer not only begs the question, but reveals the inadequacy of the codified law of war as it existed during World War II and today. It provides no guidance to military personnel planning combat operations.

As a boy, the author went to see a postseason football bowl game. This game pitted an individual who had been selected as the best running back in college football against a nationally-recognized defensive player. In the second half, the two players met in a bone-jarring collision that could be heard above the roar of the 60,000 fans. As they were carried, unconscious, from the playing field, the announcer declared that "This was a case of the irresistible force meeting the immovable object." In World War II, a similar collision occurred between the bombing doctrine and tactics of all nations and the basic humanitarian concept of discrimination; the innocent civilian suffered as a result.

How did this happen? The preceding pages have suggested some problems. Except for the fundamental prohibition on the attack of the civilian population as such—and reasonable people may differ on the degree to which this was honored—the law of war was not even on the World War II playing field, and moral principles can be asserted to support or condemn the actions that occurred. But the principal source of international law, the practice of nations, clearly illustrates the failure of the law of war to come to grips with changes that had taken place not only in weapons but in warfare itself. Warfare underwent revolutionary technological changes during the twentieth century to which the law of war has yet to adjust. Speaking of the submarine, airplane, and nuclear weapons, international lawyer Julius Stone summarized the predicament:

> A factor in the weakness of modern war-law springs from rapid technological development in new and transformed weapons, . . . [which] doubly depress the role of law. On the one hand they outmode existing rules; on the other, when the new weapons are wholly new, like the airplane or the atom bomb, the problem of regulation finds the rudimentary organs of international legislation at their most impotent. The weapons come into use in a kind of legal vacuum. The more destructive they are, the stronger is the pressure of public opinion in most countries to limit or even outlaw them. But also, the more effective they are, the more rarely can legislation by agreement be achieved, so long as only one State or block of States thinks it has or may get a decisive lead in the weapon.[192]

Thus occurred the legal vacuum that existed before and throughout World War II. Of course, the vacuum was not total. All nations agreed for humanitarian and utilitarian purposes that indiscriminate bombardment—whether by land, naval, or air forces—was prohibited. But the acknowledged and apparently accepted philosophy of discrimination was qualified by these events of World War II. A long-standing practice of nations was that collateral civilian casualties were not only an inevitable result of bombardment, but the cost to a nation of engaging in war; their avoidance was the principal responsibility of the defender, who had exclusive control over the civilian population. An equally long-standing principle was that collateral civilian casualties, as a result either of general bombardment or inaccurate bombardment, were a way in which the morale of an enemy nation could be affected, legally. Discrimination was the sole standard in law and the ethics of war. Against that vague, undefined standard were legal/moral counterarguments that efficient brutality in war deterred war or hastened the conclusion of hostilities, and a more brutal campaign could and should be waged against an unjust or immoral opponent.

Neither of these counterarguments had been rejected by the law of war at the outset of World War II. There has been some qualification of the first since World War II by the limited war theory articulated within some Western democracies, but then again none of these nations has been confronted with a threat equal to that

192. J. STONE, *supra* note 53, at 349–50.

experienced during World War II. The limited war theory has not been accepted by the non-Western World, as illustrated by actions by both sides in the Iran-Iraq War and Soviet operations in Afghanistan.[193] The second counterargument remains a valid moral point, and is a fundamental concept overriding the law of war in many non-Christian nations, as well as in Socialist military doctrine.[194] Neither counterargument can be brushed aside easily.

The principle of discrimination was at the time of World War II, and remains today, conditioned by the commingling of military objectives with the civilian population, as well as the fundamental failure of the law of war to acknowledge that the traditional distinction between the combatant and noncombatant was obsolete, and had been for the century preceding World War II. Also, legitimate actions taken by the defender, such as dispersion of war materials and/or production facilities, camouflage or other ruses, and air defenses, could result and are intended to result in a bombing force being less precise, thereby placing the defender's civilian population at greater risk.

This last point is quite important, but generally is neglected in evaluating a bombing mission or campaign, or actions taken by an attacker to compensate for the defender's efforts. For example, each major bombing campaign during World War II found the attacker forced to resort to the cover of darkness in order to minimize the effectiveness of enemy defenses, with a concomitant decrease in bombing accuracy.[195]

In this regard something must be said about "indiscriminate" bombing, as the term has been used rather promiscuously by many historians, international lawyers, and other writers. The term indiscriminate is without legal definition; a standard dictionary definition is "not marked by discrimination; not marked by careful distinction."[196] Unfortunately, such definition contributes little to answering the question as to whether the law regarding discrimination was followed by bomber forces during World War II. Three observations can be made:

1. In considering "careful distinction," the standard was one of ordinary care by

---

193. Thus while the Vietnam War was fought as a limited war by the United States, it was regarded as total war by the North Vietnamese. The 1982 Falklands-Malvinas War was fought as a limited war by both sides, but on a battlefield virtually devoid of civilians. The Arab-Israeli Wars have been fought against a background of superpower influence in which each has encouraged constraint by the combatant nations in order to avoid superpower confrontation. Use of chemical weapons—weapons regarded as prohibited under international law, and a weapon to which no nation resorted during World War II—by Iraq and Iran in their conflict, the Soviet Union in Afghanistan, Vietnam in Southeast Asia, and Cuba in Angola, and the rejection by Third World leaders of any constraint on the use of chemical weapons at an international conference convened to discuss the problem of chemical weapons, held in Paris in January 1989, *see* Tesko, *Chemical Warfare Treaty/Chemical Warfare Threats: It's Not Just the Soviets Anymore*, LXXIV NAT'L DEF. 31–33 (April 1989), not only illustrates the philosophical distinction with which non-Western nations view international law and the law of war, but the lack of an enforcement mechanism available to the law of war.

194. The law of war essentially remains a Western concept. Although the 1949 Geneva Conventions for the Protection of War Victims are law of war treaties to which more than 95% of the nations of the world are party, even these fundamental treaties enjoy limited acceptance in practice outside the Western world.

195. Although 1937 plans called for RAF Bomber Command to carry out night operations only, initial Bomber Command operations (except for leaflet dropping) were conducted in daylight, with catastrophic losses to enemy defenses. This lead to the policy of night operations. *See* I C. WEBSTER & N. FRANKLAND, *supra* note 81, at 138–39, 141; HASTINGS, *supra* note 8, at 60–61. After equally valiant daylight bombing efforts during the Battle of Britain, the Luftwaffe turned to night bombing in the winter of 1940–1941. *See* F. MASON, *supra* note 81, at 648; and J. FOREMAN, BATTLE OF BRITAIN: THE FORGOTTEN MONTHS (London, 1988). For U.S. bombing operations against Japan, *see* H. HANSELL, JR., THE STRATEGIC AIR OFFENSIVE AGAINST GERMANY AND JAPAN 183 (1986); and LEMAY & YENNE, SUPERFORTRESS: THE B–29 AND AMERICAN AIR POWER 120 (1987).

196. WEBSTER'S THIRD NEW INTERNATIONAL DICTIONARY OF THE ENGLISH LANGUAGE (1976).

a reasonable man under the same or similar circumstances. No greater standard of care has been proposed in the years that have passed since World War II.

2. In the race to condemn aerial bombardment, many have failed to take into proper account the effect of a defender's actions. If a bomb is dropped and misses the target, the bomber is guilty of indiscriminate bombing. This is an untenable position even by today's bombing standards. It holds World War II bomber crews to a higher standard of bombing accuracy than is justified by the facts, holds aerial bombardment to a higher standard than artillery or naval gunfire, and in particular fails to take into account intervening actions by a defender that prevent—and are intended to prevent—a bomber from bombing as accurately as possible.[197]

3. History also offers evidence of state practice that is not always consistent. Luftwaffe briefing photographs and documents for air raids on the A. V. Roe Supermarine aircraft factory, the Thornycroft boat building premises and the "British Mex. Petroleum Company" in Southampton in December 1940, suggest a desire properly to identify target locations.[198] Strong evidence has been offered that prior to 1942 the Luftwaffe exercised more than ordinary care in its bombing raids.[199] Yet in addition to Hitler's and Goering's view of the Luftwaffe as a weapon of intimidation and terror, plans were drawn to attack civilian populations,[200] and a leading historian of the Luftwaffe has observed that whether or not the bombing of Rotterdam was a mistake, Germany did not hesitate to note the connection between its bombing on 14 May and the surrender of all Dutch military forces the following day.[201] Similar contradictory evidence between a desire to place bombs squarely on legitimate military targets and a disdain for accuracy or care for the possibility of collateral civilian casualties can be found in the records of every other World War II air power. While state practice thus becomes important, it is difficult to ascertain a bombing policy merely by seeing where a bomb struck, because of the myriad factors that influence or may influence its eventual point of impact, as will be discussed.

Did indiscriminate bombing occur during World War II? Of course, and each

---

197. *See*, KALSHOVEN, BELLIGERENT REPRISALS 164–65, 168–69 (Leyden, 1971), in which the author concludes that the Luftwaffe bombing of London on 24 August 1940 and RAF Bomber Command's response against German cities were (based solely on results, dismissing intent, while acknowledging enemy defenses) "indiscriminate." Historically bombing accuracy diminishes by 200% once an aircraft is taken under fire. Thus, an aircraft whose normal Circular Error Probable (the radius of a circle within which half of the bombs are expected to fall) is, for example, 500 meters would increase to 1500 meters once the aircraft is taken under attack.

198. F. MASON, *supra* note 81, at 414. The book contains a number of illustrations of Luftwaffe target documents.

199. Horst Boog, "Luftwaffe and Unterschiedsloser Bombenkrieg bis 1942," at the "Conference on the Air War in World War II," Militargeschichtliches Forschungsamt, Freiburg im Breisgau, Federal Republic of Germany (Sept. 1, 1988).

200. W. MURRAY, *supra* note 85, at 21 notes that Nazi plans for the invasion of Czechoslovakia assigned the following tasks to its two air fleets: (a) destruction of the Czech air force, (b) hinderance of the mobilization and movement of reserves, (c) support of the army's advance, and (d) attack of the enemy population.

Likewise, Generaloberst Alfred Jodl in June 1940 offered three avenues for a direct attack on England: (a) an offensive by air and sea against British shipping combined with air attacks against centers of industry, (b) terror attacks by air against population centers, and (c) finally, a landing operation aimed at occupying England. W. MURRAY, STRATEGY FOR DEFEAT: THE LUFTWAFFE, 1933–1945 45 (Maxwell Air Force Base, Alabama, 1983).

In contrast, Horst Boog lists the following tasks: first, to annihilate the enemy air force by attacks on its ground organization and industrial base rather than fighting it in the air; second, to support the operations of the Army and Navy; and third, to bomb the centers of war potential in the rear of enemy territory. H. Boog *Higher Command and Leadership in the German Luftwaffe, 1939–1945*, in A. HURLEY & R. EHRHART, *supra* note 38, at 147. The last task was strategic (in the sense the term was used during World War II), and mirrors the mission of RAF Bomber Command.

201. W. MURRAY, *supra* note 85, at 40.

major participant was guilty of it at one time or another. The fundamental distinction between bombing forces was one of capability and emphasis more than intent.[202] This author agrees with the conclusion of Royse that the general measure of discrimination is tied to military utility or effectiveness, that is, that bomber forces should bomb as accurately as possible given their capabilities and opposition. Bomber forces during World War II generally endeavored to perform their respective missions at a level that made the most effective use of their capabilities, subject to conditions over the target (enemy defenses, wind, and weather). Certainly there are exceptions. Allied bomber forces exercised a greater standard of care in an effort to minimize civilian casualties in Nazi-occupied nations than they did in their attack of targets in Germany. But attempts by some critics to set a time during the war at which bombing forces could have become more discriminate are open to challenge.[203]

In this regard, even if more precise standards had existed during World War II, the law of war is not a suicide pact. It does not require that an attacker employ the most discriminate force available to him. Were that the case, RAF Bomber Command (for example) would have been obliged to fly precision-bombing missions exclusively once it demonstrated its capability to do so with the 1943 dams raids by No. 617 Squadron,[204] or a nation would be required to sacrifice commando units rather than employ bomber aircraft in attack of military objectives where there is a risk of collateral civilian casualties. No such obligation exists in the law of war.

XII. AIR WAR LAW: 1945

The destruction wrought in the process of World War II was a product not only of the condition of total war, but also the absence of clear legal standards. However, based upon the practice of nations during that conflict, and dismissing actions taken as "reprisals" (whether or not reprisals in fact) that require more detailed evaluation

202. As British historian R. J. Overy notes,

> It is worth looking at the German decision to plan for strategic bombing in more detail because this was an area of particular failure during the war. In fact so unsuccessful was it that most historians have dismissed altogether the idea that the Luftwaffe prepared for war in the same way as the Royal Air Force and the United States Army Air Forces. Yet at the Nuremberg trials Goering protested that his intention had been from the outset to create an air force for independent bombing operations, and that tactical army support was secondary.

R. OVERY, *supra* note 85, at 85, 106.

203. *See* BEST, *supra* note 8, at 280. He selects mid-1944 as that point in the war when RAF Bomber Command in particular should have been more discriminate in its attacks. *Cf.* TERRAINE, THE RIGHT OF THE LINE 678 (London, 1985), in which, speaking of a later time (February 1945), he remarks:

> [O]nly the luxury of hindsight and the detachment of non-participation can undervalue the enormous sense of that weight of time, the intense desire to bring the whole business to an end as quickly as possible, that possessed not merely Bomber Command, or the Royal Air Force, but virtually the whole nation.

The supposition also ignores other outside influences, such as weather. While U.S. B–17 crews fought valiantly to make their case for daylight precision bombing, in the closing months of 1944, using radar bombing through 10/10ths cloud, bombing accuracy decreased. Against Japan, for a variety of reasons, bombing efforts were not directed against precise industrial targets, but against urban areas—as RAF Bomber Command had been carrying out its attacks over Germany. *See* Gary J. Shandroff, The Evolution of Area Bombing in American Doctrine and Practice (New York University, 1972) (unpublished dissertation).

204. As described in BRICKHILL, THE DAM BUSTERS (London, 1951); EULER, ALS DEUTSCHLANDS DAMME BRACHEN (Stuttgart, 1978); COOPER, THE MEN WHO BREACHED THE DAMS (London, 1982), and SWEETMAN, OPERATION CHASTISE (London, 1982).

than space allows at this time, certain fundamental principles can be found interwoven throughout the aerial bombing campaigns of the warring nations:

a. The intentional attack of the civilian population generally was regarded as prohibited, in large measure owing to the military inefficiency of such attacks or greater priority of attack of specific targets related to the enemy's war effort. However, collateral injury to the civilian population or damage to civilian objects was the "price of doing business," *i.e.*, waging war. While there was some belief that such collateral injury or damage was a means for attack on the morale of the nation, this may well have been an afterthought to explain away the inherent inaccuracy of bombing.

b. To the degree that there was concern for collateral civilian casualties, it was regarded as a mutual obligation shared by the attacker, defender, and the individual civilian. The primary responsibility for protection of the civilian population rested squarely with the defender, and each nation exercised this responsibility through elaborate civil defense procedures.

c. Where collateral civilian casualties occurred, they could be attributed to myriad factors, not the least of which was the intensity of enemy defenses. Other factors included weather, enemy deception, dispersal of targets, and their commingling with the civilian population as a natural consequence of industrialization and urban growth.

d. Lawful targets were regarded as: military equipment, units, and bases; economic targets; power sources (coal, oil, electric, hydroelectric); industry (war supporting manufacturing, export and/or import); transportation (equipment, lines of communication, and petroleum, oil, and other lubricants necessary for transportation); command and control; geographic; personnel; military; and civilians taking part in the hostilities, including civilians working in industries directly related to the war effort.

If international legal standards were to be codified, it remained the responsibility of the nations of the world to do so. Subsequent negotiation of law of war treaties provided mixed help.

XIII. 1949 GENEVA CONVENTIONS

On September 4, 1945, only days after the conclusion of World War II, the International Committee of the Red Cross (ICRC) addressed a letter to the U.S. Department of State and to the foreign offices of Great Britain, the Soviet Union, China, and France, inviting each to send representatives to Geneva to discuss informally with the ICRC proposals for possible revision of international conventions relating to prisoners of war and civilian internees. Following these preliminary discussions, the ICRC planned to invite other governments to participate, to include the nations of the British Commonwealth, Belgium, Brazil, Czechoslovakia, the Netherlands, Norway, Poland, and Yugoslavia.

The ICRC had an underlying purpose for acting immediately after the cessation of hostilities. Its desire was to take advantage of the expertise developed by nations during the war and capitalize upon it before those participating specialists had returned to their civilian professions or lost sight of their wartime activities.

The U.S. Secretary of State agreed with the ICRC premise, and accepted its invitation by letter dated February 5, 1946. In preparation for the ICRC meeting, an interdepartmental Prisoner of War Committee was established. The committee was comprised of representatives from the Departments of State, War, Navy, and Justice, and the American National Red Cross. Members of the Post Office Department participated when matters relating to communications and mail were discussed. Seventeen formal meetings of the U.S. interdepartmental committee were held between July 1, 1946, and February 28, 1947. Although the committee's title suggests a primary interest in prisoner of war matters, its discussion was broader.

The ICRC held a preliminary conference of National Red Cross Societies for the study of issues related to the 1929 Geneva Conventions at its headquarters in Geneva in July 1946. Subsequently the ICRC convened a meeting of government experts who met in Geneva from April 14 to 26, 1947. Of the eighteen nations invited, sixteen accepted the invitation; fifteen (Australia, Belgium, Brazil, Canada, China, Czechoslovakia, France, Great Britain, India, Netherlands, New Zealand, Norway, Poland, Union of South Africa, and the United States) attended. The Soviet Union and Yugoslavia declined the invitation, while the Greek delegation was unable to attend when its aircraft was accidentally destroyed.

Despite the absence of the Soviet Union, the dissolution of the wartime alliance between Great Britain, the United States, and the Soviet Union was apparent, as Poland (the delegation having arrived a week late, apparently because it was awaiting instructions from Moscow) introduced a resolution condemning war and the new weapons of war. Poland made other proposals that would provide a basis for refusal to apply any prospective conventions that would be developed from any conferences on political grounds in the event of future hostilities. While unsuccessful, in retrospect the Polish effort was a harbinger of future Socialist application of the law of war.[205]

Although there was no agreement as to dates for a future diplomatic conference, the meeting of government representatives did produce reports regarding the modernization of the 1929 Geneva Conventions Relating to the Wounded and Sick in Armies in the Field and to Prisoners of War. The ICRC in turn produced four draft conventions that were introduced at the XVIIth International Red Cross Conference at Stockholm in August 1948. After their approval by that conference, the drafts were taken as the basis for discussions at the Diplomatic Conference convened by the Swiss Federal Council for the Establishment of International Conventions for the Protection of War Victims, held in Geneva from April 21 to August 12, 1949.

That conference produced four conventions that served to revise the 1929 Geneva Convention for the Relief of the Wounded and Sick in Armies in the Field; the 1907 Hague Convention X for the Adaptation to Maritime Warfare of the Principles of the Geneva Convention; and the 1929 Geneva Convention Relative to the Treatment of Prisoners of War; and to create a new treaty to deal with the protection of civilians in time of war. The four treaties are known collectively as the Geneva Conventions for the Protection of War Victims of August 12, 1949.[206] While the four 1949 Geneva

205. The preceding summary is contained in the Report to the Secretary of State of the U.S. Delegation to the Meeting of Government Experts (Aug. 26, 1947).

206. The four conventions are: Geneva Convention for the Protection of the Wounded and Sick in Armed Forces in the Field, *opened for signature* Aug. 12, 1949, 6 U.S.T. 3114, T.I.A.S. 3362, 75 U.N.T.S. 31; the Geneva Convention for the Amelioration of the Condition of the Wounded, Sick, and Shipwrecked Members of Armed Forces at Sea, *opened for signature* Aug. 12, 1949, 6 U.S.T. 3217, T.I.A.S. 3363, 75 U.N.T.S. 85; the Geneva Convention Relative to the Treatment of Prisoners of War, *opened for signature* Aug. 12, 1949, 6 U.S.T. 3316, T.I.A.S. 3364, 75 U.N.T.S. 135; and the Geneva Convention Relative to the Protection of Civilian Persons in Time of War, *opened for signature* Aug. 12, 1949, 6 U.S.T. 3516, T.I.A.S. 3365, 75 U.N.T.S. 287. The records of the negotiations are contained in Final Record of the Diplomatic Conference Convened by the Swiss Federal Council for the Establishment of International Conventions for the Protection of War Victims (Berne, 1950). *See* G. DRAPER, THE RED CROSS CONVENTIONS (1958).

Conventions primarily address war victims in the hands of a belligerent, they do include several provisions germane to this article.

Article 19 of the Geneva Convention for the Amelioration of the Condition of the Wounded and Sick in Armed Forces in the Field (GWS) provides:

> Fixed establishments and mobile medical units of the Medical Service may in no circumstances be attacked.
>
> The responsible authorities shall ensure that the said medical establishments and units are, as far as possible, situated in such a manner that attacks against military objectives cannot imperil their safety.

Similar language is contained in article 18, paragraph 5 of the Geneva Convention Relative to the Protection of Civilian Persons in Time of War (GC): "In view of the dangers to which hospitals may be exposed by being close to military objectives, it is recommended that such hospitals be situated as far as possible from such objectives."

Although the language is different, the provisions have the same intent, that is, to provide protection to hospitals and other medical equipment and establishments from the collateral effects of war. The provisions are important in their recognition of the *shared* responsibility for limiting collateral damage or, put another way, for not placing the responsibility for limiting collateral damages or injury exclusively on an attacker. The commentaries published by the ICRC on these two conventions make this clear.[207] But one commentary also noted that a hospital's "proximity must not appear to be an indirect attempt to protect a military objective from attack."[208] Article 28 of the GC is more direct, declaring that "The presence of a

---

207. COMMENTARY ON THE GENEVA CONVENTION FOR THE AMELIORATION OF THE CONDITION OF THE WOUNDED AND SICK IN ARMED FORCES IN THE FIELD [hereinafter GWS COMMENTARY] 198–99 (Geneva, 1952); and COMMENTARY ON THE GENEVA CONVENTION RELATIVE TO THE PROTECTION OF CIVILIAN PERSONS IN TIME OF WAR [hereinafter GC COMMENTARY] 152–53 (Geneva, 1958).

208. GWS COMMENTARY, *supra* note 207, at 199. Pictet, the editor of GC COMMENTARY, notes that "It will no longer be possible to change the location of many civilian hospitals already in existence. . . . In such cases the precautionary measure will consist in seeing that no military objectives are sited in the vicinity, and, if they are already there, that they are removed if possible." Pictet notes on the same page that:

> The legal protection accorded to . . . hospitals must be accompanied by practical measures to ensure that they are situated as far as possible from military objectives and to protect them from the accidental consequences of attacks on such objectives. If that is not done the protection is very likely to be illusory, even if the hospitals are clearly marked.

Id. at 153.

Pictet's statement was a fair prediction. During Linebacker II bombing operations against North Vietnam (18–29 December 1972), the Bach Mai Military Storage Complex was targeted for attack. The target was roughly twenty square miles in area, and included the Bach Mai military airfield in its center. Adjacent to the airfield was the 940-bed (unmarked) Bach Mai Hospital. A cell of three B–52 bombers was assigned the attack of the storage complex. The crews established a line of attack that paralleled (rather than passed over) the Bach Mai Hospital, in order to avoid damage to it. At the time of the attack of the military complex, the third B–52 in the cell had fallen five miles behind the other two. losing its mutual electronic countermeasures protection. As it crossed the bomb release line, it was hit by two Soviet SA–2 surface-to-air missiles. As the aircraft descended, out of control, some of its bombs struck the Bach Mai Hospital. While initial North Vietnamese reports suggested massive damage and injury to patients and staff (including some American prisoners of war), U.S. photographic assessment revealed the damage to be minimal. Subsequently North Vietnam acknowledged that the patients and medical staff had been evacuated prior to the commencement of Linebacker II operations, and that there were no American prisoners of war at the hospital at the time it was struck by the errant bombs. Nonetheless, a 1982 CBS *60 Minutes* program celebrating the tenth anniversary of the end of U.S. involvement in the Vietnam War resurrected the erroneous version of the hospital's damage. *See* Parks, *Linebacker and the Law of War*, 34 A. U. REV. 2, 22–23, 25 (Jan.–Feb. 1983).

protected person may not be used to render certain points or areas immune from military operations."[209]

The Geneva Convention Relative to the Treatment of Prisoners of War (GPW) establishes rather comprehensive protection for prisoners of war, providing:

> No prisoner of war may at any time be sent to, or detained in, areas where he may be exposed to the fire of the combat zone, nor may his presence be used to render certain points or areas immune from military operations.
>
> Prisoners of war shall have shelters against air bombardment and other hazards of war, to the same extent as the local civilian population. With the exception of those engaged in the protection of their quarters against the aforesaid hazards, they may enter such shelters as soon as possible after the giving of the alarm. Any other protective measure taken in favor of the population shall also apply to them.
>
> Detaining Powers shall give the Powers concerned, through the intermediary of the Protecting Powers, all useful information regarding the geographical location of prisoner-of-war camps.
>
> Whenever military considerations permit, prisoner-of-war camps shall be indicated in the daytime by the letters PW or PG, placed so as to be clearly visible from the air. The Powers concerned may, however, agree upon any other system of marking. Only prisoner-of-war camps shall be marked as such.

Similar language in article 83 of the GC provided like protection for civilian internees.[210]

---

209. Pictet's GC COMMENTARY makes it clear why this provision was incorporated into the GC:

> During the last World War public opinion was shocked by certain instances . . . of belligerents compelling civilians to remain in places of strategic importance (such as railway stations, viaducts, dams, power stations or factories), or to accompany military convoys, or again, to serve as a protective screen for . . . fighting troops. Such practices, the object of which is to divert enemy fire, have rightly been condemned as cruel and barbaric.

GC COMMENTARY, *supra* note 207, at 208. Pictet states that the prohibition applies "to the belligerents' own territory as well as to occupied territory, to small sites as well as to wide areas." *Id.* at 209. A dilemma surrounding this last statement is the fact that the Soviet Union and other socialist nations traditionally have asserted that the law of war does not bind them with regard to actions any of them may take in defense of their own territory, and that any claim to the contrary is not consistent with the sovereignty of the state. During the Rolling Thunder bombing campaign against North Vietnam (2 March 1965 to 1 November 1968), for example, the Government of North Vietnam made generous use of its civilian population and civilian objects, including hospitals, as a screen from attack of otherwise legitimate targets. *See* Parks, *supra* note 109, at 2–23.

210. Article 23, GPW, is contained in SCHINDLER & TOMAN, *supra* note 27, at 439; article 83, GC, is in SCHINDLER & TOMAN, *supra* note 27, at 526. The experience of the inadvertent attack of or damage to prisoner of war (POW) camps during World War II prompted the addition regarding marking. While there was some question during the negotiations as to the practicality of this requirement in the age of modern, high-speed jet aircraft, the advantage lies in being able to mark the location of prisoner of war camps on target intelligence maps for planning purposes in developing strike plans for attack of a target in the vicinity of a POW camp.

There is at least one instance of an aerial attack of a POW camp because it was not marked as such. Prisoner of War Camp Eight, located in Kang-Dong, North Korea, was struck by bombs from United Nations aircraft at 2100 on January 14, 1952. Twenty POWs were killed and fifty-five injured. A United Nations Command investigation revealed that the camp was unmarked, and had been struck while United Nations aircraft were carrying out attacks against military targets in the immediate vicinity of the camp. A strong protest was lodged by the United Nations Command, which included a demand that all POW camps and civilian internee camps be marked so as to be visible from the air. Although the North Koreans did not mark the camps, they did provide data showing the locations of their POW camps. 10 DIGEST OF INTERNATIONAL LAW 410 (Marjorie M. Whiteman, ed. 1968).

Pictet recognizes one difficulty with the requirement regarding notification of the location of POW camps, in that this may allow an enemy to stage a rescue operation against the camp. He dismisses this excuse on the basis that parties to World War II knew where each other's camps were located even

The 1949 Geneva Conventions for the Protection of War Victims contain language that is pragmatic and balanced, because they were written by individuals experienced in war. Responsibility for minimizing risk to hospitals (military or civilian), prisoner of war camps, and civilian internee camps was placed squarely in the hands of the party who could best control it, i.e., the defender, although the attacker had a clear obligation to avoid the intentional attack of any of these objects. The responsibility of the "defender," however, extended to taking action not only to avoid use of any of these protected objects as a shield for military operations, but also to minimize risk to their damage (or injury to protected persons within them) incidental to lawful military operations by an attacker.

XIV. 1954 HAGUE CONVENTION

A variety of law of war treaties contain provisions for the protection of cultural property. Damage done to cultural property during World War II prompted the Netherlands following the war to recommend the negotiation of a new convention for cultural property only.[211] A committee of government experts was convened by the General Conference of the United Nations Educational, Scientific and Cultural Organization (UNESCO) in 1952 to draft a convention. After receipt of the experts' draft, UNESCO sponsored a conference at The Hague from 21 April to 14 May, 1954. Attended by representatives from fifty-six nations, the conference produced the Hague Convention for the Protection of Cultural Property in the Event of Armed Conflict and its annexed Regulations for the Execution of the Convention.[212]

---

when they were not marked. His dismissal of this excuse does not entirely dispose of the possibility of a raid or rescue operation on a POW camp, as happened in World War II and in the 1970 American rescue mission against the abandoned Son Tay POW camp in North Vietnam. For example, on January 30, 1945, elements of the U.S. Army's 6th Ranger Battalion, reinforced by Alamo Scouts and Filipino guerrillas, rescued 511 United States and Allied POWs from a Japanese POW camp near Cabanatuan on Luzon in the Philippine Islands. The rescue mission is described in F. JOHNSON, RAID ON CABANATUAN (1978), and M. KING, RANGERS: SELECTED COMBAT OPERATIONS IN WORLD WAR II 55–71 (1985). On February 23, 1945, the U.S. Army's 1st Battalion, 511th Parachute Infantry conducted an airborne and amphibious assault on a Japanese compound at Los Banos in Luzon, where 2147 United States and Allied civilians were interned. *See* G. DEVLIN, PARATROOPER! 597–610 (1979); A. ARTHUR, DELIVERANCE AT LOS BANOS (1985); and E. FLANAGAN, JR., THE LOS BANOS RAID (1986). The 1970 Son Tay rescue mission is described in B. SCHEMMER, THE RAID (1975).

The prohibition on use of POWs to shield military objectives from attack is a different issue. On 19 May 1967, U.S. Air Force aircraft successfully attacked the Hanoi Thermal Power Plant, placing it out of commission. Immediately thereafter, the North Vietnamese established a small prisoner of war facility (nicknamed *Dirty Bird* by American POWs because of its filth) in a building adjacent to the Hanoi Thermal Power Plant, and made sure that U.S authorities were made aware of the presence of American POWs next to the power plant. One prisoner, Captain George G. McKnight, USAF, was made to work outside the *Dirty Bird* so that he would be observed by officials from the Canadian Embassy in Hanoi, as the North Vietnamese knew the Canadians would report their observations to United States authorities. It was from *Dirty Bird*'s solitary cells that Navy Lieutenant George T. Coker and Captain McKnight staged an unsuccessful escape attempt during the night of October 11–12, 1967. *See* J. HUBBELL, P.O.W. 304, 355–60 (1976). The Hanoi Thermal Power Plant remained off limits until the December 1972 Linebacker II bombing operations, when U.S. Air Force F-4 Phantom aircraft disabled the power plant using laser-guided bombs.

211. Previously protection for cultural property existed in articles in general law of war treaties, such as articles 27 and 56 of the Annex to Hague Convention IV of 1907 and article 5 of Hague Convention IX. In 1935, a regional agreement known as the Roerich Pact (SCHINDLER & TOMAN, *supra* note 27, at 737) was promulgated for the American nations. This was the first treaty devoted exclusively to the protection of cultural property in time of war.

212. Contained in SCHINDLER & TOMAN, *supra* note 27, at 745. *See* A. ROBERTS & R. GUELFF, DOCUMENTS ON THE LAWS OF WAR 339–70 (Oxford, 1982). The United States is not a party to the 1954 Hague Cultural Property Convention because of military objections made by the Joint Chiefs of Staff. However, the United States Army, which would have primary responsibility for its implementation

Protection of cultural property always has been dependent upon its not being used for military purposes. Thus article 27 of the Annex to Hague Convention IV of 1907 provides: "In sieges and bombardments all necessary steps must be taken to spare, as far as possible, buildings dedicated to religion, art, science, or charitable purposes, historic monuments, hospitals, and places where the sick and wounded are collected, *provided they are not being used at the time for military purposes.*"[213]

The language of article 27 also is significant in that it is neutral, that is, the obligation to minimize damage to cultural property is shared by the attacker and the defender. The defender's responsibility does not end merely with marking any such object with "distinctive and visible signs,"[214] but extends to other appropriate, commensense measures. Thus during the 1941–1944 German siege of Leningrad, the Russian defenders heavily sandbagged and covered with timbers the famous "bronze horseman" equestrian statue of Peter the Great, and the statues of General Mikhail Kutuzov and General Aleksandr Suvorov, conquerors of Napoleon, and took a number of other major steps to protect their cultural property.[215] Article 3 of

among the armed services, integrated the treaty into its doctrine as early as 1955. The details of the 1954 Hague Cultural Property Convention are taught in law of war and civil affairs courses offered by the United States armed services.

213. SCHINDLER & TOMAN, *supra* note 27, at 84 (emphasis added). Article 5 of Hague Convention IX Concerning Bombardment by Naval Forces in Time of War is similar, its concluding phrase stating "on the understanding that they are not used at the same time for military purposes." *Id.* at 813. Paragraph 7 of article 26 of the stillborn 1923 Hague Rules of Aerial Warfare provided that "A state . . . must abstain from using the monument and the surrounding zone for military purposes, or for the benefit in any way whatever of its military organization, or from committing within such monument or zone any act with a military purpose in view." *Id.* at 211.

214. Article 27 of Hague IV does not specify the type of distinctive or visible marking, but the second paragraph of article 5 of Hague IX states that "It is the duty of the inhabitants to indicate such monuments, edifices, or places by visible signs, which shall consist of large, stiff rectangular panels divided diagonally into two colored triangular portions, the upper portion black, the lower portion white." *Id.* at 813. The same distinctive marking was called for in article 25 of the unadopted 1923 Hague Rules of Air Warfare, but improved the provision contained in Hague IX. The former specified that the upper portion of the marking had to be black, while the Hague Air Rules anticipated the potential for confusion in combat by specifying that either could be on top, so long as the markings were the two black and white triangles.

215. H. SALISBURY, THE 900 DAYS: THE SIEGE OF LENINGRAD 176 (1969). By the ninth day of the war (July 1) more than one-third (a half million objects) of the great art treasures of Leningrad's incomparable Hermitage Museum had been packed and evacuated from the city. *Id.* at 129–30, 148–49. Salisbury further describes Russian efforts in Leningrad:

> Within a month the Leningrad Public Library had shipped off 360,000 of its most priceless items (out of a collection of 9,000,000). Voltaire's Library, the Pushkin archives and the incunabula had gone off in July [1941, the first full month of the German invasion]. Now the attic had been filled with sand and the most precious remaining books were removed to the cellars. The main reading room was closed, and a smaller room on the first floor was opened for 150 readers. The card catalogue, the information bureau, the print collections, had been put in the subbasement, and many treasures had been transferred to the gloomy subterranean galleries of the Peter and Paul Fortress and the Alexander Nevsky catacombs.
>
> Some fifty-two boxes of treasures from the great Pushkin palaces of Catherine and Alexander had been shipped out before the Germans swept in. The valuables of the Russian Museum were sent to Gorky and then . . . on to Perm by river barge.
>
> During the second half of July most of the animals in the Zoological Gardens had been evacuated. So had the Lenfilm studios, the scientific institutes of the Academy of Science and other institutes, totaling ninety-two in all.
>
> Most of the great artistic ensembles had now left Leningrad. The Philharmonic and the Pushkin Drama Theater went to Novosibirsk, the Conservatory to Tashkent, the Mariinsky Opera and Ballet to Perm, the Maly Opera to Orenburg. Two great trains, on July 1 and July 20, had carried off the treasures of the Hermitage and a third was being prepared.

the 1954 Hague Cultural Property Convention continues this obligation, stating: "The High Contracting Parties undertake to prepare in time of peace for the safeguarding of cultural property situated within their own territory against the foreseeable effects of an armed conflict, by taking such measures as they consider appropriate."[216]

Paragraph 1 of Article 4 of the 1954 Hague Cultural Property Convention codifies the mutual obligation for the protection of cultural property, providing:

> The High Contracting Parties undertake to respect cultural property situated within their own territory as well as within the territory of other High Contracting Parties by refraining from any use of the property and its immediate surroundings or by the appliances in use for its protection for purposes which are likely to expose it to destruction or damage in the event of armed conflict; and by refraining from any act of hostility directed against such property.[217]

The 1954 Cultural Property Convention makes a distinction between ordinary cultural property and cultural property entitled to special protection. The latter includes a limited number of refuges intended to shelter movable cultural property in the

---

Id. at 258. Similar actions were taken by other nations. *See* M. SIMON, BATTLE OF THE LOUVRE: THE STRUGGLE TO SAVE FRENCH ART IN WORLD WAR II (1971).

The responsibility was mutual, falling both on attacker and defender, and at times members of the attacking force had to be reminded of their obligation. For example, on December 29, 1943, General Dwight D. Eisenhower, United States Army, who was then serving as Commander in Chief, Allied Forces, circulated General Order No. 65 to all commanders regarding the protection of historical monuments in Italy:

> Today we are fighting in a country which has contributed a great deal to our cultural inheritance, a country rich in monuments which by their creation helped and now in their old age illustrate the growth of the civilization which is ours. We are bound to respect those monuments so far as war allows.
>
> If we have to choose between destroying a famous building and sacrificing our own men, then our men's lives count infinitely more and the buildings must go. But the choice is not always so clear-cut as that. In many cases the monuments can be spared without any detriment to operational needs. Nothing can stand against the argument of military necessity. But the phrase "military necessity" is sometimes used where it would be more truthful to speak of military convenience or even personal convenience. I do not want it to cloak slackness or indifference.
>
> It is a responsibility of higher commanders to determine through [Allied Military Government] officers the locations of historical monuments whether they be immediately ahead of our front lines or in areas occupied by us. This information passed to lower echelons through normal channels places the responsibility on all commanders of complying with the spirit of this letter.

10 DIGEST OF INTERNATIONAL LAW 438 (Marjorie M. Whiteman, ed. 1968). Eisenhower's order preceded the attacks on Monte Cassino, which ultimately led to the bombing of the abbey on top of the mountain on February 15, 1944. For discussion of that event, *see* M. BLUMENSON, U.S. ARMY IN WORLD WAR II, SALERNO TO CASSINO 395–418 (1969). *See also* III THE ARMY AIR FORCES IN WORLD WAR II, *Europe - Argument to V-E Day* 362–64 (W. Craven & J. Cate, eds. 1951), (Argument is a code name used during World War II); M. BLUMENSON, MARK CLARK 183–90 (1984); D. HAPGOOD & D. RICHARDSON, MONTE CASSINO (1984); and J. PARTON, *Air Force Spoken Here* GENERAL IRA EAKER & THE COMMAND OF THE AIR 359–64 (1986). The Combined Chiefs of Staff had issued a similar order on January 10, 1943, stating that "[c]onsistent with military necessity, the position of the church and of all religious institutions shall be respected and all efforts made to preserve the local archives, historical and classical monuments and objects of art." M. BLUMENSON, U.S. ARMY IN WORLD WAR II, SALERNO TO CASSINO, *supra*, at 395. While the bombing of the abbey at Monte Cassino remains one of the great controversies of World War II, the histories cited illustrate the difficulty of command decision making in the fog of war. For some further historical perspective, particularly as it relates to ground forces and their use or abuse of cultural property, *see* Haines, *Who Gives a Damn About Medieval Walls?*, 8 PROLOGUE 97–106 (Summer 1976).

216. SCHINDLER & TOMAN, *supra* note 27, at 173.

217. *Id.*

event of armed conflict, as well as centers containing monuments and other immovable cultural property of very great importance.[218] But specific conditions were placed upon providing special protection for such property. The property could receive special protection only if it is:

> situated at an adequate distance from any large industrial center or from any important military objective constituting a vulnerable point, such as, for example, an aerodrome, broadcasting station, establishment engaged upon work of national defense, a port or railway station of relative importance or a main line of communication [and is] . . . not used for military purposes.[219]

Recognizing that a cultural object may already be located in proximity to military bases or other objects that would constitute lawful targets, paragraph 5 of article 8 provides for its being given special protection "if the High Contracting Party asking for that protection undertakes, in the event of armed conflict, to make no use of the objective and particularly, in the case of a port, railway station or aerodrome, to divert all traffic therefrom. In that event, such diversion shall be prepared in time of peace."

In the event a belligerent undertakes activities that violate the provisions of the convention related to special protection, the cultural object can lose its protection. However, article 11 provides that the decision to revoke that protection "can be established only by the officer commanding a force the equivalent of a division in size or larger."[220]

The five law of war treaties (the four Geneva Conventions and the Hague Convention) negotiated during the decade following World War II, took a pragmatic view with regard to the changes in warfare brought about by aircraft as each addressed matters of concern within its respective scope. Responsibility for the protection of persons or objects in the main lay with the defender, not the attacker, in that it was recognized that the former had the greatest control over the persons or objects for whom or for which protection was sought. Each of the treaties also recognized the inevitability of collateral damage incidental to the conduct of military operations, particularly in the give-and-take between attacker and defender, and discouraged the placing of military objects in the vicinity of protected persons or objects, or vice-versa. As will be seen, this approach was abandoned in the negotiation of the 1977 Protocols Additional to the Geneva Conventions for the Protection of War Victims, and the burden essentially shifted entirely to the attacker despite clear evidence that many nations in the intervening years regularly used hospitals, cultural objects, civilian objects, and the civilian population to shield lawful targets from attack.

---

218. Article 8, paragraph 1.

219. Paragraphs (a) and (b), article 8. Paragraph 3 of article 8 states that a center containing monuments entitled to special protection "shall be used for military purposes whenever it is used for the movement of military personnel or material, even in transit. The same shall apply whenever activities directly connected with military operations, the stationing of military personnel, or the production of war material are carried on within the center." Paragraph 2 requires that "A refuge for movable cultural property may also be placed under special protection, wherever its location, if it is so constructed that, in all probability, it will not be damaged by bombs."

220. To date, very little property has been registered under the special property provisions, undoubtedly because of the high standard required of the applicant. Conversely, the level at which a decision may be taken to revoke that protection where special property is abused is relatively low, and in fact lower than the level at which the decision was made to bomb the abbey at Monte Cassino. This is not intended to suggest that Monte Cassino necessarily would have been entitled to the special protection envisioned by article 8, but rather to illustrate that the greatest responsibility for the protection of cultural property lies with the belligerent claiming that protection (and potential defender), rather than with an attacking force or belligerent carrying out military operations in the vicinity of that property.

XV. POST WORLD WAR II DEVELOPMENTS

The period following World War II led not to a permanent peace but to a number of major conflicts, including the action in Korea,[221] the Algerian war for independence,[222] the civil war in Nigeria,[223] the wars in Vietnam,[224] the guerrilla war in Malaya and other British wars,[225] the Arab-Israeli conflicts,[226] and the myriad internal conflicts that continue to plague the world.

---

221. On the use of airpower in Korea, *see* R. FUTRELL, THE UNITED STATES AIR FORCE IN KOREA, 1950–1953 (1961); AIRPOWER: THE DECISIVE FORCE IN KOREA (1957); and R. HALLION, THE NAVAL AIR WAR IN KOREA (1986).

222. *See* A. HORNE, A SAVAGE WAR OF PEACE (1978); and J. TALBOTT, THE WAR WITHOUT A NAME (1980).

223. *See* J. DE ST. JORRE, THE BROTHERS' WAR (1972); J. STREMLAU, THE INTERNATIONAL POLITICS OF THE NIGERIAN CIVIL WAR, 1967–1970 (1977); D. JACOBS, THE BRUTALITY OF NATIONS (1987); and STOCKHOLM INTERNATIONAL PEACE RESEARCH INSTITUTE (SIPRI) YEARBOOK 1968/69, 381–414 (Stockholm, 1970). Few conflicts have witnessed a more abusive use of airpower against the civilian population than Nigerian operations against the secessionist Biafra, and it revealed one of several dichotomies that was to be codified into the two 1977 Protocols. While Third World nations were anxious to incorporate into Protocol I restrictions on the use of airpower against them by other nations, they had no desire for limits on their use of airpower (or any other form of force) in their suppression of internal threats. Another dichotomy concerned the employment of mercenaries. Nigeria made extensive use of mercenaries during its civil war, including employment of many as pilots. Nigerian Air Force pilots were poorly trained, and in particular were unable to fly at night, the time when most relief shipments were flown into the beleagured Biafran nation; mercenaries were needed by Nigeria to interdict nighttime relief flights. But mercenaries fighting for Biafra left an indelible imprint on the Government of Nigeria, and it campaigned long and hard for the condemnation of mercenaries that exists in article 47 of Protocol I. Article 47 potentially limits the use of mercenaries by one nation against another, but does not prevent a nation from using them within its own territory in its defense against either an internal or external threat. *See* Parks, *Mercenaries and the Law of War*, in TERRORISM, POLITICAL VIOLENCE AND WORLD ORDER (Henry H. Han, ed. 1984).

224. The French campaigns against the Viet Minh are summarized in E. HAMMER, THE STRUGGLE FOR INDOCHINA, 1940–1954 (1954); E. O'BALLANCE, THE INDO-CHINA WAR, 1945–1954 (1961); B. FALL, STREET WITHOUT JOY (1961); J. ROY, THE BATTLE OF DIENBIENPHU (1963); B. FALL, HELL IN A VERY SMALL PLACE (1966); B. FALL, THE TWO VIET NAMS (1963); and J. BUTTINGER, VIETNAM: A DRAGON EMBATTLED (1967).

The use of U.S. airpower in the war in South Vietnam is contained in J. SCHLIGHT, THE WAR IN SOUTH VIETNAM: THE YEARS OF THE OFFENSIVE, 1965–1968 (1988); and D. MROZEK, AIR POWER & THE GROUND WAR IN VIETNAM (1989). The use of U.S. Air Force gunships throughout Southeast Asia is contained in J. BALLARD, DEVELOPMENT AND EMPLOYMENT OF FIXED-WING GUNSHIPS, 1962–1972 (1982).

The official history of the "out country" campaigns, *i.e.*, Laos, Cambodia, and North Vietnam is in preparation by Dr. Wayne Thompson, Office of Air Force History; no publication date has been announced. In 1980 Jacob Van Staaveren of the Office of Air Force History completed an official volume entitled INTERDICTION IN SOUTHERN LAOS, 1960–1968. Although cleared for open publication by the four military services, the Joint Chiefs of Staff, the Office of the Secretary of Defense, and the Central Intelligence Agency, it remains classified because of unspecified objections by the Department of State. *But see* C. ROBBINS, THE RAVENS (1987).

For the bombing campaigns against North Vietnam, *see* J. BROUGHTON, THUD RIDGE, *supra* note 109; W. MOMYER, AIR POWER IN THREE WARS (1978); U. SHARP, STRATEGY FOR DEFEAT (1978); P. MERSKY & N. POLMAR, THE NAVAL AIR WAR IN VIETNAM (1981); G. BASEL, PAK SIX (1987); J. NICHOLS & B. TILLMAN, *supra* note 109; J. BROUGHTON, GOING DOWNTOWN, *supra* note 109; M. CLODFELTER, THE LIMITS OF AIRPOWER (1989); J. ETHEL & A. PRICE, ONE DAY IN A LONG WAR: MAY 10, 1972, AIR WAR, NORTH VIETNAM (1989); Parks, *supra* note 109; and Parks, *supra* note 208.

225. The successful British campaign in Malaya is discussed in R. CLUTTERBUCK, THE LONG LONG WAR (1966); E. O'BALLANCE, MALAYA: THE COMMUNIST INSURGENT WAR, 1948–1960 (1966); N. BARBER, THE WAR OF THE RUNNING DOGS (1971) and R. STUBBS, HEARTS AND MINDS IN GUERRILLA WARFARE: THE MALAYAN EMERGENCY, 1948–1960 (1989). British military campaigns following World War II but preceding the 1974–1977 Diplomatic Conference that produced the 1977 Protocols are reported in M. DEWAR, BRUSH FIRE WARS (London, 1984).

226. *See* E. O'BALLANCE, THE ARAB-ISRAELI WAR, 1948 (London, 1956); E. O'BALLANCE, THE SINAI CAMPAIGN OF 1956 (1960); D. KURZMAN, GENESIS 1948: THE FIRST ARAB-ISRAELI WAR (1970); W. STEPHENSON, ZANEK! A CHRONICLE OF THE ISRAELI AIR FORCE (1971); E. O'BALLANCE, THE THIRD ARAB-ISRAELI WAR (London, 1972); E. O'BALLANCE, ARAB GUERRILLA POWER (1973);

Internal conflicts posed a particular problem. Primarily a product of the postwar period of decolonialization, they constitute the greatest threat to innocent civilians. The four Geneva Conventions of 1949 had taken a step to endeavor to interject the law of war into the internal conflict environment with article 3 common to each of them.[227] But more needed to be done. Moreover, a need existed to update the rules governing hostilities, rules not revised since the Hague Conventions of 1907, particularly in light of the progress that had been made in aircraft. The law clearly was far behind technology.

A. ICRC Draft Rules

In the early 1950s, the ICRC decided to extend its role beyond protection for war victims in the hands of a party to a conflict. The ICRC undertook to venture into areas regarding the conduct of hostilities that traditionally had been a part of the Hague law. In particular, members of the ICRC sought to regulate, if not prohibit, the employment of aerial bombardment beyond the immediate battlefield; in this regard the ICRC modified its traditional role of protection for war victims to take on a disarmament perspective. Disarmament and the law of war are simultaneously similar and dissimilar, and the dissimilarities would later operate to the disadvantage of advancement of the law of war in the 1977 Protocols. As will be seen, an ICRC fixation on attainment of restrictions on aerial bombardment took precedence over practical measures that might have enhanced the protection of the civilian population, to the detriment of the law of war. The early frustration of the ICRC with aerial bombing is illustrated by the following hypothetical scenario postulated by a leading member of the ICRC:

> Here are two villages in an occupied country. Detachments of the enemy are going through them. Unidentified inhabitants shoot down some fifteen soldiers. A rapid police inquiry naturally produces nothing. To identify the assailants would require long interrogations and probably torture, since it is a matter of extracting information from patriots, conscious of serving a sacred cause. Moreover, other columns are arriving and there can be no question of conducting enquiries for weeks. The [division] commander will simply consider 'the enemy' is present in these two villages. He has a few planes at his disposal; he causes one of the villages to be bombed flat and several hundred people are killed. In the case of the other, he orders . . . the execution of 25 people.
>
> Faced with these two series of homicides, what will be the attitude of justice? There is no room for hypotheses: the law is perfectly clear. The pilots who wiped out the village, and their officers, will be charged with no crime. On the other hand, the soldiers, members of the firing squad and officers who took no part in the execution . . . of the 25 inhabitants of the second village, will be found guilty of homicide.

E. O'BALLANCE, THE ELECTRONIC WAR IN THE MIDDLE EAST, 1968–1970 (London, 1974); C. HERZOG, THE WAR OF ATONEMENT (1975); E. WEIZMAN, ON EAGLES' WINGS (1976); E. O'BALLANCE, NO VICTOR, NO VANQUISHED: THE YOM KIPPUR WAR (London, 1978); T. DUPUY, ELUSIVE VICTORY: THE ARAB-ISRAELI WARS, 1947–1974 (1978); Shlaim & Tanter, *Decision Process, Choice, and Consequences: Israel's Deep-Penetration Bombings in Egypt, 1970*, 30 WORLD POLITICS 483–517 (July 1978); Y. BAR-SIMON-TOV, THE ISRAELI-EGYPTIAN WAR OF ATTRITION, 1969–1970 (1980); and C. HERZOG, THE ARAB-ISRAELI WARS (1982).

227. Common article 3 is contained in SCHINDLER & TOMAN, *supra* note 27, at 376 (for the GWS). Although it provides minimal protection for persons taking no part in the hostilities or suspected of taking part in the hostilities, it was a major step forward in the law of war. To date, however, effective implementation of this minimal protection has been limited. In fact, the record of the 1949 Geneva Conventions is open to mixed evaluation. At the time this article was written, 167 of the 171 nations of the world are parties to the four 1949 Geneva Conventions; more nations are parties to the 1949 Geneva Conventions than are members of the United Nations. However, this count is misleading, as there has been virtually no implementation of even the most basic requirements of those four treaties in 98% of those nations. Third World implementation is nonexistent in all but one or two nations.

From this state of the law there can be drawn only one precious, but amoral, axiom: Never carry out executions or destructions with the care of a craftsman. But long live wholesale massacre![228]

In 1956 the ICRC produced its Draft Rules for the Limitation of the Dangers Incurred by the Civilian Population in Time of War.[229] Following so closely on the 1949 Geneva Conventions, the draft rules were adventurous in extending their applicability equally to international armed conflicts *and* internal conflicts;[230] the ICRC clearly recognized the danger posed to the civilian population by the latter.

Discussion of several of the provisions contained in the Draft Rules germane to this article will be deferred until they are considered in the form in which they ultimately appeared in the 1977 Protocol I.[231] However, some provisions merit consideration at this time, because their form changed considerably during negotiation of the 1977 Protocols or were dropped entirely.

Article 6 of the Draft Rules provided in part:

Attacks directed against the civilian population as such, whether with the object of terrorizing it or for any other reason, are prohibited.

It is forbidden to attack dwellings, installations or means of transport, which are for the *exclusive use of*, or occupied by, *the civilian population*.

Nevertheless, should members of the civilian population . . . be within or in close proximity to a military objective they must accept the risks resulting from an attack directed against that objective. [Emphasis added]

The article is significant in two respects. First, it protected from international attack only those objects used exclusively by the civilian population, thereby recognizing the legality of attack on civilian objects, the potential use of which may be of value to a nation's war effort or which may be used simultaneously for military and

228. P. Boissier, L'Epee et la Balance 55–56 (Geneva, 1953), translation by Professor Geoffrey Best. Boissier's statement is legally incorrect while indicating the bias that existed (and continues to exist) at the ICRC regarding aerial bombardment. While the pilots have a right to carry out an order on the assumption that it is lawful unless it is patently illegal—and Boissier's hypothetical situation does not suggest to the contrary, although pilots normally would not receive a mission assignment to "bomb a village" as such—the commander who orders the mission is directing acts of murder for which he could be held accountable. At best they are reprisals against the civilian population, which are prohibited by article 33 of the 1949 Geneva Convention Relative to the Protection of Civilian Persons in Time of War (GC). The means used does not make an otherwise illegal act legitimate.

There are three other matters of interest in the hypothetical. Boissier purposely selects aircraft as the means for attack of the village, although artillery could have been used for the same (illegal) purpose; this illustrates the ICRC fixation against aerial bombardment. The hypothetical ignores customary international law and the domestic law of the nation to which the military commander belongs. Such an attack clearly would have been a violation of customary law and, in the United States, charges could have been brought against the commander in question for violations of article 118 (murder), Uniform Code of Military Justice. Finally, Boissier's suggestion that the commander in question would resort to torture of civilians in an attempt to gain information as to the identity of the attackers of his forces manifests Boissier's skepticism with the law of war as such, because torture of civilians in occupied territory is expressly prohibited by articles 31 and 32, GC.

229. Schindler & Toman, *supra* note 27, at 251–57.

230. Article 2 of the Draft Rules provides that:

The present rules shall apply:

(a) In the event of declared war or any other armed conflict, even if the state of war is not recognized by one of the Parties to the conflict. [This language is taken from article 2 common to the four 1949 Geneva Conventions.]

(b) In the event of an armed conflict not of an international character.

231. For example, use of the term "attacks" as found in article 3, the definition of "civilian population" contained in article 4, and the definition of "military objective" contained in article 7 will be discussed in conjunction with the analysis of articles 49(1), 50, and 52, respectively.

civilian purposes.[232] Second, it recognized that members of the civilian population assume a certain risk of injury incidental to combat operations when they place themselves within, or adjacent to, a military objective.

Article 10 was expressly written to prohibit target area bombing as practiced during World War II, providing: "It is forbidden to attack without distinction, as a single objective, an area including several military objectives at a distance from one another where elements of the civilian population, or dwellings, are situated in between the said military objectives." The provision is a manifestation of the ICRC desire to preclude a repetition of area bombing as it was practiced during World War II. While commendable on first impression, it fails to take into consideration steps that may be taken by a defender, such as dispersal of supplies into populated areas, that may lead to such actions by a belligerent engaged in legitimate, offensive operations. To its credit, however, the ICRC had recognized this imbalance, and incorporated the following passive precautions into article 11:

> The Parties to the conflict shall, so far as possible, take all necessary steps to protect the civilian population subject to their authority from the dangers to which they would be exposed in an attack—in particular by removing them from the vicinity of military objectives and from threatened areas.
>
> Similarly, the Parties to the conflict shall, so far as possible, avoid the permanent presence of armed forces, military materiel, mobile military establishments or installations, in towns or other places with a large civilian population.

The danger of these companion articles lay in the fact that they had begun the shift of responsibility for collateral civilian casualties from the traditional shared responsibility to placing it predominantly on the belligerent engaged in offensive operations—and with the least control over the civilian population. Thus the language concerning area bombardment was absolutely prohibitive, whereas the language regarding movement of the civilian population from the area surrounding a target was hortatory, not mandatory.

Article 13 of the Draft Rules strengthened the language contained in article 28, Geneva Convention, by providing: "Parties to the conflict are prohibited from placing or keeping members of the civilian population subject to their authority in or near military objectives, with the idea of inducing the enemy to refrain from attacking those objectives." Although this article established a clear duty, it failed to specify responsibility for collateral casualties where the duty is violated. It established a duty without a remedy, while shifting the responsibility for collateral casualties to the party engaged in offensive operations.

At this point in time, however, the issue became moot. The ICRC introduced the rules at the XIXth Red Cross Conference held in New Delhi, India, in 1957, where they were greeted by a response from governments that can be described (at best) as no reaction or (at worst) as one that was extremely negative. There were several reasons for this. First, the rules were proposed in the midst of the Cold War, when perceptions and policies between the two superpowers was markedly different from the era of *Glasnost* and *Perestroika*; the first of the postwar arms control agreements had not even seen the light of day at that time.[233]

232. Such as power plants, refineries, and lines of communication.

233. The first postwar arms control agreement was The Antarctic Treaty (12 U.S.T. 794, T.I.A.S. 4780, 402 U.N.T.S. 71), signed by the United States on December 2, 1959, with ratification advised by the Senate on August 10, 1960. It entered into force on June 23, 1961. This arms control agreement was made possible because seven nations (Argentina, Australia, Chile, France, New Zealand, Norway,

Second, article 14 specifically condemned weapons "whose harmful effects—resulting in particular from the dissemination of incendiary, chemical, bacteriological, radioactive or other agents—could spread to an unforeseen degree . . . from the control of those who employ them, thus endangering the civilian population." Both the Soviet Union and the United States saw a clear attempt by the ICRC to prohibit or regulate nuclear weapons, which neither was prepared to accept.

The third reason related directly to the second, and that concerned the role of the ICRC in armed conflict. The ICRC is a private Swiss corporation made up entirely of Swiss citizens. It has performed extremely well (given the circumstances) in endeavoring to provide protection for war victims in the hands of a belligerent. But Switzerland is a neutral nation whose citizens have not fought a military engagement since March 5, 1798, and there was a strong and justifiable reluctance to permit private individuals with little or no modern military training or experience to intercede into an area as complex as the conduct of hostilities.[234]

B. Conferences of the 1960s

The ICRC was persistent, and reintroduced its Draft Rules at the XXth International Conference of the Red Cross in Vienna, Austria, in October 1965. That conference adopted a resolution with the following language relating to the law of war:

> solemnly declares that all Governments and other authorities responsible for action in armed conflicts should conform at least to the following principles:
>
> - that the right of the parties to a conflict to adopt means of injuring the enemy is not unlimited;
> - that it is prohibited to launch attacks against the civilian population as such;
> - that distinction must be made at all times between persons taking part in the hostilities and members of the civilian population to the effect that the latter be spared as much as possible; [and]
> - that the general principles of the law of war apply to nuclear and similar weapons.[235]

Over the next two years several events were to provide the ICRC with some unexpected, if not highly questionable allies, in large measure because of the U.S. military operations in defense of South Vietnam. Consider the following three examples.

---

and the United Kingdom), were making specific claims to the Antarctic region on the basis of discovery, exploration, or geographic proximity. Eight other nations, including the United States and the Soviet Union, had engaged in exploration but had put forward no specific claims. Neither the Soviet Union nor the United States recognized the claims of other nations; hence there was a mutual interest in reaching agreement to demilitarize the continent. United States Arms Control and Disarmament Agency, ARMS CONTROL AND DISARMAMENT AGREEMENTS 19–27 (1982).

234. Switzerland is not a member of the United Nations and, accordingly, has substantially less military experience than some other neutrals (such as Sweden), whose military forces have participated in peacekeeping operations. While members of the ICRC have considerable experience carrying out their humanitarian missions in areas of armed conflict, oftentimes at great personal risk, their experience nonetheless remains that of an observer rather than a participant. They have no experience in decision making in the heat of battle or the fog of war. This affects both their ability and credibility to deal with those portions of the law of war relating to the conduct of hostilities, and frequently is manifested in proposals offered by the ICRC.

There also was some petty jealousy, as rules related to the conduct of hostilities traditionally were reserved for negotiation in The Hague, the Netherlands.

235. SCHINDLER & TOMAN, *supra* note 27, at 259–60. Editorial discussion of the resolution in the SCHINDLER & TOMAN text errs, however, in stating that "The resolution was affirmed by the United Nations General Assembly in resolution 2444." While the first three sentences quoted were contained in the General Assembly resolution, the fourth sentence relating to nuclear weapons was deleted.

From January 3–15, 1966, the first Tri-Continental Conference of Asian, African and Latin American Revolutionary Solidarity, sponsored by the Afro-Asian Peoples Solidarity Organization, was held in Havana, Cuba. Delegates to the Communist-dominated conference represented governments, opposition parties and revolutionary guerrilla movements. The major issues discussed at the conference were the Vietnam War, the 1965 U.S. stability operation in the Dominican Republic, and "colonialism and neo-colonialism throughout the world." The language of resolutions adopted by the conference mirrors that adopted by the International Conference on Human Rights at Teheran, Iran, in May 1968, and in United Nations General Assembly Resolutions cited by the ICRC in its support for a Diplomatic Conference updating the law of war.

Socialist World protests against U.S. efforts to assist South Vietnam in its resistance to conquest by North Vietnam, and especially the Socialist World's campaign against the United States bombing of North Vietnam, were carefully couched in law of war terms alleging "indiscriminate" bombing of "non-military objectives," "civilian" casualties, and the use of "illegal" weapons.

The defeat of Arab nations by Israel during the Six-Day War in June 1967, was in large measure because of Israel's effective use of its numerically smaller, but qualitatively superior air force. Resolutions passed by the United Nations Security Council and General Assembly calling upon Israel to adhere to the 1949 Geneva Conventions in the territories it occupied as a result of its victory in the June 1967, Six–Day War suggested that the Arab bloc intended to use the law of war as a diplomatic tool in its continuing conflict with Israel.[236]

It was during this time that the ICRC revisited its proposal to convene a conference to update the law of war, on the assumption that any call for a conference would have strong support in the Third World. On May 19, 1967, only days before the Six-Day War, the ICRC addressed a memorandum to all States Parties to the 1949 Geneva Conventions raising a question regarding further development of the law of war. The memorandum included a list the ICRC had prepared of what it considered to be the written and customary rules that could be considered as still in force. Its timing could not have been more propitious.

The ICRC assumption was confirmed in language adopted by the International Conference on Human Rights at its meeting in Teheran, Iran, on May 12, 1968, where its Resolution XXIII contained the following:

> Considering further that the Red Cross Conventions of 1949 are not sufficiently broad in scope to cover all armed conflicts, . . .
>
> noting also that *minority racist* or *colonial regimes* which refuse to comply with the decisions of the United Nations and the principles of the Universal Declaration of Human Rights frequently resort to executions and inhuman treatment of *those who struggle against such regimes* and considering that such persons should be protected against inhuman or brutal treatment and also that such persons if detained *should be treated as prisoners of war* . . . .
>
> 1. Requests the General Assembly [of the United Nations] to invite the Secretary-General to study:

236. Security Council Resolution 237 Concerning Humanitarian Protection for Civilians and Prisoners of War in the Area of the Middle East Conflict, June 14, 1967. S.C. Res. 237, 22 U.N. SCOR, Resolutions and Decisions of the Security Council 1967, at 5, U.N. Doc. S/INF/22/Rev. 2 (1968). General Assembly Resolution 2252 (ES-V) Concerning Humanitarian Assistance to Civilians and Prisoners of War, July 4, 1967. G.A. Res. 2252 [ES-V], U.N. GAOR, Resolutions adopted by the General Assembly during its Fifth Emergency Special Session June 17, September, 18, 1967, Supp. 1, at 3–4, U.N. Doc. A/6798 (1967).

> . . . (b) The need for additional humanitarian international conventions or possible revision of existing Conventions to ensure better protection of civilians, prisoners and combatants in all armed conflicts and the prohibition and limitation of the use of certain methods and means of warfare.[237]

Although the resolution did not limit its scope to organizations or individuals fighting against Israel, it was at this point that the effort of the ICRC to develop a new law of war treaty became inextricably intertwined with the Arab war against Israel and of other conflicts supported by the Third World. This resolution not only had an effect on the overall shape of the treaty that was to become the 1977 Protocol I, but also was related directly to the language drafted in those articles that affect aerial bombardment. Qualitatively Israel had been the principal airpower in the Middle East; the Arab nations saw a chance at the 1974–1977 Diplomatic Conference to diminish Israel's capabilities. Those efforts would pay large dividends during the 1982 Israeli incursion into Lebanon, as will be seen. Other Third World nations viewed the proposal as a means to limit external threats to their respective regimes.

Seven months later the United Nations General Assembly adopted Resolution 2444 regarding respect for human rights in armed conflicts. The resolution repeated the first three of the four points contained in the resolution adopted by the XXth International Conference, while deleting the fourth point regarding nuclear weapons.[238]

At the XXIst International Conference of the Red Cross, held in Istanbul, Turkey, in September 1969, the conferees adopted a resolution (drafted by the ICRC) urging the ICRC to convene a conference of government experts representing the principal legal and social systems of the world to review documents and proposals prepared by the ICRC in order to assess those areas of the law of war in which progress might be possible. In short, the ICRC drafted a resolution calling upon itself to convene a conference to review the documents which it had prepared.[239]

---

237. SCHINDLER & TOMAN, *supra* note 27, at 261–62 (emphasis added).

238. SCHINDLER & TOMAN, *supra* note 27, at 263–64. The resolution made an unfortunate association of the law of war with human rights. The former are specific rules relating to legal rights and obligations of a nation engaged in war, some of which involve deprivation of the most fundamental human right, the right to life, and for the violation of which individuals can be held criminally responsible. They also are frequently a product of military considerations. In contrast, the latter is largely philosophical and political, with little or no individual criminal responsibility for its breaches; in the words of one author, "even their discussion (not to mention their implementation) is dependent on political bodies and their conjectural majorities." Mario'n Mushkat, *The Development of International Humanitarian Law and the Law of Human Rights*, 21 GERMAN YEARBOOK OF INTERNATIONAL LAW 150–68 at 160 (1978). Mushkat points out that much of the marriage was intended to legitimize the use of violence by the Palestine Liberation Organization (PLO) against Israel while providing international status for the PLO, and for no other reason. This was carried over into the 1977 Protocol I.

239. There was not only a need for an update of the law of war, particularly as it related to aerial bombardment, but also some interest in new negotiations. However, the interest was not overwhelming within governments. At a meeting, such as the Conference of the International Red Cross, it is difficult for delegations to vote against general resolutions calling upon humanitarian ideals, particularly when they have no binding effect upon governments. But such apparently harmless "motherhood and apple pie" resolutions are but one step in the building block process used by the ICRC and some of its more liberal supporters, such as Sweden and Switzerland, to suggest to governments that a conference is necessary. Since the 1974–1977 Diplomatic Conference, the United States and other nations have taken a more cautious approach to resolutions proposed at Red Cross Conferences. At the XXVth Conference of the Red Cross and Red Crescent, held in Geneva in October 1986, for example, the United States and Soviet Union delegations joined with others to defeat a resolution prepared by Sweden and Switzerland condemning directed energy weapons. To illustrate further how forum shopping is used in this building block process, following defeat of this resolution, the Government of Sweden in April 1988, held an informal meeting at its Mission in Geneva to interest selected delegations from the United Nations Committee on Disarmament on the same issue. The Soviets declined to attend, while the author was sent to Geneva for the sole purpose of attending the meeting to repudiate statements made by

That same month the Institute of International Law passed a resolution regarding "The Distinction Between Military Objectives and Nonmilitary Objects in General and Particularly the Problems Associated with Weapons of Mass Destruction."[240] While the resolution takes an extreme view and does not restate customary international law, it is yet another indication of the attention that the law of war was receiving at this time, in no small measure because of the involvement of the United States in the war in Vietnam.[241] Slowly but surely, the stage was being set for a new law of war conference.

C. United Nations Resolutions 2444 and 2675

In a letter dated September 22, 1972, the General Counsel of the Department of Defense responded to a letter from Senator Edward M. Kennedy relating to the United States interpretation of the law of war. The General Counsel's letter specifically rejected the resolution of the Institute of International Law as an accurate statement of the law of war, but stated that it regarded the three points contained in United Nations General Assembly Resolution 2444 (taken from the first three points of the resolution of the XXth Red Cross Conference, quoted above) as declaratory of customary international law. However, the letter elaborated upon the United States interpretation of these broad principles, noting:

a. While armed forces must refrain from making civilians as such the object of armed attack, they are not restrained from attacking lawful targets, even though there is a risk of incidental casualties or damage to civilian objects in the vicinity of the target;

b. The third principle (distinction must be made at all times between persons taking part in the hostilities and members of the civilian population, so that civilians are spared as much as possible) addresses primarily the party exercising control over members of the civilian population. The DOD General Counsel's letter went on to state that:

> This principle recognizes the interdependence of the civilian community with the overall war effort of a modern society. But its application enjoins the party controlling the population to use its best efforts to distinguish or separate its military forces and war-making activities from members of the civilian population to the maximum extent feasible so that civilian casualties and damage to civilian objects incidental to attacks on military objectives will be minimized as much as possible.

Swedish authorities in their draft papers; this second Swedish attempt failed. This was followed by a Swedish attempt to get the matter on the agenda of the United Nations Special Session on Disarmament, held in New York in June 1986, which also did not meet with success. In February 1989, the author, along with a medical expert and a scientist, each employed by the United States Government, were invited by the ICRC to attend a meeting of "experts" at the ICRC (at ICRC expense) on directed energy warfare that paralleled previous Swedish efforts. All U.S. invitees declined their invitations, as did invitees from the United Kingdom and Canada. The latter nations sent observers to the meeting, which was held in June 1989. It is expected that the ICRC will prepare a report indicating that its "experts" supported the Swedish call for new negotiations. As with some other Swedish initiatives regarding weapons, the primary motive is economic rather than humanitarian or altruistic. Given the ICRC's purported dedication to its own principles of neutrality and independence, its support for a program by an individual nation that is based on that nation's economic and political interests is questionable and inconsistent with criteria (viz., neutrality and independence) for U.S. contributions to the ICRC (The United States is the largest contributor to the ICRC.)

240. SCHINDLER & TOMAN, *supra* note 27, at 265–66.

241. The Vietnam War focused a great deal of attention on the law of war. There were many publications produced during this time that raised an interest in the subject. Three examples are 1–4 THE VIETNAM WAR AND INTERNATIONAL LAW, (1968–1976); WHEN BATTLE RAGES, HOW CAN LAW PROTECT? (John Corey, ed. 1971); and LAW AND THE INDO-CHINA WAR (John Moore, ed. 1972).

The letter warned against "attempts to limit the effects of attacks in an unreasonable manner," expressly referring to the 1923 Hague Rules of Air Warfare as such a failed attempt. The letter closed after repeating its rejection of the resolution of the Institute of International Law.[242] Its importance lies in its statement of the law of war as it was considered to have existed prior to the 1974–1977 Diplomatic Conference.

The following year the United Nations General Assembly (UNGA) adopted Resolution 2675 (XXV) which, after "noting with appreciation" the work of the ICRC "to ensure the better protection of human rights in armed conflicts of all types," set forth the following basic principles:

> - In the conduct of military operations during armed conflicts, a distinction must be made at all times between persons actively taking part in hostilities and civilian populations;
>
> - In the conduct of military operations, every effort should be made to spare civilian populations from the ravages of war, and all necessary precautions should be taken to avoid injury, loss or damage to civilian populations;
>
> - Civilian populations as such should not be the object of military operations;
>
> - Dwellings and other installations that are used only by civilian populations should not be the object of military operations;
>
> - Places or areas designated for the sole protection of civilians, such as hospital zones or similar refuges, should not be the object of military operations; and
>
> - Civilian populations, or individual members thereof, should not be the object of reprisals, forcible transfers or other assaults on their integrity.[243]

The text of UNGA Resolution 2675 bears examination for several reasons. It correctly states the general requirement regarding discrimination in the application of force, while limiting the attack of civilian objects only to those used *exclusively* for military purposes. However, the requirement that "every effort" must be made to spare civilian populations the effects of war drifts away from the customary standard of reasonable care, while placing responsibility entirely upon military commanders without a concomitant responsibility on the part of the civilian population as such. The prohibition on reprisals exceeded that stated in the law of war at that time, in that the population of the enemy not in the hands of an occupying power remained a legitimate object for reprisals. As with all UNGA resolutions, UNGA Resolution 2675 was not binding; but it also was not authoritative as to the state of the law of war at the time. Its intended effect, however, was cumulative, in that it offered yet another "building block" on the road to the ICRC's goal of a new law of war conference.

D. Conference of Government Experts

Two years later the ICRC convened its Conference of Government Experts on the Reaffirmation and Development of International Humanitarian Law Applicable in Armed Conflicts. That conference had been preceded by a Conference of Red Cross

242. A summary of the letter is contained in Arthur W. Rovine, *Contemporary Practice of the United States Relating to International Law*, 67 AM. J. INT'L L. 122–25 (January 1973). The General Counsel's letter was coordinated with The Judge Advocate Generals of the Army, Navy, and Air Force.

243. SCHINDLER & TOMAN, *supra* note 27, at 267–68.

Experts on the Reaffirmation and Development of International Humanitarian Law Applicable in Armed Conflicts, held in The Hague from March 1–6, 1971, in which the ICRC explained its agenda and drafts to members of national Red Cross Societies.[244]

The first session of the Conference of Government Experts was conducted in Geneva from May 24 to June 11, 1971. Its basic aim was to have attendees review the lengthy set of documents and proposals submitted by the ICRC in order to assess where progress would be possible in the further development of the law of war.[245] Almost 200 "experts" from thirty-nine nations, including the United States, attended the meeting.[246] It was apparent that there was insufficient time to complete the work necessary to produce an agreed draft text, and the conferees agreed to a second session.[247]

The second session of the Conference of Government Experts was held in Geneva from May 3 to June 2, 1972.[248] Because there had been complaints that the Third World had not been adequately represented at the first conference, all states parties to the 1949 Geneva Conventions were invited to send representatives to the second session. The comments of the senior U.S. representative in his June 1, 1972, closing

244. REPORT ON THE WORK OF THE CONFERENCE OF RED CROSS EXPERTS ON THE REAFFIRMATION AND DEVELOPMENT OF INTERNATIONAL HUMANITARIAN LAW APPLICABLE IN ARMED CONFLICTS, THE HAGUE, 1–6 MARCH 1971 (Geneva, April 1971). The attendees were the senior officers of national Red Cross Societies, not experts. The United States attendees were from the American National Red Cross and knew little of the law of war. The United States delegation head, the President of the American National Red Cross, acknowledged on many occasions his skepticism regarding the efficacy of the law of war.

245. The reader will note that the ICRC had developed the term "international humanitarian law applicable in armed conflicts" to supplant the traditional *law of war*. The first step actually was taken within the United Nations, where the term "law of armed conflict" had replaced law of war, on the theory that the Charter of the United Nations had outlawed war—notwithstanding the fact that United Nations forces fought in the Korean *War*, and the general public refers to conflicts by the traditional term of *war* (*e.g.*, the 1967 Arab-Israeli War, the 1971 Indo-Pakistani War, the 1973 Yom Kippur War, the Vietnam War, the 1982 Falklands/Malvinas War, *etc.*). Moreover, combatants captured in an "armed conflict" continue to be called "prisoners of *war*" rather than "prisoners of *armed conflict*," the acronym for which (as some pundits have noted) would be the same as that of the Pentagon Officers Athletic Club. Changing *law of war* to *law of armed conflict* was a way of avoiding acknowledgment of the limits of international law. While the U.S. Navy and Air Force changed their programs to use the term "*law of armed conflict*," the overall program of the Department of Defense as well as the programs of the Army and Marine Corps have retained the traditional term *law of war*, as has the author.

The ICRC borrowed a page from the Marxist-Leninist lexicon in adding the term "humanitarian", as it suggests that anyone who opposes adoption of the rules under consideration is anti-humanitarian. The term is singularly inappropriate to those parts of the law of war dealing with combat. The author, who has taken the life of other men in combat at ranges as close as three meters, finds nothing humanitarian about such an action—which is fully condoned by the law of war.

246. Again, there were no criteria for establishing the expertise of the "experts." The majority of attendees were lawyers, not military officers from the combat arms branches. This was the case throughout the Diplomatic Conference and the subsequent Conference on Certain Conventional Weapons.

247. U.S. DEPARTMENT OF STATE, REPORT OF THE U.S. DELEGATION TO THE CONFERENCE OF GOVERNMENT EXPERTS ON THE REAFFIRMATION AND DEVELOPMENT OF INTERNATIONAL HUMANITARIAN LAW APPLICABLE IN ARMED CONFLICTS, GENEVA, MAY 24–JUNE 11, 1971 (1971); INTERNATIONAL COMMITTEE OF THE RED CROSS, REPORT ON THE WORK OF THE CONFERENCE OF GOVERNMENT EXPERTS ON THE REAFFIRMATION AND DEVELOPMENT OF INTERNATIONAL HUMANITARIAN LAW APPLICABLE IN ARMED CONFLICTS, GENEVA, 24 MAY–12 JUNE 1971 (Geneva, August 1971); COMMENTARY ON THE ADDITIONAL PROTOCOLS OF 8 JUNE 1977 TO THE GENEVA CONVENTIONS OF 12 AUGUST 1949 [ICRC COMMENTARY] xxxi (Geneva, 1957).

248. The conference was again preceded by a preparatory meeting of Red Cross national society officials. ICRC, REPORT ON THE WORK OF THE CONFERENCE OF RED CROSS EXPERTS ON THE REAFFIRMATION AND DEVELOPMENT OF INTERNATIONAL HUMANITARIAN LAW APPLICABLE IN ARMED CONFLICTS, VIENNA, 20–24 MARCH 1972 (Geneva, April 1972). The same "experts" from the American National Red Cross who attended the 1971 Hague meeting attended the Vienna meeting.

statement at the second session of the Conference of Government Experts suggest the change in atmosphere that had occurred:

> Some countries have been led by their experience, geography, industrial development, and other factors to invest in and rely on certain weapons for their military forces, and other countries have been led to invest in and rely on other weapons. Some countries rely more heavily on infantry and ground combat forces, and others rely more on fire power and mobility. A few countries happily have had little, if any, direct involvement in hostilities in recent years; others have been steadily involved. All of these differences, and others, continue to produce profoundly different views of both priorities and possibilities in the development of legal restraints on the means and methods of warfare. [249]

This was particularly true with regard to the development of rules relating to the use of airpower. The developing nations regarded the use of airpower by the developed nations as a remnant of the days of colonialism and as a continuing threat to their independence, the former with some justification. The Royal Air Force had developed and employed with considerable effect a program of air policing within the British colonies in the interwar (1919–1939) years. The comments of one of the participants in those campaigns offer an appropriate description of the divergency of views on the subject:

> The Air Method was often criticized on the score that it was brutal and caused particular resentment on the part of its victims—built up a 'legacy of hate' was a common expression. That meaningless phrase 'indiscriminate bombing' was constantly deployed. . . . The impression was put about that women and children suffered specially from air action; it was considered perfectly legitimate to *shell* a tribal village without warning, but even in an area where troops were in actual contact with a tribal enemy, villages were not allowed by the regulations to be *bombed* without special permission and the usual period of warning. . . . [O]n one occasion during a battle in Waziristan [India] when I, as Air Force Commander, was requested by the Army Commander to bomb a village from which heavy fire was holding up our advance, and had regretfully to refer him to the instructions of the Government of India on this point, I was told, 'Oh, come on, that will be all right, we'll say we shelled it.' That indeed would have been all right and in accordance with the extraordinary rules of the game. [250]

---

249. U.S. DEPARTMENT OF STATE, REPORT OF THE U.S. DELEGATION TO THE CONFERENCE OF GOVERNMENT EXPERTS ON THE REAFFIRMATION AND DEVELOPMENT OF INTERNATIONAL HUMANITARIAN LAW APPLICABLE IN ARMED CONFLICTS, GENEVA, MAY 3–JUNE 2, 1972, 54 (1972). The senior U.S. representative to the Conference of Government Experts was Ambassador George H. Aldrich. Ambassador Aldrich also served as the head of the United States delegation to the Diplomatic Conference and the subsequent United Nations Conference on Certain Conventional Weapons.

250. J. SLESSOR, *supra* note 176, at 66. On the air policing program of the RAF, *see also* A. BOYLE, TRENCHARD 365–79, 382–86, and 388–95 (London, 1962); M. DEAN, THE ROYAL AIR FORCE AND TWO WORLD WARS 35–36 (London, 1979); Beaumont, *A Lease on Empire: Air Policing, 1919–1939*, 26 AEROSPACE HIST. 84–90 (Summer/June 1979); and C. BOWYER, RAF OPERATIONS, 1918–1938, 55–235 (London, 1988). The "legacy of hate" was not directed just at Great Britain, because France and Spain had used airpower for policing purposes in their respective parts of Morocco between the wars (L. KENNETT, *supra* note 38, at 68), as had the United States in the Banana Wars in Latin America. *See* A. MILLETT, *SEMPER FIDELIS*: THE HISTORY OF THE UNITED STATES MARINE CORPS 236–63 (1980). The subsequent desire for limiting airpower expressed by developing nations at the 1974–1977 Diplomatic Conference also may have occurred in part because of the insistence of Great Britain in the course of the Geneva Disarmament Conference (1932–1934) on retaining the right to use airpower for policing purposes throughout its empire. It seemed to suggest that Great Britain was willing to abolish military and naval aircraft that might kill civilians of like culture and race, but that airpower could be employed against individuals of different cultures and races. While there may be some truth to this supposition, there also were economic factors, in that Royal Air Force operations had scaled down substantially the costs of policing the British Empire. In fact the British in 1933 unsuccessfully sought to achieve precisely what the Third World accomplished in 1977: an absence of restriction on the use of airpower for suppression of internal dissent. *See* H. HYDE, *supra* note 135, at 287–89; M. SMITH, *supra* note 135, at 118–19.

Third World nations that had waged anti-colonialism wars since 1945 had much the same experience as their pre-war predecessors in being confronted with the threat of air power. The Vietminh [in 1972 in power in the Democratic Republic of Vietnam (North Vietnam)] admitted that one of the greatest advantages held by the French during their war was airpower,[251] as also was the experience of the Front de Liberation Nationale (FLN) in the 1954–1963 Algerian war for independence from France,[252] and North Vietnam and its proxy, the Viet Cong, in the war against the government of the Republic of Vietnam (South Vietnam). Third World concern regarding airpower was fueled by the Israeli victory in the 1973 Yom Kippur War, which took place between the second session of the Conference of Government Experts and the opening of the Diplomatic Conference in 1974. The comments of the senior U.S. representative to the first session of the Conference of Government Experts were insightful in recognizing the desire of Third World nations to negate the airpower advantage of the developed nations, permitting the labor-intensive Third World nations to fight in terms of manpower rather than firepower: Third World desire to negotiate a new law of war treaty clearly had as much if not more of an arms control angle than a humanitarian interest. The ICRC fully shared the Third World view with respect to airpower.[253]

251. G. TANHAM, COMMUNIST REVOLUTIONARY WARFARE 104 (1967).

252. *See generally* A. HORNE, *supra* note 222. Third World opposition to the use of airpower by developed nations can be illustrated by one incident from the Algerian War. The guerrillas, called the FLN, were supported financially by the Arab League, and provided sanctuaries from which to conduct their military operations in Morocco and Tunisia, the latter in violation of articles 2–5 of the Hague Convention V Respecting the Rights and Duties of Neutral Powers and Persons in Case of War on Land of October 18, 1907. SCHINDLER & TOMAN, *supra* note 27, at 941–49. The FLN copied the practice of the Vietminh of neutralizing French airpower by locating its camps and training bases within villages. *See* G. TANHAM, *supra* note 251, at 108.

In six months preceding February 1958, French patrols had been involved in more than eighty shooting incidents with the FLN on the Tunisia-Algeria border. On January 11, 1958, a FLN battalion ambushed a French force, killing fifteen soldiers before fleeing back into Tunisia. Days later, a French aircraft was shot down by machine-gun fire from the Tunisian village of Sakiet, which appeared to be a fortified FLN camp. After another French plane was damaged by fire from Sakiet on 8 February, French Air Force B–26 bombers attacked Sakiet, killing some eighty people, including women and children. Undoubtedly anticipating a French response, the second FLN attack was carried out on market day, when the town was crowded with civilians. The international uproar that followed emphasized the French bombing, while neglecting the FLN use of the civilian population as a screen from attack. The intent clearly was not just to condemn the French bombing, but to take away the French airpower advantage while preserving the FLN sanctuaries outside Algeria. A. HORNE, *supra*, at 249–50, 265–70.

253. This is not altogether unusual. As Clausewitz noted, while, during war, a nation should focus on trying to achieve the optimum conditions to foster that nation's interests in the ensuing peace, a nation in peace should foster conditions most favorable to the nation's interests in any war that may ensue. Winston S. Churchill described this use of negotiations in a speech to his constituency entitled *A Disarmament Fable* on October 25, 1928:

> Once upon a time all the animals in the zoo decided that they would disarm, and they arranged to have a conference to arrange the matter. So the rhinoceros said when he opened the proceedings that the use of teeth was barbarous and horrible and ought to be strictly prohibited by general consent. Horns, which were mainly defensive weapons, would, of course, have to be allowed. The buffalo, the stag, the porcupine, and even the little hedgehog all said they would vote with the rhino, but the lion and the tiger took a different view. They defended teeth and even claws, which they described as honorable weapons of immemorial antiquity. The panther, the leopard, the puma and the whole tribe of small cats all supported the lion and the tiger. Then the bear spoke. He proposed that both teeth and horns should be banned and never used again for fighting by any animal. It would be quite enough if animals were allowed to give each other a good hug when they quarrelled. No one could object to that. It was so fraternal, and that would be a great step towards peace. However, all the other animals were very offended with the bear, and the turkey fell into a perfect panic. The discussion got so hot and angry, and all those animals began thinking so much about horns and teeth and hugging when they argued about the peaceful intentions that had brought them together that they began to look at one another in a very nasty way. Luckily the keepers were

Although some Western delegations, including the United States, recognized the need for "damage control" in limiting proposals that were unrealistic, their sincere interest in updating the codified law of war tended to obscure their veiw of the potential implications of proposed language. This remained a problem throughout the Diplomatic Conference that followed.

The clear purpose of the second session of the Conference of Government Experts was to develop two draft protocols for consideration by a Diplomatic Conference; the first would address international armed conflict, while the second would endeavor to expand the protection provided the civilian population in internal conflict. While Sweden and the ICRC devoted considerable effort to expansion of the discussion to include certain conventional weapons, this issue was not resolved until the 1978–1980 United Nations Conference on Certain Conventional Weapons, discussed *infra*. Norway pressed very strongly for a single protocol, without success. But the developing nations from the outset of their involvement stood strongly behind the proposition that "wars of national liberation" had to be considered international armed conflicts, and included in Protocol I.

The other major area of work concerned the draft articles prepared by the ICRC for the protection of civilians. Essential to this discussion was the definition of terms such as civilian, civilian population, civilian objects, and military objectives. There was a disparity of views with regard to these definitions and no agreement was reached during the session. After much open debate of the ICRC-drafted articles, the senior American representative advised the conferees that he

> expressed the desire of the United States Government to increase the protection of innocent victims of armed conflict, but emphasized certain concerns. Key among them was the fact that modern warfare includes civilians in the battlefield, and it has become increasingly difficult to prevent the intermingling of military and civilian activities and to separate and protect civilians. Under such conditions, he noted the increasing difficulty of identifying an entity called 'the civilian population.' The best approach, he suggested, was to elaborate basic guidelines, rules general enough to be understood by an ordinary soldier or a commander of regular or irregular forces and fair enough so that they would be thought of as deriving from basic requirements of law and humanity and thus consistently applied.[254]

Taking this approach, the senior U.S. delegate noted, "caused a certain amount of hostility against the U.S. position," particularly by the ICRC. Jean S. Pictet, a senior ICRC representative, turned to another U.S. delegate and declared: "If we cannot outlaw war, we will make it too complex for the commander to fight!"[255] The Conference of Government Experts concluded, still fragmented from confrontations between Western nations and their traditional views of the law of war, and the developing nations with their revolutionary ideas. The ICRC reviewed the texts produced and with an admitted degree of arbitrariness reworded many of the proposals to conform to the desires of the ICRC. A number of procedural steps were taken that would lead to the Government of Switzerland convening The Diplomatic Confer-

---

> able to calm them down and persuade them to go back quietly to their cages, and they began to feel quite friendly with one another again.

M. GILBERT, V WINSTON S. CHURCHILL, THE PROPHET OF TRUTH, 1922–1939, 305 (London, 1976). The author has no quarrel with this effort by the Third World, but does find it disingenuous for proponents of Protocol I (including the ICRC) to represent that the language of Protocol I was intended to address humanitarian concerns only.

254. U.S. DEPARTMENT OF STATE, REPORT OF THE U.S. DELEGATION TO THE CONFERENCE OF GOVERNMENT EXPERTS, *supra* note 247, at 11.

255. Comment attributed to Mr. Pictet by Waldemar A. Solf.

ence on the Reaffirmation and Development of International Humanitarian Law Applicable in Armed Conflicts (the Diplomatic Conference). While, in the words of one ICRC representative, at this point "the texts [of the two draft protocols] passed out of the hands of the Red Cross to enter a new phase in which States would have the power of decision," in truth the ICRC had an active role in the ensuing Diplomatic Conference.[256]

E. The Diplomatic Conference

Background. The Diplomatic Conference took place over the course of four sessions between 1974 and 1977.[257] There were substantial distinctions between the Diplomatic Conference and the Hague Peace Conferences of 1899 and 1907, and the 1949 Diplomatic Conference: the length of the negotiations; the number of delegations, bringing with them cultural and philosophical differences that were substantially greater than they had been previously; and the fundamental political differences between the East and the West that had begun to surface at the 1949 Geneva Diplomatic Conference.[258] Notwithstanding the very clear lesson of the failed 1923 Hague Air Rules against international lawyers exercising the lead in negotiating a treaty in which they lack subject-matter expertise, many delegations—and particularly the Western delegations—were almost exclusively comprised of international lawyers; no delegation had a military officer of the stature of a Mahan, Fisher, or Rodgers.[259] Delegates with combat experience for the most part were veterans of

256. ICRC COMMENTARY, *supra* note 247, at xxxi-xxxii. *See also* INTERNATIONAL COMMITTEE OF THE RED CROSS, CONFERENCE OF GOVERNMENT EXPERTS ON THE REAFFIRMATION AND DEVELOPMENT OF INTERNATIONAL HUMANITARIAN LAW APPLICABLE IN ARMED CONFLICTS, GENEVA, 3 MAY–3 JUNE 1972 (Geneva, 1972).

257. Four sessions were held: 20 Feb. to 29 Mar. 1974, 3 Feb. to 18 Apr. 1975, 21 Apr. to 11 June 1976, and 17 Mar. to 10 June 1977. It is not the intention of this article to discuss the Diplomatic Conference in detail. For general reference, *see* NEW RULES FOR VICTIMS OF ARMED CONFLICTS (1982); ICRC COMMENTARY, *supra* note 247; and Parks, *The 1977 Protocols to the Geneva Conventions of 1949*, NAVAL WAR C. REV. 17–27 (Fall 1978).

258. In contrast to the twenty-five nations that attended the 1899 Hague Peace Conference, one hundred twenty-six nations participated in the first session of the Diplomatic Conference. One hundred twenty-one nations attended the second session, one hundred six the third session, and one hundred nine the last session. In addition, eleven national liberation movements were present by invitation, and twenty-four international organizations were represented at the Diplomatic Conference with observer status. There also was a Working Group for the Development of Humanitarian Law comprised of representatives from twenty-seven private organizations. A complete list of attendees is contained in SCHINDLER & TOMAN, *supra* note 27, at 608–13. The official records of the Diplomatic Conference are contained in seventeen volumes. FEDERAL POLITICAL DEPARTMENT, OFFICIAL RECORDS OF THE DIPLOMATIC CONFERENCE ON THE REAFFIRMATION AND DEVELOPMENT OF INTERNATIONAL HUMANITARIAN LAW APPLICABLE IN ARMED CONFLICTS, GENEVA, 1974–1977 (Bern, 1978). The volumes are not well organized for research purposes. Professor Howard S. Levie's four-volume PROTECTION OF WAR VICTIMS: PROTOCOL I TO THE GENEVA CONVENTIONS (1979–1981) reorganizes the official record of Protocol I into an article-by-article, chronological sequence. For Protocol II, *see* LEVIE, THE LAW OF NON-INTERNATIONAL ARMED CONFLICT (1987). Another useful research tool is INDEX OF INTERNATIONAL LAW (Waldemar A. Solf and J. Ashley Roach, eds. Geneva, 1977).

259. The problem would be the same if a conference were called to promulgate a treaty on international monetary controls, and international lawyers (rather than practicing economists and bankers) made up the delegations. While doubtless there are international lawyers who have worked in the international banking business, at the time of the Diplomatic Conference few international lawyers worked in the law of war field on a day-to-day basis, or possessed knowledge or background in military affairs with regard to matters such as targeting intelligence. The U.S. military took steps to correct this in 1982, when it began an annual Military Operations & Law Symposium, wherein senior operations officers and judge advocates meet to discuss contemporary operational-legal matters. Each of the U.S. military services has developed an operational law program to educate its lawyers in this area, but few of those lawyers would feel qualified to negotiate a law of war treaty without substantial advice and assistance from the military staffs. That did not exist during the Diplomatic Conference.

One member of the U.S. delegation has stated that "The provisions [of the Protocols] were closely scrutinized by the military services and the Joint Chiefs of Staff." Solf, *A Response to Douglas J. Feith's "Law in the Service of Terror: The Strange Case of the Additional Protocol,"* 20 AKRON L. REV. 261–89, at 265 [Fall 1986]. Similarly, Ambassador George H. Aldrich, the head of the U.S. delegation to the Diplomatic Conference, has said "The Office of the Secretary of Defense and the Joint Chiefs of Staff approved our position papers for each session." Aldrich, *Progressive Development of the Laws of War: A Reply to Criticisms of the 1977 Geneva Protocol I*, 26 VA. J. INT'L L. 693–70, at 695 (Spring 1986). Both statements are highly misleading with regard to the process by which JCS approval of documents related to the Diplomatic Conference was obtained.

The delegation members prepared their position papers with little or no consultation with the military service staffs, the Office of the Secretary of Defense, or the JCS, and then submitted their position papers to the JCS for approval. The position papers seldom were written in absolute terms, instead leaving the maximum amount of latitude for the delegation in which to maneuver in the course of the negotiations. Moreover, the system for military review of delegation position papers did not lend itself to *close* scrutiny. The JCS decision-making system is a deliberative process normally used for papers no more than two or three pages in length. The delegation position papers were substantially in excess of one hundred single-spaced, typewritten legal-size pages in length, and were always submitted to the JCS for worldwide distribution (to the theater commanders and service staffs), examination, comment, and approval on very short notice.

An example of how the delegation prepared—and negotiated—issues illustrates the lack of military cognizance over the actions of the U.S. delegations. Prior to the Diplomatic Conference, a soldier caught by the enemy while wearing an enemy uniform could be tried and executed as a spy; the U.S. Army in fact executed eighteen German soldiers apprehended in U.S. uniforms during the December 1944 Battle of the Bulge. *See* C. MACDONALD, A TIME FOR TRUMPETS 32, 69, 87–89, 119, 224–27, and 451–53 (1984). [Hitler had ordered his soldiers to wear U.S. Army uniforms after being impressed with the success of American soldiers seconded (assigned) to the Office of Strategic Services (OSS) in infiltrating Aachen in September 1944.] But if a soldier wearing an enemy uniform accomplishes his mission and returns to his own lines, he has committed no war crime and would not be subject to any form of punishment if subsequently captured while wearing his own uniform. A question before the Diplomatic Conference was whether the wearing of an enemy uniform should be made a war crime; the ICRC was urging a prohibition on the wearing of enemy uniforms.

The U.S. delegate responsible for negotiating this issue unilaterally (that is, without consultation with the special operations community or the military service staffs) made the decision to accept the language contained in article 39, paragraph 2 of Protocol I making the wearing of an enemy uniform a war crime. On his return, he incorporated the prohibition into a service regulation on deception—prior to U.S. signature of the Protocols.

Subsequently, Ambassador Aldrich defended the decision on the basis that "Modern forces rarely use such tactics." Aldrich, *supra*, at 712, n. 70. This assertion is not historically sound. There exists a very long history of the wearing of enemy uniforms, as indicated by the following examples assembled from unclassified sources by the author:

WHERE	WHEN	WHO
Northeast Europe	1940	Germany
Soviet Union	1941–1943	Germany
Soviet Union, Germany	1942–1945	Soviet Union
North Africa	1942	Great Britain
France	1942–1944	Great Britain
Germany	October 1944	United States
Belgium	December 1944	Germany
Algeria	1958–1962	France
South Vietnam	1968	North Vietnam
Southeast Asia	1965–1972	United States
Southeast Asia	1971–1972	Soviet Union
Middle East	1967,1973	Israel
Zambia, Mozambique	1970s	Rhodesia
Uganda	1976	Israel
South Africa	1978	Mozambique
South Korea	June 1983	North Korea
Peru	1984	Shining Path
Libya	1985	Chad
Salvador	1985–1988	Farabundo Marti National Liberation Front
Nicaragua	1986	Sandinista government

The military review conducted subsequent to U.S. signature of the 1977 Protocols also identified a discrepancy that placed American prisoners of war at greater risk. Article 93, GPW, permits the

World War II, which had concluded twenty-nine years before the commencement of the Diplomatic Conference. In the interim there had been quantum leaps in technology, particularly in the areas of aerial bombardment and air defense, about which the delegates knew little, if anything.[260] While some military lawyers possessed some expertise in the law of war, that expertise did not extend to hostilities issues as they related to the employment of airpower; in fact, there was no delegate at the Diplomatic Conference who had dropped a bomb in anger in the quarter century preceding the conference.[261]

---

wearing of civilian clothing or enemy uniforms for the purpose of facilitating escape from a prisoner of war camp; this authority apparently was annulled by articles 39(2) [enemy uniforms] and 44(7) [civilian clothing] of Protocol I. The records of the U.S. delegation reveal that they overlooked this discrepancy during the course of the negotiations. The major commentary prepared by a member of the U.S. delegation mentions the discrepancy with regard to the use of enemy uniforms, but fails to recognize the effect on the wearing of civilian attire by escaping prisoners of war. *See* NEW RULES FOR VICTIMS OF ARMED CONFLICTS, *supra* note 257, at 214, listing the wearing of enemy uniforms by escaping prisoners of war as "*probable* unprohibited ruses," at 257.

In defense of the unilateral decision of the United States delegation, Ambassador Aldrich has illustrated the danger of delegates negotiating "by the seat of their pants." Ambassador Aldrich states: "It might be true that the provision has little value, although American soldiers who had to contend with German infiltrators wearing American uniforms during the Battle of the Bulge in 1944 might disagree, but it seems equally true that nothing significant is lost by accepting the provision." Aldrich, *supra*, at 712. Ambassador Aldrich's reference is to Operation Grief, in which members of SS-Standartenfuehrer Otto Skorzeny's 150th Panzer Brigade created chaos behind allied lines. Wearing U.S. uniforms, this 250-man unit created panic and confusion all out of proportion to its numbers. This not only suggests the military value of the tactic, but the fallacy of diplomats at a law of war conference outlawing it.

When properly employed, special operations forces are a strategic (rather than a tactical) asset. The decision by the U.S. delegation to acquiesce in the prohibition has several implications:

(1) It is generally accepted within the NATO special operations community that the Soviet Union is prepared to devote one division to hunting down each NATO special operations team (four to thirteen men) deployed within the Soviet Union. Although NATO special operations plans are highly classified, one can see that the language of article 39(2) makes Soviet security problems easier, and the survival of NATO special operations teams more problematical.

(2) Making a decision to vote for something because it caused some United States personnel a few nights without sleep in 1944 reflects a certain lack of experience and maturity. Using the same standard, a delegation member could acquiesce in a ban on artillery because he was once subjected to an artillery barrage, or decide to go along with a prohibition on intermediate-range nuclear forces because he believes they are not needed. A delegation's authority to make such decisions must be based upon authority granted after full consultation rather than personal feelings.

(3) Soviet intentions for wearing NATO country uniforms are well known. *See* M. WELHAM & B. QUARRIE, OPERATION SPETSNAZ: THE ARMS, TACTICS AND TECHNIQUES OF SOVIET SPECIAL FORCES 40 (London, 1989). *See also* V. SUVAROV, SPETSNAZ (London, 1987) and J. COLLINS, GREEN BERETS, SEALS & SPETSNAZ: U.S. AND SOVIET SPECIAL MILITARY OPERATIONS (1987). (*Spetsnaz* is the abbreviation for *Voyska Specialnoye Nazachenia*. While it stands for "special designation troops," it has become associated with Soviet special operations forces.) The prohibition contained in article 39(2) would not keep the Soviet Union and the Warsaw Pact from employing such forces, but limits NATO options.

(4) The problem within NATO may be put this way. A special operations team from a NATO nation deploys deep into the Soviet Union wearing Soviet uniforms. The team completes its mission and begins its exfiltration. It enters NATO lines through the territory of a nation party to Protocol I. Under the terms of articles 86 and 87, the host nation has an obligation to arrest the men and prosecute them for a violation of the law of war. Alternatively, a NATO staff member representing a nation that is party to Protocol I, upon hearing of the plan, would be obliged to stop the operation. The difficulties of the provision have been discussed extensively within NATO over the past decade.

The principal purpose for this lengthy discussion was to illustrate that the U.S. delegation made numerous decisions regarding provisions in Protocols I and II without an appreciation of their potential implications, and without consultation with the military services over the more than four years in which the Protocols were negotiated.

260. As suggested in the example regarding electronic warfare contained in footnote 77.

261. The United States had one of the more qualified delegations, but even it lacked experience and expertise related to aerial bombardment. For example, Major General George S. Prugh, The Judge Advocate General of the Army, was a member of the U.S. delegation for the first two sessions. An

Even had there been greater experience or expertise, it is unlikely that it would have been able to stem the tide of Third World domination of the Diplomatic Conference. The developing nations came to the conference with a very clear agenda: (a) gain international recognition for certain national liberation movements—specifically the Palestine Liberation Organization, the African National Congress, and the two principal liberation groups fighting the Portuguese government in Angola, the Angola National Liberation Front (FNLA) and People's Movement for the Liberation of Angola (MPLA);[262] (b) limit the use of military force, and particularly airpower, by another nation against them;[263] and (c) avoid restrictions that might limit their use of force to suppress internal threats. They were successful in accomplishing each.[264]

---

artillery battery commander in the Pacific during World War II, General Prugh also served as the Staff Judge Advocate, United States Military Assistance Command, Vietnam, from November 1964 to mid-1966; his law of war expertise lay in prisoner of war matters as they related to an insurgent environment. Then-Brigadier General Walter D. Reed, USAF (subsequently, The Judge Advocate General of the Air Force, 1977–1980), had been trained as a B–29 navigator in the last year of World War II, but did not see combat service; his subsequent international law work contained limited exposure to the law of war. Waldemar A. Solf, the civilian Chief of the International Law Branch of the International Affairs Division in the Office of The Judge Advocate General of the Army, had served in Europe as an artillery officer during World War II. Perhaps the most highly experienced international lawyer on the U.S. delegation, Mr. Solf had no background in matters related to aerial bombardment and did not work on the provisions in Protocol I related to that subject.

262. One example of this specific interest is that the People's Movement for the Liberation of Angola (MPLA) and Angola National Liberation Front (FNLA) were invited to, and attended, the first two sessions of the Diplomatic Conference. Once Portugal granted Angola its independence on November 11, 1975, neither organization returned to the conference. Representatives of the African National Congress attended the first three sessions but, feeling its interests had been served, did not attend the 1977 session. The Palestine Liberation Organization attended all four sessions.

Another illustration of the North-South split that overshadowed the Diplomatic Conference is United Nations General Assembly Resolution 3103 (XXVIII) of December 12, 1973, entitled *Basic Principles of the Legal Status of the Combatants Struggling Against Colonial and Alien Domination and Racist Regimes*, contained in SCHINDLER & TOMAN, *supra* note 27, at 601–03. The language contained therein raises armed conflicts in which particular national liberation movements are fighting to the level of international armed conflicts; provides prisoner of war protection for members of national liberation movements; and condemns the use of mercenaries *against* national liberation movements. Eighty-three nations voted in favor of the resolution, including the nations of Africa (except South Africa), the Middle East (except Israel), and the Socialist bloc. Thirteen voted against it, including the United States, while nineteen abstained. The same bloc of nations were able to incorporate each of these provisions into Protocol I.

263. There is evidence that members of the ICRC actively enlisted the support of a number of Third World nations in their campaign against aerial bombardment by promising support for those provisions in which the Third World had expressed interest. While this may be true, it is doubtful that the Third World nations required ICRC assistance in achieving their political goals at the Diplomatic Conference.

264. Many of the Third World delegates were diplomats stationed at their missions to the United Nations in Geneva, and veterans of work in the United Nations General Assembly in New York. They were intimately familiar with methods for fighting within a United Nations-type of conference with the developed nations. *See* B. NOSSITER, THE GLOBAL STRUGGLE FOR MORE: THIRD WORLD CONFLICTS WITH RICH NATIONS (1987). Western nations were at a disadvantage, in that they seldom presented a unified front, and were constantly concerned that they could be singled out for criticism as anti-humanitarian if they threatened to break consensus. The U.S. delegation was particularly sensitive to this during the 1977 session, given the Carter Administration emphasis on human rights. The developing nations comprised more than 60% of the delegations present, and could conceal their individual opposition behind the anonymity of group opposition. Most of them also were considerably less concerned with the possible impact of their being characterized as anti-humanitarian than were the Western democracies, and used the threat of walking out as leverage throughout the four sessions of the Diplomatic Conference. Some developing nations lost interest in the negotiations once recognition had been gained for the Palestine Liberation Organization and the African National Congress. Most continued to attend as members of the Group of 77, the so-called neutral, nonaligned nations. This group included Sweden and Switzerland which, with the ICRC, directed the efforts to incorporate constraints on airpower into Protocol I.

While the Diplomatic Conference was predominantly a North-South and Arab-Israeli struggle, there was considerable Soviet influence in that many of the leaders were Soviet trained, if not Soviet proxies.

Some additional perspective can be gained from the words of Ambassador George H. Aldrich, the head of the U.S. delegation to the Diplomatic Conference. Writing in his final report on the conference, Ambassador Aldrich stated:

> We agreed in Istanbul in 1969 to the ICRC effort that laid the foundation for this Conference, but we did so with considerable misgivings. As a country that relies for its military effectiveness more on technology, modern equipment, and firepower than on massed manpower, the United States had to approach this Conference with caution and concern. Moreover, we had seen in other contexts the risk that conferences of one hundred or more countries would be dominated by a majority of developing countries, a majority of which all too often seems to be led by radical States bearing grudges against the wealthy countries and against the United States in particular. These concerns were, in fact, justified . . . .
>
> Consistent with these concerns, we approached the Conference as more of a hazard than an opportunity . . . .[265]

The interests of the United States in the Diplomatic Conference fell into four specific areas:

a. The improvement of implementation of the existing law of war conventions, including improved procedures for the designation of a Protecting Power and for the performance of the Protecting Power's tasks by the ICRC;

b. Better procedures for dealing with the missing and dead and their effects at the end of the war;

c. Better procedures for quick battlefield evacuation of the wounded, particularly by aircraft; and

d. Increased protection for the civilian population in internal conflicts.

These interests clearly reflected the experience of the United States during the Vietnam War. As will be seen, the success of the U.S. delegation in pursuing these interests was limited, and a failure with regard to the last. Beyond this, the United States delegation had a general interest in improvement of the law of war, but recognized that important issues were at stake in connection with the protection of the civilian population, the regulation of means and methods of warfare, and the

---

See B. PORTER, THE USSR IN THIRD WORLD CONFLICTS: SOVIET ARMS AND DIPLOMACY IN LOCAL WARS, 1945–1980 (London, 1984), although the book principally addresses overt participation *vis-à-vis* covert training and support.

Some perspective can be gained from the United Nations General Assembly voting, which consistently has been anti-United States and pro-Soviet. In the 1987 United Nations General Assembly, for example, member states agreed with the United States 18% of the time, while voting with the Soviet Union 80% of the time. Ken Adelman, *One-way Fare to Geneva*, Wash. Times, December 12, 1988, at D1. The percentage ratio was worse during the years of the Diplomatic Conference. The overall problem of cultural and political differences of view between the Western nations and the Socialist bloc, including many of the developing nations, is analyzed in G. DORSEY, BEYOND THE UNITED NATIONS: CHANGING DISCOURSE IN INTERNATIONAL POLITICS & LAW (1986). Professor Dorsey illustrates the fundamental disagreement that exists among the Western nations, the Socialist bloc, and the developing nations with regard to the protection of human rights. His book provides valuable insight into the reasons for the failure of the ICRC and the Western nations to improve protection for war victims in internal conflict in Protocol II.

265. U.S. DEPARTMENT OF STATE, REPORT OF THE UNITED STATES DELEGATION TO THE DIPLOMATIC CONFERENCE ON THE REAFFIRMATION AND DEVELOPMENT OF INTERNATIONAL HUMANITARIAN LAW APPLICABLE IN ARMED CONFLICTS, FOURTH SESSION 28–29 (1977).

prohibition of weapons. Hence it was determined to exercise great caution in developing the law in these areas.[266]

In addition to the friction that existed between the United States and the developing nations, there was disagreement within the Western nations, particularly in the area related to the conduct of hostilities. Some of this disagreement has been alluded to in review of the role of the ICRC in attempting to assert a leadership role in the development of rules related to hostilities, and particularly to restrict aerial bombardment; but there is more.

Interest of Other Nations. During the two decades preceding the Diplomatic Conference, the ICRC and its supporters, neutral, nonaligned nations such as Switzerland, Finland, Austria and Sweden, had become so impressed by modern firepower that they began to advocate unconditional protection for individual civilians and the civilian population as such, unrealistic interpretations of the Just War *principle* of proportionality (expressed by these advocates as the *rule* of proportionality), and strict liability standards for the consequences of command decisions made in the heat of battle.

In addition to altruistic purposes, three other motives influenced their advocacy:

a. Inferior military powers in the isolated role of a neutral or nonaligned nation regarded the "humanitarian" law movement as another vehicle for the conventional disarmament of the superpowers. Their ends could be achieved by appealing to the less-developed nations to embrace the law of war as a method for neutralizing the advantages of technologically-advanced nations. By creating new restrictions and prohibitions on the use of modern weapons or the conduct of modern tactical operations, advocates could achieve their conventional disarmament goals through the back door, a tactic similar to that attempted by some smaller nations at the First Hague Peace Conference. Rather than confront the superpowers in overt disarmament negotiations, these advocates pursued their objective through less-publicized negotiations updating the law of war.

b. The same nations, and to some extent some members of the North Atlantic Treaty Organization (NATO), believed (and continue to believe) that a key influence for compliance with the law of war is the construction of a well-publicized regime of law that will serve as a means for bringing international public opinion to bear in time of war, which, in turn, will cause a belligerent to refrain from certain tactical options, even where they are lawful. Sweden had used this technique with great effect in limiting U.S. bombing operations against North Vietnam, and believed it could work against totalitarian nations as it did with a democracy if a proper framework were developed. That framework was to be Protocol I. Sweden was successful in enlisting the support of many of the NATO nations (who saw themselves as the battleground for any future Warsaw Pact-NATO confrontation), or in enlisting peace groups in those nations who at least could pressure the Government to support Swedish and ICRC initiatives.

c. Correlative to these two arguments was an economic interest in the continued minimization of the national defense budget in order to permit greater expenditures

266. U.S. Department of State, Report of the United States Delegation to the Diplomatic Conference on the Reaffirmation and Development of International Humanitarian Law Applicable in Armed Conflicts, First Session 25–26 (1974).

on more popular domestic social programs; hence, that which could be accomplished to limit the actions of any potential threat was "money in the bank."

Each of these factors had considerable bearing in developing the rules for aerial bombardment. These nations did not see themselves as nations involved in the projection of military power, but strictly in terms of nations that might be attacked. In this regard they saw airpower solely as an offensive tool that could be employed against them and sought protection from that threat. They shared this view with the developing nations.[267]

Conference Committees and Consensus Voting. Negotiation of the two protocols was divided among three main committees. Committee I was responsible for the general provisions of Protocols I and II; Committee II was responsible for those provisions relating to the wounded, sick, shipwrecked, civil defense, and relief; and Committee III dealt with those articles addressing the protection of the civilian population, means and methods of combat, and a proposed new category of prisoners of war. There also was a Drafting Committee and a Credentials Committee, each of which met infrequently. An *ad hoc* committee on certain conventional weapons was created and held two separate meetings in the course of the Diplomatic Conference, which will be discussed *infra.*

Voting was by consensus. This voting technique has led to a certain degree of confusion, as some authors have represented that the delegations "unanimously approved" each part of each article of the two Protocols, and some international lawyers have suggested that consensus voting equals unanimous assent by all nations, thereby creating "instant customary law."[268] This is an incorrect understanding of

267. This view of aerial bombardment is not new. The Geneva Disarmament Conference of 1932–1934 devoted much time and effort to the question of bomber aircraft and bombing because of Japanese air attacks on China. On March 19, 1932, Sir John Simon, the British Foreign Minister, circulated a paper among his colleagues proposing "the complete prohibition and outlawry in all circumstances of the dropping of bombs from any aircraft on the territory or shipping of another sovereign state." The paper was prepared by Alexander Leeper, an Australian member of the British Foreign Office, who argued that the bomber was "the most effective weapon of the aggressor," without considering its potential use in national self-defense or to support defensive operations. His proposal gained only momentary attention. H. HYDE, *supra* note 135, at 279–80.

There are other historical similarities. Much of the effort at disarmament and/or regulation of aerial bombardment in the era between World Wars I and II was driven by economic considerations of the participating nations; this was particularly true with regard to the Geneva Disarmament Conference, which coincided with the Great Depression.

Similarly, for domestic economic and political reasons the Government of Sweden in 1972 issued Defense Decision FB72, which brought a radical cut in the Swedish defense budget. A downward trend in Swedish spending for national defense continued throughout the period during which the 1977 Protocols were negotiated, with only a slight increase occurring in reaction to the 1981 incident in which a Soviet *Whiskey*-class submarine was discovered aground in Swedish internal waters, with subsequent evidence of Soviet *Spetsnaz* activity in Sweden. The very strong effort the Swedish delegation made within the Group of 77 for limitations on actions by an attacker was tied less to humanitarian concerns than to their desire to compensate for any increased vulnerability Sweden might face from the Soviet Union as the result of its unilateral disarmament. *See* Ries, *Sweden's Defense at the Crossroads*, 22, INT'L DEF. REV. 1617–21 (December 1989); *see also* M. LEITENBERG, SOVIET SUBMARINE OPERATIONS IN SWEDISH WATERS, 1980–1986 (1987).

268. *See* Veuthey, *Guerrilla Warfare and Humanitarian Law*, 234 INT'L REV. OF THE RED CROSS 115–38 (May–June 1983), where he states that, "Nearly all the articles of Protocol I were adopted by consensus; even where a consensus was not achieved, the number of negative votes was negligible; the fundamental rules embodied in the First Protocol accordingly reflect the universal *opinion juris* as to the rules of positive law which govern all international armed conflicts." This statement is factually incorrect with regard to the application of the rule of consensus as applied during the Diplomatic Conference, as explained in the text; it also is legally incorrect. *See* Sohn, *The Law of the Sea: Customary International Law Developments*, 34 THE AM. U. L. REV. 271–80 (1985), which at page 278, citing the North Sea Continental Shelf Cases, Federal Republic of Germany v. Denmark and Netherlands, 1969 I.C.J. 3, 39, 41, states that:

the consensus process at the Diplomatic Conference, as well as the authority of delegations at that conference.

A consensus vote meant that a delegation had no *substantive* objection to a particular article or provision to the degree that that delegation was willing to break consensus; it did not mean that the delegation agreed entirely with the provision under consideration, or that delegations agreed on how the provision should be interpreted. This avoided bringing a provision or article to a vote, and permitted delegations to pressure other delegations to accept an article, however imperfect it may have been, rather than break consensus. In the process, of course, the language had to be made purposely vague in order to accommodate the objections of a possible consensus breaker while not raising the possibility that other delegations would break consensus because of the changes that were made. This encouraged general, rather than specific, language in texts; it did not necessarily mean that there was agreement. The delegations agreed as to the incorporation of each article into a draft treaty for consideration by governments; however, there was no agreement that any particular article codified customary international law, or otherwise constituted an acceptable codification of a principle of international law. At the Diplomatic Conference, there was frequent, fundamental disagreement as to the interpretation of texts adopted by consensus.

The record of the Diplomatic Conference is rife with statements by delegations that "had a vote been taken, this delegation would have voted against or abstained" with regard to a particular article, or by a delegation clarifying its vote through an explanation.[269] An example will illustrate this point.

> The [International Court of Justice] is thus willing to pay attention not only to a text that has codified preexisting principles of customary international law, but also to one that has crystallized an "emergent rule of customary law." It seems, therefore, that once a consensus is reached at an international conference, a rule of customary international law can emerge without having to wait for the signature of the convention.

Professor Sohn's argument can be distinguished from the standpoint of the Diplomatic Conference and the authority granted it by the states. As noted in the text of footnote 236, provision was made in article 92 of Protocol I for a six-month delay in signature of the Protocols so that nations could review the two draft treaties and determine if they desired to sign and/or ratify them. The Diplomatic Conference delegates were well aware that they lacked the authority to promulgate rules that would bind their respective nations.

A distinction also exists between a treaty adopted by consensus that has as its purpose the codification of customary international law and one that develops principles that are contrary to customary international law. Protocol I is more of the latter than the former, particularly with regard to those rules that relate to aerial bombardment. In the dozen years that have passed since the Diplomatic Conference, the author has participated in several conferences of international lawyers that have endeavored to reach agreement on identification of the articles in Protocol I that codify customary international law. Each conference has arrived at a different list of articles or provisions.

The important point is one that Professor Sohn has stated on other occasions: that "international law has only one source—the common will of states." Sohn, *Thoughts on Customary International Law*, 1,2 RUSK CENTER NEWSLETTER 2–3 (University of Georgia School of Law, January 1984). Because of the consensus voting procedure that existed at the Diplomatic Conference, nations were merely agreeing not to disagree rather than to agree. Given the degree to which it was necessary to employ a practice of purposeful ambiguity in order to reach *consensus*, there was no manifestation of a common will.

269. For example, at the Plenary Meeting of the Diplomatic Conference that took place on May 27, 1977, the delegate from France stated that:

> Article [55] concerning the protection of the natural environment lays down rules for the conduct of war. As such, it has direct implications for the organization and management of a country's military defense against invasion. The French delegation . . . did not oppose the consensus on the adoption of the article, but wishes it be known that had there been a vote, it would have been abstained.

H. LEVIE, III PROTECTION OF WAR VICTIMS: PROTOCOL I TO THE 1949 GENEVA CONVENTIONS, 276 (1980).

Article 44, paragraph 3 of Protocol I provides that an irregular combatant (such as a guerrilla or partisan) may retain his status as a lawful combatant if he carries his arms openly "during such time as he is visible to the adversary while he is engaged in a military deployment preceding the launching of an attack in which he is to participate."

The developing nations, and particularly those who supported the actions of the Palestine Liberation Organization and the African National Congress, argued that it was not possible for a guerrilla to display his weapon until a "split second" before his attack. The Western nations, including the United States, argued that if the article were to be in keeping with the general principle that "the Parties to the conflict shall at all times distinguish between the civilian population and combatants,"[270] guerrillas or partisans must display their arms openly upon any movement toward the place of attack.[271] The article was accepted by consensus, with a number of delegations stating that had the matter been brought to a vote, they would have abstained.[272] Western nations have been explaining or qualifying their vote ever since. In this particular instance, the negotiators were miles apart in their interpretation of the article; a consensus vote accomplished nothing.

Second, delegation *acceptance* of a provision always is *ad referendum*, that is, with the understanding that its vote for particular language in a treaty represents agreement among the delegations present, while reserving to governments the decision as to acceptability for purposes of ratification or accession. With respect to the 1977 Protocols, formal signature of the two Protocols by national representatives commenced six months after conclusion of the Diplomatic Conference; this break was designed to give time for nations "to consult, in cabinets and parliaments, and decide whether they were willing to adopt the Protocols and the obligations contained therein."[273]

It is not possible here to devote the space to negotiations at the Diplomatic Conference as was done with the two Hague Peace Conferences and the 1922–1923 Hague conference that drafted the air rules. Nor is there any intent to enter into the debate that has arisen over the degree to which Protocol I has politicized the law of war, or to join the discussion of those articles not related to aerial bombardment, except where it is necessary to do so for perspective or illustrative purposes. The debate to date has been lively, but has been concerned primarily with the political reasons for the U.S. decision against ratification of Protocol I, and does not bear repetition.[274]

---

270. Article 48, Protocol I, contained in DEPARTMENT OF THE ARMY PAMPHLET 27–1–1, PROTOCOLS TO THE GENEVA CONVENTIONS OF 12 AUGUST 1949, 34–35 (1979).

271. For example, at the time of its signature of the two Protocols, December 12, 1977, the United Kingdom stated that "the Government of the United Kingdom will interpret the word 'deployment' in paragraph 3(b) of [article 44] as meaning 'any movement towards a place from which an attack is to be launched.' " The same or similar language was used by Belgium, Italy, Republic of Korea, and the Netherlands upon the ratification of Protocol I by each of those nations. SCHINDLER & TOMAN, *supra* note 27, at 717, 707, 712, 713 and 714. Some nations have added language that movement would include that which can be seen with sight-enhancement equipment (such as binoculars, night-vision goggles, or thermal-imaging devices) rather than just the naked eye, though no such phrase has appeared as yet as part of any interpretive statement on ratification.

272. H. LEVIE, *supra* note 269.

273. NEW RULES FOR VICTIMS OF ARMED CONFLICT, *supra* note 257, at 551; ICRC COMMENTARY, *supra* note at 247 at 1068–69.

274. Nor does the author intend to critique the performance of the members of the U.S. delegation on the manner in which they carried out their duties. International negotiations are complex and difficult, and it is inappropriate for one who was not there to second-guess decisions made in the midst of negotiations. A negotiator is entitled to the same standard as a battlefield commander for his decisions made in the heat of battle. However, just as a commander may be found by historians or

strategists studying a war or battle to have made a wrong decision in battle (for which he may be criticized, but should not be held criminally accountable) so may the products of the decisions of negotiations be subject to critical scrutiny.

For a general discussion of the Protocols, *see* Green, *The New Law of Armed Conflict*, ESSAYS ON THE MODERN LAW OF WAR 1–26 (1985).

For specific criticism of the political effects of Protocol I, *see* Feith, *Law in the Service of Terror: The Strange Case of the Additional Protocol*, THE NATIONAL INTEREST 36–47 (Fall 1985); Feith, *International Responses*, U. RA'ANAN, HYDRA OF CARNAGE: INTERNATIONAL LINKAGES OF TERRORISM 265–85 (1986); Feith, *Protocol I: Moving Humanitarian Law Backwards*, 19 AKRON L. REV. 531–35 (Spring 1986). In response to Mr. Feith's criticisms, *see* Solf, *supra* note 259.

The other principal articles are Roberts, *The New Rules for Waging War: The Case Against Ratification of Additional Protocol I*, 26 VA. J. INT'L L. 109–70 (Fall 1985); Aldrich, *supra* note 259; Gasser, *Agora: The U.S. Decision Not to Ratify Protocol I to the Geneva Conventions on the Protection of War Victims*, 81 AM. J. INT'L L. 910–25 (October 1987); and Sofaer, *Agora: The U.S. Decision Not to Ratify Protocol I to the Geneva Conventions on the Protection of War Victims (Cont'd)*, 82 AM. J. INT'L L. 784–87 (October 1988).

A difficulty with the Solf, Aldrich, and Gasser articles is that each provides "perfect" legal solutions to problems that are fundamentally political. An example of this form of argument (not from any of the articles) follows:

> At the time North Vietnam became a party to the 1949 Geneva Convention Relative to the Treatment of Prisoners of War (GPW), it entered the following reservation:
>
> > The Democratic Republic of Vietnam declares that prisoners of war *tried and convicted* of war crimes or crimes against humanity . . . shall not benefit from the provisions of the present Convention, as specified in Article 85. [Emphasis added]
>
> Article 2 common to the four 1949 Geneva Conventions provides in part:
>
> > [T]he present Convention shall apply to all cases of declared war or of any other armed conflict which may arise between two or more of the High Contracting Parties, even if the state of war is not recognized by one of them.

At the time the United States became a party to the GPW, it made the following declaration: "Rejecting the reservations which States have made with respect to the [GPW], the [U.S.] accepts treaty relations with all Parties to that Convention, except as to the changes proposed by such reservations."

In the course of the Vietnam War, North Vietnam never tried or convicted any U.S. military personnel in its hands. The "perfect" legal solution was fully recognized by all concerned—and simultaneously ignored by the Socialist World. As the principal scholar on POWs has concluded:

> [T]he American pilots are entitled prima facie to prisoner-of-war status under the 1907 Hague Regulations, the 1929 Geneva Prisoner-of-War Convention, and the 1949 Geneva Prisoner-of-War Convention. *In fact, it would be difficult to imagine a more clear-cut case of entitlement to such status.* [Emphasis added]

Levie, *Maltreatment of Prisoners of War in Vietnam*, in 2 THE VIETNAM WAR AND INTERNATIONAL LAW 361–415, at 383–84 (Richard A. Falk, ed. 1969). But the "perfect" legal solution does not address the political fact that North Vietnam denied POW status to captured U.S. military personnel for the entire course of the Vietnam War. *See* R. RISNER, THE PASSING OF THE NIGHT (1973); J. DENTON, JR., WHEN HELL WAS IN SESSION (1976); J. HUBBELL, *supra* note 210 and J. STOCKDALE & S. STOCKDALE, IN LOVE AND WAR (1984).

In the course of the Vietnam War the ICRC made seventy-two requests to the Hanoi Government for permission to visit American POWs in its hands. The North Vietnamese refused each, stating that the captured U.S. military personnel were not entitled to POW treatment. For the texts of the reservations to article 85 of the Socialist nations, *see* SCHINDLER & TOMAN, *supra* note 27, at 563–92. For objections to those reservations by Australia, New Zealand, the United Kingdom and the United States, *see Id.* at 565, 580, 589, 590, and 591.

As previously noted, an objective of the United States at the Diplomatic Conference was to "neutralize" the reservation of the Socialist nations to article 85, GPW, in order to prevent recurrence of the Vietnam experience. The United States effort was an attempt at yet another "perfect" legal solution to what was (and remains) a political problem; the American solution (in the words of Ambassador George H. Aldrich) "specifically outlaws a tactic used by our enemies in attempts to justify their inhumane treatment of thousands of American prisoners of war in Korea and Southeast Asia" thereby creating somewhat of a "double crime" by prohibiting something that already was clearly a breach of the 1949 Geneva Prisoner of War Convention. Aldrich, *supra* note 259, at 698. It also was unsuccessful, as will be discussed.

The Diplomatic Conference concluded on June 10, 1977, and the Protocols were open for signature in Berne, Switzerland, on December 12, 1977. The United States was present and signed the Protocols on that date. In light of the subsequent decision by the U.S. Senate not to ratify Protocol I, some light needs to be shed on the circumstances surrounding the American decision to sign as well as the steps leading the Senate to decide against ratification of Protocol I. The latter included a comprehensive military review; those articles that affected aerial bombardment will be examined.

Signing of 1977 Protocols. Upon its return to the United States, selected members of the American delegation began work on the necessary documents for a decision as to United States participation in the signature ceremony that was to occur six months later.[275] Ambassador Aldrich and the remaining members of the delegation assumed that the United States would sign and ratify both Protocols and wrote their supporting documents accordingly. This assumption was reached without consultation with any agency or official of the U.S. Government. The assumption at first blush may appear appropriate, given the record of the United States as a leader in respect for and implementation of the law of war. However, history suggests that the assumption may have been inappropriate. Although the United States ratified the 1949 Geneva Conventions, it declined to become a party to the 1923 Hague Rules of Aerial Warfare and the 1954 Hague Convention for the Protection of Cultural Property in the Event of Armed Conflict, and did not ratify the 1925 Geneva Protocol for the Prohibition of the Use in War of Asphyxiating, Poisonous or Other Gases, and of Bacteriological Methods of Warfare until 1975. Thus while the United States has found acceptable law of war treaties relating to the protection of war victims, it has been considerably more cautious in its acceptance of treaties relating to the employment of arms.

Given the vast scope of Protocol I, the decision by the delegation in favor of signature and ratification certainly was premature if not presumptuous. The delegation's decision colored the review prepared for senior American officials with regard to U.S. signature. Potential interpretation problems were played down or ignored; in many cases, the interpretation the American delegation had of a provision was the only interpretation discussed, even though it was known that others were expressed in the course of the negotiations that differed substantially from that of the U.S. delegation.

For example, article 35, paragraph 3, and article 55, paragraph 1, of Protocol 1 prohibit attacks on the natural environment that will result in "widespread, long-term and severe damage." It was clear throughout the course of the Diplomatic Conference that the language was specifically directed at certain U.S. operations during the Vietnam War, and particularly the use of herbicides.[276] The terms

275. With some notable exceptions. Brigadier General Reed was promoted to Major General and became The Judge Advocate General of the Air Force in October 1977. His participation upon return from Geneva was limited thereafter. Similarly, Captain Richard L. Fruchterman, JAGC, USN, the Chief of the International Law Division of the Office of the Judge Advocate General of the Navy until September 1976, served on the U.S. delegation as its naval representative; upon completion of the 1977 session, he ceased his active involvement with the Protocols. The author became Head of the Law of War Branch in the International Law Division of Navy JAG in October 1977, and attended all meetings of the Department of the Defense Law of War Working Group as the naval representative during the balance of the period leading up to the U.S. decision regarding signature of the Protocols.

276. *See* ICRC COMMENTARY, *supra* note 247 at 662, n. 2; H. LEVIE, *supra* note 269, at 259–77, and particularly the statements of Hungary (*id.* at 259–60) and North Vietnam (*id.* at 260). *See also* J. NEILANDS, *Harvest of Death: Chemical Warfare in Vietnam and Cambodia*, STOCKHOLM INTERNATIONAL PEACE RESEARCH INSTITUTE, ECOLOGICAL CONSEQUENCES OF THE SECOND INDOCHINA WAR (Stockholm, 1976); W. THOMAS, LEGAL AND SCIENTIFIC UNCERTAINTIES OF WEATHER MODIFICATION

"widespread," "long-term" and "severe damage" are approximately the same as the terms used in the 1977 Convention on the Prohibition of Military or Any Other Hostile Use of Environmental Modification Techniques (ENMOD),[277] except that the terms are stated in the conjunctive (and) in Protocol I but in the disjunctive (or) in the ENMOD Treaty. The terms are defined in the ENMOD Treaty,[278] but there was no agreement as to definition of the terms in Protocol I, with some delegations arguing that "long-term" could be as brief as a single season.

However, in the U.S. review prior to signature, former delegation members concluded their analysis of this provision by stating that "This article is expected to have negligible impact on U.S. military operations," inasmuch as the report of Committee III of the Diplomatic Conference stated that "long term" "was considered by *some* to be measured in *decades*, with reference made to twenty to thirty years as a minimum, and it *appeared* to be a widely shared assumption that battlefield damage incidental to conventional warfare would not normally be proscribed by this provision."[279]

In fact, the matter was not agreed upon in the course of the Diplomatic Conference. That there was a potential for substantial divergence in interpretation of these terms is indicated by the *ICRC Commentary*, which states:

> In times of armed conflict . . . the Protocol [I] and the [ENMOD] Convention, taken together, prohibit:

(1977); and WARFARE IN A FRAGILE WORLD: MILITARY IMPACT ON THE HUMAN ENVIRONMENT (Arthur H. Westing, ed. 1980), and ENVIRONMENTAL WARFARE: A TECHNICAL, LEGAL & POLICY APPRAISAL (London, 1984). For a discussion of the U.S. employment of herbicides in Southeast Asia, *see* W. BUCKINGHAM, JR., OPERATION RANCH HAND: THE AIR FORCE AND HERBICIDES IN SOUTHEAST ASIA, 1961–1971 (1982); and P. CECIL, HERBICIDAL WARFARE: THE RANCH HAND PROJECT IN VIETNAM (1986).

277. SCHINDLER & TOMAN, *supra* note 27, at 163–75. The ENMOD uses the terms "widespread," "long-lasting" and "severe," while Protocol I uses "widespread," "long-term," and "severe damage."

278. The following understanding was incorporated into the negotiating record of the ENMOD Treaty and included in the report transmitted by the Conference of the Committee on Disarmament to the United Nations General Assembly in September 1976:

> It is the understanding of the Committee that, for the purposes of this Convention, the terms "widespread," "long-lasting" and "severe" shall be interpreted as follows:
>
> (a) "widespread:" encompassing an area on the scale of several hundred square kilometers;
>
> (b) "long-lasting:" lasting for a period of *months, or approximately a season* [emphasis added];
>
> (c) "severe:" involving serious or significant disruption or harm to human life, natural and economic resources or other assets.

The Conference on Disarmament made special note that "it is further understood that the interpretation set forth above is intended exclusively for this Convention [ENMOD] and is not intended to prejudice the interpretation of the same or similar terms if used in connection with any other international agreement." SCHINDLER & TOMAN, *supra* note 27, at 168. Note, however, that this does not preclude another treaty from using the same definitions.

279. U.S. DEPARTMENT OF DEFENSE, LAW OF WAR WORKING GROUP REVIEW AND ANALYSIS OF PROTOCOLS I & II ADOPTED BY THE DIPLOMATIC CONFERENCE ON INTERNATIONAL HUMANITARIAN LAW I-35-2, 4 (Nov. 1977) (emphasis added). The author attended the meeting at which this (and other) discrepancies were raised. The decision was made that controversial matters would not be discussed in the review document, as that might preclude American participation in the signing ceremony scheduled for 12 December 1977. While there seemed to be agreement that the Protocols had to be analyzed "warts and all" in any review prior to the U.S. decision as to ratification, it was the author's experience that members of the American delegation to the Diplomatic Conference thereafter continued to avoid raising any issue that was potentially adverse to a favorable U.S. decision. They had lost their objectivity and had become advocates for U.S. ratification, whatever the cost.

> (a) Any direct action on natural phenomena of which the effects would last more than *three months or a season*
>
> (b) Any direct action on natural phenomena of which effects would be widespread or severe (for the interpretation of these terms . . . see [ENMOD Convention definitions]), *regardless of the duration*, affecting one or other of the Parties to the Convention, even if it is not a Party to the conflict.[280]

The document prepared by former members of the American delegation to the Diplomatic Conference, while lengthy, was not a review of the Protocols; it was a brief for U.S. signature.

The Joint Chiefs of Staff (JCS) met in executive session on November 2, 1977, five weeks before the date of the scheduled signing ceremony. In attendance were the Chairman of the JCS; the Chief of Staff of the Air Force; the Chief of Naval Operations; the Commandant of the Marine Corps; and, substituting for the Chief of Staff of the Army, the Vice Chief of Staff. Also present were the Director of the Joint Staff and the Chairman's Executive Assistant. Before each rested a single JCS decision memorandum. Attached to it was a typewritten document, single-spaced on legal-size paper, almost three inches thick. The JCS, the service staffs, and the worldwide theater commanders had been provided less than two weeks in which to review a complex law of war document that required six years to negotiate. Realizing that the task was impossible, another general officer was present. This was General Alexander M. Haig, USA, theater commander for U.S. forces in Europe. Accompanying him was his deputy. General Haig advised the Chairman and the service chiefs that the JCS should vote in favor of U.S. signature, because "signing doesn't mean anything and has no binding effect" on the United States. General Haig had intervened in the JCS decision at the request of his old friend, Ambassador George H. Aldrich, who feared that any hesitation on the part of the JCS would preclude U.S. participation in the signing ceremony the following month. Based upon his assurance, the JCS voted in favor of U.S. signature—on the condition that the JCS would be permitted a full military review prior to any decision as to ratification of the Protocols by the United States. That condition was accepted by the Secretaries of Defense and State. Ambassador Aldrich and the United States Ambassador to Switzerland were present at the signing ceremony and signed on behalf of the United States.[281]

---

280. ICRC COMMENTARY, *supra* note 247, at 416 (emphasis added).

281. General Haig's statement is simultaneously correct and incorrect. Under the terms of Protocol I (articles 92–94), signature alone does not bind a nation; the nation does not become a party until it deposits its instrument of ratification or accession. However, under the terms of article 18 of the Vienna Convention on the Law of Treaties, a nation is obligated once it has signed the treaty to refrain from acts which will defeat the object and purpose of the treaty, until it has made its intention clear that it does not intend to become a party to the treaty. This the Reagan Administration did in forwarding Protocol II only to the Senate for its advice and consent to ratification on January 29, 1987.

A representative of the ICRC has stated that "Washington's decision to sign the two Protocols, especially Protocol I, is of great significance. It reflected *the U.S. delegation's* positive assessment of the Diplomatic Conference." Gasser, *supra* note 274, at 916 (emphasis added). Similarly, Ambassador Aldrich has stated that "None of the defects in the Protocol [I discovered by the subsequent military and political review] should deter the United States from ratification, as they are curable by means of understandings or reservations, as both the State and Defense Departments recognized prior to the Reagan Administration." Aldrich, *supra* note 259, at 719. The former statement is closer to the truth than the latter. Neither the Secretary of State nor the Secretary of Defense was prepared to make a decision with regard to U.S. ratification until the military review promised the JCS as a condition for signature was completed and considered by the Departments of Defense, State and Justice. At the time of U.S. signature there were major differences between the military services and Ambassador Aldrich with regard to certain provisions contained in Protocol I, such as the prohibition on reprisals contained in article 51; they had not been addressed at the department level.

F. Background of Military Review of 1977 Protocols

As part of the Diplomatic Conference that negotiated the 1977 Protocols, an *ad hoc* committee considered restrictions or prohibitions on certain conventional weapons. While no treaty provisions resulted from the work of this committee, the Diplomatic Conference adopted a resolution recommending that the United Nations sponsor a separate conference on certain conventional weapons. The United Nations accepted the recommendation. Preparatory conferences were held in Geneva in August 1978, and March–April 1979, followed by formal negotiating sessions in the fall of 1979 and 1980. These sessions led to the Convention on Prohibition or Restrictions on the Use of Certain Conventional Weapons Which May Be Deemed to Be Excessively Injurious or to Have Indiscriminate Effects (UNCWC),[282] previously discussed. While some work on the 1977 Protocols took place between 1978 and 1980, preparation for and negotiation of what became the UNCWC demanded most of the time.

Between 1978 and 1980 former members of the U.S. delegation to the Diplomatic Conference prepared various drafts for submission of the two Protocols by the President to the Senate for its advice and consent to ratification. The author's review in June of 1980 of the draft commentaries prepared up to that time revealed that none had as their purpose the review promised the JCS at the time of their consent to U.S. signature. The earlier review and analysis essentially was a legislative history prepared for the limited purpose of approval of the signature decision. As previously noted, that review and analysis was cursory, and criticism of language contained in the various articles was mooted if not avoided altogether. There was no analysis of the overall impact of the Protocols on the broad spectrum of potential combat operations in which United States military forces might be involved.[283]

Moreover, the two statements suggest the basis for the American decision to sign the two Protocols and its effect. The U.S. delegation unilaterally made the decision to sign and ratify, and prepared documents supporting its decision. The U.S. signature in turn conveyed to others a misimpression of American intentions. Some allies have informed the United States that they would have been more cautious in approaching the decision to ratify the Protocols had they known in 1977 that the United States might not become a party to Protocol I. But that was not the impression conveyed to them by members of the American delegation.

282. The Canadian delegation took a portion of the title to create the acronym CUSHIE, for *C*auses *U*nnecessary *S*uffering [or] *H*as *I*ndiscriminate *E*ffects. The acronym never quite caught on, resulting in the unpronounceable acronym UNCWC for *U*nited *N*ations *C*onventional *W*eapons *C*onference.

283. A NATO Military Committee review of the 1977 Protocols during this period did consider the overall impact question, and concluded that the 1977 Protocols would have no adverse impact on alliance operations. This report was prepared by individuals who participated in the negotiation of the Protocols, and suffers from the same problems that hampered the U.S. review prior to signature. Subsequent studies by the United States and several of its Allies, as well as a decade of NATO Military Committee discussions of the Protocols, has cast doubt on the credibility of the original study.

The Strategic Studies Institute of the U.S. Army War College conducted an evaluation of the Protocols in 1978–79. The study was precipitated by concerns expressed by a senior Army judge advocate with regard to the practicality of the warfighting provisions of Protocol I (articles 48–58). The ultimate recommendation of the study was that the "Army position should be that the JCS recommend ratification of Protocols I and II," subject to two dozen recommended reservations and statements of understanding. STRATEGIC STUDIES INSTITUTE, U.S. ARMY WAR COLLEGE 25 (Carlisle Barracks, Pa. 20 March 1979).

One recommendation in the Army War College Study revealed the chameleon-like approach to interpretation of the Protocols by its proponents. In 1976 an opinion had been prepared by the principal U.S. negotiator of the provisions relating to medical aircraft (articles 24–30, Protocol I) that the language contained in article 28, paragraph 2, prohibited the use of cryptological equipment on medical aircraft (DAJA-IA 1976/1080). The same position is reflected in the document prepared by former delegation members prior to U.S. signature. Accordingly, the Army War College Study recommended:

> a. The U.S. Senate be advised of the adverse nature of the prohibition of carrying encryption equipment on board medical aircraft;

Similarly, draft commentaries prepared between 1978 and 1980 were not intended to be a critical analysis of the Protocols, but rather a compilation of statements of U.S. interpretation of the articles of the Protocols for consideration by the President and the Senate. As such, the draft commentaries did not constitute a military assessment of the Protocols; they presented them in their most favorable light only. They did not inform the service chiefs of the myriad interpretations possible of the language contained in the Protocols, some of which clearly were contrary to the American interpretation.

An argument can be made that it might have been preferable for the U.S. Senate to have ratified Protocol I as quickly as possible with appropriate reservations and statements of understanding in the hope of influencing future interpretation of its many ambiguous provisions. But advancement of such a point of view could have been made only after critical review of the treaty rather than in lieu of such a careful analysis. The approach taken prior to 1980 colored the tenor of the review and analysis prior to U.S. signature and the subsequent draft commentaries. Many potentially controversial provisions were given less than adequate analysis, if not ignored completely; other issues discovered by the subsequent military review had been papered over with highly legalistic arguments to become "non-problems."

On June 19, 1980, the author submitted a memorandum to the members of the Ad Hoc Law of War Working Group advising that the work accomplished to date was not regarded as constituting the military review of the 1977 Protocols promised the JCS,[284] suggesting that such a review be undertaken. On September 12, 1980, The

---

b. An understanding be provided the U.S. Senate prior to ratification which establishes two points:

(1) that the United States does not intend to use medical aircraft for the collection or transmission of intelligence data;

(2) that the United States intends to carry secure voice equipment and encryption materials on board medical aircraft for the purpose of protecting communications made in support of purely medical operations.

The Army War College recommendation was made for two reasons. Because of the adverse experience of the Army in Vietnam (in loss of the element of surprise because of enemy interception of U.S. transmissions), a national policy decision had been made in 1971 that all future communications would be encrypted. Moreover, medical evacuation helicopter crews employ an abbreviated format message system for reporting the number and type of casualties on board the aircraft to facilitate immediate casualty care upon arrival at a treatment facility which, if intercepted, would appear to be an encrypted message. Because of the language contained in article 28(2), either could place the medical aircraft at risk, and could subject the crew to charges of violation of the law of war if captured. Despite the fact that the U.S. delegation was the principal sponsor of the provisions related to medical aircraft, these issues had been neglected in the course of the six years of negotiations. It also serves further to illustrate the degree to which the delegation worked in a vacuum in preparing the U.S. position.

The Army War College recommendation led to an immediate reversal of the previous U.S. interpretation of article 28(2). A new opinion was prepared (DAJA–IA 1979/26), reversing the previous opinion, concluding that the article did not prohibit the use of cryptological equipment on medical helicopters. This rapid reversal of opinion was a key factor in the decision to demand a separate military review by individuals who had not been members of the U.S. delegation to the Diplomatic Conference.

The foregoing should not be read as questioning the integrity of any member of the U.S. delegation to the Diplomatic Conference. But some had been through six years of intense negotiations (beginning with the Conference of Government Experts) and had lost their objectivity with regard to the Protocols. In similar circumstances in a domestic law matter, it would have been appropriate for them to have recused themselves.

284. DAJA–IA 1980/6084. The Ad Hoc Law of War Working Group, which had been formed at the start of the 1971 Conference of Government Experts, consisted of representatives from the Office of the Legal Adviser, Department of State; the Office of the General Counsel, Department of Defense; the Office of the Joint Chiefs of Staff; the international law divisions of the Offices of The Judge Advocate Generals of the Army, Navy, and Air Force; the Office of the Director, Judge Advocate Division, Headquarters, U.S. Marine Corps; and nonlawyers from service staffs and other agencies, when required.

Judge Advocate General of the Army wrote a memorandum to the Deputy Chief of Staff of the Army for Operations and Plans recommending that final approval of the 1977 Protocols be deferred until the Chief of Staff of the Army was satisfied that he could testify before any Senate committee considering the 1977 Protocols that their ratification was in the national security interest. The memorandum recommended a critical review and analysis.[285] The Deputy Chief of Staff for Operations and Plans concurred with the recommendation of The Judge Advocate General in a memorandum dated December 8, 1980. It was not until January 1981, that a military review of the 1977 Protocols actually was begun.

As occurred in negotiation of the 1977 Protocols, much of the nuts and bolts work of the military review fell to members of the Department of Defense Ad Hoc Law of War Working Group. No assumptions were made for or against ratification of the Protocols. Where one member began to drift one way or another, either in the preparation of an analysis of a particular provision or as to the overall aspect of ratification, the inherent combativeness of the members of the group produced a counterargument by another member of the working group to offset any potential bias that might creep into any evaluation. The prevailing attitude was to provide an analysis that set forth in adequate detail the positive *and negative* aspects of a particular provision *vis-à-vis* the existing law so that decision makers at appropriate levels could make informed decisions with regard to particular articles and, ultimately, the overall decision as to U.S. ratification.

This process entailed considerable research and led to a number of questions. What did the article say in plain language? What had been said at the Diplomatic Conference, and by whom? What had the United States or other nations previously said on a particular subject? What had recognized international lawyers written on the subject? Could a practice of nations on the point in question be established? (In this regard, it was important to avoid the frequent temptation of an anecdotal view of history as necessarily being tantamount to the practice of nations. Similarly, the fact that nations had not engaged in a particular tactic or kind of operation since World War II did not necessarily mean that this former practice was now regarded by nations to be illegal.)[286] How does one establish intent absent evidence of specific acquiescence, or restraint? Did the post-World War II war crimes trials offer any assistance in defining or clarifying a provision? What impact would a proposed rule have in light of technological advances on the battlefield? What was the prospect for a particular rule gaining universal respect? Was a particular rule consistent with U.S. doctrine and tactics? At what level should a particular rule be applied? Was a particular provision susceptible to more than one interpretation? If so, what would be the interpretation of the United States? Of its allies? Of its potential adversaries? Did a particular provision in fact advance protection for the civilian population?

These and other questions were asked repeatedly through the review process.

---

285. DAJA–IA 1980/6122 (prepared by the author). The author has included this chronology because of the misimpression under which some have labored, that concerns regarding Protocol I did not arise until the Reagan Administration. *See* the discussion in *supra* note 275. The insistence upon the military review promised the JCS at the time of the U.S. signature was initiated by the author in the fall of 1980, during the term of President Carter, and would have been made earlier but for the concentration of the author and others on the negotiation of the United Nations Conventional Weapons Convention.

286. Thus, prior to the sinking of the Argentine cruiser *Belgrano* during the 1982 Falklands/Malvinas War, some international lawyers suggested that submarine warfare had become illegal because no nation had engaged in such warfare since 1945. The same suggestion has been made with regard to nuclear weapons. Were one to follow this line of reasoning, it would mean that a nuclear power would have to employ one nuclear device in each conflict in order legally to preserve its options for future conflicts.

When examining national practice in a particular conflict, an effort was made to distinguish policy decisions made by national leaders to limit the level of violence through strategic or tactical restraint from a decision based on a belief that greater or different levels of violence were legally impermissible. This distinction was not always maintained during the Diplomatic Conference.[287]

In contrast to the previous practice of sending one large document around for consideration by the military services, individual issue papers were prepared. With a single exception, these papers generally did not exceed more than five pages. Each identified the issue, analyzed it, identified possible alternative interpretations, provided options as to decisions that could be made [accept without reservation or understanding, accept with understanding (with recommended language), or reserve], and requested a decision. In the drafting phase, the draft was carefully coordinated with particular commands and those offices on the staffs of the military services with the knowledge and expertise essential to a complete examination of the issue.[288] There was considerable reliance on all-source intelligence with regard to the practice and/or intentions of other nations.[289] Not until a draft had been thoroughly examined was the paper submitted to the JCS review process, at which time it was circulated worldwide for consideration.

287. For example, members of the American delegation to the Diplomatic Conference frequently were questioned by the individuals preparing the military review as to why the United States accepted a provision in Protocol I. More times than not, the response was "because that's the way we did it in Vietnam." Although this rationale constitutes a misunderstanding of history, it served as the basis for many of the decisions related to the language contained in articles 48 to 58 of Protocol I, the specific point of reference being the U.S. air campaigns against North Vietnam *as they had been reported in the press*. Yet actions by senior American officials imposed severe operational restrictions on U.S. forces operating over North Vietnam, which the North Vietnamese openly exploited. These policy restrictions served as a considerable detriment to U.S. forces, were imposed without any consideration of the law of war, and forced U.S. units to operate well within legally permissible boundaries. *See* Parks, *supra* note 109, and Parks, *supra* note 208. (Each of these articles was prepared in large measure from classified Air Force studies available in Washington, but to which the American delegates did not avail themselves in the course of the four years of negotiations of the Protocols.)

288. For example, article 10, paragraph 1 of Protocol I states that "All the wounded, sick and shipwrecked . . . shall be respected and protected." Article 8(a) defines "wounded" and "sick" as "persons, whether military *or civilian*." The 1949 Geneva Conventions obligate the military to treat wounded and sick members of military forces only; *see, e.g.*, article 12, GWS. The review of this provision by the American delegation prior to U.S. signature stated that article 10 of Protocol I creates no new obligation, except to obligate a party to care for wounded and sick civilians "*if* [civilian] *medical resources are inadequate for that purpose*." The same statement is contained in New Rules for Victims of Armed Conflicts, *supra* note 257, at 107–08. The language of article 10 does not limit the obligation to provide civilians medical care to those cases when civilian medical resources are inadequate. Using the plain language of article 10, an ICRC publication, Alma Baccino-Astrada, Manual on the Rights and Duties of Medical Personnel in Armed Conflicts 39–40 [Geneva, 1982] and the ICRC Commentary, *supra* note 247, at 145–148, published subsequent to the completion of the U.S. military review state the obligation as unequivocal; neither is the assertion made in the U.S. delegation's review prior to signature supported by the negotiating record. Levie, Protection of War Victims: Protocol I to the 1949 Geneva Conventions, 241–311 (article 8), 333–352 (article 10) (1979). An issue paper was prepared in coordination with the Offices of the Surgeons General of the Army, Air Force and Navy, inquiring whether the United States military could assume this additional obligation; the same issue was raised in NATO meetings with alliance members. In both cases the response was resoundingly negative. Military medical facilities would be overwhelmed if obligated to treat wounded and sick civilians. All agreed that if a wounded or sick civilian were taken in by a military medical facility, that person would be entitled to equal care on the basis of medical priority. But none were prepared to assume the new obligation the ICRC claims article 10 creates.

289. Intelligence inquiries were not limited to doctrine and tactics of potential enemies. Those nations that rushed to become parties to Protocol I during the first five years it was available for ratification or accession were scrutinized to determine what steps, if any, were taken to implement that convention. With the exception of Denmark, Finland, Norway, Sweden and Switzerland, all other nations party to Protocol I had taken no steps to implement Protocol I, and had done nothing to implement their obligations under the Geneva Conventions of 1949—to which most had been parties for some years.

A detailed review in the U.S. military was possible for several reasons. There was a breadth of combat experience available within the services. In addition to the fact that officers involved in the military review had experience in World War II, Korea, Vietnam, and Grenada, they also had access to detailed analyses of the Middle East conflicts of 1967, 1973, and 1982, the 1982 Falklands/Malvinas War, the Iran-Iraq War, and Soviet military operations in Afghanistan. The later campaigns were particularly important in placing certain provisions of Protocol I in perspective on the modern battlefield, where electronic warfare has significant influence. While it is necessary to view each individual's combat service as somewhat unique to a particular war, mission, battle, or even a certain piece of terrain, combat experience is invaluable in relating the esoteric details of a law of war treaty to the practical realities of the battlefield.

A thorough military review was possible because of the degree of knowledge of international law and the law of war within the U.S. military. The Law of War Working Group established during the negotiation of the Protocols continues in operation today. The comprehensive dissemination programs established by each of the four U.S. military services in the post-Vietnam era has led not only to an increased overall awareness within the military, but to a significant cadre of military judge advocates with advanced degrees in international law and extensive experience in its teaching and practice. This practice—formalized in 1979 in part because of the requirement contained in article 82 of Protocol I[290]—has led to military lawyers providing law of war advice on a daily basis on operational matters at virtually every level of command as they review doctrine, operations plans, contingency plans, and rules of engagement; review new weapons; participate in field exercises and war games; and serve in operations centers during periods of crisis management. Military lawyers at the service level and in specified and unified commands were deeply involved in the preparation of the 1981 Worldwide Peacetime Rules of Engagement for Seaborne Forces and the subsequent Worldwide Peacetime Rules of Engagement, approved by the Secretary of Defense on June 26, 1986. Military lawyers at a variety of levels were active participants in the planning and execution of the 1983 Grenada rescue operation, the 1981 and 1986 freedom-of-navigation exercises to challenge Libya's illegal claim to the Gulf of Sidra, the subsequent air strike against terrorist-related targets in Libya, and the 1989-1990 military operations in Panama. In 1982, The Judge Advocate General of the Army established the previously-described annual Worldwide Military Operations and Law Symposium. In short, judge advocate participation in operational matters had taken a quantum leap since 1979. This improvement provided a strong system for a responsible military review of the 1977 Protocols.

The U.S. military traditionally has been consulted independent of the political leadership with regard to the acceptability of treaties relating to national security matters. There is a strength to this, for if a treaty cannot withstand critical scrutiny prior to ratification, its chances for implementation and respect are substantially diminished. Given the military commander's responsibility for accomplishment of his mission in a lawful manner, a military review of Protocols I and II was appropriate. It also was important to review these draft treaties in light of certain technological advantages enjoyed by the United States rather than in the generic sense in which they had been examined previously. Military advice is not always negative; in many

290. SCHINDLER & TOMAN, *supra* note 27, at 670. For discussion of this provision, *see* Parks, *The Law of War Adviser*, XVIII REVUE DE DROIT PENAL MILITAIRE ET DE DROIT DE LA GUERRE 359–417 (1979); and 31 JAG JOURNAL 1–52 (Summer 1980).

cases detailed military review of a treaty tends to offset visceral reaction to a treaty by political fringe groups.

G. Analysis of Impact of 1977 Protocols

The military review examined each of the Protocols from several standpoints.

Ensuring Respect for the Law of War. The United States is a party to the four Geneva Conventions of August 12, 1949. Article 1 common to those conventions states that "The High Contracting Parties undertake to respect and to ensure respect for the present Convention in all circumstances."[291] The U.S. military review examined the language contained in Protocols I and II to determine whether each contributed to the continued credibility of the law of war. While Protocol II made a minor advance in the protection of innocent civilians in internal conflicts, it was concluded that Protocol I diminished rather than advanced the law of war. Although there were several reasons for this conclusion, two principal issues will be discussed to illustrate this point.

Article 51, paragraph 6, and article 52, paragraph 1, of Protocol I prohibit reprisals against the civilian population or civilian objects of an enemy nation, respectively. These provisions are not a codification of customary international law, but, in fact, a reversal of that law. The military review considered whether surrender of these rights would advance the law of war, or threaten the continued respect for the rule of law in war. It was concluded that removal of this legal right placed any further respect for the rule of law by certain nations in jeopardy.

Reprisals historically have existed in a state of confusion. The term "reprisal" has been used by national leaders to justify actions that might be better characterized as retaliation, revenge, or legitimate acts of self-defense.[292] The term has been misused by historians,[293] resulting a doubt expressed by some regarding the effec-

291. SCHINDLER & TOMAN, *supra* note 27, at 375 in GWS.

292. Within the U.S. military, the confusion may have been caused in part by the fact that the law of war manuals of each of the services contained similar, but different, definitions for the term and criteria for the execution of a reprisal. *Cf.* the language contained in UNITED STATES ARMY FIELD MANUAL 27–10, *The Law of Land Warfare* para. 497 (1956); NAVAL WARFARE INSTRUCTIONAL PAMPHLET 10–2, *The Law of Naval Warfare* sec. 310 (1955); and AIR FORCE PAMPHLET 110–31, *International Law—The Conduct of Armed Conflict and Air Operations* para. 10–7 (1976). The military review standardized the definition of *reprisal* and the conditions for its execution. *See* NAVAL WARFARE PUBLICATION 9, *The Commander's Handbook on the Law of Naval Operations* para. 6.2.3 (1987). For a general examination of reprisals and the discussions at the Diplomatic Conference, *see* ICRC COMMENTARY, *supra* note 247, at 982–87, and NEW RULES FOR VICTIMS OF ARMED CONFLICTS, *supra* note 257, at 311–15.

293. For example, Professor D. P. O'Connell characterized the United States Navy's employment of unrestricted submarine warfare in World War II as a reprisal for the Japanese attack on Pearl Harbor. D. O'CONNELL, THE INFLUENCE OF LAW ON SEA POWER 44 (London, 1975). Naval historian Samuel Eliot Morison regarded the Japanese attack on Pearl Harbor as a basis for abrogation of article 22 of the 1930 London Treaty for the Limitation and Reduction of Naval Armaments. SCHINDLER & TOMAN, *supra* note 27, at 881–82; *Coral Sea, Midway, and Submarine Operations* IV HISTORY OF UNITED STATES NAVAL OPERATIONS IN WORLD WAR II, 190 (1949). Another historian has interpreted the United States action as a renunciation of article 22. C. BLAIR, SILENT VICTORY 106 (1975). In fact, an American campaign of unrestricted submarine warfare against Japan was planned and approved prior to the Pearl Harbor attack. *See* Talbott, *Weapons Development, War Planning and Policy: The U.S. Navy and the Submarine, 1917–1941*, 37 NAVAL WAR C. REV. 53–71 (May–June 1984). As noted by the first historian to discover this:

> The motives which impelled the United States . . . to resort to unrestricted submarine warfare . . . were the same which had activated Germany to the same tactic. They were cooly, studiously strategic: to cut off the enemy's vital overseas trade and thereby weaken his capacity to fight and win a long war. Submarines were the only American naval instrument which could reach across the Pacific at the beginning of the conflict, and they were promptly put to this prearranged task.

tiveness of reprisals.[294] The 1949 Geneva Conventions prohibit reprisals against persons protected by those conventions, in large measure because of the abuse of reprisals during World War II.[295]

Because a reprisal involves an illegal act—accomplished for the limited purpose of forcing an enemy to cease certain illegal acts—it is politically sensitive, particularly in a democracy with a history of respect for the rule of law. But reprisals or the threat thereof have proved necessary and effective in preventing violations of the law of war, and the U.S. Government was opposed to a broadening of restrictions on reprisals at the Diplomatic Conference. The American delegation was unwilling to break consensus on this matter, however, resulting in a number of provisions in Protocols I and II narrowing the objects against which a reprisal may not be taken.[296] At the time of U.S. signature of the two Protocols, a major difference existed between the U.S. Departments of State and Defense as to whether these provisions were acceptable.[297]

In the course of the military review, the provisions limiting reprisals were considered from the standpoint of ensuring respect for the law of war. The United States has threatened the use of reprisals on several occasions to prevent violation of the law of war by others, to good effect. Thus a threat by President Franklin D. Roosevelt to resort to the use of chemical weapons deterred their use by Nazi Germany during World War II.[298]

A more recent example emphasized the concerns of the Department of Defense. In the course of the Vietnam War, the Government of North Vietnam threatened "war crimes" trials of American military personnel in its hands.[299] When the Johnson Administration warned of reprisals against North Vietnam if such illegal trials were conducted, the North Vietnamese Government quickly decided to permit socialist Bertrand Russell to conduct "trials" of the United States in general rather

---

Samuel F. Bemis, *Submarine Warfare in the Strategy of American Defense and Diplomacy, 1915–1945* at 36 (unpublished paper delivered at the Naval War College, Newport, Rhode Island, November 1, 1961). Using the criteria for a reprisal contained in any one of the law of war manuals cited *supra* note 292, the U.S. employment of unrestricted submarine warfare against Japan could not be characterized as a reprisal.

294. Thus the document prepared by the American delegation in support of U.S. signature of the two Protocols stated that "[Reprisals] are not particularly efficient militarily to the extent that vital resources are diverted away from attacks against military objectives. Another problem with reprisals is the substantial existing requirements of law which regulate their execution." United States Department of Defense, Department of Defense Law of War Working Group Review and Analysis of Protocols I and II Adopted By the Diplomatic Conference on International Humanitarian Law I–51–9 (1987) [hereinafter Law of War Working Group].

295. Article 46, GWS; article 47, GWS (Sea); article 13, GPW; and article 33, GC.

296. Articles 20 (civilian medical personnel), 51(6) (civilian population in enemy hands), 52(1) (civilian objects), 53 (cultural objects), 54(4) (objects indispensable to the survival of the population), 55(2) (the natural environment), and 56(4) (works and installations containing dangerous instruments), Protocol I.

297. By way of illustration, the language quoted in footnote 294 is followed by a statement that:

> It would appear unlikely that the U.S. would have to resort to reprisals against civilian populations, as such, except in situations involving nuclear weapons . . . . On the other hand, it is possible that the U.S. might want to preserve the right of reprisal in some types of widespread conventional warfare.

The first sentence was authored by Ambassador Aldrich; the second, by Defense Department members of the U.S. delegation. Law of War Working Group, *supra* note 294, at I–51–9.

298. U.S. Department of State Bulletin, VII *Statement by President Roosevelt on the Use of Poison Gas*, 507 (8 June 1943).

299. The matter is discussed in Levie, *supra* note 274, at 382–90. *See also* J. Hubbell, *supra* note 210, at 181, 223, 267, and 274–75.

than prisoners of war in North Vietnamese hands—and far away from North Vietnam.[300] In another instance, although officially characterized as an act of self-defense against a continuing threat, the 1986 United States attack of terrorist-related targets in Libya was a reprisal that has successfully deterred Libya from acts of terrorism against American citizens for almost four years—clear evidence that reprisals can be effective.[301]

The review prepared by former members of the American delegation to the Diplomatic Conference prior to U.S. signature recommended that the United States make a statement at time of signature to the effect that

> [the United States] reserves the right, in the event of massive and continuing attacks against the civilian population, to take reprisals against the civilian population of the State perpetrating these illegal attacks for the sole purpose and only to the extent necessary to bring the illegal attacks to an end.

This statement paralleled one made by Ambassador Aldrich in explanation of the American Delegation's participation in the consensus adoption of Protocol I. However, because the disagreement between the Departments of State and Defense could not be resolved prior to the signing ceremony on December 12, 1977, no statement was made at the time of U.S. signature.[302]

The American military review recognized that the statement made by Ambassador Aldrich failed to take into consideration the abuses of U.S. prisoners of war that were widespread in the course of the wars in Korea and Vietnam.[303] It seemed highly probable that the greatest area for violation of the law of war in future conflicts was in prisoner of war abuse by Communist nations.

---

300. *See generally* AGAINST THE CRIMES OF SILENCE: PROCEEDINGS OF THE INTERNATIONAL WAR CRIMES TRIBUNAL (1968). The inaugural session of the Bertrand Russell "war crimes" trial was held in London in November 1966 to establish the major areas of concern and inquiry. The next session was held in Stockholm, 2 to 10 May 1967; and the final session in Roskilde, Denmark, 20 November to 1 December 1967. The United Kingdom and France refused to permit the "trials" to take place within their territory. *See also* B. RUSSELL, WAR CRIMES IN VIETNAM (1967). Russell invited international personalities such as Jean-Paul Sartre and Simone de Beauvoir to serve as judges along with representatives from Yugoslavia, Germany, Turkey, Italy, the United States, and Cuba. Sartre was elected executive chairman and, although a leftist, endeavored to keep an open mind during the proceedings. Sartre and de Beauvoir did not believe the United States could be charged with genocide, as Russell proposed. As de Beauvoir's biographers describe subsequent events, "The Cuban delegate, 'a lovely woman,' . . . for whom this was a political affair, found their scruples superfluous. Sartre, who always fell for a beautiful woman, let himself be convinced by the beautiful Cuban delegate. In his capacity as executive chairman, it fell to him to write the preamble to the tribunal's verdict. His text, composed in the early-morning hours, was adopted unanimously. . . . The International Russell Tribunal on U.S. War Crimes in Vietnam condemned the United States for genocide." C. FRANCIS & F. CONTIER, SIMONE DE BEAUVOIR: A LIFE, A LOVE STORY 321–23 (1985). For a critical analysis of the trials, *see* G. LEWY, AMERICA IN VIETNAM 311–13 (1978).

301. Because the United States has joined in a number of United Nations resolutions cautioning against reprisals in peacetime, the American attack was characterized as an act of self-defense against a continuing threat. One need only examine the criteria for a reprisal and the steps taken by the United States prior to and in the course of the attack to see that American actions fit both the definition of a reprisal and its criteria. *See* Parks, *supra* note 86.

302. NEW RULES FOR VICTIMS OF ARMED CONFLICTS, *supra* note 257, at 314, contains Ambassador Aldrich's statement in explanation of the U.S. participation in the consensus adoption of Protocol I. The difference of opinion between the Departments of State and Defense, and the decision against its resolution prior to the 12 December 1977 signing ceremony are based on the author's participation in the meetings that took place during the time between officials of the two departments.

303. Examples of POW abuse during the Vietnam War have been provided in previous pages of this article. For the Korean War, *see* U.S. SENATE, 83d Cong., 1st Sess., KOREAN WAR ATROCITIES (1954); and UNITED KINGDOM, MINISTRY OF DEFENCE, TREATMENT OF BRITISH PRISONERS OF WAR IN KOREA (London, 1955); T. FEHRENBACH, THIS KIND OF WAR 178, 209–10 (1963); and Levie, *Prisoners of War in International Armed Conflict*, 59 U.S. NAVAL WAR C. INT'L L. Studies 349–50 (1978).

The matter was raised in the course of several meetings with NATO allies, without resolution. Those nations that saw their territory as a potential battleground continued to express the desire they had voiced during the Diplomatic Conference to close the door entirely on any form of reprisal, regardless of the risk of violation by a potential enemy.[304] The delegate of one NATO ally suggested that a threat to carry out a reprisal was not prohibited by Protocol I—merely the act itself.[305] Another delegate stated that if the United States were to ratify Protocol I and reserve some right of reprisal, since his nation found it politically infeasible to reserve this right, he expected his nation would ask the United States to carry out a reprisal in its behalf and as its agent if its military personnel in the hands of an enemy were abused. This illustrates the political sensitivity of the issue.

Nonetheless, the American military review recognized the historic pattern for abuse of U.S. and allied prisoners of war by their enemies, and concluded that a broad reservation to the prohibition on reprisals contained in articles 51 and 52 of Protocol I was essential as a legitimate enforcement mechanism in order to ensure respect for the law of war.

A second concern with regard to the need to ensure respect for the law of war was the major change made in the law of war by the language contained in article 44, paragraph 3, of Protocol I, previously discussed.[306] Historically an individual who is not a member of regular armed forces is not entitled to combatant (and prisoner of war) status unless he is a member of an organization: (1) commanded by a person responsible for his subordinates; (2) that has a fixed distinctive emblem recognizable at a distance; (3) the personnel of which carry their arms openly; *and* (4) conduct their operations in accordance with the laws and customs of war.[307]

There was a specific humanitarian purpose for this provision: if a militia or similar organization wanted to attain legitimate combatant status for itself and its members, it had to meet the same standards as nations. Article 44, paragraph 3, of Protocol I discontinued the obligation to adhere to the law of war for selected organizations (such as the Palestine Liberation Organization and the African National Congress) while continuing to require adherence to it of nations.

The purpose for this amendment of customary international law, it was argued, is that by "providing an incentive for the irregular combatant to comply with the law, . . . [it thereby increased] the protection of both civilians and regular soldiers."[308] The alternative was prosecution of individual combatants for individual offenses.[309] Considering that the ICRC Commentary on the Geneva Convention Relative to the Treatment of Prisoners of War had described the previous requirement for organization adherence to the law of war as an "essential provision" for respect for the law

304. *See* New Rules for Victims of Armed Conflicts, *supra* note 257, at 312, n.37.

305. The same argument was raised in the course of the Diplomatic Conference. *See* F. Kalshoven, The Law of Land Warfare 65 (Leyden, Netherlands, 1973). As a treatise correctly indicates,

> The fallacy in Professor Kalshoven's argument is that a threatened reprisal will be regarded as a bluff if made by a Party which usually complies with the law of armed conflict. The credibility of such a threat is enhanced only if there is a general cynical attitude about the effectiveness of conventional restraints on the use of force.

New Rules for Victims of Armed Conflicts, *supra* note 257, at 315.

306. *See* text at *supra* note 271.

307. Article 1 of the Annex to Hague Convention IV of 1907, contained in Schindler & Toman, *supra* note 27, at 75; and article 4A(2) of the Geneva Convention Relative to the Treatment of Prisoners of War of 1949, contained in *id.* at 430–31.

308. Aldrich, *supra* note 259, at 704.

309. Solf, *supra* note 259, at 273; and Gasser, *supra* note 274, at 921.

of war,[310] it was necessary to ascertain whether the change brought about in article 44(3) or Protocol I ensured or diminished respect for the law of war.

It took little examination to realize that article 44(3) did not enhance respect for the law of war. Previously an organization had to adhere to the law of war to gain legitimacy for the organization and its members; in addition, its members could be prosecuted for violations. As noted, article 44(3) removed the first requirement.

The theory behind this change was that guerrilla organizations generally start as undisciplined groups facing difficulties of command and control, and that it was unfair to deny prisoner of war status to the individual guerrilla who wanted to comply with the law of war; that automatically to deny combatant status to a guerrilla served as a disincentive to that individual to comply with the law of war.[311] Strangely, the Diplomatic Conference delegates took the exact opposite approach in article 47 in denying prisoner of war protection to mercenaries.

The theory behind the change contained in article 44(3) is entirely inconsistent with the doctrine and practice of Communist revolutionary warfare. Communist guerrilla units are extremely well organized and disciplined; violence against the civilian population is selective and intentional, and is regarded as essential to the survival of the insurgent movement. The record of the use of intentional violence against the civilian population by Communist revolutionary organizations is long and well-established.[312] Communist revolutionary warfare employs violence against

---

310. J. PICTET, COMMENTARY OF THE GENEVA CONVENTION RELATIVE TO THE TREATMENT OF PRISONERS OF WAR 61 (Geneva, 1960).

311. This argument was voiced in the report of the U.S. Delegation to the first session of the Diplomatic Conference. FIRST SESSION, *supra* note 266, at 8.

312. The Vietnam War brought a wealth of information on Communist revolutionary warfare techniques. On the systematic, deliberate use of violence against civilians, *see* G. TANHAM, *supra* note 251, at 121–23; D. PIKE, VIET CONG (1966), chapter 13, and specifically 246–48; B. FALL, THE TWO VIETNAMS, *supra* note 224, at 359, 360, 361; W. DAVISON, SOME OBSERVATIONS OF VIET CONG OPERATIONS IN VILLAGES, RAND RM-5267/2-ISA/ARPA at vi, 28–29, 30–34 (Santa Monica, May 1968), U.S. MISSION IN VIETNAM, VIET CONG USE OF TERROR, 16–38 (rev. ed. Saigon, Mar. 1967) which contain a detailed listing of acts of terror directed at local elected officials, schoolteachers, and other prominent civilians; R. PEARCE, THE INSURGENT ENVIRONMENT, RAND RM-5533-1-ARPA 36–50, 53–54, 87–88 (May 1969); S. HOSMER, VIET CONG REPRESSION AND ITS IMPLICATIONS FOR THE FUTURE, RAND R-475/1-ARPA v–vi (May 1970); J. RACE, WAR COMES TO LONG AN: REVOLUTIONARY CONFLICT IN A VIETNAMESE PROVINCE 82–94 (1971); W. ANDREWS, THE VILLAGE WAR: VIETNAMESE COMMUNIST REVOLUTIONARY ACTIVITIES IN DINH TUONG PROVINCE, 1960–1964 51–71, 115–16 (1973); and G. LEWY, *supra* note 300, at 272–77, and table 8–1, appendix II, at 454, in which Lewy concludes that terrorism was methodical (*id.* at 272) and that "the use of these terror tactics constituted an integral part of communist strategy" (*id.* at 277). Lewy also correctly notes that the use of violence against the civilian population was not merely an opening phase of the conflict; it was a technique carried out throughout the Vietnam War. For example, "Statistics for the years 1968–1972 indicate that about 80% of the terrorist victims were ordinary civilians and only about 20% were government officials, policemen, members of self-defense forces or pacification cadres. . . . Capital punishment occasionally was carried out by disembowelment with the villagers forced to be in attendance" (*id* at 273). Further:

> A VC/NVA force of about 12,000 men seized Hue during the night of 20 January 1968 and held the old imperial city for 26 days. During this time some 6,800 civilians were killed or abducted. . . . In the first phase of the purge local communist cadres, following prepared blacklists, rounded up key civil servants, officers, educators and religious figures—the leaders of the community—and executed them. A captured VC document with the classification "Absolute Secret" states that during the occupation of Hue the Communists "eliminated 1,892 administrative personnel, 38 policemen, 790 tyrants", and an assortment of other enemies of the party.

Id. at 274.

These citations from the Vietnam War are typical of Communist Revolutionary Warfare rather than being unique to that war. Similar examples can be found in every conflict. For example, for the Algerian War and the activities of the FLN, *see* A. HORNE, *supra* note 222, at 118–19, 120–23, 134–35, 144, 184–88, 352, 425, 479, and especially chapter nine, 183–207; and J. TALBOTT, *supra* note 222, at 79–82. Other examples can be found daily in local press clippings:

the individual civilian and the civilian population as such by choice rather than as a result of indiscipline, as was misperceived by the ICRC in its effort to change the law. One of the strongest U.S. proponents for ratification of Protocol I has conceded that the relaxation of the standard contained in Hague Convention IV of 1907 and the 1949 Geneva Prisoner of War Convention was a primary goal of the Socialist World.[313] In that, they were successful.

Proponents of the change that occurred in article 44(3) have suggested that the right to prosecute the individual combatant for a violation of the law of war is sufficient to ensure respect for the law of war. That argument is historically incorrect and pragmatically unsupportable.[314] Heretofore an organization and its members

---

(1) In November 1986, the Peruvian Maoist group Shining Path killed a woman who was a candidate for the Huancayo Town Council, the day before national elections. *Peruvian Candidate Slain on Eve of Election*, N.Y. Times, Nov. 9, 1986, at 9.

(2) In 1987, a former member of the African National Congress confirmed that organization's policy of executing local elected black officials, because they are regarded as collaborators with the white-minority South African government. Morrison, *ANC Killer Recalls Haunting Existence*, Wash. Times, October 27, 1987, at A8. *See also* Jensen and Deigh, *An Insurgency with Methods Reminiscent of the Vietcong's*, 2, 10 INSIGHT 28–31 (Mar. 10, 1986).

(3) In June, 1988, Shining Path executed a United States agricultural advisor and his Peruvian colleague in their war against the Government of Peru. *U.S. Agronomist Killed in Andes by Guerrillas*, Wash. Post, June 16, 1988, at A33.

(4) In November, 1988, El Salvador's Marxist Farabundo Marti National Liberation Front (FMLN) embarked on a campaign to force civilians to take sides in the war by assassinating local elected civilian leaders. Farah, *Salvadoran Rebels Step Up the War*, Wash. Post, Nov. 26, 1988, at 1.

(5) In December, 1988, it was disclosed that the FMLN had murdered eight mayors since March 1988, and was planning on killing justices of the peace in a campaign to demonstrate their power in the face of declining international support. Gruson, *Salvador Rebels Step Up Terrorism*, N.Y. Times, Dec. 16, 1988, at A10.

(6) In December, 1988, members of the Marxist People's Liberation Front and the Patriotic People's Movement in Sri Lanka blockaded roads and entered communities, where they killed 23 civilians in an effort to prevent national elections. Crossette, *23 Killed at Hands of Sri Lanka Left*, N.Y. Times, Dec. 19, 1988, at A7.

(7) As rebels in Sri Lanka agreed to a cease-fire, it was revealed that members of the Sinhalese People's Liberation Front had killed more than 3,500 government officials and governing party members in the preceding two years. *Sri Lanka and Tamil Rebels Agree to a Cease-Fire*, N.Y. Times, June 29, 1989, at A5.

As is true of the citations to the practice of Vietnamese communists during the Vietnam War, the foregoing are considered representative of Communist Revolutionary Warfare, not isolated incidents. Supporters of organizations that rely upon terrorism to accomplish their objectives argue that "one man's terrorist is another man's freedom fighter," or note that "George Washington was called a terrorist by the British." In response to these claims, an expert on terrorism had the following comments in a recent speech:

> We see here the peculiar depravity of people who can make no distinction between confronting the regular constituted forces of a powerful nation—as George Washington did—and throwing burning gasoline on a young mother and her three infant children as happened last month in Israel. George Washington never did that.
>
> Or attacking a nursery school in Ma'alot in 1974 and killing 22 children, three older people, and wounding 66. George Washington never did that, either. . . . [Or] the hijacking of an Air France commercial liner to Entebbe in 1976 and a Lufthansa commercial liner to Mogadishu in 1977. . . . Or the murder of a cripple in a wheelchair in a botched hijacking master-minded by the Palestine Liberation Front's Abu al-Abbas, one of [Yasser] Arafat's underlings in the PLO.

Noel Koch, as quoted in *For the Record*, Wash. Post, Dec. 9, 1988, at A26.

313. Solf, *supra* note 259, at 268, where Mr. Solf states that "It is readily understandable that the relaxation of the standards for qualifications of privileged combatants was a high priority goal of those governments and authorities who employ guerrilla warfare in furtherance of political objectives."

314. As previously noted in the text supporting *supra* note 92, an attempt to hold war crimes trials following World War I was unsuccessful. War crimes trials took place after World War II because there

the allies achieved total victory over the Axis powers. *See generally* E. DAVIDSON, THE TRIAL OF THE GERMANS (1966); P. PICCAGALLO, THE JAPANESE ON TRIAL: ALLIED WAR CRIMES OPERATIONS IN THE FAR EAST, 1945–1951 (1979); B. SMITH, REACHING JUDGMENT AT NUREMBERG (1979); B. SMITH, THE ROAD TO NUREMBERG (1981); R. CONOT, JUSTICE AT NUREMBERG (1983); and A. & J. TUSA, THE NUREMBERG TRIAL (1984).

The difficulty of trials of individuals accused of war crimes during hostilities can be illustrated by one American case from World War II. On March 12, 1944, a German POW was found murdered at the United States POW camp at Papago Park, Arizona, apparently killed by fellow prisoners of war who (correctly) believed he was a turncoat. A criminal investigation identified seven suspects. In accordance with article 60 of the 1919 Geneva Convention Relative to the Treatment of Prisoners of War (SCHINDLER & TOMAN, *supra* note 27, at 339–64, at 354), United States authorities notified Germany through the Swiss Government of its intention to prosecute the seven suspects for murder. Germany then notified the United States that, quite by coincidence, it intended to prosecute an equal number of American military personnel on the same charge. United States authorities elected to proceed with the trial. The seven were convicted, and sentenced to death. In accordance with articles 65 and 66 of the 1929 GPW, this information was conveyed to Germany through the Swiss Government. A response was received that, again by coincidence, the seven Americans also had been found guilty and had received the same sentence. United States authorities deferred execution of the sentences until the end of hostilities and the repatriation of all American POWs, and on August 25, 1945, the seven German POWs were hanged at Fort Leavenworth, Kansas. *See* R. WHITTINGHAM, MARTIAL JUSTICE (1971).

In the course of the Korean War, North Korea infiltrated personnel into South Korea to be "captured" and placed in United Nations POW camps, because it had been revealed that a number of North Korean and Chinese POWs were not anxious to be repatriated once hostilities were concluded. On May 7, 1952, the infiltrated POWs staged a major riot within compound 76 on Koje Island, killing a number of fellow POWs. The United States commander was prepared to bring those responsible to trial, but was prohibited from doing so by the United States Department of State because of concern for United States and United Nations military personnel in the hands of Communist forces. H. VETTER, MUTINY AT KOJE ISLAND (1965), and W. HERMES, TRUCE TENT AND FIGHTING FRONT, UNITED STATES ARMY IN THE KOREAN WAR 233–62 (1966).

The ICRC Commentary on the Protocols, in discussing the change in article 44(3), states that "the obligation for all combatants to comply with the rules of international law applicable in armed conflict remains in its entirety, for such combatants can be punished in case of breach." ICRC COMMENTARY, *supra* note 247, at 526. In support of this position, an ICRC spokesman has cited the American experience in Vietnam, where

> members of Vietcong guerrilla units who were captured while actually engaging in combat ("carrying arms openly") were *treated* by the U.S. Military Assistance Command as prisoners of war (but not granted formal POW status), whereas a Vietcong who had committed an act of terrorism did not receive that treatment.

Gasser, *supra* note 274, at 921, citing Solf, *supra* note 259, at 273.

The statements of Gasser and Solf are incorrect and misleading in that they fail to state *why* the United States began to treat Vietcong as POWs. The history of the basis for this policy decision is described in Levie, *supra* note 274, at 391–92:

> On April 9, 1965, a Vietcong terrorist was tried, convicted and sentenced to death by a South Vietnamese court. At that time the Vietcong announced that if the sentence of execution was carried out, Gustav C. Hertz, a kidnapped civilian American [Agency for International Development] officer, would be shot. The terrorist was apparently not executed.
>
> On June 22, 1965, another Vietcong terrorist was executed by a South Vietnamese firing squad after he had been tried, convicted and sentenced for acts of terrorism by a South Vietnamese special military court. Three days later both Radio Hanoi and the Liberation Radio announced that an American soldier held as a prisoner of war (Sergeant Harold G. Bennett) had been executed in reprisal for the execution of the Vietcong terrorist.
>
> On September 22, 1965, three more Vietcong terrorists were executed in Da Nang after a trial, conviction and death sentence by a South Vietnamese court. Four days later, on September 26, the Liberation Radio announced that the Vietcong had retaliated by the executions of two American prisoners of war, Captain Humbert R. Versage [Versace] and Sergeant Kenneth M. Roraback. Once again the United States labeled these reprisal executions as "murder" and as violations of the [GPW]. It filed a protest with the ICRC which was transmitted to and rejected by the [National Liberation Front].

Thereafter, as Gasser and Solf have stated, American authorities provided POW protection (but not status) to Viet Cong captured in the field. Although Viet Cong reliance on terrorism (as documented in

could not claim combatant status until and unless the organization adhered to the law of war. Article 44(3) removed that requirement, permitting an organization to assert a claim as a legitimate belligerent while ignoring its law of war obligations. This was the precise objective of the Palestine Liberation Organization, the African National Congress, and those nations supporting their claims. This substantially diminished the likelihood of respect for the law of war.

Protection of U.S. Military Personnel. Arguments proffered thus far by proponents of U.S. ratification of Protocol I have been phrased entirely along lines of concern for the further development of the law of war. But the American military review had two other purposes, one of which was concern for U.S. military personnel taken prisoner of war by an enemy. Given threats of war crimes trials for captured U.S. military personnel during the Korean and Vietnam Wars, this was not an idle concern.

The American delegation to the Diplomatic Conference was keenly aware of this threat, and took one approach to the problem that was described previously.[315] Even if that approach were effective, however, it would merely guarantee a U.S. prisoner of war certain procedural rights were he charged with a "war crime." In that respect the approach taken by the American delegation was inadequate.

Diplomacy, it may be said, is the art of achieving agreement. It follows that in order to achieve agreement, a resort to purposeful vagueness may be necessary on occasion. Indeed, arms control agreements and other treaties are replete with language that permit more than one interpretation. The recent dispute within the U.S. Government over interpretation of the Anti-Ballistic Missile Systems Treaty[316] is

---

supra note 312) did not abate, United States and South Vietnamese prosecution of Viet Cong for acts of terrorism came to a complete halt. Reprisals against captured United States personnel—specifically prohibited by article 13 of the GPW—stopped enforcement of the law of war through the prosecution of individuals responsible for war crimes. When Viet Cong were tried in civil courts and incarcerated in civilian jails, it was for minor offenses.

The United States military procedure for determining the status of a suspected guerrilla is described by Fred K. Green in *The Concept of 'War' and the Concept of 'Combatant' in Modern Conflicts*, 10 REVUE DE DROIT PENAL MILITAIRE ET DE DROIT DE LA GUERRE 267–309 (1971). In fact, reliance on judicial hearings for determination of the status of captured personnel was limited. When used, the captured Viet Cong frequently would endeavor to characterize their actions as criminal rather than belligerent for a particular reason. While the United States had invested a great deal of money in the construction and maintenance of POW camps, little improvement had been made in the civilian jails of South Vietnam. Hence the latter generally applied a "first in, first out" rule, releasing convicted individuals on that basis regardless of the seriousness of their offense. In contrast, individuals provided POW protection could be held in a POW camp for the duration of the hostilities. Hence captured Viet Cong saw an advantage in being denied POW protection and convicted of a civil offense, as it generally meant that they could return to their guerrilla duties within six months.

In a similar instance, in June 1985 a radical Shiite Moslem group known as the Party of God hijacked a Trans World Airlines flight enroute from Athens to Rome. In the course of the hijacking a United States passenger, Robert Stethem, was murdered. One of the terrorists involved in the kidnapping, Mohammed Ali Hamadi, was apprehended with explosives in his possession at the Frankfurt, West Germany, airport in January 1988. United States authorities immediately requested his extradition. But members of the Party of God kidnapped three West Germans in Beirut in retaliation for Hamadi's arrest, threatening their execution if Hamadi was not released. West German authorities declined to extradite Hamadi, and were reluctant to bring him to trial for fear for the safety of the West German hostages. It was not until the United States established conclusively that Hamadi not only was a principal but was in fact the leader of the 1985 TWA hijacking that Bonn authorities agreed to try Hamadi, as they were legally obligated to do under the 1970 Hague Convention for the Suppression of Unlawful Seizure of Aircraft (22 U.S.T. 1641, T.I.A.S. 7192). Subsequently Hamadi was found guilty of murder, hijacking, assault, and explosives importation, and sentenced to life imprisonment.

315. *See* discussion of the negotiation of article 75, Protocol I, contained in *supra* note 274.

316. Treaty Between the United States of America and the Union of Soviet Socialist Republics on the Limitation of Anti-Ballistic Systems, May 26, 1972, 23 U.S.T. 3435, T.I.A.S. 7503, contained in U.S. ARMS CONTROL AND DISARMAMENT AGENCY, ARMS CONTROL AND DISARMAMENT AGREEMENTS 139–47 (1982).

illustrative not only of the degree to which reliance is made upon ambiguity, but of the problem that can occur as a result.[317]

Extensive reliance was made on ambiguity in the course of the Diplomatic Conference, and agreement could not have been reached were it not for purposeful ambiguity.[318] Yet a clear distinction exists between international agreements in general and law of war treaties. Although international agreements frequently permit amendment, renunciation, or abrogation in the event the agreement in question proves unsatisfactory, law of war treaties such as Protocol I provide for specific penal sanctions against military commanders who violate their provisions.[319] These sanctions necessitate specific language in such treaties. Specificity is especially critical in that potential adversaries have a long record of denying prisoner of war protection and threatening war crimes trials against U.S. and allied military and civilian personnel who fall into enemy hands.[320] In this regard, the resort to purposeful ambiguity in Protocol I is a great disservice to battlefield commanders operating in the fog of war.

The members of the military review began to examine the language of the 1977 Protocols as a lawyer viewing a contract on behalf of his client. Given the purposeful ambiguity built into the Protocols by their negotiators, the picture was not favorable.

The American delegation to the Diplomatic Conference (along with others) took the approach of obtaining language that permitted the United States certain legal rights with respect to what it could do in hostilities. In the course of the negotiations, however, in order to achieve consensus, the language of many provisions was made intentionally vague, permitting interpretations of treaty provisions that were contradictory to Western interpretations. The United States and other Western delegations did not necessarily concern themselves with any interpretation except their own. Examples previously have been provided with regard to articles 44(3) and 55; other examples will be offered in the discussion of those articles that affect aerial bombardment.

---

317. *See e.g.*, Nunn, *The ABM Reinterpretation Issue*, 10 THE WASH. Q. 45–58 (Autumn 1987); and Sofaer, *The ABM Treaty: Legal Analysis in the Political Cauldron*, 10 THE WASH. CAULDRON 59–75 (Autumn 1987).

318. Much credit for agreement is due Ambassador Aldrich, whose negotiating skills were essential to the degree of success achieved in reaching agreement in the Protocols. Ambassador Aldrich is a protege of former Secretary of State and National Security Adviser Henry Kissinger, who placed great reliance upon purposeful ambiguity in order to reach agreement. For example, in describing the 1973 agreement between the United States and North Vietnam ending the war in Southeast Asia, one historian has noted:

> At his 24 January [1973] news conference, Kissinger voiced approval of the agreement. "It is clear," he said, "there is *no legal way* by which North Vietnam can use military force against South Vietnam." The National Security Adviser then added: "Now, whether that is due to the fact that there are two zones temporarily divided by a provisional demarcation line or because North Vietnam is a foreign country with relation to South Vietnam—*that is an issue we have avoided making explicit in the agreement, and in which ambiguity has its merits*."

M. CLODFELTER, *supra* note 224, at 199, citing *Agreement on Ending the War and Restoring Peace in Vietnam: New Conference, 24 January 1973*, 9 Weekly Compilation of Presidential Documents 71 (29 January 1973) (emphasis added). The 1975 conquest of South Vietnam by North Vietnam reveals the fallacy of such diplomacy or, collaterally, an overreliance on written agreements with nations that have no regard for the rule of law.

319. Article 85, Protocol I.

320. Proponents of ratification of Protocol I argue that any ambiguities can be corrected through statements of understanding. Such statements would be of value if an American soldier, sailor, airman, or marine were to be brought to trial in a United States court, or before an impartial international tribunal; they are of dubious value in a captor's less-than-impartial court, particularly when the captor is allowed a contradictory interpretation because of vagueness introduced into the provision in question at the time of its negotiation.

The military review again identified yet another problem that poses a direct threat to the safety of U.S. military and civilian personnel who fall into enemy hands. Article 102 of Protocol I establishes that the Arabic, Chinese, English, French, Russian, and Spanish texts are equally authentic. A cursory comparison in 1985 identified discrepancies between the English and Russian texts; no independent comparison has been made of the other texts.[321] Yet ratification of Protocol I would constitute acceptance of the Protocol in each of its official languages, notwithstanding any discrepancies.[322]

In this case, the client was the American fighting man. No lawyer in good faith could advise a client to accept a contract which contained myriad major ambiguities subject to multiple interpretations by the parties (some of whom have a long record of disregard for the concept of *pacta sunt servanda*), prepared in six different languages with potential discrepancies between the texts, but by which the client would not only be legally bound but could be found criminally and civilly liable.[323]

Protection of National Security Interests. Notwithstanding attempts by some to characterize Protocol I as a humanitarian agreement, those articles that affect the conduct of hostilities are as much an arms control agreement as they are law of war provisions. A primary objective of the ICRC as early as 1953 was to force the conduct of hostilities, and particularly the employment of airpower, back onto the immediate battlefield or, stated another way, to prohibit the use of airpower beyond the immediate battlefield.[324] The ICRC clearly sought to breathe new life into the 1923 Hague Air Rules.[325] While its initial efforts took a relatively pragmatic view, it was caught up in the momentum of Third World and Western European nations' use

---

321. The term "re-identified" has been used because the author's predecessor, Waldemar A. Solf, first raised this concern in 1977 prior to U.S. signature of the Protocols. He was advised by Department of State officials not to worry about it. An official Soviet text was not available until more than a year after the Protocols were open for signature. While the ICRC has published and distributed texts of the Protocols in French, Spanish, English, and Arabic, the Russian and Chinese texts have never been made available. Nor has there been an independent corroboration of the texts.

322. Article 33, paragraph 1 of the Vienna Convention on the Law of Treaties provides that "When a treaty has been authenticated in two or more languages, the text is equally authoritative in each language." While paragraph 3 provides that "The terms of a treaty are presumed to have the same meaning in each authentic text," this presupposes that the text has been confirmed as the same, which has not been accomplished with regard to the texts of Protocols I and II. No such comparison has been undertaken by the Department of State, which has the responsibility for such action. Again, however, the point would be rather moot, for example, if a United States airman in an enemy POW camp were threatened with a war crimes trial for violation of a text that not only is ambiguous but potentially could have an entirely different meaning in the captor's language.

323. In addition to the penal sanctions contained in article 85, article 91 provides for damages (not reparations) for violations of Protocol I. Considering just the disagreement with regard to article 10 of Protocol I concerning admission of the civilian population into military medical facilities, the potential for civil litigation is considerable.

324. Claud Pilloud, a senior lawyer with the ICRC during the course of the negotiation of the Protocols, admitted this to the author during a drive from San Remo, Italy, to Geneva in 1978.

325. Thus in introducing its earlier draft rules an ICRC representative stated that, "The 1922/23 [Hague Air Rules] project would have required combatants to abstain from bombing when it might affect the civilian population, but a good text was useless if it went unsigned, unratified and unimplemented." NEW RULES FOR VICTIMS OF ARMED CONFLICTS, *supra* note 257, at 310, n.32. ICRC texts consistently give a perjorative connotation to airpower, while tending to ignore acts of terrorism carried out by guerrillas. *See Guerrilla Warfare and Its Legal Implications*, 87 ICRC BULLETIN 4 (April 6, 1983) in which it is stated: "Some chiefs of staff are inclined to regard the 'realistic' military counter to . . . [guerrilla] tactics as a strategy of aerial bombing, summary executions, if not torture and 'disappearances.' " Thus the ICRC equates aerial bombardment, which is no less lawful than artillery bombardment or other employment of arms, with three patently illegal actions—summary executions, torture, and "disappearances"—to suggest its illegality *per se*. This is representative of the ICRC fixation against the employment of airpower, and illustrates its intent closely to regulate (if not prohibit) the use of airpower beyond the immediate battlefield, and the ICRC's fundamental ignorance of modern warfare.

of the Diplomatic Conference as a means for limiting external threats posed by nations with significant airpower capabilities.

From the standpoint of the United States, there were several concerns. First, as Ambassador Aldrich acknowledged early in the negotiations of the Protocols, the United States historically has relied on its technological superiority to enhance its warfighting skills. Not the least of these is the *discriminate, accurate* employment of firepower, including airpower. The military review had to address the fundamental issue that Protocol I sought to constrain one means of warfare—airpower—while simultaneously enhancing another—guerrilla warfare—not only at increased risk to the civilian population but also to U.S. and allied combatants.

Second, the United States is a superpower with global obligations. It is not limited to fighting in a single theater; it has mutual defense commitments around the world. It must be prepared to employ military force at all levels of conflict, ranging from "peacetime" incidents such as the 1986 airstrike against terrorist-related targets in Libya to total war. The requirements of Protocol I had to be viewed in that light.

Pragmatic Standpoint. Finally, the Protocols had to be viewed from a pragmatic standpoint. War, according to a recent Marine Corps manual,

> is among the greatest horrors known to mankind; it should never be romanticized. The means of war is force, applied in the form of organized violence . . . that we compel our enemy to do our will . . . . Violence is an essential element of war, and its immediate result is bloodshed, destruction, and suffering. While the magnitude of violence may vary with the object and means of war, the violent essence of war will never change.[326]

In a word, war is something that cannot be trifled with by individuals who do not understand it. It is complex and lacking in order,[327] not given to simple rules that govern in all circumstances at all levels of conflict. The military review cast a

---

326. HEADQUARTERS, U.S. MARINE CORPS, FMFM–1, *Warfighting* 11 (1989) (FMFM–1). Or, as Clausewitz said,

> Kindhearted people might, of course, think there was some ingenious way to disarm or defeat an enemy without too much bloodshed, and might imagine this is the true goal of the art of war. Pleasant as it sounds, it is a fallacy that must be exposed: war is such a dangerous business that the mistakes which come from kindness are the very worst.
>
> This is how the matter must be seen. It would be futile—even wrong—to try to shut one's eyes to what war really is from sheer distress at its brutality.

ON WAR 75–76 (M. Howard & P. Paret, eds. 1984).

327. FMFM–1 comments on this point:

> In an environment of friction, uncertainty, and fluidity, war gravitates toward disorder. Like the other attributes of the environment of war, disorder is an integral characteristic of war; we can never eliminate it. In the heat of battle, plans will go awry, instructions and information will be unclear and misinterpreted, communications will fail, and mistakes and unforeseen events will be commonplace.

FMFM–1, *supra* note 326, at 8–9. What most concerned the author and other members of the military review group who had personal experience in combat was the degree to which the rules contained in Protocol I, and particularly articles 48–58, assumed that a combat commander has a greater grasp of his environment than is generally the case. This prompted one reviewer to recall the statement of John Galsworthy that "Idealism increases in direct proportion to one's distance from the problem."

Members of the military review were particularly concerned with the provision contained in article 81 of Protocol I that grants to the ICRC "all facilities within [the power of the Parties to the conflict] so as to enable the [ICRC] to carry out the humanitarian functions assigned to it by the [1949] Conventions and this Protocol in order to ensure protection and assistance to the victims of conflicts." This provision has been interpreted by the ICRC as blanket authority to move about the battlefield as some sort of referee, deciding when and where a commander had applied too much firepower, or the wrong kind of firepower.

The danger of the provision was manifested in the 1982 Israeli incursion into Lebanon. In its opening

critical eye at the rules contained in Protocol I with two basic questions: (a) Is United States military practice consistent with the requirements contained in Protocol I?, and (b) Is there a likelihood of universal respect for the provisions of Protocol I by all parties to a conflict, at all levels of conflict? The military review determined that positive gains claimed for Protocol I by Ambassador Aldrich in fact achieved little, if any, improvement over existing law.

One of the advances alleged was the language contained in articles 32 through 34 relating to missing and dead persons on the battlefield.[328] Given national concern for the unrecovered dead and missing in action from the Vietnam War, the guidance to the American delegation placed great emphasis on creation of an international obligation that went beyond existing law of war requirements. Comparison to articles 15 to 17 of the 1949 GWS determined that the Protocol I gain is more one of form than substance.[329] The United States forces on Grenada searched for and recovered enemy

---

phases a representative of the ICRC informed a press conference that Israeli Defense Forces (IDF) had killed more than 10,000 civilians since crossing into Lebanon. The information should have been verified before its release, inasmuch as it was received from PLO Chairman Yasser Arafat's brother. The information subsequently was found to be false, and the ICRC delegate was recalled. But the ICRC nonetheless released a statement calling upon Israel to cease the "indiscriminate" attack of civilians, ignoring the PLO's use of civilians and civilian objects such as hospitals and churches as shields from attack.

Several days later an ICRC representative called the author, asking how the United States had "permitted" the IDF to employ an American "tank" bearing the Magen David Adom, the Israeli equivalent to the Red Cross and Red Crescent. On investigation, it was determined that the "tank" was a M113 armored personnel carrier being used exclusively as a medical vehicle. The United States Army employs M113s in the same role, and numerous other nations also employ armored personnel carriers in this role. The ICRC representative lacked fundamental training in the identification of military vehicles, even though he had served in the Swiss military.

These actions revealed several weaknesses of the ICRC. First was the ignorance of ICRC delegates of military matters that they now feel prepared to judge. Second was a certain bias or inability to speak impartially. Previous statements of the ICRC historically had been generic statements calling upon all parties to a conflict to take protection for the civilian population into consideration in their operations. The 1982 announcement was disturbing because it singled out only one party to the conflict, suggesting that it was the only party that might not be in compliance with the law of war. (An official investigation by the author in 1983 revealed that the IDF had taken extraordinary steps to protect the Lebanese civilian population in the course of the IDF incursion into Lebanon.) ICRC actions also raised some questions about the ICRC looking solely at the effect rather than the cause of damage.

A senior ICRC official subsequently acknowledged that the ICRC has different "methods" (standards) for dealing with democratic nations *vis-à-vis* totalitarian states or terrorist organizations. While it chooses to emphasize "quiet diplomacy" with the latter, the ICRC will not hesitate to rely on international public pressure to address what it perceives to be infractions of the law of war by a democracy. Hence the ICRC made no public statements about the denial of its seventy-two requests to visit U.S. POWs in North Vietnam, or of Soviet violations of the law of war in Afghanistan, or of recent military operations by Syria and Iraqi-backed forces in Beirut (which have resulted in substantially greater damage and loss of civilian life than actions by Israel in 1982). But it has been very quick to criticize any action by Israel. The author recently learned that the ICRC threatened (but did not employ) critical public statements about U.S. POW camps in South Vietnam, even though privately its delegates praised American efforts. The issue is not whether such criticism is warranted, but rather the double standard the ICRC has adopted. Such an attitude is an abandonment of the ICRC's requirement for neutrality, and furnishes fuel for propaganda to totalitarian regimes. For these reasons, the language contained in article 81 is unacceptable outside the ICRC's traditional focus on respect for war victims contained in the four 1949 Geneva Conventions.

328. Aldrich, *supra* note 259, at 693.

329. Article 33, paragraph 1 of Protocol I provides that: "As soon as circumstances permit, and at the latest from the end of active hostilities, each Party to the conflict shall search for the persons who have been reported missing." In contrast, article 15 of the 1949 GWS provides that: "At all times, and particularly after an engagement, Parties to the conflict shall, without delay, take all possible measures to search for . . . the dead and prevent their being despoiled."

Thus, whereas the 1949 GWS requires that a party to the conflict search for the dead (including the missing in action) at all times, and particularly following an engagement, the language of Protocol I obligates a party to the conflict to carry out such a search only at the end of a war. (The term "active hostilities" has been interpreted to mean the end of war, not the end of a particular engagement. ICRC COMMENTARY, *supra* note 247, at 353.)

dead following the end of that operation, for example, without any reference to the language of Protocol I.[330] Comparison to the language contained in the 1973 Agreement Between the United States and Vietnam revealed the language of article 33 of Protocol I to be *weaker* than that of the agreement between the United States and Vietnam.[331] The failure of the latter in the years following the end of the Vietnam War suggests how enhancement will evolve in practical rather than legal terms; as with the GWS provisions, implementation remains dependent upon good faith of the party in question. Article 33 of Protocol I essentially is a legal solution to a problem that seldom if ever is resolved in legal terms. It constitutes no advancement over exisiting law.

Another purported enhancement is the language of articles 24 to 30 for the increased protection of medical aircraft.[332] The language is an improvement in that it provides a regime in which parties to a conflict *may* establish procedures for the safe operation of medical aircraft. But as with its predecessor language in article 36 of the GWS, such safe operation largely remains dependent upon express agreement between the parties to the conflict.[333] The medical aircraft provisions of Protocol I were unnecessary to achieve such special agreement: For example, the famous Red Cross Box in which medical aircraft of Great Britain and Argentina were allowed to operate during the 1982 Falklands-Malvinas War was achieved despite the fact that neither belligerent was a party to the 1977 Protocols at the time of the conflict.[334]

The American military analysis revealed that communication (much less agreement) between the parties to the conflict on the modern battlefield was, at best, extremely

330. In contrast, Libya—a party of Protocol I since 1978—recovered the bodies of the F-111F aircrew lost during the 1986 United States airstrike, but refused to return them to the United States. One body was returned in January 1989, when questions were being raised in the international arena about Libya's construction of a chemical weapons facility. The second remains in Libyan hands, *Libya Says It Plans to Return Body*, Philadelphia Inquirer, Dec. 25, 1988, at 20; and *Libya Offers to Accept Controls on Suspect Plant*, Wash. Post, Dec. 25, 1988, at A48. Only the most perverse would suggest that Libya's failure can be attributed to the fact that the United States is not a party to Protocol I. The ICRC has remained silent regarding Libya's conduct.

331. Article 8B of that agreement provides that:

> The parties shall help each other to get information about these military personnel and foreign civilians of the parties missing in action, to determine the location and take care of the graves of the dead so as to facilitate the exhumation and repatriation of the remains and to take such other measures as may be required to get information about those still considered missing in action.

Agreement on Ending the War and Restoring the Peace in Vietnam Between the Government of the Democratic Republic of Vietnam and the Government of the United States of America, Jan. 27, 1973 24 U.S.T. 1, T.I.A.S. 7542. *Cf.* Richburg, *Vietnam Stalls on MIAs*, Wash. Post, Mar. 20, 1987, at A30.

332. For discussion of these provisions, *see* Solf, *supra* note 77.

333. For example, article 26 of Protocol I states that "protection for medical aircraft can be fully effective only by prior agreement between the competent military parties to the conflict" when medical aircraft are operating in and over those parts of the contact zone which are either physically controlled by friendly forces or the physical control of which is not clearly established. Article 27 provides that "medical aircraft of a Party to the conflict shall continue to be protected while flying over . . . areas physically controlled by an adverse Party, provided that prior agreement to such flights has been obtained from the competent authority of that adverse Party." Only when medical aircraft are flying over their own territory is their operation not dependent upon agreement with the adverse Party. Even then article 25 provides that "For greater safety, . . . a Party to the conflict operating its medical aircraft in these areas may notify the adverse Party, . . . in particular when such aircraft are making flights bringing them within range of surface-to-air weapons systems of the adverse Party."

In contrast, article 36 of the GWS provides that: "Medical aircraft . . . shall not be attacked, but shall be respected by the belligerents, while flying at heights, times and on routes specifically agreed upon between the belligerents concerned."

334. Argentina became a party to the 1977 Protocols on 26 November 1986. Great Britain had not reached a decision as to ratification at the time this article was prepared.

unlikely due to communication security, operational security, the impact of electronic warfare, and the incompatibility of communication equipment.[335] This was particularly true for the frequency of medical evacuation sorties that are flown on a day-to-day basis. The ambiguities in article 28 relating to use of cryptological equipment placed U.S. medical aircraft and aircrews at greater risk than previously, and were totally incompatible with established U.S. policy and medical evacuation communication procedures.[336]

The articles of Protocol I were negotiated to respond to problems found in Vietnam relating to the use of medical evacuation helicopters. The American military review concluded that even if the provisions of Protocol I had been in effect during the Vietnam War, for tactical, ideological and technological reasons they would have been of no value.[337] Nor would they be of value on a modern, high-intensity

---

335. Incompatibility between U.S. and, *e.g.*, Warsaw Pact communications equipment is a fundamental problem that precludes the arrangement of the agreements contemplated by articles 25 through 29 of Protocol I. Readers familiar with the 1983 American rescue operation in Grenada will recall that communication equipment incompatibility among the forces participating in the mission precluded vital communications during that operation. Even greater communications compatibility problems arise when considering *e.g.*, NATO alliance operations, and those are compounded when *e.g.*, Warsaw Pact communications equipment is considered. In a word, the parties cannot communicate with one another. The heavy emphasis placed upon jamming of all enemy communications within the theater of operations exacerbates the matter.

Caution should be exercised to distinguish an ability to listen (*i.e.*, intercept) an enemy's transmissions *vis-à-vis* communicate with an enemy; they are not the same, and seldom, if ever, will an enemy reveal his ability to accomplish the former. Allied abilities to intercept German ULTRA transmissions remained highly classified for more than three decades following World War II, for example.

During the Vietnam War, North Vietnamese and Viet Cong forces frequently intercepted U.S. and Allied transmissions, including requests for medical evacuation aircraft, to exploit them to their military advantage. This included the attack of medical evacuation aircraft. Frequently this was accomplished through the use of captured American radios. Had the medical aircraft provisions of Protocol I been in effect during the Vietnam War, they would have been of no benefit, because the enemy would not have wanted to reveal the degree to which he could listen in on American transmissions for fear that U.S. forces would encrypt their communications (which were broadcast in the clear, or unencrypted, for most of the war). As a result of a study conducted by the United States Army after the Vietnam War into the effect on operational security of enemy intercept of American tactical communications, a formal policy decision was made in 1971 that all U.S. tactical communications thereafter would be encrypted. The provisions contained in articles 25–28 of Protocol I were negotiated by the United States delegation without knowledge of this policy change.

336. As discussed *supra* note 283.

337. As discussed *supra* note 335, the medical aircraft provisions of Protocol I would not have worked in Vietnam because of a fundamental incompatibility of radio equipment between U.S. forces and the North Vietnamese and its Viet Cong proxies. Even if there had been a method for communication, North Vietnamese forces (including the Viet Cong) would have had little incentive for communication or agreement. The former would facilitate American location and attack of enemy units through electronic intelligence, while enemy refusal to permit medical evacuation not only would have an effect on the morale of United States forces, but in certain circumstances might force a United States unit to break off contact in order to provide for its wounded.

A frequent misconception regarding the medical aircraft provisions of Protocol I is that they provide increased protection for medical aircraft; they do not. They provide that medical aircraft are protected from intentional attack upon agreement with competent authority for their operation in a particular area at a particular time for a particular mission, *i.e.*, the same data required by article 36, GWS. Blanket authorization to fly medical aircraft in the area of active operations is highly improbable, particularly given the dependency of nations on helicopter mobility for movement of light infantry forces and/or reliance upon helicopter gunships. The United States military review ascertained that the likelihood of such agreement at the battlefield level was virtually nonexistent. Local arrangements for removal of the wounded and sick from the battlefield (by the means to which the parties agree) already exist in article 15, GWS.

In this regard it is important to understand that the medical aircraft provisions of Protocol I provide no greater rights for protection than exist within the GWS. Article 24 of Protocol I provides that "Medical aircraft shall be respected and protected, subject to the provisions of this Part," *i.e.*, subject to agreement between the belligerents. Thus, if a besieged unit wishes to evacuate its wounded by medical aircraft without the permission of the besieging force, the besieging force commander has the right to fire upon those aircraft to defeat their mission. Nothing in Protocol I changes this.

conflict battlefield. The danger to medical aircraft on the latter is such that the U.S. Army does not intend to operate its medical aircraft any further forward than the division rear, an area akin to that specified in article 25 of Protocol I, in which protection for medical aircraft is not dependent on any agreement with an adverse party.[338] The Marine Corps operates no dedicated medical aircraft, while Navy and Air Force C–9 medical aircraft will operate much further to the rear. The conclusion of the American military review was that the provisions of Protocol I regarding protection of medical aircraft do not constitute any advancement over the language contained in article 36, GWS, and in fact would be totally unworkable on a modern battlefield.

The military review did find some advances, though none that could be considered major. One improvement sought by the United States is the language in article 42, paragraph 1, that "No person parachuting from an aircraft in distress shall be made the object of attack during his descent."[339] This article is intended to resolve the long-standing debate as to whether aircrew members descending by parachute from a disabled aircraft should be regarded as noncombatants until they reach the ground, at which time they are subject to capture or, in the event of their resistance or attempted evasion, attack.[340] The history behind the debate is long, and has been amply discussed elsewhere.[341]

While the decision as to whether to attack, for example, a pilot who had bailed out of his aircraft, often turned on the self-interest of the attacker,[342] a legitimate mili-

338. Chapter III of Annex I to Protocol I establishes elaborate communication procedures for medical units and transports, including medical aircraft. The military review found these procedures to be of little value because of the electronic warfare environment that exists on the modern battlefield that will virtually preclude receipt of the medical signals by any party to a conflict. The greatest danger to medical aircraft operating in the contact zones (as set forth in article 26 of Protocol I) is the risk of so-called "friendly fire" from shoulder-fired surface-to-air missiles such as the United States Stinger or the Soviet SA–7 Grail, which lack means for reception of electronic "medical" signals but which can operate at ranges that preclude recognition of the distinctive emblem. This is one of the principal reasons for the United States Army decision to operate its medical aircraft only in the area behind the division rear. Enemy medical aircraft operating without express permission of an opponent (as provided for in article 36, GWS) would be at the same risk of attack as a result of misidentification.

339. This article relates only to aircrew and noncombatant passengers, paragraph 3 expressly providing that "Airborne troops are not protected by this Article."

340. But only so long as they land in hostile territory, where they are subject to capture. Paragraph 2 of article 42 states specifically that descending airmen only remain protected until "reaching the ground in territory controlled by an adverse Party." A member of an aircrew descending over friendly territory would be subject to attack immediately upon making his contact with the ground. The potential for factual disputes as to whether a descending airman landing in friendly territory had touched the ground before being shot is readily apparent.

341. *See* J. Spaight, *supra* note 137, at 152–63. *See also* P. Meijering, Signed With Their Honor: Air Chivalry During the Two World Wars 49–59 (1988). Article 20 of the ill-fated 1923 Hague Air Rules provided that "When an aircraft has been disabled, the occupants when endeavoring to escape by means of a parachute must not be attacked in the course of their descent." Schindler & Toman, *supra* note 27, at 210.

342. There was some genuine belief by a few in the chivalry of the matter. For example, in the course of a meeting with Reichmarschall Herman Goering during the Battle of Britain, Luftwaffe ace Adolf Galland reported the following exchange:

> Experience had proved, [Goering] told us, that especially with technically highly developed arms such as . . . fighter aircraft, the men who controlled these machines were more important than the machines themselves. The aircraft which we shot down could easily be replaced by the British. Not so the pilots.
>
> There was a short pause . . . Goering looked me straight in the eyes and said: "What would you think of an order directing you to shoot down pilots who were bailing out?" "I should regard it as murder . . . ," I replied, "and I should do everything in my power to disobey such an order."

tary issue existed. In most cases, it is more difficult to replace a pilot than an aircraft.[343] Where a parachuting pilot (or aircrew member) could be captured after his descent, he usually was not at risk of intentional attack. Where he was descending in friendly territory, however, an argument could be made that he should be subject to attack. As Air Marshal Hugh Dowding noted during his Battle of Britain tenure as head of the Royal Air Force Fighter Command, "Germans descending over England were prospective prisoners and should be immune [from attack], while British pilots descending over England were still potential combatants. German pilots were perfectly entitled to fire on our decending airmen."[344]

While in most cases RAF pilots declined to attack Luftwaffe pilots notwithstanding this guidance,[345] there are recorded cases of such attacks being carried out by all

---

> Goering put both his hands on my shoulders and said: "That is just the reply I had expected from you, Galland." In the First World War similar ideas had cropped up, but were equally strongly rejected by the fighter pilots.
>
> [T]he subject was never mentioned again, not even later when aerial warfare became so gruesome.

A. GALLAND, *supra* note 188, at 120–21. Goering's views on this point have been confirmed by others. *See* R. TOLIVER & T. CONSTABLE, THE BLOND KNIGHT OF GERMANY, 169 (rev. ed. 1989); and D. IRVING, GOERING: A BIOGRAPHY 423 (1989).

While the author does not want to dispute this view, and in fact commends it, it is noted that the view was based somewhat upon self-interest, as was true during the original days of chivalry. The term "chivalry" arose during the Middle Ages. Chivalry is derived from *cheval*, (the French word for horse) and originally meant horsemanship. Knights, *chevaliers*, were mounted warriors who fought on horseback. R. DAVIS, THE MEDIEVAL WARHORSE 6 (London, 1989). In its original form, chivalry meant that a knight who had fallen from his horse should not be attacked. In addition to the obvious self-interest of all knights, whose allegiance often was dependent upon financial interests, a knight captured and held for ransom generally was of greater value than a dead knight. But the idea of refusing to attack one who was *hors de combat* did not extend to ordinary foot soldiers or to non-Christian soldiers, mounted or otherwise. As historian Richard Barber has observed,

> [B]eneath the high idealism of chivalric honor, war continues much as before, as cruel, atrocious and thoughtless as ever. Knighthood becomes a kind of guild of warriors, who may put the ordinary soldier and the civilian to the sword, but who rarely kill each other intentionally on the battlefield, and who see to it that military enterprises have a suitable financial reward. The occasional feat of arms is a diversion from the more serious business of pillage and destruction, and chivalry owes more to the pen than the sword.

R. BARBER, THE KNIGHT AND CHIVALRY 208 (1970). The distinctions made during the Middle Ages persisted during World War II, and are representative of respect for the law of war in general. While there was general respect for aircrew members in parachutes as between British, American, and German forces, the same cannot be said for combat between German and Russian forces, or for British and American forces in fighting the Japanese, and vice-versa, as will be seen in cites contained *infra* notes 344 and 347. While one author has characterized this as a racial bias in the case of the Pacific war it seems to have been more of a cultural issue on both sides. J. DOWER, WAR WITHOUT MERCY: RACE AND POWER IN THE PACIFIC WAR (1986). As is true of many aspects of the law of war, the concept of chivalry is based upon Judeo-Christian ideals, and benefits or suffers accordingly. British and American attacks on Japanese pilots in their parachutes differed little from the views of knights in the Middle Ages in providing no quarter for "non-believers," or from British desires in the 1930s to retain bombing for the policing of "savages," as discussed *supra* note 250.

343. For example, during the Battle of Britain, Great Britain was able to replace aircraft losses far more easily than pilot losses. *See* B. COLLIER, *supra* note 1, at 154–55, 162, 198, 200, 246, 250. Likewise, towards the closing months of World War II, the Luftwaffe had a surplus of fighter aircraft, but lacked trained pilots to fly them. *See* A. GALLAND, *supra* note 188, at 261, 264, and 268; R. TOLLIVER & T. CONSTABLE, *supra* note 342, at 146; and W. MURRAY, *supra* note 85, at 285–92, 296.

344. P. TOWNSEND, DUEL OF EAGLES 288 (1970); *see also* L. DEIGHTON, FIGHTER—THE TRUE STORY OF THE BATTLE OF BRITAIN 43 (1978).

345. As Peter Townsend comments "[Sergeant Dickinson] had been shot dead by a Me–109 while coming down by parachute. By the rules of war it was justifiable to kill a pilot who could fight again. But few of us could bring ourselves to shoot a helpless man in cold blood," *supra* note 344, at 378–79.

sides during World War II.[346] The practice of shooting at descending pilots was particularly prevalent in the Pacific, where it appears to have been more the rule than the exception.[347]

Cases are on record of the attack on American airmen in their parachutes as they descended over enemy territory during the Vietnam War,[348] so the United States strongly supported the prohibition on the attack of descending airmen. But the proposal met with substantial resistance, primarily from Arab nations that had the experience of watching Israeli pilots parachute safely into their own territory, only to be thrown back into combat on very short order. The case for attack of descending aircrew under certain circumstances as made by Air Marshal Dowding during the

---

In a slightly similar vein, Luftwaffe pilot Erich Rudordorffer, who ended the war with 222 victories, reported:

> Once—I think it was 31 August 1940—I was in a fight with four [RAF] Hurricanes over Dover. I was back over the Channel when I saw another Hurricane coming from Calais, trailing white smoke, obviously in a bad way. I flew alongside him and escorted him all the way to England and then waved goodbye. A few weeks later the same thing happened to me. That would never have happened in Russia—never.

L. DEIGHTON, *supra* note 344, at 211. *See also* J. SPAIGHT, *supra* note 137, at 160–61.

346. For examples, *see* J. SPAIGHT, *supra* note 137, at 159–62, and A. DE ZAYAS, THE WERMACHT WAR CRIMES BUREAU, 1939–1945 148 (London, 1989). Frequently pilots or aircrew members in their parachutes were fired upon by ground force personnel rather than enemy aircraft, often with disastrous consequences as a result of misidentification. For example, during the Battle of Britain RAF Flight Lieutenant James Nicholson and Pilot Officer M. A. King of 249 Squadron were descending over their own territory, their respective aircraft having been disabled during an engagement with Luftwaffe Me–109s. As one historian describes the action:

> An officer of a Royal Artillery detachment ordered his men to take up positions and open fire with their rifles at the two airmen—ostensibly in the belief that they were enemy parachutists. Some Local Defence Volunteers joined in the fusillade. Whether King himself was hit is not known, but some of his parachute strands parted, the canopy collapsed, and the young pilot plunged to his death.

F. MASON, *supra* note 81, at 268, 270; and L. DEIGHTON, *supra* note 344, at 138. Because French civilians often participated in shooting at parachuting airmen, frequently killing British and French as well as Luftwaffe airmen, German headquarters in Abbeville on 15 May 1940, issued instructions to its forces only to shoot at groups of at least three parachutists. DE ZAYAS, *supra*, at 148.

347. *See* T. BLACKBURN, THE JOLLY ROGERS 208 (1989); and R. PORTER, with E. HAMMEL, ACE! 121–23 (1985). In the latter reference, after a Japanese pilot was unsuccessful in his machinegun attack on a U.S. Marine Corps pilot descending by parachute, he made two additional passes, using his propeller to injure or kill the descending pilot, and doubtless would have made more had he not been driven away by the attack of a Royal New Zealand's Air Force P–40. The Marine lost a foot, but survived to fly again.

Attacks on descending airmen sometimes led to tragic results. In late 1944 or early 1945, four U.S. Navy F6F Hellcat fighter aircraft on a combat sweep engaged four Japanese fighters. In the ensuing dogfight, a Navy pilot observed a parachute only seconds after he had seen a Japanese fighter blow up. He opened fire on the parachuting pilot. Following the engagement, the Navy fighters discovered one of their aircraft missing as they returned to their aircraft carrier. During the debrief, the Navy pilot reported that he had machinegunned the parachuting Japanese pilot. The pilot credited with shooting down the Japanese fighter noted that the Japanese pilot was not able to jump from his aircraft before it blew up. Later that day, a screening U.S. destroyer recovered the body of the American Navy pilot who had died of the machinegun wounds received from his squadronmate's erroneous attack. Story related to the author by Barrett Tillman, Managing Editor, TAILHOOK magazine, 14 May 1989.

348. There does not seem to have been an enemy policy of shooting at descending aircrew during the Vietnam War. Indeed, the North Vietnamese were quick to recognize the value of capturing U.S. military personnel and established an award system for their capture. The problem appears to have been somewhat akin to that experienced by the Germans in France in 1940 (A. DE ZAYAS, *supra* note 346), as local citizens, acting unilaterally, frequently fired upon descending aircrew or assaulted them once they reached the ground, but before North Vietnamese military personnel could take them into custody.

Battle of Britain remained a strong argument against article 42(1) for many nations attending the Diplomatic Conference.[349]

H. Overriding Considerations

The preceding paragraphs provide background regarding the political environment in which Additional Protocol I was negotiated. As the earlier analysis of the 1899 and 1907 Hague Peace Conferences, 1923 Hague Air Rules, and 1949 Geneva Conventions conference revealed, politics is no stranger to law of war treaty negotiations. But in the course of negotiation of the 1977 Protocols, the law of war took a backseat to certain overriding considerations:

a. arms control: an effort by Third World nations, some NATO nations, and neutrals (such as Switzerland, Sweden, and Austria) to limit the military superiority of potential adversaries, and particularly the superpowers; and

b. political: an effort by Third World nations to achieve international recognition for selected national liberation movements (specifically, the Palestine Liberation Organization and the African National Congress) while protecting their right to suppress domestic dissent within their respective nations.

The 1977 Protocols do not constitute any advance for the law of war, and in many ways constitute a significant step backwards with respect to protection for war victims. The 1977 Protocols are a reflection of the time in which they were negotiated. Speaking of that era and the Third World domination thereof, a noted columnist observed: "The United Nations' moral authority evaporated in the 1970s when it became dominated by radical Third World regimes. Since then, the inherent, incurable trouble with the United Nations has been glaringly, blaringly apparent."[350]

349. The arguments are contained in LEVIE, 2 PROTECTION OF WAR VICTIMS, *supra* note 258, at 345–68. Democratic Yemen, Iraq, Jordan, Kuwait, Lebanon, Mauritania, Morocco, Qatar, Saudi Arabia, Libya, Somalia, Sudan, Syria, Tunisia, United Arab Emirates, and Yemen offered a qualifying amendment to article 42, paragraph 1, to the effect that a descending aircrew member would not be attacked "unless it is apparent that he will land in territory controlled by the Party to which he belongs or by an ally of that Party." The amendment was defeated by a vote of 47 against, 23 votes in favor, with 26 abstentions, following a heated debate. The debate illustrates the difficulty of balancing so-called humanitarian arguments against the realities of modern warfare, and serves to indicate that despite the codification of article 42, the issue is far from settled. For further discussion, *see* ICRC COMMENTARY, *supra* note 247, at 493–502; and NEW RULES FOR VICTIMS OF ARMED CONFLICTS, *supra* note 257 at 224–31. The latter is a bit quick off the mark in referring to the prohibition contained in article 42(1) as "custom" from the earliest days of aviation. The sources it cites to support its assertion, many of which were referred to in the preceding discussion, make it clear that the prohibition was far from universally accepted, and that there was considerable practice to the contrary. The debate at the Diplomatic Conference and the fact that this rule was not adopted by consensus also argues against any assertion that article 42(1) constitutes a codification of customary international law.

A collateral issue not discussed at the Diplomatic Conference and beyond the scope of this article concerns air-sea rescue of downed aviation personnel. An excellent discussion of this subject is Dunn, *Air-Sea Rescue Operations in Europe During World War II: Historical Perspective on a Footnote in International Law*, 21 A. F. L. REV. 602–19 (1979).

350. Will, . . . *and Terrorists*, Wash. Post, Dec. 1, 1988, at A27; *see also* D. MOYNIHAN, with S. WEAVER, A DANGEROUS PLACE (1978), which chronicles Senator Moynihan's 1975–1976 tenure as United States Ambassador to the United Nations in New York. Senator Moynihan's period of service coincided with the period during which substantial work was done in the negotiation of Protocol I and with the experience of the "tyranny of the majority" that was manifested by the Third World delegations at the Diplomatic Conference.

This environment continues, as evidenced by the ouster of the delegation of the Government of South Africa from the XXVth International Conference of the Red Cross, held in Geneva in October 1986. The author attended as a delegate representing the U.S. Government, and was witness to the proceedings. The ICRC opposed the ouster of South Africa, but was presented with an ultimatum by the Third World: find a way that will permit us to vote for the ouster of South Africa, or all of the Third World

XVI. PROTOCOL I

It was within the same context that Protocol I was negotiated, and it is necessary to keep that context in mind while examining those articles in Protocol I that relate to aerial bombardment. The section of Protocol I most directly relating to combat operations, articles 48 to 58, was the portion with which the U.S. military review found its greatest concern. The rules adopted by the Diplomatic Conference bear no relation to the way warfare has evolved over the past two centuries, and were expressly intended to return to a form of warfighting that has not been seen in this century. Any claim of a "humanitarian gain" is offset by the fact that the provisions contained in Protocol I shift the responsibility for the protection of the civilian population away from the host nation (which has custody over its civilian population, and which traditionally has borne the principal responsibility for the safety of the civilian population) almost exclusively onto an attacker.[351]

---

delegations will walk out. The ICRC acquiesced to Third World demands, and South Africa was ousted.

Subsequently the ICRC endeavored to place the incident in the best light. *See* Moreillon, *Suspension of the Government of the Republic of South Africa at the Twenty-fifth International Conference of the Red Cross*, 27,257 INT'L REV. OF THE RED CROSS 133–51 (Mar.–Apr. 1987). This analysis leaves much to be desired, from both a factual and a political standpoint. It was clear to Western observers that the ICRC is prepared to abandon its principles of *impartiality*, *neutrality*, and *universality* where politically expedient, and that it did so in October 1986. (For an explanation of the Red Cross Principles, *see* INTERNATIONAL COMMITTEE OF THE RED CROSS, INTERNATIONAL RED CROSS HANDBOOK 17 (12th ed. Geneva, 1983).

While the author questions the actions of the ICRC, it is not the author's intent to carry any brief for the South Africa policy of apartheid. The purpose in raising the 1986 incident was to illustrate the Third World's domination of the 1986 conference, which replicated its domination of the Diplomatic Conference that produced the 1977 Protocols. At every turn Diplomatic Conference attendees were faced with a threat of a walkout by the Third World delegations if those representatives did not have their way. This overriding threat took precedence over any advancement of the law of war.

351. There were two reasons for this. The first is the view of many nations that nothing in Protocol I or the law of war can be construed as hindering their conduct of military operations against an invader in exercise of their respective right of self-defense, as contained in article 51 of the Charter of the United Nations. While the ICRC COMMENTARY endeavors to explain away the distinction between the law of war *jus ad bellum* and *jus in bello*, there remains the view in many nations that sovereign rights take precedence over any international legal obligation, that is, nations have a right to place their civilian population at risk if necessary to provide for the national defense, and international law has exhibited an inability to respond to this claim. ICRC COMMENTARY, *supra* note 247, at 615–16. *See* the statement of France contained in the ICRC COMMENTARY discussion of article 48 of Protocol I to the effect that had there been a vote on article 48, the delegation of France would have abstained inasmuch as it considered the article to have "direct implications as regards a State's organization and conduct of defense against an invader." France's view was representative, not isolated. *Id.* at 599.

The option exercised in Protocol I was to shift the entire responsibility to the so-called invader that brings forward the second reason. A power (or powers) on foreign territory or otherwise engaged in offensive operations is perceived by many as an aggressor; hence his combat options should be limited. Such an assumption is historically incorrect. The allies that carried out strategic air operations against Nazi Germany, and ultimately crossed into Nazi Germany, for example, were replying to the acts of that nation, as were the sixteen-nation multinational United Nations forces that marched into North Korea in 1950 in response to that nation's invasion of South Korea. In the same vein, however, a combination of the two reasons brought the conclusion by the ICRC and many Third World nations that as (a) airpower is an offensive weapon, then (b) airpower is the weapon of an aggressor that (c) must be restricted. On this point, the members of the ICRC clearly were reflecting their views as Swiss citizens surrounded by NATO and Warsaw Pact nations. This point has been expressed to the author by a number of different members of the ICRC on numerous occasions, reflecting not only an ignorance of warfare but a bias against air operations.

These matters will be elaborated in the discussion of article 49, paragraph 1, and the use of the term "attacks." *See* text *infra* note 354.

A. Discrimination

Article 48 states the fundamental principle of discrimination, a principle with which there should be no disagreement.[352] Indeed, military efficiency calls for discrimination to the extent that it is reasonably possible, and the United States historically has used its technological superiority to endeavor to gain increased accuracy in order to be as discriminate as possible in placing munitions on target. This has been particularly true with regard to aerial bombardment, where World War II circular error probable (CEP) bombing accuracy standards (measured in hundreds and, in some cases, thousands of meters) have been diminished to today's CEP capabilities (measured in substantially less than 100 feet).[353]

While there is total agreement with the general principle of discrimination, there are several areas of disagreement that follow in elaboration of this principle in subsequent articles: (a) use of the term "attack;" (b) the definition of who is a civilian and who is a combatant; (c) the definition of what is a military objective as opposed to a civilian object; (d) the placing of equal emphasis on the protection of civilian objects as is provided civilians and, commensurately, a diminishment of the value of the lives of one's own combatants; and (e) assignment of responsibility for collateral civilian casualties between attacker and defender. Each will be discussed in the paragraphs that follow.

Attacks. Article 49, paragraph 1, provides that " 'Attacks' means acts of violence against the adversary, whether in offense or defense."[354] The ICRC *Official Commentary* acknowledgment that "It is quite clear that the meaning given here [in article 49] is not exactly the same as the usual meaning of the word" is an

352. Article 48 provides that "In order to ensure respect for and protection of the civilian population and civilian objects, the Parties to the conflict shall at all times distinguish between the civilian population and combatants and between civilian objects and military objectives and accordingly shall direct their operations only against military objectives." SCHINDLER & TOMAN, *supra* note 27, at 650.

353. Circular Error Probable (CEP) is defined by the United States Department of Defense (and the Inter-American Defense Board) as "An indicator of the delivery accuracy of a weapon system, used as a factor in determining probable damage to a target. It is the radius of a circle within which half of a missile's projectiles are expected to fall." The NATO definition is "An indicator of the accuracy of a missile/projectile, used as a factor in determining probable damage to a target. It is the radius of a circle within which half of the missiles/projectiles are expected to fall." U.S. DEPARTMENT OF DEFENSE, JOINT CHIEFS OF STAFF PUBLICATION 1, DICTIONARY OF MILITARY AND ASSOCIATED TERMS (1 June 1987).

For an illustration of the CEP measurement of one World War II bombing mission, *see* Hodges, *The 'Magic' 1000-foot Circle* 1 MIL. J. 6–10 (Sept.–Oct. 1977); MIL. J. 1 15–19 (Nov.–Dec. 1977); and 2 MIL. J. 30–32, 39 (Jan.–Feb. 1978). For illustrative discussion of the effort made to improve bombing accuracy, *see* P. DELEON, THE LASER-GUIDED BOMB: CASE HISTORY OF A DEVELOPMENT, RAND R-1312-1-PR (1974); McKnight, *Tactical PGMs: Implications in Perspective* IX PARAMETERS 32–46 (June 1979); Beaumont, *Rapiers Versus Clubs: the Fitful History of 'Smart Bombs'*, 126 J. ROYAL UNITED SERVICES INST. 45–50 (Sept. 1981); Haering, *How Tactical Air Works*, 108 U.S. NAVAL INST. PROC. (Nov. 1982); and Owens, *Pave Knife: The First Combat Use of the Laser Guided Bomb*, 2 NAVAL AVIATION MUSEUM FOUNDATION 77–84 (Fall 1988). George Haering notes that during the 1972 Linebacker operations, United States tactical aircraft operating over North Vietnam dropped sixty unguided or "dumb" bombs for every "smart" (either laser or electro-optically guided) bomb delivered, with considerably less effect, attesting to the potential value of the United States investment in more accurate munitions. In contrast, many Third World nations have turned to less discriminate surface-to-surface missiles because of their inability to operate modern fixed-wing attack aircraft effectively. Haering, *supra* at 64. *See* Zaloga, *Ballistic Missiles in the Third World: Scud and Beyond*, 11 INT'L DEF. REV 1423–427 (Nov. 1988). The Soviet R-17, better known as the SS-1c Scud B, was used extensively by Iran and Iraq during their 1988 "war of the cities."

354. SCHINDLER & TOMAN, *supra* note 27, at 650. The word "attacks" is used throughout Protocols I and II. In the context of the present discussion, it is considered as it appears in articles 51, 52, and 57. For a complete listing of the articles in which the term is used, the reader is referred to the two Protocols or to INDEX OF INTERNATIONAL LAW, *supra* note 258, at 21–23.

understatement.[355] Use of "attacks" to refer to acts of defense is etymologically inconsistent with its customary use in any of the six official languages of Protocol I. For example, the first edition (1933) of *The Oxford English Dictionary* defines attack as, "The act of falling upon with force or arms, of commencing battle; an offensive operation; an onset, an assault. The common military term; opposed to defense."[356]

The second edition (1989) of *The Oxford English Dictionary* continues the definition contained in the first edition, but also includes, "To fasten or fall upon with force or arms; to in battle with, assail, assault. (The ordinary word used to describe offensive military operations.)"[357] Similarly, the French term "attaque" is defined as "attack, assault, aggression,"[358] while the Spanish term "ataque" means "offensive works."[359]

The term "attacks" was selected by the ICRC, first appearing in its 1956 *Draft Rules*. It met with considerable objection at the 1971 Conference of Government Experts, but was accepted at the 1972 Conference with its changed composition of so-called experts. In introducing it as part of the draft Protocol I, the ICRC explained that,

> The term 'attack' . . . is related to only one specific military operation. . . . Care should be taken not to confuse the author of an attack . . . with an aggressor, that is to say, the Party that starts the armed conflict itself. The author of the attack is he who, whatever his position may be at the outbreak of hostilities, *starts a military operation* involving the use of arms.[360]

The ICRC explanation resolves but part of the difficulty with the use of the word "attacks" in that it merely addresses the issue of the aggressor; it fails to address,

355. ICRC COMMENTARY, *supra* note 247, at 603. What must be appreciated is that the ICRC remained totally in charge of the draft Protocols up until the time the Diplomatic Conference began its work in 1974. The ICRC OFFICIAL COMMENTARY acknowledges that it did not accept all views offered it during the Conferences of Government Experts, stating that "In other cases, when the requirements of the Red Cross so dictated, the ICRC had to take the initiative itself and assume full responsibility" for text preparation. *Id.* at xxxi. Although the ICRC received considerable criticism for its use of the word attacks, it disregarded that criticism because it best suited its agenda to return combat operations exclusively to the immediate battlefield, as well as the Swiss-Swedish goal of limiting offensive operations of an invader. (The close relationship of the ICRC to the Swiss-Swedish foreign policy goals during the negotiation of the 1977 Protocols is discussed *infra* note 361.

While the ICRC COMMENTARY subsequently states that it turned the draft Protocols over to the Diplomatic Conference and the States that participated in those negotiations for their deliberation, that is not entirely true. *Id.* at xxxiii. The ICRC participated in the Diplomatic Conference as more than a casual observer. It protected its agenda throughout the Diplomatic Conference, principally through representatives from Sweden, Switzerland, and the Third World, who were known and who met as the Group of 77 (indicating their number). Those nations held a majority lock on the decision-making process. Any nation that sought to make substantive amendments to any provision, such as to substitute another word or words for attacks, could do so only with the concurrence of this block—which in turn was heavily influenced in many respects by the arguments of Sweden, Switzerland, and the ICRC. With regard to the word attacks, the views of the ICRC and the Group of 77 were identical, that is, to use a word that (notwithstanding any disclaimer in article 49(1) to the contrary) would limit *offensive* operations against those nations. At the same time no Western delegation was willing to break consensus over the point and, indeed, many failed to appreciate the nuance.

The author did not participate in the negotiation of the 1977 Protocols. The record of the Diplomatic Conference provides little information on the corridor negotiations that were necessary to complete the myriad provisions therein. The preceding paragraph, as well as other portions of this text related to the manner in which the 1977 Protocols were negotiated, is based upon discussions over the past twelve years with more than three dozen participants in those negotiations, including six members of the ICRC and several members of delegations within the Group of 77.

356. THE OXFORD ENGLISH DICTIONARY 543 (Oxford, 1933).

357. THE OXFORD ENGLISH DICTIONARY 760 (2d ed. Oxford, 1989).

358. THE NEW CASSELL'S FRENCH DICTIONARY 58 (1973).

359. APPLETON'S NEW CUYAS DICTIONARY, Rev. part II 55 (1972).

360. INTERNATIONAL COMMITTEE OF THE RED CROSS, DRAFT COMMENTARY 54 (Geneva, 1973), (emphasis added). A similar statement appears in the ICRC COMMENTARY, *supra* note 247, at 603.

and in the italicized portion of its last sentence supports, the traditional use of the term in associating it with offensive operations only.

This was intentional on the part of the ICRC, and was in keeping with its intent of limiting offensive operations, particularly with regard to the use of airpower beyond the immediate battlefield.[361] A participant in the two sessions of Government Experts explains the ICRC purpose in selection of the term "attacks": "The advantage of the attack may be with the attacker, but the advantages of a propagandistic exploitation of the situation lie with the party attacked."[362]

Article 49(1) states clearly that the word "attacks" refers to both offensive and defensive military operations. This use of the word is contrary to its ordinary meaning, and its intentional selection by the ICRC for the purpose of limiting offensive military actions casts serious doubts upon the neutrality of Protocol I. Moreover, it runs afoul of the principle of war of the offensive. Its importance is emphasized in the foundation document for U.S. Air Force doctrine:

> Unless offensive action is initiated, military victory is seldom possible. The principle of offensive is to act rather than react. The offensive enables commanders to select priorities of attack, as well as the time, place, and weaponry necessary to achieve objectives. Aerospace forces possess a capability to seize the offensive and can be employed rapidly and directly against enemy targets. Aerospace forces have the power to penetrate to the heart of an enemy's strength without first defeating defending forces in detail. Therefore, to take full advantage of the capabilities of aerospace power, it is imperative that air commanders seize the offensive at the very outset of hostilities.[363]

Use of the word "attacks" in Protocol I served no humanitarian purpose, but did serve the purposes of certain nations (as well as those of the ICRC) in their desire to

---

361. A careful reading of the language contained in articles 48–58 of Protocol I with an understanding of the Swiss and Swedish strategy for defending their respective territories makes it clear that these two nations, working hand in glove with the ICRC, tailored (and maneuvered through the Group of 77) a law of war treaty that establishes the ideal conditions for those nations to defend themselves. As a neutral, neither nation intends to fight outside its borders. Each nation also has elaborate plans for use of its natural and man-made obstacles (the latter including urban areas) in its defense. Hence the desire of the Swiss and the Swedes (expressed by the ICRC) to use the word attacks, because it would have a potential for limiting offensive actions by forces operating against either nation.

Both Switzerland and Sweden have minimal (less than 1% of total strength) regular forces, but large reserves; Switzerland can fully mobilize 650,000 in less than forty-eight hours, for example. A number of reservists hold key military positions, but would be protected from attack until actually mobilized because of the language contained in article 51, paragraph 3 of Protocol I that "Civilians shall enjoy the protection . . . [from attack], unless and for such time as they take a direct part in the hostilities." Each nation uses underground shelters for critical war materials; some shelters are camouflaged as civilian objects, while others are entered through basements below civilian buildings. Use of civilian objects would assist in the protection of military headquarters and supply centers from attack because of the language contained in article 51, paragraph 3 that "In case of doubt whether an object which is normally dedicated to civilian purposes, such as a place of worship, a house or other dwelling or a school, is being used to make an effective contribution to military action, it shall be presumed not to be so used."

Using a "humanitarian" guise, the language of Protocol I contained in articles 48–58 was developed to place maximum constraints on a force engaged in offensive military operations regardless of the actions of a defender or, perhaps more appropriately, in spite of a defender's actions. It was tailor-made by Swiss and Swedish authorities working with the ICRC (but, as will be seen, without full coordination with the Swiss military) as yet another phase in the defense planning of those two nations. Switzerland and Sweden persuaded Group of 77 members of the desirability of these rules on the basis that the rules would place effective limits on offensive operations against their respective territories by an invader. The threat of superpower intervention was played upon heavily in Group of 77 discussions. Specific examples of the benefit availed a defender by these new rules will be provided in the analysis of individual articles. For a description of Swiss defense planning, *see* J. McPHEE, LA PLACE DE LA CONCORDE SUISSE (1984).

362. F. KALSHOVEN, THE LAW OF WAR 62 (Leiden, 1972).

363. HEADQUARTERS, U.S. AIR FORCE, AIR FORCE MANUAL 1-1. BASIC AEROSPACE DOCTRINE OF THE UNITED STATES AIR FORCE 2–6 (1984).

limit enemy military operations within their territory, even if the nation under attack was the initial aggressor. This attempt to use a law of war treaty for the political gain of some nations not only was inconsistent with the humanitarian purposes of the law of war, but served to undermine its continued credibility.

Civilians and Combatants. To determine who is a civilian requires the reading and analysis of no fewer than four different articles of Protocol I, as well as one of the lengthier articles of the 1949 Geneva Convention Relative to the Treatment of Prisoners of War.[364] It is not the intention of this article to attempt a detailed analysis of those various provisions.

Determination of an individual's status as a combatant or civilian using the appropriate provisions could be achieved where time is not of the essence. Using the legal standards of the time (which remain in effect for the United States), American forces during the Vietnam War developed an elaborate screening program that was praised by the ICRC for its protection of the rights of prisoners of war and detained civilians.[365] Where time is of the essence, however, as in the heat of battle, this cannot be accomplished. Writing a quarter of a century ago, in a time of slower aircraft and substantially less lethal air defenses, one author summarized the problem as it relates to the employment of aircraft in combat: "The speed of even the slowest fixed-wing aircraft is so great that the pilot has little chance of positively identifying an enemy who is not wearing a distinctive uniform, unless the latter obligingly waves a rifle or shoots at him."[366]

---

364. Article 50, paragraph 1 states that "A civilian is any person who does not belong to one of the categories of persons referred to in Article 4 A(1), (2), (3) and (6) of the Third Convention [GPW] and in Article 43 of this Protocol."

The cited provisions of article 4 of the GPW state that:

> A. Prisoners of war . . . are persons belonging to one of the following categories, who have fallen into the power of the enemy:
>
> (1) Members of the armed forces of a Party to the conflict as well as members of militias or volunteer corps forming part of such armed forces.
>
> (2) Members of other militias and members of other volunteer corps, including those of organized resistance movements, belonging to a Party to the conflict and operating in or outside their own territory, even if this territory is occupied, provided that such militias or volunteer corps, including such organized resistance movements, fulfill the following conditions:
>
> (a) that of being commanded by a person responsible for his subordinates;
> (b) that of having a fixed distinctive sign recognizable at a distance;
> (c) that of carrying arms openly;
> (d) that of conducting their operations in accordance with the laws and customs of war.
>
> (3) Members of regular armed forces who profess allegiance to a government or an authority not recognized by the Detaining Power. . . .
>
> (6) Inhabitants of a non-occupied territory, who on the approach of the enemy spontaneously take up arms to resist the invading forces, without having had time to form themselves into regular armed units, provided they carry arms openly and respect the laws and customs of war.

The reader must now return to articles 1 (4), 43 and 44 (3) of Protocol I to determine how those articles amend the provisions of article 4A, cited above, of the GPW. The United States and several of its allies regard the provision contained in article 44(3) to apply only to the conflicts contemplated by article 1(4). In the context of the Diplomatic Conference, that provision (in its final form) was intended to apply only to the Palestine Liberation Organization and the African National Congress. However, an ICRC official discussing article 1(4) has stated "That major innovation [article 1(4)] must not be necessarily confined in a limited historical context. . . . The realities of armed conflicts, very soon after the closing of the Diplomatic Conference, showed patently that certain parties intended to extend it to a dimension other than the colonial one." Veuthey, *Guerrilla Warfare and Humanitarian Law*, *supra* note 268, at 121. Indeed, there are indications that the ICRC intends to "determine" that article 1(4) (and hence Protocol I) applies to the Irish Republican Army as soon as Great Britain becomes a party to Protocol I, thereby using a "humanitarian" document for its political purposes.

365. *See* Green, *supra* note 314.

366. B. FALL, THE TWO VIETNAMS, *supra* note 224, at 349, citing J. CROSS, CONFLICT IN THE SHADOWS 98 (1963).

Several problems arise at this point. The first has been identified: the Byzantine definition contained in Protocol I clearly is not suited for battlefield employment, and it would be impossible for any nation to issue implementing instructions to its combat forces that would reduce the formula to a workable battlefield standard. But article 50, paragraph 1, of Protocol I continues: "In case of doubt whether a person is a civilian, that person shall be considered to be a civilian."

In the context of ground warfare, and particularly guerrilla warfare, this provision would be extremely difficult to accept; it is impossible in the realm of aerial operations.[367] The problem is exacerbated upon reading portions of article 51:

> 1. The civilian population and individual civilians shall enjoy general protection against dangers arising from military operations. To give effect to this protection, the following rules, which are additional to other applicable rules of international law, shall be observed in all circumstances.
>
> 2. The civilian population as such, as well as individual civilians, shall not be the object of attack.
>
> 3. Civilians shall enjoy the protection afforded by this Section, unless and for such time as they take a direct part in hostilities.

Violation of these provisions is made a grave breach by article 85, paragraph 3(a) of Protocol I.[368]

In analyzing these provisions, it is important to understand the interpretation by the International Committee of the Red Cross of the phrase "direct part in hostilities." The ICRC has stated that,

---

367. The late Secretary of Commerce Malcolm Baldridge once related an experience from his service as an infantry platoon leader during the 1945 U.S. capture of Okinawa that bears directly on the impracticality of this assumption. As dusk fell, an Okinawan woman approached Baldridge's position. A nervous member of Baldridge's unit fired, killing the woman. Search of the body revealed that the "woman" was in fact a male Japanese soldier trying to approach their position so that he could throw hand grenades into it. Had the provision cited from article 50(1) been in effect during the Okinawa campaign, Baldridge and/or several of his soldiers very likely would have been killed. Such a rule not only is impractical, but would do substantial damage to the credibility of the law of war.

This rule was of considerable concern to a number of Western delegations, not the least of which were the United Kingdom and the United States. *See supra* text accompanying notes 6 and 7 concerning the court's decision in the case of Generaloberst Rendulic's "scorched earth" policy in Norway.

Concerned about the difficult position in which soldiers and commanders would be placed by the language contained in the last sentence of article 50(1) (as well as language contained in articles 51 to 58), an effort was made to codify the *Rendulic* rule as part of Protocol I. Neither the ICRC, Third World nations, nor the Socialist bloc were willing to permit such flexibility in Protocol I. At the time of its signature of Protocols I and II, Great Britain made the statement, "military commanders and others responsible for the planning, deciding upon or executing attacks necessarily have to reach decisions on the basis of their assessment of the information from all sources which is available to them at the relevant time." SCHINDLER & TOMAN, *supra* note 27, at 717. It is the author's understanding that Great Britain plans a similar statement should it decide upon ratification of Protocol I. Belgium, Italy and Netherlands made similar statements at the time of their ratification. *Id.* at 707, 712, and 714. These statements of understanding are not binding upon other parties to Protocol I, particularly should they desire to charge a prisoner of war from the armed forces of one of these countries with a violation of the "heat-of-battle judgment call" provisions of articles 50 to 58.

368. Coupling the grave breach provision contained in article 85(3)(a) with the presumption contained in article 50(1) reverses normal battlefield procedures. While any civilian death is regrettable, it was the author's experience in Vietnam that close calls in the heat of battle leading to the death of an innocent civilian was not something for which a soldier, sailor, airman or Marine would be prosecuted. There are two practical reasons for this: (1) civilians in a combat area are expected to exercise the common sense to stay out of the way of combat operations while avoiding any action that might be construed as a threatening act by combatants; and (2) no commander can afford to have men looking over their shoulders for his or his lawyer's "blessing" before responding to a life-threatening act. The civilian population of South Vietnam understood this and such deaths were infrequent. The provision in question reverses this by placing the burden upon the combatant, regardless of the actions of the civilian(s).

> 'direct' participation means acts of war which by their nature or purpose are likely to cause *actual harm* to the personnel or equipment of the enemy armed forces. It is *only during such participation* that a civilian loses his immunity and becomes a legitimate target. Once he ceases to participate, the civilian *regains his right to the protection* under this Section, i.e., against the effects of hostilities, and he may no longer be attacked.[369]

An initial problem with establishment of combatant or civilian status lies in the new revolving door provided for by Protocol I for certain "civilians." Previously a civilian was protected from intentional attack unless he carried out specific combatant-like activities, whether it involved the gathering of intelligence, logistical support for combatant forces, or acts of violence. At that time that person might become either a belligerent (and entitled to prisoner of war protection if captured) or an unprivileged belligerent (and subject to punishment, if captured), but most certainly he became a legitimate target and could not revert to his civilian status. This is a long-standing provision in customary international law from which Protocol I has departed, to the benefit of a very few but to the danger of the ninety-five percent of the civilian population in any nation who do not take part in the hostilities. Writing in 1911, James Maloney Spaight stated:

> [I]f [civilian] populations have a war right against armies, armies have as strict a war right against them. The citizen must be a citizen and not a soldier. [T]here is no room in modern war for the resistance of unorganised inhabitants. They have had their chance of joining the armed forces of their country, and if they have not done so, then they must play loyally their part as citizens. [W]ar law has a short shrift for the non-combatant who violates its principles by taking up arms. 'It is manifest,' says Kipling's Unir Singh, Sikh of the Khalsa, trooper of the Gurgaon Rissala, type and spokesman of a breed of fighters, 'that he who fights should be hung if he fights with a gun in one hand and a *purwanna* [a permit given to non-combatants for their protection] in the other.' There is a whole chapter of war law—its history and its principle—epitomized in his words.[370]

The purpose of the rule so eloquently set forth by Spaight is clear: In order to provide protection for the greatest number of civilians, individual civilians are obligated to abstain from participating in the hostilities. Nations are obligated to take steps to keep their private citizens from taking part in hostilities in a manner that could endanger innocent civilians. And in order to protect the civilian population, an individual could not revert to being a civilian once he had crossed the line and committed combatant-like acts. The new rules of Protocol I clearly place the civilian population at greater risk by permitting individual civilians to cross and recross the line dividing the civilian population from combatants. These new provisions not only endeavor to revoke customary international law, but go so far as to make it a

369. ICRC COMMENTARY, *supra* note 247, at 619 (emphasis added). Protocol I thus provides a small group of "civilians" with the ability to have their cake and eat it too: by providing them prisoner of war protection (under article 44, paragraphs 2 and 3) if captured while engaged in hostilities, but immunity from attack (under article 50, paragraph 3) during those times in which they are planning attacks but not actually carrying them out. All of this is at the expense of protection for the majority of the civilian population that is not participating in the hostilities in any way.

370. J. SPAIGHT, *supra* note 161, at 38. *See also* G. LEWY, *supra* note 300, at 232, where he states:

> Another source of confusion in judging the matter of civilian casualties was the designation . . . of all villagers as innocent civilians. We know that on occasion in Vietnam women and children placed mines and booby traps, and that villagers of all ages and sexes, willingly or under duress, served as porters, built fortifications, or engaged in other acts helping the communist forces. It is well established that once civilians act as support personnel they cease to be noncombatants and are subject to attack.

war crime to direct an attack at an individual who, seconds before, was carrying out hostile acts but who is beyond capture.

The rule clearly was intended for a guerrilla-war context in which the individual "civilian" is a "farmer by day, guerrilla by night;"[371] and the new rules of Protocol I were written with the view that if a "civilian" has engaged in combatant-like activities, he may be captured and detained. But capture cannot always be accomplished. During Rolling Thunder (the 1965–1968 U.S. bombing campaign against the Democratic Republic of Vietnam) the North Vietnamese Government issued small arms to thousands of private citizens with the instruction that when the air raid sirens went off, they were to seize their weapons, run outside, and fire directly into the air. This small-arms barrage proved deadly and effective against American attack aircraft flying at tree-top level in an effort to avoid equally deadly antiaircraft guns and surface-to-air missiles. ICRC observers witnessing these actions warned the Government of North Vietnam that they were placing their entire civilian population at risk by using segments of their civilian population in this combatant mode; the warning was disregarded by North Vietnamese officials.

Recalling that the attack on a civilian is made a grave breach by article 85 (3) (a) of Protocol I, at what point does a civilian-combatant revert to being a civilian? In the historic scenario cited, suppose a North Vietnamese civilian has fired at a passing American aircraft, seriously damaging it and causing it to crash. Suddenly the civilian rifleman realizes to his horror that the downed pilot's wingman was following in thirty-second trail, witnessed the attack and crash, and is turning to fire on the "civilian" rifleman to protect his leader while he descends by parachute. The "civilian" throws down his weapon; by the ICRC interpretation of article 51 (2), the "civilian" rifleman has ceased to take a "direct part in the hostilities," and is protected from attack. This provision not only places the pilot of the trailing aircraft at risk of trial as a war criminal if he now fires at the "civilian," but makes a

371. The protection for guerrillas who were "farmers by day, and guerrillas by night" was an appeal for Third World support for the ICRC's efforts, as many Third World governments had come into power through the use of guerrilla warfare. Those governments could suppress future guerrilla movements within their countries through a refusal to accept limitations on actions taken against internal challenges, while legitimizing their actions in coming into power. Protection for guerrillas also had appeal for certain European nations, such as Norway and the Netherlands, which had experience with partisan warfare during World War II. Other nations with partisan experience, however, did not share this view.

The ICRC also emphasized protection for guerrillas with the argument that guerrilla warfare was a new phenomenon, though it is not. The term "guerrilla" originated during Napoleon's campaign in Spain, while the word "commando" was a Boer word for guerrilla during the Anglo-Boer War at the turn of the last century. With respect to the former war, *see* D. Gates, The Spanish Ulcer: A History of the Peninsula War (1986). With regard to the Anglo-Boer War, *see* D. Reitz, Commando: A Boer of the Boer War (1929); B. Farwell, The Great Anglo-Boer War (1976); and T. Pakenham, The Boer War (1979). The ICRC image of the "farmer by day, guerrilla by night" is itself historically flawed in that cases in which a population has organized and armed itself to overthrow an existing regime are few and far between. For example, most of the so-called guerrillas in the Republic of Vietnam during the United States war in that nation were trained in North Vietnam, then returned to South Vietnam individually or in organized military units. North Vietnam returned regular forces to South Vietnam in civilian attire as a matter of convenience and for the sake of plausible deniability of their role in that conflict, which since has been acknowledged.

The problem of guerrillas and their status *vis-à-vis* protection of the civilian population had been thoroughly considered in the Lieber Code, at the two Hague Peace Conferences of 1899 and 1907, and at the Geneva Conference of 1949. Protection for guerrillas was deemed not to outweigh the principles (a) that only nations have authority to wage war, and (b) that protection for innocent civilians outweighed protection for individuals who preferred to be a "farmer by day, and guerrilla by night." The provisions of Protocol I thus reverse more than a century of precedent, with no gain for the innocent civilian.

mockery of the line that has been so carefully drawn over the years distinguishing civilians from combatants in order to protect the former.

There is no humanitarian gain in the change made by article 51, paragraph 2 of Protocol I. Indeed, in providing protection for that very small percentage of the civilian population that uses the revolving door created by Protocol I, the entire civilian population of a nation could be placed at greater risk because of the distrust this provision will create between the civilian population of that nation and the opposing forces.

Protocol I draws a sharp line between civilians and combatants. Combatants are considered to include both uniformed combatants as well as civilians while they are taking a direct part in the hostilities (as defined by the ICRC, above). But there is a greater problem relating to the classification of combatants and civilians that Protocol I had the opportunity to address, and it is one that was evident three decades before the start of the Diplomatic Conference. Writing in 1944, Sir Hersch Lauterpacht stated that:

> Modern war has raised, and, in some respects, left unsolved the problem of reconciling the fundamental distinction between combatants and noncombatants with the advent of new weapons and with the increase of the numbers of both combatants and noncombatants engaged in work of vital importance for the war effort.[372]

The problem was identified long before World War II. Seven years before the outbreak of that conflict, J.F.C. Fuller wrote:

> In 1918 France had in the field an army of close upon 3,000,000 men, but this army would have been proved utterly useless unless the 1,700,000 workers employed in her war industries remained at work. During 1917 the French armies required 225,000 field gun shells a day. They wanted these shells to kill Germans with. The men and women who made them (and there were 900,000 employed in this work) were as deeply concerned in the problem of killing as the French gunners themselves. . . . In the kingly wars it was barbarous to slaughter the civilian population, because the people stood outside the quarrel. . . . The long and short of the matter is that a 'nation in arsenals' is obviously a legitimate war target; and the oftener a bull's-eye is scored on it the sooner will the war be over.[373]

---

372. *The Law of Nations and the Punishment of War Crimes* 21 BRITISH YEARBOOK OF INTERNATIONAL LAW 58–95, at 74–75 (1944). Similarly, international lawyer Clyde Eagleton argued in 1941 that:

> The distinction between combatant and noncombatant has always been of great importance in the law of war; but the basis of that distinction has now been destroyed, on the one hand . . . by the fact that every man, woman, or child, whether in uniform or not, can be and is used in the belligerent effort.

Eagleton, *Of the Illusion That War Does Not Change*, 35 AM. J. INT'L L. 659–62, at 660 (Oct. 1941). Regrettably, the only solution Professor Eagleton offered was to declare war to be illegal, "and to be done with it." *Id.* at 662.

373. WAR AND WESTERN CIVILIZATION, 236–237 (London, 1932). The same question was raised within the British Air Ministry in the months immediately preceding World War II. With regard to the previously-discussed British directives to attack military objectives only, one participant recalled Air Staff considerations:

> [T]he distinction between "military" and "civilian" was growing pretty thin—why, for instance, should Hans Schmidt, a fitter in the German Tank Corps servicing tanks at a base depot outside Dusseldorf, be fair game while his civilian brother Fritz, who was assembling the same tanks *in* Dusseldorf, be protected by law?

J. SLESSOR, *supra* note 176, at 213–14. As the earlier discussion (at *supra* text accompanying notes 175–78) indicates, a decision was made along policy rather than legal lines to apply a conservative, restricted interpretation. Air Marshall Slessor continues:

The ICRC recognized this problem, and sought the advice of its committee of experts at its first session in 1971. One of its original documents identified four categories of civilians, as represented in figure 1, at page 122. Obviously civilians who were not participating in military operations, the military effort, or the war effort—as a rule of thumb more than ninety-five percent of any nation's population—were protected from intentional attack at all times. The three designated categories were defined as:

> War effort: all national activities which by their nature or purpose would contribute to the military defeat of the adversary.
>
> Military effort: all the activities . . . [which] are objectively useful in defense or attack in the military sense, without being the direct cause of damage inflicted, on the military level.
>
> Military operations: movements of attack or defense by the armed forces.[374]

At the Second Conference of Government Experts, however, which involved Third World representation,[375] the ICRC backed away from this issue, and reacted with hostility to a statement by the senior U.S. representative that recognized the problem of civilians on the battlefield and called for "basic guidelines . . . general enough to be understood by an ordinary soldier or a commander of regular or irregular forces and fair enough so that they would be thought of as deriving from basic requirements of law and humanity."[376] In sum, the ICRC turned a blind eye to the issue, arriving at the standard described on the preceding pages.

Change of Role of Civilians. Prior to and during the eighteenth century, a civilian was entitled to protection from intentional attack so long as he refrained from participation in an armed conflict. The distinction between combatant and noncombatant was easily established. But just as war became more complex, so too did the line between combatant and civilian become less distinct. A host of military analysts and historians[377] have acknowledged that war and society underwent several revolutionary changes in the century and a half before 1939.

The democratization of war. Nation-states look to their entire population, rather than the uniformed military alone, to provide for the common defense.[378] Two

---

> Eventually we did issue in August 1939 instructions which defined military objectives very narrowly—Hans Schmidt was a military objective and Fritz was not. . . . I regarded it all as a matter not of legality but of expediency. We did what we could at the time . . . to limit air warfare as much as we could. We should no doubt have taken a different line if we had believed that, in the near future and with our existing equipment, we could have achieved anything like decisive results from an unlimited offense. But at the time of Munich we did not believe that.

Id. at 214.

Ultimately, of course, as RAF Bomber Command capabilities increased and the Luftwaffe capability to respond in kind diminished, the policy was amended. The German war industries worker was made a direct target—in part because of the intensity of German defenses, in part because of the inaccuracy of night bombing, but equally because (as previously explained) the line between "civilian" and "combatant" had not been drawn with any clarity in pre-World War II years. Protocol I was the first opportunity for the international community to address this question; it failed.

374. NEW RULES FOR VICTIMS OF ARMED CONFLICTS, *supra* note 257, at 294, n.6. The official ICRC COMMENTARY *supra* note 247 makes no mention of consideration of this categorization.

375. *See supra* discussion in text commencing at note 248.

376. Previously quoted and cited in its entirety *supra* text accompanying note 254.

377. *See* T. ROPP, WAR IN THE MODERN WORLD (1959); J. FULLER, THE CONDUCT OF WAR 1789–1961 (London, 1961); B. BRODIE & F. BRODIE, FROM CROSSBOW TO H-BOMB (1972); M. HOWARD, *supra* note 16; W. MILLIS, ARMS AND MEN (1981); M. PEARTON, *supra* note 22; L. ADDINGTON, THE PATTERNS OF WAR SINCE THE EIGHTEENTH CENTURY (1984); M. VAN CREVELD, TECHNOLOGY AND WAR (1989); and R. O'CONNELL, *supra* note 102.

378. The democratization of war preceded the French Revolution; the militia units formed in the British colonies in North America were based upon the same principle. *See* J. GALVIN, *supra* note 23; and W. MILLIS, *supra* note 23, at 13–71.

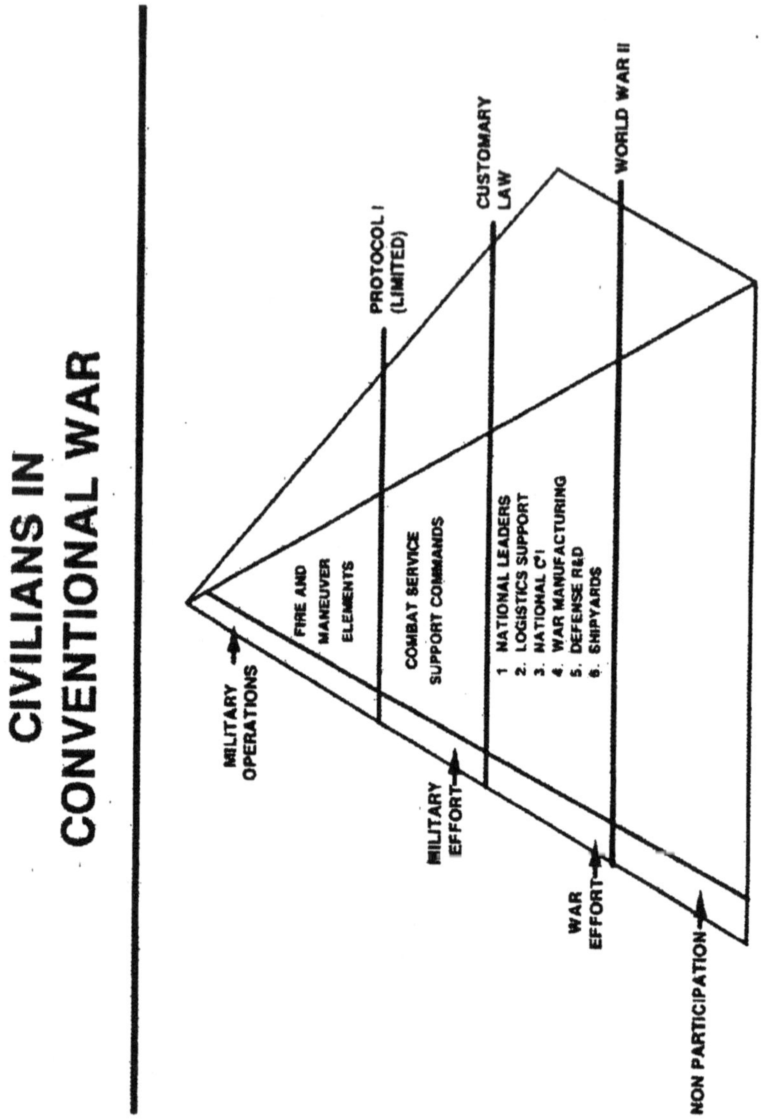
CIVILIANS IN CONVENTIONAL WAR
PROTOCOL I (LIMITED)
CUSTOMARY LAW
WORLD WAR II
FIRE AND MANEUVER ELEMENTS
COMBAT SERVICE SUPPORT COMMANDS
1. NATIONAL LEADERS
2. LOGISTICS SUPPORT
3. NATIONAL C³I
4. WAR MANUFACTURING
5. DEFENSE R&D
6. SHIPYARDS
MILITARY OPERATIONS
MILITARY EFFORT
WAR EFFORT
NON PARTICIPATION

Figure 1.

A foundation for the democratization of war lay in the commencement of conscription as a national duty. Having run short of volunteers during the winter of 1792–1793, the French National Convention first voted the conscription of 300,000 men, then on 23 August 1793 decreed that every Frenchman was permanently required for service in the armies. By the following year 1,169,000 men had registered for national military service, leading to what Theodore Ropp has described as the "first national army in modern European history." T. ROPP, *supra* note 377, at 90. *See also* Strachen, *supra* note 23; M. PEARTON, *supra* note 377, at 30; and R. O'CONNELL, *supra* note 102, at 174, 185. Speaking of the Prussian experience following the defeat of Napoleon, O'Connell notes that "Gone were the Potsdam giants and the Hohenzollern's automata professionals, replaced by a *volks* arms and a centralized military brain." *Id.* at 202. As historian John Keegan has observed:

> [T]he nineteenth-century states' enhanced powers of head-counting and tax-gathering . . . ensured that recruits could be found, fed, paid, housed, equipped, and transported to war. The institution of census-taking—in France in 1801, Belgium in 1829, Germany in 1853, Austria-Hungary in 1857, Italy in 1861—accorded recruiting authorities the data they needed to identify and docket potential recruits; with it died the traditional expedients of haphazard impressment, cajolery, bribery and press-ganging which had raised the *ancien regime* armies from those not fleet enough of thought or foot to escape the recruiting sergeant. Tax lists, electoral registers, and school rolls documented the conscript's whereabouts—the grant of the vote and the introduction of free education for all entailed a limitation as well as enlargement of the individual's liberties. By 1900 every German reservist, for example, was obliged to possess a discharge paper specifying the centre at which he was to report when mobilisation was decreed. . . . Universal conscription in the European armies took all classes willy-nilly—in Prussia from 1814, in Austria from 1867, in France from 1889—and bound them to serve for two or three years.

J. KEEGAN, THE SECOND WORLD WAR 14–15, 20 (1989).

By the time of World War I, only the United States and Great Britain did not rely on conscription for mobilization. L. ADDINGTON, *supra* note 377, at 101. A principle reason for the 1907 Hague Convention III Relative to the Opening of Hostilities lay in the European experience with mobilization during the preceding three decades, in which the very act of mobilization had come to be regarded as tantamount to an act of war. SCHINDLER & TOMAN, *supra* note 27, at 57–59.

A prime example of the mobilization of an entire population for war is Emperor Haile Sellassie's mobilization decree of October 3, 1935, on the invasion of Ethiopia by Italy:

> The hour is grave. Each of you must rise up, take up his arms and speed to the appeal of the country for defense.
>
> Warmen, gather round your chiefs, obey them with a single heart and thrust back the invader.
>
> You shall have lands in Eritrea and Somaliland.
>
> All who ravage the country or steal food from the peasants will be flogged and shot.
>
> Those who cannot for weakness or infirmity take an active part in the holy struggle must aid us with their prayers.
>
> The feeling of the whole world is in revulsion at the aggression aimed against us. God will be with us.
>
> Out into the field. For the Emperor. For the Fatherland.

J. DUGAN & L. LAFORE, *supra* note 188, at 171–72; and T. COFFEY, LION BY THE TAIL: THE STORY OF THE ITALIAN-ETHIOPIAN WAR 161 (London, 1974).

Although the original *levee en masse* in Revolutionary France was the universal conscription, a critical distinction exists between the traditional *levee en masse* and the mobilization of the manpower of a nation in that the former requires that the inhabitants of a nation "spontaneously take up arms without having time to organize themselves." (Article 2, Annex to Hague Convention IV, in SCHINDLER & TOMAN, *supra* note 27, at 75), while in the latter case the civilian population responds to formal mobilization plans.

The effect of the democratization of war is expressed in paragraph 26 of U.S. ARMY FIELD MANUAL 27–10, *The Law of Land Warfare* (1956), which states that "Under the law of the United States, one of the consequences of the existence of war between two States is that every national of the one State becomes an enemy of the other. However, it is a generally recognized rule of international law that civilians must not be made the object of attack directed exclusively at them." The term "civilian" is not defined.

The language is not new. Rules 20–22 of the Lieber Code of 1863 state:

> 20. Public war is a state of armed hostility between sovereign nations or governments.

examples can be provided from the commencement of World War II. Before the start of World War II, Great Britain had firmly reestablished its Observer Corps, a volunteer civilian organization which during that war was to grow to 32,000, including 4300 women. It had two roles: (a) to detect low-flying enemy aircraft, operating below radar coverage; and (b) report position and direction of enemy aircraft flying over Great Britain, that is, to take over the reporting of air raid tracks once the enemy aircraft had crossed the coast and no longer could be tracked by the British Chain Home radar. These individuals were an integral part of the British air defense system, not part of the civil defense structure; in a word, they were civilian volunteers augmenting the British military.[379]

As the Battle of Britain approached, and fearing a German invasion,

> [T]he Army, with the help of 150,000 civilians full-time and thousands more part-time (including schoolboys. . . .), festooned the beaches and cliffs with barbed wire, dug tank traps, set up concrete 'dragon's teeth' and pill boxes, and arranged for fire to engulf suitable stretches of shore and roadway as the enemy appeared. And behind the Army stood the unpaid Local Defence Volunteers, their number swollen by the end of June [1940] to one-and-a-half million.
>
> From the coastal districts most vulnerable (and in June proclaimed 'protected areas' forbidden to ordinary visitors), a new wave of evacuation now began. . . . Among those required to stay were members of local authorities, lifeboat crews, employees of banks, water, sewage, gas and electricity undertakings and workers on the land. These last had the heavy responsibility of obstructing their larger fields with barbed wire, disused farm machinery, tractors, commandeered old cars—anything that would make landing of airborne troops hazardous.[380]

> 21. The citizen or native of a hostile country is thus an enemy, as one of the constituents of the hostile state or nation, and as such is subjected to the hardships of war.
>
> 22. Nevertheless, as civilization has advanced during the last century, so has likewise steadily advanced, especially in war on land, the distinction between the private individual belonging to a hostile country and the hostile country itself, with its men in arms. The principle has been more and more acknowledged that the unarmed citizen is to be spared in person, property, and honor as much as the exigencies of war will admit.

SCHINDLER & TOMAN, *supra* note 27, at 6–7.

Similarly, Spaight states that "it may be taken as an axiom of modern war that the peaceful inhabitants of an invaded country, whether they are theoretically 'enemies' of the invading army or not, are in practice never treated as such." J. SPAIGHT, *supra* note 161, at 35.

The Lieber Code language and the statement of Spaight remain valid; a civilian who has not been called to serve in the military remains a noncombatant protected from attack, unless he occupies a civilian position that would render him susceptible to attack. Democratization of war alone does not establish a basis for attack of civilians. It was merely the first of several steps that led to a blurring of the relatively clear Eighteenth Century distinction between the small, professional army and the civilian population, and illustrates that the distinction has been in a state of erosion for more than two centuries.

379. *See* B. COLLIER, *supra* note 1, Appendices III and VI; F. Mason, *supra* note 81, at 96–97; and R. HOUGH & D. RICHARDS, THE BATTLE OF BRITAIN 26, 57 (London, 1989). The Observer Corps was established in 1925 for the express purpose of reporting the movements of hostile aircraft across those parts of Great Britain most vulnerable to aerial attack. B. COLLIER, *supra* at 17. As Hough and Richards note "In 1929, the War Office had relinquished control over the observer system, and the observers had become a civilian corps under Air Ministry aegis." R. HOUGH & D. RICHARDS, *supra* at 26. Civilians, though they may have been, were an integral part of the defense system of Great Britain. One official history described the Observer Corps as "the primary source of intelligence for the whole defence system about the movement over Britain of hostile aircraft." T. O'BRIEN, *supra* note 111, at 4. For its work during the Battle of Britain, the name was changed to the Royal Observer Corps in 1941.

380. R. HOUGH & D. RICHARDS, *supra* 379, at 106. Similarly, Russian civilian women are shown digging an anti-tank ditch outside Moscow in the path of the German Army Group Center's advance in October 1941 in J. KEEGAN, *supra* note 378, at 201.

As a part of its emergency measures, on 12 May 1940 British authorities agreed that "any man between the ages of sixteen and sixty-five who had fired a rifle or a shotgun and was 'capable of free movement' should be eligible" to volunteer for service in the unpaid Local Defence Volunteers. B.

The Industrial Revolution. Without the Industrial Revolution nations could not wage modern war, but it also further diminished the previous distinction between civilian objects and military objectives or targets, and between civilians and combatants.[381]

Earlier discussion of the effect of building railroads for national defense purposes is illustrative of the impact of the Industrial Revolution on national defense planning.[382] Railroads were laid along lines to support mobilization against the greatest threat to a nation's security, while Russia purposely built its railroads in a different size to thwart any foreign use of Russian railroads to support an invasion of Russia. Yet railroads were but one of several products of the Industrial Revolution that would aid national defense; others were the telegraph, improvements in weapons (such as the percussion cap, breech-loading mechanisms, magazine-fed small arms, machine-guns, and smokeless powder) and their mass production, and the use of the steam engine in naval vessels.[383]

COLLIER, *supra* note 1, at 106. The Local Defense Volunteers were renamed the Home Guard and were equipped with weapons and uniforms commencing in July 1940. R. HOUGH & D. RICHARDS, *supra* at 106.

381. As Professor Keegan has observed:

> The enormous wealth, energy and population increase released by Europe's industrial revolution in the nineteenth century transformed the world. It had created productive and exploitative industries—foundries, engineering works, textile factories, shipyards, mines—larger by far than any at which the intellectual fathers of the industrial revolution . . . had guessed. It had linked the productive regions of the world with a network of communications—roads, railways, shipping lanes, telegraph and telephone cables—denser than even the most prescient enthusiast of science and technology could have foreseen. . . . It had built the infrastructure . . . of a vibrant, creative and optimistic world civilisation. Above all, and in dramatic and menacing counterpoint to the century's works of hope and promise, it had created *armies*, the largest and potentially most destructive instruments of war the world had ever seen.
>
> The technology that built the railways also furnished the weapons with which the soldiers of the new mass armies would inflict mass casualties on each other.. . . . [T]he reason for the appearance of the fast-firing, longer-range and more accurate weapons that equipped the conscript armies between 1850 and 1900 was the particular conjunction of human ingenuity and industrial capability which made their production feasible.

J. KEEGAN, *supra* note 378, at 12, 16. *See also* P. MATHIAS, THE FIRST INDUSTRIAL NATION, (2d ed. London, 1983); M. VAN CREVELD, *supra* note 22, at 153–216; and R. O'CONNELL, *supra* note 102, at 189–211.

382. At text *supra* accompanying note 22, and the sources cited therein. Professor Keegan notes that "It is evidence of the military importance the German state and army attached to the free use of the railways that the personnel of the *Reichsban* were not allowed to unionise." J. KEEGAN, *supra* note 378, at 16, n.1.

383. *See* M. VAN CREVELD, *supra* note 377, at 170–71; R. O'CONNELL, *supra* note 102, at 190–202; and H. SPROUT & M. SPROUT, THE RISE OF AMERICAN NAVAL POWER, 1776–1918 (1959). Professor Keegan lists four significant factors:

> The first was the spread of steam power, which supplied the energy to manufacture weapons by industrial process. The second was the development of the appropriate process itself, originally called 'American' by reason of its origin in the 1820s in the factories of the Connecticut Valley, which were chronically short of skilled labor. This industrial process resulted in interchangeable parts, machined by a refinement of the ancient pantographic principle, and achieved an enormous surge of output. . . . Advances in metal engineering would have been pointless without improvements in the quality of the metal to be worked; that was assured by the development of processes for smelting steel in quantity—notably by the British engineer Bessemer after 1857. . . . The fourth ingredient of the firepower revolution was supplied shortly afterwards by European chemists, notably the Swede Alfred Nobel, who developed propellants and bursting-charges which drove projectiles to a greater distance and detonated them with more explosive effect than ever before. The effective range of infantry weapons, for example, . . . increased from a hundred to a thousand yards between 1850 and 1900.

J. KEEGAN, *supra* note 378, at 16–17.

The Industrial Revolution brought about a problem of commingling of civilian objects and military objectives; railroads that were used for the national defense also were used on a daily basis, in peace and war, for trade and civilian transportation.[384] This created problems regarding the distinction between civilian objects and military objectives, and the increased risk to the civilian population of collateral injury that will be discussed in conjunction with articles 51, 52 and 57. The immediate problem—maintaining the separation of the civilian from the combatant—also was affected by the Industrial Revolution, as the design and manufacturing of the modern weapons of war required skilled labor. While the democratization of war had brought about national conscription, the need for skilled labor necessitated a system whereby individuals or trades whose work was critical to national security could be exempted from conscription. By World War II, virtually every nation party to that conflict had enacted domestic legislation or policies that provided an exemption from military service for industrial workers, engineers, scientists, or persons possessing similar critical skills where an individual's skills were considered to be of greater value to that nation's war effort than would be his service in the military.[385] Technological

384. *See* A. MIERZEHEWSKI, *supra* note 20, for an excellent discussion of this point.

385. The problem actually began to surface during World War I. Sir Solly Zuckerman notes that:

> [T]he mobilization of scientists as scientists was anything but complete in the First World War. Some of the most brilliant young men of the day were among those who died in battle. When the young atomic physicist Moseley was killed in action in the Dardenelles, Rutherford wrote:
>
> > It is a national tragedy that our military organization at the start of the war was so inelastic as to be unable, with a few exceptions, to utilize the offers of services of our scientific men as combatants in the firing line. Our regret for the untimely end of Moseley is all the more poignant that we cannot but recognize that his services would have been far more useful to his country in one of the numerous fields of scientific inquiry rendered necessary by the war than by exposure to the chances of a Turkish bullet.

S. ZUCKERMAN, SCIENTISTS AND WAR 13 (1966) citing Rutherford, *Obituary of Henry Gwyn Jeffreys Moseley*, 96 NATURE 33 (1915).

Both the Axis Powers and the Allies established programs at the national level for screening and employment of scientists in civilian defense-related positions rather than as soldiers during World War II, as each also endeavored to do with regard to its skilled labor. *See* R. OVERY, *supra* note 85, at 147; and G. HARTCUP, THE CHALLENGE OF WAR: BRITISH SCIENTIFIC AND ENGINEERING CONTRIBUTIONS TO WORLD WAR TWO 222–24 (1970), where the author notes that:

> The first step taken was the compilation during 1937 and 1938 of a schedule of reserved occupations to provide against the mistake made in the First World War of enlisting into the forces skilled men essential for war production. Secondly, a central register of volunteers for war service with technical, professional and higher administrative qualifications was drawn up with the aid of the Royal Society, the universities and the principal technical and professional institutions. . . . By July 1939 the scientific section of the central register contained the names of 5,000 scientists.
>
> At the outbreak of war Sir Maurice Hankey was summoned by the Prime Minister to become Minister without Portfolio in the War Cabinet, one of his tasks being, as he later said, "to put science on the war map," and as a by-product of that exciting field of activity I had to assume important responsibilities in connection with higher technical and scientific manpower. . . . Eventually, over 50,000 men and women were selected for basic scientific instruction and passed to the services, research and industry. . . . Another 40,000 were engaged by the Admiralty.

See also S. ROSKILL, III HANKEY: MAN OF SECRETS 1931–1963 427–28 (London, 1974). Similarly,

> The 1942 [British] crisis in radio production was ascribed primarily to shortage of skilled labour. . . . What added to the difficulty of labour supply was the great need of the [military] Services for young radio technicians and the continuous losses which the industry consequently suffered from labour call-ups. Various attempts to deal with the problem were made. . . . The skilled labour employed by the industry—some 8,000 men and women—were "frozen," i.e., retained in the industry irrespective of age and irrespective of alternative claims on their services.

developments also led to the need for highly-trained civilian technical representatives to accompany military, naval and air forces into theaters of operations in order to maintain and repair the increasingly more sophisticated engines of war.[386]

The Scientific Revolution. Large numbers of civilian scientists have made contributions to their respective nation's war efforts that far exceeded their value in any potential uniformed military service. The scientific revolution commenced prior to World War I, but reached its first peak during that conflict.[387] Scientific research grew steadily between the wars, increased substantially during World War II, and has never looked back. It was a force multiplier; one witness illustrated this point by noting that:

M. POSTON, BRITISH WAR PRODUCTION 368–69 (London, 1952).

Similarly, on 21 June 1940 the National Resources Mobilization Act became law in Canada,

> authorizing the Governor in Council to make orders or regulations requiring persons to place themselves, their services and their property at the disposal of His Majesty in the right of Canada, as may be deemed necessary or expedient for *securing the public safety, the defence of Canada, the maintenance of public order, or the efficient prosecution of the war, or for maintaining supplies or services essential to the life of the community.* [emphasis added]

C. STACEY, ARMS, MEN AND GOVERNMENTS: THE WAR POLICIES OF CANADA 1939–1945 33 (Ottawa, 1970), On 19 August 1940, Canadian national registration began of "all persons resident in Canada over sixteen years of age, both male and female, providing sufficient basic information not only to serve as a guide for a system of compulsory service but also to use in the direction and control of labor." C. STACEY, *supra* at 123–24. Eventually, conscription was extended to age 30. *Id.* at 404. However, Stacey notes in detail the problems the Canadian government experienced in addressing the army manpower problem while protecting skilled labor. *Id.* at 403. The Committee on Labour Coordination set up a Labour Supply Investigation Committee to gain all the facts on the problem. This committee submitted a report in October 1941 that concluded in part:

> The Committee was deeply impressed by the widespread failure to regard the manpower problem as a single problem. This country is engaged in a life and death struggle in which its entire resources, *including its man-power*, must be allocated to their most effective uses. . . . [T]here is competition between the armed forces and industry, between war and non-war industries, and among the industrial concerns generally. The Committee doubts that this situation results in the most effective use of the nation's man-power.

Id. at 403 [emphasis added]. While both the Axis Powers and the Allies exempted from conscription scientists and engineers whose skills were of greater importance to their respective war efforts than service in the military, it was the British and American exploitation and employment of science and scientists that provided the critical difference between victory and defeat.

386. For example, in June 1942 No. 604 Squadron (County of Middlesex) of the Royal Air Force was equipped with Mark VII air-intercept (AI) radars for its Beaufighter night interceptor aircraft. Servicing of this new radar would have been virtually impossible but for the assignment of a civilian Scientific Officer from the RAF's Telecommunications Research Establishment to the squadron. C. RAWNSLEY & R. WRIGHT, NIGHT FIGHTER 153–55 (London, 1957). Because 604 Squadron was engaged in nightly interception of Luftwaffe intruder aircraft over Great Britain, this civilian's work was critical to the squadron's operational success. This unit was not unique in this respect; civilian technical and scientific representatives served with air, naval and ground units throughout World War II, and continue to do so today.

The importance of this civilian Scientific Officer to 604 Squadron's mission can be illustrated with a very simple scenario. If a German sniper had been able to land in England and after carrying out attacks elsewhere find his way to the 604 Squadron perimeter with only one bullet remaining, but with complete intelligence on the men and women in or supporting the unit, there is little doubt that the sniper would conclude that the most valuable target would be the civilian Scientific Officer maintaining the Mark VII AI radars. Without his expertise, the aircraft could continue to fly, but could not perform their critical nighttime interception duties. There seems to be little question that, through common sense or under the law of war standards of either World War II or today, this civilian Scientific Officer would be a legitimate target. Article 51, paragraph 3, of Protocol I would protect him from attack, and would make it a war crime [under article 85, paragraph 3 (a)] for the German sniper to attack him.

387. *See* G. HARTCUP, THE WAR OF INVENTION: SCIENTIFIC DEVELOPMENTS, 1914–1918 (London, 1988); and Pattison, *Scientists, Government and Invention: The Experience of the Inventions Boards, 1915–1918*, in HOME FIRES & FOREIGN FIELDS: BRITISH SOCIAL AND MILITARY EXPERIENCE IN THE FIRST WORLD WAR (Peter H. Liddle, ed. London, 1985).

> A bomber equipped with radar could do as much as half-a-dozen without. A Coastal Command aircraft could search the seas for enemy submarines indefinitely and fail to find them unless it had an [air-to-surface-vessel radar] set. All the courage of [RAF] Fighter Command and the skill of the Few would have been wasted, had it not been for the timely installation of the primitive radar system which saved us in 1940.[388]

Seven significant developments or devices grew to maturity during World War II. They are atomic energy, rocket propulsion, jet propulsion, radar, automation, the proximity fuse, and operational research. All involved major research and development by civilian scientists. The development of radar offers one of the better examples of the close working relationship between civilian scientists and the military, not only in the research and development stages, but in the operational employment of radar. The radar story has been told many times, and need not be retold here; it was a success for those nations which chose to exploit civilian scientific capabilities, and contributed to the loss of the war by those nations that failed to do the same, or do so to the maximum extent.[389]

388. Lord Bowden, in the Foreword to G. HARTCUP, *supra* note 385, at 11. The reference to "the Few" is to the praise of RAF Fighter Command by Prime Minister Winston S. Churchill on August 20, 1940, when he said "Never in the field of human conflict was so much owed by many to so few." R. HOUGH & D. RICHARDS, *supra* note 379, at 199; and M. GILBERT, FINEST HOUR: WINSTON S. CHURCHILL, 1939–1941 736, 742 (London, 1983). The discovery and employment of radar by the British was a critical factor in the success of "the Few"; equally critical was the Luftwaffe failure to recognize its importance.

Lord Bowden further emphasizes the value of the use of civilian scientists by noting that "Without some of the devices which this book describes, our soldiers and sailors would have been as hopeless as the troops of the Mahdi at Omdurman who were mown down by the Maxium guns of the British Army." G. HARTCUP, *supra* at 11. The 1898 battle referred to by Lord Bowden has been described by one historian as follows:

> In the opening phase of the battle thousands of Dervishes charged across an open desert in plain sight, waving their spears and screaming. Kitchener's howitzers, machine guns and rifles cut them down. Not a single Dervish reached the Anglo-Egyptian lines. Few even came as close as 500 yards. . . . An estimated 10,000 Dervishes fell, and few of the wounded survived. . . . In the subsequent phases an attack by twice as many Dervishes was defeated by an Anglo-Egyptian force 1/10th the strength of the attackers.

B. FARWELL, QUEEN VICTORIA'S LITTLE WARS 336–37 (London, 1973); and B. FARWELL, PRISONERS OF THE MAHDI (1967).

389. The proximity fuze is discussed in R. BALDWIN, THE DEADLY FUZE (1980), and G. HARTCUP, *supra* note 385, at 170–81. The proximity fuze would emit radio waves, detect their reflection from the target, and detonate the shell at the optimum point. Originally developed by British civilian scientists, the project was transferred to the United States in the course of the Tizard Committee visit in August 1941. Further development was undertaken by Dr. Merle A. Tuve, chief physicist, Department of Terrestial Magnetism, Carnegie Institution of Washington, and subsequently by the Applied Physics Laboratory of the Johns Hopkins Laboratory—in essence, by civilian scientists working in a civilian laboratory.

The first successful use of the VT-fuzed ammunition was by the U.S.S. *Helena* (CL–50) on January 4, 1943, when a Japanese Val bomber was shot down near Guadalcanal. R. BALDWIN, *supra* 234–35. The British put VT-fuzed ammunition to great effect in defending against German V–1 rockets. *Id.* at 253–71. VT-fuzed howitzer ammunition was used against ground targets commencing December 16, 1944, by U.S. Army forces during the German offensive through the Ardennes, where it was credited by General George S. Patton with winning the Battle of the Bulge. *Id.* at 279.

For the story of radar development and employment, *see* A. ROWE, ONE STORY OF RADAR (London, 1948); B. COLLIER, *supra* note 1, at 36–40; D. SAWARD, THE BOMBER'S EYE (London, 1959); R. WATSON-WATT, THE PULSE OF RADAR (1959); M. Poston, *supra* note 176, at 373–430; J. NISSEN, with A. COCKRILL, WINNING THE RADAR WAR, 1939–1945 (1987); D. FISHER, A RACE ON THE EDGE OF TIME (1988); and D. PRITCHARD, THE RADAR WAR: GERMANY'S PIONEERING ACHIEVEMENT, 1904–1945 (London, 1989).

As the Pritchard book indicates, radar was a German discovery, but one which British authorities were more successful in exploiting during World War II. The lesson is that invention alone is not enough; organization of the scientific community for national defense and exploitation of its work was a fundamental difference during World War II. As one historian has noted, "technical ingenuity was not

As a second example, operational research has been defined as "the subjection of military operations to quantitative analysis for the purpose of making a more efficient use of military force."[390] It began in World War I, but had to be re-invented

---

enough. If there was one lesson to be learned . . ., it is that at a time when all seemed lost, we survived because of extraordinary effective collaboration between the fighting men and the civilians who helped them." G. HARTCUP, *supra* at 12. British civilian scientists anticipated military requirements, developed equipment to meet those requirements, trained the military in its operation, maintained that equipment, and in some cases actually controlled its use in combat. *See, id.* at 118–21. In contrast, R. J. Overy makes the following comments regarding German collaboration with scientists:

> The people in power were unsympathetic to academic scientists, and were too technically unschooled to be able to arrive at sound scientific judgments themselves. Goering and Udet prided themselves on their amateur qualifications. Radar, for example, Goering considered "simply a box with wires." Udet could not understand, for he had never heard of it, how Heinkel's experimental jet aircraft could fly "with no engine." Even Milch for all his organizational skills was basically unsure of himself with more sophisticated equipment and was uncertain how to extract the most from the research establishment. This scientific philistinism earned the leadership the animosity and ridicule of the researchers. War-winning projects got lost in the system and the political effort of resurrecting them was often more than the researchers were willing or able to supply.

R. OVERY, *supra* note 85, at 199. Goering (at Speer's suggestion) had founded the *Reichsforschungsrat* (Reich Research Council) in 1937 as an instrument for centralizing and directing all German research. But scientific work suffered for the reasons stated above, and others. In the latter part of 1942, Hitler took steps to involve German scientists to a greater degree in the military effort. As R. J. Overy notes, however, "The reforms of the research system in 1942 came too late and were difficult to enforce." *Id.* at 198–99. *See also* S. GOUDSMIT, ALSOS—THE FAILURE OF GERMAN SCIENCE (1947). The Japanese were equally slow in exploiting radar. Guy Hartcup notes that:

> The Japanese services were rigidly conservative in outlook. There was no collaboration between the Army and Navy. . . . It was said by a Japanese scientist that a general would rather lose the war than shake hands with an admiral. The Army and the Navy each had its own radar equipment. An army radar was unable to distinguish between an enemy and friendly naval aircraft and the same confusion applied to naval radar when trying to locate enemy aircraft. Not until the autumn of 1944 did the Japanese Army and Navy set up a joint technical control committee with civilian representations, but then it was too late.

G. HARTCUP, *supra* at 30. The official history of the U.S. Army Air Force in World War II similarly states that "the Japanese possessed neither the economic potential nor the extensive skill necessary for developing and maintaining a first-class air force." W. CRAVEN & J. CATE, I PLANS AND EARLY OPERATIONS: JANUARY 1939 TO AUGUST 1942 81 (1948).

The degree to which the Axis powers failed to harness science was not total, but relative, and the radar war between Germany and Great Britain was a constant one of measures, countermeasures, counter-countermeasures, etc., all fought principally in civilian laboratories by civilian scientists working closely with the military. For a brief discussion, *see The Radar Chess Game* in M. POSTON, *supra* at 418–28; *see also* A. PRICE, INSTRUMENTS OF DARKNESS, *supra* note 110, and M. STREETLY, *supra* note 110. Poston discusses the role of the universities and industry in the development of radar. M. POSTON, *supra* at 428–30.

The references emphasize the critical value of certain civilians to a nation's ability to wage war and conduct military operations, and the necessity for a nation to organize its civilian technical and scientific expertise for national defense purposes. Most nations have undertaken this effort to some degree; distinctions can be made between those civilians performing functions critical to national defense and the private citizen who has no connection to the nation's defense. The Diplomatic Conference responsible for the negotiation of Protocols I and II failed to address this issue, however, thereby jeopardizing the safety of the private civilian through a demand of protection from direct attack for all persons not in uniform.

390. G. HARTCUP, *supra* note 385, at 25. The official Royal Air Force operational research history defines *operational research* as "numerical thinking about operations, with the aim of formulating conclusions which, applied to operations, may give a profitable return for a given expenditure of effort." BRITISH AIR MINISTRY AIR PUBLICATION 3368, THE ORIGINS AND DEVELOPMENT OF OPERATIONAL RESEARCH IN THE ROYAL AIR FORCE xvii (London, 1963), [hereinafter RAF OPERATIONAL RESEARCH]. The original terms of reference for operational research, prepared by Sir Robert Watson-Watt, were to

> examine quantitatively whether the user organization is getting from the operation of its equipment the best attainable contribution to its overall objective, what are the predominant factors governing

two decades later. Its story also has been told elsewhere.[391] One example will illustrate its importance to battlefield performance.

> [T]he paradigmatic case [for operational research] arose out of antisubmarine warfare. One of the techniques adopted by Britain to counter attacks . . . by German submarines . . . was . . . by depth charges dropped from aircraft. . . . Experience showed that the rate of destruction was sporadic and unsatisfactory.
>
> Scientists began flying with RAF Coastal Command to observe minutely the sequence of events and operations in hunting submarines over a large number of sorties. The observations were then correlated and analysed. . . . [Their] conclusions were tried out in practice . . . and the rate of successes improved. The German authorities concluded that their enemy must have a new secret weapon. In fact, the results rested on the strictly scientific analysis of what was to hand.[392]

This author went on to observe, "When scientists went on operations they ceased to

---

> the results attained, what changes in equipment or method can be reasonably expected to improve these results at a minimal cost in effort and in time, and the degree to which variations in the tactical objectives are likely to contribute to a more economical and timely attainment of the over-all strategic objective.

S. ZUCKERMAN, SCIENTISTS AND WAR: THE IMPACT OF SCIENCE ON MILITARY AND CIVIL AFFAIRS 18–19 (1967). Zuckerman lays out clearly the purpose for operational research, and who did it: "The primary purpose of operational research . . . at [RAF] Fighter Command . . . was to make the best use of the weapons and equipment the United Kingdom had. . . . [T]he work was done not by the military, who wanted the equipment, but by the scientists." *Id.* at 18.

391. RAF OPERATIONAL RESEARCH, *supra* note 390; L. THIESMEYER & J. BURCHARD, COMBAT SCIENTISTS (1947); R. CLARK, TIZARD (Cambridge, 1965); V. BUSH, MODERN ARMS AND FREE MEN: A DISCUSSION OF THE ROLE OF SCIENCE IN PRESERVING DEMOCRACY (Cambridge, 1968); and M. GORN, HARNESSING THE GENIE: SCIENCE AND TECHNOLOGY FORECASTING FOR THE AIR FORCE 1944–1986 (1988).

In October 1941, Professor P.M.S. Blackett set forth the functions of an operational research section. As the RAF OPERATIONAL RESEARCH explains:

> The first was to advise the Commander-in-Chief and his staff on matters which were not handled by the research and experimental establishments. . . . It was essential that such scientific analysis should be done in or near operations rooms, as the data on grounds of security could not be made available to the technical establishments. The chief objection to staff officers carrying out this sort of work was, firstly, that their time was largely taken up with making executive decisions and, secondly, that scientists were often better equipped to deal with certain aspects of operations, particularly those in which probability considerations and the theory of error entered. The work of an operational research section was performed at command or group headquarters, or at stations or squadrons, as circumstances dictated. The second function of an operational research section was to act as a link between the command and the technical and research establishments.

RAF OPERATIONAL RESEARCH, *supra* at xix.

Operational research within the RAF considered the following issues, among others: development of an air defense enemy aircraft reporting system; night interception of enemy aircraft; offensive operations by night; defensive operations by day; armament problems; problems relevant to the improvement of night bombing; assessment of bombing efficiency; problems affecting the cost of night bombing; problems involved in the attack of U-boats; the camouflage of antisubmarine aircraft; attack of the German "V" weapons; attacks on rail communication and shipping; and assessment of close air support operations. RAF OPERATIONAL RESEARCH, *supra* at 10–177.

The staff of an operational research section were civilian scientists. However, if they deployed overseas (permanently or temporarily), they were issued uniforms and granted honorary commissions. RAF OPERATIONAL RESEARCH, *supra* at xx.

It is the author's view that civilian scientists involved in operational research as described above clearly played a combatant role within the British military, and under customary international law could have been made the object of lawful attack. Article 51, paragraph 3 of Protocol I would protect these individuals from attack until they deployed overseas and donned their uniforms, bearing their honorary commissions. Hence though their duties would be the same, they would be subject to attack while in uniform overseas, but immune from attack while on a domestic base in civilian attire.

392. M. PEARTON, *supra* note 22, at 231–32.

be just purveyors of laboratory results to the military but participated in the making of tactical decisions."[393]

Scientists during World War II became a critical part of the war and military effort. More than ninety-five percent of the German scientists working on the V–1 and V–2 rocket programs were civilians, as were the individuals working on Project Manhattan—the development of atomic weapons—in the United States. As Maurice Pearton has observed, "The tart observation that wars were won by weapons and not by slide-rules ignored the fact that war had got to the point at which it could be lost by not using them."[394]

The predicament for the law of war was yet another increase in persons in civilian attire who were full-time participants in the military effort of their nation, even in some cases in military operations, and not with a weapon, as the ICRC *Official Commentary* suggests is necessary in order to become a combatant. These scientists were engaged in the military effort of their nation, in a capacity in which they were of greater value to their nation's war effort than they would be as uniformed soldiers. Under customary international law, there seems to be no reason why these individuals would not be regarded as combatants and subject to attack at all times; under Protocol I, they are protected from attack.[395]

Further Blurring of Civilian and Combatant. War has undergone immense change over the past two centuries. The traditional distinction between the civilian and the combatant has been blurred by myriad political and technological factors, as well as by war itself. This blurring is not unique to developed societies. During the United States' Rolling Thunder air campaign against North Vietnam, for example, the Government of North Vietnam mobilized and organized a force of more than 500,000 civilians to handle the movement of military supplies along lines of communication (LOC) and to maintain the LOC, repairing battle damage caused by the air strikes. It also mobilized another 250,000 to organize and construct its sophisticated, integrated air defense system, and to deploy and man portions of the antiaircraft defenses, while employing others to disperse North Vietnamese military supplies to minimize their risk of loss.[396]

---

393. *Id.* at 232. Similarly, the views and recommendations of civilian scientists were critical to the decision on the timing for Royal Air Force employment of the radar countermeasure "Window," metal foil strips dropped from aircraft to confuse enemy radar. Window was first employed (with substantial success) during the RAF Bomber Command mission against Hamburg on the evening of 24/25 July 1943. *See* Jones, "*Lord Cherwell's Judgment in World War II*," CVII J. ROYAL UNITED SERVICE INST. 321–27, at 325–26 (Nov. 1963); G. HARTCUP, *supra* note 385, at 148–56; A. HARRIS, *supra* note 4, at 132–34, 172–76; J. TERRAINE, *supra* note 171, at 546, n.2; A. PRICE, INSTRUMENTS OF DARKNESS, *supra* note 110, at 112–21, 124–27, 140–42, 148–49, and 151–65; G. ADERS, THE HISTORY OF THE GERMAN NIGHT FIGHTER FORCE 1917–1945 94–95 (London, 1978); and M. MIDDLEBROOK, THE BATTLE OF HAMBURG 68–70 (London, 1980).

394. *Id.* at 233.

395. For further discussion of the role of science during World War II, *see* L. THEISMEYER & J. BURCHARD, COMBAT SCIENTISTS (1949), and R. CLARK, THE RISE OF THE BOFFINS (London, 1962). The term "boffin" has been defined as "a civilian technician who advises air crew and others on specialized subjects." *Id.* at vii. Clark continues, stating that "Whatever its exact origin, "boffin" had become, long before the end of the war, a word for one particular type of scientist—the man who could understand the viewpoint of the Services, who worked with them, and who frequently shared their dangers." *Id.* at viii. His words suggest the directness of the role this nonuniformed individual played and the degree to which the RAF, perhaps more than any other service, relied upon his advice. Today that experience has been duplicated in virtually every armed service around the world.

While a boffin should be regarded as a combatant, there is of course the question as to whether he would be pursued and attacked away from the place of employment. That is a question of practicality rather than legality, *i.e.*, in most cases it would not be militarily efficient to pursue a single individual away from his place of work, whether that person is a civilian-combatant or a uniformed member of the military.

396. Parks, *supra* note 109, at 7; *see also* Cagle, *Task Force 77 in Action Off Vietnam*, 98 U.S. NAVAL INST. PROC. 76, n.10, 87 (May 1972). North Vietnamese development and employment of its

This blurring should not necessarily suggest deviousness on the part of a nation. Nations have realized that it costs more to maintain an individual in uniform than it does a civilian, and military personnel are used to perform certain national defense functions only where it is necessary for there to be a uniformed person.[397] Hence the blurring has occurred through two concurrent approaches: (a) the intentional substitution of civilians in many traditionally military positions, and (b) an increased dependence by the military upon skilled engineers, scientists, and other civilians to assist in research, development, deployment, maintenance, upgrade, and employment of weapons systems. Whether intentionally or through ignorance, the participants in the Diplomatic Conference failed to reconcile the change that has occurred over the past two centuries with the need to distinguish the true civilian from the combatant.

Clearly the work of some "civilians" has become so critical to military success that those individuals are civilians in name and garb only. They remain a very small minority, and their continued protection from attack places the innocent civilian population at risk, while greatly damaging the credibility of the law of war. Who are they, and what impact does Protocol I have upon this issue?

Figure 2 at page 133 divides the civilian population into the four categories considered by the 1971 ICRC Conference of Government Experts and illustrates those points at which certain segments of the civilian population have been the subject of attack. In the author's view, civilians working directly towards the military effort—and this would include those scientists employed on the various research projects such as radar, rockets, etc., during World War II—by the nature of their duties are far more combatants than civilians. Their civilian status should not be permitted to jeopardize the safety from attack of the innocent civilian, whose numbers make up the vast majority of any nation's population.[398]

---

highly integrated, sophisticated air defense system was accomplished through the assistance of military and civilian scientific personnel from the Soviet Union, illustrating that the technological and scientific revolutions benefit all.

Civilians were used in combatant positions throughout World War II. The United States, Great Britain, and the Soviet Union relied heavily on partisan forces to fight in the enemy's rear. *See* M. FOOT, SOE IN FRANCE (London, 1966); J. GARLINSKI, POLAND, SOE AND THE ALLIES (London, 1969); D. SCHOENBRUN, SOLDIERS OF THE NIGHT: THE STORY OF THE FRENCH RESISTANCE (1980); C. CRUICKSHANK, SOE IN SCANDINAVIA (1986); and A. BANK, FROM OSS TO GREEN BERETS (1986).

In the Pacific war, civilians, including members of the clergy, were employed as coastwatchers to provide early warning to Allied forces of approaching Japanese ships and aircraft. In addition to their intelligence-gathering, their activities included rescuing downed United States and Allied aviators, and sailors from sinking ships, including the crew of John F. Kennedy's PT–109. The work of coastwatchers in the Solomon Islands was especially critical to United States operations on Guadalcanal. Said Vice Admiral William F. Halsey of their effort: "The coastwatchers saved Guadalcanal, and Guadalcanal saved the Pacific." W. LORD, LONELY VIGIL: COASTWATCHERS OF THE SOLOMONS 292 (1977). *See also* E. FELDT, THE COASTWATCHERS (1946). The language of Protocol I fails to take into consideration the work of such individuals.

397. For example, the aircraft of the Swiss Air Force are maintained by civilians. *The Swiss Confederation*, 5 J. DEF. & DIPLOMACY 30–39, at 33 (June 1987). By the terms of Protocol I, they would be protected from attack so long as they did not pick up a weapon or, if they did, only during the time they used it.

398. For example, Sir Solly Zuckerman cites a U.S. study that concludes that five percent of the total employment in the United States is related to national defense. S. ZUCKERMAN, *supra* note 390. This number would be substantially smaller in most nations, and the number involved in the military effort (as it is defined in this article) would be substantially less, and perhaps as little as one percent of total employment. The failure of Protocol I to recognize the combatant role of that one percent in essence provides those individuals protection from intentional attack, but in so doing places the innocent ninety-nine percent of the population at risk through a loss of credibility for the law of war. The 1941 warning of Professor Philip C. Jessup bears repeating at this point: "The law often lags behind facts, but if it does not correspond to facts it is eventually nullified or modified." Jessup, *supra* note 191.

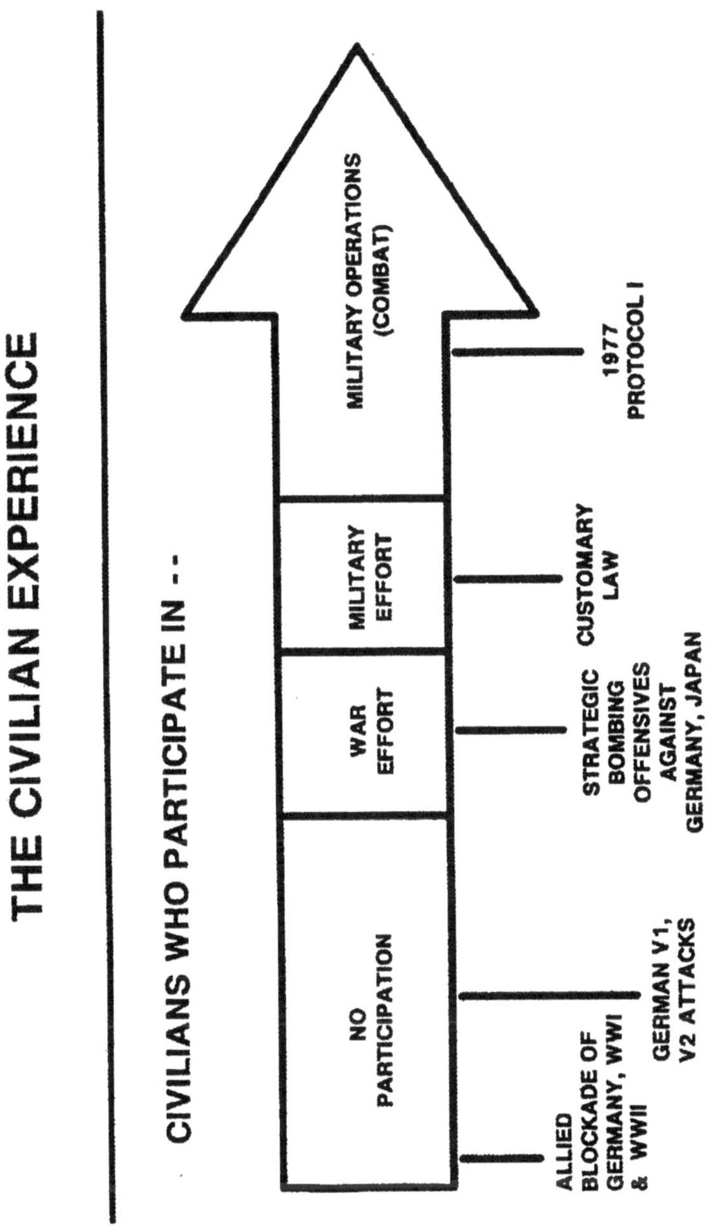

Figure 2.

Air War — 133

But Protocol I takes an extreme view, placing "civilians" at risk only when they are actually carrying out combat operations in which harm can come directly to enemy military forces. This is an unrealistic view that ignores the practice of nations, and prompted a continuous debate between two members of the United States delegation to the Diplomatic Conference that will serve to illustrate the impracticality of Protocol I:

> A civilian is driving a military truck filled with ammunition towards his front lines. If the civilian dies incidental to the attack of the truck, there is no crime; but if the driver is attacked directly, the soldier who has fired at him has committed a violation of article 51 (3) and 85 (3) (a) and must be brought to trial for a war crime.[399]

Some legal scholars have endeavored to avoid the issue by suggesting that, for example, if a military base were under attack, civilians employed thereon would be at risk from incidental injury and such injury would not be prohibited. Yet the same scholars, when asked if those civilians may be attacked directly, have stated that such intentional attack would be prohibited.

That answer may reflect the view of Protocol I, but it is not an accurate portrayal of history. For these reasons, the provisions of Protocol I related to the distinction between civilians and combatants were not militarily acceptable to the United States. In essence, a very small portion of a nation's civilian population working directly with a nation's military effort was provided protection from intentional attack to the potential detriment of the overwhelming majority of the civilian population of any nation. That was not regarded as advancing the law of war.[400]

What, then, should be the answer? In the past, that has been a policy decision made by national leaders. If one were to offer some guidelines, however, several points could be made:

> (a) if a civilian's position is important enough for him to be employed on a military base during hostilities, that civilian is at risk from attack during the time in which he is present within that objective, whether his death is incidental to the attack of the military objective or results from a direct attack;
>
> (b) the substitution of a civilian in a position that normally would be occupied by a member of the military will not make that position immune from attack;[401]

399. The debate was brought to the attention of the author by each of the participants. It was never resolved.

400. The Office of The Judge Advocate General of the Army formally addressed this issue, and concluded that war-essential civilian employees working on a U.S. military base during time of war would be subject to direct attack. Letter from DAJA-IA to Counselor for Defense Research and Engineering (Economics), Embassy of the Federal Republic of Germany (January 22, 1988).

401. For example, the Agreement Between the Government of the United States of America and the Government of the Union of Soviet Socialist Republics on the Prevention of Dangerous Military Activities signed by representatives of those nations in Moscow on June 12, 1989, entered into force on January 1, 1990, defines "personnel" as "any individual, military or civilian, who is serving in or is employed by the armed forces of the Parties." 28 INT'L LEGAL MATERIALS 877.

Article II of the agreement then proceeds to obligate each Party to "take necessary measures directed toward preventing dangerous military activities, which are the following activities of personnel and equipment of its armed forces when operating in proximity to personnel and equipment of the armed forces of the other Party during peacetime."

While the definition of personnel was intended for the limited purpose of this agreement, its purpose is clear: if a military person is prohibited from carrying out a particular activity, a Party cannot carry out that activity by employing a civilian in the place of a military person. By analogy to the point at hand, if a position normally would be occupied by a member of the military, the law of war cannot provide immunity from attack for that position if a civilian has been substituted for the military person. Protocol I fails to take this issue into account.

(c) A civilian may be subject to lawful attack if his immunity from military service is based upon the conclusion that continued service in his civilian position is of greater value to a nation's war effort than that person's service in the military.[402]

Protocol I has not resolved this important issue, but rather compounded it. Its danger is greater than a mere exclusion, however, inasmuch as its violation constitutes a grave breach for which the person responsible must be brought to trial. The matter will be resolved only with the passage of time, during which the continued practice of nations will reject the language of the treaty or by actual amendment of the treaty.

Military Objectives and Civilian Objects. Military objectives may be attacked wherever they are located and are defined in article 52 of Protocol I as being "limited to those objects which by their nature, location, purpose or use make an effective contribution to military action and whose total or partial destruction, capture or neutralization, in the circumstances ruling at the time, offers a definite military advantage."[403]

402. This is a position of employment, not an exemption from military service as the sole surviving son, *etc*. Obviously some people who are exempted from military service because of their contribution to the war effort would also be immune from attack, such as individuals involved in medical research, in the same way that medical personnel in the military are protected from attack.

The type of individual who is not a civilian in the traditional law of war sense of the word is the person who is working directly on weapons-related research or assisting in operational intelligence. An example of the latter would be Professor R. V. Jones, who served as the scientific advisor for air intelligence in Great Britain during World War II. Professor Jones informed the author that he declined to put on a uniform at the start of hostilities because he believed that his civilian stature provided him greater authority and "clout," as proved to be the case. Author's conversation with Dr. Jones, Conference on the Conduct of the Air War in World War II, Freiburg im Bresigau, Federal Republic of Germany, 2 September 1988.

As previously noted, one project in which Professor Jones had the principle hand was defeat of the Luftwaffe's *Knickebein* radio-guidance system, which he discusses at length in his MOST SECRET WAR, *supra* note 110, at 92–105, 127–45; *see also* B. COLLIER, *supra* note 1, at 157–58, and A. PRICE, INSTRUMENTS OF DARKNESS, *supra* note 110, at 19–51. The importance of Professor Jones' work is noted by Telford Taylor, who observed that "The early detection and partial frustration of *Knickebein*—a feat then known only to a few—was an early and major British victory in the Battle of Britain." T. TAYLOR, *supra* note 145, at 120. Dr. Jones' work clearly took precedence over uniformed military service, and there is no doubt that he would have been regarded as a legitimate target under customary international law, as would have been the U.S. scientists working on the Manhattan Project (development of the atomic bomb) or the German rocket developments. With regard to the latter, British historian Martin Middlebrook correctly states that "every technical man at Peenemunde was a legitimate target." M. MIDDLEBROOK, THE PEENEMUNDE RAID 218 (London, 1982). Yet all would be protected from intentional attack by Protocol I.

Consideration of the legality of attack on certain quasi-civilians (or quasi-military personnel) who are providing direct support to a nation's military effort should not be taken to the extreme of suggesting that every one of them would be pursued to their homes and attacked. It would take a person of extraordinary importance to a nation's military effort to generate such a mission by an enemy. Such persons generally would be at risk only while at their place of duty. The fundamental problem is not that these people would be sought out individually, but that their intentional attack in the course of an attack of the objective in which they are working not only is prohibited by Protocol I, but constitutes a grave breach under article 85, paragraph 3(a).

A simple example will illustrate the hypocrisy of this rule *vis-à-vis* the traditional law of war rule of protection for innocent civilians. Sergeant Jones serves as an electronic warfare technician in his nation's air force maintaining the radar intercept equipment on frontline fighters. He decides to leave the military. However, his nation recognizes that he is irreplaceable and offers him a civilian position doing the same work at three times the pay. On his last day in the military, he is working on the "black boxes" in one of these fighter aircraft. He is unable to complete the job, so the next day, as a civilian, he picks up the same tools and continues the same maintenance project he was working on the previous day. If his airbase had been attacked on his last day in uniform, Sergeant Jones lawfully could have been attacked. If the base is attacked on his first day as a civilian, an attack on Mr. Jones would constitute a grave breach under article 85, paragraph 3(a), of Protocol I.

403. Article 52 (2), SCHINDLER & TOMAN, *supra* note 27, at 652.

In contrast, article 52 establishes that civilian objects "are all objects which are not military objectives."[404] In case of doubt whether an object normally dedicated to civilian purposes, such as "a place of worship, a house or other dwelling or a school," is being used to make an effective contribution to military action, "it shall be presumed not to be so used."[405] The last requirement was a manifestation of a failure, perhaps intentional on the part of the ICRC acting in its capacity as an agent of Switzerland, to consider the practice of some nations in intentionally camouflaging military objectives to appear as civilian objects.[406] As the language of paragraph 3 would tend to favor a defender over a military force engaged in offensive operations, and encourage a defender to camouflage military objectives as civilian objects, in actual practice the provision ultimately would place the civilian population and legitimate civilian objects at greater risk.

The presumption regarding civilian objects becomes increasingly less realistic as opposing forces move to contact, in that units and personnel from each force will use civilian structures for cover and concealment from enemy observation and fire. This problem was recognized in the course of the Diplomatic Conference, where some delegations proposed that the presumption contained in paragraph 3 of article 52 be relaxed "in the contact zone where the security of the armed forces requires a derogation from this presumption."[407] One commentary explains the debate that ensued:

> The exception was urged on the ground that infantry soldiers could not be expected to place their lives at great risk because of such a presumption. It was also stated that civilian houses which

404. Article 52 (1), *id.*

405. Article 52 (3), *id.*

406. The practice of intentionally camouflaging military objectives as civilian objects should be distinguished from the commingling (intentional or unintentional) of the two.

The language of paragraph 3, article 52 must be read while bearing in mind the practice of Switzerland of camouflaging its defense positions, command centers, and storage facilities as civilian objects, or concealing them within or beneath civilian buildings. This was brought home to the author during his participation in the United Nations Conference on Certain Conventional Weapons (1978–1980), when a Swiss officer pointed out a "house" north of Nyon. The "house" is in fact a wartime military command center, carefully camouflaged as a house, complete with flower boxes and lace curtains. A photograph of the "house" is contained in Parks, *supra* note 5, at 111. The presumption benefits the "house" in Nyon; it is *not* humanitarian.

This type of action is not unique to Switzerland; the author has seen similar steps taken in Sweden, for example. Camouflaging military objectives as civilian objects is an integral part of the defense program in each nation, however, which is a principal reason why the practice is neither prohibited nor discouraged in Protocol I. It could be argued that such a prohibition would not be feasible, as a nation has the inherent right to use its property in its national defense as it pleases. This is not entirely correct, however, as illustrated by the prohibition on the use of military and civilian hospitals for acts outside their humanitarian duties, as contained in article 13 of Protocol I.

During World War II, both the Axis nations and the Allies routinely camouflaged military positions, command centers, *etc.*, as civilian objects, one of the most extensive examples being the Lockheed-Vega aircraft factory and its runway in Burbank, California, that appeared from the air to be a residential suburb—including clothes drying on outdoor clotheslines. Photographs of the aircraft plant before and after its camouflaging are contained in Parks *supra* at 110–11, and London, *Remembering Then*, 4 LOCKHEED LIFE 4–5 (Aug. 1980). For further discussion, *see* S. REIT, MASQUERADE: THE AMAZING CAMOUFLAGE DECEPTIONS OF WORLD WAR II (1978); C. CRUIKSHANK, DECEPTION IN WORLD WAR II (1979); and D. FISHER, THE WAR MAGICIAN (1983). The Reit and Cruikshank books contain numerous illustrations of military positions and equipment camouflaged as civilian objects, including an anti-tank position made to resemble an automobile service station, a pillbox camouflaged as an ice cream stand, and an aircraft hangar disguised as a gamekeeper's cottage.

One commentary has suggested that "The presumption's relation to Art. 37, Prohibition on Perfidy, may affect a not uncommon practice of camouflaging anti-tank gun emplacements to create the appearance of civilian dwellings, particularly along picturesque defiles." The fact that the author viewed the Swiss "house" in Nyon after Switzerland had become a party to Protocol I indicated that this view is speculative at best; certainly it is neither commonly held nor obligatory. NEW RULES FOR VICTIMS OF ARMED CONFLICTS, *supra* note 257, at 327.

407. NEW RULES FOR VICTIMS OF ARMED CONFLICTS, *supra* note 257, at 326–27.

happen to be in the front lines are usually used as part of the battle position. The Rapporteur recommended approval of the exception: "The presumption . . . will be a significant new addition to the law, and is of the greatest importance that it be respected in practice. It would be unfortunate to draft the provision so that it requires something we know in advance is unlikely to be lived up to."[408]

The proposed exception was rejected by a vote of 36 to 12, with 23 abstentions.[409] Refusal to recognize the realities of combat, as illustrated by this episode, continuously plagued the Diplomatic Conference.

From a military standpoint, the presumption is tailor made for a defender. He may use civilian objects in his defense, exacting significant losses from an attacker who must identify *which* civilian objects are being employed for military purposes before they are attacked. From a historical standpoint, this is a shifting of the obligations previously imposed upon both the attacker and the defender to take all reasonable measures to separate military personnel and equipment from civilian objects and the civilian population as such (as exercised during World War II through the evacuation of civilians from areas near or adjacent to potential military targets). The presumption shifts the burden entirely onto a force engaged in offensive operations. It places an unprecedented obligation on an attacker for the protection of civilian property in the hands of the defender; this obligation will not survive the harsh realities of combat. From a "humanitarian" standpoint, the placing of a higher value on an inanimate civilian object than on human life hardly can be considered humanitarian.

A potential difficulty for the use of airpower in support of troops in close contact is obvious. A beleaguered ground force commander could request close air support to assist him in holding or extricating himself from his position. The aircraft arrive overhead, but find the enemy troops concealed in civilian structures adjacent to the friendly unit positions. Under the terms of paragraph 3 of article 52, the air mission would have to abort "in case of doubt" whether the civilian structures were being used to "make an effective contribution to military action." The problem could be particularly acute where the air assets belong to a nation that is a party to Protocol I, but the nation of the supported ground troops is not, or even if both nations were party to Protocol I, if there were disagreement between the nations regarding interpretation of the presumption.

There have been several attempts at defining "military objective," each of which has been discussed previously.[410] As with consideration of other portions of Protocol I, the United States military review was concerned less with how the Diplomatic Conference arrived at a particular formula than with what it would mean in practice. The ordinary meaning of the language in a particular provision took precedent over the recollections of former members of the American Delegation to the Diplomatic Conference as to the meaning they thought the provision was intended to have at the time it was negotiated. Soldiers on the battlefield do not enjoy the luxury of consultation with the negotiating history of a treaty, and it had become clear that many of the provisions contained in Protocol I had been drafted in language that would permit different nations to come away with different ideas as to what each provision was

408. *Id.* at 327.

409. *Id.* In discussing this debate, the ICRC COMMENTARY states that "Therefore even in contact areas there is a presumption that civilian buildings located there are not used by the armed forces, and consequently it is prohibited to attack them unless it is certain that they accommodate enemy combatants or military objects." ICRC COMMENTARY, *supra* note 247, at 638.

410. See the discussion of article 25 of the 1907 Regulations to Hague Convention IV, articles 1 and 2 of the 1907 Hague Convention IX, article 24 of the unadopted 1923 Hague Air Rules, and article 8, paragraph 1 of the 1954 Hague Cultural Property Convention.

intended to mean. Of particular concern was the meaning of "military action" and "definite military advantage."

It was clear that the ICRC sought to return to the restrictions in range on combat operations sought in the 1923 Hague Air Rules, that is, to force the fighting back to the immediate battlefield. To that end the language regarding "military advantage" mirrored that contained in article 24, paragraph 1, of the 1923 Hague Air Rules. But paragraph 2 of article 24 of the 1923 Hague Air Rules contained a list of specific targets, while paragraph 3 specifically prohibited the attack of targets "not situated in the immediate vicinity of the operations of land forces." Did the ICRC intend to attempt the same range limitation through the language of article 52?

The ICRC response was provided in its *Official Commentary*. Although broader than the list contained in the 1923 Hague Air Rules, its intent clearly was to limit legitimate targets to those objectives connected to a nation's military effort rather than its war effort. The *Official Commentary* offers the following list as a model:

1. armed forces, including auxiliary or complementary organizations, and persons who, though not belonging to the above-mentioned formations, nevertheless take part in the fighting;

2. positions, installations or constructions occupied by the forces . . . as well as combat objectives (that is to say, those objectives contested in battle between land or sea forces, including airborne forces);

3. installations, constructions and other works of a military nature, such as barracks, fortifications, War Ministries (e.g. Ministries of Army, Navy, Air Force, National Defence, Supply) and other organs for the direction and administration of military operations;

4. stores of arms or military supplies, such as munition dumps, stores of equipment or fuel, vehicles [*sic.*] parks;

5. airfields, rocket launching ramps and naval base installations;

6. those of the lines and means of communication (railway lines, roads, bridges, tunnels and canals) which are of fundamental military importance;

7. the installations of broadcasting and television stations; telephone and telegraph exchanges of fundamental military importance;

8. industries of fundamental importance for the conduct of the war:

a. industries for the manufacture of armaments such as weapons, munitions, rockets, armoured vehicles, military aircraft, fighting ships, including the manufacture of accessories and all other war materiel;

b. industries for the manufacture of supplies and material of a military character, such as transport and communications material, equipment for the armed forces;

c. factories or plant constituting other production and manufacturing centres of fundamental importance for the conduct of war, such as the metallurgical, engineering and chemical industries, whose nature or purpose is essentially military;

d. storage and transport installations whose basic function it is to serve the industries referred to in (a)–(c).

e. installations providing energy mainly for national defence, e.g. coal, other fuels, or atomic energy, and plants producing gas or electricity mainly for military consumption.

9. installations constituting experimental, research centres for experiments on and the development of weapons and war material.[411]

Although the ICRC list is an improvement over the list of lawful targets contained in article 24(2) of the 1923 Hague Air Rules, it and the definition of military objective in article 52 continue to resemble the philosophy of the 1923 targeting list more than the practice of nations. Each continues to require a nexus to military operations.[412] Each fails to appreciate the necessity for attack on target systems.[413]

---

411. ICRC COMMENTARY, *supra* note 247, at 632–33, n.3. In contrast, while AIR FORCE PAMPHLET (AFP) 200–17, *An Introduction to Air Force Targeting* (23 June 1989) incorporates an amended version of the definition of *military objective* contained in paragraph 2 of article 52 of Protocol I (stating that the *military objectives* "include" rather than being "limited to" the objects described therein), paragraph 3–3a continues to state that "The key factor is whether the object contributes to the enemy's *war fighting or war sustaining capability*." [Emphasis added.]

412. As previously noted, military objectives were defined by Air Marshall Trenchard in 1928 as "any objectives which will contribute effectively towards the destruction of the enemy's means of resistance and the lowering of his determination to fight." IV C. WEBSTER & N. FRANKLAND, *supra* note 81, at 96. The practice of nations and the language of AFP 200–17, *supra* note 411, are consistent with Trenchard's definition of military objectives, and inconsistent with the definition contained in article 52, paragraph 2 of Protocol I. The discussion that follows in this text at the point at which Trenchard's definition appears illustrates the fact that the distinction between military and war effort is not always as clear as the "model" ICRC list would attempt to make it.

But the problems of targeting are even more complex. The attack of targets beyond the battlefield occurred during World Wars I and II, Korea, Vietnam, and the recent Iran-Iraq conflict to avoid repetition of the frittering away of vast amounts of manpower as occurred in the trenches of World War I. In each conflict, airpower offered a means for attacking an enemy's ability to wage war. If the enemy's ability to manufacture tanks, ships, aircraft, or small arms were thwarted, it would frustrate his ability to continue the war. Hence destruction or denial of the means to import raw materials was as important as destruction of the plants in which the engines of war were manufactured. *See e.g.*, W. MEDLICOTT, 1–2 THE ECONOMIC BLOCKADE, (London, 1952, 1959), for steps taken by Great Britain to deny critical war materials to Germany and Japan; J. TERRAINE, *supra* note 99, for German U-boat efforts against British import of war materials during the two world wars; and C. BLAIR, *supra* note 293, for U.S. submarine efforts to deny critical war materials to Japan during World War II.

Today, the issue in some conflicts is both the same, and different. Few nations can afford to manufacture all of their own weapons, choosing instead to import them from other nations. Weapons also have become substantially more expensive, and a nation at war must increase its foreign exports if it is to afford the weapons it desires. Hence targeting may emphasize the attack of materials being exported by a nation as a means for acquiring the income to purchase weapons needed to continue its war effort. This is not entirely unique to modern war; Union forces endeavored to deny Confederate export of cotton to finance its war effort during the United States Civil War. *See* F. OWSLEY, KING COTTON DIPLOMACY (1931); V. Jones, I THE CIVIL WAR AT SEA, THE BLOCKADERS 182–83 (1960), and W. SPENCER, THE CONFEDERATE NAVY IN EUROPE 1–2, 5, 94–97 (1983). This also was the case in the "war of the tankers" waged during the 1980s between Iran and Iraq, in which each sought to deny the other the ability to export oil in order to finance its purchase of new weapons. In ignoring the connections between export/import and modern warfare, or in attempting to force warfare back to the immediate battlefield, article 52, paragraph 3 of Protocol I and the ICRC "model" list fail miserably in identifying legitimate targets that will be attacked in any conflict by any nation with the means to do so.

413. Ignorance of the importance of attack of target systems is illustrated by the ICRC's limited list of military targets and by the language of paragraph 3 of article 57 of Protocol I, which states that "When a choice is possible between several military objectives for obtaining a similar military advantage, the objective to be selected shall be that the attack on which may be expected to cause the least danger to civilian lives and to civilian objects." This paragraph is totally inconsistent with the doctrine of the United States as well as targeting doctrine of NATO and the Warsaw Pact. For example, were attacks made only on "lines and means of communication (railway lines, roads, bridges, tunnels and canals) of fundamental military importance," an enemy simply would switch to other railway lines, roads, bridges, *etc*. An example would be the Allied attack on the German transportation system during World War II, which is described in the UNITED STATES STRATEGIC BOMBING SURVEY, THE EFFECTS OF STRATEGIC BOMBING ON GERMAN TRANSPORTATION, 2d ed. (1947), and in A. MIERZEHEWSKI, *supra* note 20.

Today, national funding for highway construction and maintenance is directly tied to their value to national security. For example, U.S. funding is justified in 23 U.S.C., sec. 101(b), which states:

Neither considers the importance of subcontracting in the manufacture of modern weapons systems, or of dispersion in time of war.[414] Each assumes a greater degree of certainty in the mind of an attacker as to the connection between a segment of a

---

> It is hereby declared to be in the national interest to accelerate the construction of the Federal-air highway systems, including the National System of Interstate and Defense Highways, since many of such highways, or portions thereof, are in fact inadequate to meet the needs for local and interstate commerce, for the national and civil defense.

See also 23 U.S.C., §§ 210 and 310–12. Similar provisions exist for the construction of ports, harbors, and airports. One commentary suggests that "Means of transport and communication fall into a category where their use for military purposes cannot be excluded through the presumption [of civilian use contained in paragraph 3 of article 52]." NEW RULES FOR VICTIMS OF ARMED CONFLICTS, *supra* note 257, at 326. This is evident, for example, in the use of the Autobahn in Germany as an airstrip for U.S. Air Force F–16 Falcon fighters and C–130 Hercules transport aircraft during NATO exercises such as REFORGER. The ICRC's list fails to consider the national defense basis on which much modern construction is undertaken. This appears not to be entirely accidental. Swiss construction of civilian buildings, roads and bridges is done with national defense in mind. Swiss-ICRC influence in the negotiation of Protocol I was intended to deny an enemy's right to attack structures, facilities, *etc.*, unless and until some direct connection to military use is established.

Similarly, the destruction solely of petroleum, oil and lubricants (POL) located in (using the ICRC's language) "military stores of fuel" or in "installations providing energy for the national defence" would attack far less than the entire POL system, and merely allow an enemy time to draw POL from "civilian" storage areas and installations or disperse his POL. On Swiss mobilization, for example, strategic components (including POL) normally found in concentrated storage are systematically dispersed while other POL storage is contained underground beneath "civilian" structures. J. MCPHEE, *supra* note 361, at 41.

But the Swiss example is not the only one. In late June and early July 1966, U.S. Navy and Air Force tactical aircraft attacked the Hanoi and Haiphong POL storage facilities. *See* Kasler, *The Hanoi POL Strike*, 26 AIR U. REV. 19–28 (Nov.–Dec. 1974). While the attacks destroyed substantial amounts of POL, equally substantial amounts already had been dispersed and stored in urban areas (usually near schools, hospitals, or in residential areas) and alongside earthwork dikes to shield the POL from attack. Moreover, it would be impossible to say conclusively that the POL stored in the facilities attacked was to be used for military rather than civilian use. As with food, a nation will divert POL from civilian sources to carry out its military operations, and there is no magical process by which a targeting intelligence officer may separate "civilian" POL from that of the military. For discussion of POL as a military asset in modern war and as a target, *see* U.S. STRATEGIC BOMBING SURVEY, OIL DIVISION FINAL REPORT (Jan. 1947); D. PAYTON-SMITH, OIL: A STUDY OF WAR-TIME POLICY AND ADMINISTRATION (London, 1971); R. COOKE & R. NESBIT, TARGET: HITLER'S OIL (London, 1985); and R. GORALSKI & R. FREEBURG, OIL & WAR (1987). The components of POL flow as a target system as illustrated in AFP 200–17, *supra* note 411, at 11, and include all components engaged in the extraction, transportation, distillation, storage, and distribution of POL products, whether distribution is intended for civilian or military use.

It is important to emphasize that there is a distinction between an object being a part of a target system or a lawful target and the likelihood that it will be attacked. For example, at any given time a substantial portion of gasoline for motor vehicles in the United States is located in tanks at individual service stations. In the event of a war, the United States Government could restrict sale of that gasoline through rationing, as it did during World War II, or seize or otherwise procure the gasoline for military use. That being the case, ostensibly the gasoline at private service stations would be part of the POL target system and could be attacked. In practical terms, however, individual gasoline stations would not be attacked because of the "cushion" in the target system, *i.e.*, the total number (approximately 120,000) would make such an effort militarily infeasible. Part of the role of target intelligence is to distinguish critical nodes in target systems from those parts the attack of which would be militarily infeasible. *See* Gilster, *On War, Time, and the Principle of Substitution*, 30 AIR U. REV. 2–19 (Sept.–Oct. 1979). The provisions of article 52 of Protocol I fail to comprehend the targeting process in practical terms.

414. Subcontracting for national defense was the pre-World War II inspiration of Sir Ernest Lemon in Great Britain, but was brought to a substantially higher level of efficiency by Speer in Germany as aircraft and other war materials production was dispersed in order to avoid destruction by the Allied Strategic Air Offensive. Today, for example, components of the Air Force's B–1 and B–2 bombers are built by subcontractors in almost every state of the union.

For discussion of the U.S. experience with enemy dispersion of war materials during the Korean and Vietnam Wars, *see* Haering, *How Tactical Air Works*, 108 U.S. NAVAL INST. PROC. 63, 65 (November 1982); Cagle, *supra* note 396, at 84, 85, 87 and Parks, *supra* note 109, at 8, 15.

target system and military operations than an attacker normally would possess.[415] And each is fundamentally ignorant of the modern target intelligence process.[416]

The principal problems with the definition of military objective contained in article 52 are the phrases requiring that any attack make an "effective contribution to military action" and constitute a "definite military advantage." The first requires that any destruction have a nexus to a "military" rather than strategic, psychological, or other possible advantage. In this the drafters of Protocol I displayed a serious ignorance of the art of war. As Michael Howard has noted, "Wars are not simply acts of violence. They are acts of persuasion or of discussion; and although the threat of destruction is normally a necessary part of the persuading process, such destruction is only exceptionally regarded as an end in itself."[417]

In explanation of this phrase the ICRC *Official Commentary* states that "it is not legitimate to launch an attack which only offers potential or indeterminate advantages."[418] This point is reemphasized by the phrase "under the circumstances ruling at the time," which another commentator has stated does not include "some hypothetical future time."[419] These statements suggest that leaders are possessed of a clearer vision of war and the battlefield than the experience of war reflects. Three historical examples illustrate the problem associated with this narrow view.

On April 18, 1942, twenty-six U.S. Army Air Corps B–25 Mitchell bombers took off from the aircraft carrier U.S.S. *Hornet* (CV–8) to bomb the Japanese mainland.[420] Historians are not in agreement as to the military value of the air strike, but agree that the attack provided a tremendous boost to the morale of the American people after the string of defeats U.S. forces had suffered in the preceding five months.[421]

---

415. For example, electric grids are so complex that it is not possible to ascertain whether a given power plant is "providing energy mainly for national defence," as stated in paragraph 8(e) of the ICRC model list. Even were it to be so identified, attacked, and put out of action, power would simply be transferred from another power plant. Power plants in the United States today can transfer power to other plants on the opposite side of the nation, suggesting the infeasibility of the standard contained in the ICRC model list. This capability is not unique to the United States.

416. *See* AFP 200–17, An Introduction to Air Force Targeting (23 June 1989), chapters 5, *The Target Intelligence Process*, and 6, *Target Analysis*; and the 1989 edition of this pamphlet, *supra* note 411, at chapter 5, *Target Development*. Para. 5–1 of the 1978 edition of AFP 200–17 explains the target intelligence process as "a sequence of steps by which target intelligence and target materials are produced (through the fusion and analysis of multiple sources of intelligence) and used to support operational decision-making and force employment."

417. Strategy and Policy in Twentieth-Century Warfare, Harmon Memorial Lectures in Military History 1959–1987 354 (1988).

418. ICRC Commentary, *supra* note 247, 636. Similarly, the commentary states that "the adjective ('definite') is a word of limitation denoting in this context a concrete and perceptible military advantage rather than a hypothetical and speculative one." New Rules for Victims of Armed Conflicts, *supra* note 257, at 326.

419. New Rules for Victims of Armed Conflicts, *supra* note 257.

420. The attack is described in T. Lawson, with R. Considine, Thirty Seconds over Tokyo (1943); C. Glines, Doolittle's Tokyo Raiders (1964); C. Glines, The Doolittle Raid (1988); and D. Schultz, The Doolittle Raid (1988).

421. Rodenhauser, *The Doolittle Influence on the Pacific War*, 3 Air U. Q. Rev. 25–30 (Spring 1950), concludes that the Doolittle raid had significant impact on Japanese strategy because the Japanese high command thought the raid originated in Midway, leading to the Battle of Midway, in which the Imperial Japanese Navy suffered a disastrous defeat less than two months later. *See* M. Fuchida, Midway, The Battle That Doomed Japan: The Japanese Navy's Story (1955) and S. Morison, IV Official History of United States Naval Operations in World War II, Coral Sea, Midway and Submarine Operations 69–159 (1949). Colonel Rodenhauser's conclusion was based on his interviews with key Japanese military officers as a member of the Military Analysis Division of the United States Strategic Bombing Survey (USSBS). The USSBS report entitled Japanese Air Power concludes in part that:

> The raid was too small to do substantial physical damage, but its repercussions on the planning level of the high command were considerable. . . . [A]ttention was focused on the eastern approaches

In October 1972, the North Vietnamese delegation walked away from negotiations being held in Paris with the United States in an effort to end the Vietnam War. On December 18, 1971, President Richard M. Nixon authorized the commencement

---

to the home islands, and additional impetus given the prewar plan to attack Midway and the Aleutians . . . [and] the Japanese began to implement their plans for air defense of Japan which before that time had received scant consideration. Two new Army fighter groups were organized and based in Japan, and three more were converted from a training to a defense status. A total of four Army fighter groups were held in Japan throughout 1942 and 1943 for the defense of the homeland when the Japanese Navy was urgently demanding that the Army send reinforcements to the Solomons.

UNITED STATES STRATEGIC BOMBING SURVEY, JAPANESE AIR POWER 10 (July 1946).

Colonel Rodenhauser's views are corroborated by one of the more notable histories of the Pacific war. Ronald H. Spector reports that:

> The damage actually inflicted by the raid was small, but its psychological effect on the Japanese was all that might have been desired. The army and navy had failed in their duty to safeguard the homeland and the Emperor from attack. . . . All opposition to the Midway operation on the part of the Naval General Staff abruptly ceased.

R. SPECTOR, EAGLE AGAINST THE SUN 155 (1985).

Agreeing with Professor Spector, John Keegan observes that:

> The Doolittle raid might . . . have been judged a fiasco if it had not registered with the Japanese high command. The citizens of Tokyo, to whom no public acknowledgment of the raid was made by the government, did not associate the scattering of explosions with an American attack; but the generals and admirals, as servants of the god-emperor, were horrified by the threat to his person the bombing represented.

J. KEEGAN, *supra* note 378 at 271. Similarly, Samuel Eliot Morison notes that:

> This 'answer to Pearl Harbor' did not inflict one thousandth part of the damage it was supposed to revenge; but it gave the American public . . . a great lift. The Japanese authorities . . . pinned down hundreds of planes to defend Tokyo. And, what is more important, the event expedited plans for an overextension that led to the Japanese defeat at Midway.

S. MORISON, THE TWO-OCEAN WAR 140 (1963).

The views of other historians on the effect of the Doolittle Raid are mixed. One author notes that:

> The raid had done little real damage apart from wrecking ninety buildings and causing the death of fifty civilians. But as the President had foreseen, it scored a direct hit on the morale of the United States. . . . The most far-reaching impact of the Tokyo raid was the psychological effect it had on the [Japanese] Imperial General Staff. The generals and admirals had suffered a tremendous loss of face, and their angry overreaction eventually brought a succession of strategic disasters. . . . [The raid] briefly cheered American spirits, but the Joint Chiefs of Staff, like the [Japanese] Imperial General Staff, saw it as little more than a propaganda raid. They were both to be proved wrong. In the months that followed, Doolittle's raid would prove to have initiated a chain of events through which the United States found the opportunity to dam the tide of Japanese conquest.

J. COSTELLO, THE PACIFIC WAR 235, 236, and 245 (1981). *But see* P. CALVOCORESSI, G. WINT & J. PRITCHARD, TOTAL WAR: THE CAUSES AND COURSES OF THE SECOND WORLD WAR 1030–37 (rev. 2d ed. 1989). The raid does not even receive a mention in M. GILBERT, THE SECOND WORLD WAR (1989).

There are two points that may be drawn from the Doolittle Raid that bear on consideration of the language contained in article 52, paragraph 2 of Protocol I. The first is that while some military operations may not "make an effective contribution to *military action*," as required by article 52(2), they may have significant psychological and strategic value, which is not even contemplated by article 52(2) or any other provision of Protocol I.

The second is that the requirement that an operation offer a "definite *military* advantage" suffers similar problems *vis-à-vis* psychological or strategic gains, and assumes that wartime command decisions can be made with greater certainty than usually exists. As the editor of AIR FORCE QUARTERLY REVIEW commented within the body of Colonel Rodenhauser's article, the Doolittle Raid "transformed into one of those incidents of warfare that yield rich results unplanned or undreamed of when they occur." Protocol I failed completely to consider the fog of war and the speculative nature of many decisions made in war. Rodenhauser, *supra* note 421, at 26.

of Linebacker II: bombing missions against targets in the Hanoi-Haiphong area of North Vietnam relying principally on B–52 heavy bombers. Its principal intention was not military, but to persuade the North Vietnamese to return to the negotiating table. Eleven days later, after they had exhausted their supply of 1,100 SA–2 missiles, the North Vietnamese Government indicated not only its willingness, but its desire, to return to the negotiating table and reach agreement as quickly as possible. The war ended three weeks later.[422]

In April 1986, in response to Libyan-supported terrorist attacks on the Rome and Vienna Airports and on the LaBelle Discotheque in West Berlin, President Ronald Reagan authorized an air strike against terrorist-related targets in Libya. The air strikes, carried out on the night of 15/16 April 1986, by U.S. Air Force, Navy, and Marine Corps aircraft, were intended to have more of a psychological than military purpose, to let Libya and other nations relying on terrorism as a foreign policy means know that the United States would no longer condone state-sponsored terrorism.[423]

In each of the preceding cases, the United States would have been hard pressed to state that there was a "definite military advantage" resulting from the operations described, or that the gain sought was not "potential" or "indeterminate;" the result sought in each was speculative, as are most actions in war, and more psychological than military, although each had military effects. The same may be said for many of the British commando operations and RAF Bomber Command missions in the early phases of World War II, that is, the desire by Prime Minister Winston S. Churchill to take some offensive action in order to bolster the morale of the British people.[424] Does the requirement of article 52(2) regarding a definite *military* advantage prohibit an attack where the principal purpose of that attack is psychological or political rather than military? Such an argument was raised even before the negotiation of Protocol I was completed, but the language of article 52(2) was not amended in such as a way as to address this point or rectify the identified ambiguity.

In a 1975 article, using the language of article 52(2) requiring that an attack have a definite *military* advantage, Professor Hamilton DeSaussure suggested that the 1972 United States Linebacker II bombings against military targets in North Vietnam could be regarded as illegal, as attacks "on military targets may be unjustified when the military advantage to be gained is not significant and political motives for the attack predominate."[425]

These are not the rantings of an extremist or potential enemy. This argument was made by an established international lawyer who enjoyed a long and distinguished career in the United States Air Force before taking up an equally distinguished career teaching international law. Although his argument has been refuted by other international lawyers,[426] it illustrates the ambiguity of Protocol I and the potential danger

422. *See* Parks, *supra* note 208. M. CLODFELTER, *supra* note 224; and K. ESCHMANN, LINEBACKER 61–214 (1989).

423. *See* Parks, *supra* note 86; and B. DAVIS, QADDAFI, TERRORISM, AND THE ORIGINS OF THE U.S. ATTACK ON LIBYA (1989).

424. With regard to commando operations, *see* H. SAUNDERS, THE GREEN BERET: THE STORY OF THE COMMANDOS (London, 1949); C. MESSENGER, THE COMMANDOS, 1941–1946 (London, 1985); and W. SEYMOUR, BRITISH SPECIAL FORCES (London, 1985). Early Bomber Command operations are discussed in C. WEBSTER & N. FRANKLAND, *supra* note 81; and A. VERRIER, *supra* note 183; N. LONGMATE, *supra* note 183; D. SAWARD, *supra* note 183.

425. DeSaussure & Glaser, *Air Warfare—Christmas 1972*, in LAW AND RESPONSIBILITY IN WARFARE: THE VIETNAM EXPERIENCE 119–39 (1975).

426. *See* Hoopes, *Comments*, *id.* at 140–44; Thorpe & Miles, *Comments*, *id.* at 145–49; and Fenrick, *The Rule of Proportionality and Protocol I in Conventional Warfare*, 98 MIL. L. REV. 91–127, at 123 (Fall 1982).

posed to American military personnel in the hands of an enemy. If reasonable men on friendly terms with one another can disagree as to the meaning of a treaty provision, the ability for an enemy to exploit that ambiguity in order to deny prisoner of war protection to captured American military personnel can be neither underestimated nor ignored; and no reservation or statement of understanding can rectify this problem. Refusal of the United States to ratify Protocol I will not necessarily preclude such arguments by a future opponent, but American refusal to ratify Protocol I will preclude the United States from placing its imprimatur on such ambiguous language.

Setting aside this issue, what, then, does the United States regard as lawful targets? The difference between the ICRC model list and customary international law is primarily one of range, but in that respect the two lists literally are miles apart. The practice of nations identified during World Wars I and II has continued over the half-century since the latter conflict, and the target categories previously listed remain valid.[427] The list of targets developed through the customary practice of nations and the listing contained in Air Force Pamplet (AFP) 200–17 are consistent:

---

427. *See supra* text at section XII.

428. AFP 200–17, *supra* note 411, at 9. Similarly, AIR FORCE MANUAL 1–1, *supra* note 363, at 3–2, lists as vital targets "concentrations of uncommitted elements of enemy armed forces, strategic weapon systems, command centers, communications facilities, manufacturing systems, sources of raw material, critical material stockpiles, power systems, and key agricultural areas." There are other sources. In 1987 the author was a member of the Moscow Assessment Review Panel (The Laird Commission) appointed by President Reagan to examine the security breaches in U.S. Missions in the Soviet Union. On arrival in Moscow the author received the following "Soviet Regulations on Photography." Through reverse engineering, that is, by examining those objects which may not be photographed or sketched, one may ascertain those objects the Soviet Union regards as lawful targets. The Soviet list coincides with the conclusions of the author with regard to the customary practice of nations and AFP 200–17; each is far more extensive than the ICRC's "model list."

Summary Guidance

Permitted

You are permitted to photograph or sketch, except in those specific places and locations closed to foreign travelers:

a. architectural monuments

b. cultural, educational or medical institutions

c. theaters, museums, and stadiums

d. public parks of culture and rest

e. streets, squares, and housing

f. scenes and landscapes (provided none of the objects listed in the right hand column are in the background)

You may also photograph, *after obtaining explicit permission of the management:*

a. industrial complexes producing civilian products

Prohibited

You are forbidden to photograph or sketch any of the following:

a. military equipment, installations or facilities

b. seaport harbors

c. fuel storage facilities

d. railroad junctions, tunnels, and railroad and highway bridges

e. hydroelectric installations and electric power stations

f. industrial complexes dealing with the production of military equipment

g. scientific research facilities, design offices, and laboratories

h. radio beacons and radio stations

Customary Practice	AFP 200–17[428]
Military equipment, units and bases	Military forces, equipment and facilities
Economic targets - power sources - industry - transportation	Economic targets - industrial complexes - production facilities - transportation
Command and control	Leadership targets - government centers (political)[429] - military headquarters

---

Permitted	Prohibited
b. state and collective farms	i. telephone and telegraph exchange facilities
c. tractor repair stations	j. Soviet territory from aircraft in flight
d. railroad stations	k. surface panoramic photographs and sketches of industrial complexes
e. river ports	l. in the 25-kilometer frontier (except for the places and cities which foreigners may visit, where you may photograph the objects described in the left column).
f. civilian airports	
g. educational and social organization buildings	

In contrast, open-source material indicates that Soviet KGB (Soviet Intelligence) *Spetsnaz* (Department 8) has the following guidance for targeting at the commencement of hostilities with a view toward complete and total demoralization of the targeted nation through creation of maximum chaos:
(1) key government officials and facilities, regardless of connection with the military or war effort;
(2) public utilities, regardless of connection with the military or war effort; and
(3) general population, regardless of connection with the military or war effort.
The GRU (Soviet Military Intelligence) *Spetsnaz* will attack military and/or sustainability targets. The philosophy of Soviet targeting is explained in Pipes, *Militarism and the Soviet State*, DAEDALUS 1–12 (Fall 1980), where he states that:

> The concept "correlation of forces" frequently used in Soviet literature relates to the science of war by assessing not only the balance of power narrowly conceived to include troops and weapons, but also the entire panoply of nonmilitary factors that come into play when a modern country wages war. . . .
>
> As a consequence of this approach, . . . contemporary Soviet military doctrine places the economic and "moral" cohesion of the home front quite on par with the battle readiness of the military front. The armed forces must be prepared for combat long before the outbreak of hostilities, and so must the civilian population. This line of thinking . . . requires . . . that the line that in noncommunist societies separates the military from the civilian sectors be made much less distinct.
>
> *These considerations apply, of course, not only to defensive calculations, but also to offensive ones.* Given the importance attached to industry, transport, communications, energy, and morale as factors that make for victory, Russian doctrine assigns urgent priority to strikes against these targets.

Id. at 8 (emphasis added).

While *Glasnost* may change one's view toward the probability of war between the Warsaw Pact and NATO in the near term, these lists should be viewed in the light of the worst case, *i.e.*, war, rather than the best, *i.e.*, peace, in considering a nation's thoughts on targeting.

Prior to the outbreak of World War II, the British Home Defence Committee carried out similar reverse engineering in an effort to determine those target categories most likely to be subjected to Luftwaffe attack. The list included factories; commercial oil installations; telegraph, telephone, wireless telegraph and cable systems; lighting and power plants; docks; mills; bridges; places where large quantities of food or other materials were stored, or would be stored; industrial centers; ports; naval, army and air force bases; railway junctions; and manufacturing facilities associated with the aircraft industry. B. COLLIER, *supra* note 1, at 45, 70, and 79.

429. Political targets are undefined, though generally they are regarded as members of the government infrastructure directly involved in managing the war effort. For the purpose of avoiding confusion,

Geographic	Geographic[430]

Protection for noncombatants vis-à-vis civilian objects. As previously noted, article 48 of Protocol I obligates a party to that treaty at all times to "distinguish between the civilian population and combatants and between civilian objects and military objectives. . . ."[431] As an expression of the fundamental principle of discrimination, this is a correct statement of the goal of the law of war, i.e., to take reasonable steps to minimize injury to innocent civilians and damage to civilian objects incidental to the conduct of combat operations.

But there exists in the law of war an equally fundamental distinction between the protection of life—all life, including the lives of combatants—and the degree of protection afforded civilian objects. The prohibition on the taking or abuse of human life is unequivocal. But if required by military necessity, civilian objects may be taxed, purchased, requisitioned, seized, confiscated, or destroyed, and damage or destruction incidental to legitimate combat operations is not unlawful unless it occurs as a result of wanton negligence.[432] Thus a building or other form of civilian

the author prefers the term "command and control" to "political." While a head of state may be a legitimate target in time of war, generally nations at war avoid attack of each other's leader(s) on the basis of comity. In addition, because each nation recognizes that war is not a permanent state, ultimately there must be someone with authority with whom each may negotiate.

430. In the course of its 1977 signing of the 1977 Protocols, the United Kingdom presented a statement of understanding to the effect that "in relation to Article 52, that a specific area of land may be a military objective if, because of its location or other reasons specified in the Article, its total or partial destruction, capture or neutralisation in the circumstances ruling at the time offers definite military advantage." SCHINDLER & TOMAN, *supra* note 27, at 717. An example of a geographic target is an unoccupied mountain pass through which enemy units are about to pass.

431. SCHINDLER & TOMAN, *supra* note 27, at 650. This rule is basic to the entire section (part IV, section I) of Protocol I. But though it was adopted by consensus, it was and remains the subject of disagreement on the question of responsibility between defender and attacker for collateral civilian casualties incidental to the attack of legitimate military objectives. One treatise correctly notes that the

> affirmative obligation to protect actively can have relevance only to the Party that has the capability to take the appropriate protective measures. Generally speaking, this is the Party that has control over the area in which the persons to be protected are located.
>
> The Party which controls the area in which civilians and civilian objects are located is under a strong obligation to distinguish between civilians and combatants by refraining from using the civilian population as a shield for military operations. They are also under an obligation to do what is feasible to take certain specific precautions against the effects of attacks, including the evacuation of civilians, avoiding the location of military objectives in densely populated areas, and to take other necessary precautions which are particularized in article 61 [*e.g.*, warning and evacuation]. It should also be remembered that the obligation to distinguish combatants from the civilian population is for the purpose of promoting the protection of the civilian population from the effects of hostilities. It thus follows that an important share of the responsibility for implementing the principle of distinction rests on the Party which controls the civilian population.

NEW RULES FOR VICTIMS OF ARMED CONFLICTS, *supra* note 257, at 282–84.

The ICRC COMMENTARY observes that France noted that "if there had been a vote, it would have abstained" on the grounds that the article "has direct implications as regards a State's organization and defense against an invader." The delegate from India commented (correctly, in this author's opinion) that:

> [T]his article will apply within the capability and practical possibility of each party to the conflict. As the capability of the parties to distinguish will depend upon the means and methods available to each party generally or at a particular moment, this article does not require a party to do something which is not within its means or capability.

ICRC COMMENTARY, *supra* note 247, at 599.

432. There are certain constraints on the degrees of taking of civilian objects, depending upon whether the property is public or private, movable or immovable. For example, movable cultural property may not be requisitioned, seized, or confiscated. In contrast to the protection of human life, however, *all* types of property may be destroyed in the course of military operations and without compensation if required by military necessity.

object may be destroyed to clear a field of fire or to block an enemy avenue of approach where military necessity dictates; yet military necessity may never be used as a justification for the killing of innocent civilians.[433] Article 147 of the 1949 Geneva Convention Relative to the Protection of Civilian Persons in Time of War makes this distinction in identifying those acts that are regarded as "grave breaches":

> wilful killing, torture or inhuman treatment, including biological experiments, wilfully causing great suffering or serious injury to body or health, unlawful deportation or transfer or unlawful confinement of a protected person, compelling a protected person to serve in the forces of a hostile Power, or wilfully depriving a protected person of rights of a fair and regular trial prescribed in the present Convention, taking of hostages *and extensive destruction and appropriation of property, not justified by military necessity and carried out unlawfully and wantonly*.[434]

Article 48 of Protocol I places the protection of civilian property on the same level as the protection of civilian lives. This would be a quantum leap over customary practice in protection of civilian property by any military commander, whether attacker or defender, but particularly for an attacker. Paragraphs 2 and 3 of article 57 contain language indicating a similar lack of distinction between damage to civilian property and injury to the civilian population. Paragraph 2(a)(ii) requires a military commander to "take all feasible precautions in the choice of means and methods of attack with a view to avoiding, and in any event minimizing, incidental loss of civilian life, injury to civilians *and damage to civilian objects*. . . ."[435] While paragraph 3 of article 57 states that, "When a choice is possible between several military objectives for obtaining a similar military advantage, the objective to be selected shall be that the attack on which may be expected to cause the least danger to civilian lives *and to civilian objects*."[436]

The grave breach provisions of Protocol I indicate that the lack of distinction between the protection of civilian lives and civilian objects was intended. While paragraph 3(a) of article 85 makes it a grave breach to make the civilian population or individual civilians only the object of an attack, paragraph 3(b) makes it a grave breach to launch "an indiscriminate attack affecting the civilian population *or civilian objects* in the knowledge that such attack will cause excessive loss of life, injury to civilians or *damage to civilian objects*. . . ."[437]

The domestic law of the United States, derived from English common law, clearly values life over property. In law of war practice and in common sense terms, a distinction exists between the two; civilian property has never been given the same degree of protection from damage as civilian and combatant lives from the risk of injury or death. Again, as a general rule, the language of article 48 states every pilot's ideal, that is, to place "bombs on target" while distinguishing legitimate

433. *See* 2 OPPENHEIM'S INTERNATIONAL LAW, DISPUTES, WAR AND NEUTRALITY 413 (H. Lauterpacht ed., 7th ed. London, 1952) [hereinafter LAUTERPACHT]. Destruction of a civilian object to clear a field of fire may or may not make that civilian object a military objective, as that term is defined in article 52 of Protocol I. Thus a commander setting up his defense of a position may not be sure of the direction from which the enemy is likely to attack, and may destroy civilian structures to clear a field of fire or to obstruct possible avenues of approach. Unless and until he knows precisely the direction of the enemy attack, it would be difficult for him to meet the rather stringent test that his actions offer a "definite military advantage" as required by article 52, paragraph 2. Neither the ICRC COMMENTARY (*supra* note 247, at 635–37) nor the NEW RULES FOR VICTIMS OF ARMED CONFLICTS, *supra* note 257, at 323–27, are of assistance in providing guidance.

434. SCHINDLER & TOMAN, *supra* note 27, at 547 (emphasis added). For discussion of the property phrases of article 147, *see* GC COMMENTARY, *supra* note 208, at 601.

435. SCHINDLER & TOMAN, *supra* note 27, at 654–55 (emphasis added).

436. *Id.* at 655 (emphasis added).

437. *Id.* at 671.

targets from innocent civilians and civilian objects. But as a legally binding rule, Protocol I has raised the protection of civilian objects to an unprecedented, unrealistic and unacceptable level.

The distinction in values between civilian lives and property can be illustrated by two hypothetical situations. An aircraft enroute to its target is seriously damaged by enemy anti-aircraft fire. The pilot decides that he must jettison his bombs if he is to keep his aircraft in the air. He realizes that he has two choices: if he jettisons them immediately, they will fall in a schoolyard full of children; if he delays a matter of a few seconds, his bombs will strike a farmer's barn. Assuming he has this choice, there seems to be no question but that the destruction of the barn would be of less consequence than dropping the bombs in the schoolyard, even if there were only one person in the schoolyard.

In the second scenario, a commander of an armored column pursuing a retreating enemy force finds his route of advance through a city clogged with civilian refugees. He tries in vain to move the refugees out of the way. He has two options: he may continue his advance on the road, with the refugees assuming the risk for any injuries they may incur, or he may "make a road" by destroying some of the structures in the city. (A third option, machinegunning refugees who refuse to move, clearly is out of the question.)

Once again, if all other factors in the hypothetical situation are equal, the choice remains clear: civilian lives take precedence over the protection of any form of civilian property, as they have throughout the history of warfare and of the law of war. In considering the protection of civilian property *vis-à-vis* the protection of *any* life, however, including the lives of combatants, the protection of life always will take precedence. Given a choice between the damage or destruction of a civilian building and the loss of a single life among the personnel of his command, most military commanders would opt for preserving the lives of their men. While this may not be true of all nations, most certainly it is true with regard to American values. As one historian has observed,

> To Americans, flesh and blood have always been more precious than sticks and stones, however assembled. An American commander, faced with taking the Louvre from a defending enemy, unquestionably would blow it apart or burn it down without hesitation if such would save the life of one of his men. And he would be in complete accord with American ideals and ethics in doing so. . . . If bombing and artillery would save lives, even though they destroyed sites of beauty and history, saving lives obviously had preference . . . .[438]

The practical difficulties of the presumption regarding civilian objects contained in paragraph 3 of article 52 have been discussed previously.[439] The provisions in articles 48, 52(3), 57(2)(a)(ii) and (3), and 85(3)(b) establish an intent in Protocol I

438. T. FEHRENBACH, *supra* note 303, at 234. The same distinction is made in General Eisenhower's 1943 admonishment to his forces, as quoted in full at *supra* note 215, where General Eisenhower stated that "If we have to choose between destroying a famous building and sacrificing our own men, then our men's lives count infinitely more and the building must go." The author, who has experienced the unpleasant task of writing letters to the next of kin of men in his command who died in combat, can imagine the language of a letter to an American family from the military commander of a soldier killed in action were the United States to follow the Protocol I requirements under discussion. The letter would contain a sentence to the effect that "Your son's life was lost because there was this vacant house . . . ," or "Your son gave his life not in defense of his country, but so that an abandoned barn could remain standing another day . . . ," or words to that effect. The response from the dead soldier's family (in all likelihood transmitted by way of the family's United States Senators and Congressman) would be swift and certain.

439. As discussed in conjunction with *supra* notes 407–09.

to give priority to the protection of inanimate civilian objects over the lives of combatants. In placing civilian property protection on an equal footing with civilian lives, particularly if such protection must be advanced at risk to American combatant lives, Protocol I jeopardizes the continued credibility of the law of war.[440] It also places U.S. military personnel captured by enemy forces at unnecessary risk of spurious allegations of violations of the law of war in cases where civilian property has been damaged or destroyed in the ordinary conduct of combat operations.

Responsibility for collateral civilian casualties. Two issues relate to consideration of the Protocol I provisions regarding the responsibility for collateral civilian casualties: (a) the question of responsibility as such; and (b) the so-called rule of proportionality. The two are inextricably intertwined, and must be discussed together.

Unavoidable collateral casualties among the civilian population or other protected persons are an unfortunate but inevitable part of war. Thus article 15 of the 1863 Lieber Code provides that, "Military necessity admits of all direct destruction of life or *armed* enemies, and of *other persons* whose destruction is incidentally *unavoidable* in the armed contests of war."[441]

Similarly, certain provisions in the Annex to Hague Convention IV of 1907 have been interpreted as prohibiting the use of weapons or means of warfare in a manner that would be tantamount to the intentional attack of the enemy's civilian population.[442] The difficulty has been in narrowing the ground between that which is unavoidable and that which is prohibited. Certain World War II aerial bombardment practices illustrate the necessity for narrowing the difference in order to provide better protection for the innocent civilian.[443]

Various factors have entered into the equation in the past. The first is the general attitude that collateral civilian casualties are the "cost of doing business," that is,

440. While one treatise suggests that the "military advantages" to be weighed by a commander in attacking a military objective include "the security of the attacking force" (New Rules for Victims of Armed Conflicts, *supra* note 257, at 324), the ICRC Commentary makes no such allowance.

441. Schindler & Toman, *supra* note 27, at 6.

442. For example, article 22 provides that "The right of belligerents to adopt means of injuring the enemy is not unlimited," while article 23 provides that "[I]t is especially forbidden . . . (e) To employ arms, projectiles, or material of a nature to cause superfluous injury." Schindler & Toman, *supra* note 27, at 82–83. The latter provision has been interpreted to protect the combatant from weapons that cause unnecessary suffering and to protect the civilian population from indiscriminate attack.

443. For example, while Allied aircrews generally exercised caution with regard to the jettisoning of bombs over Nazi-occupied territory (such as France, Belgium, Norway or the Netherlands) to protect the civilian population in those countries, there was a widespread practice within those same air forces of jettisoning munitions over Germany without any consideration for injury to innocent civilians. The same was true with regard to the selection of targets of opportunity. Where mission targets could not be attacked owing to weather or other difficulties, any German town could be attacked, whether it contained military objectives or not. *See* C. McBride, Mission Failure and Survival 39–40, 74, 79 (1989). *See also* Davis, *Bombing Strategy Shifts, 1944–45*, 36 Air Power Hist. 33–45 (Winter 1989), in which the following 1944 Eighth Air Force directive regarding attack of secondary and Last Resort Targets is quoted:

> 1. No towns or cities in Germany will be attacked as secondary or last resort targets, targets of opportunity, or otherwise, unless such towns contain or have immediately adjacent to them, one (1) or more military objectives. Military objectives include railway lines; junctions; marshalling yards; railway or road bridges; or other communications networks; any industrial plant; and such obvious military objectives as oil storage tanks, military camps and barracks, troop concentrations, motor transport or AFV parks, ordnance or supply depots, ammunition depots; airfields; *etc.*
>
> . . . .
>
> 3. It has been determined that towns and cities large enough to produce an identifiable return on the H2X [airborne radar bombsight] scope generally contain a large proportion of the military objectives listed above. These centers, therefore may be attacked as secondary or last resort targets by through-the-overcast bombing technique.

engaging in war; this has been discussed. Another factor is the belief that responsibility for the minimization of collateral civilian casualties lies primarily, if not exclusively, with the nation with control of the civilian population, and with the individual civilian. This is evidenced by the steps taken prior to and during World War II to develop civil defense measures in each nation, also previously discussed.

The number of civilian deaths attributable to combat operations (aerial bombardment, artillery fire, etc.), notwithstanding precautions on the part of a defender, serves as a tragic illustration of the necessity for additional measures of protection or precaution if the loss of innocent civilians is to be narrowed to an absolute, unavoidable minimum. There is little doubt that most nations agree that the death of innocent civilians accomplishes nothing in the achievement of any nation's war objectives; it strikes at the very heart of the reason for the law of war. The difficulty, however, lies in writing rules for the use of force that do not provide one side a potential advantage over its opponent, whether perceived or actual. This was the difficult task laid before the delegations at the Diplomatic Conference.

Several provisions in Protocol I relate to concern for collateral civilian casualties. The first is the requirement in article 48, for both the defender and attacker in their military operations to distinguish between the civilian population and military objectives.[444] With regard to specific requirements, paragraph 1 of article 57 provides that, "In the conduct of military operations, constant care shall be taken to spare the civilian population, civilians and civilian objects."[445]

Portions of paragraph 2 of article 57 elaborate the responsibilities expected of a military commander in providing this care:

> With respect to attacks, the following precautions shall be taken:
>
> (a) those who plan or decide upon an attack shall:
>
> (i) do everything feasible to verify that the objectives to be attacked are neither civilians nor civilian objects and are not subject to special protection but are military objectives within the meaning of paragraph 2 of article 52 and that it is not prohibited by provisions of this Protocol to attack them;
>
> (ii) take all feasible precautions in the choice of means and methods of attack with a view to avoiding, and in any event to minimizing, incidental loss of civilian life, injury to civilians and damage to civilian objects;
>
> (iii) refrain from deciding to launch any attack which may be expected to cause incidental loss of civilian life, injury to civilians, damage to civilian objects, or a combination thereof, which would be excessive in relation to the concrete and direct military advantage anticipated.
>
> (b) an attack shall be cancelled or suspended if it becomes apparent that the objective is not a military one or is subject to special protection or that the attack may be expected to cause incidental loss of civilian life, injury to civilians, damage to civilian objects, or a combination thereof, which would be excessive in relation to the concrete and direct military advantage anticipated.[446]

In an attempt to balance the responsibility for minimization of collateral civilian casualties and collateral damage to civilian objects, article 58 of Protocol I states that:

---

444. *See* discussion at *supra* note 431.
445. SCHINDLER & TOMAN, *supra* note 27, at 654.
446. *Id.* at 654–55. Paragraph 5 of article 57 admonishes that "No provision of this Article may be construed as authorizing any attacks against the civilian population, civilians or civilian objects."

> The Parties to the conflict shall, to the maximum extent feasible:
>
> (a) without prejudice to Article 49 of the Fourth Convention, endeavor to remove the civilian population, individual civilians and civilian objects under their control from the vicinity of military objectives;
>
> (b) avoid locating military objectives within or near densely populated areas;
>
> (c) take the necessary precautions to protect the civilian population, individual civilians and civilian objects under their control against the dangers resulting from military operations.[447]

Other provisions in Protocol I complement the requirements of articles 57 and 58. Paragraph 7 of article 51 provides that:

> The presence or movements of the civilian population or individual civilians shall not be used to render certain points or areas immune from military operations, in particular in attempts to shield military objectives from attacks or to shield, favor, or impede military operations. The Parties to the conflict shall not direct the movement of the civilian population or individual civilians in order to attempt to shield military objectives from attack or to shield military operations.[448]

However, in apparent recognition of the practice of some nations that would constitute a violation of article 51(7), paragraph 8 of article 51 states that, ''Any violation of these provisions shall not release the Parties to the conflict from their legal obligations with respect to the civilian population and civilians, including the obligation to take the precautionary measures provided for in article 57.''[449]

The concept of proportionality was codified into several provisions within Protocol I. The previously-quoted paragraphs 2(a)(iii) and (b) of article 57 constitute attempts to address this concept. In a related vein, paragraph 5(b) of article 51 defines as indiscriminate ''an attack which may be expected to cause incidental loss of civilian life, injury to civilians, damage to civilian objects, or a combination thereof, which would be excessive in relation to the concrete and direct military advantage anticipated.''[450] Paragraph 5 also condemns as indiscriminate ''an attack by bombardment by any methods or means which treats as a single military objective a number of clearly separated and distinct military objectives located in a city, town, village or other area containing a similar concentration of civilians or civilian

447. SCHINDLER & TOMAN, *supra* note 27, at 655–56. Article 49 of the Fourth Convention (the 1949 Geneva Convention Relative to the Protection of Civilian Persons in Time of War) provides in part that:

> Individual or mass forcible transfers, as well as deportation of protected persons from occupied territory to the territory of the Occupying Power or to that of any other country, occupied or not, are prohibited, regardless of their motive.
>
> Nevertheless, the Occupying Power may undertake total or partial evacuation of a given area if the security of the population or imperative military reasons so demand.
>
> The Occupying Power shall not detain protected persons in an area particularly exposed to the dangers of war unless the security of the population or imperative military reasons so demand.

SCHINDLER & TOMAN, *supra* note 27, at 516.

448. SCHINDLER & TOMAN, *supra* note 27, at 651–52.

449. *Id.* at 652.

450. *Id.* at 651. As noted in the text accompanying *supra* notes 17–18, the principle of *discrimination* and the concept of *proportionality* are not synonymous.

objects,"[451] while paragraph 3 of article 85 specifies those offenses that will be "grave breaches" in those instances where certain of these provisions are violated.[452]

On their face, the cited provisions appear to offer battlefield commanders a reasonable set of standards that will provide protection for civilians not participating in the hostilities[453] without unduly hindering a commander's accomplishment of his mission. But appearances can be—and are—deceiving. As with previously-discussed articles in Protocol I, the drive for consensus in articles 48–58 necessitated agreement on provisions that are purposely vague, concealing substantial differences among the delegations.[454] The problems with articles 48–58 are far more basic, however.

A fundamental problem in modern war is the commingling of the civilian population and civilian objects with military objectives, and/or the dual use of certain objects for civilian and defense-related purposes.[455] This problem has been discussed previously in conjunction with the definition of military objectives contained in article 52 of Protocol I. In that context, however, it was considered with regard to what may be considered a legitimate target. Commingling also places individual civilians and the civilian population as such at risk incidental to an opposing force's attack on legitimate targets, and it is in that context that the minimization of collateral civilian casualties requires consideration.[456] The problem was recognized prior to World War II. For example, British authorities concluded that the 1923 Hague Air

451. *Id.*

452. To wit:

(a) making the civilian population or individual civilians the object of attack;

(b) launching an indiscriminate attack affecting the civilian population or civilian objects in the knowledge that such attack will cause excessive loss of life, injury to civilians or damage to civilian objects, as defined in Article 57, paragraph 2(a) (iii); and

(c) launching an attack against works or installations containing dangerous forces in the knowledge that such attack will cause excessive loss of life, injury to civilians or damage to civilian objects, as defined in Article 57, paragraph 2(a) (iii).

Id. at 671.

453. A matter itself subject to disagreement in interpretation, as indicated previously.

454. An indication of this is the fact that more reservations and statements of understanding have been made with respect to articles 48–58 by nations that have signed, ratified or acceded to Protocol I than all other portions of the treaty combined.

455. A classic photograph from World War II is that of the magnificent Cologne cathedral standing amidst the ruins of that great city. Several different views are illustrated in E. TAYLOR, *supra* note 3, and W. RANKE, *supra* note 3; another is contained in Parks, *supra* note 5, at 99. The latter illustrates the problem of commingling. To the immediate left of the Cologne cathedral is the *Hauptbahnhof*, or principal railroad passenger terminal, through which civilian and military passengers passed, along with freight trains. The tracks progressed in one direction five hundred meters to the *Guterbahnhof Gereon*, major marshalling and switching yards. Immediately behind the *Hauptbahnhof* and the cathedral flows the Rhine River, across which runs the Mullheim railway bridge which connects the *Guterbahnhof Gereon* and the *Hauptbahnhof* to another marshalling yard. The Rhine itself was a major line of communication for the movement of bargeloads of raw materials for manufacture of military equipment, war supplies, and civilian goods throughout the war. On October 14, 1944, the Mullheim bridge was blasted into the Rhine incidental to the airstrike directed against that city, effectively interdicting Rhine River traffic at that point for the duration of the war, notwithstanding superhuman efforts to remove the obstacle. 200 UNITED STATES STRATEGIC BOMBING SURVEY, THE EFFECTS OF STRATEGIC BOMBING ON GERMAN TRANSPORTATION 2, 5 (2d ed. 1947). The inevitability of collateral civilian casualties and damage is a direct result of the commingling of civilian objects and military objectives that exists in modern society.

456. As previously indicated, the author does not accept as valid or practical the Protocol I emphasis on protection of civilian objects from collateral damage *vis-à-vis* the risk of loss of life to combatants. The Protocol I approach has little humanitarian value. The analysis that follows will concern itself only with the practical problems of minimization of collateral civilian casualties.

Rules would provide "no appreciable protection" for the civilian population because of the problem of commingling, and accordingly developed an elaborate program for the protection and/or evacuation of the civilian population.[457]

In customary international law the primary responsibility for preventing collateral civilian casualties rests with the defender and the individual civilian, with little or no responsibility imposed upon an attacker.[458] The reason for the existing rule is simple. Under most circumstances, the attacker has no idea where civilians are located and, except for a warning, has no way of controlling the location or movement of individual civilians or the civilian population; the civilian population is in the exclusive control of the defender.

The practice of *all* nations that carried out aerial bombardment operations during World Wars I and II establishes clearly that *no* nation concerned itself with the risk of injury to the civilian population of an enemy nation incidental to the conduct of military operations. Protocol I constitutes an improvement in the law of war in recognizing that an attacker should, in most cases, give consideration to minimiza-

---

457. I. O'BRIEN, *supra* note 111, at 18.

458. For example, The British Air Raid Precautions Committee (A.R.P.), which began meeting in May of 1924, determined in the 1930s that:

> "Total war" would be met, in the first instance, by democratic self-help, with responsibility placed squarely in each local community and factory to take the major part in organising its own defences. Service in the A.R.P. was to be looked upon by the individual citizen less as a new form of national service than as service to the particular community in which he lived or carried on his business.

Id. at 14, 284. State responsibility for evacuation of civilians was discussed in the text accompanying *supra* note 111. Two further illustrations are as follows:

> From June to September 1939, more than 3,500,000 British civilians were moved by authorities from areas that were believed most likely to be the targets of Luftwaffe bombing attacks. During the month of September 1939, alone, "an incredible quarter of the population [of London] had changed their address, including 825,000 schoolchildren, 624,000 mothers with children under school age, 13,000 expectant mothers, 7,000 blind people, and 113,000 schoolteachers." B. WICKS, NO TIME TO WAVE GOODBYE 32 (1988).
>
> North Vietnam issued its first order for evacuation of nonessential civilians from the vicinity of Hanoi on February 28, 1965, two days *before* the United States commenced its Rolling Thunder bombing campaign. Only 50,000 persons heeded the order, many of whom subsequently drifted back to their homes once the precise nature of Rolling Thunder was realized. In late 1967, however, as the bombing briefly intensified, mandatory evacuation decreased the civilian population of Hanoi from 600,000 to 400,000. One report stated that:
>
>> Many towns, particularly in the Hanoi/Haiphong area, with their small industry and their local government agencies, have literally moved everthing into the countryside to escape the bombing. The North Vietnamese leave for the country early in the morning and return to their homes in town in the evening. In the Hanoi area, many towns conduct their entire daily business in the suburbs and outlying regions.
>
> Butler, *Analysis and Evaluation of Enemy Capabilities to Degrade Out-Country Interdiction Tactics*, AIR. U. RES. REP. 3575, at 67 (Maxwell Air Force Base, Ala., April 1968). In the lull between the subsequent Linebacker bombing campaigns of 1972, officials on December 4, 1972, ordered the evacuation of all women, children and elderly persons from Hanoi. M. CLODFELTER, *supra* note 224, at 136, 197; Parks, *supra* note 208, at 17.

That most civilians recognize their responsibility to remove themselves from the vicinity of hostilities could be characterized as nothing more than a commonsense rule of self-preservation. It can be illustrated by the fact that in the opening days of the German invasion of France in May 1940, as many as two million Dutch and Belgian civilians and eight million French refugees left their homes to avoid the German advance and hostilities between German and French forces. A. HORNE, TO LOSE A BATTLE: FRANCE 1940 451 (1969).

Chapter VI of Protocol I (articles 61–67) provides protection for civil defense personnel and units. However, it does not obligate a nation to establish a civil defense program for the protection of the civilian population except in occupied territories.

tion of collateral civilian casualties. The issue is the degree to which an attacker should assume this responsibility. If the new rules of Protocol I are to have any credibility, the predominant responsibility must remain with the defender, who has control over the civilian population. A serious stumbling point for Protocol I is that the new rules were seen by some of its drafters, and have been seen by some proponents of the new rules (in most cases the same nations, groups or individuals), as a way of *preventing* attacks entirely. Such a view is unrealistic. Any law of war rule that offers the potential for a military advantage for the defender over the attacker, or vice-versa, is a rule doomed to failure. It not only would increase the risk to the innocent civilian, but in all likelihood would jeopardize the credibility of the law of war itself.

There is no doubt that an attacker can take certain measures to minimize collateral civilian casualties, and bears a reasonable measure of responsibility for doing so. In the 1972 Linebacker II B–52 air strikes against targets in the vicinity of Hanoi and Haiphong, for example, and in the face of the most intense and sophisticated air defenses in military history, measures were taken by aircrews that permitted them to execute and survive their missions while reducing civilian casualties to one of the lowest levels in the history of aerial bombardment.[459] Fourteen years later, U.S. Air

459. For example, Strategic Air Command B–52 radar navigators were briefed to return from their missions without dropping their bombs unless they were one hundred percent certain of their aiming point. All B–52 target maps contained the locations of schools, hospitals, and POW camps, and briefers brought such sites to the attention of a crew if its bomb run was in the proximity of any such object. M. CLODFELTER, *supra* note 224, at 191; and Parks, *supra* note 208, at 19–20. As a result of these and other precautions, the author's research and calculations reveal the following ratio of civilian deaths per ton of bombs dropped during the twelve days of Linebacker II, as compared to other historic bombing missions:

Target	Date(s)	Bomb Tonnage	Civilian Deaths	Deaths per Ton of Bombs
Guernica	26 Apr 1937	40.5	1,654	40.83
Great Britain	Battle of Britain (June–Dec 1940)	40,885	23,002	.56
Coventry	14 Nov 1940	533	568	1.06
Hamburg	24–30 July 1943	5,128.12	42,600	8.03
Remscheid	30–31 July 1943	860	1,120	1.30
Darmstadt	11 Sept 1944	979	8,433	8.61
Dresden	14–15 Feb 1945	7,100.5	25,000	3.52
Tokyo	9–10 Mar 1945	1,655	83,793	50.33
Osaka	13–14 Mar 1945	1,732.6	3,988	2.30
Linebacker II	18–29 Dec 1972	20,237	1,623	.08

For a detailed discussion of the Linebacker II missions, as well as most of these figures, *see* Parks, *supra* note 208. The figures reported therein for Linebacker II tonnage and "civilian" casualties have been amended based on additional information. Strategic Air Command B–52 aircraft delivered 15,000 tons of bombs, while Air Force, Marine Corps and Navy tactical aircraft dropped an additional 5237 tons. The original article considered only the 1318 casualties reported from Hanoi by North Vietnamese officials; another 305 died in Haiphong. M. CLODFELTER, *id.* at 195. However, the deaths per ton of bombs remained the same incredibly low .08, even accepting the North Vietnamese claim that all dead were in fact entitled to classification as noncombatants, and that all deaths could be attributable to combat actions by United States forces.

Force F–111F aircrews in April 1986 attacked terrorist-related targets in Tripoli, Libya, while operating under rules of engagement that maximized concern for collateral civilian casualties.[460] Similarly, American ground and air forces involved in the 1983 Grenada rescue operation and the December 1989 operation to install the democratically-elected government in Panama exercised precautions to protect the lives of individual civilians and the civilian population that exceeded the requirements of Protocol I.[461]

Each of these examples illustrates the basic fact that an attacker can take precautions to minimize collateral civilian casualties. But each should be considered in the context in which it was executed. Linebacker II was an operation with extremely limited objectives, and as a result targets were approved only if they were removed from populated areas, were large enough to ensure that the B–52 bomb train would fall entirely within the target, and could be approached on an axis of attack that avoided overflight of populated areas.

The 1986 Libyan airstrike also had a limited objective, that is, to dissuade Moammar Gadhafi from his continued use of terrorism as a foreign policy tool. Although a target located in a populated area was selected for attack (Aziziyah Barracks, Gadhafi's military headquarters), steps were taken to provide maximum protection to the civilian population. The target had large dimensions—roughly equivalent to the area covered by the Pentagon and its vast parking lots—and the attack was carried out late at night in part because it was known that the civilian population would be off the streets. Following the guidance provided by higher authority, aircrews established mission parameters, including weapons selection, to take all measures possible to minimize the risk of collateral injury or damage. Stringent rules of engagement for the F–111F aircraft assigned to attack Aziziyah Barracks led to a number of aircrews abandoning their mission rather than drop their 2,000-pound GBU–10 laser-guided bombs. Although the weapon itself was selected because of its extremely accurate delivery parameters, and notwithstanding the fact that the aircrews still had the capability to bomb accurately, abandonment of the mission was the result.

---

460. *See* Parks, *supra* note 86, and Parks, *Righting the Rules of Engagement*, 115 U.S. Naval Inst. Proc. (May 1989), for discussion of the United States airstrike against Libya.

461. The best analysis of the 1983 Grenada rescue operation is M. Adkin's Urgent Fury: The Battle for Grenada (1989). The United States emphasis on minimizing civilian casualties during the Panama operation is illustrated by the use of Marine Corps and Army light infantry forces and certain special operations units *vis-à-vis* firepower (artillery or airpower) to attack the Panamanian Defense Forces. This emphasis paralleled the Grenada experience. In each case, however, operations were carried out in the midst of a friendly (or at least benign, as opposed to hostile) population against relatively limited resistance.

A nation may impose limitations upon its forces that are more stringent than those contained in the law of war. For example, consider the way in which U.S. Air Force aircraft were employed in Operation JUST CAUSE, the American military incursion into Panama that commenced on 20 December 1989, to oust dictator Manuel Noreiga and to allow the democratically-elected government of Guillermo Endara to assume office. In the few minutes before U.S. Army Rangers landed near the Rio Hato barracks of the 6th and 7th Rifle Companies of the elite Battalion 2000 of the Panamanian Defense Forces (PDF), United States Air Force F–117A "stealth" fighter-bomber aircraft dropped 2000-pound bombs at the PDF barracks. Originally the barracks, and the PDF forces they housed, were the F–117A targets. The law of war unequivocally recognizes military barracks and the military personnel within them as legitimate targets. But the F–117A mission was changed to drop the bombs on a field near the barracks to confuse, stun and disrupt the PDF rather than kill them. This was because of the desire by American national leaders to accomplish the mission while minimizing alienation of the people of Panama—including PDF members and their relatives. The F–117A aircraft was selected for its precision bombing capabilities, rather than for its "stealth" characteristics. *See* Wilson, *"Stealth" Plane Used in Panama*, Wash. Post, Dec. 24, 1989, at 1; *Cheney Praises Stealth Jets' Role in Strike*, L.A. Times, Dec. 26, 1989, at 12; Morrocco, *F–117A Fighter Used in Combat for First Time in Panama*, 132 Aviation Week & Space Tech. 32–33 (Jan. 1, 1990); Wilson, *Panamanian Commanders Fled Their Posts, Thurman Says*, Wash. Post, Jan. 6, 1990, at A13; and Jehl, *Ranger Force Bore Brunt of Panama Toll*, L.A. Times, Jan. 7, 1990, at 1.

In the Grenada and Panama operations, emphasis was placed on infantry operations under circumstances where firepower (air support or artillery) normally would be employed in a conventional combat environment. This suggests the distinction that United States military and civilian authorities placed on these operations. In each case, given the limited objectives of each mission or operation, American authorities were willing to assume a greater degree of responsibility for minimization of collateral civilian casualties than required by customary law or Protocol I, or that would be acceptable in general war.

The preceding examples illustrate the fact that the United States believes an attacker should accept some responsibility for minimization of collateral civilian casualties. But rules in a law of war treaty must be capable of application across the conflict spectrum. A nation's willingness to assume a greater responsibility for minimization of collateral civilian casualties in peacetime or in a military operation where objectives are limited and national survival is not threatened is not an adequate test for new rules; rules must be considered in the context of the worst case rather than the best. In examining the rules contained in Protocol I, there are two principal difficulties in determining the degree to which an attacker must assume responsibility.

The first is the degree of responsibility, consistent with mission accomplishment and security of the attacking force. The provisions of article 57 require that a commander "do everything *feasible*"[462] or "take all *feasible* precautions"[463] in order to minimize collateral civilian casualties. Protocol I fails to define *feasible*, however. In the course of the Diplomatic Conference the NATO allies defined the term as "that which is practicable or practically possible, taking into account all circumstances ruling at the time, including those relevant to the success of military operations."[464]

At the time of their respective ratifications of Protocol I, Switzerland and Austria took reservations to paragraph 2 of article 57 to the effect that the information available at the time of the decision is decisive as to the steps required of a commander.[465] The *ICRC Commentary* rejects the NATO-nation definition with an

462. Article 57(a)(i).

463. Article 57(a)(ii).

464. Statement of the United Kingdom at the time of signature (12 December 1977), as found in SCHINDLER & TOMAN, *supra* note 27, at 717. India "expressed the understanding that Art. 57 as a whole will apply in accordance with the limits of capability, practical possibility and feasibility of each Party to the conflict. . . . These capabilities will vary, and 'this article does not require a Party to undertake to do something which is not within its means or methods or its capability. In its practical application, a Party would be required to do whatever is practical or possible.' " NEW RULES FOR VICTIMS OF ARMED CONFLICTS, *supra* note 257, at 362, n.8.

Subsequently the term *feasible* was defined in paragraph 5 of article I of Protocol III (Incendiary Weapons) of the 1980 United Nations Conventional Weapons Convention as "those precautions which are practicable or practically possible taking into account all circumstances ruling at the time, including humanitarian and military considerations." SCHINDLER & TOMAN, *supra* note 27, at 190. The statements upon ratification of the 1977 Protocol I of Belgium (*Id.* at 707), Italy (*Id.* at 712), and the Netherlands (*Id.* at 714) reflect the wording contained in this definition.

465. ICRC COMMENTARY, *supra* note 247, at 682, n.9. As indicated earlier, the Protocols were heavily influenced by Swiss diplomatic authorities, but were not the product of the closest of coordination with Swiss military authorities. The Swiss military review was highly critical of Protocol I, and the Government of Switzerland managed to obtain consent for ratification only after heavy lobbying by the ICRC and diplomatic officials who argued that it would be a substantial embarrassment if Switzerland did not ratify, because (a) the Diplomatic Conference had been financed and hosted by Switzerland, and (b) the Protocols were home grown, *i.e.*, a product of the ICRC. The Swiss reservation to paragraph 2 of article 57 was a concession demanded by the Swiss military before consenting to ratification.

explanation that repudiates the basis for the Swiss and Austrian reservations as well, stating that:

> The last-mentioned criterion [success of military operations] seems too broad, having regard to the requirements of . . . [article 57]. There might be reason to fear that by invoking the success of military operations in general, one might end up by neglecting the humanitarian obligations prescribed here . . . . What is required of the person launching an offensive is to take the necessary identification measures in good time in order to spare the population as far as possible. It is not clear how the success of military operations could be jeopardized by this.[466]

The ICRC statement illustrates a basic problem in implementation of the requirements of Protocol I. It also manifests the lack of appreciation by the ICRC of military operations. Most important, it indicates the radical shift intended by the ICRC and certain nations from the customary practice of nations with regard to responsibility for minimization of collateral civilian casualties.

A standard has been arrived at in a law of war treaty that has been praised for its "consensus"—yet there is no agreement on what the standard really means. One would hope that common sense and good faith would be the basis for the implementation of any law of war treaty. But on the battlefield, general, hortatory statements lose their value if they fail to follow common sense or established battle procedures and the principles of war. Moreover, lack of agreement places military commanders at undue risk of war crimes allegations for good-faith decisions made in the heat of battle and the fog of war.

Two essential elements appear to have been lost in the process to date. The first is the principle of war of *surprise*. It has been recognized in the codified law of war throughout this century. Article 26 of the Annex to Hague Convention IV of 1907 provides: "The officer in command of an attacking force must, before commencing a bombardment, *except in cases of assault*, do all in his power to warn the authorities."[467] This has been amended by paragraph 2(c) of article 57 of Protocol I,

---

466. ICRC COMMENTARY, *supra* note 247, at 682. As will be noted in the adoption of a similar definition in the 1980 United Nations Conventional Weapons Convention, contained in *supra* note 460, the rationale of the ICRC in opposition to this definition was rejected by this later conference. Whether the definition in the 1980 treaty will be applied by nations to the 1977 Protocol remains to be seen, although the statements on ratification by Belgium, Italy, and the Netherlands suggest that such may prove to be the case.

467. SCHINDLER & TOMAN, *supra* note 27, at 84. Article 3 of Hague Convention IX of 1907 (Concerning Bombardment by Naval Forces in Time of War) states that, "After due notice has been given, the bombardment of undefended ports, towns, villages, dwellings or buildings may be commenced." However, article 6 of the same treaty provides that: "If the military situation permits, the commander of the attacking force, before commencing the bombardment, must do his utmost to warn the authorities." *Id.* at 813. During World War II, warnings generally were not given prior to air raids in enemy territory, because enemy radar and signals intelligence generally would detect a bombing force as it assembled for a strike. Also, while perhaps not knowing the precise target, in tracking the force would be able to ascertain the approximate geographic area against which the attack would be directed. Warnings were given, on the other hand, for enemy-occupied territory, though usually for the area to be raided rather than for the target *per se*. In at least one case, the target was specified. Ninety minutes before the United States Eighth Air Force B–17 bombers attacked the Skoda armament works in Pilsen, Czechoslovakia, on 25 April 1945, the following warning was broadcast: "Allied bombers are out in great strength today. Their destination may be the Skoda works. Skoda workers get out and stay out until the afternoon." J. SPAIGHT, *supra* note 137, at 242.

A warning may be general rather than specific. Thus in 1945 the United States Twentieth Air Force dropped leaflets listing cities that would be bombed, and which were bombed subsequently. *Id.* at 242. On 23 July 1950, the following warning was broadcast by the United Nations Command to the civilian population of North Korea:

> [W]e are asking you to please leave any areas in North Korea where there are military targets, because the [United Nations] bombers will be back again and again. The United Nations planes

which states that, "Effective advance warning shall be given of attacks which may affect the civilian population, unless circumstances do not permit."[468]

The first element that has been lost in the ICRC's rejection of the suggested definition of *feasible* is the necessity for surprise. Perhaps more critical, however, is the reason behind the requirement for warning stated in Hague Conventions IV and IX, and in article 57(2)(c) of Protocol I: it enables the Government controlling the civilian population to see to its evacuation from the vicinity of military objectives that might be subject to attack; it also permits individual civilians to remove themselves and their property from high-risk areas.[469] There is little else that an attacker can do to avoid injury to individual civilians or the civilian population as such. Any attempt to increase an attacker's responsibility—particularly where a defender has failed or elected not to discharge his responsibility for the safety of the civilian population—will prove futile.

Recognizing this responsibility, and the dilemma posed by commingling, aside from the fundamental requirement imposed by article 48, two other provisions of Protocol I set out obligations for a defender. Each has been quoted previously. The

---

> have no desire to harm individuals who are not engaged in war work at military targets. Military targets are: railroads and railroad facilities, docks and harbors, bridges, power plants, factories helping the war, ships and boats, air fields and supply warehouses.
>
> If you work and live near any of these areas, get out now before it is too late. Refuse to endanger your lives.

10 DIGEST OF INTERNATIONAL LAW 140 (1968).

468. SCHINDLER & TOMAN, *supra* note 27, at 655.

469. LAUTERPACHT, *supra* note 433, at 420, deals with the matter rather unequivocally: "The purpose of notification is to enable private individuals within the locality to seek shelter for their persons and for their personal property." Similarly, in describing low-level strafing attacks on German transportation in France and Belgium in the days following D-Day (6 June 1944), the biographer of RAF hero Stanford Tuck observes that:

> Inevitably, a number of Frenchmen and Belgians were killed or injured by the strafing [Hurricanes] —the pilots knew that, but they never talked about it, because there was no foolproof way of ensuring only that Germans died. Propaganda broadcasts strove to warn civilians to stay away from possible targets, and formation leaders often risked their lives, and those of their pilots, by making "dummy runs" over factories and crowded bridges and then holding off to give people time to run clear before they attacked.

L. FORRESTER, FLY FOR YOUR LIFE 258–59 (London, 1956, and New York, 1978). A fundamental problem that many proponents of Protocol I have is an overreliance on article 57(2)(b), which states in part that:

> An attack shall be cancelled or suspended if it becomes apparent that the . . . attack may be expected to cause incidental loss of civilian life, injury to civilians, damage to civilian objects, or a combination thereof, which would be excessive in relation to the concrete and direct military advantage anticipated.

SCHINDLER & TOMAN, *supra* note 27, at 655. In the course of numerous fora on the Protocols, the author has asked an equally numerous number of proponents what an attacker is expected to do if the enemy civilian population fails to heed warning of an impending attack, or if the defender forces the civilian population to remain in or near an obvious military objective. The answer inevitably has been to rely on the language from article 57 quoted above, an answer which is altogether impractical. Such a solution would encourage certain nations to continue to fail to discharge their responsibilities to separate the civilian population from military objectives, as specified in article 48, and not to shield military objectives from attack through use of the civilian population, as prohibited by article 51(7). Read together, the quotes from LAUTERPACHT and FORRESTER illustrate that the individual civilian has an obligation to remove himself from the vicinity of a military objective, particularly after being duly warned, and that there are a limited number of things an attacker can do to separate the civilian population from a military objective, after which the individual civilian and the defender must assume responsibility for the consequences of their action or inaction.

first, article 58, admonishes a defender (a) to "endeavor to remove the civilian population, individual civilians and civilian objects under their control from the vicinity of military objectives," and (b) to "avoid locating military objectives within or near densely populated areas."[470]

In practical terms, article 58 can do little more than admonish. For hygiene, morale, communications and other reasons, military personnel and units historically have been billeted or housed in populated areas, and the doctrine of most nations provides for a continuation of this practice; it should not necessarily be viewed as sinister. Moreover, it is not always possible to remove the civilian population or individual civilians from the vicinity of a military objective for any extended period of time, particularly if there is a shortage of housing and/or the weather is severe. Nothing can be done to move immovable civilian objects in order to protect them from attack. Movable civilian objects can be removed from the proximity of military objectives, as was illustrated in the protection provided cultural property at the time of the German invasion of the Soviet Union.[471]

The provisions contained in article 58 are not obligatory. Had they been so drafted, individual nations would have fallen back upon the priority given sovereign rights over obligations incurred in an international law treaty with respect to obligations for defense of their own territory. Thus in accepting this article, the Republic of Korea offered the following statement in explanation of its vote at the Diplomatic Conference:

> [I]t is the understanding of my delegation that this provision does not constitute a restriction on a State's military installations on its own territory. We consider that military facilities necessary for a country's national defense should be decided on the basis of the actual needs and other considerations of that particular country. An attempt to regulate a country's requirements and the fulfilment of those requirements in this connection would not conform to actualities.[472]

In addition to the Korean statement, there were nations—including Switzerland—that had difficulty with article 58 following the Diplomatic Conference. The article requires separation of civilians and civilian objects from military objectives "to the maximum extent feasible." In ratifying Protocol I, both Switzerland and Austria reserved article 58, declaring that each would be bound by its provisions subject to the requirements for the defense of their national territory.[473] While many nations have become party to Protocol I without a similar reservation, the statements of Switzerland and Austria are entirely consistent with statements frequently made by Socialist nations regarding the precedent sovereignty has over law of war obligations in the defense of their territory.

Protocol I does make a distinction between a failure to separate civilians from the vicinity of military objectives and the intentional placement of military objectives in populated areas or the movement of civilians into the vicinity of military objectives in order to shield the military objectives from attack. Article 58 addresses the former to the extent that it can be resolved; paragraph 7 of article 51 (to be discussed, infra) is

470. Quoted in its entirety in the text associated with *supra* note 447.
471. As detailed in *supra* note 215.
472. ICRC COMMENTARY, *supra* note 247, at 693. France voted against article 51 on the basis that paragraphs 4, 5, and 7 would seriously hinder the conduct of defensive operations against an invader. Sixteen other nations abstained without explanation, but for the same reason. NEW RULES FOR VICTIMS OF ARMED CONFLICTS, *supra* note 257, at 317.
473. ICRC COMMENTARY, *supra* note 247, at 693; and SCHINDLER & TOMAN, *supra* note 27, at 705 (Austria) and 716 (Switzerland). This reservation is another example of the failure of coordination with the Swiss military during the course of the negotiation of Protocol I.

directed at the latter, which is the second provision setting out the obligations of a defender for minimization of civilian casualties. Jean S. Pictet's earlier comments regarding this practice of using the civilian population as a shield during World War II merit repeating:

> During the last World War public opinion was shocked by certain instances . . . of belligerents compelling civilians to remain in places of strategic importance (such as railway stations, viaducts, dams, power stations or factories), or to accompany military convoys, or again, to serve as a protective screen for . . . fighting troops. Such practice, the object of which is to divert enemy fire, have rightly been condemned as cruel and barbaric . . . .[474]

However much it may shock public opinion, the practice continues. Writing of his experience in the Korean War, a British officer reported that the North Koreans

> have concentrated, in a country which is a mass of small villages with few towns, always in the villages, where they could put their troops under cover, their trucks in houses, and their tanks in barns, and where, in a quite small village, two or three battalions could practically disappear from sight. To get them out of these hide-outs has required very extensive damage to the civilian population of Korea. It is one of the most unhappy and lamentable features of the campaign that in the effort to extract the Communists from these village strongholds, the civilian population has suffered abnormally, even worse than in wars in the West.[475]

The United States' experience during the Vietnam War was similar to that of Korea. In the Republic of Vietnam, Viet Cong routinely launched their 122mm and 140mm rockets at American and Allied positions, or cities, from the center of a village at night. They did this in the hope that American and Allied forces would initiate counterbattery fire that would destroy the village, or that the civilian population would shield their excape.[476] In the air campaigns over the Democratic Republic of Vietnam, the North Vietnamese purposely placed surface-to-air missile sites, antiaircraft gun positions, and ground-control radar equipment within or immediately adjacent to populated areas in order to shield this military equipment from attack. Convoys full of loaded military trucks were parked in full view on the streets of cities and villages during daylight hours, venturing onto the highways only under the cover of darkness, using populated areas and the civilian population as a screen from attack in daylight.[477]

---

474. GC COMMENTARY, *supra* note 208, at 208.

475. Wykeham-Barnes, *The War in Korea with Special Reference to the Difficulties of Using Our Air Power*, J. ROYAL UNITED SERVICE INST. 149–58, at 153 (May 1952). Similarly, in a statement made on August 7, 1950, United States Secretary of State Dean Acheson issued the following statement in defense of American use of airpower in response to the North Korean invasion of South Korea:

> The air activity of the United Nations forces in Korea has been, and is, directed solely at military targets of the invader. These targets are enemy troop concentrations, supply dumps, war plants and communications lines. It is well known that the Communist command has compelled helpless civilians to labor on these military sites. Peaceful villages are used to cover the tanks of the invading army.

DIGEST OF INTERNATIONAL LAW, *supra* note 467, at 140.

476. Personal knowledge and experience of the author. For example, on November 20, 1968, the author's unit headquarters was struck by 140mm rockets fired from within the outskirts of the city of Da Nang. The rockets were fired on market day—the day in which the city was packed with civilians from surrounding villages who had come to shop—in the hope that U.S. forces would overreact with counterbattery fire that would kill or injure a maximum number of civilians. We realized the enemy's intent, however, and counterbattery fire was checked.

477. See the aerial photographs contained in Parks, *supra* note 109, at 14 and 19. The author's files contain a collection of more than 100 aerial photographs taken in the course of the United States air campaigns over North Vietnam illustrating the North Vietnamese practice of using its population and

These types of activities are addressed in Protocol I by several provisions. The first, however, shifts the burden for civilian casualty avoidance entirely to an attacker. Paragraph 5(a) of article 51 makes *indiscriminate* "an attack by bombardment by any methods or means which treats as a single military objective a number of clearly separated and distinct military objectives located in a city, town, village or other area containing a similar concentration of civilians or civilian objects . . . ."[478]

Throughout the Diplomatic Conference, the United States had serious objections to this article; these objections remain. One concerns the issue of ambiguity. In the course of the Diplomatic Conference, the American delegation expressed the understanding that the words "clearly separated" referred not only to a separation of two or more military objectives which can be observed or which are visually separated, but also includes the element of a significant distance between those military objectives. Further, the distance must be at least of such a distance as to permit the individual military objectives to be attacked separately, and the American Delegation stated unequivocally that "States are responsible themselves if they misuse their own civilian population by attempting to shield military objectives from attack."[479] While some delegations agreed with the position taken by the United States, there remains a fundamental disagreement as to the interpretation of this provision.

An issue not adequately addressed in the course of the negotiation of article 51(5)(a) but having specifically to do with a defender's actions and his responsibility for collateral civilian casualties is the practice of dispersal. While there has been condemnation of so-called area bombing during World War II,[480] and article 51(5)(a) was prepared with the intent of prohibiting this practice,[481] Protocol I failed to address actions taken by a defender to disperse military equipment, industrial facilities, and similar legitimate targets among civilian objects and the civilian population as such in order to screen those military objectives from lawful attack. While area bombing during World War II was caused in part by bombing inaccuracies and the intensity of enemy defenses, an equal cause was this dispersal of legitimate targets not only to prevent their detection but also to use the civilian population as a shield to preclude their attack. In the words of one law of war treatise, area bombing

> came about during the course of the Allied attempts to destroy German war industry. Much of the industry was concentrated in comparatively small areas, particularly that of the Ruhr. By 1942, such areas were so heavily defended against air attack and military objectives so carefully concealed and camouflaged that it was practically impossible for attacking aircraft to identify and attack particular targets.
>
> In reply, the Allies evolved the tactic of target-area bombing. The idea behind this was that if the attackers cannot see their objective because of measures taken by the enemy, they will bomb the spot where they know the objective to be.[482]

---

civilian objects to shield military targets from attack. One of the author's favorites is a photograph of the Haiphong cultural center, an amphitheater, with some 200 Soviet-built trucks, laden with military equipment, parked within or on its perimeter. The photograph is used in Parks, *supra* note 5, at 109, and Parks, *supra* note 109, at 19. It may be argued that under the circumstances the Haiphong cultural center could have been attacked inasmuch as the North Vietnamese actions had caused it to forfeit its protection as a civilian object. This entirely correct legal answer must be weighed against the propaganda value the North Vietnamese would have gained from worldwide headlines declaring that the United States had bombed a "cultural center."

478. SCHINDLER & TOMAN, *supra* note 27, at 651.

479. NEW RULES FOR VICTIMS OF ARMED CONFLICTS, *supra* note 257, at 309; and Law of War Working Group, *supra* note 294, at I–51–7.

480. *See* Blix, *Area Bombardment: Rules and Reasons*, 49 THE BRITISH YEAR BOOK OF INTERNATIONAL LAW 31–69 (1978).

481. NEW RULES FOR VICTIMS OF ARMED CONFLICTS, *supra* note 257, at 309.

482. M. GREENSPAN, THE MODERN LAW OF LAND WARFARE 335–36 (1959).

The experience of World War II was repeated in Korea and in the air war over North Vietnam. Speaking of the former, one authority described the situation as follows:

> Segments of industry had located in residential sections of cities and towns, setting up dispersed production units in Korean homes. War materiel was again being manufactured . . . . This new move created a problem for U.N. commanders . . . . To destroy industry dispersed in residential areas would require area bombing of whole cities, entailing mass slaughter of thousands of innocent civilians forced to remain in the cities as a shield against attack.[483]

To remedy this problem, paragraph 7 of article 51 states that:

> The presence or movements of the civilian population or individual civilians shall not be used to render certain points or areas immune from military operations, in particular in attempts to shield military objectives from attacks or to shield, favor or impede military opertations. The parties to the conflict shall not direct the movement of the civilian population or individual civilians in order to attempt to shield military objectives from attacks or to shield military operations.[484]

Under the customary law of war, casualties resulting from a defender's use of the civilian population as concealment or cover from attack of legitimate military objectives are not the responsibility of the attacker so long as he has exercised ordinary care. Writing in the first edition of his classic *Air Power and War Rights*, James Maloney Spaight observed that,

> as a belligerent cannot allow himself to be prejudiced because the enemy locates...[military] objectives in places where they cannot be destroyed without incidental injury to civilians, he is not responsible for the resulting damage provided all due care is taken to prevent unnecessary injury. . . .[485]

Similarly, the current Air Force law of war manual states that:

> The failure of states to segregate and separate their own military activities, and particularly to avoid placing military objectives in or near populated areas and to remove such objectives from populated areas, significantly and substantially weakens effective protection for their own population. A party to a conflict which places its own citizens in positions of danger by failing to carry out the separation of military activities from civilian activities necessarily accepts, under international law, the results of otherwise lawful attacks upon valid military objectives in their territory.[486]

Professor Morris Greenspan comments that:

> Any legal justification of target-area bombing must be based on two factors. The first must be the fact that the area is so preponderantly used for war industry as to impress that character on the whole of the neighborhood, making it essentially an indivisible whole. The second factor must be that the area is so heavily defended from air attack that the selection of specific targets within the area is impracticable.

---

483. AIRPOWER: THE DECISIVE FORCE IN KOREA 131 (1950). With reference to the U.S. air campaigns over North Vietnam, the author's collection of aerial photographs contains numerous pictures of North Vietnamese dispersal of war materiel (such as barrels of oil) to the center of villages or adjacent to or on the earthwork dikes and dams of the Red River Valley.. Some of these photographs are contained in Parks, *supra* note 109, at 15.

484. SCHINDLER & TOMAN, *supra* note 27, at 651–52. Article 28 of the Geneva Convention Relative to the Protection of Civilian Persons in Time of War also is relevant to consideration of article 51 of Protocol I. It provides that "The presence of a protected person may not be used to render certain points or areas immune from military operations." *Id.* at 511.

485. J. SPAIGHT (1924), *supra* note 163, at 244.

486. DEPARTMENT OF THE AIR FORCE, AIR FORCE PAMPHLET 110–31, INTERNATIONAL LAW—THE CONDUCT OF ARMED CONFLICT AND AIR OPERATIONS 5–13 (1976).

> In such circumstances, the whole area might be regarded as a defended place from the standpoint of attack from the air, and its status, for that purpose, assimilated to that of a defended place attacked by land troops. In the latter case, the attacking force may attack the whole of the defended area in order to overcome the defense, and incurs no responsibility for unavoidable damage to civilians and nonmilitary property caused by the seeking-out of military objectives in the bombardment.[487]

But Protocol I provides no language as to the responsibility for collateral civilian casualties in the event a defender resorts to actions in violation of article 51(7), or disperses military objectives amongst civilian objects or the civilian population to create the type of situation anticipated by article 51(5)(a). Placing civilians in proximity to a military position that is likely to be attacked with the intent of shielding that object from attack differs little from lining up those same civilians and executing them by firing squad; the same premeditation is required. Protocol I avoids the question, stating only that in the event a defender undertakes actions in violation of article 51(7), "any violation . . . shall not release the Parties from their legal obligations with respect to the civilian population and civilians, including the obligation to take the precautionary measures provided for in article 57."[488]

The rationale for article 51(8) is clear: the fact that one party to a conflict is violating the law of war should not be an excuse for the other party to cease to take reasonable steps to minimize injury to the civilian population in the conduct of combat operations. However, Protocol I fails to state the fact that the illegal act—the violation of article 51(7)—is the crime that places innocent civilians at risk, while attack of a lawful target is a legitimate act authorized by the law of war. While an attacker facing a target shielded from attack by civilians is not relieved from his duty to exercise reasonable precautions to minimize the loss of civilian life, neither is he obligated to assume any additional responsibility as a result of the illegal acts of the defender. Were an attacker to do so, his erroneous assumption of additional responsibility with regard to protecting the civilians shielding a lawful target would serve as an incentive for a defender to continue to violate the law of war by exposing other innocent civilians to similar risk. But a reading of Protocol I and the *ICRC Commentary* establishes that the question of responsibility was not avoided by the delegates to the Diplomatic Conference; it was the intent of the ICRC and the Group of 77 to shift entirely to the attacker the responsibility for civilian casualties incidental to a lawful attack upon a legitimate military objective.[489]

487. M. Greenspan, *supra* note 482, at 336.

488. Schindler & Toman, *supra* note 27, at 652. Although article 51(8) states "Any violations of these provisions . . .," the ICRC Commentary, *supra* note 247, at 628 confirms that the prohibitions referred to in paragraph 8 are those contained in paragraph 7. The ICRC Commentary correctly notes (a) that a defender's violation of article 51(7) should not be regarded as a material breach for which the attacker may suspend operation of the treaty or its provisions, and (b) that an attacker may meet its obligations in part through warnings (general or specific) to the civilian population, as the United States did in its air operations over North Korea and North Vietnam, and as the Israeli Air Force did in Lebanon. But it fails to address the issue of whether an attacker must assume a greater responsibility for collateral civilian casualties where a defender has violated article 51(7). The ICRC Commentary does make reference to the fact that the attacker's responsibilities include those of article 57(2)(a)(iii), the so-called "rule" of proportionality. However, it is the author's view that the attacker's responsibility remains one of due care. Any interpretation that would provide a defender an advantage over the attacker through a violation of the law of war would be contrary to the very spirit of the law of war while placing innocent civilians at unreasonable risk.

489. Thus the ICRC Commentary, *supra* note 247, at 620 states that:

> The armed forces and their installations may be attacked wherever they are, except when the attack could incidentally result in loss of human life among the civilian population, injuries to civilians, and damage to civilian objects which would be excessive in relation to the expected direct and specific military advantage.

In this respect, Protocol I departs from historic practice and customary international law. Civilians are protected from intentional attack so long as they do not participate in the hostilities, and civilian objects are protected from intentional attack so long as they are not being used for military purposes, subject to the exceptions previously discussed. But civilians and civilian objects are at risk of injury or damage if they are in the vicinity of a legitimate target. Thus article 8 of the 1954 Hague Convention on Cultural Property provides special protection for a limited number of refuges for movable cultural property on the condition that they:

> (a) are situated at an adequate distance from any large industrial center or from any important military objective constituting a vulnerable point, such as, for example, an aerodrome, broadcasting station, establishment engaged upon work of national defense, a port or railway station of relative importance or a main line of communication;
>
> (b) are not used for military purposes.[490]

Protocol I is a conscious effort by the ICRC, Switzerland, and Sweden—working through the Third World—to shift the responsibility for collateral civilian casualties from the defender to the attacker. The reason for this attempted shift is the tone the Diplomatic Conference took in favoring actions of the defender over those of an attacker, and in endeavoring to limit lawful attacks to the immediate battlefield. Thus a leading Swedish participant in the negotiation of the 1977 Protocols, in his condemnation of aerial bombardment operations, made a careful (but historically and legally incorrect) distinction regarding risk to the civilian population incidental to combat operations between land forces (that is, on the "battlefield," in its most limited sense) and extended air operations:

> Bombardment of a whole area within which various objectives are found can be used for other purposes than those which were common in Allied bombings of German cities during the Second World War. A whole area might be bombarded—by air or artillery—in preparation for an attack by land forces. The aim in such cases is to destroy *not productive capacity, but military personnel, arms and vehicles*. Although in such cases, too, civilians and civilian objects might be much

---

The ICRC COMMENTARY makes no distinction between collateral civilian casualties incidental to legitimate military operations and those caused by a defender's action (such as in violation of paragraph 7 of article 51) or inaction (such as in violation of the fundamental principle of article 48, through a failure to evacuate the civilian population from a contested area), or those occurring as a result of actions not within the control of either the attacker or defender, such as the crash of an aircraft downed by enemy air defenses. The intent of Protocol I clearly is to shift the responsibility for collateral civilian casualties to the attacker, notwithstanding actions of the defender.

The problem is exacerbated by the prohibition on reprisals against the civilian population or civilians contained in paragraph 6 of article 51. SCHINDLER & TOMAN, *supra* note 27, at 651. Assume, for example, that a defender has shielded an important military objective from attack by placing it in the midst of a densely populated area of a city, notwithstanding warnings (radio broadcasts, leaflet drops) that targets placed in populated areas will not be immune from attack. Assume also that, despite the use of extraordinary care by the attack force, some collateral civilian casualties occur. Under customary international law the attacker would be justified in stating that the responsibility for the civilian casualties rests with the defender. He would still be able to make such an argument notwithstanding Protocol I, but the defender would be able to argue that the attacker's actions constitute a reprisal in violation of article 51(6). This may appear to be the usual propaganda battle that occurs in any conflict, but it is much more, in that the language imbalance of Protocol I has given the defender's argument the greater appearance of legitimacy.

490. SCHINDLER & TOMAN, *supra* note 27, at 749–50. Similarly, in its ratification of the 1977 Protocol I, Italy declared with respect to article 53, Protection of Cultural Property and of Places of Worship, that "If and so long as the objectives protected by Article 53 are unlawfully used for military purposes, they will thereby lose their protection." *Id.* at 713. Italy's declaration is particularly candid in light of its experience with the destruction of Monte Cassino by the Allies during World War II, as discussed *supra* note 215.

affected, this kind of area pounding or saturation bombing has hardly been criticized by modern authorities. The military need for it is evident and the humanitarian case against it is not strong. The areas that might be affected by such attacks are likely to be less numerous than the areas which might be chosen for attack, e.g. because they contain productive capacity that is deemed militarily relevant. Moreover, civilians are likely to have moved from areas which are on the verge of becoming battlefields. If, in exceptional cases, the civilian population is still present, e.g. in a city, the rules on siege would apply.[491]

This attempt is not new. Paragraph 3 of article 24 of the rejected 1923 Hague Air Rules states: "The bombardment of cities, towns, villages, dwellings or buildings not in the immediate neighborhood of the operations of land forces is prohibited. In cases where . . . [military] objectives . . . are so situated, that they cannot be bombarded without indiscriminate bombardment of the civilian population, the aircraft must abstain from bombardment."[492]

The purpose behind the language of article 24(3) of the 1923 Hague Air Rules was the same as that behind the language of articles 51(5)(a) and (b) and 57 of Protocol I, as illustrated by the comment above by the Swedish delegate to the Diplomatic Conference. Speaking of the 1923 provision, M. W. Royse wrote in 1928 that, "To interpret "indiscriminate bombardment," as laid down in paragraph 3 of article 24, on the basis of incidental damage to non-combatant populations, would thus, in effect, eliminate aerial bombardment."[493]

This was precisely the intent of the 1923 Hague Air Rules and the provisions under consideration. The fundamental problem with articles 51 and 57 and their emphasis on the minimization of collateral civilian casualties is the attempt to shift responsibility for collateral civilian casualties to an attacker, notwithstanding actions (or the failure to act) by a defender, and to attempt to make a distinction with regard to the legality of attacks in the vicinity of enemy lines as opposed to the extended battlefield. The intent of the latter was to limit the airpower capabilities of certain nations, particularly the superpowers and Israel. The effect on innocent civilians, however, can be seen in the following actions that have occurred since conclusion of the Diplomatic Conference. Viewed in this light, Protocol I loses a substantial amount of its humanitarian lustre:

— In response to the 1982 Israeli incursion into Lebanon, the Palestinian Liberation Organization (PLO) announced its intent to abide by the requirements of the four 1949 Geneva Conventions and the 1977 Protocols. It immediately shifted its defensive positions into Lebanese towns, villages, and cities, where it emplaced its artillery and antiaircraft weapons on top of or immediately adjacent to hospitals, churches, or mosques. The PLO did this in order to shield the weapons from attack or cause damage to these protected objects while attempting to negate the superiority the Israeli Defense Forces (IDF) and Israeli Air Force (IAF) enjoyed in firepower (armor and artillery) and airpower, respectively, and to increase the likelihood of heavy IDF and Lebanese civilian casualties in costly house-to-house fighting. On retreating to Beirut, the PLO positioned its weapons adjacent to foreign embassies in order to achieve the same protection. It moved other equipment and forces into the lower floors of high-rise apartment buildings, while forcing the civilian tenants of those buildings to remain in the upper floors to shield the PLO from attack.

The IAF employed certain steps and very strict rules of engagement to provide protection for the civilian population in the course of its attack of PLO fixed positions.

491. Blix, *supra* note 478, at 52–53.
492. SCHINDLER & TOMAN, *supra* note 27, at 210.
493. M. ROYSE, 1928, *supra* note 156, at 232.

These included the dropping of several million leaflets to warn the civilian population to depart anticipated areas of conflict; development of highly detailed targeting maps for built-up areas to distinguish military objectives from civilian objects and other specially-protected property; positive verification of all objects as military objectives prior to authorization of any attack; establishment of a requirement to abort any bomb run if the aircraft lost the redundancy in its bomb-aiming equipment; marking of each target to minimize misidentification; delivery of a single bomb per bomb run; dropping each bomb at absolute minimum altitudes under visual (rather than radar-bombing) conditions only, at substantial risk to aircrews; verification of bomb damage where it was believed a hit had been achieved, before continuing strikes; and use of the most accurate munitions.

Notwithstanding these precautions, which are among the highest imposed by any nation in any armed conflict, the ICRC issued a public statement on 10 June 1982 calling upon Israel *only* to cease actions which placed the civilian population at risk. The ICRC also released erroneous, unconfirmed civilian casualty figures based upon information it had obtained from the head of the Palestinian Red Crescent Society—PLO Chairman Yasser Arafat's brother.[494]

---

494. Author's personal knowledge. In May 1983 the author was sent to the Middle East by the Secretary of Defense to examine the law of war issues involved in the 1982 Israeli incursion into Lebanon, and specifically to investigate Israeli Air Force (IAF) employment of airpower in light of allegations of "indiscriminate bombing" by the ICRC and supporters of the PLO. The author had access to all-source intelligence, and met with military experts (United States and foreign) who witnessed PLO actions and IAF operations. Whatever the feelings of the observers toward Israel, and they were mixed, they were unanimous in their confirmation of the IAF's exercise of care for the civilian population of Beirut in light of the PLO's efforts at using that population as a shield from attack. The author also obtained an unpublished paper prepared by Trevor Dupuy, who witnessed Israeli Defense Force (IDF) and IAF operations, which confirmed official eyewitness accounts. For his analysis of the IAF attack of 12 August 1982 (the heaviest of the incursion) *see Journalism and the Conduct of War* in T. DUPUY & P. MARTELL, FLAWED VICTORY 167–74 (1986), which may be summed up with the following:

> The PLO gained a propaganda advantage by forcing the Israelis to fire on military targets in civilian environments that should have been protected under . . . [the law of war]. A propaganda victory was won in the western world, and even in Israel, because of the double standard applied by the news media, which—on balance—grossly distorted the facts, and failed to present all of the considerations affecting the civilian loss of life and private property damage.

Id. at 174. *See* R. GABRIEL, OPERATION PEACE FOR GALILEE 132–76 (1984), *see also* Z. CHAFETS, DOUBLE VISION 304–05 (1985). A classic example of the actions of the press was NBC's John Chancellor broadcasting from Beirut, describing the IAF air attacks on the PLO, with destroyed buildings in the background, suggesting that the destruction had occurred as a result of the Israeli air attacks on the PLO. In fact, the buildings were in an entirely different part of Beirut from the area in which the PLO was located, and had been destroyed in earlier fighting not involving Israel or its military forces during Lebanon's civil war.

The ICRC statement referred to in the body of this article is contained in ICRC Press Release No. 1444, Geneva, June 11, 1982, and states:

> Lebanon: Solemn Appeal by the ICRC on Behalf of the Population. Yesterday evening, 10 June 1982, the International Committee of the Red Cross (ICRC) appealed formally and solemnly to highest authorities of Israel, demanding that all measures possible be taken so that civilians, whatever their nationality, be spared in the conflict in Lebanon. Specific mention was made of the fighting in Beirut.

Representatives of the ICRC subsequently justified their actions on the basis of the authority provided them by article 81(1) of Protocol I, which provides:

> The Parties to the conflict shall grant to the [ICRC] all facilities within their power so as to enable it carry out the humanitarian functions assigned to it by the Conventions and this Protocol in order to ensure protection and assistance to the victims of conflicts; the [ICRC] may also carry out any

— In the days immediately preceding the 1986 U.S. airstrike against terrorist-related targets in Libya, Libyan leader Moammar Gadhafi warned that he was going to take hostage British, Italian, and American civilians working in his country, and place them within or around key military positions to shield those objectives from attack.[495]

— Upon discovery of the Libyan chemical weapon facility at Rabta in 1989, there was speculation of an attack upon it by American or other military forces to pre-empt its operation. Among those employed in its construction were 270 Thai nationals. The United States urged Thailand to remove its nationals from the Rabta construction facility so that they would not be at risk in the event of its attack. Gadhafi advised the Government of Thailand that he would expel all Thai nationals working in Libya—estimated at between 25,000 and 75,000—if Thailand acceded to the United States' request.[496] Notwithstanding the fact that Libya was the second nation to ratify Protocol I, its purpose was clear—to use the Thai nationals to shield the Rabta chemical weapons plant from attack.[497]

---

other humanitarian activities in favor of these victims, subject to the consent of the Parties to the conflict concerned.

SCHINDLER & TOMAN, *supra* note 27, at 669–70. The ICRC statement departed from the ICRC's usual practice in calling upon *all* parties to a conflict to take appropriate steps to protect the civilian population. In contrast, for example, ICRC Press Release No. 1563, released on March 10, 1988, during the Iran-Iraq "war of the cities," states:

> The indiscriminate bombing of civilians in connection with the armed conflict between Iran and Iraq has been denounced by the . . . ICRC on several occasions.
>
> The ICRC is alarmed by the resumption of such bombing.
>
> The Parties to the conflict are directly responsible for the ever more cruel suffering being inflicted on civilians in this breach of the most fundamental precepts of humanity.
>
> The ICRC once more appeals to the Parties to put an end to this tragic escalation.

In singling out Israel, the ICRC failed to recognize the actions of the PLO that were a direct cause of civilian losses, while greatly facilitating the PLO's propaganda advantage. ICRC members subsequently acknowledged that their appeal had been directed at Israel only because of Israel's use of airpower. As previously mentioned, it was the opinion of those involved in the United States military review that while the ICRC may have provided substantial contributions to the law of war for the protection of war victims as contained in the four 1949 Geneva Conventions, the ICRC and its staff for political and technical reasons is singularly *unqualified* to be entrusted with the responsibilities provided it by article 81(1) of Protocol I insofar as those responsibilities include that part of the law of war related to warfighting as such. The ICRC's singling out of one party to the conflict in its call for restraint and its reliance upon disinformation provided it by one party to the conflict are but two examples of its technical incompetency in matters relating to warfighting, its long-held bias against airpower and its abandonment of its principles of *neutrality*.

495. Dickey, *Libya Said to Order Westerners to Bases*, Wash. Post, Apr. 14, 1986, at 1, A21.

496. Ottway, *U.S. Fails to Oust Thais at Libya Plant*, Wash. Post, June 1, 1989, at A10.

497. Libya became a party to both Protocols on 7 June 1978. Some might attempt to argue that inasmuch as neither Thailand nor the United States is a party to Protocol I, Libya was not bound to apply Protocol I in any potential conflict (including a single airstrike) with the United States. Such an argument would be incorrect for at least two reasons. Libya, Thailand, and the United States are parties to the 1949 Geneva Convention Relative to the Protection of Civilian Persons in Time of War, which under the terms of article 2 would apply even to an armed conflict as brief as a single airstrike. Article 34 of that convention unequivocally prohibits the taking of hostages. SCHINDLER & TOMAN, *supra* note 27, at 511. With respect to Protocol I, article 18 of the Vienna Convention on the Law of Treaties states that:

> A State is obliged to refrain from acts which would defeat the object and purpose of a treaty when:
>
> (a) it has signed the treaty or has exchanged instruments constituting the treaty subject to ratification, acceptance or approval, until it shall have made its intention clear not to become a party to the treaty; or

Customary international law requires that an attacker exercise ordinary care in the attack of military objectives located near the civilian population, to minimize injury to individual civilians or the civilian population as such incidental to the attack. The defender's responsibility is to exercise an equal degree of care to separate individual civilians and the civilian population as such from the vicinity of military objectives. Where a defender purposely places military objectives in the vicinity of the civilian population or places civilians in proximity to military objectives, in either case for the purpose of shielding military objectives from attack, an attacker is not relieved from his obligation to exercise ordinary care. Responsibility for death or injury resulting from the illegal action of the defender lies with the defender, however. The language of Protocol I—particularly as it has been interpreted by the ICRC and many of the nations known in the course of the Diplomatic Conference as the Group of 77—casts doubt upon whether the limited credibility of the law of war relating to war-fighting *per se* will survive any serious challenge. In further consideration of the issue of responsibility for minimization of collateral civilian casualties, the second factor—the concept of *proportionality*—must be examined.

B. Proportionality

There is no question that the concept of proportionality is part of the Just War Tradition and the law of war. The classic example of a disproportionate action is the destruction of a village of 500, including its population, to destroy a single enemy sniper or machine gun position. This concept of proportionality also is consistent with fire-control procedures and the efficient use of assets and capabilities. No fire-control or air support center would approve a request to employ artillery or close air support against such a target, because it would be an inefficient use of a commander's usually-limited military assets on a battlefield that generally is target-rich with enemy objects of a higher priority. In his classic work on aerial bombardment, M. W. Royse recognized the principle when he stated, "If an act is essential, if the destruction is effective and not wanton, and if the results to be gained by such an act are not grossly disproportionate to the extent of destruction, then the act can hardly be condemned regardless of the amount of suffering and violence."[498]

The United States observes the concept of proportionality in its conduct of combat operations. An example is the 1972 Linebacker I air offensive against North Vietnam. In selecting North Vietnamese power sources for attack, target intelligence authorities identified the Lang Chi hydroelectric facility, a Soviet-built, 122,500-kilowatt electric generating plant 63 miles up the Red River Valley from Hanoi that was capable of supplying seventy-five percent of the electricity for Hanoi's industrial and defense needs. Without question, it was a valuable target.

However, it was estimated that as many as 23,000 civilians could perish if its dam were breached—a clear example of the balancing of the good to be realized by a war aim (destruction of the military objective) against the evil (civilian suffering) required

---

(b) it has expressed its consent to be bound by the treaty, pending the entry into force of the treaty and provided that such entry into force is not unduly delayed. . . .

Article 26 states the international legal concept of *Pacta sunt servanda* that "Every treaty in force is binding upon the parties to it and must be performed by them in good faith." While Libya may not have treaty relations with the United States or Thailand with respect to Protocol I, it nonetheless is bound by the provisions of Protocol I with regard to civilians in its hands, regardless of their nationality.

498. M. ROYSE, 1928, *supra* note 493, at 137.

by the concept of proportionality.[499] The question of whether the target should be attacked was taken to President Nixon. He stated that he would not authorize the target's attack unless his military advisers could provide one hundred percent assurance that the electric generating plant at the top of the Lang Chi facility could be destroyed without breach of the dam.

It is at this point that the "friction of war" entered the picture. Admiral Thomas H. Moorer, USN, the Chairman of the Joint Chiefs of Staff, sought assurances from General John W. Vogt, USAF, Commander, Seventh Air Force that the President's criteria for attack of the target could be met. General Vogt responded that he had two squadrons of F–4 Phantom crews who had become experts in delivering laser-guided bombs (LGB), but that owing to the friction of war he refused to give complete assurance that the mission could be accomplished without breach of the dam. He had enough confidence in his crews, however, that he felt that there was a ninety percent chance of mission accomplishment without breach of the dam.[500] General Vogt's response was relayed to President Nixon, who authorized the attack. The Lang Chi hydroelectric facility was attacked by Air Force F–4 Phantoms using LGB on 10 June 1972. They placed twelve 2000-pound LGB through the roof of the 50-by-100-foot building, thereby destroying the electric generating plant without breach of the dam, despite the fact that the roof of the power plant was 100 feet below the top of the dam.[501]

There is value in codifying proportionality, if for no other reason than to define a concept that has been badly abused in the past. Thus in criticizing the 1972 Linebacker II air operations against military targets in North Vietnam, Telford Taylor argued that the use of B–52 Stratofortress bombers to attack military targets was a violation of the concept of proportionality from the standpoint of the possible risk to the civilian population of North Vietnam. He also suggested that the use of B–52 aircraft was an action that was disproportionate to American national security interests in Southeast Asia, and therefore illegal.[502] Similarly, following the 1981 downing of two Libyan SU–22 Fitter aircraft by American Navy F–14 Tomcats *after* the Fitters had fired air-to-air missiles at the Navy fighters, an American Coast Guard officer suggested that it was disproportionate for the United States to employ modern F–14s against the older, slower Fitters, even though the decision to engage was that of the Fitters.[503] While U.S. involvement in the Vietnam War remains a topic of popular debate almost two decades after the Linebacker operations, the Just War concept of proportionality does not mix *jus ad bellum* and *jus in bello* unless a combatant nation's actions become so patently illegal (that is, violations of the *jus in bello*) that they jeopardize any previously lawful reason for going to war. Lawful combat actions are not subject to some sort of "fairness doctrine," and neither the law of war in general nor the concept of proportionality in particular imposes a legal

499. For a description of the concept of *proportionality* and its balancing of these conflicting values, *see* W. O'BRIEN, THE CONDUCT OF JUST AND LIMITED WAR 38–42 (1981).

500. Author's conversation with General Vogt on 1 July 1982 and Admiral Moorer on 15 Sept. 1982.

501. Parks, *supra* note 208, at 11–12; and conversation with General Vogt, *supra* note 500; and M. Porter, *Linebacker: An Overview of the First 120 Days* 37–38 Headquarters, United States Air Force Pacific (27 Sept. 1973). A post-mission photograph of the dam and its destroyed power plant is in Parks, *supra* note 5, at 116.

502. Taylor, Defining War Crimes, N.Y. Times, Jan. 11, 1973, at 39.

503. McFaul, Comment and Discussion, 108 U.S. NAVAL INST. PROC. 42 (May 1982). The author believes it inappropriate to refer to the concept of proportionality as a "*rule*," because the term suggests something far more specific and binding that it is at this time, particularly in the context of responsibility for collateral civilian casualties.

or moral obligation on a nation to sacrifice manpower, firepower, or technological superiority over an opponent.[504]

In an equally egregious example, as a student at The Judge Advocate General's School, U.S. Army, in 1973, the author first heard of the concept of proportionality when he was instructed that the "rule" of proportionality could best be described with the following hypothetical scenario:

> An enemy platoon of forty men is in a defensive position on a hill, armed only with small arms. You have been assigned the mission of capturing the hill. You have the capability of attacking the hill with a company of two hundred men, supported by artillery, tanks, helicopter gunships and close air support fixed-wing aircraft. The "rule" of proportionality requires you to eschew the use of anything more than an infantry platoon armed with small arms.[505]

In a similar light, since codification of the concept into Protocol I, a former member of the U.S. delegation to the Diplomatic Conference has taught that, "The rule of proportionality means that if it takes five bombs to destroy a target and you drop six, your action violates the rule."[506] These examples ignore the military concept of bringing a *preponderance* of power to bear on a military objective, usually at a minimum ratio of three-to-one in favor of the assaulting force. It also suggests yet another danger of the concept as it has been bandied about by some international lawyers: that in some way the concept of proportionality can be applied or was intended to be applied in combat operations between combatants on a battlefield devoid of civilians. There is no viable precedent for such an interpretation.[507]

There is another reason why codification of the concept of proportionality was appropriate. It constitutes acknowledgment in Protocol I of the fact that collateral civilian casualties are in inevitable part of war where a defender has failed to separate civilians from military objectives, as required by article 48 of Protocol I.[508]

---

504. For elaboration of the concepts of *jus ad bellum* and *jus in bello*, *see* W. O'BRIEN, *supra* note 499, at 9, 13–70.

505. The class was taught by a young Army lawyer who was long on the theory of the law of war but totally lacking in military training or experience. One-third of the class of judge advocates was made up of Army and Marine Corps officers who had served combat command tours in Vietnam. It was the consensus of those students that if the instructor were placed in a position of command in the hypothetical scenario he had posited, his view of what was *proportionality* would change markedly—provided his own men did not kill him first. His Army career did not extend beyond his initial tour of service.

506. His statement is not supported by the historical employment of force nor by the very comprehensive compilation of doctrine for weaponeering a target that exists in the multi-volume Joint Munitions Effectiveness Manual.

507. The author has heard some international lawyers pontificate various theoretical obligations combatant forces have with regard to enemy combatants, such as the erroneous interpretation of the concept of *proportionality* provided in the text at the preceding footnote. But the nations of the world wisely have elected not to attempt to legislate in this area beyond the prohibitions contained in articles 22 and 23 of the Annex to the 1907 Hague Convention IV. In this context, *proportionality* has been raised in consideration of the legality of weapons, that is, whether the suffering caused by a weapon is disproportionate to its military effectiveness. This is easier to theorize about than to articulate with specific examples, however, in that weapons development has become so expensive that nations are not prone to spend money on weapons or weapon systems that are not militarily effective. Thus, a nation today would not be inclined to develop a weapon that is indiscriminate *per se* because it would not be militarily effective. In considering weapons that might cause unnecessary suffering, the same *proportionality* test is considered. However, the nations that participated in the 1978–1980 United Nations Conventional Weapons Conference placed restrictions only on weapons with regard to their possible effect on the civilian population, and not as to the injury of combatants. Protocol I of the 1980 UN Conventional Weapons Convention prohibiting weapons utilizing fragments not detectable by x-ray was adopted by consensus as it outlawed a weapon that did not exist.

508. As the NEW RULES FOR VICTIMS OF ARMED CONFLICTS, notes, "Despite persistent criticism . . . that it sets a seal of approval on incidental civilian casualties, the ICRC persisted in proposing a codification of the principle of proportionality, recognizing that some collateral injury to civilians is inevitable." NEW RULES FOR VICTIMS OF ARMED CONFLICTS, *supra* note 257, at 361.

But in the context in which it has emerged, the concept of proportionality was—and remains—dangerously undefined. As previously noted by Just War scholar James Turner Johnson, the concept of proportionality in the context of collateral damage in modern war is a "pregnant one."[509]

The negotiation pertaining to the codification of the concept of proportionality into Protocol I will be covered only briefly, because it has been summarized in a scholarly piece by Commander William J. Fenrick and discussed in the two commentaries on the Protocols.[510] Codification was strongly opposed by most Eastern European and Third World delegations on the theory that it was contrary to the providing of immunity from attack to civilians and civilian objects;[511] for this reason, neither "proportion," "proportionate," nor "proportionality" appears in Protocol I.

As previously noted, the concept is codified in articles 51(5)(b), 57(2)(a)(iii), 57(2)(b), and 85(3)(b), the principal point of codification being article 57(2)(a)(iii). This requires that those who plan or decide upon an attack shall "refrain from deciding to launch any attack which may be expected to cause incidental loss of civilian life, injury to civilians, damage to civilian objects, or a combination thereof, which would be excessive in relation to the concrete and direct military advantage anticipated."[512]

Beyond its codification, the concept runs into difficulty. While the concepts of discrimination and proportion are distinctive in the Just War Tradition, within Protocol I proportionality seems to be offered as little more than a synonym for indiscriminate. Thus, in the Just War Tradition, proportion within the *jus ad bellum* requires that "the good to be achieved by the realization of the war aims be proportionate to the evil resulting from the war," while within the *jus in bello* "the question immediately arises as to the referent of proportionality in judging the means of war."[513] The *ICRC Commentary* states unequivocally that codification of proportionality into Protocol I was not intended to address the former,[514] but Protocol I also in large measure ignores the latter. Thus, if a nation is attacked by an aggressor and lawfully responds in self-defense, the defender may violate the Just War concept of proportionality if its response is not proportionate to the threat, or if in responding its military force engages in wholesale violations of the law of war such as the denial of quarter and/or murder of prisoners of war.

In contrast, the principle of discrimination prohibits intentional attacks on noncombatants or nonmilitary targets.[515] But the concept of proportionality is codified in article 51(5)(b), which makes an attack indiscriminate if it is "an attack which may be expected to cause incidental loss of civilian life, injury to civilians, damage to civilian objects, or a combination thereof, which would be excessive in relation to the concrete and direct military advantage anticipated."[516]

---

509. J. Johnson, *supra* note 13, at 221.

510. Fenrick, *The Rule of Proportionality and Protocol I in Conventional Warfare*, 98 Mil. L. Rev. at 91–127; ICRC Commentary, *supra* note 247, at 683–85; New Rules for Victims of Armed Conflicts, *supra* note 257, at 361.

511. *See* New Rules for Victims of Armed Conflicts, *supra* note 257, at 361. The objection by Socialist and Third World delegations is illustrative of the fact that many were (and are) more interested in a basis for charging captured military personnel with violations of the law of war (to deny them prisoner of war protection, as North Korea and North Vietnam did during their respective conflicts with Free World nations) than in protection of their civilian population.

512. Schindler & Toman, *supra* note 27, at 655.

513. W. O'Brien, *supra* note 499, at 38–39.

514. ICRC Commentary, *supra* note 247, at 683. The statement in the ICRC Commentary, "This article . . . is not concerned with strategic objectives . . . ," is itself subject to several different interpretations, as will be seen.

515. W. O'Brien, *supra* note 499, at 42.

516. Schindler & Toman, *supra* note 27, at 651.

The codified language immediately was open to question. The phrase "concrete and direct military advantage anticipated" was defined by Belgium as being "that expected from an attack considered in its totality,"[517] while Italy stated that the phrase "is intended to refer to the advantage anticipated from the attack as a whole and not from isolated or particular parts of the attack."[518] Similar statements were made by Great Britain at the time of signature and the Netherlands at the time of its ratification of the Protocols.[519] With regard to a commander's expectations in commencing an attack, the same nations felt it necessary to accept the codification of the concept of proportionality subject to the *Rendulic* rule, namely that "military commanders and others responsible for planning, deciding upon or executing attacks necessarily have to reach decisions on the basis of their assessment of the information from all sources which is available to them at the relevant time."[520]

There were other doubts. One commentary suggested that, "It is . . . doubtful that incidental injury to persons serving the armed forces within a military objective will weigh as heavily in the application of the rule of proportionality as that part of the civilian population which is not so closely linked to military operations."[521]

This statement, while appearing obvious, also raises doubts about the stringent distinction made between "civilians" and "combatants" in article 51(3), previously examined. In one of the earliest critiques of Protocol I, a member of the ICRC with considerable military training and experience in teaching the law of war expressed doubts as to the feasibility of the application of the concept of proportionality at the level of the individual soldier or small unit commander.[522] Violation of the concept of proportionality does not become a "grave breach" unless and until it involves the "launching of an attack affecting the civilian population or civilian objects *in the*

517. *Id.* at 707.

518. *Id.* at 713. The same statement was made by the delegation of Canada in explanation of its vote on articles 51 and 57 at the Diplomatic Conference. Fenrick, *supra* note 510, at 107. The statement of the Delegation of the United States was similar but substantially longer:

> It is the understanding of the United States that the references in articles 51 and 57 to military advantage anticipated from an attack are intended to refer to the advantage anticipated from the attack considered as a whole and not only from isolated or particular parts of that attack. The term "military advantage" involves a variety of considerations, including the security of attacking forces. It is further the understanding of the U.S. that the term "concrete and direct military advantage anticipated" used in articles 51 and 57 means an honest expectation that the attack will make a relevant and proportionate contribution to the purposes of the attack.

Law of War Working Group, *supra* note 294, at I–51–11.

519. SCHINDLER & TOMAN, *supra* note 27, at 717 and 714, respectively.

520. *See, e.g.*, the statement of the Netherlands to this effect in SCHINDLER & TOMAN, *supra* note 27, at 714.

521. NEW RULES FOR VICTIMS OF ARMED CONFLICTS, *supra* note 257, at 295.

522. Mulinen, *The Law of War and the Armed Forces*, INTERNATIONAL REVIEW OF THE RED CROSS 18–44, at 42–43 (Jan./Feb. 1978), where Colonel de Mulinen correctly observes that:

> One cannot imagine, to take the case of an attacking tank battalion, that each of the 30 to 40 tank leaders would, on his own, and constantly, balance "the concrete and direct military advantage anticipated" against the losses and damage which might be entailed in the civilian sector. Nor can one imagine that each of these tank leaders would interrupt the attack, that is, that he would stop his own tank in the midst of the general advance. Such estimates and the decisions resulting from them are still not conceivable at the level of the platoon (or section), the company, or the battalion. It would produce enormous confusion on the battle area, such confusion as to forbid any co-ordinated and hence successful military action, unless it were conducted in a completely desert zone.

Based in large measure on Colonel de Mulinen's objections, the Swiss ratification of Protocol I was subject to a statement of understanding that "The provisions of Article 57(2) are binding only on battalion or group commanders and higher echelons." SCHINDLER & TOMAN, *supra* note 27, at 716.

knowledge that such attack will cause excessive loss of life, injury to civilians or damage to civilian objects, as defined in Article 57, paragraph 2(a)(iii).''[523] This leads one to conclude that the concept of proportionality (as it is codified in Protocol I) is not violated unless acts have occurred that are tantamount to the direct attack of the civilian population, a violation of articles 48 and 51(2), or involve wanton negligence that is tantamount to an intentional attack of the civilian population.[524] Yet a senior legal representative of the ICRC has hailed Protocol I as important in providing the authority to prosecute military commanders for violations of the ''rule'' of proportionality, as if violations were daily occurrences.[525]

In the course of the American military review of Protocol I, it was concluded that the concept of proportionality is not a rule of customary law, as it has been represented.[526] By American domestic law standards, the concept of proportionality as contained in Protocol I would be constitutionally void for vagueness.[527] State-

523. SCHINDLER & TOMAN, *supra* note 27, at 671.

524. Such an interpretation would be consistent with the grave breach provision in the 1949 Geneva Convention Relative to the Protection of Civilian Persons in Time of War, which defines a grave breach under that convention as

> those involving any of the following acts, if committed against persons or property protected by the present Convention: wilful killing . . . wilfully causing great suffering or serious injury to body or health . . . and extensive destruction of property, not justified by military necessity *and carried out unlawfully and wantonly.*

Id. at 547 (emphasis added).

525. Hans Peter Gasser, law of war panel presentation at the annual meeting of the American Society of International Law, Boston, Massachusetts, April 9, 1987. The author was a member of the panel with Mr. Gasser. The statement by Mr. Gasser seemed particularly striking to the author, given the inability of the international community to arrive at a way in which violators of the 1949 Geneva Conventions can be brought to justice where a conflict does not conclude with total victory by one side over the other, as well as in light of the silence of the ICRC during the years 1965–1969 when it knew that U.S. prisoners of war in North Vietnam systematically were being tortured, a grave breach (article 130) of the 1949 Geneva Convention Relative to the Treatment of Prisoners of War.

526. Aldrich, *New Life for the Laws of War*, 75 AM. J. INT'L L. 764, 778 (1981); the claim that the concept of *proportionality* is part of customary law also has been made by Professor Green in *Aerial Considerations in the Law of Armed Conflict*, V ANNALS OF AIR AND SPACE LAW 104 (1980). Article 38b of the Statute of the International Court of Justice annexed to the Charter of the United Nations (59 Stat. 1055, T.S. 993, 3 Bevans 1153) defines international custom as ''evidence of a general practice accepted as law.'' Custom has been further defined as involving four elements:

> a. Concordant practices by a number of nations with reference to a type of situation falling within the domain of international relations;
> b. Continuation or repetition of the practice over a considerable period of time;
> c. Conception that the practice is required by, or is consistent with, prevailing international law; and
> d. General acquiescence in the practice by other nations.

W. FRIEDMANN, O. LISSITZYN, and R. PUGH, INTERNATIONAL LAW 36 (1969). *See also* the discussion of custom in DEPARTMENT OF THE ARMY PAMPHLET 27–161–1, LAW OF PEACE 1–5 to 1–10 (1979). The military review of the practice of nations in war found little knowledge, much less acceptance, of the concept of proportionality, and in fact a substantial practice to the contrary, particularly with regard to responsibility for minimization of collateral civilian casualties.

A frequent statement by proponents of Protocol I is that the concept of *proportionality* is a part of the teachings of all the world's great religions. One need look only as far as the conflicting passages found in the Bible that require a Christian to turn the other cheek if struck *vis-à-vis* ''an eye for an eye, and a tooth for a tooth'' to realize that the holy documents of most religions contain passages that contradict one another or are subject to more than one interpretation. The superb books by Robin Wright on the rise of Islamic fundamentalism are a vivid reminder that the bloodiest wars in history have been fought over religious differences. *See* R. WRIGHT, SACRED RAGE: THE WRATH OF MILITANT ISLAM (1985), and R. WRIGHT, IN THE NAME OF GOD: THE KHOMEINI DECADE (1989); *see also* A. MAALOUF, THE CRUSADES THROUGH ARAB EYES (1985).

527. As part of the test as to whether a statute is constitutional, the statute must be specific enough to be fair notice of what conduct is forbidden or required. People v. Kirk, 362 N.E. 329 (1977). A statute is sufficiently definite if its terms furnish a test based on knowable criteria which men of

ments made by some nations in the course of the Diplomatic Conference or in conjunction with their subsequent signature or ratification of Protocol I make it clear that there is no agreement as to what the concept means, or the level at which generally it will be applied. Following more than five years of research and attendance of numerous meetings of legal and political experts, the author in 1983 prepared a document entitled ''Proportionality in a Nutshell'' (''Nutshell'') which endeavored to provide some clarification of the concept, based upon the customary practice of nations, or at least to invite discussion among legal experts within the NATO nations, Australia and New Zealand. With respect to the issue of collateral civilian casualties, it provides:

> The intentional attack of individual civilians not taking part in the hostilities, the civilian population *per se*, or civilian objects, is prohibited. . . . Proportionality does not establish a separate standard, but serves as a means for determining whether a nation or military commander responsible for planning, deciding upon, or executing a military operation has engaged in the intentional attack of civilians not engaged in the hostilities. . . . Proportionality as used in this context constitutes acknowledgment of the inevitability of incidental or collateral damage and injury in war. Other aspects:
>
> . . . .
>
> b. The formula: The occurrence of collateral civilian casualties so excessive in nature when compared to the military advantage to be gained as to be tantamount to the intentional attack of individual civilians, or the civilian population, or to a wanton disregard for the safety of the civilian population.
>
> c. *Excluded* in determination of collateral civilian casualties are:
>
> 1. Civilians taking part in the hostilities, such as those manning air defense positions, transporting military equipment, or providing other support to military forces.
>
> 2. Civilians injured or killed while working in or immediately adjacent to a lawful target.
>
> 3. Civilians injured or killed through action . . . attributable to enemy action, or beyond the control of either party, such as civilians killed by the crash of an attacking aircraft downed by enemy air defenses; civilians killed by munitions diverted from their intended target by obscurants or electronic countermeasures of the enemy; or civilians injured or killed as a result of the enemy placing them around a lawful target in an effort to shield it from attack.
>
> d. Generally measured against an overall campaign, rather than its isolated or particular parts; generally incapable of measurement on a target-by-target basis.

The ''Nutshell'' has been the subject of discussion at several international meetings, most recently one of senior military legal experts from Australia, Canada, Great Britain, New Zealand, and the United States who are responsible for preparing their respective law of war manuals, and held at Old Sarum, United Kingdom, 8–11 May 1989. While there has been general agreement with its language, there are points that have generated heated debate, such as the first phrase in the last paragraph. Although there was disagreement as to whether responsibility should be limited to comparison to an overall campaign, there also was a lack of agreement as to the level

---

common intelligence who come in contact with the statute may use with reasonable safety in determining its command. Winters v. New York, 68 S. Ct. 665 (1948). It must be set out in terms that the ordinary person exercising common sense can sufficiently understand and comply with. It must inform persons with reasonable definiteness that any particular act is disapproved or required. This test has been reaffirmed in Wright v. New Jersey, 105 S. Ct. 8900 (1985), and Roberts v. United States Jaycees, 104 S. Ct. 3244 (1984).

at which the standard should be measured. In the days since that meeting, discussions have been directed at other ways of determining the standard, with general agreement that the standard of care of any commander is one of ordinary or due care, the terms being regarded as synonymous.

At this point, the standard cannot be defined in a way that is entirely satisfactory. But that is not the issue at this point. Following more than a decade of research and meetings of international military legal experts who are anxious to implement the language contained in Protocol I to the extent it advances the law of war and the protection of the civilian population, there remains a substantial lack of agreement as to the meaning of the provisions in Protocol I relating to proportionality. This is a rather disconcerting situation given that other lawyers are claiming that the concept of proportionality is customary international law. There are several other disturbing factors:

a. The assumption of risk by an attacker for the action or inaction of the defender. The "Nutshell" disagrees with the statement contained in the Bothe, Partsch and Solf treatise that suggests that individuals working within a legitimate military target must be considered in weighing the concept or proportionality. As has been indicated in this article, there is no precedent for such consideration with respect to the enemy civilian population, and there is a serious question as to whether these individuals are "civilians" in the context of those persons entitled to protection from attack. Any other approach would permit a defender to "cost out" an otherwise legitimate target by employing civilians exclusively at the target, and would violate the fundamental law of war obligation of discrimination codified in article 48.

b. "Results" versus intent. The "Nutshell" rejects the very dangerous tendency that has developed over the past decade or so to attribute all civilian casualties to the attacker. Thus even the scholarly article by Commander Fenrick concludes with the following:

> One might hypothesize, perhaps mythologize, a Second World War in which the rules of Protocol I were applied. The city of Dresden was bombed in February 1945 by the United States Air Force and the Royal Air Force. . . . Civilian losses are unclear, but it appears at least 25,000 people were killed. . . . Would the attack decision have been the same if, before the attack decision was made, the military commander received a draft operations order from his planning staff including a provision stating: "The military advantage we expect to derive from this attack is __________, the probable losses are __________, your direction is requested concerning whether or not the probable civilian losses are 'excessive.' "[528]

Commander Fenrick's hypothesis suggests three fundamental problems with implementation of the concept of proportionality. The first is definition of the military advantage, and the level at which a determination would or should be made. The second concerns responsibility for the probable civilian losses that will result from the operation. The last deals with the friction of war.

Certainly there will be circumstances in which a small unit commander may be able to consider the consequences that might derive from his attack, and have some idea as to the location of civilians within his tactical area of operations or, if a pilot, within the vicinity of his target. An example would in fact be that cited at the outset of this discussion regarding the destruction of a village of 500 in order to neutralize a single sniper or machine gun position.[529] As with the concept of proportionality in

528. Fenrick, *supra* note 510, at 127.

529. The ICRC COMMENTARY, *supra* note 247, at 684, provides two other examples: (a) the presence of a soldier on leave cannot serve as a justification to destroy the entire village, and (b) while conceding that an attack on a bridge in the center of a village may result in some collateral damage to civilian property, it would be disproportionate to destroy the entire village. As general examples, each is correct. But the second does not take into consideration the friction of war. The example is correct if it suggests that a commander would not be justified in attacking the entire village in order to destroy the

general, other specific examples are a little more difficult to identify. To the extent any small unit commander is possessed of information as to the location of civilians, he should exercise ordinary care to minimize collateral civilian casualties, consistent with mission accomplishment and the security of his unit, tank or aircraft. The primary responsibility for minimization of collateral civilian casualties continues to reside with the party to the conflict with control over the civilian population and with the individual civilian, however.

In many cases, small unit commanders or individual pilots will not be possessed of sufficient information to weigh a decision regarding proportion. Most small unit commanders have a limited objective that is part of an overall attack, just as individual pilots will be assigned a particular target to attack as part of an overall strike force; their latitude in achieving their objectives is limited at best. Neither may be briefed as to the value of their objective or target within the overall scheme of attack, and the value may fluctuate depending upon the success or failure of the overall attack.

For example, in the weeks preceding the 6 June 1944 Allied landing at Normandy, Allied aircraft flew thousands of sorties against targets in the Pas de Calais area to persuade the Germans that the Allied invasion would take place in that area, as well as to seal off the Normandy beachhead from Wermacht reinforcements. Assume a pilot of an American aircraft has been assigned the mission of destroying a heavily-defended bridge in the middle of a village in the Pas de Calais area. In that he will not be privy to D-Day plans as to where or when the invasion will take place, he will be unable to weigh the value of his mission against the risk to the civilian population—assuming he has any idea where the civilians in that village will be at the time of his attack. For sake of argument, assume that he does know that his mission is part of the deception surrounding the invasion plan. On an individual basis, he may feel that it is not worth risking his life or the lives of civilians in the village to attack a bridge merely for the purposes of executing a feint. But every portion of the feint may be critical to persuading the Germans that the Allied invasion may take place in the Pas de Calais, and therefore to the overall success of the operation. Only a commander at the highest level—such as General Dwight D. Eisenhower—can weigh such a decision.

The second part of the issue of military advantage is suggested by Commander Fenrick's hypothesis. That surrounds the question of the military value of (to use Commander Fenrick's example) the February 1945 attack on Dresden. This is neither the time nor place to debate the issues surrounding that attack. The overall question becomes one of the military advantage of an attack that cost 25,000 civilian dead. The *ICRC Commentary* states that codification of the concept of proportionality into Protocol I was intended for use at the tactical rather than the strategic level.[530] Yet the Dresden example illustrates the difficulty of application of proportionality at the tactical level. There is adequate evidence available to suggest that the decision to attack Dresden was made at the strategic level, where the factors weighed

bridge. However, what if both attacker and defender realize this is the *only* bridge remaining that will permit the defender to rush reinforcements to the front to repulse a major offensive by the attacker, and the defender heavily fortifies his defenses around the bridge? The value of destruction of the bridge would be substantially greater, while the intensified enemy defenses (passive and active) would have a pronounced effect on the accuracy of the attacker's bombing of the bridge. Battlefield dynamics will cause the value of an objective to fluctuate markedly, sometimes in only a matter of minutes, while the success of enemy defenses—a matter not within the control of an attacker—will have considerable influence on the degree of collateral damage around a target.

530. ICRC COMMENTARY, *supra* note 247, at 683.

included providing support for the advance of Soviet forces into eastern Germany, destruction of the lines of communication at a critical chokepoint in order to prevent German reinforcement in opposition to the Soviet advance, and possible hastening of the end of the war. No tactical commander would be possessed of adequate information or authority to weigh such a decision and, at the strategic level, a national leader would be faced with the conundrum of weighing the loss of 25,000 lives against the possibility that a successful attack might end the war sooner, thereby saving hundreds of thousands of lives. This itself is a question of proportionality, of substantially greater importance than any decision made at the tactical level.

Within the issue of responsibility for collateral civilian casualties lies the equally fundamental issue of accountability. Commander Fenrick's hypothesis suggests a dangerous fallacy in tallying the total civilian casualties from an attack and holding the commander engaged in offensive operations accountable for them in their entirety, an approach made by the North Vietnamese in threatening captured American aircrews with war crimes trials in the course of the Vietnam War.

Attack of a military objective, wherever located, is lawful. While the number of civilian casualties that occur are the result of that attack, the attack is not necessarily the cause of those casualties, nor may they necessarily be attributable to the attacker. The approach under discussion suggests that "but for the attack, these civilian losses would not have occurred; therefore the attacker is responsible." This approach would make any attack on any target, wherever located, illegal, notwithstanding the actions of the defender. It would encourage a defender to leave his civilian population in place rather than evacuate them from the vicinity of a military objective, as required by article 48, or use his civilian population as a shield from attack in violation of article 51(7). It also would permit him to "cost out" a high-value target by surrounding a target with so many civilians that the effects of the attack would be disproportionate to the perceived value of the attack. The record of certain nations and "liberation movements" indicates that they would use the civilian population for this purpose, making a mockery of the law of war. In particular, a regime or organization with a consistent record of human rights violations or resort to terrorism would think little of sacrificing civilians in its defense, as was demonstrated by North Korea, North Vietnam, and the PLO during the Korean and Vietnam Wars and the 1982 fighting in Lebanon, respectively.

The question of accounting for civilian casualties also suggests the danger of this approach. As previously noted, according to North Vietnamese count, 1318 "civilians" were killed in the Hanoi area during the Linebacker II bombing campaign that took place from 18–29 December 1972. Several questions must be raised in the course of determining responsibility for the casualties. The first is whether each "civilian" was entitled to be considered a civilian based on his activities at the time he was killed. Was a particular person engaged in military activities at the time of death so as to cause a loss of civilian status? Second, even if a civilian, was that person working within a military objective? As previously indicated, there is an assumption of risk for civilians within or adjacent to a military objective, and a question should be raised with regard to any responsibility on the part of an attacker for deaths among those "civilians." Third, what was the cause of death? Was it caused by a bomb dropped by the attacker or by actions attributable to the defender? During the Linebacker II operations, for example, the North Vietnamese fired in excess of 1100 SA–2 surface-to-air antiaircraft missiles at U.S. aircraft which resulted in the loss of only fifteen B–52 aircraft. The SA–2 missiles that did not strike their targets either exploded in the air (into pieces large enough to be lethal on impact with the ground), or plummeted back to Earth intact, where they would have exploded.

The North Vietnamese also employed thousands of large-caliber antiaircraft guns firing millions of rounds of munitions, much of which had had the proximity fuze removed. Once those rounds reached the limit of their range, they also plummeted back to Earth, where they exploded on impact or were heavy enough (particularly as they were traveling at terminal velocity) to inflict a fatal wound. How many civilians were struck and killed by the debris from these SA–2 missiles or antiaircraft munitions?

Similarly, some B–52 aircraft crashed in Hanoi or its suburbs as a result of enemy actions. How many civilians died as a result of the crash of an out-of-control aircraft downed by enemy defenses?[531]

As previously indicated, the North Vietnamese did execute somewhat of an evacuation plan in the days immediately preceding the Linebacker II operations. However, how many civilian lives might have been saved with a more comprehensive evacuation plan, or better air raid precaution steps by the defender? Similarly, individual North Vietnamese civilians who had been evacuated were known to return to their Hanoi homes without authorization. Could any of the civilian deaths have been avoided by a better, enforceable air defense precaution plan? How many civilians lost their lives because they chose to continue to live in close proximity to a legitimate military target, or because North Vietnamese authorities moved antiair defenses or other military equipment near a civilian residential area? If an attacker is exercising ordinary care to minimize collateral civilian casualties, deaths attributable to the action or inaction of the defender or individual civilians are not the attacker's responsibility.

The recently concluded operations in Panama provide another illustration of the difficulty of accountability. Estimates are that as many as 300 civilians may have died in the course of the fighting. But officials have been unable to ascertain in all cases the status of the deceased, and the circumstances of death. Many members of the deposed Manuel Noreiga's Panamanian Defense Force (PDF) chose to fight in civilian clothing, for example. As a spokesman reported, "We couldn't always say if a casualty was a PDF, a civilian or what. If a guy was shot carrying a weapon, that was a pretty good indication that he was not a friendly. But troops under fire didn't always have time to label each corpse with the location where he was found."[532]

531. The bombing of Bach Mai Hospital, described *supra* note 208, incidental to the crash of the B–52 struck by two SA–2 missiles, is illustrative of the problem. While it should be obvious that an attacker is not responsible for civilian deaths caused by aircraft that crash as a result of enemy action, the point has been lost on some in the past. During the conduct of Linebacker II, a representative of the Joint Chiefs of Staff (JCS) briefed the House Armed Services Committee (HASC) after each day's operations. The JCS took great pains to illustrate through photographs the extremes being taken at every level of command to minimize risk to the civilian population of North Vietnam, much to the chagrin of those members of the HASC who opposed the bombing. A concluding briefing was provided in January 1973. During the briefing a photograph was flashed on the screen showing damage in a residential section of Hanoi. A new member of the HASC seized upon the occasion to castigate the briefer for what appeared to be erratic bombing, demanding of the briefer that he explain the circumstances surrounding the damage. The briefer responded: "I regret . . . to say that the damage was caused by the crash of one of our B–52 aircraft after being hit by a North Vietnamese surface-to-air missile, with the loss of the entire crew." The new congresswoman was not to be denied, however, as she screamed: "Well, dammit, General! Can't you teach your pilots to crash somewhere else"? (The story was related to the author by an officer who was present at the hearing session.)

532. J. Omang & D. Priest, *Accounting for Panama's Dead: Uncertainty and Confusion*, Wash. Post, Jan. 7, 1990, at A23. A Panamanian source quoted in the same story estimated that thirty percent of the "civilian" deaths were PDF members in civilian clothing or members of Noreiga's die-hard Dignity Battalions. *See also* D. Pitt, *The Invasion's Civilian Toll: Still No Official Count*, N. Y. Times, Jan. 10, 1990, at A13; and J. Goshko, *U.S. Puts Civilian Toll at 220*, Wash. Post, Jan. 10, 1990, at A16. The two later news stories indicated that U.S. officials had put the civilian death toll at 220, while conceding that many of those "civilians" may have been members of the PDF or Dignity Battalions who were killed while fighting in civilian clothing. The New York Times story stated that the Panama-

The circumstances of death were equally difficult to establish. Some civilians died when caught looting by business owners. Others died when Noriega loyalists set fire to the poor neighborhood of Chorrillo. Still other deaths are directly attributable to actions by members of Noriega's paramilitary "Dignity Battalion," such as "drive by" shootings in which Dignity Battalion soldiers opened fire on crowds of innocent civilians as they drove by, apparently because the civilians were welcoming, rather than resisting, the American operation.[533]

The fighting in Panama prompted the American media to "round up the usual far-left critics"[534] to offer unfounded allegations that many more civilians had died.[535] Misallegations of civilian casualties for propaganda effect are a familiar part of war. A major weakness of the vaguely-worded formulae in articles 51 and 57 is that they provide both domestic critics and an enemy with an appearance of authority for charges of "indiscriminate bombing," or for target-by-target analysis of bombing results based upon alleged civilian casualties without consideration either of actual fact or cause of those casualties. This was intentional on the part of the principal drafters of Protocol I (such as Sweden, Switzerland, and the ICRC, through the Group of 77). They felt, based in part on the American experience in its bombing campaigns over North Vietnam, that claims of indiscriminate bombing would lead to considerable outcry of world public opinion that would pressure an attacker to cease or slow his actions, even if they were legal or as discriminate as possible. Soviet combat actions in Afghanistan, in which entire villages and their civilian population were destroyed by ground or air action in order to deny the Mujahadin access to the civilian population, suggest that the theory behind the purpose for the language will only have an impact in a democracy.[536] Given the United States experience in World

nian Red Cross had put the number of deaths of unarmed civilians at 129, another indication of the possibility of disagreement or discrepancy in actual numbers, let alone cause of death. A later U.S. report put the figure of civilian deaths as 202, after Panama's Institute of Legal Medicine identified eighteen of those previously included in the earlier U.S. total as being members of the PDF. *U.S. Reduces Death Toll for Civilians to 202*, Baltimore Sun, Jan. 13, 1990, at 2.

533. Thus the first article cited in the preceding footnote begins with the following:

> For most of his life, Alberto Meija, 56, was a civilian cook for the Panamanian military.
>
> . . . .
>
> He was cleaning up after cooking a late dinner for Panamanian troops guarding the airport here when U.S. forces attacked it the morning of December 20. Meija ran for cover and was shot dead by PDF forces behind him, according to his daughter, who cited witnesses.
>
> Assuming her account is accurate, Meija's death raises a key question: Was he a civilian casualty of the U.S. invasion? Was he a military casualty? Or was he a murder victim?

534. Fred Barnes, The McLaughlin Group, Jan. 13, 1990. Mr. Barnes' statement was made in response to discussion by the group of an open letter to President Bush protesting U.S. operations in Panama that appeared as a full page advertisement in the New York Times on Jan. 10, 1990, at A28. It was signed by sixty-nine left-wing politicians and activists, including well-known Vietnam War protesters Ramsey Clark, William Sloan Coffin, Richard Falk, J. William Fullbright, George McGovern, and Cora Weiss, as well as Marcus Raskin of the far-left Institute for Policy Studies and Hollywood celebrities with reputations for supporting left-wing causes such as Ed Asner, Martin Sheen, and Oliver Stone. Protocol I would offer such groups increased credibility by providing them legal authority, but in the type of vague, ambiguous language that can be easily exploited in propaganda allegations of the sort published by the New York Times. As with use of the word "attack" in article 49(1), this was intentional on the part of the ICRC, Switzerland, Sweden, and the balance of the Group of 77. In specific response to the New York Times advertisement, *see* Broder, *Panama: An Intervention That Made Sense*, Wash. Post, Jan. 14, 1990, at B7.

535. For example, The New York Times advertisement referred to (*supra* note 534) alleged that "at least 400 Panamanian civilians" had been killed.

536. *See* TEARS, BLOOD AND CRIES: HUMAN RIGHTS IN AFGHANISTAN SINCE THE INVASION, 1979–1984 (1984); *see also* Brumley, *Afghan Atrocities Charged to Soviets and Their Cohorts*, Wash. Times, Nov. 19, 1987, at A10.

War II, Korea, and Vietnam, in which American aircrews were denied prisoner of war protection and in some cases executed because of spurious allegations of "indiscriminate bombing," the greater danger is that the language of Protocol I provides an enemy captor with an authentic basis for his misallegations in future conflicts, no matter how discriminate air operations may be in fact.

The difficulty of ascertaining responsibility for collateral civilian casualties also can be attributed to the confusion of combat. Reference to one incident from the early stages of the American military operations in Panama will serve to illustrate this point. News accounts stated that the 123-member U.S. Army 988th Military Police Company had assaulted a PDF dog kennel, where unit members engaged in a "fierce firefight" lasting three hours, resulting in three PDF dead. The story became somewhat of a *cause celebre* because the company commander was a woman, who (it was reported) had "crashed" through the kennel gate in her Jeep armed with a .50-caliber machine gun to lead the assault, while another woman in the unit had captured a member of the PDF "single-handedly."

Subsequent investigation determined that the firefight had lasted only ten minutes; there were no PDF casualties; neither PDF weapons nor spent enemy shell casings were found; the company commander was a half-mile away when she received reports of action, and used her jeep to break the lock on the gate; and a captured PDF soldier was found, unarmed, cowering in the ranks of the MP company when a muster was held at the end of the "battle." Initial news accounts were characterized by a later story in a competing newspaper as "grossly exaggerated," touching off a flurry of press in-fighting over the facts of the incident.[537]

The foregoing involved the simplest of attacks, a small-unit ground force operation of short duration in territory over which the American military had control and

537. *See* Broder, *Army Says Role of Female Soldiers Was Exaggerated*, Philadelphia Inquirer, Jan. 6, 1990, at 4; Shabecoff, *Female Captain's Role is Called into Question*, N.Y. Times, Jan. 8, 1990, at B8; Richardson, *Female Heroics Set Off War of Words in Press*, Wash. Times, Jan. 10, 1990, at 1; and Gordon, *U.S. Tells Calmer Story of Woman's Invasion Role*, N.Y. Times, Jan. 9, 1990, at A14. The initial news report was based upon interviews with some members of the unit. It illustrates a rather common phenomenon known as scenario fulfillment in that combatants (particularly those going into combat for the first time) see what they are expecting to see. Apparently some of the soldiers believed they saw members of the PDF in the kennel and fired in reaction, at which time all of the unit members became engaged in a one-way firefight with a non-existent enemy force. Each member of the unit doubtless would be able to pass a polygraph that he or she had been in combat as a result of what each believes occurred that night, even though later investigation indicates that the only enemy soldier present at the kennel was unarmed and hid until the United States firefight was concluded. He was discovered in the ranks of the unit when a muster was held at the end of the action.

The author witnessed several similar non-attacks during his service in the Republic of Vietnam. The most spectacular was a three-hour firefight on the night of 22–23 February 1969 between the rear-area headquarters of two U.S. Marine units in a valley below the author's position. It was the night of the 1969 Tet Offensive in which the North Vietnamese succeeded in (among other things) infiltrating most headquarters areas of First Marine Division units located near Da Nang. The author's reaction company had secured part of the First Marine Division headquarters perimeter after brief fighting, and was situated on a hill overlooking a small Vietnamese village that was straddled by the headquarters of the 1st Motor Transport Battalion and the 26th Marines (Rear), each of which had repulsed enemy attacks with some losses earlier. It is not certain how the firefight between the two units began, but it continued until daybreak, by which time each unit had virtually exhausted its ammunition supply. In a subsequent infantry sweep through the Vietnamese village by the author's unit, no enemy soldiers were found and, miraculously, no civilians had been killed by the massive exchange of small-arms fire. Yet Marines in both units swore to the frontal assaults each had received during the time in which they had fired at one another, notwithstanding the fact that the units were approximately two hundred meters apart and neither had sent Marines out of their defensive positions.

These examples again serve to illustrate the danger U.S. officials found in providing the ICRC the authority (in article 81(1) of Protocol I) to scurry about the battlefield as some sort of referee of events. The potential for error is great, not only by combatant units but, as seen in the conflicting news stories regarding the PDF kennel "attack," by individuals endeavoring to ascertain what happened after the event.

to which a relatively supportive media had access. It serves to illustrate that it is difficult, if not impossible, to ascertain the facts related to an attack *after* it has occurred, let alone examine an attack and determine the precise number of casualties, the persons entitled to be characterized as civilians, and the cost of the attack in terms of civilian lives *vis-à-vis* its anticipated military advantage. If it is difficult to determine the facts for an operation as simple as an understrength company attack on an undefended objective, one can imagine the difficulty of determining the facts—such as accountability for a particular civilian casualty—in a complex air strike involving more than one hundred aircraft against a target defended by sophisticated air defenses. It is all the more difficult for an attacking commander to make any kind of determination *prior* to an attack, particularly when (as compared to a defender) he knows little, if anything, about the location of the civilian population or individual civilians. While battlefield intelligence capabilities are increasing, no nation possesses the capacity to locate, identify, or track civilians. Any attempt to depart from the customary practice of recognizing the defender as having the primary (if not exclusive) responsibility for separating the civilian population from military objectives while foisting the responsibility for minimization of collateral civilian casualties upon an attacker is doomed from the outset. It seriously undermines the law of war by encouraging a defender to use civilians as a point of exploitation for tactical and propaganda purposes.

One page from history will serve to illustrate the latter point. On 10 May 1940, the German city of Freiburg in Breisgau was struck by bombs from raiding aircraft. Although British officials denied any attack on or air operations in the vicinity of the city, the attack was widely exploited by Nazi propaganda officials as an example of British barbarism. Three years after the war British military author J.F.C. Fuller condemned the RAF for its attack on Freiburg.[538] Eight years later official German historians announced that they had determined that the bombing had been carried out by errant Luftwaffe aircraft.[539] The lesson from this incident is two-fold: (a) determining responsibility for an action is very difficult, particularly in war where one party controls the site at which an incident occurred, who (b) may exploit it for propaganda purposes. If a reputable military historian can commit such a serious factual error in the calm of postwar, unrushed research, it is evident that it will be difficult, if not impossible, to obtain an objective determination regarding responsibility for civilian casualties from a particular operation in the midst of a conflict. The susceptibility, apparently willing, of ICRC officials to accept without question PLO statements regarding civilian casualties during the 1982 Israeli incursion into Lebanon indicates the fallacy of such an approach. Any evaluation of an attack on the basis of reported civilian casualties is an evaluation based on substantially less than a complete picture, and the whole picture may not be ascertainable until some years later, if ever.

Very early in this article a fundamental distinction was noted between the law of Geneva and the law of The Hague. The former deals with the protection of war victims who have fallen into the hands of the enemy, while the latter addresses the

538. J. FULLER, THE SECOND WORLD WAR, 1939–45, A STRATEGICAL AND TACTICAL HISTORY 222 (London, 1948).

539. *Lost Luftwaffe Aircraft Raided German City*, N.Y. Times, Apr. 5, 1956, at 1; Hackman, *The 1940 Bombing of Freiburg: Fuller and the Writing of Military History*, 25 AEROSPACE HISTORIAN 155–58 (Fall/Sept. 1978); and G. UEBERSCHAR & W. WETTE, BOMBEN UND LEGENDEN: DIE SCHRITTWEISE AUFKLARUNG DES LUFTANGRIFFS AUF FREIBURG AM 10 MAI 1940 (Freiburg, 1981). The author is indebted to Dr. Horst Boogof the *Militargeschichtlichen Forschungsamtes* for the last reference.

use of force on the battlefield. Although there have been violations, the law of Geneva has been relatively successful because the four Geneva conventions address a situation in which the obligated party is in total control.

The opposite is true with regard to the law of The Hague. Except for the obligation to provide warning, which itself is not absolute, an attacking force has no control over the civilian population in the vicinity of enemy military objectives, and in most cases will have no idea where the civilian population or individual civilians are at the time of his attack. It is a full-time task for a commander's intelligence staff to ascertain the location and strength of the enemy threat facing a command. Even where an attacking commander exercises ordinary care to minimize collateral civilian casualties, his responsibility traditionally has been tertiary—behind that of the defending commander (who has control over the civilian population) and the individual civilian (who must exercise common sense in the face of probable risks).

A fundamental problem with articles 48 to 58 of Protocol I is that those articles appear to be developed less for combat than for a basketball free-throwing contest in which each opponent obligingly permits the other to shoot his shots. The applicability of the rules to combat would be appropriate if neither opponent had consciously slept for forty-eight hours; each is ill-fed (if fed at all); the basket is constantly moving, at times obscured by smoke or fog; and the opponent is moving about the court in unknown strength, shooting at the player trying to make his baskets, who may be using a ball that is (perhaps unbeknownst to the shooter) defective or damaged by actions of his opponent. In the midst of this, the nonshooting opponent shifts his basket into the center of the spectator seats, in violation of the rules of the competition. The player attempting to make his baskets complains about his opponent placing the basket amidst the spectators, thereby endangering them. Officials do not penalize the offender, and the spectators remain in their seats. Under the rules of Protocol I, the basket shooter is admonished that he will be held responsible for any baskets that miss and cause injury to the spectators. The words of H. L. Mencken are an appropriate description of articles 48 to 58 of Protocol I, "For every problem there is a solution that is perfectly simple, perfectly obvious, and perfectly wrong."

A fundamental problem with articles 48 to 58 of Protocol I is that those articles fail to consider what Clausewitz referred to as the friction of war. His words are timeless, and are of greater value today than they were when they were written 150 to 200 years ago, not only with respect to the failure of the participants in the Diplomatic Conference to appreciate the endeavor they were trying to regulate,[540] but to the problems of the combat commander. As Clausewitz observed:

540. Clausewitz states that:

> If one has never personally experienced war, one cannot understand in what the difficulties mentioned really exist, nor why the commander should need any brilliance and exceptional ability. Everything looks simple; the knowledge required does not look remarkable, the strategic options are so obvious that by comparison the simplest problem of higher mathematics has an impressive scientific dignity. Once war has actually been seen the difficulties become clear; but it is extremely hard to describe the unseen, the all-pervading element that brings about this change of perspective.

If CLAUSEWITZ, ON WAR 119 (M. Howard & P. Paret trans. 1976) [hereinafter CLAUSEWITZ, 1976]. Others have made similar observations. A young British officer writing almost one hundred years ago of his observations of combat in Afghanistan, roundly condemns those "serene critics who note the errors, and forget the difficulties, who judge in safety of what was done in danger, and from the security of peace, pronounce upon the conduct of war." W. CHURCHILL, THE STORY OF THE MALAKAND FIELD FORCE: AN EPISODE OF FRONTIER WAR 110 (London, 1898). Similarly, the late British naval historian Arthur J. Marder, remarking on the 31 May–1 June 1916 battle of Jutland, has written:

> Everything in war is very simple, but the simplest thing is difficult. The difficulties accumulate and end by producing a kind of friction that is inconceivable unless one has experienced war. . . .
>
> Friction is the only concept that more or less corresponds to the factors that distinguish real war from war on paper. The military machine—the army and everything related to it—is basically very simple and therefore seems easy to manage . . . . In fact, it is different, and every fault and exaggeration of the theory is instantly exposed in war. The dangers inseparable from war and the physical exertions war demands can aggravate the problem to such an extent that they must be ranked among its principal ones . . . .[541]

Friction is brought about in large measure by uncertainty, about which Clausewitz wrote, "War is the realm of uncertainty; three quarters of the factors on which action in war is based are wrapped in a fog of greater or lesser uncertainty."[542] Uncertainty is caused in part by a lack of information regarding the enemy. Clausewitz noted that, "Many intelligence reports in war are contradictory; even more are false, and most are uncertain."

For these reasons, Clausewitz rejects as "worse than useless" efforts to systematize warfare with rules and formulas, raising three objections:

> They aim at fixed rules; but in war everything is uncertain, and calculations have to be made with variable quantities.

> There has been altogether too much passion and bias in the "Jutland controversy," more particularly as regards the two British principals. . . . Throughout I have made a conscientious attempt to be dispassionate and to eschew "the lucid view afforded by hindsight," for, as Homer put it, "After the event even a fool is wise." Throughout I have also borne in mind how little those concerned in the battle really knew what was going on. To judge their actions from the comfort of an armchair, with the dispatches, a mass of elaborate and accurate diagrams, and descriptions of the battle from both sides—none of which material, of course, was available to the commanding officers at Jutland—spread out before one, and with utter disregard of the effect of smoke and mist and of what the [Commander-in-Chief] and squadron commanders knew at the time of the High Seas Fleet's strength, position, and formation, would be unjust to those officers and make a mockery of Clio, the Muse of History. The historian needs also to remember that ship-to-ship directional wireless telegraphy was then in its infancy, that air reconnaissance did not, practically speaking, exist, and that there was no radar. Where possible, I have endeavored to soften my criticism by charity for human frailty and by the knowledge that, as Captain John Cresswell has so well put it in another context, "in the stresses of a great war the Fates are often stronger than man, and man at his best; that an enterprise may fail, and fail disastrously, without the officer responsible for it necessarily deserving castigation.

III FROM THE DREADNOUGHT TO SCAPA FLOW, JUTLAND AND AFTER, vii (2d ed., London, 1978). A fundamental error of the participants in the Diplomatic Conference that drafted the 1977 Protocols was a disregard for the advice and experience of the Churchills and Marders of the world. Following more than a decade's research, including discussion of the events of the Diplomatic Conference with numerous participants, the author came to realize that this was intentional; many of the participants were striving for a strict liability standard in judging the battlefield decisions of military commanders.

541. CLAUSEWITZ, 1976, *supra* note 540, at 119–20. *See also* CLAUSEWITZ, ON WAR 24–25 (M. Howard tran. 1983) [hereinafter CLAUSEWITZ, 1983]; Cheesman, *Smart Weapons, Stressed Out Soldiers*, Wall Street J., Sept. 7, 1989, at 14; and Summers, *Where Confusion is Normal*, Wash. Times, Oct. 19, 1983, at F3, where Summers notes that:

> The military's version of Murphy's Law (except that it has far more serious implications), *friction* is an inherent part of military operations. Nothing ever goes as planned. Countless minor incidents—the kind you can never really foresee—combine to lower the general level of performance, so that one always falls short of the intended goal.

542. CLAUSEWITZ, 1976, *supra* note 540, at 101, 117. The remarks of Clausewitz are mirrored by those of Wellington, who observed that "All the business of war . . . is to endeavor to find out what you don't know by what you do. That's what I call guessing what was on the other side of the hill." Wellington's problem was lack of information. While intelligence-gathering capabilities have improved, a commander's lack of knowledge of his enemy's whereabouts, capabilities, and intentions has been exacerbated by an enhancement in deception.

> They direct the inquiry exclusively toward physical quantities, whereas all military action is intertwined with psychological forces and effects.
>
> They consider only unilateral action, whereas war consists of a continuous interaction of opposites.[543]

In considering articles 48 to 58 in the context of aerial bombardment and the friction of war, myriad factors contribute to the success or failure of an attempt of a pilot or aircrew to bomb accurately. Some are within the control of the attacking aircrew(s); some are within the control of the defender; and some are not within the control of either. The following table illustrates these factors and their normal degree of control:[544]

Factor	Control of Attacker	Control of Defender	Control of Neither
Target Intelligence	some	some	
Planning time	some		
Aircrews	some		
Crew experience	some		
Force integrity	some	some	
Distance to target	some	some	some

543. *Id.* at 136. For an analysis of Clausewitz's view of uncertainty in war, *see* Herbig, *Chance and Uncertainty in On War*, in CLAUSEWITZ AND MODERN STRATEGY 95–116 (Michael I. Handel, ed. London, 1986).

544. The ICRC COMMENTARY, *supra* note 247, at 684 makes reference to the existence of factors contributing to collateral civilian casualties, listing

> their location (possibly within or in the vicinity of a military objective), the terrain (landslides, floods, *etc.*), accuracy of the weapons used (greater or lesser dispersion, depending on the trajectory, the range, the ammunition used, *etc.*), weather conditions (visibility, wind, *etc.*), the specific nature of the objectives concerned (ammunition depots, fuel reservoirs, main roads of military importance at or in the vicinity of inhabited areas, *etc.*), technical skill of the combatants (random dropping of bombs when unable to hit the intended target).
>
> All of these factors must be taken into consideration whenever an attack could hit incidentally civilian persons and objects.

The ICRC COMMENTARY is significant in three respects: (a) it gives no consideration to the effect of enemy defenses; (b) it disregards the defender's responsibility for civilian casualties where military objectives have been commingled with civilian objects or the civilian population; and (c) it assumes (as illustrated in the last sentence of the quote) that the commander of an attacking force will be able to anticipate all of these problems in advance, and plan accordingly, or that even if he is unable to anticipate certain factors, that he will be able to do something about it. For example, General Curtis LeMay has stated that the B–29 Superfortress crews he commanded to bomb Japan in February 1945 were basically untrained, which he realized would lead to less accurate bombing than he would have preferred. However, General LeMay did not have the luxury of doing anything other than that which is referred to as "on-the-job training"—in combat. LEMAY & YENNE, SUPERFORTRESS: THE B–29 AND AMERICAN AIR POWER 120 (1987).

Factor	Control of Attacker	Control of Defender	Control of Neither
Mechanical problems	some	some	some
Weather at target	minimal		most
Enemy defenses		all	
Human factor	some		

Each of these factors will be examined briefly to illustrate their potential effect on bombing accuracy.

Target intelligence. Even in the best target intelligence systems, the quality of intelligence may range from excellent to none. The intelligence may be influenced by whether the target is fixed or mobile; confusion over the map name;[545] and by its timeliness.[546]

Planning time. Planning time is critical to mission success. The 1983 Grenada rescue operation was hampered by the minimal amount of planning time for deploying units (less than forty hours for most units from the time of receipt of their warning order to the time at which they were in combat). Conversely, delays that permitted the luxury of more planning and rehearsal proved of no value in the 1971 rescue operation to the Son Tay prisoner of war camp in North Vietnam, because the American prisoners had been moved.[547] Delays by key decision makers led to United States special operations planners planning the ill-fated 1980 Iranian rescue mission in approximate two-week cycles, rather than spending four months planning a single mission.[548]

545. For example, there was considerable confusion regarding the 16 March 1968 massacre at My Lai village because there were several villages by that name and its correct name of Song My, all in the same area. During the 1983 rescue operation in Grenada, because of the suddenness of the operation American units were operating with three different maps, all with different map coodinates. But the crowning point of confusion was caught by U.S. intelligence sources who viewed an official Soviet news report of the American landing in which the Soviet briefer was discussing the operation while pointing to the city of Granada in southeast Spain.

546. Thus one author has observed that: "Intelligence types . . . routinely (usually quite innocently) withhold information aircrews would find of inestimable value or, more often, mistakenly edit the key fact of highest value to the tactician." Commenting on timeliness, he noted that

> I vividly remember watching a major [air] strike on a heavily-defended target being briefed in May 1965 using year-old U–2 [reconnaissance aircraft] photography. The same sort of thing happened when we returned to North Vietnam in 1972, in the same war, and most available photography dated to 1967–68. In 1968, a survey of targeting materials for a different target system in a different area found that three-fourths of the photographs in them were at least two years old.

Haering, *How Tactical Air Works*, 108 U.S. NAVAL INST. PROC. 62 (Nov. 1982). The interaction of the various elements under consideration can be illustrated by the fact that target intelligence photographs only one day old may be of little value to the strike force if the defender has shifted his mobile defenses to different locations, thereby affecting the way in which the strike force responds on arrival at the target. The success of the enemy defenses in turn will have a marked effect on bombing accuracy.

547. For discussion of the Son Tay mission, *see* B. SCHEMMER, THE RAID (1976).

548. Personal knowledge of author, who served as a legal adviser for portions of the rescue mission planning. To date, no accurate narrative or analysis of the 1980 rescue mission has been published. The forthcoming account by Colonel James H. Kyle, USAF (Ret.), THE GUTS TO TRY (1990), should do much to rectify this.

Adequate planning time is critical for a number of reasons, such as better intelligence, more time for pilots/aircrews to study the route to the target and the target itself, and deconfliction of the various parts of the strike force, particularly in the target area. It becomes more critical with increasing complexity and duration of the mission. At the same time, excess planning time can lead to a "wear-down process" in which the crews flying the mission are exhausted by mission preparation before they take off. Planning time is something over which operational commanders and aircrews in a perfect world would have exclusive control, but about which generally they have little control in actuality.

Aircrews. Several factors are affected by the aircrews involved in an airstrike. The strike commander does not have complete control over this factor, in that he must accept the men assigned him, and the aircrews are affected by the aircraft assigned them.

Part of the factor involves aircrew training. As one veteran of air combat over North Vietnam learned:

> Those who have not delivered weapons from an airplane have little or no conception of the problems involved or the requisite skills. There are so many variables in the accuracy equation and the chance for error is so great as to make one wonder how fighter pilots do as well as they do.[549]

Yet the United States has learned over and over that its forces usually have not trained for the war they are called upon to fight. This was true both in Korea and Vietnam.[550] Proper training or not, however, the missions must be flown. The United States is not unique in this respect, because opponents tend to change in identification or in their tactics, as the Israeli Air Force learned to its shock in its 1973 war.[551] This in turn can have an effect on bombing accuracy.

A debate has existed for years over whether tactical aircraft should have a pilot only or be multi-seated,[552] and whether aircraft should be single, dual, or multimission in design.[553] In theory, the more missions an aircraft can fly, the fewer types of aircraft that have to be bought, reducing logistics and maintenance costs. But there is a point of diminishing return, because the more missions for which an aircrew must train—for example, air superiority, battlefield interdiction, or deep-strike—the less skilled the aircrew is with each. Recent American Navy consideration of using its F–14 Tomcat fighters as strike aircraft is technically feasible, but would cause F–14 crews to train for a mission that has not been theirs for almost two decades; the same is true for the pilots making the transition from the F–15 Eagle to the F–15E Strike Eagle. In each case, the policy decisions made are reasonable and honest, often dictated by fiscal constraints as part of the normal budgeting process. But at the cutting edge, each affects potential bombing accuracy. In exercising the precautions in the attack called for by article 57 of Protocol I, a commander cannot point to these decisions in explaining his actions. He must fight the war and fly the mission with what is on the shelf.

549. Appel, *Bombing Accuracy in a Combat Environment*, 26 AIR U. REV. 40 (July–August 1975).

550. This issue is discussed at length in J. BROUGHTON, GOING DOWNTOWN, *supra* note 109 [training for tactical airstrikes against pinpoint targets] and R. HALLION, *supra* note 221 [training for close air support missions].

551. *See* the description of IAF air losses in the opening days of that conflict in E. O'BALLANCE, NO VICTOR, NO VANQUISHED: THE YOM KIPPUR WAR, *supra* note 226.

552. *See* Flanagan, *The Fighter Force: How Many Seats?* 32 AIR U. REV. 3–21 (May–June 1981).

553. *See* Suter, *Janus: Concept for a Multipurpose Fighter*, 31 AIR U. REV. 22–41 (May–June 1981).

Crew experience. Just as flight experience (overall or in aircraft type) leads to a decrease in flying accidents,[554] combat experience affects bombing accuracy, aircrew survival, and mission accomplishment, as the following illustrates:

> attrition decreased markedly as the war progressed. This was clearly the result of an aircrew training process. . . . The most striking case involved the Hai Duong Bridge and nearby targets. We never made a strike there in 1965 [the first year of the bombing campaign] without losing at least one aircraft. That year, we lost aircraft at a rate of 39 per 1,000 attack sorties. By 1967, we had reduced attrition . . . by a factor of 13. In a randomly selected 30-day period, the attrition rate was 3 per 1,000 attack sorties. Improved hardware made a contribution and probably more important, we were striking two or three times a day in 1967 instead of once or twice a fortnight as we did in 1965. But the defenses had also improved in quality and substantially increased in quantity. The bottom line was that our aircrews had learned how to live within a defense [surface-to-air missile] and flak environment, and they learned faster than the defenders.[555]

Training programs at the Air Force's Fighter Weapons School, the Navy's Fighter Weapons School (''Top Gun''), and the Navy's Strike Warfare Center (''Strike U'') have been developed to reduce the gap in experience between peacetime training and wartime missions. As with peacetime training programs throughout the history of aviation, however, realism is conditioned by safety conditions and environmental considerations, including the objections of the local population to the noise made by high-performance aircraft and/or low-level training. These factors in turn affect a commander's ability to accomplish his mission in the most accurate manner. Ironically, some of the persons who protest realistic training in peacetime are the same ones who in all likelihood will demand the greatest precision of aircrews executing their attacks once a conflict begins. But unless those aircrews are permitted to train as they would fight, their chance for successful (and discriminate) accomplishment of their mission—and survival—is substantially diminished.

Force integrity and distance to target. These two factors are considered together, as each ultimately has an effect on the degree of accuracy an aircrew may exhibit in attack of its target, either because of force attrition as a result of enemy action or mechanical failures, or crew fatigue brought on by combat enroute to the target (and the fear of more combat during egress) or mission length. Eighth Air Force attack of ''milk run'' targets close to their bases in England, where the bomber force was protected the entire time by a heavy fighter escort, as compared to the less-accurate attacks on the Swedish-owned ball-bearing factories at Schweinfurt-Regensburg in August and October 1943, following unescorted, heavily-attacked flights to the target, illustrate this point.[556]

The capabilities of a strike force to bomb accurately today would be seriously degraded if, for example, those aircraft assigned the responsibility for suppression of enemy air defenses (SEAD) were to suffer significant losses enroute to the target either as a result of mechanical failures or enemy action. The strike force undoubtedly would continue its mission, even though attack accuracy would be affected by the increased distraction of aircrews by enemy air defenses brought about by loss of portions of the SEAD support package. Similarly, the F–111F aircraft that flew from

554. *See* Borowsky, *Pilot Flight Experience and Aircraft Mishaps*, U.S. NAVAL SAFETY CENTER; Borowsky, *Fighter Aircraft Class A F/FRM Rates vs. Pilot Experience CY 77–83*, 30 APPROACH 7 (Jan. 1985); and Borowsky, *Attack Aircraft Class A F/FRM Rates vs. Pilot Experience*, 31 APPROACH 9 (Mar. 1985).

555. Haering, *supra* note 546, at 65.

556. The latter raids are described in T. COFFEY, DECISION OVER SCHWEINFURT: THE U.S. AIR FORCE BATTLE FOR DAYLIGHT BOMBING (1977), and M. MIDDLEBROOK, THE SCHWEINFURT-REGENSBURG MISSION (1983).

the United Kingdom to attack terrorist-related targets in Libya in April 1986 suffered heavy attrition of aircraft from mechanical problems due to the distance flown to the target. While the unusually restrictive rules of engagement (ROE) prevented some aircrews from completing the mission, absent those ROE most could have attacked the target successfully, though with some degradation of their capability to bomb as accurately.[567]

Mechanical problems. Anything designed by man is destined to break, regardless of the degree of care and maintenance provided. This is particularly true of combat aircraft, which undergo considerable stress during routine flight operations. One need only read a weekly summary of military aircraft mishaps, or consider one's own experience with commercial airline flight cancellations or delays owing to mechanical difficulties, to appreciate the degree to which mechanical problems occur in a peacetime environment.[558] The likelihood of mechanical problems is compounded in military aircraft by the requirement for state-of-the-art equipment to enhance bombing accuracy and aircraft survival in an increasingly hostile air defense environment. That state-of-the-art equipment in turn may not have the same degree of reliability as equipment that has undergone reliability enhancements over a period of time. The failure of equipment due to mission duration during the 1986 Libyan airstrike has been mentioned as a way in which bombing accuracy can be degraded. Another example will further illustrate this problem.

On April 1, 1944, B–24 Liberator aircraft of the 392nd Bomb Group were part of a larger force assigned to attack the I.G. Farbenindustrie Chemical Works at Ludwigshaven, Germany. Due to human (navigational) error and weather (unexpectedly high winds), the group failed to reach its target. Instead, the group elected to attack an alternate target of opportunity, the town of Pforzheim.[559] Weather and human errors caused the group to fly into Switzerland and mistake the town of Schaffhausen for Pforzheim. As was the practice, all group aircraft would bomb on the signal of the lead aircraft. But early in the mission the crews of the lead aircraft discovered that its bomb bay doors would not open completely. In order to remedy this problem, the bomb bay door safety pins were removed by the top turret gunner. However, their removal apparently led to premature release of the bombs before the lead aircraft crossed the bomb release line. The other aircraft in the group then dropped on what they believed was the lead aircraft's signal. In this instance, a mechanical error served as a blessing, as it resulted in all of the group's bombs falling in open countryside outside of Schaffhausen.[560]

557. *See* Parks, *supra* note 86, and Parks, *Righting the Rules of Engagement*, *supra* note 460, for detailed discussion of the Libyan airstrike. While the author has seen the official reports of the causes of attrition of the F–111F force, that information remains classified other than to say that the length of the flight to the target was a major factor.

558. *See* Casto, *A Week in Naval Aviation*, Weekly Summary of Aircraft Incidents, No.35–89 (20–26 Aug. 1989), at 1–3, which in providing a collage of excerpts from a typical week's message traffic lists twenty-nine mishaps. A separate feature prepared by the Naval Air Engineering Center entitled *Things Falling Off Aircraft This Week* lists 50 pieces of equipment lost in the course of flight operations during the week. Edition No. 41–89 (1–7 Oct. 1989) lists five aircraft lost in the course of flight operations during that week. Only one loss appears attributable to human error.

559. Pforzheim contained no targets of military value, but was to be bombed simply because it was a German town, as was the practice of the time. *See* C. McBride, *supra* note 443, at 74. In this respect U.S. practice has improved markedly, as aircrews today would seek other targets of military value, jettison their bombs in nonpopulated areas, or return to base with their loads if possible.

560. C. McBride, *supra* note 443, at 77–79. Unfortunately, other aircraft bombed not only Schaffhausen but Grafenhausen, causing considerable damage and resulting in the death or injury of 100 Swiss civilians. The United States paid reparations totaling $57,000,000 for the damages, injuries, and death that resulted from the incident. *Id.* at 96–125. Regrettably this was not the only occasion in which the United States Army Air Corps bombed Swiss towns or cities by mistake. While McBride

The mechanical problems discussed thus far have occurred as a result of breakdown of equipment. They also may occur due to damage from enemy air defenses which, while not causing an aircraft to break off its attack, do result in degradation of bombing accuracy, in some cases without the knowledge of the aircrew. As will be discussed, enemy air defenses have accomplished their mission if they have caused damage that will prevent the attacking aircraft's munitions from striking the intended target. But who is accountable for the collateral casualties that occur as a result? Nations award their highest decorations for valor to aircrews who press home the attack on a target in spite of enemy defenses and/or damage to their aircraft. It would be unreasonable to think that any nation would now expect its aircrews to break off an attack due to aircraft damage from enemy fire because of the concern for collateral civilian casualties expressed in Protocol I. This is particularly true because in most cases a pilot (or aircrew) will not be aware of the precise nature of damage to the aircraft until completion of the mission and return to base.

One may always hope for a "zero defects" environment; no aircrew wishes to undergo years of training and preparation, only to fly all the way to a target and miss because of mechanical failures. Nonetheless, there will be occasions where bombs or other munitions are dropped or launched with the honest expectation that they are directed at the intended target, only to find that they miss their target due to a malfunction in the aircraft, its bomb-aiming equipment, or the munitions. A strict accountability standard for collateral damage or injuries is not attainable by any nation, because of the degree to which mechanical failures are likely to occur in a modern combat environment.

Weather at target. Weather is a critical factor for bombing accuracy, and one over which an attacking force commander exercises little or no control, other than to cancel a mission until weather improves—a luxury that war does not always permit, or which may not otherwise exist. Thus the winter overcast that settled in over most of Germany during the fall of 1944 led to abandonment of the Eighth Air Force's effort at precision through visual bombing, and resulted in less accurate radar area bombing for a substantial number of the missions that followed.[561] B–29 force bombing of industrial targets in Japan during the closing months of World War II was shifted from daytime, high-altitude bombing using optical bombsights to nighttime, low-altitude radar bombing in large measure owing to high winds and cloud cover over the targets.[562]

The 1972 Linebacker I campaign against North Vietnam relied heavily upon tactical aircraft using precision-guided munitions (PGMs). But anticipating the possi-

---

concentrates on the 1 Apr. 1944 mission in which he participated, his book discusses the other incidents as well. *Id.* at 126–30. *See also* Helmreich, *The Diplomacy of Apology*, 28 AIR U. REV. 19–37 (May–June 1977).

The 1 April 1944 bombing of Schaffhausen also illustrates the difficulty of an on-scene witness determining the cause of civilian casualties occurring as a result of combat operations. A primary cause of the misdirection of the bomb group was the fact that winds were sixty miles in excess of the winds briefed for the mission and not from the anticipated direction. The leader's bomb-aiming equipment functioned intermittently and while on bombing approach over 8/10ths clouds, the equipment failed completely. Seeing what he believed was the target (Pforzheim) through a hole in the clouds, he bombed Schaffhausen, and the other aircraft bombed on his lead.

The initial official explanation of the incident blamed "extraordinary navigation difficulties and bad weather" for the accidental bombing, which exacerbated the reaction by the Swiss inasmuch as the weather at Schaffhausen as viewed from the ground was clear. C. MCBRIDE, *supra* note 443, at 100–04. The difference in perspective can be appreciated.

561. The analysis in Shandroff, *supra* note 203, is particularly good in examining this campaign and the weather effects. *See also* C. MCBRIDE, *supra* note 443, at 22–24.

562. *See* LEMAY AND YENNE, *supra* note 196, at 87–88, 104–05, 108–09, 118–21, 130, 132–34, 141, 151–52, 154; *see also* H. HANSELL, *supra* note 195.

bility of bombing operations continuing through the monsoon months of the fall and winter, the Strategic Air Command was tasked to select targets outside populated areas that would be appropriate for attack by its B–52 aircraft using their less accurate but all-weather capabilities. Tactical aircraft continued to play an important role in the subsequent Linebacker II campaign, but the adverse effect of weather on PGMs severely curtailed their use, and resulted in some collateral damage to civilian objects and collateral civilian casualties where weather (fog, rain, mist) degraded sensor resolution in the PGM.[563]

The preceding illustrate how attackers have resorted to less discriminate methods of attack where weather precluded use of the most discriminate. But the largest impact of weather on collateral civilian casualties occurred in the firestorms that struck Hamburg and Dresden during World War II. In each, unique meteorological conditions were the principal contributing factor to the conflagrations that followed. These factors were not fully appreciated by meteorological scientists until years after the war.[564]

Weather has influenced military operations throughout history, and will continue to do so. As former Chief of Staff of the West German Air Force General Johannes Steinhoff has noted: "If the Russians come, they are unlikely to court suicide by choosing a bright summer's day with visibility to the horizon; they will come at night, exploiting the murkiest weather that their forecasters can predict and they will travel beneath a sophisticated and dense antiaircraft umbrella."[565]

As General Steinhoff indicates, military commanders are not always allowed the luxury of fighting under optimum conditions. A force facing an enemy possessed of air superiority will choose to fight under adverse weather conditions in order to degrade the air capabilities of its opponent. The force with air superiority must fight using those capabilities as best as they can be employed under the circumstances. If civilians are commingled with military objectives, or if the force bent on denying an enemy the full range of his air superiority fails to discharge his responsibilities as stated in articles 48 and 51(7) of Protocol I, adverse weather will increase the probability of collateral civilian casualties, in spite of the best efforts of the attacking air force to minimize such casualties.

Similarly, while the science of weather prediction has improved markedly over the past half century, predictions remain subject to myriad variables that preclude certainty. This is particularly true in predicting the weather over a target at the time of attack. If the weather is not such as to lead to abort of the attack or attack of an alternate target, or if military requirements necessitate the attack of a target regardless of the weather, then weather may have an impact on accuracy which is beyond the control of either the attacker or the defender. Collateral casualties occurring because of weather phenomenan or conditions are equally beyond the responsibility of attacker or defender.

Enemy defenses. Fundamental to aerial bombardment is the understanding that placing aerially-delivered munitions on target is the culmination of a very long and expensive chain of effort. This effort includes aircraft design, development, produc-

563. *See* Ziegler, *Weather Problems Affecting Use of Precision Guided Munitions*, 32 NAVAL WAR C. REV. 95–106 (May–June 1979); and Samuel, *Tactical PGMs: Implications in Perspective*, 9 PARAMETERS 32–44, at n.36 (June 1979).

564. The reader is referred to the explanation of "the firestorm phenomenon" in particular in H. BRUNSWIG, FEUERSTURM UBER HAMBURG 264–73 (Stuttgart, 1978), and G. MOSGROVE, OPERATION GOMORRAH 102–16 (London, 1981), for a precise explanation of this phenomenon.

565. As quoted in Baldwin, *European Weather and Round-the-Clock Air Operations*, 32 AIR U. REV. 67–73 (May–June 1981).

tion, and acquisition, along with all associated equipment and munitions; selection and training of aircrew; the target intelligence process; and mission planning. A sortie flown ineffectively constitutes a tremendous loss of irretrievable combat power at very high risk and cost. It is somewhat of an understatement, then, to acknowledge the desire of attacking aircrews to be as discriminate as possible in order to strike their intended target.

Enemy defenses, on the other hand, are intended to create an environment that will *cause* an attack to be less discriminate. The purpose of enemy defenses is not necessarily to cause aircraft losses; the defender has accomplished his mission if he makes the attacker miss his target. This has been accomplished in a number of ways, such as through camouflage or other forms of visual deception; electronic deception or countermeasures; and active measures, including antiaircraft guns, surface-to-air missiles, and air defense aircraft. A few examples from history will serve to illustrate the point:

a. Antiaircraft fire historically has been employed to force aircraft to fly at higher altitudes, thereby decreasing bombing accuracy, or otherwise to disrupt aircrew concentration on striking the target. Thus in the 1930s:

> The [British] Committee [on air defense] came to certain conclusions on the role to be played by A.A. [antiaircraft] guns. They were (1) to destroy hostile aircraft; (2) to co-operate with fighter aircraft by disorganizing enemy formations so that our fighters might engage them with the best possible chance of success, and by indicating the position of enemy aircraft by shell-burst; and (3) to deny hostile aircraft opportunities of . . . accurate bombing by forcing them to fly high and alter course at critical moments.[566]

In the 1986 airstrike against Libya, aircrews encountered erratic Libyan antiaircraft fire that was not caused by American SEAD measures. The Libyans were employing tracer fire at night in the hope that it would affect the situational awareness of the American aircrews, causing them to miss their targets.[567]

b. Enemy fighters historically have been used not only to down attacking aircraft, but to force them to jettison their bombs prior to reaching their target, frequently with tragic results. James Maloney Spaight lists two such incidents:

> There were some unfortunate incidents in which jettisoned bombs hit hospitals, both civil and military. One occurred on 15 November 1940, in France. It was recorded by Mr. Narracott. "One [German] Heinkel," he wrote, "chased by a [RAF] Hurricane . . . jettisoned the whole of its load on to a maternity hospital at Bethenville. . . ."
>
> On 8 February 1944, it was reported . . . that an American field hospital, clearly marked, was dive-bombed on the preceding day and that 22 were killed and 63 wounded. The report was corrected on the following day. What had happened was that a [German] dive-bomber, trying to escape from an Allied fighter, had jettisoned its . . . bombs and they had unfortunately come down on the hospital.[568]

Another author recorded a similar incident with equally tragic results that occurred during the Battle of Britain:

> Another dark drizzly evening [Stanford] Tuck stalked a lone [German] Ju.88 for close on thirty minutes. . . . He was in the white bite of the moonlight, but Tuck pounced.

566. F. PILE, ACK-ACK 59 (London, 1949).
567. Reported to the author by Navy, Marine Corps, and Air Force aircrews who participated in the airstrike.
568. J. SPAIGHT, *supra* note 137, at 393.

There was time to get in only one burst. . . . He thought he'd hit it, for just before it disappeared into the overcast again, very distinctly he saw a cluster of black dots fall from its belly. At this distance his bullets couldn't have inflicted serious damage, but it was enough to make the Ju. jettison his bomb load and abandon his mission. . . .

Very early next morning, he got a long distance telephone call. It was his father. . . .

"[B]ad news I'm afraid. It's Peggy's hubby. . . .
He was killed yesterday. . . ."

And then he remembered something . . .: John [Peggy's husband] had been moved . . . to an Army camp in South Wales [near the previous night's encounter with the Ju.88] . . . .

Terrible suspicion tightened its icy grip. . . . [He] called the Intelligence Officer [to inquire of Luftwaffe activity over Wales the day before. The Intelligence Oficer replied:]

"Very quiet day. Only one minor incident. A stick of four [bombs], late in the evening, near Porthcawl. . . . Hey, wait a minute!—that must have been from the 88 you took a crack at—yes, time coincides!"

"What about . . ." Tuck's breath wouldn't come evenly, he had to force it out. "What about Porthcawl? What was hit?"

"Oh, nothing much. The stick fell in open country, but one [bomb] was just on the boundary of the Army camp at St. Donat's Castle. Damaged a lorry and a Nissen hut."

"Casualties?"

"Well, if you must know. . . . One private killed."

[T]he astounding fact had to be faced, had to be lived with: out of all the millions of people in Britain, those jettisoned bombs had killed John King Sparks. Therefore Tuck was responsible for the death of his own brother-in-law—it was Tuck who had caused the bombs to fall.[569]

The practice of defending aircraft interdicting attacking aircraft in their bomb runs continues, and was a standard tactic of MiG pilots who faced American aircraft in the skies over North Vietnam.[570]

c. Electronic warfare (EW)[571] has a potential effect on collateral civilian casual-

569. L. FORRESTER, *supra* note 469, at 130–32.

570. ACES & AERIAL VICTORIES: THE UNITED STATES AIR FORCE IN SOUTHEAST ASIA 1965–1973 10 (J. Eastman, Jr., W. Hanak, & L. Paszek, eds. 1976).

571. Electronic warfare is defined as military action involving the use of electromagnetic energy to determine, exploit, reduce, or prevent hostile use of the electromagnetic spectrum and action which retains friendly use of the electromagnetic spectrum. There are three divisions of electronic warfare (EW):

(1) Electronic countermeasures (ECM): That division of EW involving actions taken to prevent or reduce an enemy's effective use of the electromagnetic spectrum. Electronic countermeasures include:

(a) Electronic jamming: The deliberate radiation, reradiation or reflection of electromagnetic energy for the purpose of disrupting enemy use of electronic devices, equipment or systems.

(b) Electronic deception: The deliberate radiation, reradiation, alteration, suppression, absorption, denial, enhancement or reflection of electromagnetic energy in a manner intended to convey misleading information and to deny valid information to an enemy or to enemy electronics-dependent weapons. Among the types of electronic deception are: (i) manipulative electronic deception: actions to eliminate revealing, or to convey misleading, telltale indicators that may be used by hostile forces; (ii) simulative electronic deception: actions to represent friendly notional or actual capabilities to mislead hostile forces; and (iii) imitative electronic deception: the introduction of electromagnetic energy into enemy systems that imitates enemy emissions.

(2) Electronic counter-countermeasures (ECCM): That division of EW involving actions taken to ensure friendly effective use of the electromagnetic spectrum despite the enemy's use of EW.

ties in two ways. A defender's EW actions may negate an attacker's means for accomplishing an accurate attack. Alternatively, an attacker's EW countermeasures may cause a defender's antiair munitions to go awry.

One of the earliest examples of electronic warfare occurred during the Russo-Japanese War. The Japanese armored cruisers *Kasuga* and *Nisshin* commenced a long-range bombardment of the Russian base at Port Arthur. A Japanese destroyer was positioned closer to shore to observe the cruisers' fire, and to call corrections by wireless. A Russian wireless operator, overhearing the Japanese signals, held his transmitter key down and effectively jammed further Japanese communications. As a result the bombardment caused little damage.[572]

Communications jamming is but a small part of EW. EW can prevent an attacker from acquiring a target, or jam or otherwise disrupt the signals to a munition launched from or against an attacking aircraft. Moreover, EW is silent and invisible. Hence a ground observer who sees a missile fly into a schoolhouse full of children might see that it was launched from a strike aircraft, but would have no idea whether it was caused by a defect in the missile, the defender's EW measures, or an intentional attack of the schoolhouse in violation of the law of war. The author's collection of official photographs of the air campaigns over North Vietnam, for example, contains a photograph of two Soviet-built SA–2 Guideline missiles that have been launched from a site near a small village. Missile "A" is clearly headed towards the American reconnaissance aircraft that took the photograph, but missile "B" went awry on launching and now is headed directly toward the village.[573] This may have occurred as a result of United States EW actions, or because of a malfunction in the SA–2 missile. EW is a lawful intervening act by an opposing force that prevents accurate attack of the target. But it also can result in collateral civilian casualties that are beyond the control of either party to the conflict, and in most cases cannot be attributed to a particular act by one party or the other because of the number of electronic measures, countermeasures, and counter-countermeasures that may be occurring at any given moment.

d. Consider related activities, including effect of previous strikes. In the days following May 1972, when PGMs were used to great effect during the Linebacker I operations over North Vietnam, military pundits were quick to predict the demise of the gravity or so-called dumb bomb. These predictions were quickly dashed six months later, as adverse weather forced planners to resort to use of gravity bombs to

---

(3) Electronic warfare support measures: That division of EW involving actions taken under direct control of an operational commander to search for, intercept, identify, and locate sources of radiated electromagnetic energy for the purpose of threat recognition. Thus, EW support measures provide a source of information required for immediate decisions involving ECM, ECCM, avoidance, targeting, and other tactical employment of forces. Electronic warfare support measures data can be used to produce signals intelligence (SIGINT), communications intelligence (COMINT) and electronics intelligence (ELINT).

Joint Chiefs of Staff Publication 1, DICTIONARY OF MILITARY AND ASSOCIATED TERMS 128–29 (1 June 1987). As Stephen Counts states in his novel THE MINOTAUR (1989), "Quick change is the rule in electronic warfare." S. COUNTS, THE MINOTAUR 390 (1989). The unique thing about EW with respect to the 1977 Protocols is not its dynamic nature, but the fact that the delegates to the Diplomatic Conference were totally ignorant of its existence and its potential effect on the battlefield, particularly with regard to collateral civilian casualties.

572. A. PRICE, THE HISTORY OF US ELECTRONIC WARFARE, *supra* note 110, at 4–5; and A. HEZLET, ELECTRONICS AND SEA POWER 44 (London, 1975). The reader also is referred to the incident involving the Luftwaffe bombing of Dublin during the *Battle of the Beams*, as discussed *supra* note 110 for another example of the potential effect of EW.

573. The photograph is contained in Parks, *supra* note 5, at 106.

accomplish the purposes of Linebacker II, as previously described.[574] But other factors affected the accurate employment of PGMs, and as with all advances in warfare, countermeasures were and are being developed. For example:

(1) By the time of Linebacker II, the North Vietnamese had determined that electro-optical guided bombs (EOGB) and laser-guided bombs (LGB) could be neutralized through the denial of contrast for the former and through the use of smoke to obscure the target from the latter. Key targets were painted to blend with local features to prevent the contrast required for EOGB, while smoke pots were placed around other targets to defend them against LGB. Some collateral damage and casualties doubtless can be attributed to these legitimate defensive measures by the North Vietnamese, which in all probability caused the errant LGB that struck the French Embassy in Hanoi on 11 October 1972.[575]

(2) On 21 December 1972, four Air Force F–4 Phantom II aircraft carrying LGB were dispatched to attack the Hanoi Railway Station. The first two aircraft put their bombs right on target. However, the bomb of the third missed, apparently because of the smoke from the previous strikes, instead striking the *excusado* at the Cuban chancellery across the street from the Hanoi Hilton.[576]

(3) During the 1986 Libyan airstrike, smoke from the bombs of the first aircraft apparently obscured the target for a following aircraft's LGB, causing one of them to strike the French Embassy some distance away from the target.[577]

(4) In light of increased focus on the use of PGMs by land, sea and air forces, there has been a similar increase in attention to the use of obscurants on the battlefield.[578] Obscurants have one purpose: to defeat the accuracy of precision-guided munitions by blinding the seeker head of a PGM, thereby causing it to miss the target. If the defender using an obscurant is successful, and the military objectives selected for attack are surrounded by or adjacent to civilian population centers, a likely result will be collateral civilian casualties. But because of the intervening (though legitimate) act of the defender in his use of obscurants to protect his military objective(s), those casualties are not attributable to the attacker.

To summarize, a brief scenario will be offered to suggest not only the effect of intervening acts on the most precise attacks, but the difficulty that exists in totaling up collateral civilian casualties at the end of an attack:

An attacker has launched an airstrike at a military objective located in an enemy city. Warnings have been issued by the attacker that military objectives in populated areas will not be regarded as immune from attack, thereby encouraging the defender to evacuate civilians from the vicinity of legitimate targets. The defender has carried out a limited evacuation of nonessential civilians, but continues to employ civilians at military bases and other legitimate targets, including the one selected for attack on this day. He also has upgraded his defenses, employing antiaircraft guns (AAA), some of which are manned by civilians within the military objectives on the sound of the air raid sirens; large, radar-guided SA–2 Guideline surface-to-air missiles; smaller

574. *See* the discussion *supra* note 563.

575. *See* H. KISSINGER, YEARS OF UPHEAVAL 24–25 (1982).

576. Parks, *supra* note 109, at 28, n.15.

577. The bomb strike on the French Embassy was reported in news accounts at the time and confirmed by official postmission studies.

578. *See* Bulger, *Obscurants: Countermeasures to Modern Weapons*, 62 MIL. REV. 45–53 (May 1982), and Anderson, *Army Studying Device to Blind Enemy Homing in on Target*, Wash. Post, 17 Aug. 1985, at 7. Modern obscurants are multispectral; anthracene, a standard smokepot fill, is effective at defeating visible and near infrared portions of the spectrum.

SA–6 Gainful low-to-medium altitude surface-to-air missiles; small, shoulder-fired SA–14 Gremlin surface-to-air infrared (IR) heat-seeking missiles, some of which are issued to civilian workers within military objectives; small arms, some of which are issued to civilian workers within military objectives; and smoke pots and other obscurants.

The target selected for attack is located between a school and a hospital. Because of its location, the defender has concluded that it is shielded from attack and has not evacuated either the school or the hospital. Yet the items manufactured within the target are critical to the defender's war effort, and for this reason the attacker has concluded that the target must be attacked. In order to be as precise as possible, however, the actual attack will be carried out by four aircraft carrying LGB. In order to protect them, the strike force commander has assembled a large support force of airborne jammers and air-defense suppression aircraft, the latter known as Wild Weasels. The work of the support force also will minimize the effectiveness of the air defenses, thereby enhancing the probability that the mission will be executed as successfully and precisely as possible, minimizing collateral civilian casualties.

Weather forecast is for clear skies, but with a slight change of local showers in the target area. Notwithstanding their best efforts at achieving surprise, the strike force is detected and air raid warnings are sounded in the target area. Some civilians make their way to air raid shelters, but others are drawn by the curiosity of watching a battle first-hand, and decide to remain outside. Civilian workers within the target remain at their positions, with the exception of those assigned to man their AAA guns or take defensive positions after being issued their small arms or shoulder-fired IR missiles.

The Wild Weasel aircraft precede the attack force in order to defeat those surface-to-air missile (SAM) sites along the approach corridor. As one Wild Weasel detects an activated SAM site whose radar is in the tracking phase that precedes a missile launch, he launches two high-speed anti-radiation missiles (HARM) at the radar. If the radar remains on, the HARM will fly the radar's own beam back to the radar and destroy it. The radar operator realizes this and, on detecting the HARM launch, quickly fires one SA–2 missile before shutting down his radar. The track of the HARM is broken. One HARM detects another activated SA–2 radar, acquires its track, and destroys it. The blast destroys a nearby automobile garage, killing the three mechanics within it. The second HARM's track remains broken, and the missile slams into a private residence near the original enemy radar, killing its four occupants when it explodes.

Because the radar operator shut down his radar, the SA–2 he launched receives no command guidance, and its semi-active radar homing capability has been defeated by the attack force jamming. It goes out of control after its launching, and crashes into a high-rise civilian apartment building. Because of its short flight it remains full of solid liquid rocket fuel, which explodes when the 286-pound warhead detonates on impact. Thirty civilians in the apartment building are killed immediately, and another seventeen die from smoke inhalation before the building is evacuated and the resulting fire is brought under control.

The air defenses have been fully activated as the full strike force approaches the target area. The defender has launched a number of SA–2 and SA–6 missiles at the force. The missiles are unsuccessful in striking any of the aircraft, however, due to the attacker's jamming. Some of the missiles fall back into civilian areas, killing another thirty civilians. Because the attacker's jamming has defeated the radar guidance of the defender's antiaircraft guns, the crews manning the guns resort to barrage fire. As the AAA rounds reach the end of their ascent, they detonate or continue on their trajectory, exploding on impact with the ground; in either case, they rain deadly fragments onto the civilians who remained outside to watch, and another thirty are killed by this debris.

Wild Weasel aircraft immediately precede the strike aircraft over the target area, dropping antipersonnel munitions on the AAA guns and civilian employees standing outside firing small arms and launching SA–14 missiles at the Wild Weasels. Only with such suppression can the attack be as accurate as possible. The Wild Weasel attack kills twenty-seven "civilians" engaged in their various, assigned air defense missions, and most of the remaining "civilians" run back into the target building to evade the effects of the antipersonnel munitions. Some remain, however, to launch SA–6 and SA–14 missiles at the strike aircraft. The Wild Weasels and attack aircraft launch chaff and flares to defeat the guidance of these missiles, which in turn land in neighboring civilian areas, where another nine civilians are killed.

At last the strike aircraft begin to deliver their laser-guided bombs. Anticipating this, the defender has lighted smoke pots around the target and employed other obscurants. The bombs from the first attacking aircraft are right on target, however, destroying much of the target and killing fifty-seven "civilian" scientists working on the defending nation's most important weapons research within the building. All but one of the LGB from the remaining strike aircraft miss, either because of smoke from the first strike, the smoke and obscurants used by the defender, or a light rain squall that drifts through the target area just as the weapons are being delivered. One of the strike aircraft is struck by AAA fire just as it has launched its LGB; its guidance equipment is destroyed, causing its bombs to fall out of control, and the aircraft crashes shortly thereafter. The defender's actions have decreased the damage to the target, but the missed LGB and the crashing aircraft fall on the adjacent school and hospital, resulting in another sixty-three deaths.

The strike force fights its way out of the target area. Its duel with enemy defenses is not over, and in the ensuing give and take, another aircraft is lost. Its crash in a residential area and errant defender missiles and antiaircraft munitions cause another twenty-two civilian losses before the airstrike is completed.

Total civilian casualties from the airstrike are 292. How many of these individuals are in fact civilians? Those who died as the result of the strike of the defender's missiles and antiaircraft munitions certainly are not the responsibility of the attacker, nor are those who died as a result of intervening actions by the defender that caused the attacker's bombs or missiles to go awry, or his aircraft to crash. In the end, none of the casualties can be attributed to any illegal action of the attacker. If there was any action that may be regarded as illegal, it was the defender's failure to separate a military objective from his civilian population. His actions in defense of the target were otherwise lawful, but affected by the intervening, lawful actions of the attacker.

Were there an impartial observer in the midst of this carnage, he would not see any of the intervening factors that led to civilian deaths, except for the flares dispensed by the attacking aircraft to draw off infrared missiles. He might see the attacking aircraft, the bomb and/or missile release, and the damage and casualties that would appear to have occurred as a result of "indiscriminate" bombing on the part of the attacker. If he were to visit the emergency room of the hospital, or the morgue, he would see 292 persons in civilian clothing; their precise status at the time of the attack would not be known to him. No defender could avoid the propaganda opportunity offered him by this airstrike, the invisible characteristics of modern warfare, and the ambiguities regarding responsibility for these casualties presented by the language of Protocol I. It is difficult enough to find any humanitarian gain presented to potential civilian victims by this ambiguity. It is substantially less than humanitarian to think of the risk to which aircrews will be exposed due to spurious allegations of war crimes as a result of this ambiguity.

The foregoing illustrates some of the problems facing an aircrew endeavoring to accomplish its mission in the most accurate manner possible. Wars essentially are "come as you are" affairs which must be fought by the forces at hand, regardless of their training or equipment. But even where it is the best—though few commanders ever feel it as good as it should have been—those aircrews still must contend with the efforts of the enemy to defeat their placing munitions on target, as well as the myriad factors that affect bombing accuracy, including human error. The forms of enemy defenses are in themselves intervening factors that must be taken into account when raising questions about civilian casualties ostensibly caused by an airstrike. Protocol I fails to consider the give and take of warfare, instead freeze-framing the action to look at the results at the end of a mission or at another particular instance.

Any proposal to guarantee proportionality by mandating prior estimation of military advantage and civilian losses before an attack is launched is inappropriate for several reasons. First, it fails to take into account the failure of a defender to separate his civilian population from a military objective, as required by customary international law and articles 48, 51(7), and 58 of Protocol I. Second, it asks a question no commander can anticipate, in part because the attacking commander will not know where the defender's civilians are, and has a right to assume that a defender will carry out his responsibility to separate civilians from military objectives, particularly where a warning has been provided. Moreover, the same strike might have been carried out with no civilian casualties, had (for example) surprise been complete—and the conclusion is reached that individuals employed within the target are not regarded as civilians protected by the law of war while employed within that a military objective. Third, as the preceding scenario indicates, it is possible that none of the civilian deaths can be attributed to any actions of the attacker, which in and of themselves were entirely lawful. Finally, even if all of the civilian casualties could be attributed to the attacker—and under the circumstances described in the scenario, they could not—there remains a question of the value of that particular target to the defender's overall war effort. While few targets can be regarded as "panacea" targets or "war stoppers," the possibility that such a target may be struck and prompt the defender to call for a ceasefire and negotiations, thereby preventing further deaths, cannot be dismissed out of hand.

The idea of tallying up the results at the end of an airstrike or any other military operation to determine its success based upon the number of civilian deaths that occurred as a result of actions beyond the control of the attacker smacks of a return to a portion of the Just War doctrine. That provision, renounced by article 1 common to the 1949 Geneva Conventions, was that for example, combatants may be denied prisoner of war protection if their cause is not regarded as just by its opponent—or, as in this case, if the end result of a day's combat activities suggests that an opponent is employing means that are illegal.[579] No action employed by the attacker in the

579. Common article 1 states that "The High Contracting Parties undertake to respect and ensure respect for the present Convention *in all circumstances*." SCHINDLER & TOMAN, *supra* note 27, at 429 (emphasis added). ICRC commentator Jean S. Pictet has stated that:

> The words "in all circumstances" refer to all situations in which the Convention has to be applied, and these are defined in article 2. It is clear . . . that the application of the Convention does not depend on whether the conflict is just or unjust. Whether or not it is a war of aggression, prisoners of war belonging to either party are entitled to the protection afforded by the Convention.

scenario constituted an illegal act, and ideas that there must be some accountability for each civilian casualty, or that intervening acts by an opponent may be ignored, are fundamentally flawed.

Human factor. As complex as the picture at this point in time may be, there is still one more factor that enters into this equation—the human factor. The earlier reference to the comments by Clausewitz on friction and uncertainty offer a peek at the potential for problems caused by the human factor. In the confusion of war, mistakes are made. In addition to collateral civilian casualties, the history of warfare has recorded countless instances in which friendly forces have caused casualties within their own ranks. A few examples will serve to illustrate the human factor in war:

— 6 September 1939: In an episode known as the Battle of Barking Creek, Royal Air Force (RAF) Spitfires intercepted and shot down at close range RAF Hurricanes over the English Channel.[580]

— 28 June 1940: Italian antiaircraft guns at Tobruk shot down the Savio-Marchetti 79 piloted by Italo Balbo, Italian aviation hero and Supreme Commander of Italian Forces in North Africa.[581]

— February or March 1941: German Bf–109 fighters dispatched to strafe the RAF base at Ramsgate in England attacked Galland field (a Luftwaffe base) in Calais-Mark, France.[582]

— 15 March 1944: U.S. Army Air Force heavy bombers supporting Allied operations against Cassino caused 140 civilian casualties in a town fifteen miles away from the fighting, with one stick of bombs straddling an Allied corps headquarters. The official investigation concluded that the errant bombing was caused by "poor air discipline on the part of two new groups, malfunction of bomb-racks in one formation, lack of specific aiming points, and the heavy pall of smoke and dust which obscured the target after the first few attacks."[583]

In further description of the incident, another historian stated that:

> Some heavy bomber pilots were unable to identify the target, and twenty-three returned to their bases with their bombs intact; two jettisoned their loads in the sea. Rack failure on the leading

COMMENTARY ON THE GENEVA CONVENTION RELATIVE TO THE TREATMENT OF PRISONERS OF WAR 18 (Geneva, 1960); Pictet's discussion of article 2 in his COMMENTARY on each of the other three 1949 Geneva Conventions is similar. During the United States air campaigns over North Vietnam, one basis for North Vietnamese denial of POW protection to captured American aircrews was that inasmuch as civilians had been killed in the course of the United States airstrikes (regardless of cause of death), the captured aircrews were not entitled to POW protection. The interpretation of Protocol I being applied by the ICRC and others to the issue of collateral civilian casualties repeats the North Vietnamese philosophy, and takes it to its next illogical step by suggesting criminal responsibility for collateral civilian casualties that are caused by actions not within the control of the attacker.

580. F. MASON, *supra* note 81, at 93, n.2; D. FISHER, *supra* note 389, at 84–94; and R. HOUGH & D. RICHARDS, *supra* note 342, at 66–67. The author is indebted to Sebastian Cox of the British Ministry of Defence's Air Historical Branch for first bringing this incident to the author's attention.

581. C. SEGRE, ITALO BALBO: A FASCIST LIFE 392–401 (1987).

582. Letter to author from Generalleutnant D. Walter Krupinski (28 Aug. 1989), who took part in the mission. General Krupinski ended the war with 197 victories, as a pilot in Adolf Galland's JV–44 *Squadron of Experts*, flying the Me–262 jet fighter. He subsequently served in the postwar Luftwaffe, rising to the rank indicated. *See* A. GALLAND, *supra* note 188, at 353, and J. STEINHOFF, THE FINAL HOURS 183–84 (1985).

583. J. TERRAINE, *supra* note 171, at 591.

plane of one formation sent forty bombs into Allied-held areas, killing and wounding civilians and troops. These short bombs and others inflicted about 142 casualties—28 were killed—among the allied units in the Cassino area. Ten air miles away, several planes bombed Venafro by mistake, killing 17 soldiers and 40 civilians, and wounding 79 soldiers and 100 civilians. The bombing errors were an 'appalling' tragedy that [Lieutenant] General [Mark W.] Clark attributed to 'poor training and inadequate briefing of crews.'[584]

— 24–25 June 1944: In the use of Allied heavy bombers to support the Allied breakout from the Normandy beachhead, a total of 136 American soldiers were killed and 621 wounded through errant bombing.[585]

— 24 July 1944: Eighth Air Force heavy bombers killed between 101 and 118 American soldiers while wounding approximately 500 others in support operations for Operation Cobra, the attack that led to the breakout across France. One historian provides an explanation for the casualties which illustrates the nature of human error in war:

> The friendly casualties occurred in three instances. A bombardier accidently toggled his bomb load on an Allied airstrip when another plane in the formation was destroyed by [German] flak . . . , destroying planes and equipment; a lead bombardier experienced 'difficulty with the bomb release mechanism' and part of his load dropped, causing eleven other bombers to drop thinking they were over the target; and, finally, a formation of five medium bombers from the Ninth Air Force dropped seven miles north of the target, amid the 30th Infantry Division. . . . The next day, in better weather, Cobra was undertaken, again with three unfortunate friendly bombings, by B–24's. In the first case, a lead bombardier failed to synchronize his bombsight properly, so that when he dropped—and eleven other bombers dropped on his signal—a total of 470 100-lb high-explosive bombs fell behind the lines. The second occurred when a lead bombardier failed to properly identify the target and took the easy way out—bombing on the flashes of preceding bombs. A total of 352 260-lb fragmentation bombs fell in friendly lines. In the third case, a command pilot overrode his bombardier and dropped on previous bomb flashes; previous bombs had been off target but within a safe 'withdrawal' zone. The pilot's bombs fell within friendly territory.[586]

— 19 August 1944: RAF Bomber Command, attacking in daylight, caused nearly 400 British casualties, including 65 killed. It appears that someone had omitted to inform Bomber Command that the Army's standard color for marking its position was yellow; this was also Bomber Command's target-indicating color, and 77 aircraft which had gone astray proceeded to bomb on yellow marks—"the more the troops burnt yellow flares to show their position the more the errant aircraft bombed them."[587]

— 1 January 1945: During Operation Bodenplatte, a major operation employing 875 Luftwaffe fighters to attack Allied airbases in Europe, a substantial portion of the more than 200 Luftwaffe losses have been attributed to German antiaircraft guns.[588]

584. M. Blumenson, *supra* note 215, at 441.

585. J. Terraine, *supra* note 171, at 658.

586. R. Hallion, Strike from the Sky: The History of Battlefield Air Attack, 1911–1945 206–10 (1989).

587. J. Terraine, *supra* note 171, at 661; B. Horrocks, with E. Belfield & H. Essame, Corps Commander 44–45 (London, 1977); and L. Ellis, I Victory in the West, The Battle of Normandy 430–31 (London, 1962).

588. W. Girbig, Six Months to Oblivion: The Eclipse of the Luftwaffe Fighter Force 73–114 (London, 1975); Krupinski letter, *supra* note 582.

— 8 January 1973: Two U.S. Navy A–7 Corsair II aircraft and two U.S. Marine A–6 Intruders rendezvoused with a Thailand-based U.S. Air Force Phantom II for a LORAN-guided bombing mission, only to bomb the American air base at Da Nang, Republic of Vietnam, wounding nine American servicemen and one Vietnamese, due to entry of erroneous data into their computers.[589]

— 8 October 1973: In their first day of combined operations, four Iraqi MiG–21 aircraft were shot down by the Syrian air defense barrier.[590]

— October 1973: Of 514 Egyptian and Syrian aircraft lost in the Yom Kippur War, fifty-eight were shot down by their own forces.[591]

— 1 May 1982: Captain Garcia Cuerro, flying an Argentine Mirage III, was shot down over Port Stanley by Argentine antiaircraft fire while attempting to land his damaged aircraft. His was the first of three Argentine aircraft lost to Argentine antiaircraft fire during the Falklands/Malvinas War.[592]

— 8 June 1982: The civilian tanker *Hercules*, sailing 500 miles from the Falklands/Malvinas, and 600 miles from Argentina, despite regular notifications to British and Argentine authorities of the ship's name, international call sign, registry, position, course, speed and voyage destination, was attacked repeatedly over a period of three hours by Argentine fighter aircraft. Severely damaged, she eventually was scuttled.[593]

---

589. Whitney, *Da Nang Bombing Error Embarrasses U.S. Aides*, N. Y. Times, Jan. 9, 1973, at 12.

590. E. O'Ballance, No Victor, No Vanquished, *supra* note 226, at 294–95.

591. C. Herzog, The War of Atonement, *supra* note 226, at 260.

592. Letter to author from Sebastian Cox, Ministry of Defence Air Historical Branch (27 Sept. 1988), with enclosures.

593. The circumstances of the attack are discussed in detail in Argentine Republic v. Amerada Hess Shipping Corporation, 57 US Law Week 4121 (Jan. 23, 1989), ____ U.S. ____(1989). Paragraph 4 of article 57 of Protocol I provides that:

> In the conduct of military operations at sea or in the air, each Party to the conflict shall, in conformity with its rights and duties under the rules of international law applicable in armed conflict, take all reasonable precautions to avoid losses of civilian lives and damage to civilian objects.

Schindler & Toman, *supra* note 27, at 655. The author has elected not to discuss this particular provision, the 1 September 1983 Soviet downing of Korean Air Lines flight 007, the 3 July 1988 downing of Iran Air flight 655 by the U.S.S. *Vincennes* or similiar incidents such as the equally mistaken 21 October 1989 downing of a Turkish civilian survey aircraft twelve miles within Turkish territory by two Syrian MiG–21s, because this article's topic is aerial bombardment rather than air warfare in general. While some of the examples in the body of the article do not involve aerial bombardment, they are used to illustrate the immediate point rather than broaden the overall scope of the article. For discussion of the Soviet downing of KAL 007, *see* S. Hersh, The Target is Destroyed (1985); for the *Vincennes* incident, *see* U.S. Department of Defense, Investigation Report, Formal Investigation into the Circumstances Surrounding the Downing of Iran Air Flight 655 on 3 July 1988 (28 July 1988); and Friedmann, *The Vincennes Incident*, 115 U.S. Naval Inst. Proc. 72–75, 76, 78–79 (May 1989). The Syrian downing of the Turkish survey plane is reported in *Syria Apologizes for Downing Plane*, Wash. Times, Oct. 23, 1989, at 2.

The author would note that the standard used in paragraph 4 of article 57 of "reasonable precautions," which the author believes is the customary law standard for all military operations, is less stringent than the "all feasible precautions" standard that Protocol I applies to land-based operations. The brief discussion of paragraph 4 of article 57 in the ICRC Commentary, *supra* note 247, at 687–88, reinforces the author's view that the ICRC lacks the expertise to address matters related to the use of force. That discussion states in part that

> one could conceive that hostilities between adverse fleets could endanger the civilian population . . . because missiles could miss their target. . . . Similarly, fighting between adverse military

— 11 April 1989: Syrian helicopter gunships attacked two small Soviet vessels in international waters near the Syrian port of Taurus, wounding seven Soviet sailors.[594]

— 22 April 1989: An Egyptian Alpha jet on final approach (wheels down) to the Baghdad International Airport for the Iraqi-sponsored International Military Fair was shot down by Iraqi air defenses.[595]

These incidents are but a brief glimpse at the human factor and its effect in modern war.[596] The overall effect of the explanation contained in the preceding pages is to emphasize the point made by Clausewitz at the outset: that war is a world of uncertainty and confusion in which even the best efforts to place bombs on target may be thwarted by myriad factors, and in particular by the efforts of a defender to cause an attacker's munitions to strike *anywhere but on the target*. If the defender has failed to separate the civilian population from military objectives, he has made a conscious decision to leave them at risk.

Customary law requires that an attacker exercise ordinary care to minimize collateral civilian casualties. The provisions contained in articles 48 to 58 of Protocol I clearly were intended to raise the standard of care for the attacker while lowering it

---

aircraft could have incidental repercussions on the civilian population—for example, when a crippled aircraft crashes.

The ICRC's comments indicate rather clearly that whatever good the organization may do with regard to the protection of war victims protected by the 1949 Geneva Conventions, its members have no competency with regard to the give and take of modern combat operations. The last phrase in the quoted passage bears a vague resemblance to the comment of the Congresswoman contained *supra* note 531. With regard to the ICRC statement that some "missiles could miss their target," the reader need only note that inasmuch as the North Vietnamese fired in excess of 1000 SA–2 Guideline missiles at U.S. aircraft during the 1972 Linebacker II operations, downing only 15 B–52s, a very large number of missiles missed their target. The Guideline, which measures 35.4 feet in length, carries a 286-pound warhead, and when fully loaded with its solid liquid rocket fuel weighs 5070 pounds at time of launch, obviously could cause considerable damage or death if it or any major part thereof were to descend upon an area in which civilians are present. JANE'S BATTLEFIELD AIR DEFENCE 1988–89 187 (T. Cullen & C. Foss eds., London, 1988).

In a rather notable incident during the Vietnam War, in July 1972 actress Jane Fonda visited Hanoi in support of the North Vietnamese war effort against the United States Linebacker I campaign. In addition to photographs taken of her sitting on a North Vietnamese antiaircraft gun, gazing skyward through its gunsights, other photographs were taken of her outside Hanoi, standing in a huge crater allegedly caused by a bomb from a United States B–52 bomber. The intended inference was that the blast had done considerable damage in a civilian residential area. As B–52s up to that time had not operated further north than Vinh, American intelligence analysts were asked to examine the photograph in order to ascertain the source of the crater. They determined conclusively that it had been caused by a SA–2 Guideline missile.

On the modern electronic battlefield, the likelihood that missiles will miss their intended target is substantially greater than the possibility that they will hit that target. *See also* the discussion *supra* note 208 regarding the damage to Bach Mai Hospital caused by the bombs of a crashing aircraft that had been struck by two SA–2 missiles, as well as the subsequent text discussion of the difficulty of accounting for the 1318 Hanoi dead from the Linebacker II operations and assigning responsibility for their deaths. The ICRC remarks are a classic example of the adage that "fools rush in where angels fear to tread." The ICRC is singularly unqualified to offer intelligent comments on battlefield matters; its conduct during the 1982 Israeli incursion into Lebanon, as discussed *supra* note 494, also not only is a manifestation of its ignorance of military matters, but raises serious doubts about its neutrality. Had the political leadership of the United States expressed a desire to recommend Protocol I for ratification, the American military would have insisted on the strongest reservation to article 81(1) disavowing the ICRC of any role relating to operational matters.

594. Remnick, *Syrian Copters Fire in Error at Soviet Ships; 7 Wounded*, Wash. Post, Apr. 14, 1989, at A22.

595. Wilson, *Iraq Downs a Visiting Egyptian Jet*, Wash. Post, Apr. 28, 1989, at 33.

596. A rather comprehensive study of the problem is contained in Shrader, *Amicicide: The Problem of Friendly Fire in Modern War* (Fort Leavenworth, Kansas: Combat Studies Institute Research Survey No. 1, Dec. 1982).

for the defender, thereby shifting the burden for minimization of collateral civilian casualties to the party to the conflict with the least control over the civilian population that may be near military objectives. Protocol I exacerbates the problem by confusing the status of persons working within military objectives, commingling them with innocent civilians who have no connection whatever to the military effort of the defender. Its attempt to establish an unrealistic form of accountability for civilian casualties that occur incidental to legitimate military operations is useful only as a propaganda tool. It serves no humanitarian purpose, and endangers the already-tenuous credibility of the law of war.

C. Article 56: Dams, Dikes, and Nuclear Electrical Generating Stations

Recognizing a potential risk to the surrounding population from the breach of dams, dikes, or nuclear electrical generating plants, article 56 creates a new, special standard for this limited class of objects under certain circumstances. Article 56 does not prohibit the attack of this limited class of objects in all circumstances, but only if the attack may cause the release of a target's "dangerous forces" and result in "severe" losses among the civilian population. Also protected from attack are any military objectives located at or in the vicinity of these specially protected facilities if their attack may cause the release of the dangerous forces of those facilities, and severe losses among the civilian population. Most radically, however, article 56 provides protection from attack for military forces and equipment assigned to the protection of these facilities.[597]

---

597. In its entirety, article 56 states:

1. Works for installations containing dangerous forces, namely dams, dikes, and nuclear electrical generating stations, shall not be made the object of attack, even where these objects are military objectives, if such attack may cause the release of dangerous forces and consequent severe losses among the civilian population. Other military objectives located at or in the vicinity of these works or installations shall not be made the object of attack if such attack may cause the release of dangerous forces from the works or installations and consequent severe losses among the civilian population

2. The special protection against attack provided by paragraph 1 shall cease:

a. for a dam or dike only if it is used for other than its normal function and in regular, significant, and direct support of military operations and if such attack is the only feasible way to terminate such support;

b. for a nuclear electrical generating station only if it provides electric power in regular, significant and direct support of military operations and if such attack is the only feasible way to terminate such support;

c. for other military objectives located at or in the vicinity of these works or installations only if they are used in regular, significant and direct support of military operations and if such attack is the only feasible way to terminate such support.

3. In all cases, the civilian population and individual civilians shall remain entitled to all the protection accorded them by international law, including the protection of the precautionary measures provided for in article 57. If the protection ceases and any of the works, installations or military objectives mentioned in paragraph 1 is attacked, all practical precautions shall be taken to avoid the release of the dangerous forces.

4. It is prohibited to make any of the works, installations or military objectives mentioned in paragraph 1 the object of reprisals.

5. The Parties to the conflict shall endeavor to avoid locating any military objectives in the vicinity of the works or installations mentioned in paragraph 1. Nevertheless, installations erected

It was clear in the course of the American military review of Protocols I and II that the U.S. military shares the concerns of others with regard to the unwarranted release of "dangerous forces." If anything, with revelations of the 2 December 1984 release of toxic chemicals into the atmosphere at Bhopal, India, the 26 April 1986 incident at the Soviet nuclear power plant at Chernobyl, in which radioactive material was released into the air, and the 1988 discharge of toxic chemicals into the Rhine River by several major Swiss industrial companies, it would appear that article 56 perhaps did not go far enough. Military commanders are particularly alert to the fact that their units may have to operate in the vicinity of such facilities, and, therefore, would be at risk from the release of any form of dangerous forces. The reviewers also felt that any unnecessary loss of life in any combat operation should be avoided, whether the lives of the civilian population of the nation in which a conflict is being engaged or of American combatants. The question was whether a proper balance had been made between military necessity and unnecessary suffering, and whether the provisions in article 56 were balanced between attacker and defender.[598] As was true of most of the language contained in articles 48 to 58, article 56 was found to be balanced against the former in favor of the latter, particularly where the latter is operating on its own territory. Any humanitarian gain, which was slight, was lost when compared to the tactical advantage provided a defender and the risk to American military personnel from enemy air or ground defense systems that (under article 56) would be protected from attack. There also was concern, based upon the experience of the air campaigns over North Vietnam, that the article's language would provide the basis for spurious allegations of war crimes against captured American personnel.

Historically, dams and dikes have been legitimate military targets where military necessity required their destruction. The *ICRC Commentary* offers the following historical explanation for article 56:

> [I]t will be remembered that in the seventeenth century the Dutch, despite protests from the peasants, did not hesitate to flood part of their cultivated land by breaching the dikes in order to

---

> for the sole purpose of defending the protected works or installations from attack are permissible and shall not themselves be made the object of attack, provided they are not used in hostilities except for defensive actions necessary to respond to attacks against the protected works or installations and that their armament is limited to weapons capable only of repelling hostile actions against the protected works or installations.
>
> 6. The High Contracting Parties and the Parties to the conflict are urged to conclude further agreements among themselves to provide additional protection for objects containing dangerous forces.
>
> 7. In order to facilitate the identification of the objects protected by this article, the Parties to the conflict may mark them with a special sign consisting of a group of three bright orange circles placed on the same axis, as specified in article 16 of Annex I to this Protocol. The absence of such marking in no way relieves any Party to the conflict of its obligations to this article.

SCHINDLER & TOMAN, *supra* note 27, at 653–54.

598. An adage frequently cited by international lawyers is that military commanders may not consider *military necessity* when weighing the requirements of a law of war treaty provision, as military necessity already was considered in the negotiation of the treaty provision. This certainly is true with regard to certain provisions. Thus, a commander may not consider military necessity as a basis for execution of prisoners of war, in violation of articles 13 and 130 of the 1949 Geneva Convention Relative to the Treatment of Prisoners of War. SCHINDLER & TOMAN, *supra* note 27, at 435, 476. It is not so clear with regard to treaties that attempt to regulate war fighting. Thus of the 1907 Hague Convention IV and its annexed regulations, Michael Glover has said that "absent from the Hague Rules was any acknowledgment of military necessity." M. GLOVER, *supra* note 87, at 14. It was equally clear throughout the United States military review of Protocols I and II that military necessity was given little consideration in the negotiation of Protocol I, and particularly articles 48 to 58.

> prevent the advance of adverse troops. In 1938 the Chinese authorities breached the dikes of the Yellow River near Chang-Chow to stop the Japanese troops, resulting in extensive losses and widespread damage. In 1944, again in the Netherlands, German troops flooded many thousands of hectares of agricultural land with sea water to prevent the advance of the enemy.
>
> It was also during the Second World War that deliberate attacks were mounted against hydro-electric dams. The best known are those which destroyed the dams in the Eder and the Mohne in Germany in May 1943. These operations resulted in considerable damage; 125 factories were destroyed or seriously damaged and in addition 3,000 hectares of cultivated land were lost for the harvest of that year, 1,300 persons were killed, including some deported persons and allied prisoners, and finally, 6,500 head of livestock were lost.
>
> During the war in Korea aircraft attacked dams used for irrigation in the north of the country. In the Viet Nam War attacks were mounted against dams and dikes, though the United States declared that the damage caused, insofar as this was established, was accidental or secondary. According to the delegate from the Democratic Republic of Viet Nam at the Diplomatic Conference, 661 sections of dike had been either damaged or destroyed during the course of the war.[599]

Care must be exercised in reading the *ICRC Commentary* text. The damage listed is not inconsistent with lawful military operations. The fact that 125 factories in the Rhine Valley were destroyed by water incidental to the 1943 RAF Bomber Com-

599. ICRC COMMENTARY, *supra* note 247, at 667. The precise number of persons who died in the 1943 RAF dams raid is 1,294, most of whom were near the Mohne dam at the time of its breach. THE BOMBER COMMAND WAR DIARIES 386–88 (M. Middlebrook & C. Everitt, eds. London, 1985). As the Middlebrook/Everitt book explains,

> The town of Neheim-Husten, which was situated five miles downstream of the Mohne Dam, took the full impact of the flood and at least 859 people died there. By one of those tragedies which periodically struck foreign [forced] workers and prisoners of war whose camps were near targets in Germany, 493 foreigners—mostly Ukranian women landworkers—died near their camp at Neheim-Husten.

Id. at 388. To place this in today's context, it should be noted that the Ukranian women would be considered civilian internees, and that article 83 of the 1949 Geneva Convention Relative to the Protection of Civilian Persons in Time of War provides that:

> The Detaining Power shall not set up places of internment in areas particularly exposed to the dangers of war.
>
> The Detaining Power shall give the enemy Powers, through the intermediary of the Protecting Powers, all useful information regarding the geographical location of places of internment.
>
> Whenever military considerations permit, internment camps shall be indicated by the letters IC, placed so as to be clearly visible in the daytime from the air. The Powers concerned may, however, agree upon any other system of marking.

SCHINDLER & TOMAN, *supra* note 27, at 526. With respect to the POWs who died as a result of flooding caused by the RAF dams raid, article 9 of the 1929 Geneva Convention Relative to the Treatment of Prisoners of War states in part that, "No prisoner may at any time be sent to an area where he would be exposed to the fire of the fighting zone, or be employed to render by his presence certain points or areas immune from bombardment." *Id.* at 343. That the Germans had emplaced and manned antiaircraft guns on the Mohne dam makes it clear that the possibility of its attack by aircraft was contemplated, and they in turn were obligated to remove POWs from areas downstream. The situation is clouded, however, by the fact that the POWs apparently were Russian, and the Union of Soviet Socialist Republics was not a party to the 1929 Geneva Conventions. The antagonism that existed between Nazi Germany and the Soviet Union over this particular point led to the loss of life of thousands of German and Russian POWs during World War II.

A fundamental point of the preceding discussion is that the ICRC COMMENTARY, *supra* note 247, again is misleading in stating that *x* lives were lost as a result of the RAF airstrike against the Rhine dams without discussing the concomitant responsibilities a defender has to remove protected persons from harm's way, particularly when a defender has anticipated an attack through emplacing air defense equipment around a particular target.

mand dams raid is an indication of success of the mission rather than an illegal act, because the factories were engaged in war-supporting manufacture. The fact that 1300 persons were killed is of little informational value, until it can be ascertained whether those persons were civilians or combatants and, if the former, whether they died while working in the factories producing the war materials or otherwise were carrying out tasks that might have made them susceptible to attack. Finally, what would have been the value of a successful attack on the dams if the German capability to continue production had been damaged to a degree that the war ended sooner, at a savings of far more lives than were lost?[600] The same is true with respect to the attacks on dams and dikes during the Korean and Vietnam wars; none involved any great loss of civilian life and, as will be shown, they were completely consistent with lawful military operations. Thus while the *ICRC Commentary* states that "661 sections of [the North Vietnamese dike system] had been either damaged or destroyed during the course of the war," a study by a highly-respected historian of the Vietnam War found that, "Reconnaissance photographs showed bomb craters on several dikes, but these were all in close proximity to other targets of high military value; no major dike was breached or significantly damaged and the high-water season [in 1972] passed without significant flooding. . . ."[601]

A statement such as found in the *ICRC Commentary* that destruction has occurred must be placed in proper context, for war is about destruction and loss of life. The distinction that must be made is with regard to *unnecessary* destruction that would be regarded as prohibited. The *ICRC Commentary* fails to make this distinction in its discussion of article 56 or, for that matter, in its discussion of most of the prohibitions contained in articles 48 to 58 of Protocol I.

In addition to the fact that the text is misleading, the *ICRC Commentary* also is

600. Which apparently almost was the case. Alfred Speer, German wartime Minister of Armaments and Munitions, writing after the war, in commenting on the RAF dams raid stated that, "employing just a few bombers, the British came close to a success which would have been greater than anything they had achieved hitherto with a commitment of thousands of bombers." A. SPEER, INSIDE THE THIRD REICH 281 (1970). The Middlebrook/Everitt book states that

> The German view is that, if the aircraft which were allocated to the Eder had been switched to the Sorpe dam, the effect upon the Ruhr's industrial production would have been extremely serious, but the Sorpe's construction was of a nature which made it a difficult target for the Wallis bomb, hence its low priority in the raid. The Sorpe dam just managed to keep the Ruhr supplied with water until the Mohne dam was repaired.

THE BOMBER COMMAND WAR DIARIES, *supra* note 599, at 386–87. The United States Strategic Bombing Survey notes that:

> The German electric-utilities system was vulnerable to bombing because of the continuous critical shortage of electric energy, the lack of reserve capacity, the relative ease with which the electric generating and transmission equipment can be seriously damaged, much of it being of a fragile nature, the relative difficulty of repairing bomb damage or replacing destroyed facilities, the inability to transfer any appreciable amount of current, and thus to shift power losses, and the absolute dependence of industry on electric energy for its operation.
>
> . . . In the state of critical shortage in which industry found itself, any loss of production would have directly affected essential war production, and the destruction of any substantial amount would have had serious results. The Germans themselves admit this and Speer has stated that a loss of forty percent would have been dangerous and a loss of sixty percent would have caused the collapse of the war economy.

UNITED STATES STRATEGIC BOMBING SURVEY, OVERALL REPORT, EUROPEAN WAR 84–85 (30 Sept. 1945). However, the German power system, except for isolated raids such as the 1943 RAF dams raid, was never a target as such during the Allied strategic air offensive. *Id.* at 14.

601. G. LEWY, *supra* note 300, at 411.

historically incomplete. The following list of attacks on dams and dikes, though not entirely complete, is more extensive than that offered by the *ICRC Commentary*, and provides additional details regarding the basis for the attacks from past conflicts:

Dates/Footnote	Target	Summary
16/17 May 1943[602]	Mohne, Eder, Sorpe Schwelme dams in Ruhr Valley	Attacked by RAF 617 Sqdn. Purpose: loss of hydroelectric power for major German industrial area. Mohne and Eder breached; attacks on Schwelme and Sorpe were unsuccessful.
23/24 Sep 1943, 4 and 21 Nov 1944, 1 Jan 1945	Banks of parallel branches of Dortmund-Ems Canal (DEK)	Six-mile stretch of canal was drained as breaches were made in banks of both branches at a point near Ladbergen, N of Munster.
26 Oct 1944, 6 Nov 1944, 21 Nov 1944, 6 Dec 1944, 1 Jan 1945[603]	Mittleland Canal (MLK)	Like DEK, major transportation artery, particularly for coal for war manufacturing and energy demands. Attacked by 8th AF B–24s at Minden; breach drained canal, unleashing water that created sandbar in Weser River. Re-attacks by 8th AF (6 Nov, 6 Dec 44) were unsuccessful, but RAF Bomber Command attacks at Gravenhorst near the junction with DEK succeeded in draining about 30 kilometers on each occasion. Impassable from 21 Nov–11 Dec 44 and 1 Jan 45 to V-E Day.
3 Oct 1944[604]	Walcheren Island/ Westkapelle sea wall	Coastal gun batteries dominated port of Antwerp. Breach of sea wall would submerge some of guns and hamper German defense against ground attack. Sea wall breached (100 yards).

602. *See* cites contained *supra* note 204 and H. RUMPF, *supra* note 1, at 64–77; C. WEBSTER & N. FRANKLAND, *supra* note 81 Vol. I, at 168–78, 289–92, and Vol. IV, at 375, 392; earlier but less detailed volumes on the raid are G. GIBSON ENEMY COAST AHEAD (London, 1943), and P. BRICKHILL, THE DAM BUSTERS (London, 1952).

603. The best discussion of the attacks on the DEK and MLK canals is contained in UNITED STATES STRATEGIC BOMBING SURVEY, 200 THE EFFECTS OF STRATEGIC BOMBING ON GERMAN TRANSPORTATION, 1–5, 17–31 (2d ed. Jan. 1947); *see also* THE BOMBER COMMAND WAR DIARIES, *supra* note 599, at 430–31, 588, and A. COOPER, BEYOND THE DAMS TO THE TIRPITZ 20, 124–26 (London, 1984).

604. The attack on the seawall at Walcheren Island is discussed in the Official History of the Canadian Army in the Second World War by C. STACEY, III THE VICTORY CAMPAIGN: THE OPERATIONS IN NORTH-WEST EUROPE, 1944–1945 301–422 (Ottawa, 1960), and in the official British series by L. ELLIS, II VICTORY IN THE WEST, THE DEFENSE OF GERMANY 10, 23, 59, 81–82, 109–23 (London, 1968); and A. COOPER, *supra* note 603, at 126. Each official history contains an excellent discussion of the balancing of competing requirements with which a commander is faced, with regard to the protection of the lives of his own forces while accomplishing the mission *vis-à-vis* the degree of destruction that may occur in that operation. Thus, STACEY, *supra* at 374–75 states that:

> The project of flooding Walcheren by bombing the dikes . . . had to be examined from two points of view: its practical feasibility and its political desirability. . . . It is ironical that we subsequently

Dates/Footnote	Target	Summary
7 Oct 1944[605]	Kembs Dam (on Rhine, north of Basle)	Held back quantity of water that German defenders could release to defeat Allied advance. RAF 617 Sqdn. bombed dam gates, releasing water.
20 Oct 1944[606]	Etang de Lindre Dam, France	Constructed in 17th Century as part of Vauban system for defense of Metz. German breach would flood valley, cutting off U.S. forward units. USAAF P–47s, using 1,000-lb bombs, breached the dam, removing the threat.
8, 11 Dec 1944	Urft Dam	At the head of Roer Valley, in German hands. Same concern as Kembs and Etang de Lindre. Two attacks by RAF failed to breach. Germans permitted to fall into U.S. hands without breach, for reasons related to Schwammenauel Dam (below)
9 Feb 1945[607]	Schwammenauel Dam	At the head of Roer Valley, in German hands. Same concern as Urft Dam. During U.S. ground assault, German defenders partially breached in order to release no major cascade of water but to create a long-lasting flood in the Roer Valley to slow Allied advance.
30 Apr 1951[608]	Hwachon Dam	Dam and reservoir located 50 miles NE of Seoul; as U.N. forces advanced towards Seoul, Communist-held dam

> brought this calamity upon the Dutch. We did so, not for a fleeting purpose, but to accelerate an operation designed to shorten the war and, thereby, the ordeal of the Dutch themselves. Flooding Walcheren offered the prospect of an earlier opening of Antwerp and the saving of Allied soldiers' lives; these were decisive weights in the balance in favor of the admittedly terrible device of letting the salt sea into the island and thereby ruining its rich farmlands and orchards for years to come.

This discussion must be placed in the context of many World War II operations, in that the degree of consideration given the matter undoubtedly was higher because the objective under consideration was in the Netherlands and not in Nazi Germany.

605. A. COOPER, *supra* note 603, at 126–27; THE BOMBER COMMAND WAR DIARIES, *supra* note 599, at 597.

606. H. COLE, THE LORRAINE CAMPAIGN, 295–97 (1950).

607. The Urft and Schwammenauel dams are discussed at length in C. MACDONALD, THE SIEGFRIED LINE CAMPAIGN 323–28, 596–615 (1963), and C. MACDONALD, THE LAST OFFENSIVE 70–84 (1973); *see also* A. COOPER, *supra* note 603, at 160, and THE BOMBER COMMAND WAR DIARIES, *supra* note 599, at 629.

608. M. CAGLE & F. MANSON, THE SEA WAR IN KOREA 241–42 (1957); J. FIELD, JR., HISTORY OF UNITED STATES NAVAL OPERATIONS—KOREA 347 (1962); R. RAUSA, SKYRAIDER 38–39 (1982); and Tillman & Handelman, *The Hwachon Dam and Carlson's Canyon: Air Group 19's Princeton Deployment of 1950–51*, 12 THE HOOK 32–38 (Spring 1984).

Dates/Footnote	Target	Summary
		could flood roads, destroy roads and bridges. Gates of dam destroyed by torpedo attack by VA–195 and VC–35 AD–4 Skyraiders from USS *Princeton* (CV–37).
23–24 June 1951[609]	Suiho hydroelectric facility	Major power source for Manchurian industry, and to run North Korean radar network and factories. U.S. Navy airstrike from USS *Boxer* (CV–21), *Princeton* and *Philippine Sea* (CV–47) destroyed two of five primary transformers while damaging a third. Dam was untouched.
24–27 June 1950[610]	Kyosen, Fusen, and Choshin power plants	Hydroelectric systems providing power to eastern portion of North Korea. As war-related industry was dispersed into North Korean homes, power plants became viable alternative target in lieu of attack of dispersed war industries. Fusen and Choshin attacked by 5th AF and USMC TACAIR; reattacked on 24, 26 June; Choshin again on 27 June.
13 May 1953[611]	Toksan, Chasan, Kuwonga, Kusong, and Toksang irrigation dams	Major irrigation dams in North Korea attacked by USAF F–84 fighter-bombers. Destruction intended to apply military pressure to North Korea in stalemated peace talks, while waters released would destroy principal military supply routes and rice crops being grown by North Korea for export to finance war. Air attacks successful in execution and accomplishment of intended purposes; Korean War armsistice signed less

609. M. CAGLE & F. MANSON, *supra* note 608, at 441–50; J. FIELD, *supra* note 608, at 436–39; R. FUTRELL, THE UNITED STATES AIR FORCE IN KOREA, 1950–1953 481–89 (1953); AIRPOWER: THE DECISIVE FORCE IN KOREA 119–39 (J. Stewart ed. 1957); P. MEID & J. YINGLING, V U.S. MARINE OPERATIONS IN KOREA, 1950–1953, OPERATIONS IN WEST KOREA 64–65 (1972); Cressman, *The Fighting Phil Sea: An Operational History of USS Philippine Sea (CV–47), 1946–1971*, THE HOOK 32, 35 (Fall 1988).

610. R. FUTRELL, *supra* note 609; J. STEWART, *supra* note 609.

611. R. FUTRELL, *supra* note 609, at 666–72; J. STEWART, *supra* note 609, at 166–88. The latter contains a number of excellent maps and aerial photographs to illustrate the nature of damage caused by the air strikes.

Dates/Footnote	Target	Summary
		than one month later, with terms North Koreans had adamantly refused to accept [including voluntary repatriation of POWs] during preceding two years of negotiations.
10 Jun 1972[612]	Lang Chi	122.5 megawatt hydroelectric plant 63 miles up Red River Valley from Hanoi. Attacked by 7th AF F–4s using LGBs, destroying plant's turbines and generators without breach of dam.
May–Dec 1972[613]	Red River Valley dikes and dams	Major, comprehensive earthwork dike and dam system to contain water in Red River Valley area surrounding Hanoi and Haiphong, North Vietnam. Antiaircraft guns and ground-control intercept (GCI) radar were placed on top of the dams and dikes, and dispersed POL stored adjacent to dikes. AAA and GCI only were attacked to suppress fire against U.S. strike forces, using antipersonnel munitions that would cause no structural damage.

Examination of the events listed above offers some degree of explanation for previous attacks on facilities that contained "dangerous forces." At no time has a dam or dike been attacked for the purpose of injuring the civilian population. Each target has been attacked because its destruction or breach was of legitimate military value, with the exception of the Red River Valley dams and dikes, where special care was exercised not to breach the dams or dikes while attacking antiaircraft guns and GCI radar equipment that had been placed on top of the dams or dikes to shield them from attack. In several instances dams were breached to pre-empt the defender's use of the dangerous forces to impede an attacker's advance. The latter suggests a return of the dilemma posed earlier with regard to the rules contained in Protocol I: a defender may argue that the language contained in article 56 is superseded by his sovereign rights to defend his own territory, thereby placing an attacker at an immediate disadvantage *vis-à-vis* a defender with his finger on the trigger for the release of dangerous forces. Finally, in none of the attacks listed above were civilian casualties "severe" though, as will be seen, the term eludes definition or translation into a standard that can be used effectively by battlefield commanders or national

612. Author's conversations with General Vogt and Admiral Moorer, *supra* note 500, and M. Porter, *supra* note 501.
613. Parks, *supra* note 208, at 12–16.

decision makers. The inability of the participants at the Diplomatic Conference to maintain a distinction between fact and hysteria seriously affected the ultimate language in article 56.

In the course of the negotiations, a number of nations, including fifteen Arab states, sought a total ban on the attack of any facility containing dangerous materials, including oil production installations.[614] Although such facilities can be attacked by ground forces, the intent of some delegations clearly was to limit the use of air power against targets critical to a nation's war effort. While the more extreme proposals did not meet with success, the language finally accepted by the delegations has much the same effect with regard to the facilities protected.

The American military review had four specific concerns with article 56. Before discussing each, it is important to indicate what article 56 does not protect. It does not protect any of the facilities listed therein unless the civilian population is at risk from its breach. Virtually any breach of a nuclear reactor would have this potential, but the breach of a dam or dike that causes the release of the water it contains would not necessarily be precluded unless it would result in severe losses to the civilian population.[615] Neither would it preclude the attack of a nuclear electrical generating station that is not yet in operation. Article 56 does not protect nuclear facilities being used for any purpose other than the generation of power, such as for the manufacture of materials for nuclear weapons. For both reasons, the 7 June 1981 Israeli Air Force attack on Iraq's Osirak reactor would not have been prohibited by article 56.[616] Nor would article 56 have protected the facility at Vermork, in Nazi-occupied Norway, which was being used by the Germans to produce the heavy water required for development of their atomic bomb, and which was the subject of several attacks in the course of World War II.[617]

The U.S. military review was concerned with the standard of "severe" civilian casualties. "Severe" obviously was less than the "excessive" standard contained in article 51(5)(b), article 57(2)(a)(iii), article 57(2)(b), and article 85(3)(b). Indeed, no grave breach occurred unless an attack was launched against one of the facilities so protected *in the knowledge* that the attack would cause *excessive* (rather than "severe") loss of life.[618] But the term otherwise is undefined, and is subject to a variety of interpretations. Thus while the *ICRC Commentary* describes "severe" as meaning "important" or "heavy,"[619] the commentary prepared by three former members of the American and West German delegations defines the term as meaning "massive."[620] While the *ICRC Commentary* states that the standard of "common sense" must be "applied in good faith,"[621] the second reference states that the

614. NEW RULES FOR VICTIMS OF ARMED CONFLICTS, *supra* note 257, at 351, and ICRC COMMENTARY, *supra* note 247, at 668.

615. Article 56, paragraph 1.

616. The purpose of the IAF airstrike was to pre-empt Iraqi acquisition of the materials necessary to develop a nuclear weapon capability. In this regard, *see* S. WEISSMAN & H. KROSNEY, THE ISLAMIC BOMB 3–21, 227–91 (1981). Although the Iraqis have denied that the Osirak reactor was to be used for this purpose, Israeli intelligence was to the contrary. In any case, the IAF attack would not have been prohibited inasmuch as the reactor was not operable at the time of its attack. *See* D. MCKINNON, BULLSEYE—ONE REACTOR (1987), and S. NAKDIMON, FIRST STRIKE (1987).

617. D. IRVING, THE GERMAN ATOMIC BOMB: THE HISTORY OF NUCLEAR RESEARCH IN NAZI GERMANY 125–70 (1967); T. GALLAGHER, ASSAULT IN NORWAY: SABOTAGING THE NAZI NUCLEAR BOMB (1975); and R. WIGGAN, OPERATION FRESHMAN: THE RJUKAN HEAVY WATER RAID 1942 (London, 1986).

618. Article 85(3)(c) of Protocol I, as contained in SCHINDLER & TOMAN, *supra* note 27, at 671.

619. ICRC COMMENTARY, *supra* note 247, at 669.

620. NEW RULES FOR VICTIMS OF ARMED CONFLICTS, *supra* note 257, at 353.

621. ICRC COMMENTARY, *supra* note 247, at 669.

standard is absolute rather than relational.[622] The term has not been clarified and, contrary to the statement contained in the second reference, the concept of "severe" civilian losses can be viewed in relative terms in a good faith interpretation of the provision by commanders tasked with the mission to attack such a facility.

Thus, would the 1943 breach of the Mohne dam have been prohibited had article 56 been in effect at the time? The decision would have been a relational one in weighing the potential civilian casualties, however severe, against the possibility that the war might be concluded sooner, and the lives that would have saved.

And yet that raises a second problem that has plagued Protocol I at every turn. The party carrying out the attack would not be able to ascertain in all cases whether his attack would lead to "severe" civilian casualties, in that the attacking party has no control over or knowledge of the location of the civilian population that might be endangered by a breach of a facility such as those protected by article 56. He might be able to issue warnings, as was done prior to the attack of Walcheren Island in 1944.[623] Even were he to do so, however, experience teaches that his warning could lead to one of several results: (a) the civilians could be evacuated, (b) they could be left in place, or (c) additional civilians, refugees, civilian internees, or prisoners of war could be moved into the area to raise the "cost" of attacking the target. However one may argue that this would violate various provisions of the 1949 Geneva Conventions and Protocol I of 1977, it is a cold hard fact that the latter has occurred in the past and is likely to occur in the future. The language of article 56 is an invitation for some nations to use its civilian population to shield high-value targets from attack. Ambiguity of terms such as "severe" also increases the risk of spurious war crimes charges for United States personnel captured while carrying out an attack on such a protected facility, notwithstanding the more restrictive language contained in article 85 with regard to the attack of such facilities.

The second objection to the language contained in article 56 is that it prohibits the attack of such facilities or military objectives in the vicinity of such facilities if an attack *may* cause the release of dangerous forces and consequent severe losses among the civilian population. While some delegations supported use of the words "is likely to," the word "may" was chosen. The *ICRC Commentary* explains use of the term in conjunction with the attack of military objectives in the vicinity of a protected facility:

> As an example, the Rapporteur cites a hydroelectric power station incorporated in a dam or located in the immediate vicinity. If such an installation has become a military objective under the terms of article 52 . . . as a result of the circumstances of the conflict, *it cannot be attacked if such an attack could lead to the destruction of the dam.*[624]

622. NEW RULES FOR VICTIMS OF ARMED CONFLICTS, *supra* note 257, at 353.

623. C. STACEY, *supra* note 604, at 376, states that:

> on 27 September, Field-Marshal Montgomery's headquarters has requested SHAEF [Supreme Headquarters Allied Expeditionary Forces] to drop leaflets warning the population of the Scheldt islands of the imminence of heavy bombardment, [the message stating that] 'Leaflets should stress danger of flooding and urge immediate evacuation of islands or if this not possible of military objectives and low lying ground.'

624. ICRC COMMENTARY, *supra* note 247, at 670. The COMMENTARY continues:

> It is conceivable that a dam, dike, or nuclear electrical generating station is situated in the immediate vicinity of some civil engineering works, for example, a bridge or railway line, and that, in the circumstances of conflict, that bridge or a section of that line could become an important military objective. In this case too, no attack may be undertaken against such a bridge or railway line if the attack could affect the dam, dike or nuclear electrical generating station, and in this way cause the release of the dangerous forces.

Id. at 670.

With the use of the term *may*, the total prohibition on the attack of any such facility sought by many delegates has been accomplished. As General Vogt stated to Admiral Moorer prior to the successful attack on the Lang Chi hydroelectric facility in June 1972, nothing is certain in combat; earlier pages of this article illustrate the truth of this statement. Recalling the facts describing the attack on the Lang Chi plant, it is clear that if that attack had been required to meet the test of article 56 of Protocol I, it would have been prohibited. Article 56 gave pause to the American military review because it demanded the unrealistic assurance of 100% certainty in combat operations, something that cannot be achieved.

The protected facilities may lose the special protection provided them by article 56 if they (or military objectives situated near them) are used in "regular, significant and direct support of military operations" and if a military attack is the only feasible way to terminate such support.[625]

Regarding the use of any of the protected facilities in the "regular, significant and direct support of military operations," it was recognized at the time that due to the complexity of modern power grids this was a standard that would be virtually impossible to prove.[626] Most such protected facilities in all likelihood would never be used in direct support of military operations, because power for equipment used in military operations generally is provided by portable generator.[627] Thus an enemy's use of such a facility to shield military equipment from attack could legally be accomplished until and unless it was exposed by a prospective attacker as equipment that was being used for military operations. The first sentence of paragraph 5 of article 56 merely admonishes a defender from storing military equipment adjacent to such protected facilities, rather than prohibiting it.[628]

Examination of historic attacks, such as those carried out against the Mohne dam in 1943, the attacks in Korea, and the attack of the Lang Chi hydroelectric facility, indicates that seldom have such facilities been attacked because of their influence on military operations. Their value lies more at the level of war support, as was the case with regard to the Mohne dam and the branches of the Dortmund-Ems and Mittleland Canals, or in their political value, as was the case with regard to the attack of the irrigation dams in North Korea. Certainly they also can be of value in military operations, as was the case in the attack of the Westkappolle sea wall on Walcheren Island, breach of the Etang de Lindre Dam, the attack of the Roer Valley dams, and the torpedoing of the gates of the Hwachon Dam in Korea.

With regard to the latter basis for attack, however, the defender is left with a distinct military advantage, because the provisions of article 56 purposely use the word "attack" rather than "destroy" (as was contained in the original ICRC proposal) in order to preserve the right of a defender to release dangerous forces to repel an attacker, regardless of the consequences of the attack with respect to the civilian population.[629] As is true of other portions of Protocol I, sovereignty took precedence

625. SCHINDLER & TOMAN, *supra* note 27, at 653–54.

626. *See* NEW RULES FOR VICTIMS OF ARMED CONFLICTS, *supra* note 257, at 355.

627. One member of the U.S military review group, noting that military schools teach blocks of instruction on "the infantry platoon in the offense," "the artillery battalion in the defensive," "armor in the night attack," *etc.*, facetiously suggested that these same schools would have to add periods of instruction on the "nuclear power plant in the offensive," *etc.*, if a party to the conflict ever could establish that his opponent was using protected facilities to support military operations.

628. SCHINDLER & TOMAN, *supra* note 27, at 654.

629. Article 49 of the original ICRC draft rules prohibited the attack or destruction of such facilities. The word destroy was deleted at the insistence of the Dutch and Belgian delegations. ICRC COMMENTARY, *supra* note 247, at 668, n.6, and NEW RULES FOR VICTIMS OF ARMED CONFLICTS, *supra* note 257, at 353.

over humanitarian concerns. In the process, however, it compounded the problems of a military commander engaged in offensive operations in a foreign nation. The breaching operations by U.S. and Allied forces carried out against the Etang de Lindre Dam, the Roer Valley dams, and the Hwachon Dam would be prohibited, leaving a defender with a potentially devastating trump card. This was not regarded as militarily acceptable.

Perhaps the greatest objection to the language contained in article 56 is that in paragraph 5, which states in part that:

> [Military] installations erected for the sole purpose of defending the protected works or installations from attack are permissible and shall not themselves be made the object of attack, provided that they are not used in hostilities except for defensive actions necessary to respond to attacks against the protected works or installations and that their armament is limited to weapons capable only of repelling hostile action against the protected works or installations.[630]

The protection provided combatants and military equipment is unprecendented, notwithstanding claims by some experts to the contrary.[631] Providing protection to combatants and combatant equipment raises (at a minimum) two serious questions.

The prohibition contained in article 56 restricts attacks of this special property, even if it is a military objective, "if such attack may cause the release of dangerous forces and consequent severe losses among the civilian population." Assume the national leadership has decided that a particular facility must be attacked, but it wants to take every measure to ensure that its dangerous forces are not released in the course of the attack. The decision is made that a special operations (commando) team will be employed, because there is no chance that its weapons (small arms) can release the dangerous forces. After assaulting and securing the objective, the team will destroy portions of the facility that will put the facility out of action indefinitely without releasing the dangerous forces.[632]

The special operations team is confronted with two problems, however. Under article 56(5), the defender is entitled to employ forces with more than small arms to defend the facility, which means that it may be facing a heavily-armed force equipped with crew-served weapons. Worse, however, under article 56(5), the persons and equipment defending the targeted facility are protected from attack. Assume the attack is launched, and the American special operations force is defeated and captured after performing gallantly. In the course of battle, a number of soldiers in the defending force are killed or wounded. Could the captured American soldiers be charged with a violation of the law of war, to wit, paragraph 5 of article 56? The answer rather conclusively is yes.

There is another but equally dangerous problem with article 56(5) in that it places no range or limitation on the weapons to be used in defense of a facility, a problem

630. SCHINDLER & TOMAN, *supra* note 27, at 654.

631. Thus in NEW RULES FOR VICTIMS OF ARMED CONFLICTS, *supra* note 257, at 356, an analogy is made to the authority provided in article 22, paragraphs 1 and 2 of the 1949 Geneva Convention for the Amelioration of the Condition of the Wounded and Sick in Armed Forces in the Field, for armed sentries protecting a medical facility from marauders or bandits. These personnel are provided for internal and local security only, and generally are authorized to carry small arms only; such medical facilities also are subject to search by enemy forces, which is not the case with the facilities protected by article 56. As is conceded by both the NEW RULES FOR VICTIMS OF ARMED CONFLICTS and the ICRC COMMENTARY there is a qualitative difference in the defensive arms permitted sentries around medical facilities and units and the weapons that are likely to surround a facility provided special protection by article 56.

632. In the case of a nuclear power plant, for example, this could be accomplished through destruction of the turbine building (which is outside containment), the switchyards, and the transmission lines.

which both the *ICRC Commentary* and that of the former U.S. and West German delegation members conceded is ripe for controversy.[633] The problem is a rather simple one: a defender employs a sophisticated, integrated air defense system to protect his principal industrial and military areas. Within that area is a single protected facility (dam, dike, or nuclear power plant). Under article 56, he is entitled to claim that the entire air defense system is intended for the protection of that single facility. He is entitled to fire upon any aircraft approaching any target within that area because he may feel that the intended target is the protected facility. And the attacker is not entitled to attack any portion of that integrated air defense system, because he cannot prove that the intention of the defender was or is other than to protect that single protected facility.[634] If a portion of a strike force attacking another target were fired upon by any portion of that integrated defense system, and aircraft tasked with suppression of enemy air defense (SEAD) responded by attacking those portions of the air defense system that posed a threat to the strike force mission, the aircrew of a downed SEAD-mission aircraft would be faced with credible war crimes charges.

Examining article 56 in an historical context can be done through a look at the dams and dikes of the Red River Valley in North Vietnam. The Red River Valley is that part of what (at the time of the U.S. conflict) was then North Vietnam in which the major industrial areas of North Vietnam are located, including its capital of Hanoi and the major port city of Haiphong. The terrain of the Red River Valley running from the northwest to southeast has been described as a giant drainboard as the water from the monsoon seasons rushes to the Gulf of Tonkin. To meet the floodwater, which usually crests between July and September, the North Vietnamese over the centuries have constructed a complex system of almost 2500 miles of earthen dikes, dams, and sluice gates. Other dikes prevent seepage of sea water into crop-growing areas, while many primary dikes are backed up by a second line of dikes. The system was expanded by fifty percent between 1953 and 1972, with many previous dikes growing in width and height. The increase vastly complicated

633. Thus the ICRC COMMENTARY states that:

> If the works or installations are at a distance from the combat area, it is mainly a matter of defending them against attacks mounted by combatants who have been infiltrated or parachuted, or against attacks by guided missiles or projectiles dropped from aircraft. Thus there will be needed, on the one hand, a military guard equipped with light individual weapons, and on the other hand, anti-aircraft artillery. In the second case such artillery may only be used against aircraft which are out to attack the protected works or installations, but not against aircraft flying over the works or installations on their way to attacking another military objective. *It cannot be denied that this would pose serious difficulties of judgment.*

Supra note 247, at 674 (emphasis added). Similarly, the NEW RULES FOR VICTIMS OF ARMED CONFLICTS, *supra* note 257, at 356 states with regard to the language of article 51(5) that:

> It is apparent . . . that the present provision extends to the defense against hostile aircraft and raises some practical problems as to how the crews of anti-aircraft installations will be able to distinguish approaching enemy aircraft merely intending to pass the protected object en route to another military objective, from those intending unlawfully to attack the protected installation.

634. The NEW RULES FOR VICTIMS OF ARMED CONFLICTS, *supra* note 257, at 356–57 states that, "If they [the defender] launch surface to air missiles against such aircraft by mistake, a protective reaction by the adverse Party's aircraft may be expected and would be justified." This response is questionable. Paragraph five makes no distinction regarding the protection for forces defending any specially protected property, and the defender could (and undoubtedly would) argue that he was entitled to fire to defend himself against the attack. As is brought out in the body of this article, the NEW RULES answer doubtless would be of little comfort to a pilot who was downed and captured by the defender's forces while flying the "justified" protective reaction strike.

maintenance, already a constant preoccupation of the North Vietnamese Government and its people.

In 1971, a year during which the United States carried out no bombing operations over the Hanoi/Haiphong/Red River Valley area,[635] the Red River Valley suffered its worst flooding in three decades. One thirty-mile section of the dike system was breached. The force of water unleashed through this and other breaches on the primary dikes caused wide-spread erosion, cut long stretches of irrigation canals, and washed out many pumping stations. Prolonged inundation undermined both its primary and secondary dike systems. More than one million acres of riceland were flooded and the crops destroyed, forcing North Vietnam to import food from the Soviet Union and China.[636]

Because much of the effort of the civilian population normally dedicated to dike maintenance had been diverted to support the war effort, the Government of North Vietnam faced the 1972 flood season with ill-maintained dikes and the possibility of residual stress from the 1971 floods. Partly in the attempt to rally international public opinion against the Linebacker I bombing campaign that began on 9 May 1972, but primarily to increase the efforts of its people to maintain the dikes and to absolve itself of responsibility for failure to repair the system since the 1971 floods, the North Vietnamese commenced a major propaganda campaign in June 1972 alleging the intentional attack of the Red River Valley dams and dikes by American air forces.

Attack of the North Vietnam dam and dike system never was seriously contemplated during American operations against that nation. In a memorandum dated 18 January 1966, Assistant Secretary of Defense for International Security Affairs John T. McNaughton proposed destruction of the Red River Valley dams and dikes to shallow flood the rice fields, thereby leading to "widespread starvation" of the civilian population of North Vietnam, which the United States could offer to rectify "at the conference table."[637] Secretary of Defense Robert S. McNamara rejected the McNaughton recommendation.

There were legitimate reasons for attacking the dike system. The country's major transportation waterways—the Red River, the Thai Binh River, and the connecting Canal des Rapides and Canal des Bambons—were vital lines of communication between the major urban centers of Hanoi and Haiphong and lesser cities. Raw materials, such as coal from the Cam Pha and Mao Khe mines for use in the nation's thermal power plants, were moved by waterborne logistics craft (called WBLC, or "wiblix" by United States personnel during the Linebacker campaigns) along the waterways. As the northwest and northeast rail lines with China were cut by American bombing operations, military use of the waterways increased. Breach of the dams or dikes outside of populated areas would have been one way to attack this vital line of communications, just as allied heavy bombers had attacked the Dortmund-Ems and Mittleland canals in Germany during World War II. American national decision makers rejected this option, however, choosing instead to employ air-delivered bottom-laid mines and armed reconnaissance missions against the WBLC.

---

635. The United States Rolling Thunder bombing campaign ended on October 31, 1968. Until the Linebacker campaigns began on May 9, 1972, American air forces flew only reconnaissance missions over the southernmost portions of North Vietnam, in accordance with the informal agreement reached between North Vietnamese and U.S. authorities. Protective reaction strikes were flown to protect the reconnaissance aircraft.

636. Hersh, *Dikes in Hanoi Represent 2,000-Year Effort to Tame Rivers*, N.Y. Times, July 14, 1972, at 6.

637. IV Pentagon Papers 43 (Gravel Edition 1971).

This program, begun in the final year of the Rolling Thunder campaign and renewed during Linebacker I, was effective for military and law of war reasons. Sunk WBLC blocked waterways and required more effort to salvage than that necessary to repair breaks in the dikes while minimizing the likelihood of collateral injury to the civilian population of North Vietnam.

Initial allegations of the bombing of the Red River Valley dikes and dams had been made at the beginning of the Rolling Thunder campaign in 1965. The United States conveyed diplomatic messages through intermediaries to assure the Government of North Vietnam that the United States would not bomb the dams and dikes. The North Vietnamese responded by storing critical war material, such as dispersed petroleum, oil, and lubricants (POL) in containers on or immediately adjacent to the dikes,[638] and by placing ground-control intercept (GCI) radar and antiaircraft guns on top of or adjacent to the dikes.[639] In addition, many of the dikes or dams also were a part of major lines of communications moving military supplies by rail or truck into the Hanoi area, then south to the battlefields in the Republic of Vietnam.

There is no doubt that under customary international law, as evidenced by the practice of nations in the wars of this century, the dams, dikes, rail lines and roads of North Vietnam were legitimate targets. There also is no doubt that the North Vietnamese brilliantly exploited the American decision not to attack the dams and dikes of the Red River Valley. Damage did occur to the dams and dikes incidental to the lawful attack of legitimate military objectives in the vicinity of the dams and dikes, including attacks using antipersonnel munitions against antiaircraft guns positioned on the dikes and dams. This damage was acknowledged by American officials in the course of the Linebacker campaigns in response to the North Vietnamese allegations.[640]

Herein lies a fundamental consideration of the United States with regard to whether it should ratify Protocol I. The restraint in attack on the North Vietnamese dikes and dams exercised by U.S. national authorities was a policy decision, based upon the limited nature of the conflict in Vietnam as it was viewed by the national leadership. Article 56 has taken an American policy decision in a limited conflict and made it into a legally binding prohibition for all future wars, regardless of the level of the conflict. Just as North Vietnam exploited to its military advantage the restraint exercised by the United States—at a cost of hundreds of American lives and aircraft, if not the war—article 56 offers an avenue of exploitation which few, if any, future opponents would be likely to ignore.

In the course of such exploitation, the United States would not have any recourse. Any attack to induce the enemy to cease using his dams, dikes, and nuclear power plants as a shield for military objectives would be characterized by the defender as a reprisal. And reprisals against such facilities and the military objectives protected by article 56 are prohibited by paragraph 4 of that article.[641]

---

638. An aerial photograph of one such storage site is contained in Parks, *supra* note 109, at 15.

639. Aerial photographs of which can be found in Parks, *id.* at 18.

640. Gwertzman, *U.S. Issues Report to Rebut Charges of Dike Bombings*, N.Y. Times, July 29, 1972, at 1, and *Text of Intelligence Report on Bombing of Dikes in North Vietnam*, N.Y. Times, July 29, 1972, at 2, which states in part:

> All identified points of dike damage are located within close range of specific targets of military value. Of the twelve locations where damage has occurred, ten are close to identified individual targets such as petroleum storage facilities, and the other two are adjacent to road and river transport lines. Because a large number of North Vietnamese dikes serve as bases for roadways, the maze they create throughout the delta makes it almost inevitable that air attacks directed against transportation targets cause scattered damage to dikes.

641. SCHINDLER & TOMAN, *supra* note 27, at 654.

However, the greatest difficulty lies in the ambiguity of paragraph 5, which (as indicated above) both major commentaries on the Protocols acknowledge. Returning to the context of the Rolling Thunder and Linebacker I and II campaigns against military targets in North Vietnam, figure 3 is a map of Southeast Asia, particularly North Vietnam. The irregular-shaped area encompassing the cities of Hanoi, Vinh, and Haiphong is the range of the SA–2 Guideline missile envelope for missiles sited around those cities. This is the area in which existed the most important military objectives; this also is the area of the Red River Valley delta, with its earthwork dikes and dams. It also houses most of the North Vietnamese MiG airfields. The air defense envelope would be substantially larger if the North Vietnamese had been provided with SA–5 Gammon missiles, whose range is substantially greater than that of the SA–2 Guideline.[642]

Suppression of enemy air defenses (SEAD) is critical to the bombing accuracy of any air strike. Yet a reasonable interpretation of paragraph 5 of article 56 would prohibit any SEAD mission against any of the surface-to-air missile sites, antiaircraft guns, or the MiG airfields because the North Vietnamese could have claimed

SOUTHEAST ASIA

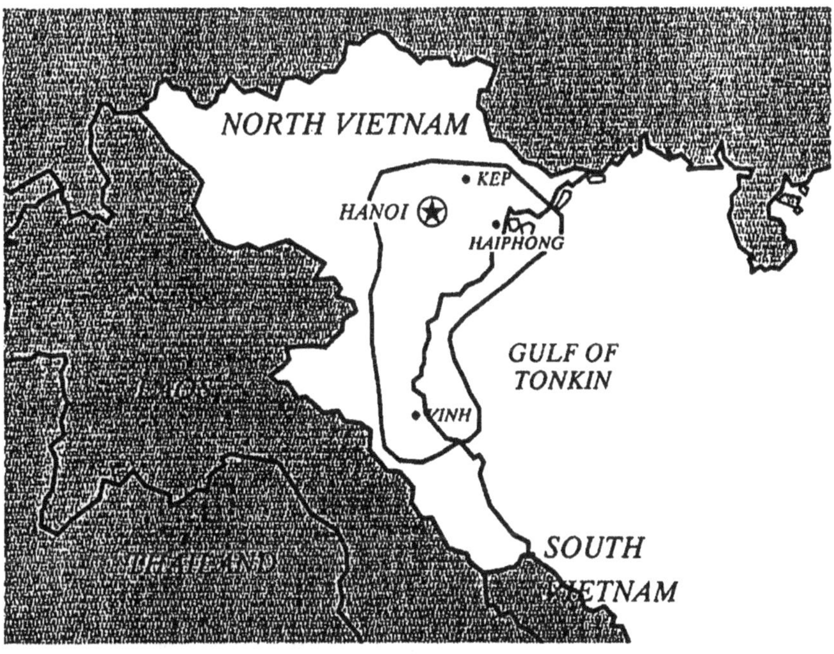

Figure 3.

642. Sources differ in describing the range of each missile. The SA–2 is credited with a range of 80 kilometers (48 miles), while the SA–5 is claimed to have a range of 240–300 kilometers (144–180). JANE'S BATTLEFIELD AIR DEFENCE 1988–1989, *supra* note 593, at 187, 190. Another source credits the SA–5 with a maximum effective range of 100 nautical miles. I WORLD WEAPON DATA BASE, SOVIET MISSILES 548, 570 (B. Wright, ed. 1986).

(assuming that Protocol I had existed at the time of the American bombing campaigns over North Vietnam) that all of its air defense net existed to protect its fragile dam and dike system. All other military objectives near the dams and dikes likewise would have been protected from attack. In essence, there could have been no bombing campaigns against North Vietnam because of the prohibitions contained in article 56. The language of article 56, which one independent analysis has described as a mixture of "ambiguity and contradiction,"[643] illustrates not only a serious problem the American military review found with article 56, but with the entire tenor of Protocol I. It favors the defender while placing U.S. aircrews at risk for alleged violation of the law of war in the execution of what previously had been lawful missions.

D. Protocol I: Conclusion

During the course of the Diplomatic Conference that produced Protocols I and II, the delegate from Togo proposed a rule that in a war between a nation with an air force and a nation without an air force, the nation with an air force would be prohibited from using it.[644] Although its proposal died in committee, Togo's attempt to use a law of war treaty to protect its economic and national security interests differed from the practice of many of the other nations present at the conference only in degree. In particular, it is characteristic of the effort made by many delegations to use Protocol I to restrict the range and nature of lawful offensive air operations. Cloaked in a humanitarian guise, the articles of Protocol I were drafted with a view to off-setting any military advantage a superior enemy force might have—particularly an air power—in attacking another nation within that other nation's territory.

In doing so, Protocol I endeavors to shift responsibility for minimizing collateral civilian casualties from the defender (where it traditionally has reposed) to the attacker, regardless of any action taken by the defender. Humanitarian concern of a defender for the lives of innocent civilians evidently ceased where (a) those civilians could be used as a shield for a military objective or their lives could be sacrificed for propaganda purposes in the course of the defense of a nation, or (b) a regime was threatened by internal conflict.

Protocol I also suffers from the intentional ambiguities of its language, which places combatants carrying out lawful combat operations at an increased risk from spurious allegations of violations of the law of war if captured. This in turn could result in a repetition of the American experience in Korea and Vietnam where United States military men were denied the fundamental prisoner of war protections to which they were legally entitled. The experiences of American aircrews in World

643. Ramberg, *Nuclear Plants—Military Hostages?*, BULL. ATOMIC SCIENTISTS 17–25, at 19 (Mar. 1986). Subsequent to the United States military review, General Rafael del Pino, formerly a senior Cuban air force officer who defected to the United States, disclosed that had the United States commenced a blockade of Cuba in the course of the 1983 Grenada rescue operation, President Fidel Castro intended to launch Cuban fighter bombers to attack nuclear power plants in Florida, presumably those at Turkey Point, twenty-four miles south of Miami. *Cuban Defector Says Castro Weighed Airstrike Against U.S.*, Wash. Post, Dec. 29, 1989, at A9. Cuba became a party to Protocol I on 25 November 1982.

644. At the time of the Diplomatic Conference, Togo's Force Aerienne Togolaise was obsolete to the point of being virtually nonexistent. As with many proposals made during the Diplomatic Conference, Togo's was driven by economic rather than humanitarian concerns. Following the decade of law of war negotiations in the 1970s, Togo rebuilt its air force's combat capability, acquiring six Embracer EMB–326 Xavantes and five Dassault Alphajets. 1987 WORLD MILITARY AIRCRAFT FORECAST 1101 (P. Sanna, ed. 1986). The size of its air force further suggests the rationale behind Togo's proposal.

War II, Korea and Vietnam serve as a fair indication that some opponents will undertake such illegal actions regardless of the state of the law of war. The ambiguities of Protocol I will greatly facilitate similar illicit efforts in future conflicts, while its limitations on reprisals will undermine a nation's ability to ensure respect for the law of war where breaches occur or are threatened. United States ratification of Protocol I would have provided unwarranted credence for the ambiguities and contradictions of that treaty, while severely hampering the already limited options for enforcement of the law of war.

Although the ICRC has been criticized in the preceding pages for some of its actions in conjunction with Protocol I, this criticism does not diminish the author's very high regard for that organization's work in implementation of the 1949 Geneva Conventions, and for its unflagging efforts to modernize the law of war. But just as a military commander may be critiqued by historians for his tactical or strategic decisions, the ICRC's efforts with regard to Protocol I are open to question.

As the preceding pages have illustrated, the ICRC is unqualified to draft provisions regarding the regulation of modern war. And while some of the "experts" who attended its preparatory conferences in 1971 and 1972 may have known something about the law of war, their knowledge of modern warfighting was weak. The draft provisions bring to mind John Galsworthy's statement that, "Idealism increases in direct proportion to one's distance from the problem." The distance of the ICRC and its "experts" was substantial, both in terms of space and time. Many of the provisions in the ICRC's draft rules and the subsequent Protocol I fail to take into consideration the myriad revolutionary and evolutionary changes in doctrine, strategy, and the institution of war as such, many of which have been heavily influenced by changes in the ability of nation-states to mobilize manpower and industry in their defense. Not only did Protocol I fail to stay abreast of technology, but it erred in endeavoring to develop rules that apply at the tactical, operational, and strategic levels of war, across the entire spectrum of conflict. In truth, it is unlikely that its provisions can be followed whatever the level of conflict, even if each party to the conflict believes in *pacta sunt servanda*.

In this respect the ICRC's composition (as a private organization of private citizens in a neutral nation) betrayed it, through lack of knowledge of modern warfighting, and through the ICRC's alliance throughout the drafting and negotiating process with the governments (though not the military) of Switzerland and Sweden. The latter nation had its own agenda during this time, reflected in the choice of the word "attack" in article 49(1) and in the language described and analyzed on the preceding pages that favors a defender over a force engaged in offensive operations. Notwithstanding claims to the contrary, Protocol I was not intended to protect the innocent civilian so much as it was developed as a vehicle for providing maximum psychological advantage to a defending nation in the arena of world public opinion.

Finally, the ICRC undertook a major and commendable step—though a calculated risk—to introduce the law of war to the Third World. Its effort failed miserably, for instead of requiring the nations of the Third World to rise to certain minimum standards of conduct in combat, the law of war succumbed to the tyranny of the majority. The old law of war—including the 1949 Geneva Conventions—largely had been ignored within the Third World for a variety of reasons, mainly for convenience, but with the excuse that it was a Christian, Western European phenomenon. The new law of war contained in Protocols I and II regrettably takes a step back by reverting to concepts regarding the justness of one's cause that were expressly rejected by the 1949 Geneva Conventions, rather than judging a nation's or combatant's conduct on the battlefield. This unfortunate mixture of *jus ad bellum* and *jus in bello* is a significant failure in the ICRC's effort to introduce the law of war into the Third World.

The Third World's insistence upon a high threshold for application of the very limited rules of Protocol II—substantially higher than that for common article 3 of the four 1949 Geneva Conventions—is testimony to the ICRC's failed effort, for which the innocent civilian suffers daily in the myriad internal conflicts being waged around the world. While the ICRC likes to note that there are more nations party to the 1949 Geneva Conventions than there are members of the United Nations, and while its efforts over the past decade have run up a lengthy list of parties to Protocols I and II, ratification or accession to a treaty is of little value if there is no implementation of or respect for that treaty. The record within the Third World with regard to implementation of and respect for the 1949 Geneva Conventions, much less the more complex provisions of Protocols I and II, is not impressive.

The American military review of Protocols I and II was the most comprehensive of any nation. During the time of the review the ICRC heavily lobbied senior United States officials to abandon the military review and ratify as quickly as possible.[645] The civilian leadership, which had serious objections to the Protocol I politicization of what previously had been an apolitical subject, patiently permitted the military review to continue unimpeded. For a number of military reasons, many of which have been discussed in the preceding pages, the JCS unanimously recommended that the United States not become a party to Protocol I.[646] The senior civilian leadership of the United States—including the Secretaries of State and Defense, and the Attorney General—agreed with the analysis of the JCS and joined in their recommendation against submission of Protocol I to the Senate for its advice and consent to ratification, and in favor of submission of Protocol II for Senate advice and consent. On January 29, 1987, President Ronald Reagan forwarded Protocol II to the United States Senate for that purpose.[647] Describing Protocol I as "fundamentally and irreconcilably flawed," President Reagan also requested an expression of the sense of the Senate that it shares the view that the United States should not ratify Protocol I.[648] Documents accompanying President Reagan's transmittal letter reaffirmed the American belief in and support for the law of war by expanding the application of Protocol II, beyond the very limited scope demanded by Third World delegations at the Diplomatic Conference, to any conflict in which common article 3 of the 1949 Geneva Conventions would be applicable.[649]

There were several reactions to the American decision against ratification of Protocol I. Former U.S. delegation members who were protective of their work product could articulate reasons why an objectionable provision could be interpreted in a way that placed it in its most favorable light, often referring to a statement made by a member of the American delegation during the course of the Diplomatic Conference. But this is not a record of trial that is being argued before a domestic appellate court. Reference to the negotiating record may occur only where the

645. Personal knowledge of author.

646. L. Gelb, *War Law Pact Faces Objection of Joint Chiefs*, N.Y. Times, July 22, 1985, at 1.

647. MESSAGE OF THE PRESIDENT OF THE UNITED STATES TRANSMITTING THE PROTOCOL II ADDITIONAL TO THE GENEVA CONVENTIONS OF AUGUST 12, 1949, AND RELATING TO THE PROTECTION OF VICTIMS OF NONINTERNATIONAL ARMED CONFLICTS, CONCLUDED AT GENEVA ON JUNE 10, 1977, 100TH CONG., 1ST SESS., (1987) [hereinafter PRESIDENT'S TRANSMITTAL].

648. PRESIDENT'S TRANSMITTAL, *id.* at iv–v.

649. Letter of Submittal to the President of Secretary of State George P. Schultz, in PRESIDENT'S TRANSMITTAL, *id.* at vii–viii.

ordinary meaning is ambiguous or obscure, or leads to a result which is manifestly absurd or obscure.[650] The problem was slightly different in that much of the language of Protocol I was made purposely vague and subject to several interpretations, including those of an opponent. In the case of war crimes allegations against captured American personnel, few prisoners of war will be afforded the right to review the seventeen volumes of the negotiating record of the Diplomatic Conference to suggest differences in interpretation of the articles they are charged with violating. The assurances of former U.S. delegation members were neither reassuring nor convincing.

Officials of the ICRC and other proponents of American ratification argued that any concerns regarding the language of Protocol I could be remedied with appropriate reservations or statements of understanding.[651] These suggestions apparently were made without an appreciation for the extent of the concerns raised by the military review, in that the military objections are not fully explained in the documents forwarding Protocol II to the Senate.[652]

Discussion of many of the military concerns with former members of the American delegation who favored ratification of Protocol I, as well as with representatives of the ICRC, revealed that the foundation for their suggestion was political rather than legal. Proponents of ratification argued against specific reservations (a) because agreement on the objectionable article or provision purportedly had been critical to the entire treaty negotiation, and thus would constitute a breach of trust with the other delegations,[653] (b) the reservation would be incompatible with the object and purpose of the treaty,[654] or (c) the reservation would violate the language of article

650. Vienna Convention on the Law of Treaties, articles 31 and 32.

651. Gasser, *supra* note 274, at 923; and Aldrich, *supra* note 259, at 719. Ambassador Aldrich stated: "None of the defects in the Protocol should deter the United States from ratification, as they are curable by means of understandings or reservations, as both the State and Defense Departments recognized prior to the Reagan Administration." As previously stated, the last phrase is fundamentally false. Even in the years preceding the Reagan Administration, there had been no agreement as to ratification of Protocols I and II or on the statements of understanding or reservations that would be required for American ratification. The decision on ratification was subject to the military review promised the JCS in getting their agreement to United States signature of the Protocols on December 12, 1977. There was a serious difference of opinion between Ambassador Aldrich and DOD officials (including the JCS) with regard to the need for a reservation to some of the prohibitions on reprisals contained in Protocol I. However, that had not been raised to the highest levels of each department at the time the Carter Administration left office.

652. *See, e.g.*, Gasser, *supra* note 274, at 923.

653. Thus proponents of ratification objected to the American military recommendation that the United States reject articles 1(4), 44(3) and 47 on the basis that each had been agreed to only after Group of 77 compromises on other provisions. But none could provide a *quid pro quo* in the form of humanitarian or other gains in return for American acceptance of the objectionable language found in those provisions.

654. Article 19 of the Vienna Convention on the Law of Treaties prohibits a reservation to a treaty if: (a) the reservation is prohibited by the treaty; (b) the treaty provides that only specified reservations, which do not include the reservation in question, may be made; or (c) in cases not falling under sub-paragraphs (a) and (b), the reservation is incompatible with the object and purpose of the treaty.

The original draft Protocol I contained a provision (article 85) prohibiting any reservation to certain listed articles. However, during the fourth and final session of the Diplomatic Conference it became clear that consensus would not be possible unless this provision was eliminated, leaving the issue of reservations to article 19(c) of the Vienna Convention. A provision that would have prohibited reservations to twenty-two specific articles was defeated in Committee I by a majority vote. A subsequent proposal to prohibit reservations to articles dealing with wars of national liberation (such as articles 1(4) and 44(3)) was defeated in the Conference plenary session. U.S. Dep't. of State, Report of the United States Delegation to the International Humanitarian Law Applicable in Armed Conflicts, 4th Sess., Geneva, Switzerland, Mar. 17–June 10, 1977 at 7–8 (1977). The foregoing serves as further illustration of the fact that consensus acceptance of the text of Protocol I by the delegations participating in the Diplomatic Conference was merely acceptance *ad referendum*, *i.e.*, subject to approval by national governments, rather than endorsement *per se* by nations, as some have inferred. *See*, e.g., Gasser, *supra* note 274, at 915, 924.

60, paragraph 5 of the Vienna Convention on the Law of Treaties, which protects "provisions relating to the protection of the human person contained in treaties of a humanitarian character, in particular to provisions prohibiting any form of reprisals against persons protected by such treaties."[655] Public writings by proponents of ratification of Protocol I were contradicted by their private statements. No solution could be found to address the myriad military and humanitarian concerns expressed by the JCS as a result of their comprehensive military review.

The question then is raised concerning the effect of Protocol I in light of the many ratifications by other nations to date. A partial response is that many nations ratified for other than humanitarian reasons, with little or no knowledge of the contents of Protocol I, and have done little, if anything, to implement their obligations.[656] Some nations party to Protocol I, including some within the NATO alliance, have begun to face the harsh realities of the requirements of Protocol I that were not considered prior to ratification. In bilateral or multilateral discussions with American officials they have stated that the provisions of Protocol I will be inapplicable to them or their allies in defense of their own territory.

War games conducted during the past decade have proved repeatedly that Protocol I will be one of the first casualties in a mid-to high-intensity conflict; it will be ignored. In joint war games conducted by Australia and the United States in 1986 and 1987 specifically to evaluate Protocol I, its provisions were found to be a "war stopper" if followed scrupulously by a party to the conflict. That is, any military commander or force adhering to the requirements of Protocol I would be defeated by an opponent not following them. For this and other reasons, Australia in 1989 postponed its decision as to ratification of Protocol I.

Because of its decision against ratification of Protocol I, the United States has undertaken a two-track program to ensure and enhance continued respect for the law of war. The comprehensive military review identified a need to update and significantly expand American military law of war manuals. A new Navy manual was published in 1987,[657] and the new Army law of war manual will be completed in 1990.[658] In preparation of the latter, discussions have been held with other nations in

655. Thus the American military recommendation of a reservation to the prohibition on reprisals against civilian objects contained in article 52 (in order to protect U.S. POWs in enemy hands) would be prohibited by the provision quoted.

656. Thus the Arab nations were quick to ratify Protocol I because of its recognition of the PLO, while many African nations became parties to Protocol I because of its recognition of the ANC and the PLO. Few have taken any steps to implement their obligations under the 1949 Geneva Conventions or the 1977 Protocol I.

In a Pentagon meeting with ICRC officials on May 30, 1986, Jacques Moreillon, then Director of the Department of Principles and Law of the ICRC, laughingly told the story of how one African national leader had decided to ratify Protocol I after ICRC officials pointed out the language of article 1(4) and 44(3), without further consideration of the contexts of Protocol I or its contents. That nation deposited its instrument of ratification within the month. Another African nation reached the same decision after the article on mercenaries (article 47) was brought to the attention of its leaders. And the Republic of Korea ratified Protocol I after ICRC representatives advised South Korean government officials that ratification of Protocol I would enhance its human rights image before it hosted the 1988 Summer Olympics.

In his 1986 meeting with DOD officials, Mr. Moreillon acknowledged that most Third World nations had no appreciation of the concept of *pacta sunt servanda*, and looked upon treaties (particularly Protocol I) as nothing more than political acts, expedient for the moment. The ICRC was exploiting this to enroll as many parties to Protocol I as possible so as to pressure Western nations to ratify.

657. THE COMMANDER'S HANDBOOK ON THE LAW OF NAVAL OPERATIONS (Naval Warfare Publication 9).

658. The revised U.S. Army Field Manual 27–10 will be entitled THE LAW OF WAR. The author of this article is its author as well.

an effort to reach common agreement on many aspects of the law of war that were beclouded by Protocol I.[659]

On a complementary but separate track, the United States and other governments have undertaken the preparation of a separate statement of principles. This would identify those provisions in Protocol I that are regarded as a codification of customary international law, and otherwise articulate what constitutes the customary law of war where the language of Protocol I is inadequate. This program, begun in 1986, continues.

The 1977 Protocols were the product of many long years of complex negotiations. The products of those negotiations leave much to be desired. Certain political organizations and groups came to the Diplomatic Conference specifically to alter the law of war to serve politics rather than for any humanitarian gain. They were successful, at great cost to the war victims whom the law of war is intended to protect—specifically, the innocent civilian *and* the combatant who has fallen into enemy hands. The very high threshold of Protocol II establishes that most nations, particularly those from the Third World, placed national security interests above humanitarian concerns.

For the most part the differences at the Diplomatic Conference were expressed along North-South rather than East-West lines. The narrowing of political differences between East and West in recent months has served to re-emphasize the differences between developed and developing nations. Considering that most wars today are internal rather than international armed conflicts, the failure of the Diplomatic Conference to develop effective rules for these lesser but equally deadly conflicts looms all the larger.

In the slightly more than two dozen "big" wars (that is, wars that claim more than 1000 civilian lives per year) currently being waged around the world, more than three million people, mostly civilians, have died. While any civilian death is unfortunate, the deaths attributed to aerial bombardment during the total war of 1939–1945 pale in comparison; the figures also suggest the lack of proper focus that befell the Diplomatic Conference.

Two points emerge from this. As one experienced military analyst has correctly concluded, "If the United States (and, for that matter, the Soviet Union as well) disappeared from the face of the earth tomorrow, most of these [internal] wars would continue unabated."[660] Second, the products of the 1974–1977 Diplomatic Confer-

---

659. As previously noted, meetings have been held with senior military judge advocates from the United Kingdom, Canada, New Zealand and Australia. New Zealand is a party to Protocol I, and Canada has stated its intention to become a party. Thus participants have been doing their utmost to narrow the differences between those governments party to Protocol I and those not, in the process clarifying the vague and contradictory language of Protocol I. This process is not a complete remedy, however, as the discussions have been among friends of a common heritage and culture.

660. Summers, *Wars and Rumors of Wars*, Wash. Times, Apr. 7, 1988, at F3. Two brief examples illustrate this point:

— During the decade of civil war within Lebanon, more than 100,000 persons, mostly civilians have died.

— In suppression of internal dissent within Liberia in January 1990, more than 500 civilians were rounded up by Liberian forces and machinegunned to death.

With regard to the former, since conclusion of the Diplomatic Conference, the ICRC has "discovered" a form of conflict falling between international armed conflict and internal armed conflict: the "internationalized non-international armed conflict" in which an internal conflict is receiving direct, external support. *See, e.g.*, Gasser, *Internationalized Non-International Armed Conflict*, 33 The American U. L. Rev. 145–59 (1983).

ence produced nothing that might bring some hope of amelioration of the suffering to the victims and potential victims of these conflicts. As with many law of war conventions, Protocol I in many respects addressed a war of the past. With respect to Protocol I and aerial bombardment, its language looked to an experience of total war which the world has not witnessed for almost a half century.

What, then, will become of Protocol I? A legal scholar, endeavoring to describe the law of war as it applied to aerial bombardment in the years immediately preceding the Diplomatic Conference, provided some hint as to the likely effect of Protocol I on the law of war:

> International law . . . has for its principal source the actual practice of nations. . . . It is significant that the Hague [Air] Rules of 1923 were never ratified by a single power. For this a number of reasons may be advanced. First, the Rules would have restricted the potency of a formidable weapon against the general trend which, ever since the unsuccessful attempt of the medieval Popes and Councils to ban the cross-bow, has been to confine prohibitions to methods of war which were either obsolete or not yet fully developed, but were in any case ineffective in addition to being cruel. Secondly, if mere indiscriminateness were to be made the criterion of an unlawful raid, it would be difficult to measure the degree of lack of discrimination involved and thus to decide whether the responsibility (if any) should be laid at the door of the planners of the raid or of the airmen charged with its execution—a matter of critical importance should one of the latter be shot down and accused of a war crime. Third, there was the point made by Lord Trenchard, and never really answered, that, if a belligerent could secure immunity for his war industries by locating them in a city, it would be equivalent to making such city neutral territory—a position the other belligerent could not possibly accept.[661]

Protocol I has been ratified by a number of nations, but it will be the actual practice of nations that determines its fate. Its contradictions of the practice of nations over the past century are not accidental, in that the drafters of Protocol I mistakenly endeavored to resurrect the failed provisions of the 1923 Hague Air Rules. For the reasons stated in this article, it is unlikely that its efforts to regulate the conduct of hostilities will meet with any greater degree of success than did the 1923 Hague Air Rules.[662]

XVII. CONCLUSION

For as long as there have been aircraft, there have been efforts to regulate their effect in war. Some efforts have been carried out because of the aversion to that which is new to war, which has been the case with virtually every innovation in weaponry. Some have been attempted because of the military advantage an airpower

---

This form of conflict existed before the Diplomatic Conference. Thus, the United States and Allied military assistance to the Government of the Republic of Vietnam created such a conflict with regard to some of the activities of the National Liberation Front (the Viet Cong), although the North Vietnamese invasion of South Vietnam simultaneously made the conflict international in character. The problem of the "internationalized non-international armed conflict" is best illustrated by the regrettable incident that occurred at My Lai on March 16, 1968, when American Army soldiers murdered several hundred unarmed, unresisting South Vietnamese civilians of all ages. The murder of civilians of an ally suggests a gap in the law of war. That gap was not closed by Protocols I and II, but was covered with regard to U.S. forces by their liability to prosecution for violations of article 118 of the Uniform Code of Military Justice (murder).

661. Johnson, *The Legality of Modern Forms of Aerial Warfare*, 72 THE AERONAUTICAL JOURNAL OF THE ROYAL AERONAUTICAL SOC. 685–92, at 688–89 (Aug. 1968).

662. This article has been concerned with aerial bombardment only. As Professor M. W. Royse explained more than sixty years ago, in most cases the accuracy of bombing aircraft will be greater than alternative means, such as surface-to-surface missiles or indirect artillery fire. *See* Royse, *supra* note 156, at 167–73. This article should not be interpreted as suggesting otherwise merely because of its limited focus.

gained over a nation that had not developed (or did not have the economic and technical resources to develop) a matching or superior capability. Some have been genuinely humane. These legislative attempts have been successful to the extent that they have not permitted one nation to gain an advantage over another, or to offset an opponent's military advantage, and to the degree that they have followed common sense. Regrettably, the latter has been missing far more often than it has been present.

The purpose of the law of war is to protect innocent persons from intentional or incidental injury to the extent they can be avoided. Responsibility for the latter, in the order of priority, historically has rested (a) with the nation exercising control over the civilian population, (b) the individual civilian, and (c) with the force attacking legitimate military objectives, to the extent that an attacker reasonably can ascertain where the civilian population is located and can influence its removal from the proximity of the military objective to be attacked. He cannot be expected to do more.

With regard to the nature of war in general and the use of air power in particular, myriad factors beyond the control of the attacking force influence or affect its ability to attack its target(s) accurately. Not the least of these are the actions of the defending force, which is making every effort to cause the attacker's munitions to miss their intended target. Many of these actions by the defender are intervening factors over which the attacker has no control and, in some cases, over which neither party has control. Proposals to "count civilian casualties" at the end of an airstrike or air campaign are of no value because of the various factors that influence an attack, and the fact that it is impossible to attribute a particular casualty to a particular act, especially within the unseen world of electronic warfare on the modern battlefield.

The employment of airpower will continue because of its military value; it is a classic example of *military necessity*. Air crews will always desire to bomb accurately because they represent the end product in the tremendous investment their nation has made in the development and acquisition of an airpower capability. The attempts at legislation of airpower over the past ninety years have been unsuccessful because each has failed to recognize this. Protocol I of 1977 was the last effort to regulate airpower as such;[663] its shortcomings have been discussed in detail in the preceding pages. It is the last word, and is likely to be for some time, in a century-long evolution. As in the beginning of aviation, the story of its regulation in war remains as vague, complex, and perplexing as warfare itself. The future codification of the law of war as it relates to aerial bombardment will succeed only where proper expertise is employed and the subject approached in a balanced matter. As this article has illustrated, this is far easier said than done.

663. Because of the extended length of the present article, the author regrettably has elected to forego discussion of the United Nations Conventional Weapons Conference that took place from 1978 to 1980 and in which the author participated as a member of the United States delegation.

Name Index

For Product Safety Concerns and Information please contact our EU representative GPSR@taylorandfrancis.com
Taylor & Francis Verlag GmbH, Kaufingerstraße 24, 80331 München, Germany

www.ingramcontent.com/pod-product-compliance
Lightning Source LLC
LaVergne TN
LVHW080801011026
849160LV00015B/1500

* 9 7 8 1 1 3 8 3 7 8 6 2 9 *